TEMPLES OF THE ANCIENT WORLD

Ritual and Symbolism

Edited by
Donald W. Parry

Illustrations directed by
Michael P. Lyon

Deseret Book Company
Salt Lake City, Utah
and
Foundation for Ancient Research and Mormon Studies
Provo, Utah

Library of Congress Cataloging-in-Publication Data

Temples of the ancient world : ritual and symbolism / edited by Donald W. Parry.
 p. cm.
 "Most of these essays were presented originally at a conference sponsored by the Foundation for Ancient Research and Mormon Studies (F.A.R.M.S.) held in February 1993 at Brigham Young University"— Introd.
 Includes bibliographical references and index.
 ISBN 0-87579-811-X
 1. Temples, Mormon—Congresses. 2. Temples—Congresses. 3. Ritual—Congresses. 4. Symbolism—Congresses. 5. Middle East—Religions—Congresses. 6. The Church of Jesus Christ of Latter-day Saints—Doctrines—Congresses. 7. Mormon Church—Doctrines—Congresses. I. Foundation for Ancient Research and Mormon Studies.
 BX8643.T4T456   1993
 246'.95893—dc20   93-36629
                                                CIP

Printed in the United States of America

10 9   8   7   6   5   4   3   2   1

Contents

Illustrations

Key to Abbreviations

AAHB   Geo Widengren, *The Ascension of the Apostle and the Heavenly Book: King and Saviour III* (Uppsala: A. B. Lundequistska, 1950)

AAM   Anton Moortgat, *The Art of Ancient Mesopotamia* (London/New York: Phaidon, 1969)

AMM   Ithamar Gruenwald, *Apocalyptic and Merkavah Mysticism* (Leiden: E. J. Brill, 1980)

ANET   James B. Pritchard, ed., *Ancient Near Eastern Texts Relating to the Old Testament,* 3rd ed. (Princeton: Princeton University Press, 1955)

ANT   M. R. James, ed., *The Apocryphal New Testament* (Oxford: Clarendon, 1924)

BSAF   John M. Lundquist and Stephen D. Ricks, eds., *By Study and Also by Faith: Essays in Honor of Hugh W. Nibley,* 2 vols. (Salt Lake City: Deseret Book Company and F.A.R.M.S., 1990)

CWHN   *The Collected Works of Hugh Nibley,* 12+ vols. (Salt Lake City: Deseret Book Company and F.A.R.M.S., 1986–)

EM   *Encyclopedia of Mormonism,* 5 vols., ed. Daniel Ludlow (New York: Macmillan, 1991)

ES   Henri J. M. Claessen and Peter Skalnik, eds. *The Early State* (The Hague: Mouton, 1978)

ET   *Encyclopedia Talmudica,* ed. Sholomo J. Zevin (Jerusalem: Talmudic Encyclopedia Institute, 5729 [1969])

FK   Robert S. Ellwood, *The Feast of Kingship* (Tokyo: Sophia University Press, 1973)

HC   Joseph Smith, *History of The Church of Jesus Christ of*

Latter-day Saints, 7 vols., 2nd ed. rev. (Salt Lake City: Deseret Book Company, 1978)

HCSE   Robert McCormick Adams, *Heartland of Cities, Surveys of Ancient Settlements and Land Use on the Central Floodplain of the Euphrates* (Chicago: University of Chicago Press, 1981)

IGL   A. Falkenstein, *Die Inschriften Gudeas von Lagaš* (Rome: Pontificium Institutum Biblicum, 1966)

JD   *Journal of Discourses*, 26 vols. (Liverpool: F. D. Richards and others, 1855–86)

KG   Henri Frankfort, *Kingship and the Gods* (Chicago: University of Chicago Press, 1978)

LJ   Louis Ginzberg, *The Legends of the Jews* (Philadelphia: Jewish Publication Society of America, 1937)

M   Mishnah

NIV   New International Version of the Bible

OSAPE   Ronald Cohen and Elman R. Service, eds., *Origins of the State, the Anthropology of Political Evolution* (Philadelphia: Institute for the Study of Human Issues, 1978)

OTP   James H. Charlesworth, ed., *The Old Testament Pseudepigrapha*, 2 vols. (Garden City, New York: Doubleday, 1983)

PG   J. P. Migne, ed., *Patrologiae Cursus Completus . . . Series Graeca*, 161 vols. (Paris: Garnier, 1857–66)

PL   J. P. Migne, ed., *Patrologiae Cursus Completus . . . Series Latina*, 221 vols. (Paris: Garnier, 1844–64)

PWJS   Dean C. Jessee, ed., *The Personal Writings of Joseph Smith* (Salt Lake City: Deseret Book, 1984)

RCC   Charlotte B. Moore, ed., *Reconstructing Complex Societies* (Cambridge: American Schools of Oriental Research, 1974)

SAK   F. Thureau-Dangin, *Die Sumerischen und Akkadischen Königsin Schriften* (Leipzig: Hinrichs, 1907)

T   Tosephta

TB   Babylonian Talmud

THPBT   Avraham Biran, ed., *Temples and High Places in Biblical*

Times (Jerusalem: Nelson Glueck School of Biblical Archaeology, 1981)

TPJS   Joseph Fielding Smith, comp., *Teachings of the Prophet Joseph Smith* (Salt Lake City: Deseret Book Company, 1976)

TTS   Menahem Haran, *Temples and Temple-Service in Ancient Israel* (Winona Lake, Indiana: Eisenbrauns, 1985)

TY   Talmud Yerushalmi (Jerusalem Talmud)

WJS   Andrew F. Ehat and Lyndon W. Cook, eds., *The Words of Joseph Smith—The Contemporary Accounts of the Nauvoo Discourses of the Prophet Joseph* (Orem, Utah: Grandin Book Company, 1992)

When references to works from antiquity are given, names of canonical books appear in roman type, while names of non-canonical books appear in italic type. References from the Old and New Testaments are quoted from the King James Version, unless otherwise noted.

Introduction

The Meaning of the Temple

The Saints have always been a temple-building people (see D&C 124:39). From the Kirtland Temple to the sacred structures of today, the Latter-day Saints have built temples wherever they have been. This great concern for sacred houses of the Lord has been shared by the people of God in past dispensations as well. "What was the object of gathering the Jews, or the people of God in any age of the world?" Joseph Smith asked. "The main object was to build unto the Lord a house whereby he could reveal unto his people the ordinances of his house and the glories of his kingdom."[1]

The temple was so important to the ancient Israelites and the other people of the ancient Near East that it played a prominent role not only in their religion, but also in their government, economy, art, and social structure. The Tabernacle of Moses was important to the Israelites, to the point that it served as a mobile sanctuary, carried about in their wanderings. The Temple of Solomon in Jerusalem became a political and religious focal point for the kingdom of Israel under the reigns of the early Israelite kings. The temple of Herod held significance for Jesus during his mortal ministry—it was a place where he both learned and taught. Herod's temple was also a place known to the early apostles and Christians (see Acts 2:46). The Nephites built a temple patterned after the Temple of Solomon soon after their arrival in the New World, and it was at the temple in Bountiful that the resurrected Lord visited and taught the Nephite faithful.

The recent popularity of Hugh Nibley's *Temple and Cosmos* indicates that LDS readers today are vitally interested in temples and information related to temples. The information in this volume builds on and goes beyond the discussions in *Temple and Cosmos* by dealing with temple ritual, symbolism, sacred versus profane space, temple architecture, sacral time, temple vestments, temple building motifs, and the setting of the temple in the ancient state. In addition, this volume presents new and significant material pertaining to the temple in the Book of Mormon and temple imagery in the Revelation of John, the book of Hebrews, and the epistles of Peter.

Definition of *Temple*

Many of the chapters in this volume examine the temple from an ancient Near Eastern—and particularly Israelite—perspective.[2] In the Old Testament the principal root from which the English word *temple* originates is *QDŠ, which denotes the "separation" or "withdrawal" of sacred entities from profane things.[3] The root *QDŠ is used with reference to God[4] (Exodus 15:11; Leviticus 20:3); God's temples (Exodus 38:24; 40:9; 2 Chronicles 29:5; Ezekiel 42:14); persons directly associated with temples, such as the priests (Leviticus 21:6) and the people of Israel (Jeremiah 2:3; Psalm 114:2); temple furniture (Exodus 30:29; 2 Chronicles 35:3); altars (Exodus 29:37; Deuteronomy 9:24); anointing oil (Exodus 30:25); incense (Exodus 30:35); priestly vestments (Leviticus 16:4); bread of the presence (1 Samuel 21:5); Jerusalem, the city of one of God's temples (Isaiah 48:2); and holy days and festivals connected to the temple (Isaiah 58:13; Exodus 35:2).[5]

A second Hebrew word commonly translated as "temple" is the term *bayit*, "house," which may be expressed simply as *bayit*, or in the explicative formula *beit Elohim*, "the house of God" (Judges 17:5), or *beit YHWH*, "the house of Yahweh" (Deuteronomy 23:19). The term "house" refers in more than one hundred instances to the Temple of Solomon and in some fifty-three instances to Ezekiel's temple. The expression "house of the temple" (2 Chronicles 36:17) appears once in the Bible. During the late Second Temple Period the temple was often called "house of the temple" and "temple,"[6] but more often "the house," the "second house" (i.e., the second temple), and the "mountain of the house" (i.e., mountain of the temple).[7]

An early mention of the Latin word *templum* (from which the English *temple* is derived) is found in the classical literature, where Varro notes the cosmic associations of the word.[8] The word *templum* signifies a "space marked out by an augur for taking observations."[9] Originally, an augur was a priest who participated in religious rites of fertility.[10] The cutting of the ground by the augur consisted of an intersection of two lines at right angles. The two intersecting lines were called the *cardo* and *decumanus*,[11] and the exact point where the lines intersected ofttimes represented the center point of the *templum*, known in various religious traditions as the navel of the earth, the *omphalos*, the cosmic mountain, the sacred tree, and the holy of holies. The two intersecting lines divided the space or area into four equal regions. Corresponding to this is the popular temple-related concept of *Himmelsrichtung*, the four corners of the earth, or the four cardinal directions.[12]

Templum then dissects the land, divides it into portions or zones, and creates disjunctions and partitions between sacred space and profane space. Israel was commanded to "distinguish *(lahabdîl)* between the holy and the profane, and between the impure and the pure" (Leviticus 10:10, translation by the author)—the temple aided them in that process.

Standing in antithesis to *temple* is the concept of the *profane*. The Latin word *profanum* (English "profane") literally means "before" or "outside" of the temple, formed from *pro* (meaning "outside") and *fanum* (meaning "temple").[13] The equivalent Hebrew word is *ḥōl*, which, according to Jastrow, has the meaning of "outside of the sanctuary, foreign, profane, common."[14] If the temple is the consecrated place created "by marking it out, by cutting it off from the profane space around it,"[15] then the profane space represents unconsecrated space, the area which remains after the sacred has been removed. By the time of the Second Temple period the Jews were well aware of the rigid lines that separated the sacred from the profane.[16]

To sum up, then, the idea of the temple, as it took shape throughout its long history, accepted the express characteristics of the root **QDŠ* and the terms *bayit* and *templum*.[17] The temple as *bayit* first and foremost became a "house" where Deity "tented" or "tabernacled"[18] among the people. It became the "House of Yahweh," where the symbols of Israelite religion—the ark of the covenant, the great altar, the lampstand, the tables of shewbread, and other sacred appurtenances and vessels—were established. The temple *(*QDŠ)* had etiological origins, a set of sacred stories that made a particular well-defined area "separate" or "withdrawn" from the surrounding profane and chaotic space. At some point in the history of the Israelite temples all things that were directly associated with the temple—space, persons, vestments, utensils, furniture, other appurtenances, and time—became "separate" or "withdrawn" from the profane. The Israelite temples conjoined with various cosmological elements possessing four corners and a well-defined center.

The Temple—A System of Rituals and Symbols

In a number of studies, Hugh Nibley, John M. Lundquist, Mircea Eliade, Geo Widengren, and others have examined closely temple rituals and symbols.[19] Lundquist, for instance, outlined the typological patterns extant among ancient Near Eastern temples by listing eighteen typological points.[20] Later George E. Mendenhall suggested that Lundquist add a nineteenth type to his list.[21] The following statement, adapted from the writings of Lundquist, presents a summary of his nineteen typological points while at the same time setting forth the rituals and symbols of the temple.

> The temple is an association of symbols and practices that are connected in the ancient world with natural mountains/elevated places (the temple par excellence), edifices, and other sacral, set-apart places dedicated for the worship of God. The set of symbols and practices include, but are not exhausted by, the following: the cosmic mountain, the primordial mound, priestly officiants and their vestments, the waters of life, the tree of life, sacred architecture, and the celestial prototype of the earthly temple. These emphasize spatial orientation and the ritual calendar; the height of the mountain/building; revelation of the divine prototype to the king or prophet by Deity; the concept of 'center,' according to which the temple is the ideological, and in many cases the physical, center of the community; the dependency of the well-being of society on the proper attention to the temple and

to its rituals; initiation, including dramatic portrayal of
the cosmogonic myth and sacred marriage; extensive
concern for death and the afterlife; sacral (covenant-
associated) meals; revelation in the holy of holies, including the use of the tablets of destiny; formal covenant
ceremonies in connection with the promulgation of law;
animal sacrifice; secrecy; and the extensive economic and
political impact of the temple in society.[22]

Temple—Placing God and Righteous Individuals in the Center

The temple is a sacred place that emphasizes God's
great plan of salvation (see D&C 109:4) and Jesus Christ's
divine atoning sacrifice, both of which were given for the
benefit and blessing of humanity. God and Jesus are the
spiritual focus of the temple—it is the place where God's
glory (see D&C 84:5; 109:12; Ezekiel 43:4) and Divine
Presence (see D&C 97:16–17; Habakkuk 2:20) exist. It is the
place where God dwells (see 2 Samuel 7:5; D&C 124:27).
The temple is connected with the divine name of God, for it
is called after God's name (see Jeremiah 7:11). His name will
be there (see 1 Kings 8:29), the sacred work accomplished
there is performed in his name (see D&C 109:9, 17–19), and
the temple is built in his name (see D&C 97:15; 124:24, 40).
The temple is the "house of God" (D&C 88:119, 130), the
"house of glory" (D&C 88:119), and the "house of order"
(D&C 88:119) that is hallowed (see 1 Kings 9:3), consecrated
(see D&C 58:57; 124:44), and dedicated as a place of holiness
by God (see D&C 109:13, 20; 84:3; 109).

One chief purpose of the temple is to permit qualified
individuals, after participating in certain rituals called gestures of approach[23] (also called threshold rituals), to
approach the temple's most sacred spot and there receive
great blessings from God. The temple is designed for the

benefit of mankind, for it is a "house of prayer" (D&C 88:119; Isaiah 56:7; Matthew 21:13), a "house of fasting" (D&C 88:119), a "house of faith" (D&C 88:119), a place of revelation (see D&C 124:39), and a "house of learning" (D&C 88:119; 109:14; Jacob 1:17; cf. Luke 2:46; Matthew 12:4–8). It is a place where families are welded together by keys of authority (see D&C 128:17–18), where the Holy Ghost is manifest with great power (see D&C 109:15), and where the gifts of the Spirit can be received in great abundance (see D&C 109:36–37). It is the holy house where the pure in heart may visit (see D&C 97:15; Psalms 15, 24) and receive visitations from Jesus Christ (see 3 Nephi 11:1; 24:1; D&C 36:1, 8; 97:16; 110:7; Malachi 3:1).

The Saints receive power in the temple (see D&C 109:13, 22, 35). The expressions "power from on high" and "endowed with power" (see D&C 38:32, 38; 43:16; 95:8; Luke 24:49) are common scriptural formulas dealing with power and the temple, and the temple is the place where the "fulness of the priesthood" may be received (D&C 124:28).

Sacred ordinances aid individuals in the process of gaining eternal blessings from God (see D&C 124: 29–31, 40). The ordinances include work for the dead (see D&C 128:28, 54), endowments (see D&C 105:33, 11–12), and others listed in Doctrine and Covenants 124:39:

> your anointings, and your washings, and your baptisms for the dead, and your solemn assemblies, and your memorials for your sacrifices by the sons of Levi, and for your oracles in your most holy places wherein you receive conversations, and your statutes and judgments, for the beginning of the revelations and foundation of Zion, and for the glory, honor, and endowment of all her municipals, are ordained by the ordinance of my holy house.

Contents of This Volume

The majority of the chapters of this volume have never been published before, and never has one book contained so many original contributions by Mormon scholars to our understanding of ancient temples. Approximately one-half of the chapters were presented at a conference sponsored by the Foundation for Ancient Research and Mormon Studies (F.A.R.M.S.) held in February 1993 at Brigham Young University.

The chapters in this volume have been arranged into eight sections dealing with temple systems from a variety of geographic locations, gospel dispensations, and socio-religious cultures. The first part, entitled "Reflections of the Modern Temple," features four chapters that examine aspects of the temple of the present era. Elder Marion D. Hanks, General Authority Emeritus and former president of the Salt Lake Temple, sets the tone for the entire volume as he shares his vast experience with the temples of this dispensation. He describes in precise terms the many blessings that can come from temple attendance and its import to the Latter-day community. Other chapters of this section examine Doctrine and Covenants 109 as a temple document par excellence, ask the question "who shall ascend into the hill of the Lord?" (and answer this question by discussing the manner in which present-day temple visitors should make significant preparations before temple participation), and show connections between the temple and the atonement of Jesus Christ.

Part 2 examines a number of temple-related concepts from the Hebrew Bible (Old Testament) and the ancient Near East. Many such temples were known to Adam, Moses, Solomon, Isaiah, Ezekiel, and other Old Testament prophets and the communities with which they associated.

Essays of the section present a definition of what a temple is in terms of what is shared by or is common to all temples in the ancient Near East, provide insights into how the creation story was used in the ritual setting of ancient temples in that region, point out a number of temple symbols that existed in the Garden of Eden, and compare the temple-building motifs of the ancient world that coincide to some extent with the building patterns of the Kirtland Temple.

Temple, covenant, law, and kingship are four themes found in Part 3. Chapters there show that the establishment of a temple aided the legitimization process of a newly created state in the ancient Near East; that the temple was connected to divine kingship, including coronation and enthronement ceremonies; and that the concepts of temple, covenant making, and the creation of laws in the Hebrew Bible and ancient Near East are intimately related.

The fourth part of the book examines the temple in the setting of the Book of Mormon and ancient America. Many authors of the Book of Mormon make both explicit and implicit references to the temple. One chapter in this section examines the religious place of the three major temples of the Book of Mormon—the temple of Nephi, the temple of Zarahemla, and the temple of Bountiful; a second discusses the temple experience of Jared as recorded in the book of Ether; and a third sets forth the significance of temples of ancient America.

Part 5 investigates the Temple of Herod from the Jewish perspective, or according to Judaism during the late Second Temple Period. This is the temple known to Jesus, John the Baptist, the twelve Apostles, and the early Saints. Sacred and profane space is compared and contrasted, and various grades of holiness, as established by the rabbis, are examined. Additionally, strands of the practices and beliefs attached to the Second Temple system remained with Judaism throughout the centuries and were woven into the theology of early medieval Jewish mystics.

As Part 6 sets forth, the New Testament contains numerous references to both the earthly and the heavenly temples, which are mentioned on numerous occasions by the writers of the Gospels, Paul, Peter, and other New Testament writers. In addition, temple esoterica, imagery, and symbolism are hidden from many in the New Testament texts. For instance, Peter's epistles describe a number of aspects of the temple and create inspired images of the temple scene. The book of Hebrews contains a number of teachings that are relevant to the Latter-day Saints and their understanding of the temples in this dispensation. Further, the Revelator describes the structure of the temple in heaven and explains its significance for those who accept Christ.

The part titled "The Real and the Symbolic" features three chapters. The first chapter examines a host of symbolic elements from the temple in both its ancient Near Eastern and restored settings, including, among many others, the "terrible questions" that the temple endowment answers; the great gap intended to separate temple participants from the world; the creation drama; names, signs, and seals; laws and covenants; and the veil. The second chapter asks the question "what is reality?" and answers the question by providing a complete definition of reality and its connections to the temple and to God. The final chapter of this section also investigates symbolic aspects of the ancient temple, including an examination of the concept of sacral time in light of the temple systems of the ancient Near East.

Part 8 presents two chapters that provide a word picture of sacral vestments of antiquity and their direct connection to the temple. The usage and symbolism of priestly clothing in the Hebrew Bible and other religious literature is the concern of one author; a second author examines the history, symbolism, and significance of the garment of Adam, especially in light of Jewish and Islamic traditions.

I wish to thank the dedicated and faithful LDS scholars who devoted so much time, energy, and insight into the research, writing, and public presentation of the papers that form this volume. Special thanks are also due to Michael Lyon, whose love of the temple and diligent study of its ancient forms are reflected in the illustrations that he gathered and created. Together we hope that from the contents of this volume, LDS readers will gain a greater appreciation for the temples of old and, at the same time, come to more fully understand the temples of the present era as revealed through Joseph Smith, the first Prophet of the Restoration.

DONALD W. PARRY

Notes

1. *HC,* 5:423–24.

2. From a different point of view, see the definitions of temple presented by Menahem Haran, *Temples and Temple Service in Ancient Israel* (Oxford: Clarendon Press, 1977), 13–15; and G. R. H. Wright, *Ancient Building in South Syria and Palestine* (Leiden: Brill, 1985), 1:225–26.

3. Francis Brown, S. R. Driver, and Charles A. Briggs, *A Hebrew and English Lexicon of the Old Testament,* tr. Edward Robinson (Oxford: Clarendon Press, 1977), 871; Ludwig Kochler and Walter Baumgartner, eds., *Lexicon in Veteris Testamenti Libros* (Leiden: Brill, 1953), 825–26. For a discussion of the word *QDŠ see Donald W. Parry, "Ritual Anointing with Olive Oil in Ancient Israelite Religion," in *The Allegory of the Olive Tree,* ed. Stephen D. Ricks and John W. Welch (Salt Lake City: Desert Book and F.A.R.M.S., 1994): 272–75.

4. God, of course, is the reason all other things may become separate or withdrawn from profane things, as shown by Sigmund Mowinckel, *Religion and Cult,* tr. John F. X. Sheehan (Milwaukee: Marquette University, 1981), 54–55; and Rudolph Otto, *The Idea of the Holy,* tr. John W. Harvey (London: Oxford University Press, 1958).

5. *A Hebrew and English Lexicon of the Old Testament,* 871–72; cf.

Roger Caillois, *Man and the Sacred*, tr. Meyer Barash (Westport: Greenwood, 1980), 20.

6. Marcus Jastrow, *A Dictionary of the Targumim, the Talmud Babli and Yerushalmi, and the Midrashic Literature* (New York: Judaica, 1985), 829.

7. Ibid., 168.

8. See Varro, *De Lingua Latina* VII, 6–9.

9. *The Concise Oxford Dictionary of English Etymology*, ed. T. F. Hoad (Oxford: Clarendon Press, 1986), 485. Corbin defines *templum* in similar terms: "It is significant that the Latin word *templum* originally meant a vast space, open on all sides, from which one could survey the whole surrounding landscape as far as the horizon. This is what it means to contemplate; to 'set one's sights on' Heaven from the temple that defines the field of vision" (Henry Corbin, *Temple and Contemplation*, tr. Philip Sherrard [London: Islamic, 1986], 386, first published in 1980 under the title *Temple et contemplation*). See also the linguistic approach to the word *templum* by Palmira Cipriano, *Templum* (Roma: Prima Cattedra di Glottologia Università, 1983). Further, on the etymological relationship between the words *tempus* and *templum* see Hermann Usener, *Goettername* (Bonn: F. Cohen, 1929), 191–93.

10. See Albrecht Blumenthal, "Templum," *Klio* 27 (1934): 1–13, admits that there is little known about the Roman augur. The Varronic formula on the temple may have been influenced in part by Cicero, who was an augur. Blumenthal adds that the expression "templa tescaque" denotes the observing of space. See also the comments in Kurt Latte, "Augur und Templum in der Varronischen Augurformel," *Philologus, Zeitschrift für das Klassische Altertum* 97 (1948): 143–59.

11. The intersecting lines, *cardo* and *decumanus*, are discussed in Werner Müller, *Die heilige Stadt, Roma quadrata, himmlisches Jerusalem und die Myth vom Weltnabel* (Stuttgart: W. Kohlhammer, 1961), 9–21; Hesselmeyer, "Decumanus," *Klio* 28 (1935): 133–79; and Stefan Weinstock, "Templum," *Römische Mittheilungen* 47 (1932): 100–103.

12. William Kroll's statement in "Mundus" in Pauly-Wissowa, *Realencyclopaedie der classischen Altertumswissenschaft* (Stuttgart: Metzler, 1893), 16:1.563, demonstrates the connection between the four cardinal directions and the temple, "hence where the four regions come together."

13. *Concise Oxford Dictionary of English Etymology*, 372.

14. Jastrow, *Dictionary of the Targumim*, 433.

15. Mircea Eliade, *Patterns of Comparative Religion* (New York: Sheed and Ward, 1958), 368.

16. The profane consisted of unclean persons (lepers, menstruants, those with a flux), unclean places (graveyards and Gentile lands), things (vessels, animals), and time (weekdays versus Sabbath or Festivals); or to sum up, the profane consisted of things that were unrelated or unassociated with the greater temple area.

17. "Thus sacralized, the word *templum* finally came to mean the sanctuary, the sacred building known as temple, the place of a divine Presence and of the contemplation of this Presence. Thus, the Latin templum became the appropriate word with which to translate the Hebrew and Arabic expressions that we met with at the start, *Beth ha-miqdash, Bayt al-Maqdis*" (Corbin, *Temple and Contemplation*, 386).

18. The Hebrew verb *šākan*, derived from the root *ŠKN*, from which also come the related words *miškān*, ("tent," "tabernacle") and *šǝkînāh* ("Divine Presence"), signifies, according to Davies, to "tabernacle, dwell among" (Davies, G. Henton, *Exodus* [London: SCM Press, 1967], 197); and according to Cross, "to tent," or "to encamp" (Frank M. Cross, "The Tabernacle," *Biblical Archaeologist* 10 [Sept. 1947]: 66). The word is used with reference to Mount Sinai (see Exodus 24:16), the tabernacle (see Numbers 5:3), the Solomonic temple (see Joel 3:17, 21; Isaiah 8:18), and the temple of Ezekiel (see Ezekiel 43:9).

19. For Hugh W. Nibley, see "What Is a Temple" in *Mormonism and Early Christianity,* in *CWHN*, 4:355–90. For Lundquist, see his doctoral dissertation, "Studies on the Temple in the Ancient Near East," University of Michigan, 1983, the chief parts of which have appeared in published form. See for example, Lundquist, "The Common Temple Ideology of the Ancient Near East," in *The Temple in Antiquity*, ed. Truman G. Madsen (Provo: BYU Religious Studies Center, 1984), 53–76; Lundquist, "The Legitimizing Role of the Temple in the Origin of the State," in *Society of Biblical Literature Seminar Papers* 21 (1982): 271–97; and Lundquist, "What Is a Temple? A Preliminary Typology," in *The Quest for the Kingdom of God: Studies in Honor of George E. Mendenhall*, ed. H. B. Huffmon, F. A. Spina, and A. R. W. Green (Winona Lake, Indiana: Eisenbrauns, 1983), 205–19. For Eliade, whose works have dealt with temple-related themes, such as sacred space, a definition of reality, the cosmic mountain, and others, see Douglas Allen and Dennis Doeing, *Mircea Eliade, An Annotated Bibliography* (New York: Garland Publishing, 1980). For Geo Widengren, who has produced a listing of the primary elements found in temple worship of the ancient Near East, see "Aspetti

simbolici dei templi e luoghi di culto del vicino oriente antico,"
Numen 7 (1960): 1–25, later summarized in his work *Religionsphänomenologie* (Berlin: Walter de Gruyter, 1969), 328–39.

20. See Lundquist's "What Is a Temple? A Preliminary Typology,"
in this volume, *Temples of the Ancient World*.

21. The nineteenth type, a contribution made by Mendenhall, is
summarized as follows: "The temple plays a legitimizing political
role in the ancient Near East" (Lundquist, "What Is a Temple?" 188),
or, "The ideology of kingship in the archaic state is indelibly and
incontrovertibly connected with temple building and with temple
ideology" (Lundquist, "The Legitimizing Role of the Temple," in this
volume, *Temples of the Ancient World*, 274–75).

22. The definition of *temple* is adapted from Lundquist, "The
Legitimizing Role of the Temple" and "What Is a Temple? A
Preliminary Typology."

23. For a treatment of gestures of approach, see Donald W. Parry,
"Ritual Anointing with Olive Oil," 275–78.

PART 1

Reflections on the Modern Temple

1

Christ Manifested to His People

Marion D. Hanks

My thanks to Dr. Cowan for his kind and generous introduction. I have nurtured similar feelings of appreciation for him and his significant contributions to the work over many years.

I am truly delighted to be with you this morning and really somewhat surprised to see that so many of you have braved the splendid snowstorm to attend this seminar. The schedule of substantive scholarly presentations planned for you following these opening remarks bodes well for fulfilling your hopes and expectations in coming.

Your energetic and conscientious chairman, Dr. Parry, directed me to an appropriate parking space, noting construction problems in nearer parking lots but assuring me it would be only a five-minute walk or so for one so energetic and young as I. With deep snow on slippery sidewalks and with shoes suited to sliding, it turned into a more Book of Mormon-like day-and-a-half journey for a Nephite. I was retrieved from a snowbank or two by generous students and stand before you this morning slightly damp and a scant red-eye airplane ride from the South Seas, where a few hours ago I was gazing upon a peaceful blue ocean with banyan and palm trees framing a beautiful scene of water and sky blending in bright sunshine.

Nonetheless, I am grateful to be here to express my

appreciation for temples and the blessing of worshiping and learning in them. I am grateful for students and scholars who pursue matters relevant to temple history and purpose and meaning, and who couple their searching with consistent temple *acquaintance* and temple *experience* and temple *worship*. This each must do if anything of significant value personally or to the work is to be accomplished through these labors.

Rufus Jones, Quaker teacher and mystic, wrote once of "two ways of dealing with the nature of things." He spoke of (1) the method of observation and description, the "spectator method," and (2) the method of "vital experience, the discovery of reality by *living your way* into the heart of things."[1]

Your subject matter for the day is of great interest to me, and I sincerely wish I could enjoy participation in every session. There is no concern in my soul about such search and discovery; there is encouragement in my heart for honest inquiry. But I do mean to emphasize that I believe, consistent with Rufus Jones's declared principles, that we need to be personally in touch with the spirit and blessing of *temple worship* while we learn all we can *about* temples and their historical meaning and purpose and importance.

We must always keep this in mind about a temple: The temple is the House of the Lord. He has accepted it as his house and promised that his name, his eye, and his heart would be in his temple perpetually. His power and Spirit may be felt there.

Why is a temple so important to us? What blessing is there for those who are spiritually and mentally attentive and sensitive in temple worship?

It is not my purpose this morning to consider at any length or in detail the theme perhaps most frequently related to the temple in the minds of many, the redemption of the dead. My special emphasis will be the blessings of the temple to the *living* who work and worship there.

Yet a thoughtful journey once more through the sense and sweetness of vicarious work in temples for the honored dead, particularly our own lineage, would be very good for the most knowledgeable or sophisticated among us. If commitment to Christ and his atoning love and his teachings is essential for all of God's children, and if God is loving and just, then some provision must be made in his plan for reaching and teaching those who died without knowing the truth and having a chance to comply with the commandments. The scriptures are clear and compelling. *No other answer* than gospel provision for family and temple work has been put forward by the religious world, the Christian "mainstream," to answer this critical question.

The effort to identify individually and do the work necessary to open the door for the dead to exercise their choices in matters of eternal progression is of great importance to us. But my attention this morning is centered in the *value and blessing* of temple work and worship *for the living*.

An excerpt from a well-known and honored statement from Elder John A. Widtsoe says:

> There is a feeling abroad that the benefits of the temple are primarily for the dead. This is not so. While the dead, if repentant, are able through our efforts to enter into a larger salvation, yet the work itself has a most beneficial effect upon the living who serve as proxies for the dead. . . . The response of the spirit of man to the ordinances of the House of the Lord stimulates every normal power and activity and helps greatly in the accomplishment of our daily tasks; more joy enters into the daily routine of life, . . . spiritual vision . . . love . . . peace

tempers the tempests of life, and we rise to higher levels of thought and action.[2]

President Gordon B. Hinckley adds, "Surely these temples are unique among all buildings. They are houses of instruction. They are places of covenants and promises. . . . In the sanctity of their appointments we commune with him and reflect on his Son, our Savior and Redeemer, the Lord Jesus Christ, who served as proxy for each of us in a vicarious sacrifice in our behalf."[3]

It is in this setting of instruction and reflection concerning our Lord, and thus our Heavenly Father, that we can, if we will, come to know them and to begin to glimpse our own eternal possibilities and present imperfections. Many of us who come to a temple to receive our own blessings bring "shallow vessels" to dip in the deep wells of our Lord; we walk with a certain bewilderment, many of us, but as we return on repeated occasions to serve others vicariously, even as he served us in ways we could not accomplish for ourselves, we begin to comprehend the meaning.

He "manifests himself" to us in his house (see D&C 109:5), and we come to revere him the more and to accept his invitation, extended to us as well as to the ancient people of this continent as he visited them after his resurrection: "Behold I am the light; I have set an example for you. . . . Therefore, hold up your light that it may shine unto the world. Behold I am the light which ye shall hold up— that which ye have seen me do" (3 Nephi 18:16, 24).

For me every proceeding and principle of the temple points to Christ, the only name given under heaven among men whereby we can be saved. Testimony is offered of the glory of the temple, of the transcendent and the supernal, and many experience some measure of the revelation, peace, thanksgiving, comfort, and faith to be enjoyed there.

Yet many who come turn away and never come again. That which is supposed to happen apparently, obviously, does not happen for them. Perhaps we could do more to prepare those who are missing the blessings.

Temple Building Commanded

In the dedicatory prayer of the first temple of this last dispensation, at Kirtland, Ohio, in 1836, a prayer revealed by God to the Prophet, it was noted that the "Lord God of Israel" had "commanded" them to build a house to his name (D&C 109:1–2). As it is recorded in section 124, verse 31, he later commanded them to build "a house unto me" in Nauvoo. In that same revelation it is noted, "For, for this cause I commanded Moses that he should build a tabernacle, that they should bear it with them in the wilderness, and to build a house in the land of promise, that those ordinances might be revealed which had been hid from before the world was" (verse 38).

The reference is, of course, (1) to the beautiful, small, portable structure fashioned under commandment in their wilderness wandering—a tabernacle, also called a "temple" and a "house of the Lord" in Samuel and elsewhere in scripture (1 Samuel 1:7, 9, 24; 3:3); and (2) to the first temple built by the Israelites in the promised land—called the Temple of Solomon. Other temple construction followed. Further, it is declared in the revelation that his people "are always commanded to build [temples] unto my holy name" (D&C 124:37–39). Temple work and worship are part of God's eternal plan and thus of the restored gospel!

The Order of the Temple Revealed

The Prophet Joseph recorded the restoration of temple understanding in his history of the Church. He notes that

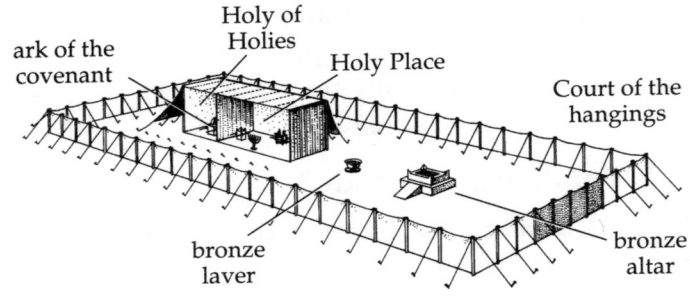

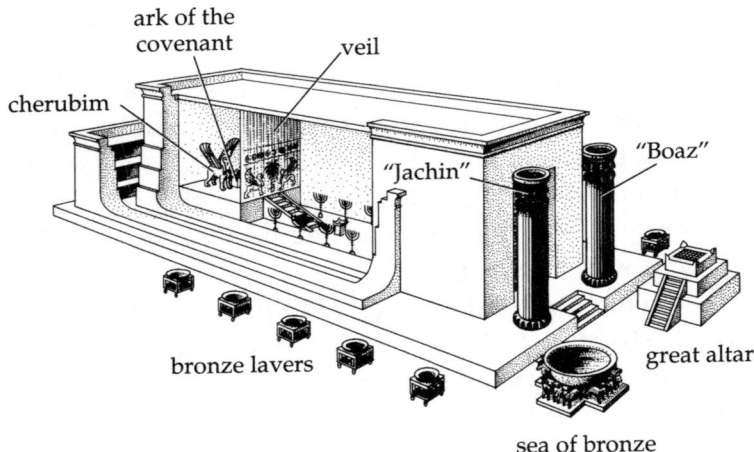

Figure 1. Top, the Tabernacle of Moses, also called the Tent of the Congregation. Bottom, the Temple of Solomon, which doubled the dimensions of the Tabernacle. (See Hebrews 8:5; 1 Chronicles 28:11–12, 19.)

he spent the day of Wednesday, May 4, 1842, in meetings in his private office above his store in Kirtland with a number of the brethren. He wrote that he was "instructing them in the principles and order of the Priesthood, attending to washings, anointings, endowments," and teaching of the keys pertaining to the Aaronic and Melchizedek Priesthood, and "setting forth the order pertaining to the Ancient of Days [Adam], and all those plans and principles by which any one is enabled to secure the fullness of those blessings which have been prepared for the Church of the First Born, and come up and abide in the presence of the Eloheim in the eternal worlds. *In this council was instituted the ancient order of things for the first time in these last days.*"[4]

He wrote that the truths taught that day to the brethren had been received by revelation and would be shared by all the Saints as they were prepared to receive them, in a place prepared to communicate them. It was urged therefore that "the Saints be diligent in building the Temple, and all houses which they have been, or shall hereafter be, commanded of God to build."[5]

Thus, in the day of restoration was declared anew the concern of the Almighty with temples and their availability and purposes. This was earlier expressed to Moses on the Mount (see Exodus 25:9, 40) and to David concerning the temple he intended and prepared to build but was prevented by the Lord from undertaking. His son Solomon was nominated to construct the temple instead, and David passed on to him the detailed pattern he had received *"by the spirit"* (1 Chronicles 28:12, italics added; see verses 2–3, 6, 11–12). Solomon's Temple was the product of this appointment by the Lord and instruction "by the spirit."

Revelation of Symbolic Meaning

The scriptures themselves bear a fascinating account of the communication of certain commandments and understanding to Adam and Eve after their expulsion from the Garden. In Moses, chapter 5, it is recorded that

Adam and Eve, his wife, called upon the name of the Lord, and they heard the voice of the Lord from the way

toward the Garden of Eden, speaking unto them, and
they saw him not; for they were shut out from his presence. And he gave unto them commandments, that they
should worship the Lord their God, and should offer the
firstlings of their flocks, for an offering unto the Lord.
And Adam was *obedient unto the commandments of the
Lord.*

And after many days an angel of the Lord appeared
unto Adam, saying: *Why dost thou offer sacrifices unto the
Lord?* And Adam said unto him: *I know not, save the Lord
commanded me.*

And then the angel spake, saying: This thing *is a
similitude of the sacrifice of the Only Begotten of the Father,*
which is full of grace and truth.Wherefore, thou shalt *do
all that thou doest in the name of the Son,* and thou shalt
repent and call upon God in the name of the Son forevermore.

And in that day the Holy Ghost fell upon Adam,
which beareth record of the Father and the Son, saying: I
am the Only Begotten of the Father from the beginning,
henceforth and forever, that as thou hast fallen *thou
mayest be redeemed, and all mankind, even as many as will*
(verses 4–9; italics added).

To this was added the exultation of spirit in Adam and
Eve as they expressed gratitude for their new and treasured
understanding of the plan and of their significant part in it
(see Moses 5:10–12), and the affirmation that "thus the
Gospel began to be preached, from the beginning. . . . And
thus all things were confirmed unto Adam, by an holy ordinance, and the Gospel preached, and a decree sent forth,
that it should be in the world, until the end thereof; and
thus it was" (Moses 5:58–59).

Thus temples do have strong *historical* roots; the building of them is *commanded;* and the meaning and even the
detail of them *revealed* (see Exodus 25:9, 39; 1 Chronicles
28:12). And as with Adam and Eve, the elements of temple

worship are *symbolic*, they are *covenant-centered*, and they bless us, as Adam and Eve learned, with the wonderful privilege of *association and instruction and education in the mission and in the principles of eternal progression central in the life of the Lord Jesus Christ*. It is with this latter point that I desire to be chiefly involved this morning.

House of Learning, Instruction, and Peace

The classic language of scripture as the Lord instructed his Saints to "establish a house" is powerful. The temple is declared to be a "house of prayer, a house of fasting, a house of faith, a house of *learning*, a house of glory, a house of order, a house of God" (D&C 88:119; 109:8; italics added). Then, in the revelation recorded in Doctrine and Covenants 97, it is declared that the Lord's House should be a "place of thanksgiving for all saints, and for a place of *instruction*" (verse 13; italics added). Anciently, the "Lord of Hosts" declared the temple to be a place where he "will . . . give peace" (Haggai 2:9).

As the scriptures *point us to the temple* and invite us to learn there, and what to learn, so does the temple *point us to scripture*. In the revealed dedicatory prayer of the Kirtland Temple is this petition: "And do thou grant, Holy Father, that all those who shall *worship* in this house may be taught words of wisdom *out of the best books*, and that they may seek *learning even by study*, and *also by faith*, as thou hast said" (D&C 109:14; italics added).

In a magnificent scriptural teaching perhaps less well known than some others, the story of Jonah and his love for the temple and its meaning in his life (and in ours if we choose) is made clear. Jonah has been called on a mission, which he tries to evade. When Jonah flees on a ship headed for Tarshish, his purpose is made known as the ship is about to founder, and he is cast into the sea and swallowed up by a "great fish," in which he remains for three days and three nights. The remarkable record in chapter 2 of Jonah is less known than this early story and the part that follows his being cast out upon dry ground and being called a second time to the mission that he has sought to avoid. I read to you the brief ten verses of Jonah chapter 2:

> Then Jonah prayed unto the Lord his God out of the fish's belly, and said, I cried by reason of mine affliction unto the Lord, and he heard me; out of the belly of hell cried I, and thou heardest my voice. For thou hadst cast me into the deep, in the midst of the seas; and the floods compassed me about: all thy billows and thy waves passed over me.
>
> Then I said, I am cast out of thy sight; yet *I will look again toward thy holy temple.* The waters compassed me about, even to the soul: the depth closed me round about, the weeds were wrapped about my head. I went down to the bottoms of the mountains; the earth with her bars was about me for ever: yet hast thou brought up my life from corruption, O Lord my God. When my soul fainted within me *I remembered the Lord: and my prayer came in unto thee, into thine holy temple.*
>
> They that observe lying vanities forsake their own mercy. But I will sacrifice unto thee with the voice of thanksgiving; *I will pay that that I have vowed.* Salvation is of the Lord (Jonah 2:1–9; italics added).

It is then recorded that "the Lord spake unto the fish, and it vomited out Jonah upon the dry land" (Jonah 2:10).

For Jonah the temple was a place where he, repentant, sorely repentant, could find comfort and forgiveness and mercy. It was to the temple that his thoughts turned in his dire need, and to his commitments to God in the temple, the vows that he had vowed. He looked to the temple for restoration and a spiritual future.

I love that whole story. I wish the moving part in it relevant to the temple were more broadly understood and shared.

A Place of Light

For my own self I add one other term of description and warmth to those noted: to me the temple is a *place of light* because it is the place, together with the scriptures, of our possibilities for a most fruitful relationship with the Lord Jesus Christ, and thus with his Father, whose will he came to do. He *taught* what he had heard from his Father, he said and *did* what he had seen his Father do, was *sent in his Father's name,* was perfectly unified in every way with his Father, and was one with the Father, even as he prayed that his disciples might be one with him and he with them. He declared that the Father was "in him" and prayed that in like manner he might be "in" the disciples: "I in them, and thou in me, that they may be made perfect in one; and that the world may know that thou hast sent me, and hast loved them, as thou hast loved me. . . . And I have declared unto them thy name, and will declare it: that the love wherewith thou hast loved me may be in them, and I *in* them" (John 17:23, 26; italics added).

Not only did he plead for those whom he had called to serve and sacrifice with him, but for all who should believe on him through them. His plea was that they all might be one as he and the Father were one (see John 17:20–23).

He was not, of course, praying for the loss of their individuality or identity, any more than he was suggesting that about himself. He was praying for them to have the perfect unity enjoyed by him and his Father. As he began the powerful petition to his Father that is sometimes called the "great intercessory prayer," Jesus reaffirmed with his Father that he had given him power to "give eternal life," this "greatest of the gifts of God," to those for whom he had stewardship. "And this is life eternal," he said, "that they might know thee the only true God, and Jesus Christ, whom thou hast sent" (John 17:3).

One of the most significant and satisfying blessings of temple worship is the clear affirmation of the relationship of the Father and the Son. The *scriptures* teach this truth plainly. The vision of Joseph Smith clarified for us once and for all their uniqueness and individuality. And the *temple* fully attests this monumental truth and leaves no doubt about their complete unity. They are one in character and quality, in purpose, in their work and glory. So perfect is their spiritual maturity, so perfect their unity, that if one speaks, it is as if the other spoke. Thus Christ comes *in the Father's name,* saying, "I and my Father are one" (John 10:30); yet he declared that "my Father is greater than I" (John 14:28).

The First Presidency and Twelve in a doctrinal exposition in 1916, during the presidency of Joseph F. Smith, made a declaration that is helpful in our understanding: "In all His dealings with the human family Jesus the Son has represented and yet represents Elohim His Father in power and authority. . . . Thus the Father placed His name upon the Son; and Jesus Christ spoke and ministered in and through the Father's name; and . . . His words and acts were and are those of the Father."[6]

The Mission of the Church

All of us are conscious I trust of President Benson's forceful declaration at the conclusion of the April 1988 general conference of the mission of the Church "to invite all to come unto Christ." His concluding statement was, "May we all go to our homes rededicated to the sacred mission of the Church as so beautifully set forth in these conference sessions—to 'invite all to come unto Christ' (D&C 20:59), 'yea, come unto Christ; and be perfected in him' (Moroni 10:32)."[7]

The mission of the Church is glorious, to invite all of us to come unto Christ through proclaiming the gospel, perfecting our lives, and redeeming our dead. As we come unto Christ, we bless our own lives, those of our families, and our Father in Heaven's other children, both living and dead.

Recall the words of the Lord: "For I will raise up unto myself a pure people, that will serve me in righteousness" (D&C 100:16). In explanation of the process of purification and sanctification, the Lord gave these remarkably pertinent words for those who seek to understand the meaning and value of a temple:

> Therefore, sanctify yourselves that your minds become single to God, and the days will come that you shall see him; for he will unveil his face unto you, and it shall be in his own time, and in his own way, and according to his own will. . . . And I give unto you, who are the first laborers in this last kingdom, a commandment that you assemble yourselves together, and organize yourselves, and prepare yourselves, and sanctify yourselves; yea, purify your hearts, and cleanse your hands and your feet before me, that I may make you clean (D&C 88:68, 74).

This responsibility to purify, to sanctify themselves, was wonderfully accomplished under difficult conditions of persecution and affliction in the time of Helaman and his son Nephi: "Nevertheless they did fast and pray oft, and did wax stronger and stronger in their humility, and firmer and firmer in the faith of Christ, unto the filling their souls with joy and consolation, yea, even to the purifying and the sanctification of their hearts, which sanctification cometh because of their yielding their hearts unto God" (Helaman 3:35).

As the mission of the Church is to "invite all to come unto Christ," so I believe, in its clearest and loveliest sense, that this is *also the mission of temples*, where we not only undertake the sacred service of work for redemption of the dead, to open the door for them, but where the choicest of all opportunities exists to learn of Christ, and to come to know him and commune with him and to purify our own hearts.

It is also the setting where the messengers who go forth to proclaim the gospel are meant to be prepared: "And we ask thee, Holy Father, that thy servants may go forth from this house armed with thy power, and that thy name may be upon them, and thy glory be round about them, and thine angels have charge over them; and from this place they may bear exceedingly great and glorious tidings, in truth, unto the ends of the earth, that they may know that this is thy work, and that thou hast put forth thy hand, to fulfil that which thou hast spoken by the mouths of the prophets, concerning the last days" (D&C 109:22–23).

The perfecting of the Saints is one of those functions through which we come unto Christ. I believe that the temple provides the best of all settings for the purification and sanctification process basic in the perfection of the Saints. Recall the moving direction of the Lord to the early leaders noted in the verses above and note also the power and promise of section 109:11–13:

> In a manner that we may be found worthy, in thy sight, to secure a fulfilment of the promises which thou hast made unto us, thy people, in the revelations given unto us; that thy glory may rest down upon thy people,

and upon this thy house, which we now dedicate to thee, that it may be sanctified and consecrated to be holy, and that thy *holy presence may be continually in this house;* and that all people who shall enter upon the threshold of the Lord's house may feel thy power, and feel constrained to acknowledge that thou hast sanctified it, and that it is thy house, a place of thy holiness (italics added).

Elder John A. Widtsoe blessed us with a beautiful statement about these verses and Doctrine and Covenants 110:7–8:

It is a great promise that to the temples God will come, and that in them man shall see God. What does this promised communion mean? Does it mean that once in a while God may come into the temples, and that once in a while the pure in heart may see God there; or does it mean the larger thing, that the pure in heart who go into the temples may there, by the Spirit of God, always have a wonderful rich communion with God? I think that is what it means to me and to you and to most of us. We have gone into these holy houses, with our minds freed from the ordinary earthly cares, and have literally felt the presence of God. In this way the temples are always places where God manifests himself to man and increases his intelligence. A temple is a place of revelation.[8]

Only through Christ

I well recall one of the first anxious and earnest conversations with a temple attender after my service as temple president began in the Salt Lake Temple. A very thoughtful young lady had read through the relevant verses concerning the function of the temple as a house of learning and of instruction. She was perceptive enough to recognize that to know God and Christ, "the only true God, and Jesus Christ, whom thou hast sent," is "life eternal" (John 17:3). She knew also that we learn to know our Father and ultimately

return to him *through Christ*. All the standard works so
teach. For instance:

> Redemption cometh in and through the Holy
> Messiah; for he is full of grace and truth. Behold he offer-
> eth himself a sacrifice for sin, to answer the ends of the
> law, unto all those who have a broken heart and a con-
> trite spirit; and unto none else can the ends of the law be
> answered. Wherefore, how great the importance to make
> these things known unto the inhabitants of the earth, that
> they may know that there is *no flesh that can dwell in the*
> *presence of God, save it be through the merits, and mercy, and*
> *grace of the Holy Messiah*, who layeth down his life accord-
> ing to the flesh, and taketh it again by the power of the
> Spirit, that he may bring to pass the resurrection of the
> dead, being the first that should rise (2 Nephi 2:6–8; italics
> added).

> Jesus saith unto him, I am the way, the truth, and the
> life: *no man cometh unto the Father, but by me* (John 14:6;
> italics added).

My testimony to her was that for me *everything* in the
temple points ultimately to Christ and to our Father. The
efficacy of the ordinances and covenants is in his atoning
love and delegated authority—the authority of "the Holy
Priesthood, after the order of the Son of God" (D&C 107:3).
But she had not yet made a clear connection in her own
mind and heart *how temple worship can become a critical key to*
knowing the Lord.

Christ, Scriptures, Temple, Home

And where do we learn of Christ? It is written that all of
the prophets understood and testified of him. For instance:

> Behold, my soul delighteth in proving unto my
> people the truth of the coming of Christ; for, for this end
> hath the law of Moses been given; and *all things which*

have been given of God from the beginning of the world, unto man, are the typifying of him (2 Nephi 11:4).

I said unto him: Believest thou the scriptures? And he said, Yea.

And I said unto him: Then ye do not understand them; for they truly testify of Christ. Behold, I say unto you that none of the prophets have written, nor prophesied, save they have spoken concerning this Christ. And this is not all—it has been made manifest unto me, for I have heard and seen; and it also has been made manifest unto me by the power of the Holy Ghost; wherefore, I know if there should be no atonement made all mankind must be lost (Jacob 7:10–12).

Where do we learn of him and thus of the Father? My answer is through prayer, through the scriptures, and through the temple.

The first, prayer, is personal and can be understood only through the *practice* of prayer. The second, scripture study, is also personal, and can be realized only through earnest effort and searching and studying and pondering. The home, with the assistance of Church instruction and the sacrament, should offer the greatest assistance and strength in these undertakings. "Therefore, go ye unto your homes, and ponder upon the things which I have said, and ask of the Father, in my name, that ye may understand, and prepare your minds for the morrow, and I come unto you again" (3 Nephi 17:3).

The temple is of utmost importance in providing the setting for purifying and therefore sanctifying ourselves, which, as we learn about Christ, can lead us to that personal knowledge of him and witness of him that lead to the most precious of life's gifts. In learning and appreciating the principles upon which his holy life was based, the path of principle which he trod, we can truly appreciate his sacred gift, his atoning death, and the pattern of his holy life.

How can this be accomplished in the temple? Note the yearning of the Psalmist thousands of years ago: "One thing have I desired of the Lord, that will I seek after; that I may dwell in the house of the Lord all the days of my life, to behold the beauty of the Lord, and to enquire in his temple" (Psalm 27:4).

The ancient worshiper wanted to be worthy of being in the temple—perhaps the equivalent of qualifying worthily for a temple recommend and being permitted to attend regularly in our time—where for him then there were two marvelous blessings and privileges: (1) to behold the beauty of the Lord and (2) to inquire in his holy temple. In complete consistency with this wish, and in fulfillment of it, was the declaration in the revelation of the Kirtland Temple dedicatory prayer that temples are provided in order that "the Son of Man might . . . manifest himself to his people" (D&C 109:5). Temple learning and worship can be the university of eternal life through Jesus Christ. In the prayer of dedication at Kirtland, this petition was offered to the Lord: "Do thou grant, Holy Father, that all those who shall worship in this house may be taught words of wisdom . . . ; and that they may grow up in thee, and receive a fulness of the Holy Ghost (D&C 109:14–15).

Is this accomplished by ceremonies and ritual? Yes, in part, if we understand the purpose, the symbolism, even as Adam and Eve were brought to understand it in the earliest days of mortality. But basically we learn through the *substance* of the message, the principles of eternal progression, of eternal life. It is around a few simple principles that we make covenants with the Lord. All who understand the temple declare them to be of highest importance in our eternal journey back into the presence of Deity. Recall Paul's statement to the Romans that we are reconciled to God by Christ's death, and saved "by his life" (Romans 5:10). To me this says that the principles of his holy life lead us to that fullness of salvation known as exaltation—loving, learning, serving, growing, *creative life* on a Godly level with loved ones and with the Father and the Son. In the temple we can learn to live as Christ lived on earth and as he and the Father live.

Central Principles of Christ's Life

What are those principles which are central in his life that are taught in the temple and that relate to the covenants we make with the Lord? He came, he said, *to do the will of his Father.* Many times he repeated this concept, including those moments in Gethsemane, as he approached the cross, when he prayed that if it be possible, this cup might pass from him, but that nevertheless the will of the Father be done and not his own. His life was geared to *giving,* in the pattern of his Father. God so loved that he gave; Christ so loved that he gave. To serve, to share, to offer the supreme example of unselfishness, even at the cross—this was central in his life.

He *loved* in a way that perhaps only he and the Father really yet understand. But we are here to learn that, to learn to love enough to give. On battlefields and in hospital rooms and in the quiet heroic circumstances of unselfish devotion to parent or child, it has been demonstrated for me that there are people who have learned truly to love and sacrifice in his way.

Of his *loyalty,* his *fidelity,* the *purity of his life,* there is no question, nor is there any question about our own responsibility to be true and faithful, to learn through heartache and heartbreak to purify our hearts as we purify our lives in order *that he may save us.* For him, to *seek first the kingdom of his Father* was the motivating and directing power of his life. He laid it all on the line, he who could have called legions of angels to his side, he who had all power given him in heaven and in earth.

The Holy Exemplar

These principles are taught in the temple; perhaps there remains only a question or two to be asked. Who of all who ever lived, of all whom we know, was the highest and holiest exemplar of these principles? Who in any measure, like he, faithfully did the will of his Father at all costs, served and shared and loved and gave without stint, was without sin, totally loyal to his commission and his commitments; who "being reviled, reviled not"; and who laid everything on the line for the work, for the Father and the Father's children?

Ultimately in a temple we kneel at a sacred altar and there covenant and, in the manner of temple symbolism, once more have our attention pointed toward him and how he died, how much he had to love God's children to suffer what he suffered for us.

For me there is no way to conceive a better and more glorious learning opportunity than the temple provides. The scriptures are full of these remarkable instructions and his holy example. Yet in the temple there is distilled in a simple way in a few moments the essence of the pattern of his holy life. We are in fact reconciled to God through his redeeming and atoning death, and we are saved in the highest and holiest sense by following the pattern of the pure and wholesome principles that were the heart of his life.

In Moroni 7 we read some of Mormon's instructions to

his son: "Charity is the pure love of Christ, and it endureth forever; and whoso is found possessed of it at the last day, it shall be well with him. Wherefore, my beloved brethren, pray unto the Father with all the energy of heart, that ye may be filled with this love, which he hath bestowed upon all who are true followers of his Son, Jesus Christ; that ye may become the sons of God; that *when he shall appear we shall be like him,* for we shall see him as he is; that we may have this hope; *that we may be purified even as he is pure"* (Moroni 7:47–48; italics added).

What Outcome?

There is yet another question to be asked as we rejoice in what we learn about the Father and the Son and the plan of life. What should happen to us through the experience of temple going and temple understanding and temple worship?

In Doctrine and Covenants 109:15 is one powerful answer: through temple worship we can grow up in the Lord, receive a fullness of the Holy Ghost, organize our lives according to his laws, and be prepared to obtain every needful thing. Other answers relate to the first and second great commandments and our mature growth in them. The parable of the sheep and the goats taught in Matthew 25:31–46 and a host of consistent and supportive scriptures emphasize the vital place of our efforts to help those who have needs. The temple should strengthen our preparation to receive the gifts of his atoning love (see D&C 88:32, 33) and to follow his example in caring for the downtrodden and needy.

In short, in the temple we learn the path of principle of which he was the glorious Exemplar. "Ye shall pray for them, and shall not cast them out; and if it so be that they come unto you oft ye shall pray for them unto the Father, in my name. Therefore, hold up your light that it may shine unto the world. Behold *I am the light which ye shall hold up— that which ye have seen me do*" (3 Nephi 18:23–24; italics added).

The Kind of People We Are

What really matters is the kind of people we are, the kind of people we become as we return to the temple to serve others and to ponder our own progress in the principles that were critical in his life—to learn and do the will of the Father, to serve and share, to love and mercifully give and forgive, to be loyal, to be clean and pure, to give to his work whatever we are privileged to give. In short, the mature experience of temple worship ideally has the power to produce—and sometimes does—a new and different kind of person who knows the path of principles followed by the Savior and gives them application in his or her personal life.

Love is more than a word or a feeling: "My little children, let us not love in word, neither in tongue; but in deed and in truth" (1 John 3:18). Brotherhood and sisterhood go beyond the desire to be kind and considerate. Good intentions, given light and life by association with the pattern of the Savior's example, by the spirit of concern and kindness taught and felt in the temple, do make a difference in many lives.

The Heart of the Gospel

As we choose and follow a course of giving, of caring, of graciousness and kindness, we come to understand that this is not an optional element of the gospel, it is the heart of it. Decency and honor, unselfishness, good manners and good taste are expected of us. What really matters, after all, is *what kind of people we are,* what we are willing to give and do "more than others." This we decide daily, hourly, as we learn and accept the direction of the Lord.

After the crucifixion, resurrection, and ascension of the Savior, something happened to the surviving disciples, led by Peter, who in a time of stress had failed him. Pentecost occurred—the coming of the Spirit—and those who had wavered stood strong in testimony and testifying. Periodically they were detained and brought before the "council." They were warned, threatened, beaten, and released. Chapters 1 to 5 of the book of Acts tell the story. The last verses of chapter 5 have dramatic impact. Gamaliel has intervened with his associates to give the disciples another chance, a little more time. So they are warned again to cease teaching and preaching Christ, are beaten once more, and released. The record says they departed the premises rejoicing that they were found worthy to suffer for Christ's sake. Then, "daily in the temple, and in every house, they ceased not to teach and preach Jesus Christ" (Acts 5:42).

In like manner something should happen *to us* as we depart the temple in the spirit of 3 Nephi 17:3: "Therefore, go ye unto your homes, and ponder upon the things which I have said, and ask of the Father, in my name, that ye may understand, and prepare your minds for the morrow, and I come unto you again."

A purifying spirit can cause us, acquainted now in a special way with the path followed and lighted by the Lord—and loving him—to be new persons, practicing love and brotherhood, rallying to the will of the Lord, serving, sharing, loving, loyal to wholesome standards, seeking first the kingdom of God.

We need to purify our family lives and make our homes places where we "teach and preach" Jesus Christ daily but follow him always. Our homes, our families, our individual lives should become centers of learning, centers of unselfishness and service. In the words of Rufus Jones, "Saints are not made for haloes and for inward thrills. They are made to become focus points of light and power. The true saint is a good mother, a good neighbor, a good constructive force in society, a fragrance and a blessing. The true saint is a dynamic Christian who exhibits in some definite spot the type of life which is fully realized in heaven."[9]

To conclude, consider again what to me is a clear and forceful key to the meaning of temples and temple worship. The Lord revealed to the Prophet Joseph Smith in 1836 the prayer that was offered at the dedication of the Kirtland, Ohio, Temple. The prayer became section 109 of the Doctrine and Covenants. For me it remains the standard and remarkable example of dedicatory prayers. One who sincerely desires to understand basic temple meaning could well read it over and over, especially its first touching, powerful two dozen verses. Verse 5 is a beautiful statement that merits deep consideration: "For thou knowest that we have done this work through great tribulation; and out of our poverty we have given of our substance to build a house to thy name, *that the Son of Man might have a place to manifest himself to his people*" (D&C 109:5; italics added).

How does he manifest himself to his people in the temple?

Chiefly, I believe, through the beauty and compelling cogency of temple principles, ordinances, and covenants, through temple worship—through the spirit of revelation and other blessings of the Spirit available there for those whose minds and hearts are in tune, and who are patient and anxious to learn and to move their own lives toward Christlike ideals (see 3 Nephi 27:21, 27).

One example may suffice in illustrating the spiritual strength that comes to those who persevere in the service of the Lord in temples. I came into the temple one morning about 4:30 A.M., grateful to have been able to plow through heavy snow from our home to get there. In a secluded room, sitting thoughtfully as he leaned forward on his cane, I chanced upon an older, deeply admired friend. Like I, he was dressed in white, temple workers' white. I greeted him cheerily and inquired what he was doing there at that hour of the morning.

He said, "You know what I am doing here, President Hanks. I am an ordinance worker here to fulfill my assignment."

"I do know that," I said, "but I am wondering how you got here through the snow storm. I just heard on the radio that Parley's Canyon is closed to all traffic, indeed barricaded."

He said, "I have a four-wheeler that will climb trees."

I said, "So do I, or I would not be here, and I live only a few miles away."

I then asked him how he had managed to get through the barricades that the news announcements had said were in place in the canyon. His answer was not atypical of this rancher/stake president whom I had first seen as a robust, strong man astride his horse when I spent an afternoon with him prior to stake conference meetings. Arthritis and age had literally shrunk him now and would soon take his life. He had much pain in moving about. His answer that morning was, "Now, President Hanks, I have known those highway officers, many of them, since they were born. They know I must get through and that if necessary I might try

to go overland! They also know my truck and my experience, and they just move their barricades if they need to."

He was there, faithful and loyal at that hour of the
morning, to begin his sacred work. It is such individuals
with such faith and devotion that temples help to develop.
For this all of us should be forever grateful.

Notes

1. Rufus Jones, *Rufus Jones Speaks to Our Time* (New York:
Macmillan, 1961), 111.

2. John A. Widtsoe, "Beginning of Modern Temple Work,"
Improvement Era 30 (Oct. 1927): 1079.

3. Gordon B. Hinckley, *Temples of The Church of Jesus Christ of
Latter-day Saints* (Salt Lake City: Ensign Press, 1988), 5.

4. *HC*, 5:1–2; italics added.

5. Ibid., 2.

6. "The Father and the Son: A Doctrinal Exposition by the First
Presidency and the Twelve," as quoted in James E. Talmage, *Articles
of Faith* (Salt Lake City: Deseret Book Company, 1982), 424–25.

7. Ezra Taft Benson, "Come unto Christ, and Be Perfected in Him,"
Ensign 18 (May 1988): 84.

8. John A. Widtsoe, "Temple Worship," *Utah Genealogical and
Historical Magazine* 12 (April 1921): 56.

9. *Rufus Jones Speaks*, 199.

2

A House of Glory

Hugh W. Nibley

There are many aspects of the temple that we could talk about; some of these may be freely discussed in public, others may not.[1] But we seem to forget that for over one hundred fifty years the Church has published, proclaimed, and circulated the most enlightening treatment of the subject, and to this no one seems to pay any attention. That is the dedicatory prayer of the Kirtland Temple. Let us briefly analyze Section 109 of the Doctrine and Covenants.

Verses 1–4. The temple has been built by express command as a means of administering salvation to the children of men. The Saints have responded, and as the Lord has called them, they now call upon the Lord. We are never passive in these matters, and here the Prophet initiates the next action. In our dealings with the Lord we are expected to move of our own volition: "Ask, and it shall be given you; seek, and ye shall find; knock, and it shall be opened unto you" (Matthew 7:7). Or, as the Jews say, there must be a stirring below before there can be a stirring above; one does not ask a blessing over an empty table. The temple exists for training us: What kind of house can we build you, asks Solomon at the dedication of his temple, since the heaven is your throne and the earth is your footstool?

But let us get down to business.

Verse 5. First of all, the temple is a place in which God

Figure 2. These 1870 photographs (above and facing page) are among the earliest known photographs of the Kirtland Temple. The School of the Prophets met together in the attic story.

manifests himself, a place of appointment, a meeting place. You will go to the tabernacle, the Lord says to Moses, "and there I will meet with thee" (Exodus 25:22; cf. 29:42). When Jesus manifested himself to all the apostles after the Resurrection, he arranged ahead of time, as he instructed Mary and as the angel instructed some of the apostles, that they should all meet him at a certain time in Galilee (see Matthew 28:7, 10, 16; Mark 16:7). So the temple is where the people come together at a particular prescribed time and place. The next question is, what people?

Verse 6. The answer is all the Saints in "solemn assembly." This makes them a special society that is to initiate the work of bringing all things together—a sort of grand unifying theory toward which all the sciences seem to be looking today, bringing everything together in one. It is in the

Figure 3. This photograph shows the western end of the Lower Court and the pulpits of the Melchizedek Priesthood. The hinged sacrament table at the front is raised, and the rollers for the privacy veils can be seen on the ceiling. It was on Sunday, 3 April 1836, after the sacrament was passed and the veils were lowered, that Joseph Smith and Oliver Cowdery beheld the great vision of the Savior (see D&C 110).

temple we are taught expressly that all truth may be encompassed within a single whole.

Verse 7. They are to bring their brains with them. That is the first qualification, that your brain and intellect may be clear and active. For they are here to *seek* diligently, to *seek* out of the best books, to *seek* learning. This is our initiative. We are to "teach one another words of wisdom; . . . [to] seek learning even by study and also by faith." And from what sources? Out of the best books? Where is the list? Why no syllabus? Because we are to do the seeking. It is we who must decide which are the best books, and to do that we must "prove all things [and] hold fast that which is good"

(1 Thessalonians 5:21). We must make our own syllabus as part of organizing ourselves and preparing "every needful thing," as it expressly tells us in the next verse. The temple is to be a place of study and learning, a school of real mental discipline. The temple marks the universal meeting place of all great societies. It is actually the source of everything that makes civilization.[2]

Verse 8. First of all, it is a *house of prayer*. That is most important—to make your cosmic connections and establish lines of communication with intelligence greater than ours. The main function of the temple is to supply a binding link between the worlds. Without that, it is nothing but a civic social center or a senior citizens' club.

Next it is a *house of fasting*. Fasting is the most effective way to slacken the grasp of this telestial world on the mind and to move toward another ambience. To fast is to do without some normal necessities; your everyday considerations must be put aside because you will be doing other things that require a totally different mind-set. To fast is to disengage from the temporal and wasteful activities of the "real world."

It is a *house of faith*. Without that, those who go through the motions are hypocrites, as the Lord told the Jews in the temple: "Destroy this temple and in three days I will raise it up" (John 2:19)—that would test their faith as to whether it was really God's house. You find yourself in the temple on faith, not exactly sure whether all this is real or whether your work will be accepted, though I must say that in the temple more than anywhere else my doubts disintegrate.

Next, it is a *house of learning*. Is this a surprise? If we are supposed to be studying and teaching diligently, thinking deeply, we must have something to think about, as well as something to show for our mental effort. That is called

learning. We are suspicious of too much learning in the
Church Educational System where it is viewed as "unspiri-
tual," but if anyone was ever more passionately dedicated
than Brigham Young to learning all he possibly could about
everything he possibly could, it was Joseph Smith.

It is also a *house of glory*. This must come next in order.
And what is glory? How do you generate that intangible
quantity? Glory, we are told, is intelligence (see D&C 93:36).
Can we be more specific? That says it all, but what is intelligence? Intelligence is defined as problem-solving ability,
i.e., intelligence is as intelligence does. What problem does
it solve? It is the supremely difficult problem of endowing
weak and foolish man with immortality and eternal life.
God says this is his "work and [his] glory—to bring to pass
the immortality and eternal life of man" (Moses 1:39)—that
we return to his presence and with him partake of eternal
life and exaltation. Since his glory is intelligence, he shares it
with us. Glory is shared intelligence. The temple is certainly
the place for that.

Order comes next. What crimes have been committed in
its name! We have noted that the temple is a place of disci-
plined thought and action, but regimentation? When I ask
what the temple teaches me, the answer is loud and clear:
to control my actions. That is self-discipline and that is what
I promise to exercise with every covenant. The law of sacrifice requires me to do things I could more easily not do; the
law of the gospel requires self-control in everyday situations, avoiding the same unseemly acts as are condemned
in the instructions of the Dead Sea Scrolls, such as laughing
too loudly, gossiping, and immodest dress. That chastity is
nothing but self-control needs no argument. And the hardest of all, the law of consecration, can only be faced against
sore temptation, and still confronts us with unresolved

dilemmas. What I promise to do with every covenant is to order my life and, specifically, as it is fully laid out in the Book of Moses for all the world to see, to do all that I do in the name of the Son, to "repent and call upon God in the name of the Son forevermore" (Moses 5:8). Note that the covenant is between me and the Father. I am to order my life, and no one else is to do it for me; the only judge of my behavior is the Father. Only the two of us know how I really qualify in this. We establish our agreement in the temple because it is a *house of God*. He takes over completely. It is in no sense an ordinary house. This should be borne in mind at all times, even to the forgetting of time and place.

Verse 9. This makes the temple a very special place set off from the world. When you enter and leave, you pass from one sphere to another. "That your incomings may be in the name of the Lord, that your outgoings may be in the name of the Lord, that all your salutations may be in the name of the Lord, with uplifted hands unto the Most High." This is not rhetoric, it is very clear. The raised hands announce your entering and leaving the sacred place. They are a sign of recognition, as well as of praise. Common courtesy even in ordinary society demands signs of polite recognition upon entering or leaving a company. Like a military salute whenever the general enters and leaves, everyone rises and salutes and he salutes too, announcing their presence to each other and getting down to business. Hence, all these greetings are "unto the Most High" for *He* is the General, *He* is the one in command. This puts everything into perspective. The next verse makes this clear.

Verse 10. "We ask thee to assist us . . . in calling our solemn assembly, that it may be done to thine honor and to thy divine acceptance." Things must not subside into everyday routine, the light of common day. People in the temple are aware of something unusual, something definitely more than mere formal or offhand routine. This requires a discipline and concentration that may try our capacity, and so we ask God to assist us in it, in this common effort between the worlds.

Verse 11. This is made clear in the *manner* in which things are carried out. The state of mind is all-important. President Joseph F. Smith said that much temple work would likely have to be done over again because of the slip-shod manner in which it was done.[3] The day before yesterday I got his meaning when I enjoyed participating in just one initiatory ordinance. It was performed in such an off-hand and perfunctory manner that I told one of the officiators that if I had not known the words by heart, I could not have understood a word he was saying.

Verse 12. The basic meaning of "sanctified" and "consecrated"—*hagios, kadosh, sanctus,* holy, etc.,—is "fenced off from the world." That is the permanent condition of the temple: "that thy holy presence may be *continually* in this house." Many holy places are open to secular use throughout the year except during the formal set times of assembly and celebration. Not so with the temple; there everything that happens is removed from the everyday world.

Verse 13. All people feel *power* at the threshold of the Lord's house; it "constrains" them. It is something not self-induced. Throughout history temples have enlisted the aid of incense, dance, mantras, drums, drugs, hypnosis, exhausting fasts, processions, tapers, stunning architectural settings, etc., to convince their devotees of supernatural forces. In the temple the Word of Wisdom alone secures stone-cold sobriety. John Chrysostom warned against all such stimulants, including paintings and images, as imposing an artificial discipline on the church and striving for theatrical and emotional effect. You cannot see, hear, smell, taste, or touch power, but you can feel it, and you cannot deny what you feel, nor can you prove it to anyone else. Is not all feeling awareness of an indefinable energy? St. Augustine urged the Christians to stop depending on promptings of the Spirit because they were too vague, unpredictable, and beyond our control, and suggested putting in their place office and ceremony, "forms and observances," which can be directed and employed at will.[4]

Verse 14. After these initiatory statements we get down to business: what do we *do* in the temple? Answer: We are "taught words of wisdom out of the best books," we "seek learning even by study, and also by faith, as *thou* hast said." But do we do that in the temple? Apparently we do, for this is equivalent to "worship in this house." The School of the Prophets was held in the temple. Central to all great temples was the great library. The temple is definitely a school, a very high school of intense study, as temples in the past have been. It was in the temple that the child Jesus astounded the wise men with his knowledge of scripture. Study is personal, but your own thoughts that may be helpful to others should be exchanged as you "teach one another"—learning is a two-way process. Lest you be keeping something of value locked in your bosom, the temple gives you the opportunity to share what excites you. The classic words for school are *schole* and *ludus;* both have the basic meaning of play and denote a place of liberal education, where we do not concern ourselves with the business of making a living but are free to sit down, relax, and exchange ideas.

Verse 15. This verse is the classic statement of the purpose of education: "And that they may *grow*," but here a special kind of growth: to "grow up in thee, and receive a fulness of the Holy Ghost, and be organized according to thy laws, and be prepared to obtain every needful thing." Growth, fulness, organization, not organization for organization's sake, but to expedite "obtain[ing] every needful thing." To do this we are instructed to stay alert, pay attention, and to come often. We are not to sit like bags of sand but to receive a fulness—nothing left out, "every needful thing," in short, all that one is able to receive. The Lord has much to say about fulness. If I could do more than I am doing, or carry more than I am carrying, and learn more than I am learning, etc., I am quite literally rejecting the fulness. This is a situation ominously set forth in 3 Nephi 16:10–12, where, speaking of the church in our day, the Lord says, "If they . . . shall reject the fulness of my gospel, behold, saith the Father, I will bring the fulness of my gospel from among them . . . and I will bring my gospel unto them"—i.e., another branch of Israel, the descendants of Lehi. Is the phasing out or neglecting of certain temple activities a rejection of the fulness? That is not for me to decide.

Verse 16. The next verse recapitulates: A house of prayer, of fasting, of faith, of glory, of God. These things all belong together. They are steps to exaltation; the ordinances mark distinct degrees or steps. This concept of *gradus ad Parnassum* is the root of civilization.

Verses 17–19. With incomings and outgoings in the name of the Lord and salutations with holy hands uplifted, we find ourselves in a very special society; here we are really entering into things. All temples are marked by boundaries, stations, levels, doors, stairs, passages, gates, veils, etc.—they all denote rites of passage going from one condition or state to another, from lower to higher, from dark to light, a complete transition from one world, telestial

Figure 4. A scene from Mozart's *Magic Flute,* in which a priest leads Prince Tamino to his trials. The opera portrays several motifs familiar to Latter-day Saint audiences, such as temple instruction concerning the meaning of life and initiation to become like the gods.

or terrestrial, to another, ultimately the celestial. At certain crucial passages one must identify oneself by an exchange of names and tokens and show oneself qualified by an exchange of words. This was characteristic of all ancient temples. It is the origin of the Hermetic tradition, which comes down to us in such altered but interesting forms as Free Masonry and such fanciful presentations as the *Magic Flute,* in which Mormon audiences recognize familiar motifs.

Verses 20–21. No unclean thing is permitted to come into the House and pollute it. Uncleanness and pollution, as we are increasingly aware today, are not only unpleasant but dangerous. One of the most striking doctrines of the Egyptian temple and funerary literature is that "pollution" is the name of the telestial world. We live in pollution. We take from the terrestrial world, the world as God made it, only what we find wholesome, pure, and delicious—"of every tree of the garden thou mayest freely eat" (Genesis 2:16). But what do we make of it? What do we return to the earth? Sewage!

In these verses we see the two-fold function of the temple. It repels evil and pollution of the carnal world, like Teflon, while at the same time it exercises a gravitational pull upon transgressors, an urge to "clean up their act," to wit, to "repent and return . . . and be restored." The suggestion of the expanding or contracting universe, the ever-conflicting and creative functions of radiation and gravitation are reinforced in the next verse.

Verse 22. Here we see the temple like some supernova, expanding irresistibly in all directions as "thy servants . . . go forth from this house armed with thy power, and that thy name may be upon them, and thy glory be round about them, and thine angels have charge over them"; i.e., the angels are there to supervise the operation, keeping everything running properly—an ancient Jewish and Christian teaching.

Verse 23. The great expansion goes out to the limits of time and space "unto the ends of the earth," bearing "exceedingly great and glorious tidings . . . that thou hast put forth thy hand, to fulfil that which thou hast spoken."

Verses 24–28. Meantime, in this world it must serve as a fortress, a "safe house," sheltered place or marshaling area—note the buttresses and battlements and the garden walls of all our older temples. The security is guaranteed by God himself, who will both decide and execute whatever smiting and fighting needs to be done. We have neither the time nor the energy to engage in combat, and contention has been strictly forbidden in all circumstances. All the world has felt a sort of unassailable aloofness about our temples.

Verse 29. The state of the opposition is to be one of astonishment and confusion. The work is bound to invite comments and vicious fictions. This part of the prophecy has been fulfilled strangely, no matter what position the Church has found itself in—it seems that as long as the project goes forward, it will excite animosity and resistance. It is the work of the temple more than anything else, as Brigham Young noted, that sets all the bells of hell to ringing—"I want to hear them ring again!" he said.[5]

Verse 30. But the resistance shall be frustrated—again no comment is necessary, but there is a hint of things to come in the upheavals of our time when we are told that their works shall be "swept away by the hail." That is ominous and by no means so fantastic as it sounded not so long ago. Hail is the infallible indicator of atmospheric extremes such as the world is experiencing today for the first time of which we are aware.

Verses 31–33. This is the historical part, something of an established pattern of recurrent events where the temple is concerned. The Saints do not enjoy a glory of the eternities cheaply; theirs is a heavy yoke to bear. This comes almost as a relief when we realize that we too are required to exert to the utmost in participating. When the building of the Provo Temple was turned over to contractors who put up signs banning all but company employees from the building site, many Latter-day Saints who remembered the building of other temples felt cheated. Since the most ancient times the building of the temple has been a work in which all, from king to peasant, joyfully participated. This could lead to riotous confusion unless the work was skillfully coordinated and directed, which it was. It was precisely the exercise demanded and inspired by the building of temples which produced the planning and discipline that gave us all the world's great civilizations. The prompt and eager oversubscribing of money to the building of every temple shows how everyone yearns to be part of the action.

Verse 34. "As all men sin forgive the transgressions of thy people." The history of the temple at Jerusalem was one of recurrent sinning and forgiving. It was while he was gazing at the temple that Jesus remarked to the apostles, "O Jerusalem, Jerusalem, . . . how often would I have gathered [you] . . . as a hen gathereth her chickens under her wings, and ye would not!" (Matthew 23:37). Again we have no real cause to complain; we know where we have fallen short. These sad conditions merely emphasize the vast importance of the issues at stake.

Verse 35. To carry us over, we receive "anointing . . . sealed . . . with power from on high." Without that power we have nothing, as we clearly see when we try to put on our own show, such as Church films of various kinds, including much sentimental kitsch with professional, non-LDS actors waxing emotional about situations that they have never experienced. Illustrations in study manuals, tear-jerking stories, photographs of sacred ordinances suffused with frosted light to make them spiritual—do we need all this rhetorical and theatrical Hollywood and Disneyland if we have the real thing? The most impressive temple sessions I have attended have been at Manti, where elderly farm people put on a far more intelligent display than the slick professionals. Do we take the real thing seriously enough?

Verse 36. "The gift of tongues . . . , even cloven tongues as of fire." This is a strange figure. To cleave means both to stick together, glue, *kleben,* etc., and also to split or separate. A cloven tongue is a loosened and articulate tongue. The image here employed recalls both the two-edged sword which is the word of or tongue of God, which "is quick and powerful, sharper than a two-edged sword, to the dividing asunder of the joints and marrow, soul and spirit" (D&C 33:1),[6] and the fiery sword of the cherubim (*kherev* means sword) that turned every which way, guarding the way of the tree of life.

Verse 37. The next verse confirms the use of metaphors, where "tongues *as* of fire" is matched by the filling of the house "*as* with a rushing mighty wind." Was there real fire or a real wind? No, but there was something real that can best be described in those terms. Everything about the temple is symbolic and yet, like the equations of the scientists, goes beyond mere symbols, bidding us to look to something that lies beyond. We know that things really happened in the Kirtland Temple, where we read also of a sound *as* of rushing waters and hair *as* white wool.

Verse 38. The covenant prepares the Saints to hold up in the day of trouble. Here the words *sealing* and *binding* are significant. "Seal up the law"—you seal a thing up for preservation from the elements, the accidents, and the ravages of time. That is the situation here, for the world is going to be a dangerous place. The temple is holding open the door, so to speak, during this climactic dispensation. Is there more trouble coming? Where is the happy ending? It is here and now! As long as we have the temple, "in the world ye shall have tribulation: but be of good cheer; I have overcome the world" (John 16:33). As long as we know the happy ending, we can anticipate a better world to come in our visits to the temple.

Verse 39. We are gathering up the righteous out of the

world from the cities of the world into the city of Zion. From the earliest times even wandering tribes have had their holy centers that quickly became cities. The cities where the elders have success are to serve as feeders into Zion, while the destroying angels are held back and the skies darken.

Verse 40. We ask God to hold off while the gathering is going on. This is the basic principle with the Jews, the Sodom and Gomorrah situation—as long as there are righteous people to be saved, God extends the time of a wicked world. It was "in process of time" that Enoch's converts were taken up to Zion—it lasted many years (Moses 7:21).

Verse 41. But in due time and after due warning to everyone, judgment descends.

Verse 42. Here we can clearly understand that it is going to be a very close call.

Verse 43. And now comes a surprise—the acid test of the righteousness and sincerity of the Saints. They pray for the wicked mob, "O Lord, we delight not in the destruction of our fellow men; their souls are precious before thee." We do not fall into the easy, almost irresistible temptation to classify the human race as good guys and bad guys. As long as the selection is going on, we should be as impartial as possible.

Verse 44. The decision is left entirely up to the Lord: "Thy will be done, O Lord, and not ours."

Verse 45. There can be no doubt that "in the last days . . . thou wilt pour out thy judgments, without measure."

Verse 46. Under these horrendous conditions it is necessary to "enable thy servants to seal up the law, and bind up the testimony, that they may be prepared against the day of burning." We seal and bind up things to keep them safe from fire and flood, or, in nautical terms, we "batten down the hatches" for what is to come, in this case a burning—can this also be partly metaphor? It makes little difference. The words *sealing* and *binding* are not vague theological jargon; they actually mean putting things in such a condition as to resist destructive forces.

Verses 47–54. Here we see just such a situation in the grim business of Jackson County. After all that has happened, Joseph can pray, "Have mercy, O Lord, upon the wicked mob, . . . that they may repent of their sins if repentance is to be found" (verse 50). In such a climactic condition the decision is of course entirely with the Lord (see verses 51–52). He is asked to "have mercy . . . upon all nations" (verse 54).

For our part we have invaluable inside support in the "principles . . . [of the] Constitution." Joseph has explained the Bill of Rights as the expression of those *principles* and the rest of the Constitution as providing a flexible means of their implementation. Whether an election is held on a Monday or Tuesday, whether a state has two or three senators, whether a majority or two-thirds shall decide an issue, these are not eternal and unchanging principles, such as free assembly, freedom of religion, freedom of speech, etc., in short, free agency.[7]

Verses 55–56. Verse 55 is a blessing on all the human race from "the kings [and] princes" to all "the poor, the needy, and afflicted ones of the earth." To soften their hearts, "that their prejudices may give way before the truth, and that thy people may obtain favor in the sight of all." The Prophet does not ask for their destruction but for a change of heart. We all must live together, and the temple should not alienate anyone.

Verses 57–59. The servants are going to the ends of the earth and everywhere seek out the lost sheep; this is no time to be blasting the planet. Not only Judah but the other eleven tribes shall build the Holy City, and the faster the stakes grow the shorter will be the time. This is the gathering of Israel on a grand scale. But the whole thing will be "cut short in righteousness." One thing is certain here. We are never going to develop Zion out of the present order of things, as many are tempted to believe during our short periods of prosperity.

Verses 60–61. The gathering is on a number of fronts. Though we "are identified with the Gentiles," there are many "children of Jacob, who have been scattered upon the mountains." The gathering is a complex operation entailing the cooperation of the Gentiles, Israel, the Jews, and the very mixed blood of Lehi. This refers us to Doctrine and Covenants 49:24–26: "But before the great day of the Lord shall come, Jacob shall flourish in the wilderness, and the Lamanites shall blossom as the rose. Zion shall flourish upon the hills and rejoice upon the mountains, and shall be assembled together unto the place which I have appointed. . . . Go forth as I have commanded you." And so we have come full circle.

Verses 62–64. This was the very time that saw the founding of Zionism at the first stirrings of the final return of the Jews to Palestine, "that Jerusalem, from this hour, may begin to be redeemed, . . . and the children of Judah may begin to return to the lands which thou didst give to Abraham, their father."

Verses 65–66. "That the remnants of Jacob [the Indians] . . . be converted from their wild and savage condition to the fulness of the everlasting gospel." Wonderfully prophetic: "At that day when the Gentiles shall sin against my gospel, and shall reject the fulness of my gospel, . . . behold, saith the Father, I will bring the fulness of my gospel from among

them. And then will I remember my covenant which I have
made unto my people . . . , and I will bring my gospel unto
them. . . . The Gentiles shall not have power over you; but I
will remember my covenant unto you, O house of Israel,
and ye shall come unto the knowledge of the fulness of my
gospel" (3 Nephi 16:10–12).

Verse 67. This refers to *"all* the scattered remnants of Israel, who have been driven to the ends of the earth." There
is no need to look in just one place, or to argue about where
they are.

Verses 68–74. This is the work of Joseph Smith and his
brethren in leading their part of the gathering "out of the
wilderness of darkness . . . [to] shine forth fair as the moon,
clear as the sun, and terrible as an army with banners; . . .
adorned as a bride for that day when thou shalt unveil the
heavens." The apocalyptic imagery here has always suggested more than mere imagination. The grandiose
panorama of the work that is going on is more magnificent
than anyone could suppose. This is followed by an equally
impressive picture of the state of the world. The Saints have
had a part to play in this process, to be responsible to the
Church when being leaders entailed particular danger—
"Remember, O Lord, . . . all the presidents of thy church . . .
and their immediate connections." Hence the presidents
and their families require particular consideration.

Verse 74. Flowing mountains and exalted valleys have
always sounded extravagant, but today as we view our science documentaries and see the instability of the elements
with tectonic movements and massive volcanic distur-
bances, we are not so sure.

Verses 75–76. Here we get the final break with this world
as we know it. The separation and the joining are both

finally completed, and so we find the Saints in glory after they have been caught up to another sphere.

Verses 77–78. Adam's prayer is repeated three times—we have come full circle and reached "an infinity of fulness." Since there is no end to fulness, there will be no end to what we are capable of receiving—as long as we do not reject it!

Verses 79–80. Here is the end and object of it all—to mingle with the Gods, to return to God's presence and partake of eternal life.

Notes

1. See, for example, *Ensign* 23 (March 1993), which discusses a number of aspects of the temple.

2. Hugh Nibley, "Looking Backward," in Truman G. Madsen, ed., *The Temple in Antiquity* (Provo: BYU Religious Studies Center, 1984), 39–51.

3. Cf. Bruce McConkie, ed., *Doctrines of Salvation: Sermons and Writings of Joseph Fielding Smith,* 3 vols. (Salt Lake City: Bookcraft, 1955), 2:208–9.

4. Hugh Nibley, *The World and the Prophets,* in *CWHN,* 3:243–48.

5. *JD,* 8:355–56.

6. Cf. Doctrine and Covenants, sections 6, 11, 12, and 14, the second verse in each case.

7. See *TPJS,* 147–48, 326–27.

3

"Who Shall Ascend into the Hill of the Lord?" Sesquicentennial Reflections of a Sacred Day: 4 May 1842

Andrew F. Ehat, 4 May 1992

In December 1844, Apostle Willard Richards began again the writing of the "History of the Church." Six months before, the martyrdom of the Prophet Joseph Smith and Patriarch Hyrum Smith interrupted this six-year-old project. During the lifetime of the Prophet, the "History" was completed to August of 1838—with Brother Richards's year-and-a-half effort responsible for everything from 1831 to 1838. Now the mourning time was past. It was time to start again. It was time to write the history of the still-incomplete Nauvoo era. The home of Elder Richards became the make-do "Church Historian's Office." Many Saints supplied their journals, notes, and records: anything that might have the slightest historical significance for this monumental undertaking. For the first two months of the winter of 1844–45, he and the tireless Thomas Bullock assembled, analyzed, and sorted the disparate sources that would comprise the compilation. On 17 February 1845, Brother Bullock began copying the apostle's final draft, starting with the entry for 6 August 1838. Two months later, after unprecedented progress, Elder Richards was ready to write the history for May of 1842. It may have seemed like just another day of work on the draft manuscripts of what would become the *History of the Church*, but like many times before during this challenging compiling process, his task was to flesh out not merely the memory, but also the meaning and message of an event in Church history. This time, however, he had the formidable task of describing and explaining what had happened on 4 May 1842, the day our holy endowment was first administered as given in our temples today.[1]

What did he have at hand? Nothing, save a scant entry from the "Book of the Law of the Lord," the only contemporary account of the events of that important day.[2] Why did none of the nine present write in their diaries of the events of this glorious day? The Prophet Joseph Smith had asked each participant *not* to record the specifics of what they had heard and seen that day. Six weeks later, in a letter to his fellow apostle Parley P. Pratt, Heber C. Kimball wrote that these favored few had received "some precious things through the Prophet on the priesthood that would cause your soul to rejoice." However, he added, "I cannot give them to you on paper for they are not to be written."[3] They were just too sacred.

While Elder Richards may have had nothing more on paper to aid him in composing this entry, he did have it written in his heart (cf. Jeremiah 31:31–34). He had been one of the chosen individuals called by the Lord to receive these precious priesthood principles that day. And from the abundance of his heart, he put down in writing the single most sweeping and succinct explanation of the *meaning* of the endowment in our written literature.[4]

In the following reading, I have chosen to unmask Elder Richards's modesty and restore his account to a first-person rendering of the events of 4 May 1842. As with many other diary entries that he so seamlessly included in the *History of the Church*, he humbly wrote the record as if it contained the words of the Prophet Joseph Smith. When he could find a diary containing information relating to the Prophet Joseph that was found nowhere else, he benignly revised and inserted into the *History* the words of others as if they were the Prophet's own. He knew Joseph did not have the time to record these things for himself.[5] In fact, Elder Richards kept the personal diary of the Prophet for the last year-and-a-half of his life. But in the case of the endowment, Elder Richards had been an eyewitness of the events. So the words he would choose for this entry would reflect as much the impact of the events on himself as well as the enlarged understanding of the endowment he had personally gained in the ensuing three years. From the original account on file in the LDS Church Archives, written in his hand but now restored as his own words, you can read these words that are more than mere description:

> 4 Wednesday May 4– I spent the day in the upper part of [Joseph's Red Brick] Store (IE.) in the private office [of the Prophet Joseph Smith] (so called, because in that room [he] keeps [his] sacred writings, translate[s] ancient records, and receive[s] revelations) and [also] in [the] general business office, or Lodge room (IE) where the Masonic fraternity met occasionally for want of a better place), in council with Gen James Adams, of Springfield, Patriarch Hyrum Smith, Bishops Newel K. Whitney, & Geo. Miller, . . . ~~Wm Marks, Wm Law~~ & Prests Brigham Young Heber C. Kimball. [With these brethren, I was] instruct[ed by the Prophet Joseph Smith] in the principles and order of the priesthood, [and from him received my] washings & anointings, ~~&~~ endowments, and the communications of keys, pertaining to the Aaronic Priesthood, and so on to the highest order of the Melchisedec

Priesthood, setting forth the order pertaining to the Ancient of days & all those plans & principles by which any one is enabled to secure the fulness of those blessings which has been prepared for the church of the firstborn, and come up ~~into~~ and abide in the presence of ~~God~~ the Eloheim in the eternal worlds. [Joseph Smith] in this council instituted the Ancient order of things for the first time in these last days. And the communications I [received in] this Council were of things spiritual, and [are] to be received only by the spiritual minded: and there was nothing made known to [us by the Prophet] but [what] will be made known to all Saints, of the last days, so soon as they are prepared to receive, and a proper place is prepared to communicate them, even to the weakest of the Saints: therefore let the Saints be diligent in building the temple and all houses which they have been or shall hereafter be commanded of god to build, and wait their time with patience, in all meekness and faith, & perserverance unto the end. knowing assuredly that all these things referred to in this council are always governed by the principles of Revelation.[6]

This, Willard Richards's draft for the Prophet's "History" entry for 4 May 1842, is, as I indicated, actually the most comprehensive statement made by an original participant, providing us Joseph Smith's explanation of the meaning of the endowment.

Especially note these words: "The communications I [received in] this Council were of things spiritual, and [are] to be received only by the spiritual minded: and there was nothing made known to [us by the Prophet] but [what] will be made known to all Saints, even to the weakest of the Saints of the last days, so soon as they are prepared to receive [them], and a proper place is prepared to communicate them, [in] . . . the temple."[7] I wish to focus our attention to these final words of entreaty, to the need for preparation, in my reflections on this incredibly important event: the day the Ancient Order was first revealed in this last dispensation.

The Prophet Joseph Smith did many things publicly to prepare the Saints for the promised blessing of the endowment. Just the record of his public sermons would serve us well in the quest for preparation.[8] Let us look at only one of these public sermons in which the Prophet Joseph refers to an ancient example of the sacred endowment.

Three days before first administering the endowment, the Prophet Joseph spoke to the assembled thousands in the grove on temple hill near the emerging Nauvoo Temple. There, in his Sunday sermon on 1 May 1842, he spoke of the endowment blessings to be poured out when the temple was completed. In this public sermon, he told them that the endowment would confer on them "the keys of the kingdom. . . . The keys are certain signs and words by which false spirits and personages may be detected from true, which cannot be revealed to the Elders till the Temple is completed. The rich can only get [the endowment keys] in the Temple, the poor may get them on the mountain top as did Moses."[9]

The one obvious question is, "Where is recorded and when did Moses receive his endowment?" Certainly, his experience recorded in Exodus 3, when he by foot ascended the mount and saw the fiery, burning bush, was a portion of an endowment. In fact, sacred experiences in the Spirit have an infinite spectrum of manifestations, all constituting a true endowment. Any true outpouring of the Spirit becomes a sacred trust, regardless of comparative intensity. But what we speak of here as Moses' endowment was the profound spiritual experience that occurred many years later. The record of this endowment begins in Moses 1 in our Pearl of Great Price.

This chapter—a restored chapter not found in the traditional scriptures—gives us far greater insight into Genesis. From Moses 1 we learn that Genesis is not merely a general history written by Moses or a pseudepigraphic story of the Hebrews allegedly written in Moses' name. Instead Moses 1 sets Genesis up as a highly personal revelation to Moses— an essential endowment of knowledge and power given prior to his mission to Egypt to reclaim lost Israel (see verses 25–26). He did not compile history as Elder Richards did: he was shown the history. Moses 1 begins as each endowment begins, with heaven and earth joining. This time, Moses ascended, not by foot but by the transporting power of the Spirit.[10] He was caught up into a mountain the name of which is not now known to us (see verse 42). There he spoke with God face to face. Once this outpouring of the abundance of the Spirit subsided, Moses found himself on his back for many hours. When he came to his strength again, he exclaimed, "Now . . . I know that man is nothing, which thing I never had supposed" (verse 10). Think of him, reflect on the fact that for the first forty years of his life, he had been primped, pampered, and prepared as a prince, even to become a king in Egypt. For all he had known, he was a member of the royal family, even a god. He had access to the greatest knowledge and library in the world. And now, at age eighty, forty years after his experience at the burning bush, having received the fulness of the endowment for the first time, he realized that he had not been fully prepared for this endowment.

As Moses' case demonstrates, the actual endowment is not a mere representation but is the reality of coming into a heavenly presence and of being instructed in the things of eternity. In temples, we have a staged representation of the step-by-step ascent into the presence of the Eternal while we are yet alive.[11] It is never suggested that we have died when we participate in these blessings. Rather, when we enter the celestial room, we pause to await the promptings and premonitions of the Comforter. And after a period of time, mostly of our own accord, we descend the stairs, and resume the clothing and walk of our earthly existence. But there should have been a change in us as there certainly was with Moses when he was caught up to celestial realms and saw and heard things unlawful to utter.

The book of Moses is what the Lord permitted him to write of his endowment experience. The scriptural recounting continues with his confrontation with the adversary. When it began, he did not have the keys to detect him. But upon calling on the Lord four times, finally, with sufficient faith, Moses was endowed with the power to cast out Satan. The Lord intervened again. He told Moses that his inquiry to know of all things in the universe could not then be completely fulfilled—that he could then only receive an account of the creation of this earth and its inhabitants. Nonetheless, the Lord gave Moses the grand gestalt of the universe as he explained his ultimate purpose: a purpose that transcends the boundaries of this earth and applies to all worlds: "This is my work and my glory—to bring to pass the immortality and eternal life of man" (Moses 1:39). And then his endowment continued when he was given an account of the creation of our eternity and our earth. He saw the scenes of the Garden of Eden. He saw the encounter between Adam, Eve, and the great adversary. With this intelligence, and much more, he could return to Egypt with a new identity and power. Who can deny that in the ensuing months Moses proved he had been empowered from on high? As Jehovah's instrument, he confounded the wizards of Egypt and led the children of Israel from bondage.[12]

Now, how prepared were the children of Israel for an endowment of power? When they were brought out of Egypt with a "stretched out arm," one explicit purpose was for them to assemble and offer sacrifice unto the Lord (see Exodus 3:18; 5:3, 17; 8:8, 27–29; 10:25). Three months after the Exodus, when they arrived at Sinai, at the request of the Lord, Moses ascended the hill again. There he was instructed to prepare Israel to receive their endowment three days later. He returned to the people. He charged them to wash themselves clean, to keep themselves pure, to not go in unto their wives for those three days: for it appears that once this charge was given, the Lord did not want anyone in Israel conceived before he came down with his presence on the holy mount to reveal his covenant (see Exodus 19).

Moses directed the administration of their preparatory cleansings. On the third day, each one heard the call to come to the foot of the mount. They had been charged not to come up into the mount or the Lord would break through and destroy them. Obeying the charge and avoiding the appointed penalty, they did not go further up the mount. However, unlike the dramatic display of Cecil B. DeMille's inaccurate but spectacular production, Moses was not alone, and the law was not first written in stone by the finger of the Lord. Rather, all Israel heard with their own ears God himself speak each of the words of the Ten Commandments. The trials of ensuing months and years would test whether those words were written in their hearts. But all that generation of Israel participated in that preparatory endowment (cf. Exodus 19:1–24:11 with Deuteronomy 5:22–27 [1–33]).

Yet, as President Brigham Young once put it, had they

followed the teachings of Moses, it would not have been
one year after the Exodus before they would have received
their full endowment.[13] As revealed in the Joseph Smith
Translation of the Bible, they rejected the higher law (see JST
Exodus 34:1–2; D&C 84:19–25). Therefore, the holy order,
and the ordinances thereof, were taken from among them.
A beautiful, yet lesser order, the Levitical order of the priesthood, was introduced. Dutiful offerings of sacrifice would
characterize this order, a service first in the tabernacle and
later in the temple. To set themselves apart not only from
the world, but from any other tribe of Israel not permitted
to bear the priesthood, the Lord revealed special clothing
they would wear only in the precincts of sacred space. As
recorded in Exodus 28–30, the Lord gave to Moses in the
mount the divine pattern of the sacred garments of the holy
priesthood. In particular, Aaron and his successor sons had
the privilege of wearing the beautiful garments of the
priesthood that only the High Priest of ancient Israel could
wear.

Let us briefly look at two other endowment occasions.
First, the endowment of the disciples of Jesus: they who had
been charged by the Savior on the night of the Resurrection
to tarry in Jerusalem until they be endued with power from
on high. Conventional Christianity mistakenly believes that
the powerful outpouring on the day of Pentecost recorded
in Acts 2—the mighty rushing wind, the cloven tongues of
fire over the heads of each of the disciples while they spoke
in tongues—was all the endowment they were to receive.
But, when read more closely, the scriptures reveal that the
disciples' endowment took place in a house (probably an
upper room) and was interrupted by a multitude of curious
men (see Acts 2:1–6). The rude interference turned out well
in the end: Peter gave his first sermon evidencing his own

anointing, a sermon that explained the last great mystery the Savior had posed to his detractors, a sermon instrumental in adding more than three thousand souls to the church that day.[14]

But their endowment pales in comparison with what the Savior from behind the veil and out of the heavens taught the Nephites of the baptism of fire and of the Holy Ghost, that which the righteous received when the Lord appeared among them (see 3 Nephi 9 [cf. especially verses 19–20 with Helaman 5]; 3 Nephi 17; 3 Nephi 19:8–36). In fact, the Lord tactfully explained to the twelve Nephite apostles that there were none in Palestine then prepared to receive the endowment that the Nephite disciples received (see 3 Nephi 19:35–36; cf. 3 Nephi 15:14–16:4).

Throughout the ages, the endowment has been a difficult experience for which to prepare. No specific length of time assures proper preparation. Not until he was eighty years of age was Moses prepared enough to receive his endowment. The children of Israel, through four hundred and thirty years of conditioning, were ill-prepared to receive their endowment even though they had passed through three months of torturous travel in the desert and had benefited from the daily, visible protection of the glory of God! And even though Jesus' disciples had had the direct presence of the Lord during the three years of his personal ministry, the Lord allowed only his twelve apostles in Jerusalem to receive as much of an endowment as they were prepared to and did receive on the day of Pentecost. The Nephite faithful received the full endowment only after the trial of their faith. Even for some of the Kirtland Saints, the seemingly interminable five-year wait for the endowment was not enough. For many of the Nauvoo Saints, another five years was not enough.

In our day, instances of lack of preparation have been cited by our prophets. When the Los Angeles temple building program was commenced, President McKay called a meeting of the stake presidents of the temple district. During this meeting, President McKay took occasion to express his feelings about the holy endowment. He indicated how some years before, a niece of his had received her ordinances in the house of the Lord. He had learned that she only recently before that had received an initiation into a sorority at the local university. She had had the crassness to say that she found the sorority initiation superior in effect and meaning to her than the endowment. President McKay was open and frank with them about the experience of one in his own family with the endowment. He wasn't worried about their audible gasps. With characteristic aplomb, he paused, and then said, "Brothers and sisters, she was disappointed in the temple. Brothers and sisters, I was disappointed in the temple. And so were you." Then he said something incredibly important that should be engraven on all our souls. "There are few, even temple workers, who comprehend the full meaning and power of the temple endowment. Seen for what it is, it is the step-by-step ascent into the Eternal Presence." Then he added, "If our young people could but glimpse it, it would be the most powerful spiritual motivation of their lives!"[15]

Let me add to this the testimony of another modern prophet regarding the influence the endowment could have on the youth. I will never forget this statement made by President Spencer W. Kimball shortly after he became President of the Church. Speaking at a fireside held in the Tabernacle on Temple Square—a fireside deemed important enough to be broadcast live on TV—President Kimball spoke to the youth of the Church in the Salt Lake Valley. As I listened to the fireside, I was awed by his assurance: "If you understood the ordinances of the House of the Lord, you would crawl on your hands and feet for thousands of miles in order to receive them!"

Indeed, we must prepare spiritually for the powerful principles of the temple, for it is in proper preparation that we qualify for its promised blessings. Each one who receives these blessings is challenged to search into and contemplate the deep meaning of the eternal truths that constitute the endowment. No one ever comprehended them at first experience. The temple holds out an ideal that only time, experience, faith, and the will of the Lord can fulfill for mortals. So when—not if—a challenge surpasses our current spiritual level, we must return for further revelation. Because of the unique gift granted to us in this dispensation, the privilege of proxy service, many can return and refresh their spirits in that holy place. Yet to those barred from its physical precincts due to distance and expense, they too can also take solace in the Savior's assurance: "[The Holy Spirit] shall teach you until ye come to me & my Father."[16] Regardless of our circumstance, we must make the effort while in the temple to sear and seal these sacred truths on our souls so the Spirit can teach and train us during private moments. To fathom its depths, to pursue its principles, to cherish its consistent call to come unto Christ, we must truly "dwell [upon] the house of the LORD for ever" (Psalm 23:6).

From the scriptural history of the endowment of this and past dispensations, may I conclude by suggesting seven prerequisite, *continuous* preparations required for those who seek these sacred blessings: (1) *Experience,* especially experience with the Spirit of the Lord; (2) *service,* as shown by a willingness to serve as a witness of the Savior, not simply by the sacrifice of worldly, but also of other worthy yet less-important enjoyments; (3) *purity*, in body, in mind, in spirit; (4) *prayer and study*, particularly about the promises and previous outpourings of such blessings in this as well as in prior dispensations; (5) *obedience and repentance*, specifically in forsaking your own sins and in forgiving others'; (6) *humility, meekness, integrity through fasting*, expressed foremost in a willingness to receive and remain true to God's covenants and promises during succeeding trials of faith; and (7) *faith in coming unto Christ for new birth*, by prayer, by a broken heart, by boldly petitioning only from him the power revealed through his ordinances. As the Psalmist succinctly asked and answered the great questions of preparation, "Who shall ascend into the hill of the Lord? or who shall stand in his holy place? [Only] he that hath clean hands, and a pure heart; who hath not lifted up his soul unto vanity, nor sworn deceitfully. He shall receive the blessing from the LORD, and righteousness from the God of his salvation. This is the generation of them that seek him, that seek thy face" (Psalm 24:3–6).

Notes

1. This sketch is based on the detailed research of Dean C. Jessee reported in "The Writing of Joseph Smith's History," *Brigham Young University Studies* 11 (Spring 1971): 466–68, as well as by consulting the diaries of Willard Richards and Thomas Bullock, the journals of the Church Historian's Office, and the draft sheets of the *Manuscript History of the Church* (all found in the LDS Church Archives).

2. The brief entry in the "Law of the Lord" is as follows: "In council in the Presidents & General offices with Judge Adams. Hyram Smith Newel K. Whitney. William Marks, Wm Law. George Miller. Brigham Young. Heber C. Kimball & Willard Richards. [blank] & giving certain instructions concerning the priesthood. [blank] &c on the Aronic Priesthood to the first [blank] continuing through the day" (Dean C. Jessee, ed., *Papers of Joseph Smith, Volume 2: Journal, 1832–1842* [Salt Lake City: Deseret Book Company, 1992], 2:380, where [blank] refers to an erased word or words). Indicating that a priest-

hood bestowal of unprecedented importance was conferred that day is the equally important entry for the next day, 5 May 1842: "Judge Adams left for Springfield the others continued in Council as the day previous & Joseph & Hyrum were [blank]" (*Papers of Joseph Smith*, 2:380). Only when new priesthood ordinances and powers were being bestowed would the persons who previously *bestowed* blessings, in turn, *receive* them back from them to whom they first administered the blessings. This was in accordance with the pattern established when John the Baptist commanded Joseph Smith to first baptize Oliver Cowdery, and then Oliver Cowdery to baptize Joseph Smith after they had been ordained by this heavenly messenger, 15 May 1829 (see Joseph Smith–History 1:70–72).

3. Heber C. Kimball to Parley P. Pratt, 17 June 1842, Heber C. Kimball Papers, LDS Church Archives.

4. In contradistinction to Elder Richards's brief but comprehensive summary, Helen Mar Whitney, in her serial "Scenes in Nauvoo, and Incidents from H. C. Kimball's Journal," *Woman's Exponent* 12 (1883): 10, 14, 26, 34, and 42, published excerpts from the four Sunday lectures given to new initiates in the Nauvoo Temple (7, 14, 21, and 28 December 1845). These lectures, even in their appropriately edited form, are the most beautiful and detailed explanations of the endowment services published. They are our best window on just what the Prophet Joseph Smith taught a favored few in sacred meetings held in his "Red Brick Store," when he tutored and trained the first temple workers of our dispensation during the last two years of his life, especially from 28 September 1843 until his death in June of 1844.

5. See Jessee, "The Writing of Joseph Smith's History," 440, 470, 472–73.

6. Draft sheet of the *Manuscript History of the Church*, in the hand of Willard Richards, 4 May 1842, Historian's Office Church Records Group. Canceled words, punctuation, and spelling have been retained as in the original, except noun and pronoun references have been modified to reflect Willard Richards's authorship.

7. Ibid.

8. See 2 April, 16 April, 17 May, 11 June, 16, 23 July, 13, 27 August, 9 October 1843; 21 January, 10 March, 7 April, 16 June 1844 sermons as recorded in *WJS*, 168–73, 194–99, 202–4, 209–16, 232–36, 238–42, 243–47, 252–55, 317–19, 327–36, 340–62, 378–83.

9. See the "Law of the Lord" account of the 1 May 1842 sermon in *WJS*, 119–20 (cf. *Papers of Joseph Smith*, 2:379).

10. The temporary transporting of an individual into the presence of the Lord is a fundamental characteristic of the endowment (see

D&C 76:5–10, 114–19). For examples, see, in chronological order, Ether 3:13–20; Genesis 28:10–22; 35:6–15; Isaiah 6:1 (1–8); Ezekiel 37:1; 1 Nephi 1:8 (8–14); 11:1 (chapters 11–14), 2 Nephi 4:25; Helaman 5:44–50; Matthew 17:1–9 (cf. 2 Peter 1:16–18); 3 Nephi 28:13–16, 36–40 (cf. D&C 84:33); Acts 7:55–56; 2 Corinthians 12:1–4; Revelation 1:10, 4:1–2; D&C 88:63–69 (45–75); 93:1.

11. See the classic comment of Oliver Cowdery (but attributed to Joseph Smith) in *TPJS*, 51; and David O. McKay, cited by Truman G. Madsen, "House of Glory," 10–Stake Fireside Address, March 1972, reprinted in *The Highest in Us* (Salt Lake City: Bookcraft, 1978), 103.

12. Moses 1:1–4:32 was received by Moses only a short while before his return to Egypt. Perhaps had Joseph Smith not been interrupted in the process of the translation of Genesis, its translation would clearly show that it was entirely revealed to Moses prior to the return to Egypt.

13. "If they had been sanctified and holy, the children of Israel would not have travelled one year with Moses before they would have received their endowments and the Melchisedec Priesthood. But they could not receive them, and never did. Moses left them and they did not receive the fulness of that Priesthood. . . . The Lord told Moses that he would show himself to the people; but they begged Moses to plead with the Lord not to do so" (Brigham Young, *JD*, 6:100–101).

14. The sermon is recorded in Acts 2:14–40. He gave the answer to the mysterious question of the Savior—the question that forever silenced his critics from asking questions again (see Matthew 22:41–46)—recounted in verses 25–36, especially verses 33–36. See Acts 2:41 for the number of converts added to the Church that day.

15. Madsen, "House of Glory," 102–3.

16. *WJS*, 15.

4

The Temple and the Atonement

Truman G. Madsen

Daily for the past two years I have looked out from the Jerusalem Center on the Mount of Olives to the vista of the ancient city of Jerusalem. Every day in my mind's eye I have seen a temple that is not there. It is a temple of prophecy. The Jews speak of it as the third temple. Anciently a temple stood on that mount, built by the son of David, Solomon. After its destruction another temple, Zerubbabel's, was built, often called Herod's temple because he helped the Jews enlarge and enhance it. That too was destroyed. Many doves, many pigeons, many lambs died on the altar of the temple in graphic symbolic promise of the future redeemer. Many Israelites came and went, missed the point, and missed the Messiah.

In the time of Jesus the annual celebration of the Day of Atonement, Yom Kippur, culminated in the temple. On that day a high priest chosen for this specific role led the people into the outer temple courts. After preparatory prayer he daubed sacrificial blood of the flawless and slain lamb on the four horns of the altar, ascended the steps to the veil of the temple, and alone went into the Holy of Holies. There— the only time each year when the sacred name was spoken aloud—he pronounced the actual name of God. At that

---

This chapter is condensed and revised from an address given under F.A.R.M.S. sponsorship in San Diego, California, October 1993.

moment all present prostrated themselves in prayer.[1] The high priest represented them all, a disparate group of people, yet they saw Israel as one person. The sin of any was considered the sin of all; the righteousness of any as the righteousness of all. Standing now before God through their high priest, they were being judged. He was to "cleanse the sanctuary" and thus symbolically cleanse them.

The high priest called down from God the power of atonement. The people believed that on that day their destiny was fixed. If they came to the temple contrite and repentant, they would be blessed in the coming year. If not, they might not live another year. They were also taught that the time could come when, because of their persistent sinfulness and degeneracy, the sanctuary could not be cleansed. At such a time the efforts of the high priest would be unavailing, and the people would be rejected of God, along with their sanctuary, and the temple would be destroyed.[2]

The high priest prepared carefully for Yom Kippur ceremonies and during the prior week lived away from his family in the temple.[3] You may remember that Luke says of Jesus, speaking of his last week, that he "abode in . . . the mount of Olives" (Luke 21:37). On that Mount and in the moon-shadow of the desecrated temple, Jesus later bled, bled as a human scapegoat, bled in vicarious sensitivity, bled in soul-wracking anguish of what it feels like to err and sin and deceive and alienate beyond all hope of renewal.

Future Temple of Jerusalem

Today only a small minority in the Jewish world still hope for a new temple, though the expectation has been voiced daily in their prayers and rituals for nearly two thousand years. Many Jews as well as Christians think we no longer need a temple. But Joseph Smith was taught from on high, and he taught, "We need the temple more than anything else."[4] Why? Because we need the Christ more than anything else.

In the future temple in Jerusalem, priests and Levites will administer. The Levites will offer again (which means they once did) "an offering unto the Lord in righteousness" (D&C 13; see also Malachi 3:3; D&C 128:24). That will involve, according to our sources, the offering of blood sacrifices, which will be "restored and attended to in all their powers, ramifications, and blessings."[5] The whole purpose of the sacrificial patterns passed down from before the days of Moses was "to point the mind forward to Christ,"[6] who would become himself the great atoning sacrifice. When the Levites and priests are purified, the Prophet taught, then shall "the offering of Judah and Jerusalem be pleasant unto the Lord as in days of old and as in former years." And "as Israel once was baptized in the cloud and in the sea, so shall God as a refiner's fire and a fuller's soap purify the sons of Levi" (see D&C 128:24).[7] Through them, in turn, he will purify the people. In the new temple of Jerusalem they will perform these sacrifices after recognizing and lamenting that they persecuted their king. They will accept and apply his atoning power, and thus become a holy people. The consuming fire, the celestial burnings in which God dwells,[8] will permeate his holy temple. "Then also cometh the Jerusalem of old; and the inhabitants thereof, blessed are they, for they have been washed in the blood of the Lamb" (Ether 13:11).

These events are to occur in what is called the old world. Counterpart events will occur in the New Jerusalem of the new world, "which should come down out of heaven, and the holy sanctuary of the Lord" (Ether 13:3).

All this will be the Divine preface to "a new heaven and a new earth" (Ether 13:9).

The Atonement and the Temple

I have walked at night from the traditional room of the last supper, on Mount Zion, to and through the Valley of Kidron. In the days of Jesus that lonesome valley was at least forty feet deeper, a veritable canyon. He would have had to walk northward past two tombs, one known as the Tomb of Absalom, the other the Tomb of Zechariah. I have wondered if he said to himself as he passed, "I am going to open these tombs. And all tombs!" Then on to the garden known as *Gat-shemen*, Gethsemane. That night Christ fathomed the depths. Jesus atoned to bring about at-one-ment to restore the lost, to reunite the separated, to heal the breaches of this life.

We all have anxiety about the death *of* the body. To Mary, just before he resuscitated Lazarus, Jesus said, "I am the resurrection, and the life" (John 11:25). He came to overcome physical death. And that is completely out of our hands. The death of the body will come to all of us, and it is not much to be feared. Our worn-out tenement will be requickened and transformed.

But the scriptures speak of other kinds of death, deaths *in* the body, living deaths. These are the worst kind, deadening and desolating. Thus, for example, we die by degrees intellectually as we suppress the light within us and close our minds to spiritual things. We die emotionally and lapse into deceitfulness and hard-heartedness when we sin or shun the Christlike life. Further, we die in our powers of creation and, modern revelation adds, procreation when we ignore and flout the very source of life, who is Jesus Christ. All living deaths require atonement and healing. The atonement of Christ, through the ordinances of the house of the Lord, "reverses the blows of death."[9] Christ cannot reach us inwardly if the very core of us is willfully corroded and corrosive. As we persist in sin, the result is a dulled mentality, a seared conscience, a closed and hardened heart, and stifled creativity.

Christ's atonement extends to fragmented and traumatized families and the family of man. Fragmented families represent another kind of death. If his healing of wounds is the beginning, then his sealing of families is the end. He will not rest until these are achieved. Temple teachings echo Jewish traditions concerning "the merit of the fathers" and conversely "the merit of the children." Jewish tradition says that somehow the righteousness of Abraham, Isaac, and Jacob and of Sarah, Rebecca, Rachel, and Leah was so exceptional that one may come to God in their name and receive beyond any present worthiness . . . a bridge to and through the generations.[10] On the other hand children may by their lives become a redeeming force in the redemption of their ancestors and ancestresses. This parallels Joseph Smith's repeated rationale, a "bold doctrine," for proxy service in the temple: "we without them cannot be made perfect," nor they without us (D&C 128:9, 18).

This leads to the perennial questions: Why go to the temple to be married? What difference does it make where or by whom you are married? One response is that temple marriages and temple families can last forever, but there is a prior issue. The temple is designed to sacramentalize love and marriage so that it is *worth* perpetuating. The quality of love, husband for wife and wife for husband and parents for children, is enhanced in the temple as nowhere else. One first makes solemn covenants with the living God and his Christ. Then and then only can the partners kneel with divinely sanctioned confidence at an altar and commit to each other in whole-souled consecration. Then, if they walk in the light, such couples are secure from the idolatries, the competing gods, that clamor for their allegiance in a turbulent and sinister world. God becomes part of the marriage, and he covenants irrevocably to remain so. He promises that such marriages "shall be visited with blessings and not cursings, and with my power, . . . and shall be without condemnation on earth and in heaven" (D&C 132:48). If we see marital disillusionment, division, discord all about us, those are witnesses to this implicit temple truth: without Christ's one-making power, marriages and families feud and fade. The commitment, the intensity, and the quickening influences of marriage are ultimately dependent on our relationship with Christ.

In these and other ways, temple ordinances are designed to penetrate all levels of our consciousness, to dig into our frail flesh, and to melt and meld our hearts into oneness with ourselves, each other, and with him. "Herein is the work of my Father continued, that he may be glorified" (D&C 132:63). In this world when we become enamored of someone, we say, "Your wish is my command." Through temple covenants we demonstrate to him, "Your command is my wish." He does not command what he has not himself been through. In preparation for his atonement—and in culmination of it—he received all the ordinances, the last being his resurrection. As John personally saw and recorded, "He received not of the fulness at first, but continued from grace to grace." John saw that he finally received the fulness and that "the glory of the Father was with him, for he dwelt in him" (D&C 93:13, 17).

Perhaps prior to his resurrection, his highest point was on the Mount of Transfiguration. Joseph Smith said, "View him . . . on the Mount transfigured before Peter and John, there receiving the fulness of priesthood or the law of God. . . . After he returned from the Mount, did ever language of such magnitude fall from the lips of any man? Hearken him, 'All power is given unto me both in heaven and the earth.'"[11]

Of such transcendent temple blessings, the Prophet once said, "The rich can only get them in the temple—the poor may get them on the Mountain top as did Moses."[12] Christ opened the way, walked the way, and now is the Way (see John 14:6). And his way leads through his temple: "If a man gets the fulness of God he has to get [it] in the same way that Jesus Christ obtain[ed] it and that was by keeping all the ordinances of the house of the Lord."[13]

Jesus the Temple, Man the Temple

Many interpreters of the New Testament outside of this Church espouse the view that when Jesus Christ came, he replaced, once and for all, the temple.[14] So is it really necessary to have a stone-on-stone temple? Or is Christ the temple? Or, as Paul writes, is man a temple? (see 1 Corinthians 3:16; 6:19). Modern revelation confirms the neglected biblical message—all three are true, and the atonement of Jesus Christ is the living link that brings all three together. That truth is taught symbolically in the New Testament, with symbols that have both temporal and spiritual meaning.

Let me illustrate.

"Destroy this temple," Jesus said, enraging the listeners who supposed he spoke blasphemously of the Herodian temple, "destroy it and I will rebuild it in three days" (cf. John 2:19). He spoke of his body. Just as clearly Paul has said, "Ye are the temple of God," and an utterly defiled temple will be destroyed. Indeed, our very elements are the tabernacle of God, yea, even temples (see D&C 93:35). He prophesied not only that one stone of the Jerusalem Temple would not be left upon another (see Matthew 24:2), but also that a new temple would rise, as it were, from its ashes.

He puzzled and then inspired the Samaritan woman at Jacob's well: I am the "living water" (John 4:10). Likewise, he taught that we are, or can become, living waters. "He that believeth on me, as the scripture hath said, out of his belly shall flow rivers of living water" (John 7:38). He and his temple will flow with life-giving waters to heal even the most polluted and decadent of waters and bring fruitfulness like unto Eden to the whole earth (see Revelation 22:1–2).

He said to the famished multitude, most of whom saw only the loaves and fishes, "I am the bread of life" (John 6:35). He likewise said to Peter and his brethren, "Feed my sheep . . . feed my lambs" (John 21:15–17), and they came to understand that they were to be, like him, the providers of the bread of life. His temple is a house of nourishment, likened by the Jews to the *omphalos,* the navel connecting heaven and earth.[15] Those who enter these precincts, hungering and thirsting, are to find the feast of feasts and be filled. Having freely received, they will be strengthened to freely give (see Luke 22:32; D&C 108:7).

He said while the entire Temple Mount was lighted, all ablaze with oil lamps for the Feast of Tabernacles, "I am the light of the world" (John 8:12). And elsewhere to his disciples, "Ye are the light of the world" (Matthew 5:14). His temple is a house of light: "My glory shall rest upon it" (D&C 97:15), "more glorious than the first."[16] He is the light that shines in darkness (see John 1:5), even the deepest darkness.

"I am the door of the sheep," he testified on the Temple Mount, and "I am the good shepherd" (John 10:7, 14), not a timid hireling, but the person willing to live and die for the sheep (see John 10:11–15). Just as clearly he taught, "He that entereth in by the door is the shepherd of the sheep" (John 10:2) and "that which ye have seen me do even that shall ye do" (3 Nephi 27:21). We are to be willing to give our lives (see D&C 123:13) for him and for the sheep. His temple enables us to so covenant unto the death.

He names himself the stone of Israel, the chief cornerstone and promises that "he that buildeth upon this rock shall never fall" (D&C 50:44; Ephesians 2:20). Likewise, he refers to his apostles and prophets as the foundation (Ephesians 2:20).[17] His temple is built on solid bedrock, the center and centering place, where, or near where, tradition says, the first land emerged from the surrounding waters of Creation.[18] And where father Abraham and then Christ manifested a love for the Father that meant a determination to serve him at all hazards.[19]

He said after submitting himself to the menial, even slavish, task of foot washing, "I am the true vine" and, "[Ye] cannot bear fruit . . . except [ye] abide in the vine." He likewise said, "Ye are the branches" and "I have chosen you, and ordained you, that ye should go and bring forth fruit" (John 15:1–5, 16). His temple is for the "called, and chosen, and faithful" (Revelation 17:14). It is a house of abundance, the place of planting, the place of the regained and transformed tree of life (see Revelation 2:7; Exodus 15:17).[20]

He said, "I was in the beginning with the Father." He likewise said, "Ye were also in the beginning with the Father." He said, "[I] am the Firstborn." He likewise said, "And all those who are begotten through me are partakers of the glory of the same, and are the church of the Firstborn" (D&C 93:21–23). Christ the Creator of worlds has revealed that some of us were partners in the Creation (see Abraham 3:23–24; 4). However, through the temple, he makes all of us partners in procreation. The Only Begotten is the only begetter of life eternal. His "life and light and spirit and power" are sent forth by the will of the Father.[21] As in baptism, so in baptism for the dead, his blood is sanctifying power. "By the water ye keep the commandment; by the Spirit ye are justified, and by the blood ye are sanctified" (Moses 6:60). "Being born again," the Prophet taught the modern Twelve, "comes by the Spirit of God through ordinances."[22] The rebirth that climaxes all rebirths is in the House of the Lord. As Elder George F. Richards put it, "The ordinances of the Gospel have virtue in them by reason of the atoning blood of Jesus Christ, and without it there would be no virtue in them for salvation."[23]

Receiving the Fulness

The Atonement saves us *from* death, sin, hopeless ignorance, and lasting estrangement from those we have the capacity to love, but it also saves us *for* an abundance of life, blessings that the scriptures call "the fulness." He who was described as having an "infinity of fulness" (D&C 109:77) promises his fulness to those who come to him. Thus, for example, these fulnesses are associated with temple worship and temple covenants:

—a fulness of the earth (see D&C 59:16). This earth is to become heaven, a celestial orb. And worship is defined as coming "unto the Father in my name, and in due time receiv[ing] of his fulness" (D&C 93:19). Each time we dedicate a temple, we remove part of the curse on the earth.[24]

—a fulness of truth (see D&C 93:26). The principles of

intelligence—of light and truth such that one may be "glorified in truth"—are latent and manifest in the temple. All the functions of intellect are there to be mined: memory, imagination, lucid and coherent reasoning powers, and anticipatory knowledge. Of course, learning can be had from many sources. But the light and truth that "groweth brighter and brighter until the perfect day" (D&C 50:24) are in the House of the Lord.

—a fulness of the Holy Ghost (see D&C 109:15).

—a fulness of the priesthood (see D&C 124:28).

—a fulness of the glory of the father, "which glory shall be a fulness and a continuation of the seeds forever" (D&C 132:19; see Abraham 2:9–11). In the temple the powers of godliness are called down, and we are told they are otherwise not manifest unto men in the flesh (see D&C 84:20–21). Joseph Smith commanded, "Go to and finish the temple, and God will fill it with power, and you will then receive more knowledge concerning this priesthood."[25] Further he said that the Melchizedek Priesthood was "not the power of a Prophet nor apostle nor Patriarch only but of King & Priest to God to open the windows of Heaven and pour out the peace & Law of endless Life to man."[26] This is the vital reenactment of the promises to Abraham, Isaac, and Jacob, a posterity not only numerous but radiant like unto the stars.

—a fulness of joy that is related to all of these (see D&C 93:33–34). Joseph Smith said, "The mighty anchor holds the storm, so let these truths sink down in our hearts, that we may even here begin to enjoy that which shall be in full hereafter."[27] In the midst of a multitude filled with celestial wholeness at the temple in Bountiful, Jesus said, "Now behold, my joy is full. And when he had said these words he wept" (3 Nephi 17:20–21). There heaven came so close

even the children spoke with the tongue of angels. It was an
ineffable outpouring. In Hebrew the root word for "joy" is
tied to ʿăḇôḏāh, works, specifically temple service. The word
originates with feasting, partaking of the sacrificial meal, in
the temple. Here is the foreshadowing of the Messianic
feast, the "marriage supper of the Lamb," the future sacramental partaking of new wine in his kingdom (see D&C
27:5–14; 133:10). It is the glorious foundation of the reminding, enlivening, and covenant-making process we call the
sacrament.

Jesus—Keeper of the Gate

Modern scripture promises that all the pure in heart
who come into this house (one yet to be built in America,
namely in the New Jerusalem), "all the pure in heart that
shall come into it shall see God" (D&C 97:16). The late Elder
John A. Widtsoe was born in Norway, to a mother who was
a lonely convert. As a boy he was assured by a roving patriarch that he would have great faith in Jesus Christ even
unto the day of face-to-face communion. Linked to that
promise was another: "Thou shalt have great faith in the
ordinances of the Lord's house." These are inseparable;
strong and vivifying faith in Christ inevitably draws us
toward his sanctuary. Widtsoe was called early as a special
witness of Jesus Christ. He taught that for most of us this
temple promise does not always mean face-to-face communion; it means a "wonderfully rich communion with God"[28]
that will prepare us for that consummation.

We are never required to make covenants except in a
setting where Divine grace, the extension of Christ's atonement, is promised to assist us in fulfilling them. With
the covenants of baptism comes the baptism of fire and
the Holy Ghost. With the covenant of sacrament comes the

promise of his Spirit to be with us "always." With the oath and covenant of the priesthood and its heavy responsibilities comes the conferral of priesthood gifts. With the solemn covenanting of temple worship comes "an endowment of power," Christ's power.

A small sculpture on a wall at the Garden of Gethsemane depicts Jesus Christ drawn out against what appears to be a stone altar.[29] One is gripped by the total exhaustion of Christ's body kneeling there under the weight of the world. It is comforting to me that he, even he, could not bear it all alone. A moment came, the record says, when as "he prayed more earnestly" an angel came "strengthening him" (Luke 22:43–44), and he received power from on high. To those of us who would follow him, the message is, Our all is required. Faint and tentative and half-hearted vows will not avail. Nothing less than our all must be brought to the altar. But our all is not enough. It must fuse with his all. And his all he continues to give. Only he can lift us to the full measure of our potential.

At temple dedications we are blessed to stand for the hallowed and hallowing Hosannah Shout. This tribute of acclamation might well be "to Father and Son." The phrase is more pointed and poignant: "To God and the Lamb." As he rode down the Mount people cried in dawning awareness of his Messianic role, "Hosanna," which literally means "O, save us!" "Blessed is the King of Israel that cometh in the name of the Lord" (John 12:13). John's chronology allows us to conclude that lambs were being brought down the Mount of Olives for sacrifice in the Passover temple service at the very time Jesus hung on the cross (John 19:14).

We are privileged to cry, at the crescendo of faith amidst the dedication of his temple, "Oh, atone for us!" It is a plea for his mercy as from the multitude near the temple in the ancient world. "O have mercy, and apply the atoning blood of Christ that we may receive forgiveness of our sins, and our hearts may be purified" (Mosiah 4:2). In that exultant shout, and at every upward step through the temple, "the Lamb slain from the foundation of the world" is summoned, invoked, pled with (Revelation 13:8). Hence the great reassurance of divine acceptance at the Kirtland Temple: "I will manifest myself to my people in mercy in this house" (D&C 110:7).

With almost his last breath Jesus said from the cross, "It is finished," to which the Joseph Smith translation adds four words, "Thy will is done" (John 19:30; JST Matthew 27:54). Other theologies teach that Christ is now beyond, utterly beyond, any passion or feeling. Typically also the last week of Jesus is singularized as "the passion of Jesus." Joseph Smith changes that word in the book of Acts to "sufferings" (Acts 1:3; JST Acts 1:3). His sufferings are not absolutely finished. That day is still future. It will not come until "Christ shall have subdued all enemies under his feet, and shall have perfected his work" (D&C 76:106). The perfecting of his work is the perfecting of his people. Are any perfected? Only those who are "*made* perfect through Jesus the mediator of the new covenant, who wrought out this perfect atonement through the shedding of his own blood" (D&C 76:69; italics added).

"When he shall deliver up the kingdom, and present it unto the Father, spotless, saying: I have overcome and have trodden the wine-press alone, even the wine-press of the fierceness of the wrath of Almighty God. Then shall he be crowned with the crown of his glory, to sit on the throne of his power to reign forever and ever" (D&C 76:107–8). "And then shall the angels be crowned with the glory of his might, and the saints shall be filled with his glory, and receive their inheritance and be made equal with him" (D&C 88:107). And then it will be said, "It is finished; it is finished! The Lamb of God hath overcome and trodden the wine-press alone, even the wine-press of the fierceness of the wrath of Almighty God" (D&C 88:106).

Until that day there is within him the penetrating awareness that causes the heavens to weep: in the world is human suffering and needless suffering and the seemingly universal choosing of the way of death. Can we begin to imagine what he feels in his depths to have paid that awful price in order to reach to our very core and then have us turn our backs on him?

We demonstrate that we have been touched with his mercy, for "mercy hath compassion on mercy" (D&C 88:40), by going to the house of the Lord. Many of us go, sometimes wounded and groping in our inner and outer lives, yet seeking to act in love for those others who lived before us and to whom we owe much. They struggled through mortality, often with much less light and certainly much less of the blessings of this world than we. We can do something for them that they cannot do for themselves.

As the "keeper of the gate" (2 Nephi 9:41), Jesus the Christ summons us, "Come unto me" in my holy sanctuary (Matthew 11:28; see 2 Chronicles 30:8; D&C 110:7–9), and he promises, "Whoso knocketh, to him will [I] open" (2 Nephi 9:42). He is in his sanctuary; "he employeth no servant there" (2 Nephi 9:41). We who put off our shoes to walk on holy ground need not be put off by the fact that mere mortals administer these divine ordinances. They may be familiar and ordinary persons from just around the corner. Yet they represent the Lord himself. Christ himself is blessing us, reaching down to us through those ordinances. The

Lord himself is waiting for us beyond the veil. It is he who voices and magnifies and endows the temples with a summation of human experience that is a step-by-step ascent into his presence. May we go to him in his temple. May we serve as he served. May we live as he lived. I so pray in the name of Jesus Christ, amen.

Notes

1. See M *Yoma* 3:8 in *The Mishnah: Oral Teachings of Judaism,* tr. Eugene J. Lipman (New York: Viking Press, 1973), 111, 116.

2. Jewish sources state that the temple was destroyed because of the transgressions of Israel (see TB *Sanhedrin* 64a, TB *Shabbat* 33a, *Lamentations Rabbah* 1:39, *Exodus Rabbah* 31:10; *Leviticus Rabbah* 19:6; *Numbers Rabbah* 21:14). According to *Lamentations Rabbah* 2:4, "seven transgressions were committed by Israel on that day: they killed a Priest, a prophet, and a judge, they shed innocent blood, they profaned the Divine Name, they defiled the Temple Court, and it happened on the sabbath which was also on the Day of Atonement."

3. M *Yoma* 1:1.

4. *HC,* 6:230.

5. *TPJS,* 173.

6. *TPJS,* 60.

7. *WJS,* 66, based on Malachi 3; spelling and punctuation have been standardized.

8. See *TPJS,* 346–48, 367; Zechariah 6:12–13; Isaiah 33:10–22.

9. Hugh Nibley, *The Message of the Joseph Smith Papyri* (Salt Lake City: Deseret Book, 1975), 108–11.

10. See Solomon Schechter, *Some Aspects of Rabbinic Theology* (New York: Macmillan, 1923), 170–98.

11. *WJS,* 246, spelling corrected and punctuation added. See also Matthew 28:18; D&C 93:17.

12. *WJS,* 119–20.

13. *WJS,* 213, spelling corrected. See the expanded version of this statement in *TPJS,* 308.

14. See R. J. McKelvey, "Christ the Cornerstone," *New Testament Studies* 8 (1961–62): 352–59; and *The New Temple: The Church in the New Testament* (London: Oxford University Press, 1969), 75–84.

15. See Josephus, *Jewish War* 3:52.

16. At the Manti Temple dedication in May of 1888, Lorenzo Snow prayed "that they may rebuild their city and temple, that the glory of

the later house may be greater than that of the former house" (*Selected Manifestations*, ed. David M. Reay [Oakland, California: n.p., 1985], 122).

17. The verse reads in part, "And are built upon the foundation of the apostles and prophets, Jesus Christ himself being the chief corner stone."

18. See John M. Lundquist, "The Common Temple Ideology of the Ancient Near East," in Truman G. Madsen, ed., *The Temple in Antiquity* (Provo: BYU Religious Studies Center, 1984), 60–66.

19. See *TPJS*, 150.

20. See Truman G. Madsen, "The Temple and the Restoration," in *The Temple in Antiquity*, 13.

21. See *HC*, 1:171–72.

22. *TPJS*, 162.

23. Conference Report, April 1916, 54.

24. "The Prophet Joseph said the curse would not be taken off the earth all at once" (Eliza R. Snow, *Woman's Exponent* 7 [July 30, 1878]: 50).

25. *TPJS*, 323.

26. *WJS*, 245.

27. *WJS*, 196; punctuation and spelling corrected.

28. Widtsoe, "Temple Worship," *Utah Genealogical and Historical Magazine* 12 (April 1921): 56.

29. B. H. Roberts describes the Salt Lake Temple as an altar "unto God" (Conference Report, October 1928, 86; see also "Testimonies in Bronze and Stone," Conference Report, October 1913, 26).

PART 2

The Temple in the Hebrew Bible and the Ancient Near East

5

What Is a Temple?
A Preliminary Typology

John M. Lundquist

As we attempt to determine what constitutes a temple and its ritual in the ancient Near East, it becomes evident that we find in the temple[1] of Solomon many kinds of archaeological problems, ones that involve architecture, interior and exterior furnishings, ritual installations, arrangements of courtyards, and relationships to other buildings—and yet, there are no archaeological remains of Solomon's Temple. The accounts of Solomon's Temple also present us with philological or text problems. We find in the Bible descriptions of building procedures and descriptions of the cult carried out within the temple. And yet the biblical material is beset with problems: it is diffuse, separated chronologically, and in some cases contradictory within itself, as is the case with the descriptions given in 1 Kings and 2 Chronicles of various architectural details.[2] Rare indeed is an instance anywhere in ancient western Asia where we have the union of standing or excavated temple remains and texts that can be unequivocally related to the ritual practices of that temple.[3] When we face these

This chapter originally appeared in H. B. Huffman, F. A. Spina, and A. R. W. Green, eds., The Quest for the Kingdom of God: Studies in Honor of George E. Mendenhall (Winona Lake, Indiana: Eisenbrauns, 1983).

deficiencies with regard to the temple of Solomon, we are led inevitably to the comparative method, and we attempt to relate architectural remains and ritual texts from surrounding cultures to those descriptions given in the Old Testament.[4] As unsatisfying as the comparative approach often is, it can yield positive results if kept "within closely adjacent historical, cultural or linguistic units," and if "the comparison be between a total ensemble rather than between isolated motifs."[5]

When using the comparative method, the issue of cultural continuity versus discontinuity must be considered. In the light of the extraordinary cultural disruptions in the ancient world,[6] it is important to note that there were areas of equally extraordinary cultural, historical, and religious continuity.[7] I believe that the temple as an institution and the cult associated with it constitute one of the most interesting examples of such continuity.[8] The following list of motifs attempts to focus on this continuity. It does not purport to be a complete motif list (hence the word "preliminary" in the title), nor to have identified all examples to which a given motif may apply. Nor is it my intention to claim that a common "pattern" can be applied indiscriminately to all ancient Near Eastern temples without regard to time, space, and cultural uniqueness. The full extent to which such a list can be applied to various temple traditions is a task worthy of continued research.[9]

Proposition 1. The temple is the architectural embodiment of the cosmic mountain.

This theme is extremely common in ancient Near Eastern texts.[10] From the time of Sargon II onwards, the cult room of Assur in the temple of Assur, Éd Aššur, was "House of the Great Mountain of the Lands."[11] This perception is very common in the Old Testament, as is seen in

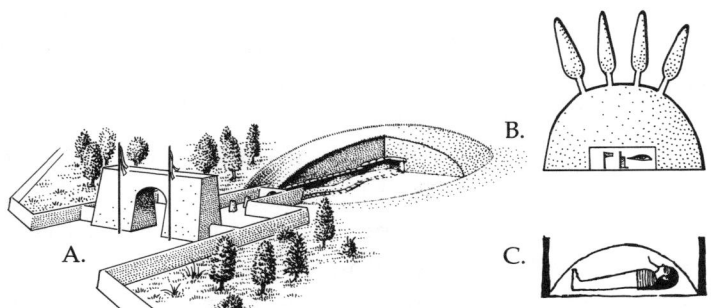

Figure 5. In Egypt, the primeval mound that emerged from the waters of creation became identified with the burial mound of the god-king Osiris, as in this reconstruction of the Middle Kingdom temple (A) at Medamud. Later hieroglyphic representations of this mound show trees growing upon it (B) as well as the mummy of Osiris (C) within.

such passages as Isaiah 2:2 and Psalm 48:2. These conceptions of Zion as a holy mountain go back ultimately to the inner-Israelite experience at Sinai. The temple of Solomon would seem ultimately to be little more than the architectural realization and the ritual enlargement of the Sinai experience.

One need not be dealing with an actual building in order to be in what I would call a "temple" setting in the ancient Near East.[12] Ancient religious texts are permeated with temple symbolism. In many cases the texts describe an encounter between the deity and a person that did not take place within a building, and yet it bears all the earmarks of the "temple" relationship. Basic to temple ideology is the act of appearing "before the Lord." As Menahem Haran states it: "In general, any cultic activity to which the biblical text applies the formula 'before the Lord' can be considered an indication of a temple at the site, since this expression stems from the basic conception of the temple as a divine dwelling-place and actually belongs to the temple's technical terminology."[13] In spite of the many vagaries involved in the textual analysis of Exodus 19–24,[14] it would seem that in this case the "temple at the site" is the mountain itself. Geo Widengren compares the Sinai theophany with the text describing the enthronement of Enmeduranki of Nippur in the temple of Ebarra: "ascension to God, a meeting between Moses and God and a handing over to Moses of the tablets belonging to God." He further mentions the sacral meal that Moses and the elders ate in the presence of God (see Exodus 24:11) following the sealing of the covenant with blood (see Exodus 24:8).[15]

Proposition 2. The cosmic mountain represents the primordial hillock, the place that first emerged from the waters covering the earth during the creative process.

In Egypt, for example, all temples are seen as representing the primeval hillock.[16] "Practically every temple or shrine of this period [Late Period] was considered a replica of the first temple, built upon the primaeval mound in the midst of the water of the Nun."[17]

The Eninnu temple, built by Gudea, is depicted as arising up out of the primeval waters *(apsu)* and raising its head to heaven.[18] This same temple is called the "foundation of the abyss"—*temen abzu*—and the "house of the abyss."[19] The Gudea Cylinders are filled with the motif of the house (= mountain) rising up out of the primordial waters. Indeed, it seems to me that the Gudea Cylinders are social and religious documents of inestimable value. They provide us the full scenario of temple building as it must have been perceived by many ancients. Parts of this scenario can be attested elsewhere,[20] but perhaps nowhere else in such complete form.[21]

A.

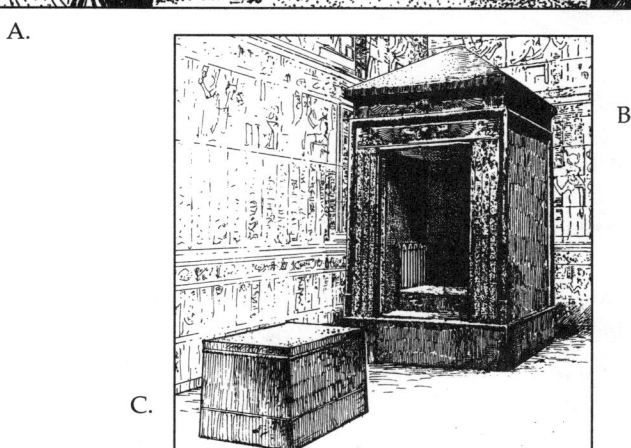

B.

C.

Figure 6. In the temple of Horus at Edfu (A), massive columns represent the aquatic plants growing up from the primeval waters. This is
also represented by the papyrus and reeds engraved within the black
granite shrine (B), where a golden image of Horus stood behind closed
doors. The shrine is surmounted by a pyramidion representing the primordial hillock. The altar (C) originally supported a sacred boat in
which the image of the deity was carried on the shoulders of priests in
procession down this corridor past the columns, as if the boat and
image were floating on the waters of the first morning of creation.

Figure 7. In the Dura Europos synagogue (c. A.D. 150), Moses is shown striking the rock to bring forth living water from a wellhead before the menorah in the Tabernacle. The water flows to the entrance of the tents of each of the twelve tribes, just as the Torah was said to flow as living water.

Proposition 3. The temple is often associated with the waters of life that flow forth from a spring within the building itself—or rather the temple is viewed as incorporating within itself or as having been built upon such a spring.

The reason such springs existed in temples is that they were perceived as the primeval waters of creation—Nun in Egypt, Abzu in Mesopotamia. The temple is thus founded on and stands in contact with the primeval waters. According to Hugh Nibley, "at every hierocentric shrine stood a mountain or artificial mound and a lake or spring from which four streams flowed out to bring the lifegiving waters to the four regions of the earth."[22] Geo Widengren

A.

B.

Figure 8. The Taj Mahal (A) is the most famous example of the Persian-style paradise gardens where the four rivers of Eden flow from the center, as also illustrated by this contemporary (c. 1650) Islamic map of paradise (B).

connects the water, tree, temple basin, and a sacred grove.[23] The theme occurs in Ezekiel 47:1 and, in all probability, in Psalm 29.

Proposition 4. The temple is built on separate, sacral, set-apart space.[24]

Excavations at Eridu and Uruk and the Diyala Valley document the practice of incorporating the foundations of earlier temples into the platform of later ones. This practice was achieved by filling in the surviving chambers of the earlier temple with mud brick.[25] This same practice has been documented more recently in Syria.[26] Mount Moriah, the place where Solomon built his temple, carried of course the association of Abraham's sacrifice of Isaac. But the

Figure 9. Even today in the Near East, the farmer rides a wooden sledge in order to crush and separate the kernels from the chaff on the threshing floor, as shown in this 1897 engraving. This circular, hard-packed surface was frequently the scene of harvest festivals and ritual drama. King David bought the threshing floor of Araunah the Jebusite and offered the oxen and threshing instruments as an atoning sacrifice. This spot later became the site of Solomon's Temple (2 Chronicles 3:1).

threshing floor, which David purchased from Araunah the Jebusite, may carry overtones more significant for the erection of a temple. And de Vries points out that "the threshing floor is an *omphalos*, at once a navel of the world (with the hub of ears in the middle) and a universe-emblem (a round piece of earth, with the earth in the middle, and the sun-oxen going round)."[27]

The process of excavating an enormous trench, which is then filled with sand, the whole serving as the foundation for the temple, is known not only from Early Dynastic Mesopotamia (the Temple Oval at Khafaje), but also in Late-Period Egypt. Late-Period Egyptian texts give the mythological rationale behind this practice: the bed of sand represents the primeval mound, which is founded in the

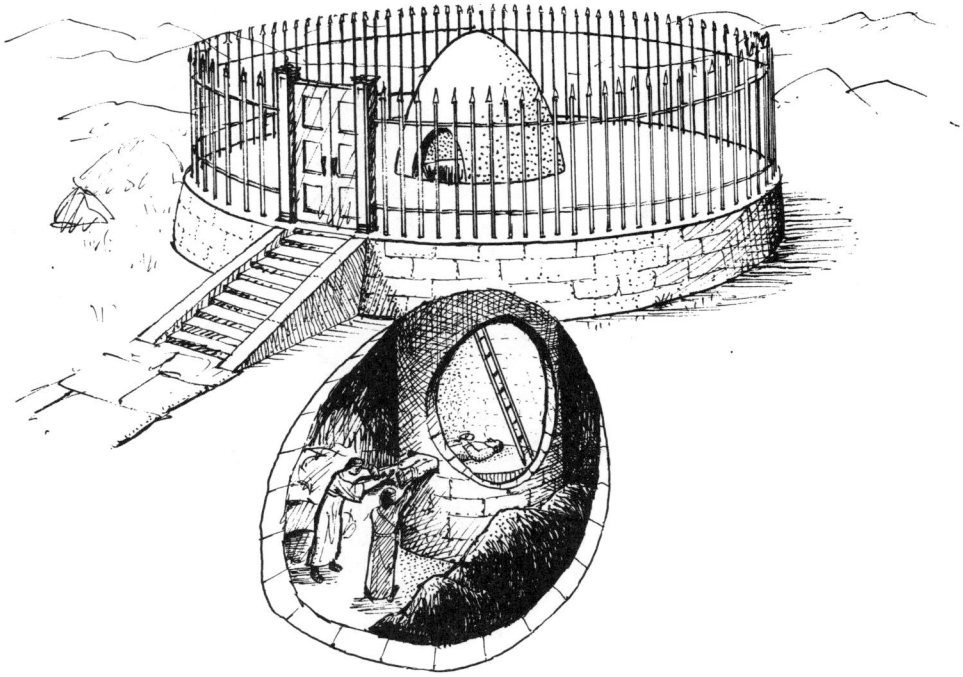

Figure 10. Pausanias (c. A.D. 150) recorded his experience of consulting the oracle of Trophonios, where he fasted; crossed a river; was bathed, anointed, and clothed in a white robe; and climbed the sacred mountain. He then descended through the center of a marble platform "like a threshing floor," where he experienced the divine mystery, which he was forbidden and unable to describe.

primeval waters of Nun.[28] A similar "mythological" setting for the practice documented at Khafaje would seem to be present in the temple of Enki at Eridu, which was also believed to have been founded in the primeval waters, in this case Abzu.[29] As A. J. Spencer states, "The effect of religious beliefs on architecture was not, as some have claimed, a vague symbolism, but was an important part of the construction of the temples, necessary for the buildings to fulfill their symbolic role."[30]

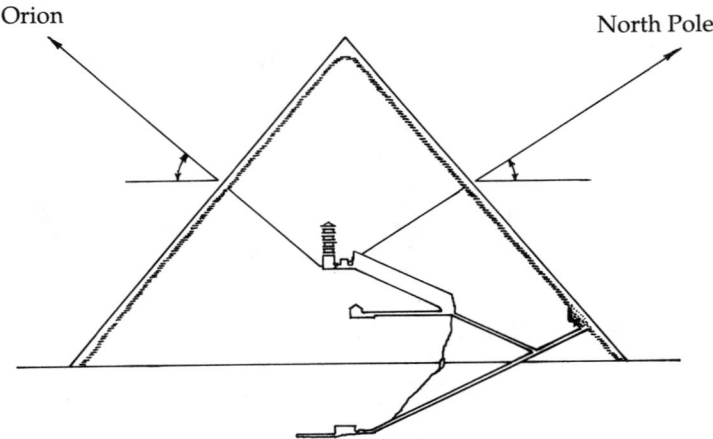

Figure 11. The Great Pyramid of Khufu is oriented to the four directions with astonishing accuracy. The northern so-called "air shaft" points to the North Pole and the pole star of that time (c. 2600 B.C.), Alpha Draconis, while the southern channel points to Osiris/Orion at culmination. They could not have been used as sighting tubes, but were intended for the passage of the Pharaoh's soul *(ka)* to the eternal stars.

Proposition 5. The temple is oriented toward the four world regions or cardinal directions, and to various celestial bodies such as the polar star.

As such it is, or can be, an astronomical observatory where sightings are made, the purpose of which is to help those who come to the temple orient themselves in the universe. The buildings might face the rising sun or other celestial bodies, for example.

There is an example of a long-maintained tradition of orienting the corners of temple buildings to the cardinal directions, as in the prehistoric temples of levels 11 through 6 at Eridu (Tell Abu Shahrain) and the partly contemporaneous northern Ubaid period temples of levels 14 through 12 at Tepe Gawra.[31] The burials discovered in the Ubaid period cemetery at Eridu were oriented in the same

Figure 12. This reconstruction of the Neo-Sumerian ziggurat of Ur (c. 2100 B.C.) expresses the desire to re-create the cosmic mountain on the plains of Mesopotamia.

direction as the temples.[32] A Seleucid period tablet for a temple ritual at Uruk reads in part, in A. Sachs's translation: "In the first watch of the night, on the roof of the topmost stage of the temple-tower of the Resh temple, when the star Great Anu of Heaven rises and the star Great Antu of Heaven rises in the constellation Wagon, (he shall recite the composition beginning? . . .)." And further on in the same text, "Upon seven large golden trays, you shall present water (for washing) hands to the planets Jupiter, Venus, Mercury, Saturn, Mars, the moon, and the sun, as soon as they appear."[33]

Proposition 6. Temples, in their architectonic orientation, express the idea of a successive ascension toward heaven.

The Mesopotamian ziggurat or staged temple tower is an excellent example of this architectural principle. It was constructed of three, five, or seven stages or levels.

Monumental staircases led to the upper part of the tower, to a small temple that stood at the top.[34]

Proposition 7. The plan and measurements of the temple are revealed by God to the king, and the plan must be carefully carried out.

Nabopolassar stated that he took the measurements of Etemenanki, the temple tower in the main temple precinct of Babylon, under the guidance of Shamash, Adad, and Marduk and that he kept the measurements in his memory as a treasure.[35] Gudea's well-known dream, which he received while in the temple of Baga, revealed to him the plan of the temple to Ningirsu, which he was to build. He was shown a lapis-lazuli tablet with the temple plan on it and was given a sacred brick mould that contained the bricks to be used in the building.[36] Moses was given the plans for the building of the tabernacle directly by God (see Exodus 25:9), and God appeared to Solomon at Gibeon before the building of the temple commenced (see 1 Kings 3:4–15) and after it was finished (see 1 Kings 9:3–9). Although the text does not say so explicitly, Kapelrud interprets the passages concerning Solomon in the light of the dream/revelations of Gudea and assumes that the plans of the temple must have been revealed to Solomon on the first occasion.[37]

Proposition 8. The temple is the central, organizing, unifying institution in ancient Near Eastern society.

Solomon's dedicatory prayer for the Jerusalem temple in 1 Kings 8:22–54 is an extraordinarily clear expression of this idea. The same concept comes through clearly in the Gudea Cylinders.[38] Jonathan Smith says of the ancient world: "On three things the world stands: on the law, on the temple service, and on piety," and adds the comment that "the temple and its ritual serve as the cosmic pillars or the

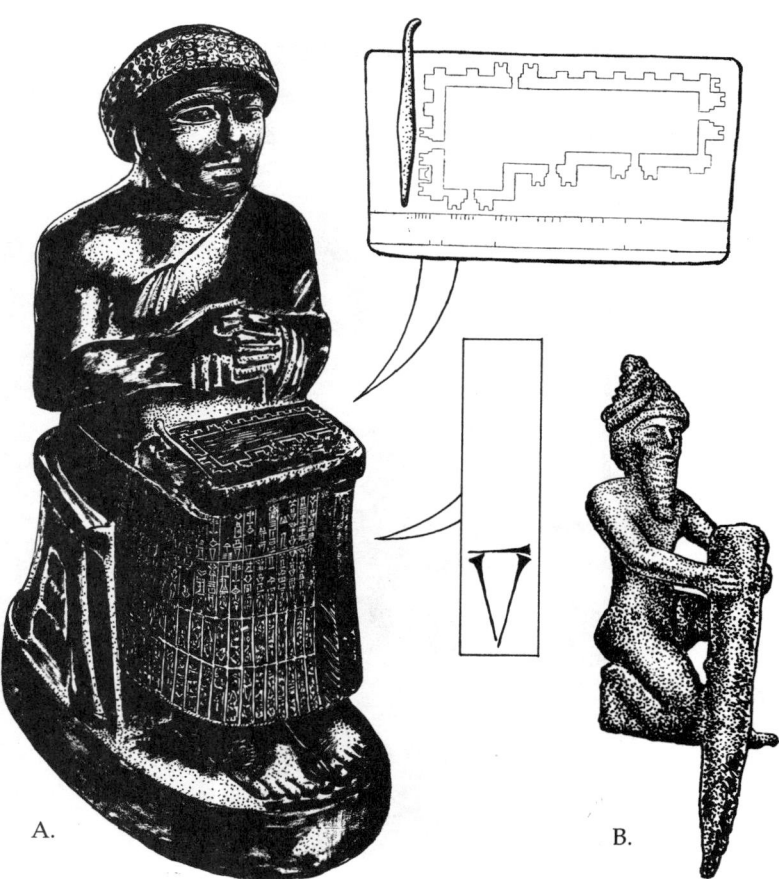

Figure 13. This image of Gudea of Lagash (A) would have been placed in a temple. It shows him with hands clasped in prayer, with a tablet and stylus on his lap. The tablet is delicately incised with the ground plan of a temple as well as a divine standard of measure along the edge. One of the frequently used cuneiform symbols in the lengthy inscription represents a peg, *dù* or *gag,* meaning "to build," since pegs and rope were used in laying out the ground lines, as shown by the small bronze figure of a kneeling god (B) holding such a peg.

Figure 14. At the dedication of the Jerusalem temple, Solomon lifted up his arms to heaven and said, "The heavens, even the highest heaven, cannot contain you. How much less this temple I have built!" (1 Kings 8:27, NIV). This 1858 engraving from a Hebrew prayer book shows Solomon on his knees before the great three-tiered altar, with the wheeled bronze lavers for water on either side. The Hebrew inscription on the arch is from verse 30: "And hearken thou to the supplication of thy servant, and of thy people Israel."

'sacred pole' supporting the world. If its service is interrupted or broken, if an error is made, then the world, the blessing, the fertility, indeed all of creation which flows from the Center, will likewise be disrupted."[39]

Proposition 8a. The temple is associated with abundance and prosperity, indeed is perceived as the giver of these. Conversely, the destruction or loss of the temple is seen as calamitous and fatal to the community in which the temple stood.

One reads that abundance shall come from heaven when the foundation of the temple is laid, that there will be a fullness of water, oil, and wool and that harmony and light will influence people's lives.[40] The destruction is viewed as the result of social and moral decadence and disobedience to God's word. This latter idea is seen quite clearly in Lamentations and Haggai and in the Sumerian "Lamentation over the destruction of Sumer and Ur,"[41] where, however, the destruction brought on Sumer and her temples and people is caused not so much by the people's wickedness as by a decree of Enlil that political power be shifted to another people.[42] The Sumerian historiographic poem "The Curse of Agade" is another well-known example of the view that the desecration of a temple by a king (in this case Naram-Sin) brings destruction on his entire people.[43]

Proposition 9. Inside the temple, images of deities as well as kings, temple priests, and worshipers are washed, anointed, clothed, fed, enthroned, and symbolically initiated into the presence of deity, and thus into eternal life. Further, during the New Year rites, texts are read and dramatically portrayed that recite a pre-earthly war, the victory in the war by the forces of good, led by a chief deity, the creation and establishment of the cosmos, cities, temples, and social order. The sacred marriage is also carried out at this time.

Figure 15. This reconstruction of the interior of the Old Assyrian Ishtar temple at Assur shows devotional statues dedicated by worshipers on benches against the wall, so that they would always be in attendance on the goddess located on the central axis. A raised slab in the center perhaps received sacrificial blood, while a hand basin stands at the right, with three stepped altars before the deity itself.

Images were manufactured, washed, anointed, clothed, and initiated.[44] The clothing of the goddess in a "priestly garment" is described in the "Blessing of Nisaba by Enki."[45] The washing and clothing of Inanna in "garments of power" in preparation for the sacred marriage rite and of Shulgi in the *me* garment along with a "crown-like wig" are described.[46] Exodus 29 and Leviticus 8 and 16 describe the washing, anointing, and clothing in priestly garments, including the Urim and Thummim, which Widengren associates with the Tablets of Destiny of Babylonian traditions of the Aaronide priests of Israel.[47] The "people" are involved

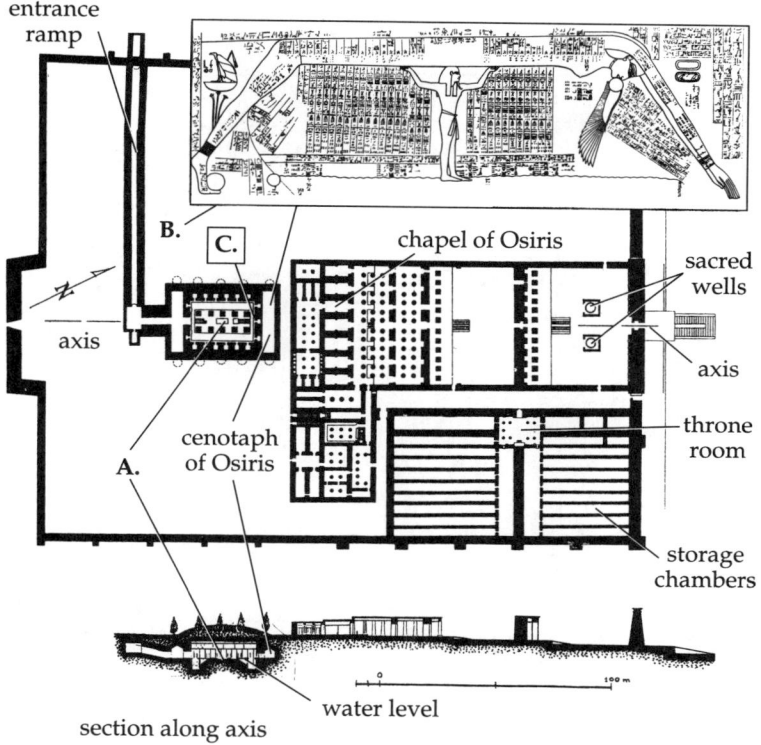

entrance
ramp

B.

C.

chapel of Osiris

sacred
wells

axis

axis

throne
room

cenotaph
of Osiris

A.

storage
chambers

section along axis

water level

Figure 16. The temple complex of Osiris built by Seti I at Abydos is one of the most beautiful monuments of the New Kingdom, combining an underground island (A), surmounted by a mound planted with trees, with a vast temple built along the same axis. The roof of the cenotaph chamber (B) shows the sky-goddess Nut swallowing the winged sun disk, which will be reborn in the east. Though there is no direct passageway between the temple and tomb, their construction on the same axis demonstrates their unity in the minds of the designers.

in washing and clothing rituals at Sinai, just as they are involved in the covenant ceremony that follows the giving of the law (see Exodus 19 and 24).

The question of the temple as a locus of initiation into divine life, something that has long been associated with

axis

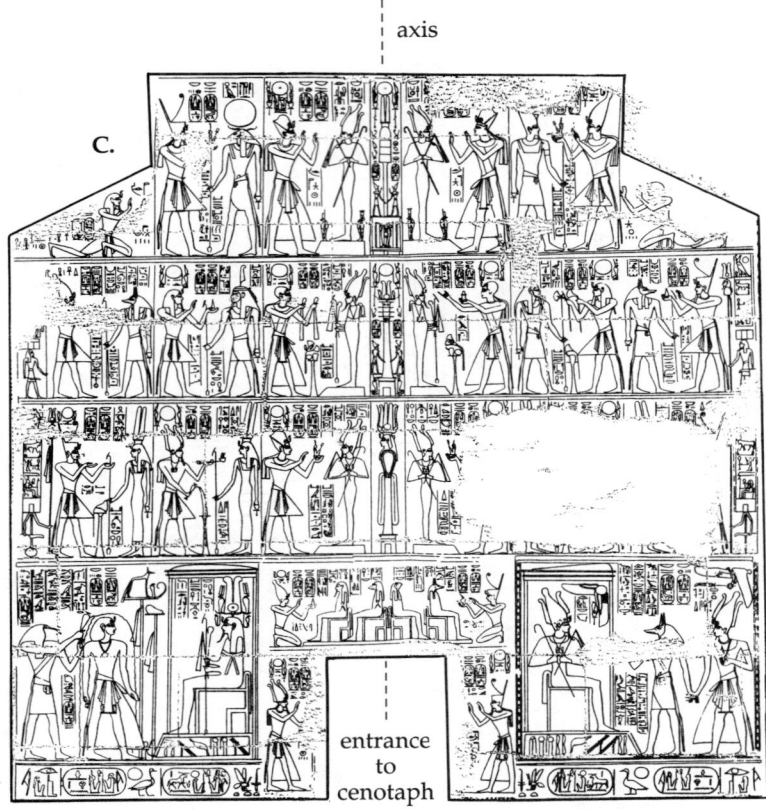

C.

entrance
to
cenotaph

Figure 17. The east wall of the subterranean central hall of the temple complex at Abydos shows symbols of Osiris and his sister/wife Isis along the central axis. The human forms of the deities always stand with their backs toward this axis, while the Pharaoh, wearing various crowns, moves toward it. The bottom register shows him being led into the divine presence, while the upper registers show him making offerings of cloth (a) and incense (b) and using his little finger to anoint with oil (c).

Egyptian religion, is a question intertwined with the issue of the temple as a locus of vicarious cult drama. That such was the case in Egypt is well established.[48] It has long been assumed that the *Enuma Elish* was the "text" of the

Babylonian New Year's festival carried out in the Esagila temple and in the *akītu* festival house, that is, that it was recited there.[49] That it was the text of a dramatic presentation, a dramatic recreation of the war in heaven, Marduk's victory, the creation of mankind, and the organization of the cosmos and of the earth has been assumed by some and doubted by many others.[50] An Assyrian building inscription of Sennacherib (K. 1356) states that the *bīt akītu* festival house in Assur had bronze door plates on the central entryway that depicted the battle between Assur (taking Marduk's place) and Tiamat. Sennacherib is himself identified as a substitute for Assur in the battle.

Pallis affirms that the "king acts the part of the leading deity in the battle drama" and that "we cannot doubt that a religious battle drama took place in bit Akitu during the Akitu festival, in which the king acted the part of the divine victor." He further emphasizes that to assume that the bronze door plates described above are "a mere artistic decoration, independent of the cult, is out of the question here."[51] H. Sauren attempts to demonstrate that the Gudea Cylinders form the text for a seven-day "mystery play," carried out each year at the temple dedication feast. He assumes that groups of actors, perhaps extending beyond priestly circles, would have been carefully chosen for each year's enactment.[52]

The view has been fairly widespread that the Baal cycle from Ras Shamra, found along with the other mythological texts in the library or scribal rectory on the temple acropolis, was used by the priests of Ugarit as the text of a dramatic presentation carried out in the temple of Baal.[53] The presence in the Baal texts of the themes of council in heaven, battle between deities, creation, temple building, and sacral meal, among others, when coupled with the find spot of the

A.

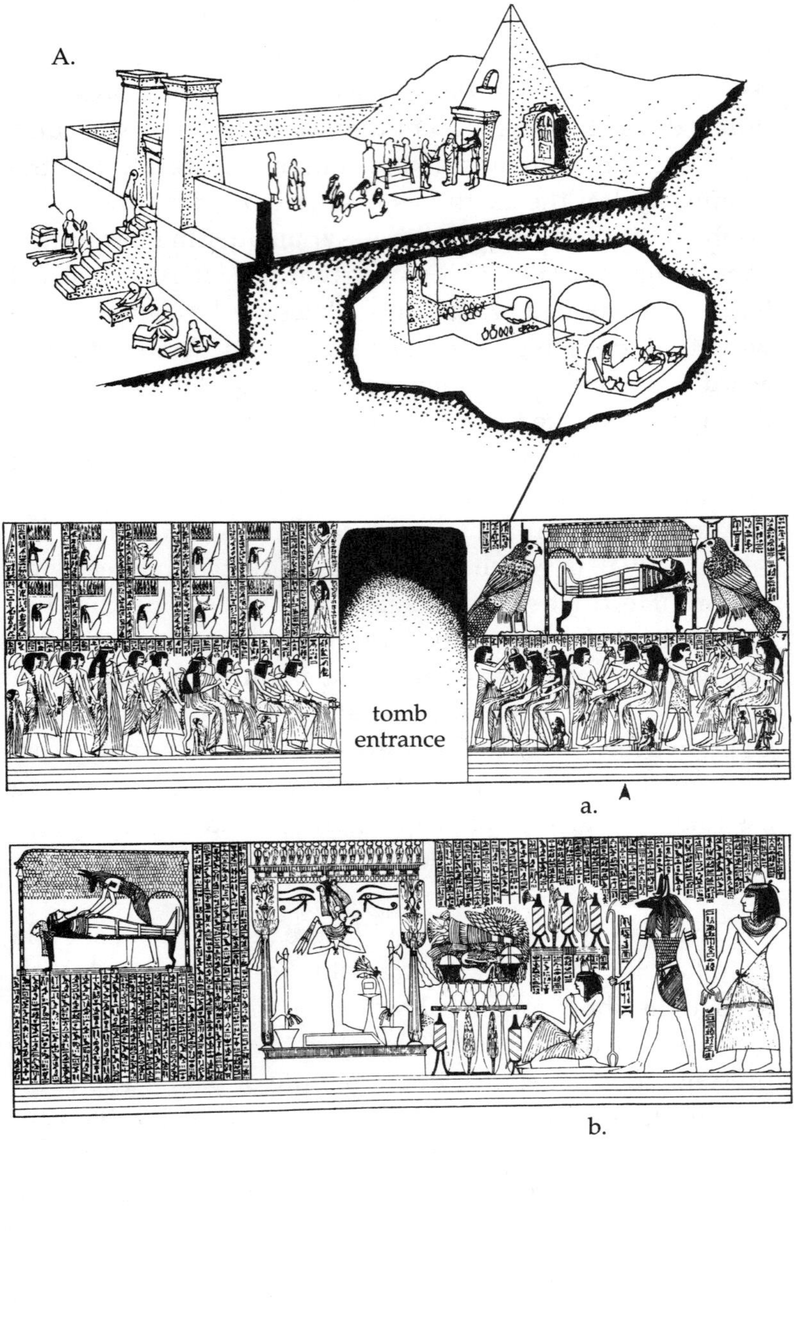

tomb
entrance

a. ▲

b.

B.

Figure 18. In this depiction of the Opening of the Mouth ceremony (A) at the tomb of Sennedjem (c. 1250 B.C.), his mummy is held upright by a priest wearing an Anubis mask before a small pyramid chapel representing the cosmic mountain. Afterwards he will be taken down into his "Room of Gold" or burial chamber, where the murals show him and his wife (a) seated with their ancestors on one side as their descendants face them in a joyous family reunion, complete with children playing under their chairs. On the opposite wall, Anubis leads Sennedjem by the hand into the presence of Osiris (b). Similarly, in this catacomb painting (B) of more than a thousand years later, the Roman matron Vibia is led *(inductio)* into the great feast of the next life.

tablets and the analogies with *Enuma Elish* and its role in the Babylonian New Year's festival, would seem to point in this direction, but we cannot certainly decide such an issue.[54] It seems to me that the Ur III and earlier cylinder seals that depict the "presentation, by an intermediary, of a worshipper to a god or a deified king," would prove to be a most interesting study from the point of view of their ritual setting. It is possible that the last preserved part of the Seleucid tablet from Uruk may be relevant in this regard.[55]

Proposition 10. The temple is associated with the realm of the dead, the underworld, the afterlife, the grave.

The unifying feature here is the rites and worship of ancestors. The temple is the link between this world and the next. It has been called "an antechamber between the worlds." Tombs can be—and in Egypt and elsewhere are—essentially temples (compare the cosmic orientation, texts written on the tomb walls that guide the deceased into the afterlife, etc.). The unifying principle between temple and tomb is resurrection. Tombs and sarcophagi are "sacred places," sites of resurrection. In Egyptian religion Nut is depicted on the coffin cover, symbolizing the cosmic orientation (i.e., "Nut is the coffin").[56] One of the chapels in the Eninnu temple was called "é.nì.ki.sè 'the house in which one brings offerings for the dead.' " It carried the further description "it is something pure, purified by Abzu."[57] There is an intimate connection between burials and temples VIII and XI at Tepe Gawra, the latter of which, according to Arthur Tobler, "attracted considerable numbers of burials to its precincts."[58]

Proposition 11. Sacral, communal meals are carried out in connection with temple ritual, often at the conclusion of or during a covenant ceremony.

Having attempted to establish the temple background of Exodus 19–24 above in discussing Proposition 1, I would like now to introduce 24:11, the meal that directly follows the covenant ceremony of Exodus 24:8, as the prime example of this point. The Gudea Cylinders end with the conjunction of a festive meal attended by all of the gods and the fixing of the destinies.[59] Pallis states that "the akitu festival was concluded by a great sacrificial meal of which all, the gods, the king, the priests, and the people, partook."[60] *Enuma Elish* III 128–38 contains the account of the gods entering the sacred chamber where the destinies are decreed, at which time they partook of a festive banquet.[61] We have the recurring theme here of formal act and sacral meal, the same phenomenon that we see in 1 Kings 8 where,

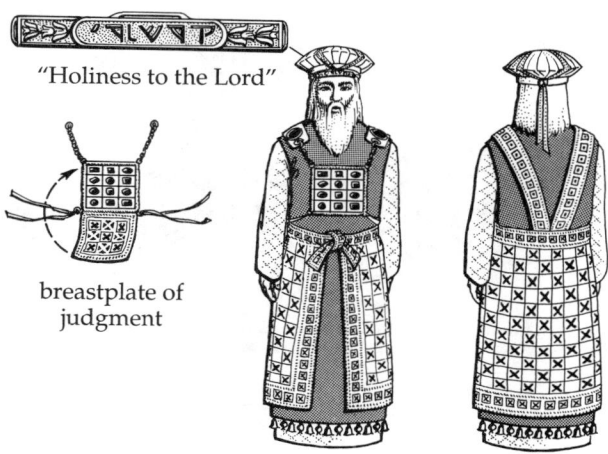

"Holiness to the Lord"

breastplate of
judgment

Figure 19. The Urim and Thummim were sacred stones used in an oracular fashion still not completely understood. When not in use, they were kept in a pouch formed by folding up the embroidered panel of the Breastplate of Judgment.

following Solomon's dedicatory prayer for the Jerusalem temple (a prayer carried out "with his hands spread up to heaven"), the king held a feast. This prayer fits in remarkably well with the form and the religiosity expressed in the Babylonian psalm cycle *su-ila*.[62]

Proposition 12. The tablets of destiny ("tablets of the decrees"[63]) are consulted both in the cosmic sense by the gods, and yearly in a special chamber, in the Eninnu temple of Gudea's time.[64]

It is by this means that the will of the deity is communicated to the people through the king or the prophet for a given year.[65] The association of sacred meal and setting of the destinies in *Enuma Elish* and in the Gudea Cylinder B has been pointed out above in discussing Proposition 11. Widengren has an excellent discussion in which he interprets the association of heavenly council, enthronement,

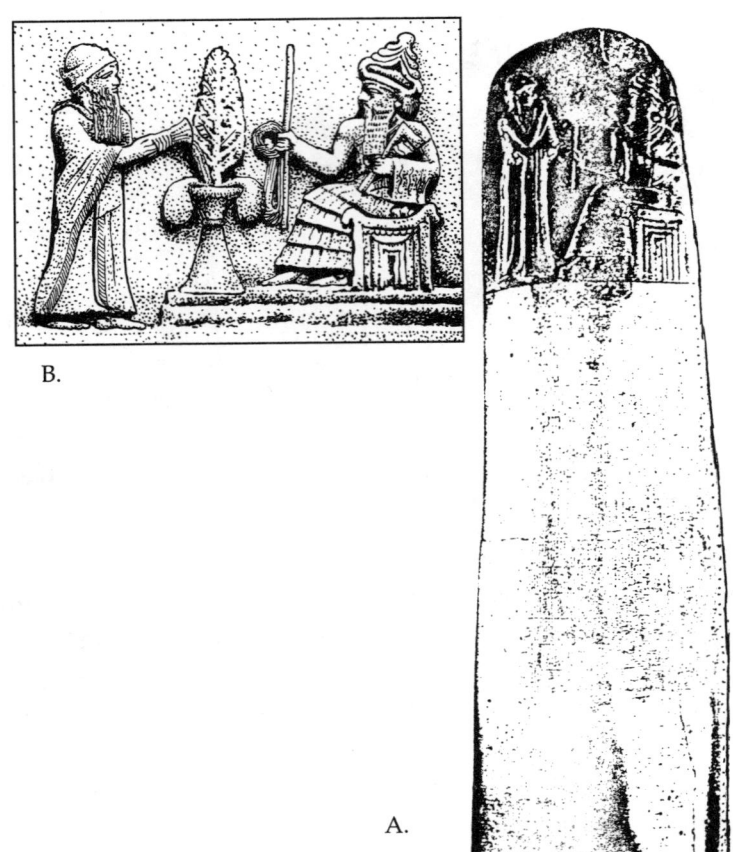

B.

A.

Figure 20. The famous basalt Stele of Hammurabi (A), c. 1700 B.C., depicts the actual ceremony that took place in the Holy of Holies of the Esagila where the sun god Shamash gives Hammurabi the ring and staff of dominion. The detail (B) from the Neo-Sumerian Urnammu Stele shows a close-up of the *canon*, or measuring rod (cf. Ezekiel 40:3), and the ring of coiled cord used in the process of laying out the temple ground plan.

and tablets of destiny. He writes that "the tablets of Law, as well as the Urim and Thummim, play the same role as the tablets of destiny in being the instrument by which the will of the deity is communicated to the leader of the people, be it Moses or the king."[66] Both the Urim and Thummim and the tablets of destiny are fastened in a pouch on their possessor's chest.[67]

Proposition 13. There is a close interrelationship between the temple and law in the ancient Near East.

The building or restoration of a temple is perceived as the moving force behind a restating or "codifying" of basic legal principles and of the "righting" and organizing of proper social order. The Old Testament "clearly associates the conceptions of 'covenant' and 'law' with one another in a definite relationship."[68] I would add "temple" to this pair. The act of Moses' appearing "before the Lord" in Exodus 19–24 produced the law, or rather what Mendenhall would call "policy."[69] The action that gives rise to the "codification" of the ancient collections of "royal judgments," or "just laws"[70] is, in my opinion, rebuilding or rededicating of a temple, or the appearance of the king in the temple early in his reign. The Prologue of the Code of Hammurabi places great emphasis on his concern for the temples and cult centers under his sway and finally states, just before the "laws" proper begin: "When Marduk commissioned me to guide the people aright, to direct the land, I established law and justice in the language of the land."[71] This commission from Marduk would presumably have come to Hammurabi in Esagila, where in fact a stela containing the laws was placed.[72] The Epilogue also states, "I, Hammurabi, am the king of justice, to whom Shamash committed law."[73] This is not to revive the largely outmoded ideas of Henry Maine and others that law derives from religion;[74] it is simply

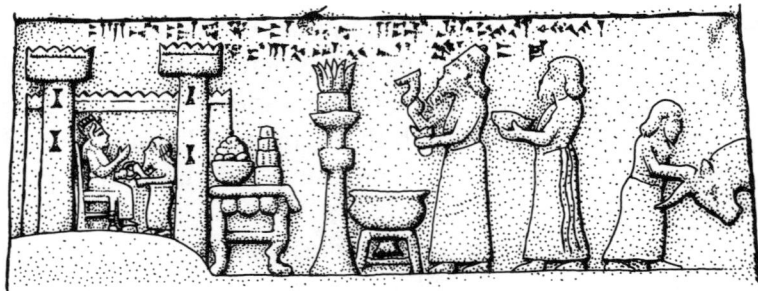

Figure 21. One of the panels from the White Obelisk shows a calf at the far right being led to sacrifice before the altar. The enthroned goddess, left, bestows power upon her worshiper in another "ring and rod" ceremony as she sits in her temple, with its two pillars, on the usual raised mound.

to look more carefully at what the texts themselves say, which is, I believe, that the impetus by the king to compile the existing body of judicial precedents was seen to come as a result of duties connected with the temple.[75]

Proposition 14. The temple is a place of sacrifice.

The ubiquity of this aspect of temple worship in the ancient Near East is such that its mention here may seem superfluous. And yet sacrifice has been one of the most difficult, least understood, and most discussed of all religious phenomena.[76] In northern Mesopotamia the recent excavations at Tell Chuera in northern Syria have yielded one of the most important archaeological evidences for a sacrificial practice in ancient times. The Akkad period Nord-Tempel yielded remains of an offertory stairway at the east entrance along with what appeared to be an offering table and an adjacent *Wanne,* which would have received the blood of the offerings. The excavators of Tell Chuera compare the remains of this installation with the well-known scene of the White Obelisk of Assurnasirpal I, which shows an

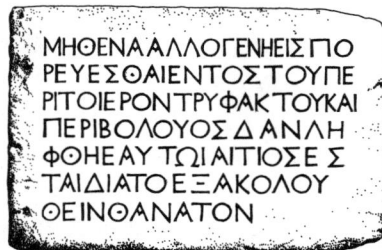

ΜΗΘΕΝΑ ΑΛΛΟΓΕΝΗ ΕΙΣ ΠΟ	No Gentile shall enter
ΡΕΥΕΣΘΑΙ ΕΝΤΟΣ ΤΟΥ ΠΕ	inward of the partition
ΡΙΤ ΟΙΕΡΟΝ ΤΡΥ ΦΑΚΤ ΟΥ ΚΑΙ	and barrier around the temple,
ΠΕΡΙΒΟΛΟΥΟΣ Δ ΑΝ ΛΗ	and whoever is caught
ΦΟΗΕ ΑΥ ΤΩΙ ΑΙΤΙΟΣ Ε Σ	shall be responsible
ΤΑΙ ΔΙΑΤΟ Ε Ξ ΑΚΟΛΟΥ	to himself for his
ΘΕΙΝ ΘΑΝΑΤΟΝ	subsequent death.

Figure 22. The rare surviving marble sign, part of the *soreg*, or encircling fence around the temple precinct, warned Gentiles not to enter the inner courts of the temple of Jerusalem during the late Second Temple Period.

elaborate cult installation of sacrificial offering in front of a temple.[77]

Proposition 15. The temple and its ritual are enshrouded in secrecy.

This secrecy relates to the sacredness of the temple precinct and the strict division in ancient times between sacred and profane space. Exodus 19:12–13, 21–24 apply here: there are certain precincts that are "off limits." To trespass sacred precincts, or to approach sacred objects without being ritually prepared, can result in disaster (see 1 Samuel 6:19–20). A second century A.D. Aramaic inscription from Hatra invokes "the curse of Our L[ord] and Our Lady and the Son of our Lord and Shaharu and Baasham[en] and Atargatis [be] on [anyone] who enters past this point into the shr[ine]."[78] The Neo-Babylonian tablet that describes the ritual for the consecration and induction of a divine statue concludes with the warning "let initiate instruct initiate, he shall not let the uninitiated see: it is a thing forbidden of Enlil, the elder, [and] Marduk."[79]

The problem of secrecy relates of course to the question of who was allowed access to the temple precincts, or, rather, to what extent the general populace was allowed access to the temple ritual. A series of inscriptions on doors of the Ptolemaic temple at Edfu in Egypt relates access to the temple to moral worthiness: "Everyone who enters by this door, beware of entering in impurity, for God loves purity more than millions of possessions, more than hundreds of thousands of fine gold." And again, "Do not come in sin, do not enter in impurity, do not utter falsehood in his house." And the admonition to secrecy: "Do not reveal what you have seen in the mysteries of the temples."[80]

Of course, these admonitions are directed to priests, for, as Fairman writes: "It is clear that for the majority of the people there was not direct contact with either daily service or with many festivals, and no participation in any intimate or sacred rites."[81] During the ceremonies connected with the New Year festival and the rededication of the temple, "the doors of the temple were shut while they were being celebrated, and no member of the general public witnessed them."[82] In Egypt, as well as in Israel and Mesopotamia, the primary way that the general populace would have taken part in temple ritual was through attendance at the great processionals and the public banquets that would take place at the end of a ritual period.[83] But all Israelite males were commanded to "appear before the Lord God" three times during the year (Exodus 23:17; 34:23), and this was expanded to include all members of the family, as we see in Deuteronomy 16:1, 14 and 31:11–12.[84] Inscriptions on the south gate of the *temenos* of the Edfu temple give further insight into what access the common people would have had to the temple, and what role it would have played in the religion of the people: "It is the standing place of those who have and those who have not in order to pray for life from the Lord of Life. . . . The place for hearing the petitions of all petitioners in order to judge Truth from Falsehood. It is the great place for championing the poor in order to rescue them from the strong. . . . The place outside which offerings are made at all times consisting of all the produce of the servants."[85]

The Epilogue of the Code of Hammurabi states that a stele containing the Code was placed in Esagila, where any oppressed person could read the pertinent passages of the laws and thus understand his cause. But as Wiseman writes, it is unlikely that common Babylonians could have come into the sacred precincts of Esagila to examine the stele.[86] Copies of the stele would presumably have been available elsewhere. Yet another insight into the extent to which common people would have had access to temples comes from the countless votive sculptures that archaeologists find in the excavation of temple ruins. Such statues, meant to represent their human offerers, often inscribed, and presumably manufactured, in a temple workshop and available for purchase by the donor, would be placed in the temple, presumably by priests, and stationed on benches in the sanctuary, in an adjoining room, or in a courtyard. The statue would then stand perpetually before the effigy of the deity, representing the blessings the offerer hoped to obtain.[87] The Early Dynastic temples in the Diyala Valley give us classic architectural examples of temple precincts that are successively cut off from their immediate surroundings and made inaccessible to passersby by means of thick walls and elaborate series of courtyards.[88]

Notes

1. I am not going to discuss the meaning of the term *temple* itself. For a rather standard definition of the term, see W. B. Kristensen, *The Meaning of Religion* (The Hague: Nijhoff, 1960), 369. It should be noted that the Greek root *temno*, from which *temenos* derives—"a piece of land marked off from common uses and dedicated to a god, precinct" (*Liddell-Scott-Jones Greek English Lexicon* [Oxford: Clarendon Press, 1968], 1774)—has a predecessor in Sumerian *temen* (Anton Deimel,

Sumerisch-Akkadisches Glossar [Rome: Verlag des Päpstl. Bibelinstituts, 1934], 206), which appears, for example, in the inscriptions of Gudea of Lagash. See *SAK,* 76 (= Statue C III 8), 78 (= Statue E II 13). For a discussion of Babylonian equivalents of *temple,* see Edmond Sollberger, "The Temple in Babylonia," in *Le Temple et le Culte* (Istanbul: Nederlands Historisch-Archeologisch Instituut) 20 (1975): 31–34.

2. For an excellent discussion of the various problems related to the study of the temple of Solomon, see Jean Ouellette, "The Basic Structure of Solomon's Temple and Archaeological Research," in *The Temple of Solomon,* ed. J. Gutmann (Missoula: Scholars, 1976), 1–20.

3. Such is not the case with Egypt, where a prominent example can be found in Eve A. E. Reymond, *The Mythological Origins of the Egyptian Temple* (Manchester: Manchester University Press, 1969).

4. See Theodor A. Busink, *Der Tempel von Jerusalem,* 2 vols. (Leiden: Brill, 1970).

5. Jonathan Z. Smith, *Map Is Not Territory* (Leiden: Brill, 1978), ix.

6. See George E. Mendenhall, "'Change and Decay in All Around I See': Conquest, Covenant and the Tenth Generation," *Biblical Archaeologist* 39 (1976): 152–57.

7. Mendenhall has also been in the forefront of documenting such continuity. See "The Ancient in the Modern—and Vice Versa," in *Michigan Oriental Studies in Honor of George G. Cameron,* ed. Louis L. Orlin (Ann Arbor: Department of Near Eastern Studies, University of Michigan, 1976), 227–53.

8. See Arvid S. Kapelrud, "Temple Building, a Task for Gods and Kings," *Orientalia* 32 (1963): 56–62.

9. In compiling the following list of motifs, I have learned much from Hugh Nibley, "What Is a Temple?" in *Mormonism and Early Christianity,* in *CWHN,* 4:355–90.

10. See *SAK,* 113 (= Gudea Cylinder A XXI 23), 141 (= Gudea Cylinder B XXIV 9); "Hymn to the Ekur," in *ANET,* 582–83 ("The great house, it is a mountain great / The house of Enlil, it is a mountain great / The house of Ninlil, it is a mountain great," etc.).

11. G. van Driel, *The Cult of Assur* (Assen: Van Gorcum, 1969), 34–36.

12. See Kristensen, *The Meaning of Religion,* 257–58.

13. Menahem Haran, *Temples and Temple Service in Ancient Israel* (Oxford: Clarendon, 1978), 26.

14. See Martin Noth, *The Laws in the Pentateuch and Other Studies* (Edinburgh/London: Oliver and Boyd, 1966), 36–41.

15. *AAHB,* 24.

16. For Egypt, see Reymond, *The Mythical Origin of the Egyptian Temple*, 46–47, 59, 266, 305. See also J. A. Wilson, in *ANET*, 4 n. 7A.

17. J. Spencer, "The Brick Foundations of Late-Period Peripteral Temples and Their Mythological Origin," in *Glimpses of Ancient Egypt (Fs. H. W. Fairman)*, ed. John Ruffle, G. A. Gaballa, and Kenneth A. Kitchen (Warminster: Aris and Phillips, 1979), 133. See also M. el-Din Ibrahim, "The God of the Great Temple of Edfu," in *Glimpses of Ancient Egypt*, 170–73.

18. See *SAK*, 113 (Cylinder A XXI 18–27).

19. *SAK*, 113 (Cylinder A XXII 11) and 127 (Cylinder B V 7), respectively.

20. See Kapelrud, "Temple Building."

21. See also A. Falkenstein and Eva Strommenger, "Gudea," *Rivista Istituto di Archeolgia* 3 (1971): 676–87.

22. Hugh Nibley, "The Hierocentric State," *Western Political Quarterly* 4 (1951): 235.

23. See Geo Widengren, "Early Hebrew Myths and Their Interpretations," in *Myth, Ritual and Kingship*, ed. S. H. Hooke (Oxford: Oxford University, 1956), 168. For this theme at Ras Shamra, see Richard Clifford, "The Temple in the Ugaritic Myth of Baal," *Symposia*, ed. F. Cross (Cambridge: American Schools of Oriental Research, 1979), 145. For an Egyptian example, see H. W. Fairman, "Worship and Festivals in an Egyptian Temple," *Bulletin, John Rylands Library* 37 (1954–55): 177.

24. See *AAM*, 20 (the Temple Oval at Khafaje), 19 (fixing the building immovably in the earth by means of foundation figures).

25. See Joan Oates, "Ur and Eridu, the Prehistory," *Iraq* 22 (1960): 45.

26. See G. van Driel, "De Uruk-Nederzetting op de Jebel Aruda: een Voorlopig Bericht (Stand eind 1976)," *Phoenix (Vooraziatisch-Egyptisch Genootschap "Ex Oriente Lux")* 23 (1977): 46.

27. *Dictionary of Symbols and Imagery*, 2nd ed. (Amsterdam/London: North-Holland, 1976), 464. (I am indebted to Michael Lyon for suggesting this latter connection.)

28. See Spencer, "The Brick Foundations," 133.

29. See E. Douglas Van Buren, "Foundation Rites for a New Temple," *Orientalia* 21 (1952): 293, and the discussion of Proposition 7.

30. Spencer, "The Brick Foundations," 133.

31. See Ann Louise Perkins, "The Comparative Archaeology of Early Mesopotamia," *Studies in Ancient Oriental Civilization* 25 (1949): 67–70, 87.

32. See Max Mallowan, "The Development of Cities from Al-'Ubaid to the End of Uruk 5," *Cambridge Ancient History*, 3rd ed., 2

vols./2 parts (London: Cambridge University Press, 1970), 1/1:347. For the possibility of a temple observatory at Akkad in the time of Sargon the Great, see John D. Weir, *The Venus Tablets of Ammizaduga* (Istanbul: Nederlands Historisch-Archeologisch Instituut, 1972), 40–47. For an extensive discussion of possible cosmic symbolism in the temple of Solomon, see W. F. Albright, *Archaeology and the Religion of Israel*, 5th ed. (Garden City: Doubleday, 1968), 144–50. For an interpretation of evidence from Egypt and Mesopotamia in this light, see Andrzej Wiercinski, "Pyramids and Ziggurats as the Architectonic Representations of the Archetype of the Cosmic Mountain," *Katunob* 10 (1977): 71–87. (I am indebted to Professor John Sorenson for this reference.) For the orientation of the Ziggurat of Nanna at Ur, see *AAM*, 56.

33. *ANET*, 338. For a discussion of the cosmic orientation of the Israelite tent shrine, see Hugh Nibley, "Tenting, Toll, and Taxing," *Western Political Quarterly* 19 (1966): 603–5. For an attempted refutation of the view that Solomon's Temple was oriented toward the sun, see H. Van Dyke Parunak, "Was Solomon's Temple Oriented toward the Sun?" *Palestine Exploration Quarterly* 110 (1978): 28–33.

34. See *SAK*, 77, 79 (Gudea Statue D II 11, Statue E I 16 = "e.PA, Temple of the seven zones"); but see also *IGL*, 132–34, which casts doubt on the traditional meaning (that is, a seven-tiered building) ascribed to these and similar passages. For the *gigunû* as the most holy and secret sanctuary of the sacred marriage, placed atop the seven-staged ziggurat, see E. Douglas Van Buren, "Foundation Rites for a New Temple," 301–2. And for a Sumerian sacred marriage text expressing the imagery of an ascent toward the chapel that stands atop the ziggurat, see Thorkild Jacobsen, *The Treasures of Darkness* (New Haven/London: Yale University, 1976), 126.

35. For Nabopolassar's text, see Stephen Herbert Langdon, *Die neubabylonischen Königsinschriften*, Vorderasiatische Bibliothek 4 (Leipzig: Hinrichs, 1912), 62–63. And see E. Douglas Van Buren, "Foundation Rites," 293 for an explanation of the "ordinances and ritual of Eridu," the "precisely ordained rites" that must be carried out in the construction of a temple in Mesopotamia.

36. See *SAK*, 89–97 (= Cylinder A I–VII). See also *AAHB*, 30.

37. See Kapelrud, "Temple Building," 59–61.

38. As for example *SAK*, 101–3 (= A XI 18–27), and *SAK*, 123 (= B I 10).

39. Jonathan Smith, referring to *M'Abot* 1:2, in *Map Is Not Territory*, 118. For an excellent discussion of the economic and social role of the Mesopotamian temple, see J. N. Postgate, "The Role of the Temple in

the Mesopotamian Secular Community," in *Man, Settlement and Urbanism,* ed. P. J. Ucko, R. Tringham, and G. W. Dimbleday (Cambridge: Schenkman, 1972), 811–25.

40. See *SAK,* 101 (= Gudea Cylinder A XI 1–27).

41. *ANET,* 611–19.

42. See *ANET,* 646 n. 6.

43. See *ANET,* 646–51.

44. See Sidney Smith, "The Babylonian Ritual for the Consecration and Induction of a Divine Statue," *Journal of American Oriental Society* (1925): 37–60; O. R. Gurney, "Babylonian Prophylactic Figures and their Rituals," *Annals of Archaeology and Anthropology* 22 (1935): 31–96; Edmond Sollberger, "The Temple in Babylonia," 33; and Fairman, "Worship and Festivals," 173, 180.

45. W. W. Hallo, "The Cultic Setting of Sumerian Poetry," in *Actes de la XVII Rencontre Assyriologique Internationale,* ed. Andre Finet (Bruxelles: Comite Belge de Recherches en Mesopotamie) 17 (1970): 129.

46. S. N. Kramer in "The Dumuzi-Inanna Sacred Marriage Rite: Origin, Development, Character," *CRRA* 17 (1970): 136–40.

47. *AAHB,* 27.

48. See the texts in *ANET,* 4–6 and 329–30, and Fairman, "Worship and Festivals," 193–96.

49. As we see in *ANET,* 332.

50. See Svend Aage Pallis, *The Babylonian Akitu Festival* (Copenhagen: Bianco Lunos, 1926), 248–67; W. G. Lambert, "The Great Battle of the Mesopotamian Religious Year, the Conflict in the Akitu House," *Iraq* 25 (1963): 189–90.

51. *The Babylonian Akitu Festival,* 260–65, and Walter Andrae, *Das Wiedererstandene Assur* (Munich: C. H. Beck, 1977 reprint [orig. 1938]), 223.

52. See H. Sauren, "Die Einweihung des Eninnu," *CRRA* 20 (1975): 95–103.

53. For a recitation of the views of many scholars who held this or similar views, see Ivan Engnell, *Studies in Divine Kingship in the Ancient Near East,* 2nd ed. (Oxford: Blackwell, 1967), 103–5.

54. See Richard Clifford, "The Temple in the Ugaritic Myth of Baal," 145; Loren R. Fisher, "Creation at Ugarit and in the Old Testament," *Vetus Testamentum* 15 (1965): 313–24. And for a very important Ugaritic text that combines the themes of enthronement, mountain (temple), creation, ritual battle, and sacred marriage, among others, see Loren R. Fisher and F. Brent Knutson, "An Enthronement Ritual at Ugarit," *Journal of Near Eastern Studies* 28 (1969): 157–67.

55. See *AAM,* 68; *ANET,* 339. For an extensive discussion of the

themes of baptism, anointing, clothing, enthronement, and initiation into divine life in Mandean religion, and the Syrian and Mesopotamian background of such customs, see Geo Widengren, "Heavenly Enthronement and Baptism, Studies in Mandaean Baptism," in *Religions in Antiquity, Essays in Memory of Erwin Ramsdell Goodenough*, Studies in the History of Religions, vol. 14, ed. Jacob Neusner (Leiden: Brill, 1968): 551–82. Finally, for the sacred marriage drama in an Egyptian temple, see Fairman, "Worship and Festivals," 196–200.

56. Kristensen, *The Meaning of Religion*, 372–73. For the Hittite sphere, see O. R. Gurney, *Some Aspects of Hittite Religion* (Oxford: Oxford University, Schweich Lectures, 1977): 61–63. For Egypt see Fairman, "Worship and Festivals," 200.

57. *IGL*, 131. For a discussion of a sepulchral chamber to Marduk in Etemenanki in Babylon, see Pallis, *The Babylonian Akitu Festival*, 104–5, 108–9.

58. Arthur Tobler, *Excavations at Tepe Gawra* 2 (Philadelphia: University of Pennsylvania, Museum Monographs, 1950), 98–101. At Ur, however, where we might expect spectacular support for such a connection, Woolley is at pains to dampen such speculation; see C. L. Woolley, *Ur Excavations* 2, *The Royal Cemetery, Text*, Publications of the Joint Exped. of the Brit. Mus. and the Mus. of the Univ. of Penn. to Mesopotamia (New York: Trustees of the Two Museums, 1934), 12–14. Isaiah 65:3–4 would seem to be relevant here, but see the discussion of W. Boyd Barrick, "The Funerary Character of 'High Places' in Ancient Palestine: A Re-assessment," *Vetus Testamentum* 25 (1975): 565–95. He does not, however, discuss this passage.

59. See *IGL*, 120.

60. Pallis, *The Babylonian Akitu Festival*, 173.

61. See *ANET*, 64–66.

62. See Erich Ebeling, *Die Akkadische Gebetsserie 'Handerhebung'* (Berlin: Akademie Verlag, 1953). See also *AAHB*, 24. For a Hittite text that conjoins the themes of blood, sacral meal, and covenant, see Gurney, *Some Aspects of Hittite Religion*, 29–30.

63. Thorkild Jacobsen, *The Treasures of Darkness* (New Haven: Yale University Press, 1976), 178–79.

64. See *IGL*, 141–42.

65. Note *Enuma Elish* IV 22.

66. *AAHB*, 27.

67. See Geo Widengren, "Early Hebrew Myths and Their Interpretation," in *Myth, Ritual, and Kingship*, ed. S. H. Hooke (Oxford: Oxford University Press, 1956), 167; see also Pallis, *The Babylonian Akitu Festival*, 193–94.

68. Noth, *The Laws in the Pentateuch*, 39.

69. George Mendenhall, "Ancient Oriental and Biblical Law," *Biblical Archaeologist* 17 (May 1954): 26–28.

70. See F. R. Kraus, "Ein zentrales Problem des altmesopotamischen Rechtes: Was ist der Codex Hammurabi?" *Genava* 8 (1960): 285–88.

71. *ANET*, 165.

72. See *ANET*, 178.

73. *ANET*, 178.

74. See William Seagle, *History of the Law* (New York: Tudor, 1946), 117–30.

75. Mendenhall, "Ancient Oriental and Biblical Law," 11.

76. For an excellent summary of the *status questionis*, see Kristensen, *The Meaning of Religion*, 444–52 and 458–96. For a selection of sacrificial practices over a widespread geographical area, see, for Egypt, Fairman, "Worship and Festivals," 178, 180–84, 191, 198–202; for Assyria, van Driel, *The Cult of Assur*, 86–119; for Asia Minor, Gurney, *Some Aspects of Hittite Religion*, 24–43.

77. See Anton Moortgat, *Tell Chuera in Nordost Syrien, Vorläufiger Bericht über die dritte Grabungskampagne 1960* (Wiss. Abh. der Arbeitsgem. für Forsch. des Landes Nordrhein-Westfalen, 24; Köln/Opladen; Westdeutscher Verlag, 1962): 13–14, with Plan II and Abb. 9–10. See also Dennis J. McCarthy, "The Symbolism of Blood and Sacrifice," *Journal of Biblical Literature* 88 (1969): 166–76.

78. Delbert R. Hillers, "*Mskn* 'Temple' in Inscriptions from Hatra," *Bulletin of the American Schools of Oriental Research* 207 (1972): 54–56.

79. Smith, "The Babylonian Ritual for the Consecration and Induction of a Divine Statue," 51–52.

80. Fairman, "Worship and Festivals," 201.

81. In ibid.

82. Ibid., 187.

83. Ibid., 202–3; J. N. Postgate, "The Bit Akiti in Assyrian Nabu Temples," *Sumer* 30 (1974): 57–62; and 1 Kings 8:62–66.

84. See also Haran, *Temples and Temple Service*, 290–94.

85. Fairman, "Worship and Festivals," 203.

86. See D. J. Wiseman, "The Laws of Hammurabi Again," *Journal of Semitic Studies* 7 (1962): 166.

87. See Henri Frankfort, *Sculpture of the Third Millennium B.C. from Tell Asmar and Khafajah*, Oriental Institute Publication no. 44 (Chicago: University of Chicago, 1939), 10–11.

88. See *AAM*, 20–25.

6

Liturgy and Cosmogony: The Ritual Use of Creation Accounts in the Ancient Near East

Stephen D. Ricks

In his luminous study of the Egyptian background of the Joseph Smith papyri, Hugh Nibley notes that the creation story constitutes a focal point in Egyptian religious literature and in the temple ritual.[1] The most notable among these is, perhaps, "the oldest Egyptian text of all, the Shabako story of the Creation," which appears to have been the script of "a drama in which certain key scenes were presented by actors, while the story as a whole was recited and explained to the temple audience by a lector-priest," referred to in this instance as a "Theaterdirektor" by the Egyptologist Kurt Sethe, who studied the Shabako Stone extensively.[2] This phenomenon was not, however, restricted to the Egyptians among the peoples of the pre-Christian Near East.[3] A similar liturgical use of the creation story, often in conjunction with temple worship, was made in Mesopotamia, Persia, and in Israel of the Second Temple period.

The *zagmuk* or *akītu* (New Year's) festival figures as the central cultic event in the Mesopotamian religious calendar. It constituted "the confluence of every current of religious thought, the expression of every shade of religious feeling"

among the Babylonians and Assyrians.[4] The *akītu* festival
served to reestablish the proper pattern of nature, with
order prevailing over chaos, and to reaffirm the gods, the
king, and his subjects in their respective roles in the cosmic
order. Reflections of the festival are to be found as early as
the third millennium B.C. in the yearly rites of the Sumerian
city-states of Ur and Erech, but no extensive evidence exists
for its celebration until the time of the Late Assyrian and
Late Babylonian kingdoms (750–612 B.C. and 650–539 B.C.
respectively).[5] Among the documents recovered from this
late period are priestly liturgical commentaries, "order of
service" manuals prepared to guide the priest in the proper
performance of the lengthy and complex rituals of the *akītu*
festival, which lasted through the first twelve days of Nisan,
the first month of the Babylonian calendar.[6] On the fourth
of Nisan, in the temple of Marduk (the temple serving as a
symbol of the ordered cosmos in the ancient Near East[7]), the
priest was instructed to read the *Enuma Elish*, the Babylonian creation myth, which recounts the victory of Marduk
over the powers of chaos personalized in Apsu and Tiamat
and his creation of the world, and concludes with a hymn
extolling the kingship of Marduk.[8] In the later stages of the
festival the victory of Marduk over Tiamat was ritually
reenacted.[9]

Among the ancient Persians the ritual recitation of the
birth of the gods was customary on sacrificial occasions.
Herodotus reports in his *Histories* that after the one who
was offering sacrifice had cut the animal victim into pieces
and had boiled them, he spread them "on the softest
grass."[10] Thereupon a Magian, the Persian priest whose
presence was obligatory at such sacrifices, chanted the
account of the birth of the gods *(theogoniēn)* "as the Persian
tradition relates it."[11]

Figure 23. This bas-relief is believed to represent Marduk holding three-pronged thunderbolts in each hand, fighting the chaos monster, Tiamat.

It has been suggested that the creation account of Genesis 1:1–2:4 was used in the temple liturgy of Israel at the New Year's Festival before the Babylonian exile, when the enthronement of the Lord was celebrated, and possibly on other occasions as well.[12] The didactic-liturgical nature of the creation account itself, with its constant refrains, "and God saw that it was good,"[13] "and the evening and the morning were the first day,"[14] etc., strengthens the case for its ritual use.[15] Although this hypothesis is attractive, in the absence of "order of service" manuals (such as those found in Mesopotamia) or of descriptions of the Israelite rituals from external sources (such as Herodotus's description of the Persian sacrifices), it must remain tentative.[16]

Whereas we lack internal and external sources that

Figure 24. From this royal tomb in Kurdistan (c. A.D. 350), we see a typical Persian sacrificial altar. The men each carry a bow symbolic of royalty and wear white face masks to protect the sacred fire from contamination, as do the modern Parsis in India. The enthroned god moves in a lunar boat within the circle of the sun in a relief above the altar, while a four-winged seraph moves before him on the left and an unusual eleven-pointed star follows on the right.

concern the liturgical use of the creation account in pre-Exilic Israel, we have both for the Second Temple Period. In the Mishnaic tractate *Ta⁽anit* (committed to writing, along with the rest of the Mishnah, by Judah the Prince ca. A.D. 200, but probably representing far older traditions), various items of information and instruction are given regarding the temple duties of the twenty-four courses of laymen *(anshē ma⁽amad)*, priests, and Levites (mentioned in 1 Chronicles 24). The laymen are given the responsibility of reading sections of the Genesis creation account while the priests and Levites perform the sacrifices.[17] The laymen belonging to the course currently serving in the temple who had not been able to go up to Jerusalem were charged with the duty of reading the creation account in their own towns.[18] Theophrastus may be referring to the same practice in his *De Pietate* when he remarks that the Jews "now sacrifice victims according to their old mode of sacrifice. . . . They do it fasting on the intervening days.[19] During the whole time, being philosophers by race, they converse with each other about the deity and at nighttime they make observations of the stars, gazing at them and calling upon God" (a possible allusion to a recital of the creation account).[20] Even in modern Judaism the Genesis creation account is accorded an honored place in the liturgy, being read *in toto* on Simḥat Torah (the final day of the Feast of Tabernacles) and in part (Genesis 2:1–3) on Friday evening, twice during the service and once at *kiddush*, when the Sabbath is solemnly blessed following six days of labor.[21]

These brief remarks have been confined to the use of the creation account as liturgy in the ancient Near East. However, it is a phenomenon far more widespread than that, as the researches of Mircea Eliade amply illustrate.[22] Ritual repetition of the past is not restricted to the recitation of the creation account. As just two examples, the Christian ordinances of baptism and the sacrament both involve a ritual recollection of the death and resurrection of Christ. The apostle Paul makes explicit this connection when he writes in 1 Corinthians 11:26, "For as often as ye eat this bread, and drink this cup, ye do shew the Lord's death till he come." Based upon the individual's worthy participation—and Paul warns in the strongest terms possible against unworthily participating in the sacrament of the Lord's supper: "Whosoever shall eat this bread, and drink this cup of the Lord, unworthily, shall be guilty of the body and blood of the Lord" (1 Corinthians 11:27)—these ordinances have a saving value ("that they may always have his Spirit to be with them"—Moroni 4:3; D&C 20:77; see Moroni 5:2; D&C 20:79).[23]

Clearly, the primal creative acts (and hence their recitation or reenactment) were viewed by the peoples of the ancient Near East and a host of others as possessing a dynamic (even sacramental) and not a static quality. "What happened in the beginning," writes Raffaele Pettazzoni, "has an exemplary and defining value for what is happening today and what will happen in the future."[24] By becoming a participant in the victory of the forces of order in the creation through reciting or reenacting the creation, the individual or community also becomes a participant in the fruits of that victory.

Notes

1. See Hugh Nibley, *The Message of the Joseph Smith Papyri* (Salt Lake City: Deseret Book, 1965), 129–32.

2. Ibid., 131; cf. Kurt Sethe, *Das "Denkmal memphitischer Theologie": Der Schabakostein des Britischen Museums* (Leipzig: Hinrichs, 1928), 17.

3. Nibley has also noted, in *Message of the Joseph Smith Papyri*, 257–58, 260–61, 264, 275, the probable ritual use of the creation account in the Qumran community and the liturgical use of the early Christian *Odes of Solomon* and *Pistis Sophia*, each of which contains extended references to the creation. These documents will not be considered in this study.

4. *KG*, 319.

5. See ibid.

6. See W. G. Lambert, "Myth and Ritual as Conceived by the Babylonians," *Journal of Semitic Studies* 13 (1968): 106.

7. L. R. Fisher, "The Creation at Ugarit and in the Old Testament," *Vetus Testamentum* 15 (1965): 320: "The temple is symbolic of the ordered cosmos and at the same time makes it possible to maintain order." Cf. Mircea Eliade, *Cosmos and History* (New York: Harper and Row, 1959), 17: "The very conception of the temple as the *imago mundi*, the idea that the sanctuary reproduces the universe in its essence, passed into the religious architecture of Christian Europe."

8. See F. Thureau-Dangin, *Rituels accadiens* (Paris: Leroux, 1921), 136, lines 279–84. Lambert, "Myth and Ritual," 107, points out that a recently studied Babylonian liturgical commentary also calls for the reading of the *Enuma Elish* on the fourth of Kislimu, and suggests that it may have been read on the fourth of each month.

9. The date for this rite is variously given in the sources as the eighth, tenth, and eleventh of Nisan (Lambert, "Myth and Ritual," 107; see also W. G. Lambert, "The Great Battle of the Mesopotamian Religious Year: The Conflict in the Akitu House," *Iraq* 25 [1963]: 189–90).

10. Herodotus, *Histories* I, 132, tr. A. D. Godley, 2 vols. (London: Heinemann, 1960), 1:173.

11. Ibid.

12. See E. O. James, *Creation and Cosmogony: A Historical and Comparative Inquiry* (Leiden: Brill, 1969), 29.

13. See William F. Albright, "The Refrain 'and God saw *kî ṭôḇ,'* " in *Melanges Bibliques redigés en l'honneur de André Robert* (Paris: Bloud and Gay, n. d.), 22–26.

14. Loren R. Fisher, "An Ugaritic Ritual and Genesis 1:1–5," *Ugaritica* 6 (1969): 197–205, notes that a recently published cultic text from Ugarit ends each section with the refrain "day one," "day two," etc., in a manner strikingly similar to the language of the Genesis creation account.

15. See Arieh Toeg, "Genesis 1 and the Sabbath" (in Hebrew), *Bet Miqra* 50 (1972): 290. Moshe Weinfeld, "Sabbath, Temple Building, and the Enthronement of the Lord" (in Hebrew), *Bet Miqra* 69 (1977): 188–89, points out the striking parallels in the language and structure between the Genesis creation account and the account of the construction of the tabernacle in Exodus 39–40 and suggests that there was an intimate relationship between the creation and the temple (which, as we have noted above, is symbolic of the ordered cosmos) in the mind of the Hebrews. Similarly, Peter J. Kearney, "Creation and Liturgy: the P Redaction of Ex 25–40," *Zeitschrift für die Alttestamentliche Wissenschaft* 89 (1977): 375–78, analyzes the close structural relationship between the Genesis creation record and Exodus 25–31, which contains the divine instructions for the erection of the desert tabernacle and the establishment of the cult.

16. Similarly, there are some striking resemblances in the cult and mythology of the Hittites, Ugaritians, and Babylonians. However, the absence of any clear indication of the liturgical use of a creation myth among the Hittites and people of Ugarit during their festivals (where

evidence exists for the Babylonians' use of it) must make us cautious against including them among those who do.

17. M *Ta‘anit* 4:2–3.

18. M *Ta‘anit* 4:2.

19. This may refer to the practice, recorded in M *Ta‘anit* 4:3, of the laymen *(anshē ma‘amad)* fasting on certain days during their week of service.

20. Theophrastus, *De Pietate, apud Porphyrius, De Abstinentia* II, 26; quoted in Menahem Stern, *Greek and Latin Authors on Jews and Judaism* (Jerusalem: Israel Academy of Sciences and Humanities, 1974), 8.

21. See Toeg, "Genesis 1 and the Sabbath," 293.

22. See *Myth and Reality* (New York: Harper and Row, 1968), 28–34.

23. See S. G. F. Brandon, "Ritual Perpetuation of the Past," *Numen* 6 (1959): 112–29, for further examples from other religions.

24. *Essays on the History of Religions* (Leiden: Brill, 1954), 256.

7

Garden of Eden: Prototype Sanctuary

Donald W. Parry

The Garden of Eden pericope (Genesis 2–3) contains a number of powerful symbols that are related to and represent archetypal depictions of subsequent Israelite temple systems. In a cogent manner, the Garden of Eden, as it is referred to throughout the Bible, Pseudepigrapha, and rabbinic writings, served as the prototype, pattern, and/or originator of subsequent Israelite temples, "a type of archetypal sanctuary."[1] The garden was not a sanctuary built of cedar or marble, for it is not necessary for a temple to possess an edifice or structure; but rather it was an area of sacred space made holy because God's presence was found there. Mircea Eliade has stated that the Garden of Eden was the heavenly prototype of the temple,[2] and the *Book of Jubilees* 3:19 adds that "the garden of Eden is the Holy of Holies, and the dwelling of the Lord." This essay will examine these claims.

Eleven prototypical aspects of the Garden of Eden will be examined. They are

(1) The tree of life was located both in the garden and in the temple.

(2) Both the garden and the temple were associated with sacred waters.

(3) Eastward orientations played a role in the garden story and in subsequent Israelite temples.

(4) The cosmic mountain was symbolically affiliated with the garden and temple.

(5) The account of the earth's creation is closely connected with the Garden of Eden pericope and the temple.

(6) Cherubim, or heavenly beings, function as guardians of the garden and the temple.

(7) Revelation was an essential part of the garden and the temple.

(8) Sacrifice existed in the garden and in subsequent temple systems.

(9) Similar religious language existed in both the garden and the temple.

(10) Sacred vestments were associated with Adam and Eve in the garden and with the priesthood in the Jerusalem temple.

(11) Abundance was associated with the garden and the temple.

(1) The Tree of Life

Much attention is given to the tree of life by the author of Genesis 2–3. It is referred to on three occasions. The first citation to the tree is recorded in Genesis 2:9, where it is stated that God planted "the tree of life in the middle of the garden."[3] In this account the tree is a definite tree (preceded by the definite article, hence called "the tree"), and it is located at the center of Eden's garden. The tree stands opposite the "tree of knowledge of good and evil," or the tree of death.[4] It is found in the same context as the river of Eden. The second and third references to the tree of life are found in connection with God's desire to protect the tree from the hands of Adam and Eve (Genesis 3:22–24). We learn that Adam and Eve, had they been permitted to partake of the fruit of the tree of life, would have lived forever.

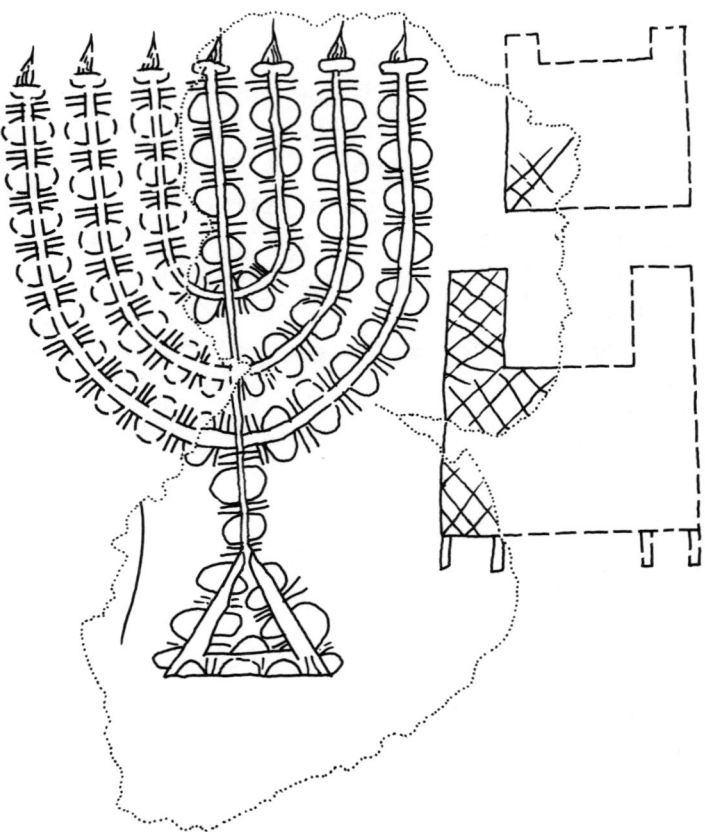

Figure 25. During the existence of the Temple of Herod, someone scratched this drawing into the wall plaster of a house in the Herodian quarter only five hundred meters away. Though crudely done, it shows the elaborate ornaments described as "knops and almond flowers" in Exodus 25:31–40. The objects on the right are thought to be stylized representations of the golden altar of incense that stood before the veil and the table of shew-bread.

To prevent access to the tree, God established cherubim and a flaming sword at the east entrance of the garden.

The continuity of the tree of life icon in Israelite temple

society is evident when one considers the nature of the tabernacle menorah or seven-branched lampstand. The menorah, as an important religious symbol for the Israelite community, is given due consideration in the Pentateuch. Its construction (Exodus 25:31–40; 37:17–24), consecration (Exodus 30:27; 40:9), placement in the tabernacle (Exodus 25:37; Numbers 8:2–3), and the manner of transporting it (Numbers 3:31; 4:9) are items of discussion in the scriptures. The sacred object was also located in the Solomonic temple (1 Kings 7:49), wherein a total of ten menorahs were used, all made of pure gold, five standing on the north and five standing on the south side of the holy place of the temple. The second temple possessed a lampstand, although the sources regarding this situation are unclear and often contradictory.[5]

That the menorah was a stylized tree of life is made clear in the description produced in Exodus 25:31–40.[6] The menorah must have had the appearance of a tree, possessing seven branches (a number of symbolic significance to the Israelite community) and a number of flowers (almond blossoms?). It may be concluded that the actual, living tree of life was present in the garden, and symbolic representations of the tree of life, in the form of lampstands, were present in later Israelite temples.

(2) Sacred Waters

Several analogous scriptural narratives employ imagistic descriptions of sacral waters originating and flowing from the temple. The prophet Joel explicitly asserts that "a fountain shall come forth from the house of the Lord" (Joel 3:18). After providing a lengthy description of the future temple of Jerusalem (see Ezekiel 40–46), Ezekiel presents a statement regarding a river that would flow from the threshold of the temple, through the courtyard, and out of the city of Jerusalem, finally reaching the Dead Sea. The prophecy states that the temple river will heal the putrid waters of the Dead Sea, bless fishermen with an abundance of fish, and increase fruit-bearing vegetation in the deserts. In short, the temple river will bless mankind with a paradisiacal earth (see Ezekiel 47:1–12). John the Revelator beheld a vision that hearkens back to the original paradisiacal state of the Garden of Eden. Speaking of the temple in heaven, the seer describes "a pure river of water of life, clear as crystal, proceeding out of the throne of God and of the Lamb" (Revelation 22:1–4). The throne of God, of course, is situated in the Holy of Holies of the temple.

The book of Daniel describes a different type of river, also issuing from a throne. After receiving an eschatological vision, Daniel provides a description of the Ancient of Days sitting upon his throne of "fiery flame." Flowing from the throne was a "fiery stream" (Daniel 7:9–11). Two pseudepigraphic passages recall Daniel's statement. The first, *3 Enoch* 36:1–2, reads, "A river of fire . . . flows beneath the throne of glory"; and the second, *1 Enoch* 14:15, says, "Beneath the throne were issuing streams of flaming fire." Enoch, similar to John's and Daniel's portrayal, describes the waters as coming from the throne, suggesting that God is the source of the waters.

The rivers of Eden, described in Genesis 2–3, represent the quintessential sacred waters. Originating, according to *3 Enoch* 18:19, "opposite the throne of glory," these pure waterways separate into four rivers and go forth from Eden to water the entire earth (see Genesis 2:10).[7] It is evident that Eden's sacral waters served as a model for subsequent temple rivers.

Figure 26. As late as 1450, artists like Giovanni di Paolo were still trying to reconcile biblical and classical models of the universe. On the left, God sets the rainbow-colored spheres with the Zodiac in gold spinning round the island earth with the mountain of God at the top. The four "heads" of the rivers of Paradise occur twice; once on the left at the mountaintop where they flow down to water the whole earth and again on the right under the feet of Adam and Eve as the angel firmly pushes them out of Eden.

(3) Eastward Orientation

Spatial orientation played a vital role in the architectural setting of ancient Near Eastern temples.[8] So too, the Mosaic tabernacle and the temples of Jerusalem were directionally situated so that the entrance of the tabernacle or temple faced eastward. The Garden of Eden, possessing a number

of templelike qualities, produced the prototypical pattern
for subsequent Israelite temple orientation.[9] East appears to
be *the* direction of import in Eden. Three biblical statements
reveal a concern for orientation in Eden:[10]

(1) The fact that God planted the garden in the east section of Eden (see Genesis 2:8) suggests a primacy for the
direction. Although the purpose for this location in Eden is
not explicitly stated, it is generally accepted by scholars that
east, possessing a number of symbolic meanings, is the
sacred direction in Israelite religion.

(2) The second designation of "east" in the garden pericope is mentioned in connection with the four rivers of Eden.
It is likely that the four rivers of Eden (see Genesis 2:10–14)[11]
flowed outward from Eden toward the four cardinal directions—north, east, south, and west. Eden is depicted as being
established at the center of the four rivers, perhaps providing
the water source for the four rivers. The etymological meaning of the word *templum* (English "temple")[12] has a direct connection with the four cardinal directions, a concept that has
been well established by a number of authors.[13] Of special
note in the narrative description of the rivers is that all four
rivers are mentioned by name—Pison, Gihon, Hiddekel,
Euphrates—but only one of the four directions is mentioned
by name. River number three flowed eastward, writes the
author of Genesis. The directional flow of the other three
rivers is unknown.

(3) Once more *east* takes a prominent position in the garden story. After Adam and Eve were expelled from the
garden, God placed cherubim and a flaming sword at "the
east of the garden of Eden" (Genesis 3:24; Alma 12:21) to
prevent the fallen couple from an unauthorized return to
the garden. This celestial blockade suggests that there
existed an entrance to the garden established at the east end

of the garden. If no such entrance existed, then why would a blockade be necessary? Or, if other entrances were found to the garden, then why did God not establish cherubim and swords at other locations around the garden? Once more the eastward orientation of the Garden of Eden parallels the eastward orientation of the Mosaic tabernacle and Jerusalem temples, having entrances at the east.

(4) Cosmic Mountain

Every Near Eastern temple symbolically recalls a mountain,[14] but the first temple complex (i.e., the Garden of Eden) possessed a mountain in actuality. The biblical Garden of Eden account alludes to the presence of a mountain. Be it remembered that a river originated in Eden that divided into four heads, and flowed outward (i.e, downward) into the four parts of the world. Assuming that the natural laws of gravitation were in effect during this primordial era, the rivers of Eden would have flowed downward, suggesting that Eden was located at an elevation higher (i.e., a mountain) than surrounding territories.

Placing assumptions aside, however, biblical evidence delineates a mountain in Eden. In Ezekiel 28:11–16 the king of Tyre is metaphorically compared to Adam. The king is told: "Thou hast been in Eden the garden of God. . . . Thou art the anointed cherub that covereth; and I have set thee so: thou wast upon the holy mountain of God. . . . Thou wast perfect in thy ways from the day that thou wast created, till iniquity was found in thee. . . . Thou hast sinned: therefore I will cast thee as profane out of the mountain of God" (vv. 13–16). The terms "garden of God," "Eden," and "cherub" and the concept of sin are express Edenic themes found in Genesis 2–3. Ezekiel employs Edenic typology, explaining that Tyre (Adam) was perfect while in the Garden of

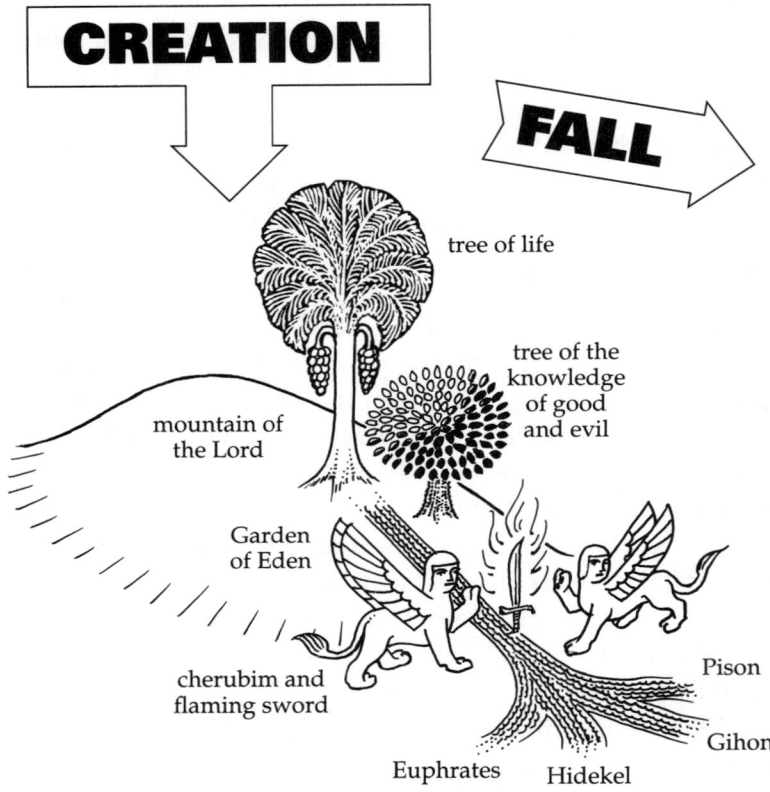

Figure 27. This schematic drawing attempts to depict the sacred land-scape of Genesis in simplified form. The first land to arise from the waters became the Mountain of the Lord, where the Lord created Adam. It is from this divine center that creation begins and extends out in all directions. The Hebrew for *east* means "faceward or frontward"; thus, driving Adam from before his face is part of the continuing east-ward movement (see Alma 42:2).

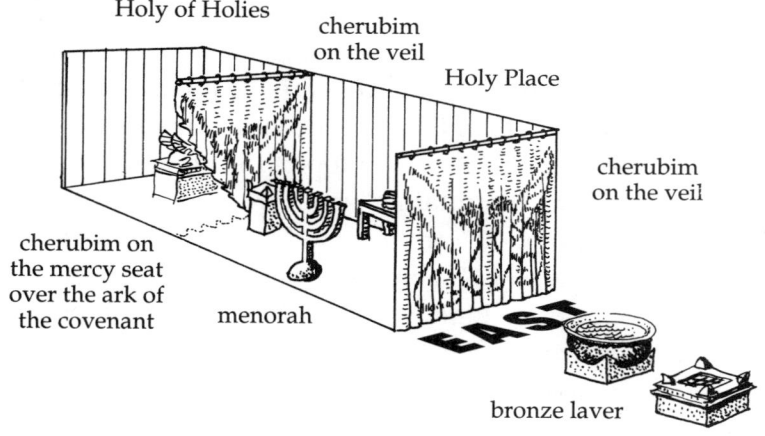

Once a year on Yom Kippur, the Day of Atonement, Adam's eastward expulsion from the Garden is reversed when the high priest travels west past the consuming fire of the sacrifice and the purifying water of the laver, through the veil woven with images of cherubim. Thus, he returns to the original point of creation, where he pours out the atoning blood of the sacrifice, reestablishing the covenant relationship with God.

Eden, was anointed, and for a period of time dwelt on the mountain of God. But he sinned and was thrown from the mountain, or cast from the temple, since no unclean thing was allowed in the temple. Important for our purposes is the notion that a mountain existed in Eden.

Pseudepigraphic *1 Enoch* 18:6–12, 24–25 provides a description of the mountains in Eden. During a panoramic vision of paradise, Enoch beheld several extraordinary mountains. All of them were "dignified and glorious" and made of precious and ethereal stones. And, more importantly, the mountains (which were in groups of three) were not arranged across the horizon as are the typical adjacent-type mountains. Rather, Enoch noticed that the mountains were stacked three high, one on top of the other, escalating heavenward. The mountains "were pressing into heaven like the throne of God" and reached skyward "where the heavens come together." This idea of mountains one on top of the other, or three high, is the apotheosis of "successive ascension toward heaven."[15]

These concepts hearken back to the ancient Near Eastern idea of the primordial mound[16] or the primordial hillock. According to the Babylonian tradition, for example, the Eninnu temple, which was built by Gudea, is representative of the primordial hillock that arose out of the chaotic waters (*apsu*).[17] Regarding the Egyptian view of the primordial mound, Lundquist writes that "in Egypt . . . all temples are seen as representing the primeval hillock."[18] The primordial mound projects backward into history to the period of the creation of the earth, where, according to one Hebrew tradition, the primordial mound was the first land that emerged from the waters of chaos during the creative period (cf. Genesis 1:9–10).[19] Identified as the consecrated *topos*, the primordial mound represented order and definition amidst the unruly chaotic waters.[20]

From the rudimentary concept of the primordial hillock developed the idea of the cosmic mountain (i.e., the temple), with its careful delimitation, well-defined borders, and clear-cut spaces. The transition from a raw natural mountain to a synthetic physical temple edifice seems to have been quite natural. In the first place, temple buildings retained their distinct mountain character by being constructed of natural indigenous materials, many times coming from the mountains themselves. Persons who stood before the lofty components of the temple would naturally look heavenward, similar to one who stands before a striking mountain. In this regard the temple became "the architectural embodiment of the cosmic mountain."[21] More importantly, however, the temple building was constructed upon a mountain or hillock of known importance. The temples of Jerusalem (Solomon's, Zerubbabel's, and Herod's), all being constructed upon the identical mount, were part of a continuing tradition of sacred events that occurred there. What was once a sacred *topos* now became a sacred *topos* with sacral architecture superimposed upon it.

(5) Creation

Significantly, the garden story immediately follows the creation pericope in the book of Genesis. As has been shown elsewhere in this volume, there is a direct connection between the creation of the cosmos and ancient Near Eastern ritual. Several scholars, including Weinfeld and Kearney, have noted the connection between the creation of the cosmos and the Israelite temple. Weinfeld juxtaposes the creation account (Genesis 1–2) with the chapters of Exodus that deal with the construction of the Tabernacle (see, especially, Exodus 39–40), and then presents several points of comparison between the two accounts. He notes that after six days of divine creative activity, God rested on the seventh day. Similarly, after the construction of the Tabernacle, which also took six days, Deity rested.[22]

Carrying the point a step further, Fisher reveals that the temple of Solomon was built in seven years (see 1 Kings 6:38), precisely as the world was created in seven days. Fisher concludes that "one must speak of ordering the cosmos in terms of seven even as the construction of the microcosm must be according to the same pattern."[23] Hence, it may be determined that the construction of the Mosaic tabernacle and Solomonic temple recall the formation of the earth. Just as chaos became organized and orderly, so the temple brings order and organization unto the world.

P. J. Kearney also draws a number of comparisons between the creation account (Genesis 1–2) and the Tabernacle pericope (Exodus 25–31).[24] Both God and Aaron brought forth light—God brought forth light unto the world (see Genesis 1:2–3); Aaron produced light for the Tabernacle precinct (see Exodus 30:1–8). In Genesis, God created the seas and placed the *topos* within the waters; in the temple the bronze laver or molten sea was constructed according to God's instructions and became part of the temple precinct (cf. Genesis 1:9–10 and 1 Kings 7:23). Kearney believes that temple building in the ancient world was a natural consequence of and built upon the creation of the world.[25]

One additional correspondence between the creation of the cosmos and the construction of the temple may be added to the list—Deity acted as overseer for both activities. At the completion of his creative work of the cosmos, God declared the work to be "good" (Genesis 1:10, 12, 18, 21, 25), and then God blessed and sanctified the seventh day (see Genesis 2:3).

(6) Cherubim

In the biblical writings the first mention of *cherubim* (Hebrew plural form of *cherub*) is found in the Edenic account. God "drove out the man; and he placed at the east of the garden of Eden Cherubims, and a flaming sword which turned every way, to [guard] the tree of life" (Genesis 3:24). Symbolic likenesses of the cherubim were later embroidered into the veil of the tabernacle (see Exodus 26:31) and carved into the walls, doors, and panels of the temple of Solomon (see 1 Kings 6:29–35; 7:29, 36).[26] In addition, two large cherubim were placed on either side of the throne of God in the Holy of Holies (see 1 Kings 6:23–28; Exodus 25:18–22; 1 Samuel 4:4; 2 Samuel 6:2). The cherubim were identical in size and possessed great wings that extended from one wall of the Holy of Holies to the other. Each cherub was made of olive wood, which was overlaid with gold. Ezekiel also mentions cherubim in his description of Jerusalem's future temple (see 41:18–25).

A primary mission of the cherubim, together with the flaming sword, was to protect the tree of life so that man, in his unworthy state, would not partake of the fruit of the tree (cf. also Alma 42:2–3).[27] The locale of the representations of the cherubim in the temples held significance. They were located on either side of the throne of God (mercy seat), embroidered into the veil, and situated along the path that led to God's presence. The cherubim functioned as divine sentinels, guarding the path leading to the presence of God, preventing the trespass by unauthorized persons.

(7) Revelation

One of the many boons of the ancient temple setting was that direct communication between God and man was possible. The prophetic theological stance of the era was

A.

B.

Figure 28. These two bronze cherubim (A) from Northern Syria (c. 800 B.C.) were probably made for a divine or royal throne such as the one on this ivory fragment (B) from Megiddo. In Psalm 99:1, the Lord "sitteth between the cherubims." In traditional teachings, they represented the powerful servants of God, combining the intelligence of mankind with the strength of the lion's body and the freedom to move as an eagle (cf. D&C 77:4).

directional prayer, wherein temple worshipers directed their prayers toward the Jerusalem temple (see 1 Kings 8:42; Psalms 5:7; 138:2; Daniel 6:10; Jonah 2:4). Similarly, revelation was extant in the Garden of Eden, for "communication with Heaven was easy *in illo tempore*," and the meeting between the gods and man took place in actuality.[28] Communing with God was a simple matter for man, because man could climb the mountain of Eden, then the tree of life, and ascend to heaven.[29] 2 *Enoch* 31:2 states that in the beginning God gave Adam "open heavens" so that the first man could "look upon the angels."

Examples of divine conversation (or direct revelation) between God and man in the Garden of Eden abound in Genesis 2 and 3:

2:16 "and the Lord God commanded the man, saying"
2:18 "and the Lord God said"
3:8 "and they heard the voice of the Lord God"
3:9 "and the Lord God called unto Adam"
3:11 "and he [God] said"
3:13 "and the Lord God said unto the woman"
3:16 "unto the woman he [God] said"
3:17 "and unto Adam he [God] said"
3:22 "and the Lord God said"

Both Adam and Eve received numerous personal communications from God in the garden setting. After the Fall, however, the couple prayed at an altar, and revelation became much less frequent, and it took place in different forms and at different places.

(8) Sacrifice

It is well known that animal sacrifices formed a considerable portion of ancient Israelite temple ritual.[30] Entire sections of the Bible are dedicated to the various types of sacrifices, outlining the rules and commandments regarding the sacrifices. The numerous laws of sacrifice as revealed to Moses were not known in the Garden of Eden. However, the biblical text implies that sacrifice did exist before Adam and Eve were cast out of the garden. After God cursed Adam and Eve, he made garments of animal skins for the couple and then "clothed them" (Genesis 3:21). It is significant that God used an animal skin to clothe Adam and Eve. To acquire the skin, an animal had to be slain, and perhaps the animal was slaughtered as part of a sacrificial ceremony.

Is it possible that God himself performed the sacrifice? And do we know what type of animal was sacrificed? If God did not perform the sacrifice on behalf of Adam and Eve, who did? And if a lamb (or bullock) were not used for the coats of skin, then what type of skins did Adam and Eve wear? Certainly, they would not have used the skin of a camel or swine or other animal considered to be unclean to the later Israelites. Inasmuch as lambs were slaughtered by the thousands as part of the law of Moses, the skin of a lamb was the logical choice. Conceivably, God sacrificed a lamb, typically pointing forward to the moment when the Lamb of God would be slaughtered as an atoning sacrifice on behalf of all mankind. It is also noteworthy that God himself "clothed" Adam and Eve with the garments. Such personal attention by Deity to the matter of the coats of skins underscores the liturgical import of the garments. Candlish, who believes that animal sacrifice originated in the garden, has noted that since God "concerned himself with the materials" of the garments, something "higher and holier" was intended, some spiritual meaning and purpose for the skins.[31]

Apparently the animal sacrifice conducted by God in the Garden of Eden represented only one type of sacrifice, for extracanonical scriptures identify sacrificial concepts with the garden. A passage from the *Books of Adam and Eve* implies that Adam and Eve practiced a form of sacrifice before they were cast from the garden. After the fall of Adam, the first man pled with the angels: "Behold, ye cast me out. I pray you, allow me to take away fragrant herbs from paradise, so that I may offer an offering to God after I have gone out of paradise that he hear me."[32]

(9) Esoteric Language

Frequently the descriptive language of the scriptures regarding the Israelite temples recalls the Garden of Eden experience. Three specific phrases, found in connection with the Garden of Eden, are also used by later biblical writers while describing the tabernacle or temple. Each of the three phrases will be examined.

1. Adam was told to "dress it and keep [the garden]"

God commanded Adam to "dress" (work) and "keep" the garden (Genesis 2:15). Two Hebrew terms utilized in this statement, *ʿābad* (work) and *šāmar* (keep), are also found in descriptive statements having reference to the later Israelite temple system. For instance, the Levites were instructed to "keep (*šāmar*) all the vessels of the tabernacle" and "to work (*ʿābad*) the work" of the tabernacle (Numbers 3:8; author's translation; see also Numbers 8:26; 18:5–6). Noting these parallels, Gordon Wenham has written that "if Eden is seen then as an ideal sanctuary, then perhaps Adam should be described as an archetypal Levite."[33] *Genesis Rabbah,* a rabbinic commentary on the book of Genesis, saw a parallel between the garden and the temple. According to *Genesis Rabbah* 16:5, the phrase "to work and keep it" (Genesis 2:15; author's translation) points to an early sacrificial order.[34]

Special attention should be paid to the Hebrew term *ʿābad*. Its root meaning in Hebrew is connected with the concepts of service and labor, both secular and religious. In a religious sense, the term expressly points to constructing the tabernacle (see Exodus 35:24), repairing the temple (see 2 Chronicles 34:13), and working with fine linen (see 1 Chronicles 4:21).[35] According to one Hebrew lexicon, *ʿābad* means "to worship" or "to perform a cultic rite."[36] During the late Second Temple period, the term was also associated with temple worship, but often mentioned in connection with a sacred tree.[37] Whether or not this concept recalls the sacred tree of life of the Garden of Eden is a matter deserving further study.

2. God walked about Eden and the temple

The method by which God moved about in Eden (see Genesis 3:8) and the tabernacle (see 2 Samuel 7:6–7; Leviticus 26:12; Deuteronomy 23:14) was identical. The biblical authors describe God's movement in both sacred places using the Hebrew *hithpaʾel*, a verbal form of *hālakh*. The masculine singular participial form, found only eight times in the Hebrew Bible, may be translated as "walking about" or "walking himself." Thus, God both "walked about" in the garden and "walked about" in the tabernacle. Inasmuch as the same rare verbal form is employed in several statements regarding the temple, a connection seems to be implied between the Garden of Eden and the temple.

3. In the presence of the LORD

Menachem Haran has argued that the phrase "before the Lord" (*lipnê Yahweh*) indicates a temple setting. He writes that "in general, any cultic activity to which the biblical text applies the formula 'before the Lord' can be considered an indication of the existence of a temple at the site, since this expression stems from the basic conception of the temple as a divine dwelling-place and actually belongs to the temple's technical terminology."[38] The phrase is recorded in Genesis 3:8, where it is stated that "Adam and his wife hid themselves from [before] the LORD God [*mippₔnê Yahweh*]."[39] Again, identical language is employed at both the Garden of Eden and the Jerusalem temple.

(10) Sacred Vestments

The vesting of temple worshipers and officiants with sacral vestments was customary in the Israelite temple system.[40] Entire chapters, such as Exodus 28–29, describe the sacred vestments to be worn by Aaron and his sons while ministering in the temple. The ordinary priestly vestments consisted of four parts: breeches, a headpiece, a girdle, and a tunic. The high priestly vestments consisted of eight pieces: in addition to the four vestments belonging to the priest, the high priest wore an ephod, robe, breastplate, and frontplate.

Adam and Eve, while in the garden, possessed two items of clothing that apparently held ritual meaning: the apron (see Genesis 3:7) and the garment of skins (see Genesis 3:21). The apron, perhaps made from fig leaves of the same tree of which they had unlawfully eaten,[41] no doubt held some sort of ceremonial significance for the first couple. The garments of skins were made by God himself (see Genesis 3:21), a fact that adds to the significance and import of the sacral clothing. It is quite likely that these vestments, belonging to Adam and Eve and obtained while in the garden, served as archetypes for later sacral vestments belonging to the Israelite temple system.

(11) Abundance and Prosperity

While creating a list of motifs common among ancient Near Eastern temples, John Lundquist has determined that one conventional motif found among temple systems is that "the temple is associated with abundance and prosperity."[42] So, too, with the situation at Eden—prosperity and abundance existed there as standard conditions.[41] The garden was planted by God himself (see Genesis 2:8), and perhaps for this reason Ezekiel called Eden the "garden of God" (28:13). Interestingly, the word *Eden* means "luxury" and "delight."[42] Thus Eden connotes a situation of abundance. Noteworthy also is the idea that the garden was deemed a sacral place ritually fit and ceremonially clean (a prerequisite for Israelite temples), pure enough for God to walk about in (see Genesis 3:8–10).

Furthermore, God planted "every tree that is pleasant to the sight, and good for food" (Genesis 2:9). Apparently all or many of the trees of the garden bore fruit, for God told Adam that "of every tree of the garden thou mayest freely eat: but of the tree of the knowledge of good and evil, thou shalt not eat of it" (Genesis 2:16–17). Also, God gave "every herb bearing seed, which is upon the face of all the earth, and every tree, in the which is the fruit of a tree yielding seed; to you it shall be for meat. And to every beast of the earth, and to every fowl of the air, and to every thing that creepeth upon the earth, wherein there is life, I have given every green herb for meat" (Genesis 1:29–30). The garden was watered by a river (see Genesis 2:10).

For later biblical prophets, the Garden of Eden became a byword for prosperity and fruitfulness (see Isaiah 51:3; Ezekiel 36:35; Joel 2:3). Each of these elements—God's hand in the planting of the garden, his divine presence there, the fruit and herbs designed as food for both man and beast, and the river of water that provided a source of life for the plants—denote a place of abundance and prosperity.

Conclusion

First and foremost, the Garden of Eden became sacred space because it was created by Deity, and his presence was found there. It remained sacred (like temples) because God cast out those who had profaned it (i.e., Adam and Eve). The Garden of Eden, as described in the book of Genesis and elsewhere, contained a number of features present in subsequent Israelite temples. These features include symbolic representations of the primordial landscape: the tree of life, the sacred waters, and the cosmic mountain. In addition, the Garden of Eden and those who occupied it, similar in many respects to the Israelite temples, possessed an eastward orientation, cherubim, and sacred vestments, and it was associated with prosperity and abundance. The garden was associated with divine revelation, sacrificial ordinances, and the creation of the earth. Finally, similar religious language described both the Garden of Eden and subsequent temples.

Notes

1. Gordon J. Wenham, *Genesis 1–15*, vol. 1 of *Word Biblical Commentary* (Waco, Texas: Word Books, 1987), 86.

2. See Kurt Sethe, *Patterns in Comparative Religion* (New York: New American Library, 1958), 282.

3. Here I read the Hebrew term *bətôk* as "middle," rather than the traditional reading of "midst" (see Francis Brown, S. R. Driver, and Charles A. Briggs, *A Hebrew and English Lexicon of the Old Testament*, trans. Edward Robison [Oxford: Clarendon, 1977], 1063). Other sources, both primary and secondary, place the tree at the center of paradise (see, for example, Esther C. Quinn, *The Penitence of Adam* [University of Mississippi: Romance Monographs, 1980], 113; and Mircea Eliade, "The Yearning for Paradise," *Daedalus* 88 [1959]: 257–60). Eliade has written much about the mythical center of the universe and its relationship to religion and temples. He places the sacred tree at the center or navel of the world, which becomes the center pole or *axis mundi* of the universe. The sacred tree is always found on the top of a holy mountain, and the two landscape features,

mountain and tree, connect heaven and earth, enabling mankind to commune with the gods.

4. On the "tree of knowledge of good and evil" as the tree of death, see Ingvild Saelid Gilhus, "The Tree of Life and the Tree of Death," *Religion: Journal of Religion and Religions* 17 (Oct. 1987): 337–53.

5. See Carol L. Meyers, *The Tabernacle Menorah* (Missoula: Scholars, 1976), 36–38.

6. See also ibid., passim.

7. Cf. *3 Enoch* 19:4.

8. On the subject of spatial orientation, see John D. Wilkinson, "Orientation, Jewish and Christian," *Palestine Exploration Quarterly* 116 (1984): 16–30; L. A. Snijders, "L'orientation du temple de Jerusalem," *Oudtestamentische Studiën* 14 (1965): 214–34; Hans J. Klimkeit, "Spatial Orientation in Mythical Thinking as Exemplified in Ancient Egypt: Considerations toward a Geography of Religions," *History of Religions* 14 (1975): 266–81; B. Diebner, "Die Orientierung des Jerusalemer Tempels und die 'Sacred Direction' der frühchristlichen Kirchen," *Zeitschrift des Deutschen Palästina-Vereins* 87 (1971): 153–66; and Bezalel Porten, "The Structure and Orientation of the Jewish Temple at Elephantine—A Revised Plan of the Jewish District," *Journal of the American Oriental Society* 81 (1961): 38–42.

9. The word *orient* has etymological ties to the term *east.* F. Landsberger has explained that "etymologically, 'orientation' signifies a turning toward the east" ("The Sacred Direction in Synagogue and Church," *Hebrew Union College Annual* 28 [1957]: 181).

10. In addition to the biblical implications that deal with the eastward orientation of the garden, two passages from the pseudepigrapha make connections to the same (see *Sibylline Oracles* 3:24–26 and *2 Enoch* 30:13–14).

11. Cf. *3 Enoch* 18:19; 19:4.

12. On the meaning of *templum,* see *The Concise Oxford Dictionary of English Etymology,* ed. T. F. Hoad (Oxford: Clarendon, 1986), 485; Henry Corbin, *Temple and Contemplation,* trans. Philip Sherrard (London: Islamic, 1986), 386, first published in 1980 under the title *Temple et contemplation.* See also the linguistic approach to the word *templum* by Palmira Cipriano, *Templum* (Roma: Prima Cattedra di Glottologia Universita, 1983). Further, on the etymological relationship between the words *tempus* and *templum,* see Hermann Usener, *Goettername* (Bonn: Cohen, 1929), 191–93; Albrecht Blumenthal, "Templum," *Klio* 27 (1934): 1–13; Kurt Latte, "Augur und Templum

in der Varronischen Augurformel," *Philologus: Zeitschrift für das klassische Altertum* 97 (1948):143–59.

13. Wilhelm Kroll's statement in "Mundus" in Pauly-Wissowa, *Realencyclopaedie der classischen Altertumswissenschaft,* 24 vols. (Stuttgart: Metzler, 1893), 16:1.563, demonstrates the connection between the four cardinal directions and the temple, "hence where the four regions come together." The intersecting lines, *cardo* and *decumanus,* are discussed in Werner Müller, *Die heilige Stadt, Roma quadrata, himmlisches Jerusalem und die Myth vom Weltnabel* (Stuttgart: Kohlhammer, 1961), 9–21; Ellis Hesselmeyer, "Decumanus," *Klio* 28 (1935): 133–79; and Stefan Weinstock, "Templum," *Romisch Mittheilungen* 47 (1932): 100–103.

14. The publications dealing with the cosmic mountain in the ancient Near East are extensive. See, for example, Richard J. Clifford, "The Cosmic Mountain in Canaan and the Old Testament," *Biblica* 55 (1974): 443–46; Robert L. Cohn, *The Shape of Sacred Space: Four Biblical Studies* (Chico: Scholars, 1981); W. Gaerte, "Komische Vorstellungen im Bilde prähistorischer Zeit: Erdberg, Himmelsberg, Erdnabel und Weltenströme," *Anthropos* 9 (1913): 956–79.

15. John M. Lundquist, "What Is a Temple? A Preliminary Typology," in this volume, *Temples of the Ancient World,* 93–94.

16. Many modern authors have investigated the different aspects of the primordial mound. Maurice A. Canney, "The Primordial Mound," *Journal of the Manchester University Egyptian and Oriental Society* 20 (1936): 25–40, investigates remnants of the primordial mound tradition throughout the ancient and postbiblical Near Eastern world, including the Egyptian, Babylonian, Samaritan, Jewish, and Christian cultures (see also E. A. E. Reymond, *The Mythical Origin of the Egyptian Temple* [New York: Barnes and Noble, 1969], 46–47, 59, and 266; and Lundquist, "What Is a Temple?" 84–86).

17. See Canney, "The Primordial Mound," 25–40.

18. Lundquist, "What Is a Temple?" 86.

19. See ibid., 86–87. Lundquist's summary proposition is correct that "the cosmic mountain represents the primordial hillock, the place that first emerged from the waters covering the earth during the creative process" (86).

20. See ibid.

21. Ibid., 85–86.

22. Moshe Weinfeld, "Sabbath, Temple, and the Enthronement of the Lord: The Problem of the 'Sitz im Leben' of Genesis 1:1–2:3," *Melanges Bibliques et Orientaux* (1981): 501–12.

23. Loren R. Fisher, "The Temple Quarter," *Journal of Semitic Studies* 8 (1963): 41.

24. See P. J. Kearney, "Creation and Liturgy: The P Redaction of Exodus 25–40," *Zeitschrift für die alttestamentliche Wissenschaft* 89 (1977): 375–87.

25. Ibid., 384–87.

26. Ancient Assyrian religion had the equivalent of the Israelite cherubim. Menahem Haran, "The Ark and the Cherubim: Their Symbolic Significance in Biblical Ritual," *Israel Exploration Journal* 9 (1959): 30–38, 89–94, identifies the cherubic-type beings that belong to the Mesopotamian religions (92–94).

27. For various approaches to the status and nature of the cherubim, see R. H. Pfeiffer, "Cherubim," *Journal of Biblical Literature* 41 (1922): 249–50; Édouard (Paul) Dhorme, "Les Cherubins," *Revue biblique* 35 (1926): 328–58, 481–95; and William F. Albright, "What Were the Cherubim?" *Biblical Archaeologist* (1938): 1–3.

28. Mircea Eliade, "Yearning for Paradise," 1959: 260.

29. Ibid., 256.

30. On the meaning and symbolism of sacrifice in the Bible, see Baruch A. Levine, *In the Presence of the Lord* (Leiden: Brill, 1974); and N. Kiuchi, *The Purification Offering in the Priestly Literature: Its Meaning and Function* (Sheffield: Sheffield Academic Press, 1987). On the social aspects of sacrifice, see Gary A. Anderson, *Sacrifices and Offerings in Ancient Israel: Studies in their Social and Political Importance* (Atlanta: Scholars, 1987), 27–55.

31. Robert S. Candlish, *Studies in Genesis* (Grand Rapids: Kregal, 1979), 82.

32. *Books of Adam and Eve* 9:3–4; cf. 29:4; *Jubilees* 3:27–28; Exodus 29:18; 30:34.

33. Gordon Wenham, "Sanctuary Symbolism in the Garden of Eden Story," *Proceedings of the Ninth World Congress of Jewish Studies,* Jerusalem, August 4–12, 1985 (Jerusalem: World Union of Jewish Studies, 1986): 21.

34. The rabbinic commentators saw other connections between the temple and the garden. For instance, *Genesis Rabbah* 21:8 likens the expulsion of Adam and Eve from Eden to the destruction of the temple.

35. R. Laird Harris, ed., *Theological Wordbook of the Old Testament,* 2 vols. (Chicago: Moody, 1980), 2:640.

36. *Lexicon in Veteris*, 670–71, citing Exodus 13:5. Cf. also the use of ʿābād in Zechariah 3:8, where the messianic title *Branch* is found. ʿĀbād

is an "Arab root meaning to 'worship, obey' (God)' (*Theological Wordbook of the Old Testament*, 2:639).

37. According to Jastrow, the term *avodah* (from *ʿābād*) has reference to "space required for attending to a plant" (Marcus Jastrow, *A Dictionary of the Targumim, the Talmud Babli and Yerushalmi, and the Midrashic Literature* [New York: Pardes, 1950], 1036). My thanks to Robert C. Robbins, one of my Hebrew students, for pointing this source out to me.

38. *TTS*, 26.

39. The reading of the King James Version is also correct: "from the presence of the LORD God."

40. One of Lundquist's typological motifs includes "inside the temple, . . . worshipers . . . are clothed" (Lundquist, "What Is a Temple?" 97).

41. See *Books of Adam and Eve* 20:5.

42. Lundquist, "What Is a Temple?" 97.

43. According to pseudepigraphic materials, during the pristine state found in Eden, all animal life could talk (see *Book of Jubilees* 3:28) and all beings enjoyed communion with God (see *Testament of Adam* 1:10; 2:7). Darkness was not known to its inhabitants, for they had perpetual light (see *2 Enoch* 31:2). Neither did they know pain, sickness, disease, or death, for the fruit of the vegetation offered continuous life.

44. Brown, Driver, and Briggs, *Hebrew and English Lexicon of the Old Testament*, 726.

8

Temple-Building Motifs:
Mesopotamia, Ancient Israel,
Ugarit, and Kirtland

Stephen D. Ricks and Michael A. Carter

Introduction

In his study "Temple Building, a Task for Gods and Kings," Arvid Kapelrud notes the striking similarity among the numerous accounts of temple construction in the ancient Near East. He focuses his attention particularly on temple-building accounts in the cylinder of Gudea (2125 B.C.), in the Ugaritic myths (ca. 1300–1200 B.C.), and in the temple of Solomon, about which he outlines the following features in common:

> In the cases where a king is the actual temple builder the following elements are most often found: 1. Some indication that a temple has to be built; 2. The king visits a temple over night; 3. A god tells him what to do, indicates plans; 4. The king announces his intention to build a temple; 5. Master builder is engaged, cedars from Lebanon, building-stones, gold, silver, etc., procured for the task; 6. The temple finished according to plan; 7. Offerings and dedication, fixing of norms; 8. Assembly of the people; 9. The god comes to his new house; 10. The king is blessed and promised everlasting domination.[1]

No less than in the ancient Near East, temple construction has been a formative activity in the restored Church, and the construction of its temples follows a pattern that corresponds in many regards to that found in the ancient Near East. This can be seen in the building of the Kirtland Temple. Following the pattern outlined by Kapelrud, we consider in this essay features in the motif of temple building in the ancient Near East—especially Mesopotamia, Ugarit, and the Bible—and compare it with the construction of the Kirtland Temple.

1. Some Indication Is Given That a Temple Has to Be Built

Mesopotamian texts are particularly rich in references to this element of the temple-building motif. An unusually dry spell indicated to Gudea that the Lord Ningirsu wanted a temple at Lagash built:

> In the nightly vision, as Gudea
> Saw that day his master Lord Ningirsu,
> (t)he (latter) spoke to him about his house
> and the building thereof,
> turned to him about Eninnu's offices,
> which are all great.[2]

Other Mesopotamian texts tell a similar story. From a religious text describing the building of the Ekur (the temple of Enlil in Nippur), we learn that "The 'Great Mountain' Enlil" commanded Urnammu (ca. 2112–2096 B.C.) to rebuild his temple. Urnammu immediately set out to build the temple by preparing bricks.[3] We read from a clay cone inscription from Warad-Sin (ca. 1834–1823 B.C.), king of Larsa, that the temple of Nannar, the moon god, was rebuilt "when the god of the new moon, his favorable sign permitted my eyes to see, by his life-giving vision he illumined me, and to build his temple to restore its place he directed me."[4] Similarly, on an alabaster block found in the

Figure 29. Urnammu, King of Ur, had this small figure cast in bronze, showing him carrying a basket of mortar and inscribed with his name and titles. It was then buried in the foundation deposit to preserve a record of his personal participation in the building of the temple of Enlil at Nippur.

Ashur temple at Ashur, there appears an inscription in "mirror-writing" from Shalim-ahum (ca. 1975 B.C.) declaring "the god Ashur *requested of him* a temple."[5] An alabaster tablet written during the reign of Tukulti-Ninurta I (ca. 1244–1208 B.C.) reports that Ashur-Enlil requested Tukulti-Ninurta to build him "a cult center on the bank opposite" Ashur.[6] In an octagonal clay prism inscription, it is reported that when Tiglath-Pileser I (ca. 1115–1077 B.C.) ascended to power, An and Adad "commanded" Tiglath-Pileser to rebuild their temple that had fallen into ruins.[7]

The Ugaritic texts thus far discovered tell us little about temple construction.[8] However, much is made of palace building among the gods, which closely parallels the motif of temple building. In the Baʿal cycle of myths, Yam and Nahar challenge the authority of the gods. El, the head of the pantheon, even orders the artisan god Kothar wa-Khasis to build a palace for them. However, Baʿal finally overcomes them and asks that a palace be built for him (significantly the word for palace in Ugaritic, *hkl*, is cognate with the Hebrew *hêkāl*, which means both palace and temple). This palace of the god in heaven is equivalent to the construction of his temple on earth.[9]

In ancient Israel, the stories of the construction of both the tabernacle and the temple contain commands from God to construct those edifices. God commanded Moses to tell the Israelites that they "make me a sanctuary; that I may dwell among them" (Exodus 25:8). When David indicated a desire to construct a more permanent dwelling for the Lord, the prophet Nathan initially approved his plan (see 2 Samuel 7:1–3). Later, however, Nathan learned (in a pointed and significant word-play) that, while the Lord would build a house (i.e., dynasty, Heb. *bayit*) for David, David's son would be the one to build a house (Heb. *bayit*) to the Lord (see 2 Samuel 7:4–17). This may explain why no specific command is given by the Lord to Solomon himself to construct the temple.

In a revelation called the "olive leaf . . . plucked from the Tree of Paradise," received on December 27 and 28 of 1831,[10] Joseph Smith was commanded by the Lord to build a temple. Joseph's associate, Frederick G. Williams, gave the following account of how the revelation was received:

> Bro[ther] Joseph arose and said, to receive revelation and the blessing of heaven it was necessary to have our minds on God and exercise faith and become of one heart and of one mind. Therefore he recommended all present to pray separately and vocally to the Lord for [him] to reveal his will unto us concerning the upbuilding of Zion & for the benefit of the saints and for the duty and employment of the Elders. Accordingly we all bowed down before the Lord, after which each one arose and spoke in his turn his feelings; and determination to keep the commandments of God. And then proceeded to receive a revelation concerning the duty [of the Elders as] above stated. 9 oclock P.M. the revelation not being finished the conference adjourned till tomorrow morning 9 oclock a.m. [28th]. met according to adjournment and commenced by Prayer thus proceeded to receive the residue of the above revelation [D&C 88] and it being finished and there being no further business before the conference closed the meeting by prayer in harmony with the brethren and gratitude to our heavenly Father for the great manifestation of the holy Spirit during the setting of the conference.[11]

In the revelation we find an indication that the temple has to be built: "Organize yourselves; prepare every needful thing; and establish a house, even a house of prayer, a house of fasting, a house of faith, a house of learning, a house of glory, a house of order, a house of God; that your incomings may be in the name of the Lord; that your out-goings may be in the name of the Lord; that all your saluta-tions may be in the name of the Lord, with uplifted hands unto the Most High" (D&C 88:119–20).

2. The King Visits the Temple Overnight

Of course, an overnight visit to a temple by the king or builder of the new temple is found only where such sanctu-aries already exist. Thus, while no specific parallel is to be found for this feature in the construction of the Kirtland Temple (even though there are at least five accounts of Joseph Smith receiving revelations through dreams),[12] sev-eral instances can be found in the ancient Near East.

The god Ningirsu's first message to Gudea (cited above) was confirmed by the goddess Nanshe:

> Being that the man—
> . . .
> was surely my brother Ningirsu,
> he will have spoken to you
> about the building of his shrine Eninnu.[13]

Gudea was advised to offer a chariot to Ningirsu, which he did. Thereafter, he entered the "shrine Eninnu," where he spent several days and nights.

After remaining on Mount Sinai for forty days and nights, Moses received instructions in constructing the tabernacle[14] (see Exodus 24:18; 25:8–9). If, as Donald Parry has convincingly shown, Sinai is to be understood as a temple type, Moses' lengthy sojourn on the mountain may be seen as a kind of overnight stay in the temple.[15] Fol-lowing his accession to the throne, Solomon frequently offered burnt offerings upon the altar of Gibeon. During the night, while he slept at the place, the Lord appeared to him and spoke to him, asking him to name whatever he wished (see 1 Kings 3:5). Solomon responded that he wished wisdom. While the examples in 1 Kings 4:29–34 of the wisdom with which Solomon was blessed focus on his rule, the emphasis in 1 Kings 5 shifts abruptly to preparations for building the temple. While the link in this section is less explicit than in other ancient Near Eastern texts in connecting a night visit to a shrine and temple building, "the building order may lie hidden in the narrative about Solomon's visit to the high place in Gibeon."[16]

3. God Tells Him What to Do, Indicates Plan

While Gudea was in the Eninnu shrine, Ningirsu instructed him in the manner of constructing his temple:

> O you who are to build for me,
> ruler who are to build for me my house,
> Gudea—for building my house
> let me give you the signposts
> and let me tell you the pure stars above,
> (the heralds) of my appointed tasks.[17]

The account of Nabopolassar (626–605 B.C.) of building in the main temple precinct in Babylon records that before beginning the construction of a temple tower, he consulted an oracle. In response to his query, Nabopolassar not only received divine approval for his task, but was also provided by the gods the measurements of the temple tower as well. According to the text, Nabopolassar "kept the measurements in his memory as a treasure."[18]

There is no specific mention of directions being given to Solomon by God for the construction of the temple, but it seems likely that this was the case, particularly since a great deal of attention is focused in 1 Kings 6 and 7:13–51 on the details of constructing and furnishing the temple. On the other hand, most of Exodus 25–40 is presented as commands given by the Lord to Moses on Sinai for the construction of the tabernacle, the preparation of its furnishings, and the consecration of its functionaries, not as an account of the carrying out of the Lord's directives. Note how these chapters are introduced: "Then have them make a sanctuary for me, and I will dwell among them. Make this tabernacle and all its furnishings exactly like the pattern I will show you" (Exodus 25:8–9, NIV).

Much is said in early Latter-day Saint sources concerning God's instructions for the building of the Kirtland Temple. According to Brigham Young: "Joseph not only received revelation and commandment to build a Temple, but he received a pattern also, . . . for without a pattern he could not know what was wanting, having never seen one, and not having experienced its use."[19] Orson Pratt stated: "When the Lord commanded this people to build a house in the land of Kirtland, he gave them the pattern by vision from heaven, and commanded them to build that house according to that pattern and order; to have architecture, not in accordance with architecture devised by men, but to have everything in that house according to the heavenly pattern that he by his voice had inspired to his servants."[20]

Truman Angell, who was intimately involved with the construction, stated:

> Joseph received the word of the Lord for him to take his two counsellors Williams and Rigdon and come before the Lord and he would show them the plan or model of the House to be built: We went upon our knees, called on the Lord, and the Building appeared within viewing distance: I being the first to discover it. Then all of us view it together. After we had taken a good look at the exterior, the building seem to come right over us, and the Makeup of this Hall seems to coincide with what I there saw to a minutia.[21]

Once, while Truman Angell was working on the finishing touches on the first floor of the temple, Frederick G. Williams entered it. When he was asked how it looked to him, "he answered that it looked like the model he had seen. He said President Joseph Smith, Sidney Rigdon and himself were called to come before the Lord and the model was shown them. He said the vision of the Temple was thus shown them and he could not see the difference between it and the House as built."[22] The early Mormon leaders Heber C. Kimball, Edward W. Tullidge, and Erastus Snow all similarly state that the command to build the Kirtland Temple and the pattern used were revealed by God.[23] Even non-Mormon sources made mention of the divine origin of the pattern of the Kirtland Temple. A letter, dated 16 March 1836, in the *Ohio Atlas* reported: "Their temple, in Kirtland, is a huge misshapen edifice, that comes nearer to the Gothic than any other style of architecture. The pattern . . . was given by direct revelation from Heaven, and given to those individuals separately."[24]

4. The King Announces His Intention to Build a Temple

Following the dream in which he had received instructions from Ningirsu to build a temple, Gudea awoke and immediately "gave instructions to his city as to one single man."[25] Similarly, the building inscription of Esarhaddon (680–669 B.C.) reflects this element of the temple-building motif. Esarhaddon expresses his desire to build the Esagila in Babylon by summoning "artisans and the people of Karduniash (Babylonia) in their totality" for that purpose.[26]

The very structure of the tabernacle passage in Exodus, in which God reveals to Moses what he is to say to the children of Israel, presupposes an announcement to the people by Moses that the temple is to be built (see Exodus 24:18–25:6). Similarly, in his letter to Hiram, Solomon announces his intention to build the temple, "Now the Lord my God has given me peace on every side, and there is no adversary or disaster. I intend, therefore, to build a temple for the Name of the Lord my God, as the Lord told my father David" (1 Kings 5:4–5, NIV).

It is difficult to determine the degree of publicity that attended the announcement of the building of the Kirtland Temple. However, in an early 1833 letter to leaders of the Church in Missouri, Joseph Smith stated: "The Lord commanded us, in Kirtland, to build a house of God, and establish a school for the Prophets[;] . . . the Lord helping us, we will obey."[27]

The building of the temple and the creation of the School of the Prophets were closely tied objectives. The original direction to institute the temple and the school came in the same revelation (see D&C 88). On March 8, 1833, another revelation was received that again emphasized that the School of the Prophets should be established (see D&C 90). On May 4 "a committee to obtain subscriptions, for the purpose of erecting such a building" was appointed, and on June 1 a circular discussing the building of the temple where the School of the Prophets might meet was issued to the various branches of the Church.[28] Clearly, Joseph Smith made public his intentions to commence with the temple.

5a. Master Builder Is Engaged

Gudea is depicted as a tireless overseer of the construction of the temple of Eninnu:

> Building with silver, the ruler
> sat with the silversmiths,

Building Eninnu with precious stones,
he sat with the jewelers,
building with copper and tin
Ninturkalamma directed before him the craftsmen
     and metal casters.[29]

Indeed, continues the account, "for the sake of building the house for his master, he slept not nights, nor rested the head at noon."[30]

In rebuilding the temples of Babylon, Esarhaddon made use of "wise architects and skilful builders."[31] When Sennacherib came to power, a temple known as "the Temple of the New Year's Feast of the Desert" (the *bīt akīti*), located outside the walls of Ashur, had fallen into disrepair. According to the inscription on the foundation stele, Sennacherib sought "the aid (*lit.* work) of master-builders" in his construction of the temple.[32] In the Ugaritic myth of Baʿal, Kothar wa-Khasis is the master builder who is given charge of the construction of Baʿal's palace by El:

And the Bull Ilu, his father, said:
["Ha! Kotharu, (you) builder!]
[Build] a man[sion] quickly,
[set up a palace quickly]
in the middle of [the highlands of Sapanu]
[on the mountain of Baʿlu].[33]

In the construction of the Tabernacle, Moses was commanded by God to commission Bezalel and Oholiab, "master craftsmen and designers," as the "master builders" of the tabernacle (Exodus 35:30–35). They were endowed with "skill and ability to know how to carry out all the work of constructing the sanctuary" (Exodus 36:1, NIV). Apparently there were others as well who were "given skill" to carry out the construction of the tent and the fashioning of all of its accoutrements (see Exodus 31:6–7). In the case of the construction of Solomon's temple, it is uncertain whether he or another acted as the master builder. However, he clearly appears to be in charge of the building operations: he chose "thirty-three hundred foremen who supervised the project and directed the [150,000] workmen" (1 Kings 5:16, NIV).

Artemus Millett, V. W. Upham, and H. C. Summerset were engaged as building supervisors for the construction of the Kirtland Temple. In the "Temple Ordinance Chronology" chart, Artemus Millett was recorded as the Master Builder. He was baptized by Elder Brigham Young and confirmed a member by Elder Joseph Young in Canada in January 1833, and Brigham announced that he had a mission for him. Brigham said that the Prophet Joseph wanted him to go to Kirtland, Ohio, and take charge of the mason work on the temple they were going to build there. So he closed out his business, and in April 1834 he moved to Kirtland, where he worked on the temple from the laying of the cornerstones until its completion. He had the full superintendency of the building, including charge of the plastering and cementing of the building, both inside and out.[34]

5b. Cedars from Lebanon, Building-Stones, Gold, Silver, etc., Procured for the Task

The Gudea cylinders devote considerable attention to the materials from which the temple to Ningirsu is made. "*Haluppu* oaks, ebony, and *abba* wood" were transported for use in the construction of the temple. Gudea also went to Lebanon ("the mountain of cedars") in order to obtain wood.[35] Other Mesopotamian inscriptions also regularly mention the use of the finest materials—silver, gold, and cedars—in the construction of temples. Entemena (ca. 2404–2375 B.C.), the *ensi* of Lagash, records that he constructed a temple for Ningirsu and "with gold and silver he adorned it."[36] Shamsi-Adad I (ca. 1813–1781 B.C.) roofed the temple of Ashur-Enlil in Ashur with "cedar beams" and "erected in the rooms cedar doors *with* silver and gold *stars*," and overlaying the walls of the temple with "silver, gold, lapis lazuli, (and) carnelian; cedar resin, best oil, honey, and ghee I mixed in the mortar."[37] In the inscription of Tiglath-Pileser I, the gods An and Adad specifically command that cedars from Lebanon be used in the construction of the temple.[38] In the Ugaritic Baʿal epic, the Baʿal's palace was built on Mount Saphon "of silver and gold," as well as lapis lazuli.[39] Further, Kothar wa-Khasis

> went to the Lebanon for its trees,
> to the Shiryon for the choicest of its cedars
> yes, (to) the Lebanon for its trees,
> (to) the Shiryon for the choicest of its cedars.[40]

Great attention is paid that the finest materials available be procured for Solomon's temple. These included "cedars of Lebanon" (1 Kings 5:6, NIV), "pine logs" (1 Kings 5:8, NIV), quarried stone for the foundation, and "pure gold" (1 Kings 6:21) for the interior.

The builders of the Kirtland Temple used the very finest materials available in its construction. At the time, some suggested that the temple be made of local timber, but Joseph Smith insisted that the building be made only from quarried stone.[41] Although this was a financial hardship and posed difficulties for the few men available, Smith's directions were followed, and a sandstone quarry was purchased and used.[42] The exterior plaster of the temple was made from crushed glass, bone, and other materials at great sacrifice. According to several reports this gave the building a beautiful and "striking appearance."[43]

The choice of materials used in the sacred edifice were

much like those commanded to be used in the building of the next Latter-day Saint temple: "Come ye, with all your gold, and your silver, and your precious stones, and with all your antiquities; and with all who have knowledge of antiquities, that will come, may come, and bring the box-tree, and the fir-tree, and the pine-tree, together with all the precious trees of the earth; and with iron, with copper, and with brass, and with zinc, and with all your precious things of the earth; and build a house to my name, for the Most High to dwell therein" (D&C 124:26–27).

6. The Temple Finished according to Plan

After the description of the construction of the temple in exquisite detail in the final columns of Gudea Cylinder A, the beginning of Cylinder B reports that, with the work done, "the people were laid off, and by and by the people went away."[44] Thereafter, the local (Annunaki) gods came to admire the structure, and the house was readied (with the aid of the gods) for the visit of its lord, Ningirsu.

As the final step in the completion of the temple, Solomon commanded that the ark be brought to "its place in the inner sanctuary of the temple. . . . Then Solomon said, 'The Lord has said that he would dwell in a dark cloud; I have indeed built a magnificent temple for you, a place for you to dwell forever'" (1 Kings 8:6, 12–13, NIV).

The Kirtland Temple was completed in accordance with a revealed plan in the spring of 1836. The Reverend Truman Coe gave the following description of the new temple:

> The completion of the temple, according to the pattern shown to Joseph in vision, is a monument of unconquerable zeal. The imposing splendor of the pulpits, the orders of the Melchisedec and the Aaronic priesthoods, and the vails which are let down or drawn by machinery, dividing the place of worship into several apartments,

presents before us a strange compound of Jewish antiquity and Roman Catholic mummery. The reproof which
the prophet addresses to ancient Israel . . . can never be
applied to these Mormons.[45]

7. Offerings and Dedication, Fixing of Norms and 8. Assembly of the People

At the conclusion of the building of the temple of
Sargon II at Dur-Sharrukin, the king invited "Assur, the
father of the gods, the great lord, the gods and goddesses
who abide in Assyria" into their temple. Various items were
offered to them, including "bright silver . . . sleek bullocks,
fat sheep, (barnyard) fowl, geese (?), doves, the brood of fish
and birds, the immeasurable wealth of the deep (*apsu*), wine
and honey, the products of the gleaming (snow-capped)
mountains." The people also gathered at the temple amidst
"jubilation and feasting."[46] When Baʿal's palace was finished, Baʿal slaughtered small cattle, bulls, rams, calves, and
lambs and summoned all the other gods to his new house,
and a great banquet took place:

> [Baʿal] slaughtered oxen,
> and small stock as well.
> He slew bulls
> and the fattest of rams,
> yearling calves,
> sheep, a multitude of lambkins.
> He invited his brothers to his mansion,
> his kin inside his palace,
> he called the seventy sons of Athiratu.
> . . . They ate, the gods drank,
> and they were supplied with a suckling,
> with a salted knife they carved a fatling.
> They drank beakers of wine,
> from golden cups blood from the trees.[47]

For the final ceremony of the placement of the Ark within the temple, "Solomon summoned into his presence at Jerusalem the elders of Israel, all the heads of the tribes and the chiefs of the Israelite families. . . . All the men of Israel came together to King Solomon at the time of the festival in the month of Ethanim, the seventh month" (1 Kings 8:1–2, NIV). When the priests withdrew from the Holy Place where they had placed the Ark, "the cloud filled the temple of the Lord. And the priests could not perform their service because of the cloud, for the glory of the Lord filled his temple" (1 Kings 8:11–12, NIV). Thereafter, Solomon addressed his people and offered the prayer of dedication (see 1 Kings 8:14–66).

As was the case with Near Eastern temples, standards and norms were set for the Kirtland Temple. Before meetings were conducted in the new temple, rules and regulations to be observed in the sacred edifice were drafted by the Prophet and his colleagues.[48] Following the fixing of norms, the people gathered for the dedication of the temple. Like several Old Testament cases, the people met in a "Solemn Assembly" for the dedication.[49] An early Church leader, George A. Smith, recalled the assembly: "When the Temple was completed there was a great manifestation of power. The brethren gathered together to its dedication. We considered it a very large building. Some nine hundred and sixty could be seated, and there would be room for a few to stand, the congregation was swelled to a little over a thousand persons at the time of the dedication."[50]

Joseph Smith offered a dedicatory prayer before the Saints assembled in the temple and, at the conclusion, he earnestly solicited the Lord:

> O hear, O hear, O hear us, O Lord! And answer these petitions, and accept the dedication of this house unto

thee, the work of our hands, which we have built unto thy name; and also this church, to put upon it thy name. And help us by the power of thy Spirit, that we may mingle our voices with those bright, shining seraphs around thy throne, with acclamations of praise, singing Hosanna to God and the Lamb! And let these, thine anointed ones, be clothed with salvation, and thy saints shout aloud for joy. Amen, and Amen (D&C 109:78–80).

Immediately following the dedication, the assembly participated in the ordinance of the sacrament.[51] According to the Doctrine and Covenants, the sacrament is an ordinance wherein one offers a "sacrifice unto the Lord thy God in righteousness, even that of a broken heart and a contrite spirit" (59:8). The Latter-day Saint sacrament is clearly perceived as an "oblation" and an "offering" (see D&C 59:12).

9. God Comes to His New House

Following vigorous preparations by Gudea and the gods,
The warrior Ningirsu entered the house,
the owner of the house had come,
a very eagle catching sight of a wild bull!
The warrior's entering his house
was a storm roaring into battle.
Ningirsu roamed through his house,
it was (the sound of) the Apsû temple precincts
when festivals are celebrated.[52]

During and after the dedication on 27 March 1836, there were numerous supernatural occurrences in the temple at Kirtland. It was reported by several members of the congregation that during the dedication angels and the apostle Peter appeared.[53] Some spoke in tongues, and others had visions. On the evening following the dedication (Monday), there was a special priesthood meeting. According to one account men prophesied and the temple was filled with angels. The temple glowed in the evening sky, and in astonishment, people ran to the building and asked, "What is happening? Is the temple on fire?" On March 29 (Tuesday), the apostles John the Beloved and Peter both appeared in the temple to Church members. On the following day, March 30 (Wednesday), twelve men reported that they saw "the Savior and angels in the temple."[54]

The most important report, however, regarded the experience of Joseph Smith and Oliver Cowdery on 3 April 1836. According to Cowdery, he and Smith went together into a partitioned section of the temple to pray. After arising from prayer, they received the following vision:

> The veil was taken from our minds, and the eyes of our understanding were opened. We saw the Lord standing upon the breastwork of the pulpit, before us; and under his feet was a paved work of pure gold, in color like amber. His eyes were as a flame of fire; the hair of his head was white like the pure snow; his countenance shone above the brightness of the sun; and his voice was as the sound of the rushing of great waters, even the voice of Jehovah, saying: I am the first and the last; I am he who liveth, I am he who was slain; I am your advocate with the Father. Behold, your sins are forgiven you; you are clean before me; therefore, lift up your heads and rejoice. Let the hearts of your brethren rejoice, and let the hearts of all my people rejoice, who have, with their might, built this house to my name. For behold, I have accepted this house, and my name shall be here; and I will manifest myself to my people in mercy in this house. Yea, I will appear unto my servants, and speak unto them with mine own voice, if my people will keep my commandments, and do not pollute this holy house. Yea the hearts of thousands and tens of thousands shall greatly rejoice in consequence of the blessings which shall be poured out, and the endowment with which my servants

have been endowed in this house. And the fame of this house shall spread to foreign lands; and this is the beginning of the blessing which shall be poured out upon the heads of my people. Even so. Amen (D&C 110:1–10).

10. The King Is Blessed and Promised Everlasting Dominion

Following the acceptance of the temple by the gods and its outfitting with all kinds of gifts, there is a lengthy encomium to Ningirsu, and then to Gudea, who is characterized as

> a fine *mēsu* tree
> made to sprout forth in Lagash
> by Ningirsu,
> he has indeed established your name
> from the south to the north.
> You . . . are an ab[le ru]ler, for whom the house
> has determined a [good] fate:
> Gudea son of Ningishzida,
> life is verily prolonged for you![55]

Whereas most of the Mesopotamian inscriptions end with a prayer for blessing from the god, in some—the Urnammu and Esarhaddon inscriptions, for example—the god bestows the blessing. When Urnammu finished the temple to Enlil, a banquet was held in which the god honored and blessed Urnammu.[56] Following the completion of a temple by Esarhaddon and the offering of sacrifices to the gods, "these gods (then) sincerely bestowed a blessing upon my royal rule."[57]

After the dedication of the temple, the Lord spoke to Solomon, promising him, quite literally, an everlasting dominion: "I have heard the prayer and plea you have made before me; I have consecrated this temple, which you have built, by putting my Name there forever. My eyes and my heart will always be there. . . . If you walk before me in integrity of heart and uprightness . . . and do all I command and observe my decrees and laws, I will establish your royal throne over Israel forever" (1 Kings 9:3–5, NIV).

After the Lord appeared to Joseph Smith and Oliver Cowdery, the "vision closed," and Moses, Elias, and Elijah appeared to them. Each of these supernatural beings gave Smith and Cowdery special priesthood rights and authority. The most noteworthy of these is the "sealing" key or "fullness of the priesthood." Joseph Smith taught that one who receives the "fulness of the priesthood" holds the office of a "king and priest of the most high God"; he is promised everlasting life with the gods, godly dominion, and the highest priesthood power.[58]

Conclusion

In his insightful study of the temple and meetinghouse types of sacred space, Professor Harold Turner notes the striking resemblance of the temples of the Latter-day Saints to other temples, ancient and modern, which he contrasts with the meetinghouse type of structure:

> As a final example representing a modern Western community we refer to the great granite temple of the Church of the Latter Day Saints at Salt Lake City, Utah. *The plan for this was revealed in a dream to the then leader of the Mormons, Brigham Young, so establishing it as a divinely-given sanctuary.* Although the public were admitted before its consecration, to show that it contained no fearsome secrets, it then became distinguished from Mormon chapels and tabernacles by being confined to those deemed ready to receive the mysteries of advanced religious teaching. *In no sense is it a Mormon congregational meeting place.* It is reserved for special functions which all seem to have cosmic reference. In one chamber is the great copper tank where Mormons may be baptized for,

and so united for all eternity with, deceased non-Mormon ancestors (hence the great concern with genealogies); here also is the marriage room where unions regarded as holding through all eternity are celebrated. The splendid classrooms are each devoted to consideration of one of the four great periods in cosmic history; the teaching and the murals help one to understand and meditate upon first, the primeval era, then the paradisal world of Eden, followed by the disordered world as we know it, and finally the perfected celestial realm. The increasing number of Mormon temples in other areas throughout the world show similar features which in their own peculiar way reveal some of the marks of the temple type and make the term entirely appropriate.[59]

Aside from some vocabulary that might strike the Latter-day Saint reader as odd, Turner's brief analysis contains several important insights: (1) The temple type of architecture and function is distinct from the meetinghouse type. (2) Temples are built on set-apart space that is not accessible to all equally. Those who do enter are expected to have (to borrow a well-known phrase from a psalm that is also concerned with temple worship) "clean hands, and a pure heart" (Psalm 24:3–6; cf. Psalm 15; Isaiah 33:14–16). (3) Temples have a cosmic reference point. This may be seen in temples' directional orientation: the ceremonial main entrance to the temples of the Latter-day Saints (indicated by the inscription "Holiness to the Lord" above the entrance) is generally on the east side. This cosmic orientation is further shown by the divisions within the temple that embrace the dead, the world of the living, and deity. Consider, for example, the baptismal font in Latter-day Saint temples, which was "instituted as a similitude of the grave, and was commanded to be in a place underneath where the living are wont to assemble, to show forth the living and the dead, and that all things may have their likeness, and that they may accord one with another" (D&C 128:13). The cosmic orientation in Latter-day Saint temples is also indicated by their ceremonial concern with the events that surround the creation. (4) As Turner notes, and as we have also seen in this essay, the plans for temples are revealed by deity.[60]

All of these features concerning the temples of the Latter-day Saints mentioned by Turner are also found among the elements in Lundquist's typology of temples in the ancient Near East (discussed at length elsewhere in this volume[61]). The similarity in features and functions in temples of the ancient Near East and temples of the Latter-day Saints—of which the commonalities in temple building are merely one example—is not the result of serendipity, but it occurs because those temples resemble a pattern that goes back to the beginning. As Hugh Nibley notes about Latter-day Saint temples: "Here for the first time in many centuries men may behold a genuine temple, functioning as a temple should—a temple in the fullest and purest sense of the word."[62]

Notes

1. Arvid S. Kapelrud, "Temple Building, a Task for Gods and Kings," *Orientalia* 32 (1963): 62. We wish to thank Bruce Satterfield for providing access to his excellent unpublished paper "Ancient Mesopotamian Temple Building in Historical Texts and Building Inscriptions" for the preparation of this essay.

2. Thorkild Jacobsen, "The Cylinders of Gudea," in Jacobsen, *The Harps That Once . . .: Sumerian Poetry in Translation* (New Haven, Connecticut: Yale University Press, 1987), 389; cf. Kapelrud, "Temple Building," 57.

3. See *ANET*, 583–84.

4. George A. Barton, *The Royal Inscriptions of Sumer and Akkad* (New Haven: Yale University Press, 1929), 319, 321.

5. A. Kirk Grayson, *Assyrian Royal Inscriptions*, 2 vols. (Wiesbaden: Harrassowitz, 1972–76), 1:6; italics added.

6. See ibid., 1:116.

7. Ibid., 2:18.

8. Translations of the Ba‘al mythological cycle may be conveniently found in G. R. Driver, ed. and trans., *Canaanite Myths and Legends*, 2d ed., ed. John C. L. Gibson (Edinburgh: Clark, 1978); Michael D. Coogan, ed. and trans., *Stories from Ancient Canaan* (Philadelphia: Westminster, 1978); Johannes C. de Moor, ed. and trans., *An Anthology of Religious Texts from Ugarit* (New York: Brill, 1987).

9. See Kapelrud, "Temple Building," 58–59; cf. M. Dietrich, U. Loretz, and J. Sanmartin, eds., *Die Keilalphabetischen Texte aus Ugarit* (Neukirchen-Vluyn: Neukirchener Verlag, 1976), 1.1.II, 1.4.II. For a cautious approach to myth as a paradigm of societal organization, see R. A. Oden, Jr., "Method in the Study of Near Eastern Myths," *Religion* 9 (Autumn 1979): 182–96.

10. *HC*, 1:316.

11. Frederick G. Williams, "Kirtland Council Minute Book," 3–4, cf. "Kirtland Revelation Book," 47–48, cited in Lyndon W. Cook, *The Revelations of the Prophet Joseph Smith* (Provo: Seventy's Mission Bookstore, 1981), 181.

12. See *HC*, 5:254–55; 6:194, 461, 609–10; *WJS*, 170.

13. Jacobsen, "Cylinders of Gudea," 396.

14. Forty in the Bible is typically a period of preparation. Cf. Wilhelm Roscher, *Die Zahl 40 im Glauben, Brauch, und Schrifttum der Semiten: Ein Beitrag zur vergleichenden Religionswissenschaft, Volkskunde, und Zahlenmystik, Abhandlungen der Königlichen Sächsischen Akademie der Wissenschaften, Leipzig*; Philologisch-historische Klasse 27:4 (1909); and Wilhelm Roscher, *Die Tesserakontaden und Tesserakontadenlehren der Griechen und anderer Völker, Berichte über die Verhandlungen der Königlichen Sächsichen Akademie der Wissenschaften, Leipzig*; Philologisch-historische Klasse 61:2 (1909): 15–206. See also Eduard König, "Die Zahl 40," *Zeitschrift der Deutschen Morgenländischen Gesellschaft* (1907); Friedrich Heiler, *Erscheinungsform und Wesen der Religion* (Stuttgart: Kohlhammer, 1961), 173–74.

15. See Donald W. Parry, "Sinai as Sanctuary and Mountain of God," in *BSAF*, 1:482–500; cf. David N. Freedman, "Temple without Hands," in *THPBT*, 21–30.

16. Kapelrud, "Temple Building," 60.

17. Jacobsen, "Cylinders of Gudea," 399.

18. Stephen Langdon, *Die neubabylonischen Königsinschriften* (Leipzig: Hinrichs, 1912), 63.

19. *JD*, 2:29, citation taken from the cornerstone-laying oration of April 6, 1833.

20. *JD*, 14:273; cf. *JD*, 13:357.

21. Recorded in Truman O. Angell Journal (typescript), Brigham Young University Library, Special Collections, cited in Cook, *Revelations*, 198.

22. Truman O. Angell to John Taylor, letter, 11 March 1885, LDS Church Archives, cited in Cook, *Revelations*, 322.

23. See Heber C. Kimball, *Times and Seasons* 6 (15 January 1845): 77 (article citation taken from the Heber C. Kimball Journal); Edward W. Tullidge, *Life of Joseph the Prophet* (Plano, Illinois: Reorganized Church of Jesus Christ of Latter Day Saints, 1880), 187–89; official record of a public address given by Erastus Snow, St. George Stake Historical Record, November 20, 1881, LDS Church Archives (H. D. C.), #97707.

24. Cook, *Revelations*, 322. This letter was reprinted in the *Painesville Telegraph*, 20 May 1836.

25. Jacobsen, "Cylinders of Gudea," 403.

26. David D. Luckenbill, *Ancient Records of Assyria and Babylonia*, 2 vols. (Chicago: University of Chicago Press, 1927), 2:244.

27. Letter from Joseph Smith to William W. Phelps, 14 January 1833, in *HC*, 1:316.

28. *HC*, 1:342–43, 349–50.

29. A.xv.25–30, in Jacobsen, "Cylinders of Gudea," 408.

30. A.xvii.7–9, in ibid., 409.

31. Luckenbill, *Ancient Records*, 2:251.

32. Ibid., 2:185.

33. Dietrich, Loretz, and Sanmartin, *Die Keilalphabetischen Texte aus Ugarit*, 1.1.II:26–29, in de Moor, *Anthology*, 23.

34. See Artemus Millett, "Autobiographical Sketches," typescript, n.d., LDS Church Archives.

35. A.xv.16, 18, in Jacobsen, "Cylinders of Gudea," 407.

36. Barton, *Royal Inscriptions*, 53.

37. Grayson, *Assyrian Royal Inscriptions* 1:20.

38. See ibid., 2:26, 28; cf. the inscription of Ashur-Nasir-Apli (883–859 B.C.) concerning the temple of Mamu at Imgur-Enlil, in ibid., 179; and the "Black Obelisk" inscription of Shalmaneser III (858–824 B.C.), in Luckenbill, *Ancient Records*, 1:201.

39. See Dietrich, Loretz, and Sanmartin, *Die Keilalphabetischen Texte aus Ugarit*, 1.4.V.18–19; cf. de Moor, *Anthology*, 55.

40. Dietrich, Loretz, and Sanmartin, *Die Keilalphabetischen Texte aus Ugarit*, 1.4.VI:18–21, in de Moor, *Anthology*, 58.

41. See Lucy M. Smith, *History of Joseph Smith by His Mother* (Salt Lake City: Steven and Wallis, 1945), 230.

42. See *JD*, 2:214.

43. Harlan Hatcher, *The Western Reserve: The Story of New Connecticut in Ohio* (Cleveland: World, 1966), 119.

44. B.i.10–11, in Jacobsen, "Cylinders of Gudea," 425–26.

45. Truman Coe, in *The Ohio Observer*, 11 August 1836.

46. Luckenbill, *Ancient Records*, 2:38.

47. Dietrich, Loretz, and Sanmartin, *Die Keilalphabetischen Texte aus Ugarit*, 1.4.VI.41–45, 55–59, in de Moor, *Anthology*, 60–61.

48. See *HC*, 2:368–69.

49. See *HC*, 2:410–28.

50. *JD*, 11:9.

51. See *HC*, 2:427.

52. Jacobsen, "Cylinders of Gudea," 429.

53. See Lyndon W. Cook, "The Apostle Peter and the Kirtland Temple," *Brigham Young University Studies* 15 (Summer 1975): 550–52.

54. Barrett, *Joseph Smith*, 248–51.

55. Jacobsen, "Cylinders of Gudea," 444.

56. See G. Castellino, "Urnammu: Three Religious Texts," *Zeitschrift für Assyriologie und vorderasiatische Archäologie* 53 (1959): 108–10.

57. Alexander Heidel, "A New Hexagonal Prism of Esarhaddon," *Sumer* 12 (1956): 35.

58. Joseph Smith Diary, 28 September 1843; see also public address of Joseph Smith, 10 March 1844, in "Wilford Woodruff Journal," 10 March 1844 (Sunday), cited in *WJS*, 327–38, 243–48; *HC*, 5:527; Heber C. Kimball Journal, entry of 26 December 1845; D&C 76:51–58; 121:28–29.

59. Harold W. Turner, *From Temple to Meeting House: The Phenomology and Theology of Places of Worship* (New York: Mouton, 1979), 46; italics added.

60. Further, see Stephen D. Ricks, "Temples through the Ages," in *EM*, 4:1463–64.

61. See John M. Lundquist, "What Is a Temple? A Preliminary Typology," in this volume, *Temples of the Ancient World*, 83–117.

62. "What Is a Temple?" in Hugh Nibley, *Mormonism and Early Christianity*, in *CWHN*, 4:368.

PART 3

Temple, Covenant, Law, and Kingship

9

The Legitimizing Role of the Temple in the Origin of the State

John M. Lundquist

If the ancient Mesopotamian historian is to give any meaningful account of his materials at all he must of a necessity relax the stringent claim of "what the evidence obliges us to believe," for it is only by taking account of evidence which is suggestive, when the suggestion is in itself reasonable, rather than restricting himself to wholly compelling evidence, that he will be able to integrate his data in a consistent and meaningful presentation. In replacing "what the evidence obliges us to believe," with "what the evidence makes it reasonable for us to believe" the historian—at the peril of his right to so call himself—leaves, of course, except for details of his work, the realm of knowledge to enter that of reasonable conjecture. This may not be altogether palatable to him, but since the nature of his materials allows him no other choice the best he can do is to accept it as gracefully as possible and with full awareness of its consequences in terms of limited finality of the results possible to him.[1]

I may be accused here of ideationalism, or something vile like that, but that is all right with me. My current research centers on religious systems expressed in art. In my estimation, there was strong ideological motivation in these early societies, particularly as embodied in

This paper originally appeared in Society of Biblical Literature Seminar Papers *21 (1982): 271–97.*

religious systems, and this is something that materialist archaeologists tend to ignore. If some of these scholars found themselves transported to some of these societies they pretend to reconstruct, they would not recognize, I suspect, much around them.[2]

Part I

The thesis of this paper is that the state, as we presently understand that term as applying to archaic societies (I will presently give a number of attempts to define this term), did not come into being in ancient Israel—indeed, could not have been perceived to have come into being—before and until the temple of Solomon was built and dedicated. Solomon's dedicatory prayer and the accompanying communal meal represent the final passage into Israel of the "divine charter" ideology that characterized state polities among Israel's ancient Near Eastern neighbors. (I will discuss shortly the implications of the Deuteronomic dating of 1 Kings 8 for the above claim.)[3]

In the ancient Near East, temple building/rebuilding/restoring is an all-but-quintessential element in state formation and often represents the sealing of the covenant process that state formation in the ancient Near East presumes.[4] We find significant vestiges of temple symbolism (as discussed in "The Typology" below) in earlier moments in Israelite history, at the mountain in the time of Moses, during the time of the Conquest, as recorded in Joshua 8 and 24, and, in fact, according to Menahen Haran: "In general, any cultic activity to which the biblical text applies the formula 'before the Lord' can be considered an indication of a temple at the site, since this expression stems from the basic conception of the temple as a divine dwelling place and actually belongs to the temple's technical terminology."[5] However, only with the

completion of the temple in Jerusalem is the process of imperial state formation completed, making Israel in the fullest
sense "like all the nations" (1 Samuel 8:20).[6] The ideology of
kingship in the archaic state is indelibly and incontrovertibly
connected with temple building and with temple ideology.

Definitions of State

It is important to note at this stage that I am not attempting to introduce the temple as the central feature in a
"prime-mover" hypothesis concerning state origin. The
process of early state formation is a fluid one, a process that
can go either forward or backward.[7] I am introducing the
temple more as an integrative, legitimizing factor that symbolizes, and, I believe, in the ancient mind would have symbolized, the full implementation of what we today call the
state.

Relatively rare in scholarship is the attempt to define
analogues to the term state from ancient sources. For
Mesopotamia we have Thorkild Jacobsen's description of
"primitive democracy" for the Protoliterate period, for
which he chooses "the relatively noncommittal term 'Ken-
gir League'" in place of "state" or "nation."[8] He recognizes
the state primarily as the "monopoly of violence," or, quoting Max Weber, a community becomes a state when it "successfully displays the monopoly of a legitimate physical
compulsion."[9] For Jacobsen, in Mesopotamian myth Anu
and Enlil "embody, on a cosmic level, the two powers
which are the fundamental constituents of any state:
authority and legitimate force."[10] Similarly R. M. Adams
wrote from the evidence of remains from the preliterate
Uruk period found in the central Euphrates floodplain:
"Among its features were: deities whose cults attracted pilgrimages and voluntary offerings; intervals of emergent,

centralized, militarily based domination of subordinate centers that had been reduced to the status of clients, alternating with other intervals of fragile multicenter coalition or local self-reliance."[11] "A better case can be made that the primary basis for organization was of a rather more traditional kind: religious allegiance to deities or cults identified with particular localities, political subordination resting ultimately on the possibility of military coercion, or a fluid mixture of both."[12]

Dr. Mendenhall's characterization of the transition from the Federation to the State in ancient Israel purports that "when a population emerges from a community to a political monopoly of force, it almost inevitably imitates models best known and most accessible to it."[13] He further writes: "The foundation of the community had nothing to do with a social agreement concerning divine legitimacy of social power structures—this entered from paganism with David and Solomon—but with common assent to a group of norms which stemmed from no social power."[14] His definition of the state which Israel took over from its neighbors during the period of the united monarchy is then "the maximization of human control. It is the divine power incarnate in the state or even the person of the king, which guarantees the success of the daily economic activities of the subjects, just as it is the king who guarantees the military protection with the same divinely delegated authority."[15]

Perhaps the most suggestive formula for an ancient definition of the state comes from the Sumerian King List, which yields this formula: the state = a king (invested with kingship by the gods) + a (capital) city.[16] This introduces us to the controversial problem of the role of urbanism in the origin of the state, an issue to which I will return later.[17]

Buccellati found that texts from Syria, including the Old Testament, come closer to the Sumerian than to the Akkadian formulas of expressing what I call above a definition of state polities in the ancient Near East. Although I will introduce highly sophisticated evidence below for the proposition that Israel did not achieve state formation until the monarchy, and thus that the period of Judges cannot be considered a time of state formation in Israel, it is probable that the Old Testament gives us this very picture in a manner highly reminiscent of the stylistic simplicity of the Sumerian King List. The very refrain of Judges, "in those days there was no king in Israel, but every man did that which was right in his own eyes" (17:6; see also 18:1; 19:1; 21:25), tells us that this period cannot be considered the time of Israelite state formation, either according to ancient views, or our own, while the theme of 1 Samuel 8, "we will have a king over us; that we also may be like all the nations" (verses 19–20), alerts us to the fact that, in the view of the ancients as well as in the views of modern research, a state polity is being introduced.

Part II

Recently I have been engaged in an attempt to identify commonalities in the temple practices/ideologies of the various ancient Near Eastern traditions. My main purpose in such an endeavor has been to construct a model or typology that will assist scholars in understanding "the social foundations of ancient polytheism,"[18] insofar as ancient temples can be seen to embody and to express central and crucial elements of such systems. The purpose of such a typology is to allow for "explanatory power in dealing with a set body of data." It will "point beyond the surface to the underlying patterns and processes; it will explain as well as identify."[19] It is true that I conclude that the main elements, if not all, of the following typology were accepted by and taken into the religious system of ancient Israel, and this at a time far antedating the introduction of the monarchy. Folker Willesen wrote many years ago that "if the temple ideologies of the different nations are able to display certain traits, common throughout the whole ancient world, it may be a special branch of the Chaos-Cosmos ideology."[20]

Perhaps a more succinct definition of what I mean by "ideology" is the following by Edward Shils:

> The central value system is constituted by the values which are pursued and affirmed by the élites of the con-stituent sub-systems and of the organizations which are comprised in the sub-systems. By their very possession of authority, they attribute to themselves an essential affin-ity with the sacred elements of their society, of which they regard themselves as the custodians. By the same token, many members of their society attribute to them that same kind of affinity. . . . The élites of . . . the ecclesi-astical system affirm and practice certain values which should govern intellectual and religious activities (includ-ing beliefs). On the whole, these values are the values embedded in current activity. The ideals which they affirm do not far transcend the reality which is ruled by those who espouse them. The values of the different élites are clustered into an approximately consensual pattern.[21]

This is the ideology that I attempt to identify and describe in what follows. I introduce the typology here because it will play an interpretive role later in this paper.[22]

The Typology

1. The temple is the architectural embodiment of the cosmic mountain.

2. The cosmic mountain represents the primordial

hillock, the place that first emerged from the waters that covered the earth during the creative process. In Egypt, for example, all temples are seen as representing the primeval hillock.

3. The temple is often associated with the waters of life that flow forth from a spring within the building itself—or rather the temple is viewed as incorporating within itself or as having been built upon such a spring. The reason such springs existed in temples is that they were perceived as the primeval waters of creation (Nun in Egypt, Abzu in Mesopotamia, Tehôm in Israel). The temple is thus founded on and stands in contact with the waters of creation. These waters carry the dual symbolism of the chaotic waters that were organized during the creation and of the life-giving, saving nature of the waters of life.

4. The temple is associated with the tree of life.

The first four items, taken together, constitute what I call a "primordial landscape," which we can expect to see reproduced architecturally and ritually in the ancient Near Eastern temple tradition.[23]

5. The temple is built on separate, sacral, set-apart space.

6. The temple is oriented toward the four world regions or cardinal directions, and to various celestial bodies such as the polar star. Astronomical observation may have played a role in ancient temples, the main purpose of which was to regulate the ritual calendar. Since earthly temples were viewed as the counterparts of heavenly temples,[24] this view also would have contributed to the possible role of temples as observatories.

7. Temples, in their architectonic orientation, express the idea of a successive ascension toward heaven.[25] The Mesopotamian ziggurat or staged temple tower is the best example of this architectural principle. It was constructed

of various levels or stages. Monumental staircases led to the upper levels, where smaller temples stood. The basic ritual pattern represented in these structures is that the worshipers ascended the staircase to the top, the deity was seen to descend from heaven, and worshipers and deity were then thought to meet in the small temple that stood at the top of the structure.

8. The plan and measurements of the temple are revealed by God to the king or prophet, and the plan must be carefully carried out. The Babylonian king Nabopolassar stated that he took the measurements of Etemenanki, the temple tower in the main temple precinct at Babylon, under the guidance of the Babylonian gods Shamash, Adad, and Marduk, and that he kept the measurements in his memory as a treasure.

9. The temple is the central, organizing, unifying institution in ancient Near Eastern society.

10a. The temple is associated with abundance and prosperity; indeed, it is perceived as the giver of these. These ideas are clearly expressed in Neo-Sumerian temple hymns, particularly in the Cylinder inscriptions of Gudea of Lagash and in the Keš Temple Hymn.[26] Many years ago Julius A. Bewer wrote an article in which he compared the religious and social role of the temple as it is depicted in the Cylinder inscriptions of Gudea with similar associations in the prophecies of Haggai. Gudea attributes wide-reaching social, legal, and economic reform as well as agricultural abundance to the building of the temple.[27]

10b. The destruction or loss of the temple is seen as calamitous and fatal to the community in which the temple stood. The destruction is viewed as the result of social and moral decadence and disobedience to God's word.

11. Inside the temple and in temple workshops, images of deities as well as living kings, temple priests, and wor-

shipers are washed, anointed, clothed, fed, enthroned, and symbolically initiated into the presence of deity, and thus into eternal life. Further, New Year rites are held, at which time texts are read and dramatically portrayed that recite a pre-earthly war in heaven; the victory in the war by the forces of good—led by a chief deity; the creation; and establishment of the cosmos, cities, temples, and the social order. The sacred marriage is also carried out at this time.

11. The temple is associated with the realm of the dead, the underworld, the afterlife, the grave. The unifying features here are the rites and worship of ancestors. Tombs can be and, in Egypt and elsewhere, are essentially temples (cf. the cosmic orientation, texts written on tomb walls that guide the deceased into the afterlife, etc.). The unifying principle between temple and tomb can also be resurrection. In Egyptian religion the sky goddess Nut is depicted on the coffin cover, symbolizing the cosmic orientation (cf. "Nut is the coffin").

12. Sacral, communal meals are carried out in connection with temple ritual, often at the conclusion of or during a covenant ceremony.

13. The tablets of destiny (or tablets of the decrees) are consulted both in the cosmic sense by the gods and yearly in a special temple chamber, *ubšukinna* in the Eninnu temple, in the time of Gudea of Lagash. By these means the will of deity was communicated to the people through the king or prophet for a given year.

14. God's word is revealed in the temple, usually in the holy of holies, to priests or prophets attached to the temple or to the religious system that it represents.

15. There is a close interrelationship between the temple and law in the ancient Near East. The building or restoration of a temple is perceived as the moving force behind a

restating or "codifying" of basic legal principles and a "righting" and organizing of proper social order.

16. The temple is a place of sacrifice.

17. The temple and its rituals are enshrouded in secrecy. This secrecy relates to the sacredness of the temple precinct and the strict division in ancient times between sacred and profane space.

18. The temple and its cult are central to the economic structure of ancient Near Eastern society.

It is evident that at least one major function of ancient temples is missing from this list.[28] The most obvious feature that is missing is the political function of the temple in the ancient Near East. In terms of the present paper, the temple plays a legitimizing political role and serves as "the ritual functioning system that establishes the connection between deity and king."[29] I will thus add to the typology an additional item:

19. The temple plays a legitimizing political role in the ancient Near East, or, as stated above, the ideology of kingship in the archaic state is indelibly and incontrovertibly connected with temple building and with temple ideology. It is this latest addition to my typology that I will now continue to develop in the present paper.

Part III

It is necessary now to discuss the issue of state formation as it relates to ancient Israel. Theories of state formation have been widely tested on ancient and ethnographic populations[30] but have only recently begun to be applied to ancient Israel. I am not aware of any published archaeological field projects within Palestine that have gone into the field with an explicit research strategy in which hypotheses of state origins in the country were tested, in the way, for example, that Henry Wright has field tested and refined his ongoing hypotheses in Iraq and Iran,[31] or in the way that Robert McCormick Adams has tested and refined theories of state origins over many years of surface survey in Iraq.[32]

Israelite Society as Chiefdom

A number of recent publications have succeeded in demonstrating that Israelite society during the period of the Judges should be classified as a chiefdom, taking the three-fold evolutionary schema developed by Elman Service (tribe, chiefdom, archaic civilization) as a model.[33] Mendenhall, for example, characterizes Israel during this period as "an oathbound unity of the village populations of ancient Palestine that was oriented first toward the realization of the ethical rule of Yahweh as the only Suzerain, and secondly toward the avoidance of the reimposition of the imperialism of the foreign-dominated regimes of the Palestinian power structures—the city-states."[34]

In one of the most interesting and challenging claims made in recent years for the ability of field archaeology to reconstruct the social structure of ancient societies, Colin Renfrew presented a list of twenty features characteristic of chiefdoms, "not one of . . . which cannot be identified in favorable circumstances from the archaeological record."[35] This list includes the following items:

1. A ranked society.
2. The redistribution of produce organized by the chief.
3. Greater population density.
4. An increase in the total number of societies.
5. An increase in the size of individual residence groups.
6. Greater productivity.
7. More clearly defined territorial boundaries.

8. A more integrated society with a greater number of sociocentric statuses.

9. Centers that coordinate social and religious as well as economic activity.

10. Frequent ceremonies and rituals serving broad social purposes.

11. The rise of priesthood.

12. Relation to a total environment (and hence redistribution), i.e., to some ecological diversity.

13. Specialization, not only regional or ecological but also through the pooling of individual skills in large cooperative endeavors.

14. The organization and deployment of public labor, sometimes for agricultural work (e.g., irrigation) and/or for building temples, temple mounds, or pyramids.

15. An improvement in craft specialization.

16. The potential for territorial expansion associated with the "rise and fall" of chiefdoms.

17. A reduction of internal strife.

18. A pervasive inequality of persons or groups in the society associated with permanent leadership, effective in fields other than the economic.

19. Distinctive dress or ornament for those of high status.

20. No true government to back up decisions by legalized force.

James W. Flanagan concluded his study by commenting, "Most of the elements of Renfrew's list of twenty characteristics of chiefdoms cited above can be documented in Israel. These indicate both the presence of chiefs and the absence of a strong centralized monopoly of force equipped with laws during the time of Saul and the early years of David."[36]

Theories of State

Numerous theories have been propounded to define the state and to account for its emergence. These theories can be roughly divided into two classes: (1) the "prime mover" theories, according to which a single variable, such as irrigation works, population growth, religious influence, trade, or environmental factors, is posited as the primary moving force in the development of complex social organization;[37] (2) theories that are cybernetic or systemic in nature, "in which multiple possible sets of causes in the ecology, economy, society and intersocial environment may singly or in combination produce more permanent centralized hierarchies of political control."[38] Claessen and Skalnik offer the following working definition of the state: "The early state is the organization for the regulation of social relations in a society that is divided into two emergent social classes, the rulers and the ruled." They then offer the following "main characteristics of the early state":

1. There are a sufficient *number* of people to make possible social categorization, stratification, and specialization.

2. Citizenship is determined by residence or birth in the *territory*.

3. The *government* is *centralized* and has the necessary sovereign power for the maintenance of law and order, through the use of both authority and force, or at least the threat of force.

4. It is *independent*, at least de facto, and the government possesses sufficient power to prevent separatism (fission) and the capacity to defend its integrity against external threats.

5. The productivity (level of development of the productive forces) is developed to such a degree that there is a *regular surplus* which is used for the maintenance of the state organization.

6. The population shows a sufficient degree of *social*

stratification that emergent social classes (i.e., rulers and ruled) can be distinguished.

7. A *common ideology* exists, on which the legitimacy of the ruling stratum (the rulers) is based.[39]

Gregory Johnson has defined the state as "a differentiated and internally specialized decision-making organization which is structured in minimally three hierarchical levels."[40] In an essay published in 1978, Henry Wright defined the state as "a society with specialized decision-making organizations that are receiving messages from many different sources, recoding these messages, supplementing them with previously stored data, making the actual decisions, storing both the message and the decision, and conveying decisions back to other organizations. Such organizations are thus internally as well as externally specialized."[41]

This definition, by the way, underlines the extraordinary role of record keeping in early states and points us toward a recognition of the complexity of the bureaucratic structure that we can expect to find. It also raises the question of the place of writing in the origin of the state. Certainly in the ancient Near East we have writing in each example of state formation. As Adams has written, writing and other forms of craftsmanship guaranteed that "a highly significant segment of the population must have been given or won its freedom from more than a token or symbolic involvement in the primary processes of food production."[42] Mendenhall has emphasized the great dependence that the burgeoning monarchy of Israel would have had on an extensive scribal bureaucracy, the lack of which in traditional Israelite society would have necessitated David and Solomon turning to the well-established Jebusite bureaucracy to fill this need.[43] On the role of writing in general as a concomitant of state origins, Lawrence Krader has written, "The relation between the formation of the state and the development of script, of writings, is not a chance correlation, but a coordination with interacting consequence in the service of the former."[44] Finally, Ronald Cohen's recent definition of the state emphasizes it as

> a centralized and hierarchically organized political system in which the central authority has control over the greatest amount of coercive force in the society. Sub-units are tied into the hierarchy through their relations to officials appointed by and responsible to a ruler or monarchical head of state. These officials maintain the administrative structure of the system and attempt to ensure its continuity by having among them a set of electors who choose and/or legitimate a new monarch.[45]

According to Service, "there seems to be no way to discriminate the state from the chiefdom stage." He then quotes Sanders's and Marino's *New World Prehistory*: "Differences between chiefdoms and states are as much quantitative as they are qualitative."[46] Claessen and Skalnik distinguish the state from chiefdoms in the latter's lack of a "formal, legal apparatus of forceful repression," and also its incapacity to prevent fission.[47] Cohen sees fission as the main feature that distinguishes chiefdoms in comparison with states: "The state is a system that overcomes such fissiparous tendencies. This capacity creates an entirely new kind of society. One that can expand and take in other ethnic groups, one that can become more populous and more powerful without necessarily having any upper limits to its size or strength."[48]

If we compare Renfrew's list of characteristics of chiefdoms, above, with the definitions of the state that have been cited, it would be possible to conclude that the only, or perhaps better, the major, features that distinguish the two would be the presence of stratified society in the state, in the place of ranked society in the chiefdom,[49] and the inability of the chiefdom to enforce its will legally or by force; in other words, the chiefdom lacks the monopoly of force (Renfrew's point 20, but see below). Otherwise it would probably be fair to say, à la Sanders and Marino, that the state constitutes "more of the same." This comes out in a rather interesting way in Wright's successive working models of his field work in southwestern Iran. His figure 5 emphasizes, for example, "increasing population" and "increasing competition for land," while figure 6 develops a model of "*increasing* population," "*increasing* demand for goods," "*increasing* interregional exchange," and "*increasing* competition." His figure 7, his working model for 1970, emphasizes "*more* specialization in herding," "*more* demands by nomads for goods and food," "*more* raiding," "*more* grain production in lowlands."[50] Thus it seems that even though the variables that he tested changed as his successive field work established certain variables as untenable or irrelevant, the field work also apparently demonstrated an evolutionary increase in these variables in the development from a chiefdom to a state.

Kaminaljuyu as a Model

One of the most interesting, archaeologically based studies of the transition from chiefdom to statehood in recent years, and one that I feel has great potential for application to field-work-based tests of hypotheses of state formation in ancient Israel's homeland (evidently it will demand this type of field testing, following the example of Henry Wright, Adams, and others, before major progress will be made in bringing ancient Israel into the orbit of primary state formations), is that of William T. Sanders and Joseph Michels and others on the Kaminaljuyu Project, at the site of Kaminaljuyu, in the Valley of Guatemala. Sanders gave a tentative summary of some of the results of the field work, especially as they relate to the problem of state formation, at the conference on Reconstructing Complex Societies.[51] I am going to summarize what appear to be the main points of Sanders's article, especially as they relate to his views of chiefdoms and the state. I will also make reference to comments that Martin Diskin made on Sanders's paper at the conference.[52]

The majority of Sanders's conclusions that will be quoted here refer to the following archaeological phases at Kaminaljuyu: Terminal Formative (Verbena-Arenal Phases—100 B.C.–A.D. 300); Early Classic (Aurora Phase—A.D. 300–500); Middle Classic (Amatle I—A.D. 500–700); Late Classic (Amatle II—A.D. 700–1000).[53] To begin with, Sanders introduces the problem of the relationship between civilization and the state. He defines civilization as

> a large, internally complex society. By internally complex we mean that a civilization is a society composed of many sub-societies, each with its own value systems and life styles, and that these distinctions are based primarily on differences in occupation, wealth, and political power. By large, we mean societies at least with populations in the tens of thousands. There is also a growing tendency among cultural anthropologists interested in complex societies to consider a state level of political organization as one of their fundamental characteristics.[54]

Thus "civilization" implies "the state." Thus also Anatolii M. Khazanov: "Civilization is a broader concept than the state. Aside from the latter it also embraces a written language . . . and the concept of towns. . . . The obvious fact is that the contemporary state, like any more or less developed state of the past, presupposes a civilization."[55] Sanders defines the state "as a political system involving adjucative [sic] power and explicit manifestation of force."[56]

Sanders evidently sees the chiefdom stage of political development prevailing at Kaminaljuyu through the Terminal Formative period, at which time the transition to the state begins, with full state formation completed by Late Classic times. Several features stand out as characterizing a chiefdom form of political development at Kaminaljuyu: Chiefs can often mobilize much greater expenditure of public resources for the building of temples and tombs than on personal residences for themselves. It is toward the end of the Terminal Formative that larger expenditures of labor begin to be devoted to the building of "elite residential platforms." In general though, it is the ability of the leader of a state to exercise "adjudicative rather than mediating functions," to "command the control of strategic resources (particularly agricultural land)," and to demand a greater "scale and sophistication of civic buildings" that distinguishes the state from a chiefdom. Further, the chiefdom seems to place a much greater emphasis on the funerary cult, "with the implications that ancestral spirits or chiefs themselves were the main objects of worship rather than high gods." This pattern would support the assumption that "the political system was still structured primarily along kinship lines."[57]

Sanders argues that a series of ceremonial platforms of the Arenal Phase, although implying "the ability of a leader to amass labor for ceremonial construction" (and thus implying the state), nevertheless "strongly suggests that these were funerary temples dedicated to dead chiefs or lineage ancestors rather than to high gods" (thus implying a chiefdom).[58] As matters develop during the Terminal

Formative, population increases considerably, a situation that leads to political instability in a chiefdom, because of its tendency "to be stable only on the lowest levels of political integration." At this point we reach the stage of a "paramount chiefdom," involving a much greater population, when "unusually able and vigorous men with great charismatic power achieve a paramount position during their own lifetime, and sometimes this paramouncy survives through the reigns of a number of succeeding chiefs, but generally involves a period of less than 100 years in total length."[59]

One of the most interesting phenomena, appearing during Early/Middle Classic times and heralding the advent of the state, is the introduction of large, centralized monumental building projects, with the architecture modelled after a major adjacent culture. Sanders writes that the style of the architecture is a "slavish imitation of the architecture of the great site of Teotihuacan in central Mexico implying a very close, special relationship between the two sites."[60] Along with a deemphasis on the funerary cult, there seems to be the introduction of high gods, "particularly the imported god Tlaloc, from Teotihuacan," and a corresponding "reorganization of ceremonialism towards temple construction."[61] Sanders writes in general of a major ideological change during this time, apparently attributable to the influence of cultural and religious influences coming from Teotihuacan. In response to a question posed during the discussion period at the conference "whether the similarity in architecture between Teotihuacan and Kaminaljuyu was the result of foreign invasion of people living there or a result of imitation by the local people," Sanders replied

that there was a drastic architectural reorganization. There was a sudden shift from the style of the buildings

in the main civic center of a community, which had a
long tradition of elite culture with its own sculptural and
architectural style. The centers were abandoned; and the
new center, a massive acropolis, was built in foreign
style. Simultaneously with this was the introduction of
the Tlaloc religious cult from Teotihuacan. But whereas
at Teotihuacan there were several avatars of Tlaloc, there
was only one of these versions found in foreign areas;
and it is the same one whether at Tikal or Kaminaljuyu.
There seems to have been a highly organized religious
system which came in and replaced the native religion,
and many of the religious artifacts disappeared.[62]

More generally, Sanders speaks of enormous increases
in population from Middle Formative to Late Classic times,
necessitating great structural changes "if the society were to
hold together." One such change was "the disappearance of
the ranked lineage type pattern,"[63] a situation expanded by
Martin Diskin in his comments to Sanders's paper: "But the
shift from rank society . . . to stratified society is best seen in
the economic sphere where specialization and exchange
mechanisms signal class or caste distinction and mobility is
increasingly curtailed."[64]

During the Late Classic period, population in the Valley
of Guatemala doubled, but at the same time "there is clear
evidence of a retraction of population, in which many slope
areas were abandoned and settlement was concentrated in a
few prize agricultural portions of the valley, where soils
were deep and fertile and where erosion was a minor problem."[65] Intensive agricultural practices are introduced at this
time. It appears that the people of the Late Classic occupied
perhaps 35 percent of the land that had been farmed during
the Terminal Formative. This led to a social setting in the
Late Classic of "intense competition over land resources; on
the intrasocial level this would produce unequal access to

land, patron-client relationships, and social stratification. On the intersocietal level competition would lead to intense warfare and increasing centralization of political authority."[66]

Martin Diskin elaborated these developments by positing "political control and monopoly of power . . . over the producers"; the "peasant group . . . subject to the superior power of a political elite," and "its alternatives are severely restricted"; "with the growth of new social forms, the costs are borne by ever increasing levies in the forms of taxes, services, and what Wolf generally calls 'rent.' This condition, that of rent payer, becomes irreversible. Usually this is so not only because of the power of the state . . . but because local production patterns become 'adjusted' to state needs and less and less toward self-sufficiency."[67] In his response to the comments on his paper, Sanders elaborated the theory behind such developments:

> One of the interesting things that archaeologists have indicated in many chronological sequences, or cultural historical sequences, is a general reduction in the quality of the average technology of individuals as one proceeds through time; . . . as the political system gets more highly stratified, as the holdings of the peasants get smaller, and as they contribute more and more to the system, obviously their purchasing power declines, and one may get an overall decline in peasant technology."[68]

Sanders then generalized this principle into a distinguishing feature defining one of the differences between a chiefdom and a state. We would note the movement "from a chiefdom level, where the individual still has a fair amount of independent action and the farmer, in particular, an ability to produce surpluses to a highly evolved political state where there is a class of people who are really living on the bare subsistence level, getting very close to Wolf's caloric minima and replacement level."[69]

The implications for ancient Israel of some of the patterns of cultural evolution at Kaminaljuyu, as suggested by Sanders, seem very obvious to me, although it is not my purpose in this paper to attempt to draw out these implications. Especially important seem the problems of marshaling strategic resources, particularly for public building, in the chiefdom and the state; the role of funerary cult in Palestine during chiefdom and state,[70] with the attendant implications for the worship of ancestors in a kin-based religious setting; massive architectural undertakings under foreign aegis in connection with major ideological readjustment as the society is transformed from a chiefdom into a state; population trends and changes in social structure, especially at the top; the introduction of charismatic leaders during the "paramount chiefdom" stage, at a time when population has increased considerably (of course, the issue of charismatic leadership during the period of the Judges in Israel has been extensively studied);[71] comparative agricultural usage in chiefdom and state, and patterns of land-use intensification; the comparative role of peasants in chiefdom and state, including the resource flow between rulers and ruled and other evidence of class division; and technology at the village peasant level in chiefdom and state.[72]

Finally, the study of the political evolution has suggested that "the structure, functioning and evolution of early states of all times and places show marked similarities. These findings give us reason to believe that it may be possible to develop a generally acceptable definition of the early state and to infer some of its basic characteristics."[73] While we must observe the cautions of Flanagan that "human societies are not so easily typed, and thus the factors interrelating processual phenomena militate against facile generalizing,"[74] we can still welcome the extent to which ancient Israel's cultural history has been brought into the general pattern and discussion of tribe–chiefdom–state, and applaud continued attempts to refine our knowledge of this process.

Part IV

In introducing the temple as an institution of ancient Near Eastern society[75] and its role in state formation, I want to emphasize a fundamental principle laid down by Barbara Price: "By definition the processes of state formation—pristine or secondary—involve major institutional transformations resulting in turn from significant bioenergetic change."[76] Price relies primarily on two types of data, architecture and settlement patterns, to provide reliable measures of the extensive bioenergetic changes that state formation represents.

> The greater the energy encapsulated in a piece of data, the more reliable will be its evidence, the greater the number of problems for which its application will be relevant and valid. . . . Stronger evidence of social, political, and economic [I would add, religious] processes can be derived from other kinds of material evidence, such as architecture, assuming that it is its scale or mass rather than its style that is emphasized. [And finally,] "A building," if appropriately analyzed, is thus theoretically capable of providing information on a fairly wide range of problems.[77]

Similarly for Sanders and Marino, who rely heavily on the evidence of architecture, settlement patterns, and craft specialization to measure the evolution of civilization, "civic architecture clearly relates to the institutional characteristics of any culture, so that the changing patterns of civic architecture of archaeological sites in a given area should provide important clues."[78]

The introduction of the concept of civic architecture as an important clue to some of the central distinguishing features of ancient civilization must at the same time introduce us to the "tell" as the main target configuration of a given ancient civilization that the archaeologist will be interested in investigating.[79] Of course this does not mean that the archaeologist explores the tell to the exclusion of its hinterlands—its resource area. An effective approach to the understanding of complex society in its formative periods requires a balance between the investigation of the "central city or the urban complex," and "the relations of the urban center to its surroundings and the effects of the urban system on the entire region."[80] An archaeological study of the temple in the ancient society will, however, in general, locate us on the mound itself, perhaps indeed on an acropolis within or on the mound itself, since acropolises have often, but not always, been located at the rough geographical center of the mound.[81]

What I am getting at here is that the temple stands at the "center" of ancient Near Eastern societies, not necessarily at the geographical center, for, as Edward Shils writes: "The central zone is not, as such, a spatially located phenomenon. It almost always has a more or less definite location within the bounded territory in which the society lives. Its centrality has, however, nothing to do with geometry and little with geography." (The ideological or sociological center of ancient societies does not necessarily stand at the geographical center.) "The centre, or the central zone, is a phenomenon of the realm of values and beliefs, which govern the society. It is the centre because it is the ultimate and irreducible; and it is felt to be such by many who cannot give explicit articulation to its irreducibility. The central zone partakes of the nature of the sacred."[82] It is in this sense that I believe that temples often stood at the "center" of ancient Near Eastern society, including Israelite society in the time of the Temple of Solomon.[83]

Role of Temples in State Formation

It should be noted, however, that none of the studies of the origins of the state, referred to above, had any role for the temple in the process of state formation. Although I want to reemphasize that I am not introducing the temple as a prime-mover hypothesis for state origins, I do feel that its exclusion in state-formation hypotheses is a mistake. In response to the opening quotation of this paper, which originally appeared as a criticism by Michael Coe of William Sanders's "materialist" ignoring of religious systems, Sanders replied that he ignored these factors "since this type of study does not lead to scientific generalization."[84] Combining the influence Sanders grants to civic architecture with the textual evidence that we have for the importance of the temple in ancient Near Eastern society, we can indeed formulate testable hypotheses with regard to the role of the temple and other religious/ideological values in ancient society. Perhaps this is what Robert Adams had in mind in faulting the reconstructions of Wright and Johnson for omitting "in the face of overwhelming evidence not only of its importance as a historic force elsewhere but of incontrovertible archaeological evidence that it was the predominant preoccupation precisely in the Uruk period, . . . any concession of a special role for religion and religious institutions."[85]

The central position of temple building/rebuilding/restoring in the royal inscriptions of the kings of ancient

Western Asia is well known.[86] In general, the pattern for these kingdoms would seem to be similar, a pattern that would also fit the Israelite state under Solomon: the state is not necessarily fully formed immediately upon the accession to kingship of a given charismatic figure. As with Israel in the time of David, state formation began in that time, but it was not finalized until the reign of his successor. Further, the process of temple building/rebuilding/dedication does not necessarily take up the king's main attention in the first year or two of his reign. If we may take the Babylonian year names as an example of this, in most cases the first few years were taken up with building and rebuilding walls, defeating remaining enemies, and in general solidifying control over the kingdom. Then, in the case of Sumuabum, the first king of the First Dynasty of Babylon, for example, it is the fourth year that bears a name connected with temple building; in the case of his successor, Sumulael, it is the seventh; in the case of his successor Sabium, the eighth; in the case of Hammurapi, it is the third.[87]

In most cases under discussion here, we will be dealing, strictly speaking, with secondary state formations and not with pristine states. And, as I suggested above, this is in all probability the correct designation also for Israel under David, Solomon, and their successors. But, as Price maintains, "all by definition are equally states."[88] The examples that I will refer to here for the role of the temple in state formation will come from polities that in my opinion can bear either the pristine or secondary state designation.

Khafaje as a Model

To begin with I would like to introduce two examples that represent a conflation of evidence for the importance of temples in the state from two different periods of the history of southern Iraq during the third millennium B.C. I am referring to the Temple Oval at the Early Dynastic I–II site of Khafaje in the Diyala Valley (an archaeological example) and the cylinder inscriptions of Gudea of Lagash (ca. 2143–2124 B.C.), which describe the process of building a temple to the god Ningirsu.

Although separated in time, these two bodies of evidence both bear the same witness to what Mallowan calls "the fantastically extravagant effort Early Dynastic man was prepared to go" to please his god.[89] The site of Khafaje, of which Mound A was excavated by an Oriental Institute team during the 1930s, lies just to the east of Baghdad, on the Diyala River. The extraordinary development of this temple-dominated city plan fits into the late Early Dynastic I and Early Dynastic II, when so many changes took place that were to characterize the era of "primitive monarchy" of the earliest historical Sumerian states. The "implosive" process of urbanization,[90] the building of the first city walls at Uruk, large-scale palace architecture, and monumental temple platforms further characterize the Early Dynastic I and II periods in southern Mesopotamia. This was a period of major state development.[91] As far as Gudea is concerned, he was the second governor of the most important post-Akkad, pre-Ur III state in southern Mesopotamia. The building materials for the temple he built came from as far away as the Amanus Mountains, Ebla, and the Jebel Bishri.[92]

The Temple Oval at Khafaje dominated a city settlement that was surrounded by a six- to eight-meter-wide defense wall. A number of other important temples, chief among them the many levels of the Sin Temple, and sections of private houses were also excavated. The building process involved in the ancient construction of the Temple Oval was truly phenomenal. The Oval is surrounded by a double wall that enclosed an area of about eight thousand square meters. This area was prepared for the construction of the temple by being excavated to a depth of over eight meters. Then clean, sandy soil was brought into the excavation site from elsewhere and laid into the pit. The excavators estimated "a volume of not less than 64,000 cubic meters [of sandy soil], the equivalent of 6 1/2 million basket loads as soil is carried nowadays." The foundation walls of the oval were then raised on the sand base, the sand being limited to the area encompassed by these walls.[93] The original excavation for the foundations of the Temple Oval cut through earlier, apparently Early Dynastic levels of houses, but there was also evidence that parts of the foundations had been founded on a reclaimed swamp. This "staggering amount of labor" was "entirely preliminary to the brickmaking and the erection of the massive structure itself."[94]

What was the meaning of such a procedure? Ellis writes that "I know of no ancient text that explains the reason for this."[95] I have attempted elsewhere to connect such a practice with temple ideology attested to in Egypt at a much later period.[96] A. J. Spencer has written of the enormous expenditure of labor that went into fulfilling the "mythological requirements" of temples in the Late and Ptolemaic Periods:

> The construction of the vast temple enclosure walls in undulating brickwork is an obvious example. Another effect, closely related to the substructure of the peripteral temples, is the development of a new style of foundation for large cult temples in the Late Period. . . . The entire area to be occupied by a Late-Period temple was dug out into an enormous rectangular pit, which was then lined with strong brick retaining walls and filled up to the top with sand. Over this sand bed were laid several courses

of stone to create a platform on which to build the temple.[97]

Attested examples of this type of structure have been found in the Delta and in Upper Egypt. Fortunately, this building procedure is given a mythological foundation in an Edfu text which describes the building of the temple there: "He excavated its foundation down to the water, it being filled up with sand according to the rule, being constructed of sandstone as an excellent work of eternity." Thus, "The temple had to rest on a bed of sand, as a representation of the primaeval mound, and it was desirable that this sand should extend down to the subsoil water, as the Mound had stood in the Nun." Thus in this case we have a textual attestation for the enormous amount of work that Egyptians in this period were prepared to undertake in order to fit the temple building to mythological presuppositions. As Spencer writes, "The effects of religious belief on architecture were not, as some have claimed, a vague symbolism."[98]

The same holds true, I believe, for a case such as the Temple Oval, particularly when we consider the extent to which mythological traditions of ancient Mesopotamia viewed temples as being founded in and arising out of the sweet waters of the abyss, the home of the god of wisdom Enki. I have given considerable evidence for this connection elsewhere.[99] A fairly common Sumerian phrase states that the temple's *temen* (foundation) "is sunk into the *abzu*."[100] One Neo-Sumerian hymn exhibits a kind of inner or chiastic parallelism of the first two words of two successive lines which, as I have tried to show elsewhere,[101] very possibly approaches the primeval mound-temple ideology of Egypt. Line 4 of this hymn begins "Abzu, shrine," (*abzu èš*), while

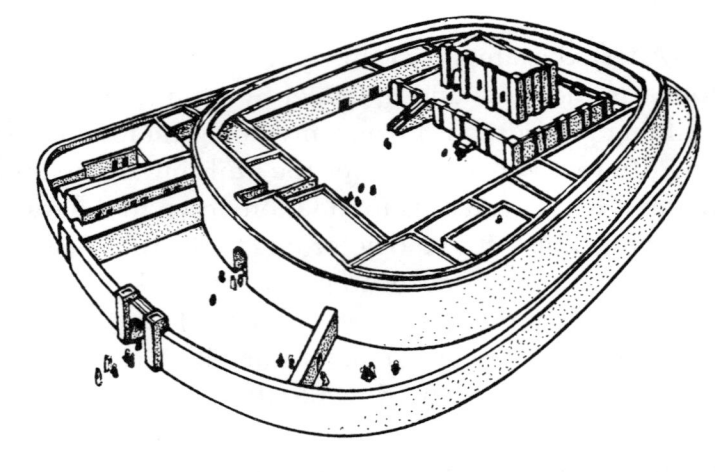

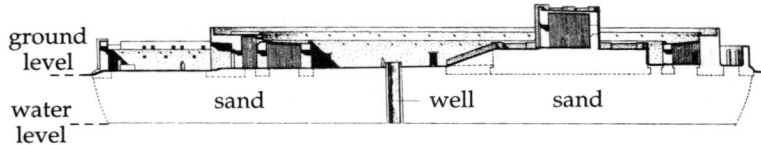

Figure 30. The temple of the goddess Inanna at Khafaje (c. 3000–2500 B.C.) was begun by excavating down to the groundwater level and placing sixty-four thousand cubic meters of purified sand as the foundation for the structure above, a massive earth-moving task even today. The temple is built in successive platforms, evoking the "mountain of God."

line 5 begins "House, holy mound," (*é du₆-kù*), where *èš* and *é* are synonymous and *abzu* and *du₆-kù* are synonymous.[102] The reclaimed swamp on which the Temple Oval was built could thus take on a greater significance in light of the above.

Mesopotamian Temples as Models

The Gudea hymns "give a vivid picture of the ideology behind the temple building, and they are the best examples which can be found on Sumerian soil."[103] Many scholars have recognized the relevance of the Gudea inscriptions to the Old Testament.[104] Kapelrud has pointed out the main parallels between traditions of temple building in which "the gods" are the main protagonists, as in the *Enuma Elish*, and the Baal Cycle from Ras Shamra, and those in which kings are the center of attention, as with Gudea, Moses, and Solomon.[105] With the former the main elements are

> 1. A victorious god after battle; 2. He wants to have his own temple; 3. Permission asked from the leading god; 4. Master builder set to work; 5. Cedars from Lebanon, building-stones, gold, silver, etc., procured for the task; 6. The temple finished according to plan; 7. Offerings and dedication, fixing of norms; 8. A great banquet for the gods.[106]

In those instances where kings are depicted as temple builders, Kapelrud found the following elements:

> 1. Some indication that a temple had to be built; 2. The king visits a temple overnight [incubation]; 3. A god tells him what to do, indicates plans; 4. The king announces his intention to build a temple; 5. Master builder is engaged, cedars from Lebanon, building-stones, gold, silver, etc., procured for the task; 6. The temple finished according to plan; 7. Offerings and dedication, fixing of norms; 8. Assembly of the people; 9. The god comes to his new house; 10. The king is blessed and promised everlasting domination.[107]

(One would have to add to this list, also, a great banquet for all the people.)

For the purposes of this paper, the most important aspect of temple building—its legitimizing role in the establishment of a dynasty—is most clearly expressed in the Gudea Cylinder B. Once the temple had been completed, it was necessary that its god, Ningirsu, should be led inside and formally installed as "king."[108] Ningirsu had in the meantime been carried to the Temple of the Abyss of Enki in Eridu, the most ancient and honored temple in Sumer, to receive the legitimizing approval of Enki for the temple that Gudea was building in Lagash.[109] Ningirsu then returned from Eridu and was majestically ushered into his temple during the New Year festival. During this festival, the sacred marriage rite was carried out between Ningirsu and Bau, the destinies were fixed, and a communal meal was shared by the inhabitants of the city.[110] The gate through which Ningirsu would have been led into the temple was at the same time one of the city gates. This was the *kà.ki.lugal.ku$_4$*, "the gate through which the king (Ningirsu) enters." Next to this gate stood a pillar (*^{giš}ti*), "a heavenly *nir* that extends to heaven."[111]

To return to Cylinder B, Gudea, depicted as a priest who leads the processions, prayers, and sacrifices, receives his kingship in perpetuity from Ningirsu. One of the key passages is B.VI.14–18, which reads, in Falkenstein's translation, *"dass (Ningirsus) Stadt, das Heiligtum Girsu, Gereinigt, der 'Thron der Schicksalsentscheidung' aufgestellt, dass Szepter langer Tage geführt werde, dass der Hirte Ningirsu für Gudea das Haupt (wie) eine schöne Krone zum Himmel erhebe."*[112] Another passage, which is important for the thesis presented here, is B.VIII.13–19, where Ningirsu is presented as having returned from Eridu (again, the introduction of Eridu as the main, legitimizing temple center in the ideology that underlies the Gudea Cylinders), and *"der Thron in der 'wohlgebauten' Stadt gefestigt werde, dass für das Leben des guten Hirten Gudea die Hand (zum Gebet) an den Mund geführt werde."*[113] Here we have the ultimate "legitimizing" connection, bringing together all the main factors that I believe were involved in the establishment of the "divine charter" ideology in ancient Near Eastern state polities: the god in his temple, which temple was built by divine instruction by the king of the city after it was duly authorized and approved by Enki of the "Temple of the Abyss" in Eridu; then the king, the "good shepherd," was handed a scepter of perpetual rule, guaranteeing the authority and legitimacy of his throne; all of this carried out, of course, in the temple itself (which of course, as mentioned above, underscores the priestly functions of the king, at least in this tradition).[114]

Thus we have an ancient theory of state origins, centered around the building of a temple to the main deity of the city, and the establishment of a dynastic system through this means. The Gudea inscriptions give us perhaps the clearest view of this process (the fact that they may give us a fanciful and idealized picture[115] does not detract from their value as a theoretical statement of an ideology, a "constitution," if you will, a statement of how things should be, as viewed through the eyes of temple poets, the intellectuals of that day). The site of Khafaje, as an example, begins to show us how this theory would have been carried out architecturally, and how the architecture of the temple would have related to the city plan as a whole. Note here, for example, that the best-preserved city gate at Khafaje was found situated just to the northwest of the Temple Oval, so that entry into the city gate at this point would have given one a direct view of the gate of the Temple Oval itself.[116] Khafaje also shows us what the implications of this arrangement would be for the economic role of the temple in the city.[117]

Leaving the evidence introduced above, we should mention in passing that two of the most famous religious epics of ancient Near Eastern literature, the *Enuma Elish* and the Baal Cycle from Ras Shamra, give us a similar temple-

centered view of state origins, a view in which the legitimizing decisions of the cosmic deities are transferred to
earth and to the earthly monarch, the whole process symbolized by and centered in the building of a temple. Of
great interest here is a point made by Jonathan Z. Smith in
his critique of Mircea Eliade's views of "Center" symbolism: "Eliade has not, to my knowledge, dwelt on the significance of the fact that the Babylonian creation epic,
Enuma Elish, is not so much a cosmogony as it is a myth of
the creation of a temple."[118] With regard to the Baal Cycle,
we have the recent statement of Frank Moore Cross: "Baʿl
founded his temple on Mount Ṣāpōn in order to make manifest his establishment of order, especially kingship among
the gods. The earthly temple of Baʿl manifested not only
Baʿl's creation of order, but at the same time established the
rule of the earthly king. There is thus a tie between the
temple as the abode of the king of the gods and the temple
as a dynastic shrine of the earthly king, the adopted son of
the god. The temple and kingship are thus part of the
'orders of creation,' properly the eternal kingship of the god
of order, the eternal dynasty of his earthly counterpart."[119]

If we thus use the above statement of Cross as a summary description of the temple-centered state polity, keeping in mind the evidence from Gudea and the evidence of
the extraordinary, "fantastically extravagant" (Mallowan)
building practices associated with temples, as at Khafaje,
referring at the same time to my typology above, especially
points 1–4 (the "primordial landscape"), then I think that
we can begin to answer the question of how a building can
play such an important role in legitimizing centralized,
monarchical, dynastic authority in the ancient Near Eastern
state.

Of course, the "fantastically extravagant" effort that

went into the temple building meant corvée labor and extensive oppression of the masses by the ruling classes, which is what we expect in the early state, at least at certain levels of its evolution.[120] But remember point seven in Claessen and Skalnik's "main characteristics of the early state," above: "A *common ideology* exists, on which the legitimacy of the ruling stratum (the rulers) is based." Elsewhere they elaborated this point, adding that the "basic concept [of the common ideology] is the principle of reciprocity between the ruler in the center and his subjects living for the greater part in agrarian communities."[121] We would assume that the oppressive labor requirement imposed by the building of the Temple Oval would have transgressed this "principle of reciprocity," and, of course, in the matter of the succession to the kingship of Israel, following Solomon's death, we know that this principle was broken, and we have a record of the acrimonious negotiations that accompanied its breaking and the subsequent division of the kingdom (see 1 Kings 12). But we must also remember two important factors that relate to this point: (1) "By their very possession of authority, they [the elites] attribute to themselves an essential affinity with the sacred elements of their society, of which they regard themselves as the custodians. By the same token, *many members of their society attribute to them that same kind of affinity*";[122] and (2) "the common man, lastly, remains an unknown, the most important unknown element in Mesopotamian religion."[123] Therefore we must assume the probability that temples played unifying, integrating, positive, genuinely pious roles in the ancient community, and that, to some extent, perhaps impossible to define, even corvée would not have been viewed as an entirely onerous duty in connection with temple building.[124]

Figure 31. King Bel-Harran-bel-usur erected this stele to commemorate his independence. He is shown adoring the symbols of the gods: the shovel of Marduk, the stylus of Nabu, the winged sun of Shamash, the moon of Sin, and the star of Ishtar.

Two Other Temples as Models

Before leaving this section I would like to refer to two additional pieces of evidence that support the thesis of the paper. First is the stele of the Assyrian noble Bel-Harran-bel usur, who, sometime during the reign of Shalmaneser IV, founded his own, presumably independent, city in the desert west of Niniveh. So great was the weakness of the central power at this time that Bel-Harran-bel-usur was able to claim total independance on his stele, calling in the first instance on the Babylonian gods Marduk and Nabu, ignoring Ashur and ignoring the Assyrian king. He himself claims to have established the freedom of the city, exempting it from certain taxes and establishing certain endowments. We can safely call this foundation a secondary state, I believe. In the stele itself, after he has named the gods who have authorized his new city, we read:

> Bel-Harran-bel-usur . . . who fears the great gods, they have sent and,—the mighty lords, at their exalted word and by their sure grace, I founded a city in the desert, in a waste. From its foundation to its top I completed it. A temple I built and I placed a shrine for the great gods therein. Its foundation I made firm as the mountains are set down, I established its foundation (walls) for all eternity. Dur-Bel-Harran-bel-usur I called its name,—in the mouth of the people, and I opened up a road to it. I inscribed a stele, the images of the gods I fashioned on it, in the divine dwelling place I set it up.[125]

This seems, to me at least, to point out the centrality of the temple building in state formation, even in so ephemeral a polity as was Dur-Bel-Harran-bel-usur.

The second piece of evidence that I would like to introduce here is the thesis of the very important recent article of Richard D. Barnett.[126] Barnett, starting off with Solomon's prayer of dedication of the Jerusalem temple (see 1 Kings 8), examines evidence from Hittite and neo-Hittite gateway reliefs that illustrates the process by which the gods of these cities were ritually and ceremoniously invited into the city and installed and whereby they took up their residence in the city's temples. The reliefs generally show a procession of nobles and soldiers, male and female worshipers, approaching the seated deity of the city, where a feast is in process. In the case of Carchemish, the "worship at the gate" motif appears to have terminated at the chief temple itself, although the excavations were not able to demonstrate this conclusively. Especially interesting is the building inscription of Azitawadda which states at one point, "Having built this city and having given it the name of Azitawaddiya, I have established Ba'l-*Krntryš* in it. A sacrific[ial order] was established for all the molten images. . . . May Ba'l-*Krntryš* bless Azitawadda with life, peace, and mighty power over every king."[127] I have pointed out above the possibility that the temple gate at Lagash through which Ningirsu was introduced into the Temple was also one of the main city gates, and the fact that the Temple Oval was built directly adjacent to a main city gate. The process of memorializing the introduction of a city's gods into their temples—in some cases temples that were built just inside the city gate (as at Alaca Huyuk for example)—by means of wall reliefs that depict a sacral procession with banquet[128] further supports the thesis that temple building was central to the ancient state formation process.

Part V

Ancient Israel developed from a chiefdom to a (in all probability, secondary) state during a period of about two generations, covering the span of the Iron Age IC period (about 1000–918 B.C.). As I suggested above, the process of evolution from chiefdom to state is graphically recounted in the Old Testament, in terms that are familiar to the modern student of such processes in ancient societies. From the refrain that ends the book of Judges,[129] to Samuel's admonitions concerning the institution of kingship in 1 Samuel 8,[130] to Nathan's (first) oracle to David in 2 Samuel 7 informing him that he should not build a house for Yahweh,[131] to the night vision/dream of Solomon during the incubation at the high place of Gibeon where he presumably received the instructions that he should build the temple,[132] to the actual building and dedication of the temple, the Old Testament gives us an extraordinary and apparently unmatched ancient narrative of the tensions, debates, and political and theological arguments that accompanied the advent of the dynastic state. Again, the state was not "caused" by the introduction of the temple and the accompanying divine charter ideology; the temple is a symbol of a "major institutional transformation," resulting "from significant bioenergetic change,"[133] and thus signals to us, as I believe it did to the Israelites of that period and to their neighbors, that they had achieved a state, "like all the nations" (1 Samuel 8:20).[134] We might as well take the ancient record at its own word.

The Temple of Solomon in State Formation

But what of the Temple of Solomon? The "cosmic-universal rule"[135] implied by the Israelite monarchy demanded a temple that incorporated the same cosmic symbolism as did temples in the surrounding region. I believe that Albright's description and interpretation of the various cosmic features in the Temple of Solomon, such as the two pillars, Jachin and Boaz, the Sea, the twelve bulls, the altar of burnt offerings, and the platform, *kîyôr*, on which, according to the Chronicler, Solomon stood while uttering the prayer of dedication (see 2 Chronicles 6:12–13), have not been effectively either superseded or refuted.[136] In spite of whether Jachin and Boaz served as structural columns within a *bit Ḥilani* porch, or whether they were free-standing pillars, which has been the opinion of most scholars,[137] it is undeniable, in my opinion, that they had a major symbolic purpose in relationship to the sanctuary. Pillars built with such symbolic purpose would probably point us toward free-standing structures, and we can generally agree with S. Yeivin that "a custom of erecting twin columns in front of the facades of temples (without any architectural relation to the building) was current in the western part of the Fertile Crescent (the area of Israel, Phoenicia, Syria) at least since the XIIIth century B.C.E. and till the IInd century C.E."[138]

The symbolic purposes played by such pillars could well have included those mentioned as possibilities by Albright, namely, "they may have been regarded as the reflection of the columns between which the sun rose each morning to pour its light through the portico of the Temple into its interior," or that, "like the Egyptian, *djed* symbol they may also have denoted 'endurance,' 'continuity,' in which case their dynastic role would become self-evident."[139] It is this latter that I think is especially important in the light of the thesis of this paper. I assume that the pillars played a major role in legitimizing the temple and the dynasty of David in the minds of the people. In other words the pillars, Jachin on the south, carrying the message that Yahweh had established the dynasty and the temple, and Boaz on the north, carrying the message that the power that emanates from the sanctuary is that of Yahweh.[140]

A suggestion by R. B. Y. Scott made several years ago

seems most interesting and relevant here. Scott drew upon an example from Cylinder A of Gudea of Lagash, as well as other Near Eastern evidence, to demonstrate the hypothesis that the words "Jachin" and "Boaz" were parts of two inscriptions, "of which the opening words came to designate the pillars on which they appeared."[141] The relevant passage in Gudea is A.XXII.24–XXIV.7, where Gudea has stones brought into the temple precinct and fashioned into six steles, each of which bears a sentence name. These were set up on the temple terrace, apparently surrounding it, at various gates leading into the temple, and inside the temple itself. One of these, which was stationed at the *ká.sur.ra.* gate, was called, in Thureau-Dangin's translation, *"der Herr des Sturmes Enlil, welcher nicht seinesgleichen hat, blickt mit günstigem Auge auf Gudea, den Gross-priester [en] Ningirsus."* The next stele mentioned, stationed toward the rising sun, bore the name *"der König der (brausenden) Wirbelwinde Enlil, der Herr, der nicht seinesgleichen hat, hat in seinem reinen Herzen erwählt Gudea, den Grosspriester Ningirsus."*[142] The following stele, erected at *šu.ga.lam*, the main entrance to Eninnu, bore the name *"der König, durch den die Welt ruht, hat befestigt den Thron Gudeas, des Grosspriester Ningirsus."*[143] Thus each of these steles bore an inscription that identified the ruling dynast with the chief god of the city and, particularly in the case of the stele at the *šu.ga.lam* gate, specifically legitimized the throne of Gudea.

R. B. Y. Scott's suggested reconstruction for the inscription on Jachin was "He (Yahweh) will establish the throne of David, and his kingdom to his seed forever." And for Boaz, "In the strength of Yahweh shall the king rejoice," or some such, drawing on language well known from the Psalms.[144] In Scott's more recent discussion of the same problem, he wrote that "it seems probable that the names of the pillars in Solomon's royal temple, where he officiated as high priest, were derived from the initial words of dynastic inscriptions like that of Gudea."[145] This view seems to me by far the most reasonable and the most likely explanation of the pillar's significance, adding more evidence for the legitimizing political role of the temple and its appurtenances and allowing us to see more clearly just how a building could have played such a role in ancient societies.

One additional role played by pillars in the ancient Near East, that of witnesses of covenant ceremonies, can be proposed. Widengren has pointed out the central role of the king in Israelite covenant making during the period of the monarchy. He found three main elements present in such ceremonies: (1) the king plays the central role, calling the assembly and reading from the book of the law; (2) the king himself appears "before the Lord," thus assuming the role of high priest; and (3) "the covenant is made in the temple."[146] I have argued elsewhere for the centrality of the role of the temple in ancient Near Eastern covenant rituals.[147] Covenants are sealed in temples or near pillars standing near temples, and thus they derive their binding efficacy on the ancient society from the temple's authoritative, legitimizing position within the society. We have a classic example of the role of a pillar, presumably either Jachin or Boaz, in the covenant renewal ceremony of Josiah, as recorded in 2 Kings 23:2–3: "The king went up into the house of the Lord, and all the men of Judah and all the inhabitants of Jerusalem with him, and the priests, and the prophets, and all the people, both small and great: and he read in their ears all the words of the book of the covenant which was found in the house of the Lord. And the king stood by a pillar and made a covenant before the Lord."[148] "On the evidence of the association of the pillars with the covenant in the two passages in Kings, Jachin and Boaz might be survivals of the standing stones of witness to the covenant at the central sanctuary, cf. Josh. 24.26f."[149] The pillar must play here the same legitimizing role that I have described for the state itself.

The process of "state renewal" in Israel, which is after all what the covenant-making process is during the period of the monarchy, and what we have also on other occasions where the pillars play a similar role (see 2 Kings 11:12–14), derives its power from the temple. Of course, when the kingdom split and Solomon's temple ended up in the new, southern kingdom, it was obvious that Jeroboam would have had to establish new temples in the northern kingdom that would legitimize his dynasty, also under the aegis of Yahweh, as he intended. His choice of shrine centers and of symbols represents an archaizing attempt to establish a temple cultus that would have all the appearance of legitimacy in the eyes of his subjects that the Jerusalem temple held.[150]

Solomon finished the temple in his eleventh year (ca. 959 B.C.), in the eighth month (Bul), and dedicated it the following year in the seventh month (Ethanim). The eleven-month delay between completion and dedication could well be attributed to Solomon's wish to dedicate the temple at the New Year, during the Feast of Tabernacles. Johannes de Moor noted that "he was obeying a venerable Oriental tradition according to which sanctuaries had to be dedicated preferably on New Year."[151] We must distinguish here between spring and fall New Year's festivals. In Israel there was an older spring New Year and a more recent fall New Year; the latter, "falling on the New Year common to Canaan and Egypt, in Israel became the great feast of the era of kingship."[152] Generally speaking, the New Year in the

Mesopotamian tradition began in the spring, with the modification that there may have been a cultic year that began in the fall. The Babylonian Akitu Festival, for example, took place mostly in Nisan, earlier in Adar.[153] Thus while it is technically correct that "sanctuaries are dedicated at the Near Year," according to De Moor, we must distinguish temple dedications/festivals that took place at the spring New Year, such as the Gudea Eninnu Temple and the *Enuma Elish*/Akitu in Babylon, and those that took place during the fall New Year, such as the Baal Temple at Ras Shamra and the Temple of Solomon.[154]

With regard to Solomon's prayer of dedication of the Jerusalem Temple itself, most authorities agree that large parts of the prayer in 1 Kings 8 are the work of the later Deuteronomic editor. Gray sees verses 1–11 as preserving an authentic account of what actually happened on that occasion and verses 62–66 as reflecting "a genuine tradition of the significant assembly of the sacral community Israel at the dedication of the new central sanctuary, but this is the work of the Deuteronomistic compiler."[155] Montgomery sees "the original elements of the story" contained in verses 1, 3, 5, and 6.[156] It is important here to note the importance of post-dedication, post-New Year public feasts in all the traditions that have been discussed above: Gudea, Babylonian (*Enuma Elish*), Ugaritic, etc.[157] Most authorities assume that verses 62–66 have been worked over by the Deuteronomic editor and that the numbers are too large. Note that 2 Chronicles 29:31–36 depicts a similar event with more manageable numbers.[158] Weinfeld sees verses 12–13 of 1 Kings 8 as a summary of the original prayer, which he compares with similar statements in the dedicatory prayers of Gudea and Esarhaddon.[159]

An important Deuteronomic element in the prayer of

Solomon is the "name theology," as seen in verses 17–20, 44, 48, where the temple is seen as having been built to the "name" of Yahweh, rather than as his actual dwelling place. Contrast this with Psalms 74:2 and 76:2, where the Temple on Mount Zion is seen as the dwelling place of Yahweh, "an earlier conception," more in line with Near Eastern views of temples.[160] Another Deuteronomic feature of the prayer that stands out strongly is the view that the temple is a house of prayer, rather than a cultic center, the actual dwelling of Yahweh. First Kings 8:41–43 is especially important here, where Yahweh will listen to the prayers of foreigners who come to the temple to honor his name.[161] The important point that I want to make, in the light of the Deuteronomic argument, is that the pre-Deuteronomic sources of the Old Testament that make reference to the Temple of Solomon place that edifice in the pattern well known to us from other ancient Near Eastern temple traditions.[162] To put it another way, the Deuteronomic argument is largely irrelevant as far as the main thesis of this paper is concerned: the Israelite state (a pre-Deuteronomic polity) was capped by a legitimizing temple/cult system that was intimately related to other such systems in the Near East.[163]

Notes

1. Thorkild Jacobsen, "Early Political Development in Mesopotamia," in *Toward the Image of Tammuz and Other Essays on Mesopotamian History and Culture,* ed. William L. Moran (Cambridge: Harvard University Press, 1970), 133–34.

2. Michael Coe, "Comments on Professor Sanders' Paper," in *RCC,* 117.

3. See George E. Mendenhall, "The Monarchy," *Interpretation* 34 (1975): 166–68.

4. "The ideal of the covenant is then prevalent everywhere in the traditions of this occasion, and we may thus conclude that Solomon at the dedication festival actually renewed the covenant with

Yahweh" (Geo Widengren, "King and Covenant," *Journal of Semitic Studies* 2 [1957]: 8).

5. *TTS*, 26.

6. See Mendenhall, "Monarchy," 157.

7. See the views of Richard N. Adams, "The Early State: Theories and Hypotheses," in *ES*, 22; George E. Mendenhall, *The Tenth Generation* (Baltimore: Johns Hopkins University Press, 1973), 188–89. For summaries of the various prime-mover theories of state origins, see J. Stephen Athens, "Theory Building and the Study of the Evolutionary Process in Complex Societies," in *For Theory Building in Archaeology*, ed. Lewis R. Binford (New York: Academic Press, 1977), 353–57, with a valuable chart on page 354.

8. Jacobsen, "Early Political Development," 140.

9. Thorkild Jacobsen, "The Cosmos as a State," in *Before Philosophy, The Intellectual Adventure of Ancient Man* (Baltimore: Penguin Books, 1972), 156; see also "Foreword," in *HCSE*, xiv.

10. Jacobsen, "The Cosmos as State," 156.

11. *HCSE*, 81.

12. Ibid., 78.

13. Mendenhall, "Monarchy," 159.

14. Mendenhall, *Tenth Generation*, 195.

15. Ibid., 192.

16. This most important point can be deduced, I believe, from Giorgio Buccellati, "The Enthronement of the King and the Capital City in Texts from Ancient Mesopotamia and Syria," in *Studies Presented to A. Leo Oppenheim*, ed. R. D. Biggs and J. A. Brinkman (Chicago: Oriental Institute, 1964), 54–61.

17. For the present, see *HCSE*, 52–129, and especially 75–81.

18. Mendenhall, *Tenth Generation*, 192.

19. Lee D. Snyder, "Modeling and Civilization: Can There Be a Science of Civilization?" Abstract for International Society for the Comparative Study of Civilization, Typescript, 1982, 1–2.

20. Folker Willesen, "The Cultic Situation of Psalm LXXIV," *Vetus Testamentum* 2 (1952): 290.

21. Edward Shils, "Centre and Periphery," in *Selected Essays by Edward Shils* (Chicago: Center for Organization Studies, Department of Sociology, 1970), 3.

22. This list is a revision of what appears in my chapters "What Is a Temple? A Preliminary Typology," in this volume, *Temples of the Ancient World*, and "The Common Temple Ideology of the Ancient Near East," in Truman G. Madsen, ed., *The Temple in Antiquity*

(Provo: BYU Religious Studies Center, 1984). Both studies provide validations for the typology.

23. For the presence of such a "landscape" in the mythical texts from Ras Shamra, see Frank Moore Cross, "The Priestly Tabernacle in the Light of Recent Research," in *THPBT*, 170–72.

24. See Bruno Meissner, *Babylonien und Assyrien* (Heidelberg: Winter, 1925), 2:107–12, 409–10; for this imagery in the Old Testament and in the texts from Ras Shamra, see David Noel Freedman, "Temple without Hands," in *THPBT*, 21, 28; and Cross, "The Priestly Tabernacle, 170.

25. "The Sumerians and their successors found a special significance in the height of the temples" (Eric Burrows, "Some Cosmological Patterns in Babylonian Religion," in *The Labyrinth*, ed. S. H. Hooke [London: Society for Promoting Christian Knowledge, 1935], 60).

26. For the latter see Gene B. Gragg, "The Keš Temple Hymn," in *The Collection of the Sumerian Temple Hymns*, ed. Ake W. Sjöberg and E. Bergmann (Locust Valley: Augustin, 1969), 168, lines 22–30, and 173, lines 90–95. For Gudea, see F. Thureau-Dangin, *Die Sumerischen und Akkadischen Königsinschriften* (Leipzig: Hinrichs, 1907), 86–141.

27. Julius A. Bewer's article, "Ancient Babylonian Parallels to the Prophecies of Haggai," *American Journal of Semitic Languages and Literatures* 35 (1919): 128–33, retains considerable value. Of course, some claims of prosperity in temple hymns and building dedications may be fictional, as has been proved, for example, by the prices claimed by Shamshi-Adad I in his dedicatory inscription for the "Enlil" temple in Ashur. In this case, we are dealing not with genuine piety, but with political propaganda (see Albert K. Grayson, *Assyrian Royal Inscriptions*, ed. Hans Goedicke [Wiesbaden: Harrassowitz, 1972], 20–21).

28. Of course, there may be many such missing; but as Snyder, "Modeling and Civilization," pages 1–2, writes: "A good model need not be perfect in every detail as long as it stimulates empirical testing and refinement, but until the model is relatively complete, effective testing is impossible."

29. George E. Mendenhall, private communication.

30. See *ES*, 109–530; Henry T. Wright, "Toward an Explanation of the Origin of State," in *OSAPE*, 49–68.

31. See Wright, "Toward an Explanation of the Origin of State," 57–66.

32. See *HCSE*, 27–51. Evidently the researches of Professor Lawrence Stager on the distinctions between highland and lowland

villages during Iron Age Palestine will go far to correct this deficit, once they are more fully published.

33. See Elman R. Service, *Origins of the State and Civilization* (New York: Norton, 1975), 303–8; James W. Flanagan, "Chiefs in Israel," *The Journal for the Study of the Old Testament* 20 (1981): 47–73; Frank S. Frick, "Religion and Sociopolitical Structure in Early Israel: An Ethno-Archaeological Approach," in *Society of Biblical Literature 1979 Seminar Papers*, ed. Paul J. Achtemeier, vol. 2 (Missoula: Society of Biblical Literature/Scholars Press, 1979): 233–53; George E. Mendenhall, "Social Organization in Early Israel," in *Magnalia Dei, Essays on the Bible and Archaeology in Memory of G. Ernest Wright*, ed. Frank Moore Cross et al. (Garden City: Doubleday, 1976), 132–51.

34. Mendenhall, "Social Organization in Early Israel," 136.

35. Colin Renfrew, "Beyond a Subsistence Economy: The Evolution of Social Organization in Pre-historic Europe," in *RCC*, 73.

36. Flanagan, "Chiefs in Israel," 69. We must keep in mind the very vigorous opposition that was raised against Renfrew's claims for archaeology at the conference in Cambridge where he presented the above list of features. Ruth Tringham rejected outright the ability of archaeologists to recognize ten of the items on the list from the archaeological record, and granted the remaining items only with "very rigorous backup information on the environment, economy, and technology." On a more general level, she accused Renfrew of "very simplistic use of ethnographic analogy which would make many an anthropologist shudder" (ibid., 88–89). As such, Tringham was mirroring the stinging criticisms made against what she considered the overoptimistic and naive use of ethnographic data by archaeologists like Edmund Leach, in his now famous "Black Box" summary lecture at the 1971 Sheffield seminar on the explanation of culture change (in *The Explanation of Culture Change: Models in Pre-history*, ed. Colin Renfrew [Pittsburgh: University of Pittsburgh Press, 1973], 761–71). Leach's criticisms were answered by D. H. Mellor at the same conference ("Do Cultures Exist?" in ibid., 59–72). The point is that biblical scholars and Syro-Palestinian archaeologists should exercise care and discrimination in the extent to which they adopt models from other disciplines for application to biblical problems. There is always the danger expressed by Coe ("Comments on Professor Sanders' Paper," 116), who said that "archaeologists tend to be somewhat retrograde in the models which they adopt from other fields of study."

37. See Athens, "Theory Building," 353–57; Wright, "Toward an Explanation of the Origin of State," 49–52.

38. Cohen, "State Origins: A Reappraisal," 70; see also Wright, "Toward an Explanation of the Origin of State," 49–68.

39. Adams, "The Early State," 21, italics in original; see also 639–40.

40. Quoted in *HCSE*, 76.

41. Wright, "Toward an Explanation of the Origin of State," 56.

42. *HCSE*, 80.

43. See Mendenhall, "Monarchy," 159–62; see also Cohen, "State Origins: A Reappraisal," 36–37.

44. Lawrence Krader, "The Origin of the State among the Nomads of Asia," in *ES*, 104.

45. Cohen, "State Origins: A Reappraisal," 36.

46. William T. Sanders and Joseph Marino, *New World Prehistory*, 9, cited in Service, *Origins of the State and Civilization*, 304.

47. Adams, "The Early State," 22.

48. Cohen, "State Origins: A Reappraisal," 35. Any more formal study of the development of the state in ancient Israel than the present one will have to deal with the issue of fission with regard to the breakup of the Israelite monarchy in the time of Jeroboam. What does this say for the nature of the Israelite state? Does it disqualify the monarchy of David and Solomon from the category of early state? Flanagan, by the way, sees David "on the boundary line between chiefdom and kingdom" ("Chiefs in Israel," 67).

49. For this distinction, see Service, *Origins of the State and Civilization*, 44–46, quoting Fried.

50. Wright, "Toward an Explanation of the Origin of State," 60, 62, 64; italics added. Of course, his working models are much more complicated and extensive than the excerpts given here.

51. William T. Sanders and Joseph Marino, "Chiefdom to State: Political Evolution at Kaminaljuyu, Guatemala," in *RCC*, 97–113, 118–19.

52. See Martin Diskin, "The Costs of Evolution," in *RCC*, 113–16.

53. Sanders and Marino, "Chiefdom to State," 97.

54. Ibid.

55. Anatolii M. Khazanov, "Some Theoretical Problems of the Study of the Early State," in *ES*, 89.

56. Sanders and Marino, "Chiefdom to State," 98.

57. Ibid., 109–10.

58. Ibid., 103.

59. Ibid., 111.

60. Ibid., 106.

61. Ibid., 111.

62. Ibid., 121.

63. Ibid., 111.

64. Diskin, "The Costs of Evolution," 115.

65. Sanders and Marino, "Chiefdom to State," 107.

66. Ibid., 113.

67. Diskin, "The Costs of Evolution," 114.

68. Sanders and Marino, "Chiefdom to State," 118.

69. Ibid.

70. See W. F. Albright, *Archaeology and the Religion of Israel*, 5th ed. (Garden City: Doubleday Anchor, 1968), 102–4, with notes; W. Boyd Barrick, "The Funerary Character of 'High Places' in Ancient Palestine; A Reassessment," *Vetus Testamentum* 25 (1975): 565–95, and Abraham Malamat, "King Lists of the Old Babylonian Period and Biblical Genealogies," *Journal of the American Oriental Society* 88 (1968): 173 n. 29.

71. See Abraham Malamat, "Charismatic Leadership in the Book of Judges," in *Magnalia Dei*, 152–68. Malamat writes, interestingly, of the process of the "Routinization of charisma" (164) that results in the monarchy.

72. Many of these issues are treated at some length by Mendenhall, particularly in "Monarchy," and in "Social Organization in Early Israel." Also valuable is Flanagan's "Chiefs in Israel," and Frick, "Religion and Sociopolitical Structure in Early Israel," whose study is the first, as far as I am aware, to apply a theory of Israelite chiefdom to the archaeological evidence. Especially interesting in Frick's study is his discussion of Iron Age I agricultural practices, which appear to have been oriented toward subsistence, rather than toward the needs of a centralized bureaucracy, which fits the picture from Kaminaljuyu (see 244–46). Also of great interest is Norman K. Gottwald, "Early Israel and the 'Asiatic Mode of Production' in Canaan," in *Society of Biblical Literature 1976 Seminar Papers*, ed. George MacRae (Missoula: Society of Biblical Literature/Scholars, 1976), 145–54. Gottwald's discussion can benefit by seeing the Asiatic mode of production within the wider theory of state origins, as is done, for example, in *ES*, 643, 647–49, and by being more specific in placing "Early Israel" at some defined point along the chiefdom-state spectrum, as Flanagan, Frick, Mendenhall, and I have attempted to do. Also of interest here is the view of Barbara Price concerning the data from Kaminaljuyu, that Kaminaljuyu represents a secondary state, developing from a ranked society under pressure from the primary state, centered at Teotihuacan. Is it possible that the Israelite monarchy, is, technically, an example of a secondary state, developed

from a ranked society under the pressure of the Philistine/ Phoenician states that surrounded it? (see Barbara Price, "Secondary State Formation: An Explanatory Model," in *OSAPE*, 170–79). Such a view could be read into Mendenhall, "Monarchy," 157–60. Claessen and Skalnik add this: "State formation is not caused by war, but is greatly promoted by war, or by the threat of war and by social stress" ("Limits: Beginning and End of the Early State," in *ES*, 626). See also Malamat, "Charismatic Leadership in the Book of Judges," 164; G. W. Ahlstrom, "Where Did the Israelites Live?" *Journal of Near Eastern Studies* 41 (1982): 133–38.

73. Adams, "The Early State," 5.

74. Flanagan, "Chiefs in Israel," 49.

75. One of the "Great Organizations" described by A. Leo Oppenheim in *Ancient Mesopotamia, Portrait of a Dead Civilization*, comp. Erica Reiner, rev. ed. (Chicago: The University of Chicago Press, 1977), 95–101, 106–9.

76. Price, "Secondary State Formation," in *OSAPE*, 166.

77. Ibid., 164–65.

78. Sanders and Marino, "Chiefdom to State," 98.

79. See G. Ernest Wright, "The Tell: Basic Unit for Reconstructing Complex Societies of the Near East," in *RCC*, 123–30.

80. Charles Redman, "Research Design for a Regional Approach to Complex Societies," in *RCC*, 133, 136.

81. For sketch views of a variety of configurations that major mounds in Syria have assumed, especially noting the relationship of an acropolis to the remaining area encompassed within the fortification wall, see W. J. van Liere, "Capitals and Citadels of Bronze Age Syria in their Relationship to Land and Water," *Annales Archeologiques Arabes Syriennes (Damascus)* 13 (1963): fig. 3A–C.

82. Shils, "Centre and Periphery," 1.

83. See also Jonathan Z. Smith, *Map Is Not Territory* (Leiden: Brill, 1978): 98–101, 107–19, 186–89.

84. Sanders and Marino, "Chiefdom to State," 119.

85. *HCSE*, 77.

86. See Oppenheim, *Ancient Mesopotamia*, 108–9.

87. See A. Ungnad, "Datenlisten," *Reallexikon der Assyriologie und vorderasiatische Archäologie* 2 (1938): 174–78; for the surviving year names of the Sargonic Dynasty, which, along with the First Dynasty of Babylon, can be considered a secondary state, see ibid., 133–34.

88. "Pristine states achieve this level of integration through systemic operation of essentially autochthonous processes; secondary states, as defined, reflect regular processes of interaction/competi-

tion of expanding states vis-à-vis non-state organized populations"
(Price, "Secondary State Formation," in *OSAPE*, 170).

89. Max E. L. Mallowan, "The Early Dynastic Period in Mesopotamia," *Cambridge Ancient History* 1/2 (1971): 270.

90. See *HCSE*.

91. See Edith Porada, "The Relative Chronology of Mesopotamia,
I," in *Chronologies in Old World Archaeology*, ed. Robert W. Ehrich
(Chicago: The University of Chicago Press, 1965), 161–63; Robert
McCormick Adams, "Patterns of Urbanization in Early Southern
Mesopotamia," in *Man, Settlement and Urbanism*, ed. Peter J. Ucko et
al. (Cambridge: Schenkman, 1972): 735–50; William W. Hallo and
William Kelly Simpson, *The Ancient Near East: A History* (New York:
Harcourt Brace Jovanovich, 1971), 42–46.

92. See Adam Falkenstein and Eva Strommenger, "Gudea,"
Reallexikon der Assyriologie und vorderasiatische Archaologie 3 (1971):
676–78.

93. Henri Frankfort, *Oriental Institute Discoveries in Iraq, 1933/34,
Fourth Preliminary Report of the Iraq Expedition* (Chicago: University of
Chicago Press, 1935), 32–33. (Unfortunately, I was unable to consult
the final report for the Temple Oval, OIP, 53). See also Pinhas
Delougaz, Harold D. Hill, and Seton Lloyd, *Private Houses and Graves
in the Diyala Region*, OIP 88 (Chicago: University of Chicago Press,
1967): 24–25.

94. See Henri Frankfort, *Progress of the Work of the Oriental Institute
in Iraq, 1934/35, Fifth Preliminary Report of the Iraq Expedition* (Chicago:
University of Chicago Press, 1936), 15–17.

95. Richard S. Ellis, *Foundation Deposits in Ancient Mesopotamia*
(New Haven: Yale University Press, 1968), 12, and 6–34, for descriptions of various building rites connected with temples.

96. See Lundquist, "What Is a Temple?" 83–117.

97. A. J. Spencer, "The Brick Foundations of Late-Period Peripteral Temples and Their Mythological Origin," in *Glimpses of Ancient
Egypt, Studies in Honor of H. W. Fairman*, ed. John Ruffle, G. A.
Gaballa, and Kenneth A. Kitchen (Warminster: Aris & Phillips, 1979),
133.

98. Ibid., and see point 2 in my typology, pages 186–87.

99. See Lundquist, "Common Temple Ideology," drawing on the
temple foundation hymns of Gudea and on Neo-Sumerian temple
hymns. The same picture is found in the *Enuma Elish*.

100. A. Falkenstein, *"Sumerische Bauausdrücke," Orientalia* 35 (1966):
236.

101. See Lundquist, "Common Temple Ideology."

102. Ake W. Sjöberg and E. Bergmann, *The Collection of the Sumerian Temple Hymns, Texts from Cuneiform Sources* 3 (Locust Valley: Augustin, 1969), 17, 50. For du_6-*kù,* "shining (holy) mound," see A. Deimel, *Sumerisches Lexikon* II/3 (Rome: Verlag des Päpstl, Bibelinstituts, 1934), 459.

103. Arvid S. Kapelrud, "Temple Building, A Task for Gods and Kings," *Orientalia* 32 (1963): 58.

104. In addition to Kapelrud, "Temple Building," and Bewer, "Ancient Babylonian Parallels," cited above, see Richard D. Barnett, "Bringing the God into the Temple," in *THPBT*, 11, and Moshe Weinfeld, *Deuteronomy and the Deuteronomic School* (Oxford: Clarendon, 1972), 35, 248–50.

105. "Moses is 'to a great extent depicted in royal categories'" (Kapelrud, "Temple Building," 61, quoting Ivan Engnell).

106. Ibid.

107. Ibid., 62.

108. See B.II.5, B.V.1.

109. See A.II.11, B.III.9; see also E. Douglas van Buren, "Foundation Rites for a New Temple," *Orientalia* 21 (1952): 293, 296–97, and Ellis, *Foundation Deposits,* 7–8.

110. *IGL,* 120.

111. References to the Gudea Cylinders are taken from *SAK;* see also *IGL,* 121, 137, and Gudea Cylinder A.XXV.5–8. According to Deimel, ^{giš}ti is a *"biegsame Stange; Rippe; Pfeil (mit Bronze dazu verarbeitet),"* (*Sumerisches Lexikon,* II/1, 150).

112. A. Falkenstein and W. van Soden, *Sumerische und Akkadische Hymnen und Gebete* (Zurich: Artemis, 1953), 170.

113. Ibid., 172.

114. Of course, Gudea is not strictly a *lugal,* "king," but an *ensi,* "governor." For a discussion of the evolution of these terms in ancient Sumerian texts, along with an emphasis upon the priestly functions of the *en,* see Jacobsen, "Early Political Development in Mesopotamia," 375.

115. See Samuel N. Kramer, *The Sumerians, Their History, Culture and Character* (Chicago: University of Chicago Press, 1963), 137–40.

116. See OIP 88, 24–25 and plate I.

117. This is a question that I am not discussing here, although it is well known that temples served, among other things, as treasuries, and that they were often looted, either by the local king in order to pursue warfare or other foreign policy ventures (see 2 Kings 16:8), or by conquerors (see 1 Kings 14:25–26). The Eninnu, built by Gudea, had a "treasury," which apparently served both as his own royal

treasury and as a temple treasury. It is described as being filled with various precious and semiprecious stones and metals (see *IGL*, 131). According to Edmond Sollberger, the possibility exists that there was a "marked evolution from simplicity to luxury" in the furnishings and treasures found in temples during the third millennium B.C. (see "The Temple in Babylonia," in *Le Temple et le Culte* [Istanbul: Nederlands Historisch-Archeologisch Instituut, 1975], 34).

118. Smith, *Map Is Not Territory*, 99.

119. Cross, "The Priestly Tabernacle," 174. I have devoted considerable space in Lundquist, "What Is a Temple?" 83–117, to validations derived from *Enuma Elish* and the Baal Cycle.

120. See Adams, "The Early State," 20–21.

121. *ES*, 640.

122. Shils, "Centre and Periphery," 3; italics added.

123. Oppenheim, *Ancient Mesopotamia*, 181.

124. For a view of the positive, pious aspects of Mesopotamian temple establishments, see J. N. Postgate, "The Role of the Temple in the Mesopotamian Secular Community," in *Man, Settlement and Urbanism*, 813–18, 820–21. Postgate gives evidence for the general horror that would have been felt in the community at the sacking of the temple treasuries (see 815 and n. 18).

125. D. D. Luckenbill, ed., *Ancient Records of Assyria and Babylonia* (Chicago: The University of Chicago Press, 1926–27), 1:295–96; see A. T. Olmstead, *History of Assyria* (Chicago: University of Chicago Press, 1951), 167–69, 203–4, for Bel-Harran-bel-usur's decline under Tiglathpileser III.

126. See Barnett, "Bringing the God into the Temple," 10–20.

127. *ANET*, 654.

128. See point twelve of the typology above, page 189, and Lundquist, "What Is a Temple?" 104–5, for a description of the role of sacral meals in covenant ceremonies.

129. See Robert G. Boling, *Judges, Introduction, Translation, and Commentary* (Garden City: Doubleday, 1975) 256, 258, 273, 293; but see also Weinfeld, *Deuteronomy and the Deuteronomic School*, 169–70, with notes. The debate over the editorial strand to which these passages should be assigned and the view of the monarchy that they represent are irrelevant to my argument, which is simply that the passages reveal self-knowledge on the part of the Israelite editors of various stages of political evolution and the implications of these stages for the Israelite community.

130. See Weinfeld, *Deuteronomy and the Deuteronomic School*, 169–70; William McKane, *I and II Samuel, Introduction and Commentary*

(London: SCM, 1963), 66–69; and P. Kyle McCarter, Jr., *I Samuel, a New Translation* (Garden City: Doubleday, 1980), 156–62. I have suggested above, note 72, the possibility that Israel represents a secondary state that was formed under the pressure of the Philistine/Phoenician states surrounding her. McCarter writes that "it might be argued that a king is requested out of military necessity. Israel's premonarchical institutions have become inadequate to cope with new political realities, especially the Philistine threat" (*I Samuel*, 160). But he rejects this explanation.

131. See McKane, *I and II Samuel*, 217–19; Weinfeld, *Deuteronomy and the Deuteronomic School*, 194, for the presumed Deuteronomic editing of verses 13a and 247–48. See also Frank Moore Cross, *Canaanite Myth and Hebrew Epic, Essays in the History of the Religion of Israel* (Cambridge: Harvard University Press, 1973), 241–64.

132. See Kapelrud, "Temple Building," 59–60; Weinfeld, *Deuteronomy and the Deuteronomic School*, 250–54.

133. Price, "Secondary State Formation," in *OSAPE*, 166.

134. See McCarter, *I Samuel*, 160–62; Cross, *Canaanite Myth and Hebrew Epic*, 243; and Mendenhall, "Monarchy," 157.

135. See Cross, *Canaanite Myth and Hebrew Epic*, 265.

136. See Albright, *Archaeology and the Religion of Israel*, 138–50, with notes.

137. See Jean Ouellette, "The Basic Structure of Solomon's Temple and Archaeological Research," in *The Temple of Solomon*, ed. Joseph Gutmann (Missoula: Scholars, 1976), 7–11, with notes.

138. S. Yeivin, "Jachin and Boaz," *The Palestine Exploration Quarterly* 91 (1959): 20. But note also the bronzed pillar that stood near the gate through which Ningirsu would have been led into the Eninnu temple in Lagash (see note 111 above). The phenomenon is not limited to the Levant.

139. Albright, *Archaeology and the Religion of Israel*, 143, and notes. See also H. Van Dyke Paranuk, "Was Solomon's Temple Oriented toward the Sun," *The Palestine Exploration Quarterly* 110 (1978): 28–33.

140. See John Gray, *I and II Kings, a Commentary*, 2d ed. (Philadelphia: Westminster, 1970), 187.

141. R. B. Y. Scott, "The Pillars Jachin and Boaz," *The Journal of Biblical Literature* 58 (1939): 146.

142. *SAK*, 115.

143. *IGL*, 140–41. I would also like to recall the "bronzed" pillar that stood outside the gate "through which Ningirsu enters" the temple (see note 111 above).

144. Scott, "The Pillars Jachin and Boaz," 148–49.

145. R. B. Y. Scott, in *The Interpreter's Dictionary of the Bible*, 2:781.

146. Widengren, "King and Covenant," 3.

147. See Lundquist, "What Is a Temple?"

148. See Widengren, "King and Covenant," 5–7. See also George E. Mendenhall, "Covenant Forms in Israelite Tradition," *Biblical Archaeologist* 17 (September 1954): 50–76: "Provision for deposit in the temple and periodic public reading"; with the accompanying explanation, "Since the treaty itself was under the protection of the deity, it was deposited as a sacred thing in the sanctuary of the vassal state."

149. Gray, *I and II Kings*, 188; see also Widengren, "King and Covenant," 12–17.

150. See Cross, *Canaanite Myth and Hebrew Epic*, 73–75.

151. *New Year with Canaanites and Israelites, Part One: Description* (Kampen: Kok, 1972), 18. See also Gray, *I and II Kings*, 206–8; and James A. Montgomery, *The Book of Kings, A Critical and Exegetical Commentary*, ed. Henry S. Gehman (New York: Scribner's, 1951), 186–88. Montgomery would excise *behag* "as a back reference from v. 65" (ibid., 187).

152. Cross, *Canaanite Myth and Hebrew Epic*, 123, with notes, and 238.

153. See Svend A. Pallis, *The Babylonian Akîtu Festival* (Copenhagen: Bianco Lunos Bogtrykkeri, 1926), 27–30; and H. Hunger, "Kalender," *Reallexikon der Assyriologie und Vorderasiatische Archaologie* 5 (1977): 297–303.

154. For Ras Shamra, see further Johannes C. de Moor, *New Year with Canaanites and Israelites, Part Two: The Canaanite Sources* (Kampen: Kok, 1972), 5. See also H. W. Fairman, "Worship and Festivals in an Egyptian Temple," *Bulletin, John Rylands Library* 37 (1954–55), 187: "The traditional time for the dedication of a temple was either on the eve of New Year's Day, or on New Year's Day. . . . The ceremonies on the temple roof on New Year's Day included the annual rededication of the temple and its gods: the union with the sun not only brought renewal of fertility and welfare to Egypt, it renewed for another year the life and powers of Edfu, Horus, and the gods who lived with him in the temple."

155. Gray, *I and II Kings*, 203.

156. Montgomery, *The Book of Kings*, 186.

157. See Lundquist, "What Is a Temple?" and item twelve of my typology, page 189.

158. See Montgomery, *The Book of Kings*, 199–200, for additional examples.

159. See Weinfeld, *Deuteronomy and the Deuteronomic School*, 35–37.

160. Ibid., 194–98; see also Cross, *Canaanite Myth and Hebrew Epic*, 254.

161. See Weinfeld, *Deuteronomy and the Deuteronomic School*, 37, 195–99.

162. See ibid., 250–55; Kapelrud, "Temple Building."

163. See Norman K. Gottwald, *The Tribes of Yahweh, A Sociology of Liberated Israel* (Maryknoll: Orbis Books, 1979), 371–74 in particular. Also of exceptional value is G. W. Ahlstrom, "Heaven on Earth—At Hazor and Arad," in *Religious Syncretism in Antiquity, Essays in Conversation with Geo Widengren*, ed. Birger A. Pearson (Missoula: Scholars, 1975), 67–83, with many references.

10

King, Coronation, and Temple: Enthronement Ceremonies in History

Stephen D. Ricks and John J. Sroka

Introduction

A central feature of nearly every ancient and medieval society was kingship—rule by divinely appointed kings—an institution whose origins are lost in the mists of time. In the view of the ancient Egyptians, kingship was coextensive in time with the world itself;[1] to the Sumerians, kingship was a gift of the gods.[2] Indeed, as one scholar has recently noted, "Chronicles of kingship from Egypt, to Mesopotamia, to Persia, to China, to Italy, to northern Europe, to pre-Columbian Mexico all trace the line of kings to the first king, a supreme cosmic deity who founded the kingship rites. . . . The accounts [of the creation] speak of a creator, a first man, and a first king—all referring to the same cosmic figure."[3]

A central ritual associated with kingship was the coronation ceremony: that series of acts, performed in a temple or other sacred space, by means of which the king accedes to the throne and is endowed with the power and authority by which alone his rule is possible. Features of these coronation ceremonies, which have been attested to among numerous and often widely separated cultures, display remarkable similarities. The cultural anthropologist Arthur Hocart was the first to isolate the common features of coronation ceremonies and to synthesize the available evidence, which he published in his ground-breaking work *Kingship*.[4] Subsequent specialized studies of kingship and coronation patterns in Africa,[5] India,[6] Japan,[7] and the ancient Near East[8] have served only to confirm the general outline of Hocart's findings, but there has been no synthesis of the accumulated evidence.

In this study, we consider some of the more widely attested features of the coronation ceremony, especially in the ancient Near East. Relevant material from other cultures, where detailed studies of enthronement rites have been made, is also considered. Given the amount of evidence available and the number of ritual acts in the coronation ceremony that have been isolated, not all of the features can be dealt with in the body of the text. They are summarized in Appendix A. In Appendix B all the features of the coronation ceremony that are attested to in selected cultures—Africa, Egypt, England, Fiji, India, Israel, Japan, and Siam (Thailand)—are noted.

A note on methodology is appropriate. Comparative studies in religion and anthropology have been popular during the past century. These works are often memorials to the extraordinary erudition and insight of their authors, but have subsequently, and often justly, been criticized for their lack of critical acumen. These studies are elaborately descriptive but often fail to explore the meaning of parallels, even within a single cultural setting. While these criticisms have been important in tempering the excesses of "parallelomania" by emphasizing the distinction between the formal similarities of ritual acts and the contextual meaning of those acts, comparative studies do retain their value, because they delineate the contours of broader cultural patterns. While the primary purpose of this study is to outline the striking resemblances in coronation rites throughout the world by detailing formal similarities among the various ceremonies, we remain aware of the differences in meaning that each of the ritual acts may have in its own context.

Individual Elements of Coronation Rites

Sacred Place

In the ancient Near East, in particular, coronation ceremonies were frequently carried out in temples. Joash's consecration, for example, took place in the temple (see 2 Kings 11:4–14; 2 Chronicles 23:3–12). Roland de Vaux thinks that "the consecration of the other kings of Judah after Solomon took place" there.[9] According to Alan Gardiner, the coronation of certain Egyptian kings, such as Haremhab, took place in the temple.[10] Further, as Henri Frankfort notes, both Sumerian and Assyrian texts describe coronation ceremonies performed in the temples of Erech and Aššur.[11] In ancient Persia as well, the enthronement rites of the king generally took place in a temple at the ancient capital of Pasargadae.[12]

Secrecy

Secrecy—the insistence that the ritual acts constituting the coronation ceremony be viewed only by the initiated— is an important feature of several of the rites, especially modern ones, for which we have detailed accounts. In the Japanese enthronement rite, for example, "the Daijō enclosure certainly keeps out all non-participants, and it was guarded by traditional groups such as the Ōtomo, Mononobe, etc."[13] Similarly, women, children, and commoners

Figure 32. In this drawing by an eyewitness to Hirohito's *Daijōsai* on the midnight of 14 November 1928, the emperor is shown walking on a reed mat unrolled on white silk before him. A ceremonial umbrella-shaped crown is held over his head to indicate his central position in the cosmos. When he is alone in the shrines, he will eat a sacred meal in the presence of his ancestors, thus demonstrating the continuity of the divine mandate. Sixty-three years later, his son Akihito, the present emperor of Japan, enacted the same ceremony in his "Feast of Kingship."

were all excluded from the Indian coronation ceremony.[14] In Thailand, the traditional rite of the king's consecration was "distinctly private."[15] This same secrecy is also a part of the African[16] and Fijian[17] coronation ceremonies that we have examined.

Secrecy seems to be an almost universal feature of initiation ceremonies. The Egyptologist C. J. Bleeker notes that "initiation presupposes a religious secret which is only known to the initiated."[18] These secrets include, according to Mircea Eliade, "the myths that tell of the gods and the origin of the world, the true names of the gods, [and] the role and origin of the ritual instruments employed in the initiation ceremonies."[19]

The secrecy surrounding initiation rites in general and enthronement ceremonies in particular also characterizes the rituals at temples and other sanctuaries. Among the Mesopotamians, temple rites were a jealously guarded secret.[20] The ancient Egyptians were strictly forbidden to reveal what they had seen in the temple.[21] In ancient Greece, the secrecy surrounding the rituals performed in the sanctuary at Eleusis was so rigorous that in 200 B.C., when two young men from the distant town of Akarnania innocently entered the sanctuary at Eleusis during the enactment of a mystery festival and betrayed themselves by asking questions about the rites, they were promptly executed.[22] Of the Eleusinian mysteries, George Mylonas writes that "the last Hierophant carried with him to the grave the secrets which had been transmitted orally for untold generations, from one high priest to the next."[23]

Of secrecy in religious traditions in general, Irach Taraporewala writes:

> In considering the history of any religion we get, first of all, either authenticated Scriptures compiled by the followers of that Faith or else descriptions left by contemporary outsiders narrating how these doctrines and beliefs affected them. In the second place, there is a certain amount of what might be called "floating tradition" and folklore embodied in the varied rites and ceremonies practiced by the believers in that Faith. And thirdly, there is a certain amount of "sacred" or "mystic" tradition and teaching known to only a few, and which was jealously guarded from the "profane" who were likely to scoff at it. This "sacred," and therefore secret, lore was known only to a few initiates, but in order that the memory of these may not be completely lost most of this secret teach-

ing was embodied in some sort of symbolic ritual which could be performed openly before the public.[24]

Ablutions

Ablutions—ceremonial washings that were believed to avert evil, give life and strength, and symbolize rebirth— were a regular part of the coronation ceremonies and of other ritual occasions as well in the ancient Near East.[25] Even as a child, the Egyptian crown prince was sprinkled with water by officials in order that he might be endowed with divine qualities and be reborn.[26] In his daily preparations for entrance into the temple, the pharaoh was sprinkled with holy water, an act that endowed him with life, good fortune, stability, health, and happiness. For the purpose of performing these ritual acts of ablution, a pool or lake was connected with many Egyptian temples.[27] During the Sed festival, the recurring feast celebrating the pharaoh's kingship, the pharaoh would have his feet ceremonially washed.[28]

It is still uncertain whether ablutions were part of the ancient Israelite coronation ceremonies. However, since purification in water is mentioned in Exodus 29:4 in connection with the anointing and investment of Aaron and his sons (cf. Exodus 40:12), Geo Widengren thinks that "it is probable that certain water-purifications had a place in the Israelite royal consecration."[29] St. Cyril of Jerusalem may have based his comments on an extrabiblical tradition when he said, in his lecture *On the Mysteries*, "When the High Priest raised Solomon to the kingship, he anointed him after washing him in the waters of Gihon."[30] Although there is no explicit mention in 1 Kings 1:38–39 of a ritual ablution in connection with King Solomon's coronation rites, the Talmud records that "our Rabbis taught: The kings are anointed only at a fountain."[31] The presumption in favor of the existence of ablutions in the Israelite coronation ceremony is also strengthened by the symbolic placement of the temple—the site of many Israelite coronations (e.g., the coronation of Joash in 2 Kings 11:4–14)—over the center of the world, where the "Water of Life" flowed.[32]

Ablutions are also widely attested in coronation ceremonies in other parts of the world. During many African coronations, kings were either washed or sprinkled with water, which both cleansed the king and enabled him "to see a part of the divine life."[33] In Japan, the emperor entered a building called the Kairyu-den, or Ablution Hall, where he took his bath of purification. After entering the bath, the Emperor folded his arms and stooped down while the officiants poured water over him.[34]

In general, the available descriptions of the coronation rites give few particulars concerning the ablution ceremony. Reports of other initiation rites, however, provide us a fairly detailed insight into the procedures involved. For example, according to reports concerning the ceremonial ablutions among the Mandaeans of Iraq and Iran, the hands, face, forehead, ears, nose, lower part of the body, mouth, knees, legs, and feet are all washed.[35] During the initiation ceremony of the Bektashi order of Sufi Muslims, the meaning of each act of the ablution rite is explained:

> He washes his hands in order to be freed from all the prohibited things to which he has stretched his hands before; he rinses his mouth in order to cleanse it from all falsehood and fault that may have issued from it; he rinses his nose to cleanse it from whatever forbidden things he has smelt; he washes his face in order to be absolved from every shameful thing; his feet in order to be cleansed from every instance of having walked in rebellious and mistaken paths; while he wipes his head

and ears he wishes to be absolved from every unreasonable thing which is counter to the religious law, and further, while wiping his face from all the acts of disobedience which he has committed. Kadri adds that this ablution differed from the ordinary ablution in so far as it was effective forever. This meaning is quite clear: it is the complete removal of all that is sinful and unclean and belongs to his former life.[36]

Anointing

Anointing the king with oil is a significant element of the coronation ceremonies in the ancient Near East, as elsewhere in the world. From extant sources it is clear that the Hittite accession ceremony included "anointing with oil, clothing in special garments, coronation, and the bestowal of a royal name."[37] Further, although there is no clear evidence that the Egyptian king was anointed at the time of his accession to the throne, the sources indicate that he was anointed every morning prior to entering the temple in order to perform the daily liturgy there.[38]

The Old Testament records the anointings of six Israelite kings: Saul (1 Samuel 10:1), David (2 Samuel 5:3), Solomon (1 Kings 1:39), Jehu (2 Kings 9:6), Joash (2 Kings 11:12), and Jehoahaz (2 Kings 23:30). In addition, it is recorded in 2 Samuel 19:10 that Absalom was anointed to be king. Indeed, the very name "Messiah," used with reference to several of the kings of ancient Israel, means "anointed," and it doubtless refers to the rite of anointing the king at his installation as monarch.[39] Later Jewish legend had it that the idea of anointing began with the first man. According to this story, when Adam was 930 years old, he knew that his days were coming to an end. He therefore implored Eve, "Arise and go with my son Seth near to paradise, and put earth upon your heads and weep and pray to God to have mercy upon me and send his angel to paradise, and give me of the tree out of which the oil floweth, and bring it [to] me, and I shall anoint myself and shall have rest from my complaint."[40]

Anointing as part of coronation rites is also well attested in India, Cambodia, Siam, and throughout Europe.[41] R. M. Woolley, who examined European enthronement ceremonies, found anointing to be an integral part of the rite in Byzantium, Russia, England, France, Hungary, Spain, and Germany. Some of the anointings of these coronations were quite complex. One of the more elaborate anointings was received by the Russian czar. According to Woolley: "The Anointing takes place after the Communion hymn. Two bishops summon the Czar, who takes his stand near the Royal Gates, the Czarina, a little behind him, both in their purple robes, and there the Czar is anointed on the forehead, eyes, nostrils, mouth, ears, breast, and on both sides of his hands by the senior Metropolitan, who says: "The seal of the gift of the Holy Ghost.' "[42]

New Name

According to Arthur M. Hocart, at his coronation the king "usually acquires a new name, either a title or the name of a predecessor; so do priests very frequently, for instance Popes and monks in Europe."[43] Perhaps no element of coronation rites is more widely known (and taken for granted) than the monarch's receipt of a new name or throne name at the time of his (or her) accession to the throne. During the Middle Kingdom, the Egyptian king, who had no less than five names in all, received one of these, the praenomen or throne name, at the time of his accession.[44] In Mesopotamia, the new name was given at the time of the king's accession "when the choice of the gods became effective in the world

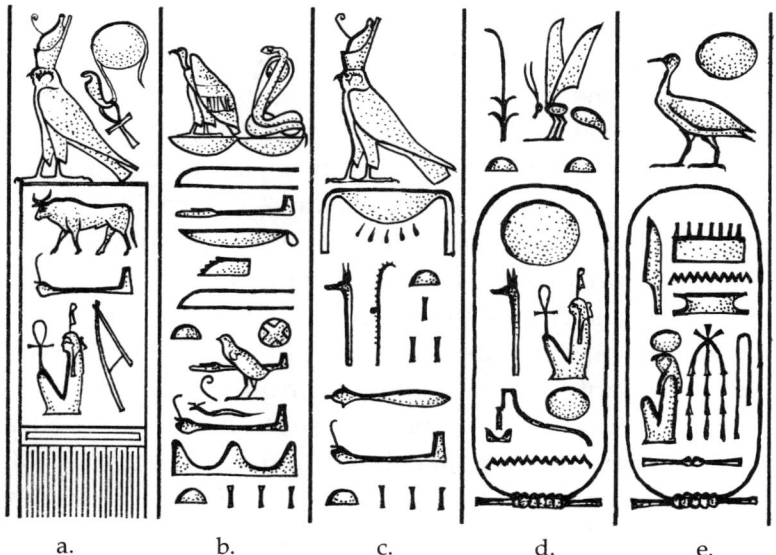

Figure 33. This is the full titulary of the five names of Ramses II:
  a. Palace name: Victorious Bull, Beloved of Maat, the Goddess of
     Truth;
  b. Two Ladies: Protector of Egypt, his two arms victorious over the
     nations;
  c. Golden Horus: Strong of Years, Great of Victories;
  d. Upper and Lower Egypt: Strong in the Sun God Re and Maat,
     chosen of Re;
  e. Son of Re: Beloved of Amun, Born of Re.

of men."[45] Before his accession, the king in Mesopotamia
bore a different name, the "name of smallness."[41] Similarly,
Parthian kings assumed the throne-name Arsak at the time
of their coronation, a fact that has complicated the process of
identifying individual rulers.[46] Since several Israelite kings
had two names—the "birth name" and the "regnal name"—
Roland de Vaux believes that it is likely, though not certain,
that the kings of Judah received a new name when they succeeded to the throne.[47]

This practice of assigning a new name at the time of the

king's enthronement is also well attested in other parts of the world. The new name or title added to the Siamese king's personal name after his coronation was inscribed on a golden plate and was "neither known nor understood by the common people."[48] Similarly, during the Japanese enthronement rite, the emperor receives a new name—the era title.[49]

Kings were not the only ones to receive new names. Biblical history is replete with examples of men (and in one case, a woman) who received new or changed names, frequently in association with a transition (usually, though not invariably, of a spiritual nature) in their lives. Thus Abram became Abraham (Genesis 17:5), his wife Sarai became Sarah (17:15), Jacob was renamed Israel (32:28), and Joseph became Zaphnath-paaneah (41:45). In the New Testament, Jesus gave Simon the name Cephas, whose Greek reflex is Peter (Matthew 16:17–18; John 1:42), while Saul took on the Latin name Paul, indicative of his role as missionary to the Gentiles (the name Paul is first mentioned in Acts 13:9, at the beginning of his first missionary labors among the Gentiles). The receipt of a new name is promised to all the faithful in Revelation: "He that hath an ear, let him hear what the Spirit saith unto the churches; To him that overcometh will I give to eat of the hidden manna, and will give him a white stone, and in the stone a new name written, which no man knoweth saving he that receiveth it" (2:17).[50]

Rebirth

Rebirth rituals—which include acting as one who is new to the world, being swallowed by a monster, acting like a newborn babe, being endowed with divine qualities, going through a burial ceremony, or simply being reawakened—are frequent concomitants of coronation ceremonies.

Figure 34. To avoid the unpleasant necessity of their own ritual execu-
tions, kings developed the custom of the "Mock King," or substitute
who ruled for a day and then was killed. This allowed the real king to
emerge reborn and invigorated for another cycle. However, the roles
were sometimes unexpectedly reversed, as recorded in the Babylonian
Royal Chronicles (2029–2006 B.C.): "That the dynasty might not come to
an end, King Erra-Imitti placed the gardener Enlil-Bani as a substitute
figure on his throne. Erra-Imitti died in his palace while sipping a hot
brew. Enlil-Bani, he who was on the throne, did not arise [from it] but
was himself installed as king [and went on to rule for twenty-four
years]."

Rebirth is also implicit in certain of the other elements of
the coronation ceremony: ablution, anointing, giving of the
new name, and the bestowal of a garment. Thus in Egypt,
according to Samuel A. B. Mercer, the "ritual act of ablutions—washing and sprinkling—symbolized new birth."[51]
In the view of Tor Irstram, the idea of death and rebirth
may provide the explanation of the custom of the king
assuming a new name upon his accession to the throne.[52]
In ancient Babylon, during the period of the Late Empire,
the king's death and rebirth were probably portrayed on
the fifth day of the great *Akītu* (New Year) festival, when

the king was divested of his royal insignia and apparel, ritually humiliated, and reinstated.[53] Henri Frankfort remarks on this event, "It is . . . clear that his renewed investiture with the insignia of royalty signified a renewal of kingship."[54]

There may be an intimation of the notion of rebirth in the accounts of the ancient Israelite kings. It is recounted of Saul that the Spirit of the Lord came upon Saul following his anointing, whereupon he became a new man (see 1 Samuel 10:6, 10). Similarly, the Spirit of the Lord came upon David immediately following his anointing to be king (see 1 Samuel 16:13). In later Jewish tradition, the association of coronation with rebirth became explicit: in the Talmud it is said that the king becomes on the day of his coronation "like a one year old babe who has not known the taste of sin."[55]

Creation

The time of the king's coronation was frequently associated with the creation of the world. This is particularly apparent in ancient Egypt. There, the crown prince's accession to the throne took place on the morning following the death of the former king, a moment chosen not merely to secure as easy and peaceful a dynastic succession as possible, but also because of its religious significance. By ascending to the throne in this manner, the crown prince "actualized the mythic deed of the sun-god, his ideal father, who in mythic times climbed the primeval hill, thus causing the day to break."[56] The installation of the Indian king, the *rajasūya*, included the re-creation of the universe.[57] And according to A. M. Hocart, the installation ceremony of the Fijian king was called the "creation of the world," "fashioning the land," or "creating the earth."[58]

Ritual Combat

This world is a place of continuing conflict between the powers of order and chaos, of good and evil, of light and darkness. In Egypt, for example, "the victory of light at creation . . . is not a final one. Darkness is not defeated once and for all, it has only been pushed back and surrounds this world of lights, continuously threatening to encroach upon its dominion."[59] Even the king at his coronation might not be exempt from a struggle for his throne. In many sacred traditions this conflict goes back to the creation itself. The contest between the opposing forces is ceremonially represented by the ritual combat or sham fight, "a fight or battle enacted in a ritual in order to illustrate a battle told of in a myth; the result of this battle is the [temporary] destruction of the enemies of the cosmic order or of the life of the community."[60]

The ritual combat sometimes represents the struggle between opposing seasonal forces, sometimes the primeval contest for control of the cosmos, or the conflict at the New Year, or the battle between forces loyal to the newly enthroned king and his enemies. The ritual combat is performed either for "the riddance of whatever is conceived as hostile," for "the enhancement of whatever is conceived of as favorable to life,"[61] or to produce a large amount of supernatural power "in the form of excitement."[62] Thus, for example, "among the Malayans a mock combat takes place every three or four years in order to expel demons," while the same ceremony is also thought "to introduce new life and vitality."[63] Similarly, Tor Irstram notes that, in Africa, "anarchy—chaos—was the natural state until the new king had fought the ritual sham fight in connection with his coronation." According to Irstram, the ritual combat represented the turning point in the mythical battle in which the god brought an end to the state of chaos, overcame the powers of anarchy, and created the cosmos—the ordered world.[64]

Many mock combats, particularly in the ancient Near East, contained reminiscences of primal battles between the gods. In ancient Iran, where the earth was "seen as the battleground of two divine powers,"[65] the New Year's festival was "the great mythic-ritual occasion of the year. . . . At this festival the king functions as a dragon-killer, slaying the mythical monster Azi Dahaka, thereby creating fertility in the world."[66] The Babylonian New Year (Akītu) festival may have included a mock combat that dramatized the battle between Marduk and Tiamat before the world was created.[67] The Egyptians may have ritually represented the primordial battle between Horus and Seth (Typhon), where the monster Apophis, depicted by a rope, is cut into pieces.[68] There appears to have been a ritual combat at the New Year Festival in ancient Ugarit. "During the first four days of the New Year Festival," de Moor informs us, "there was a ritual battle in the plains between Ma'hadu (Minet el-Beida) and Ugarit (Ras Shamra) and later on in the sanctuary of the goddess. A princess representing the goddess ʿAnatu engaged in a mock battle with the soldiers from the two cities. . . . Between the fights the soldiers seem to have regaled at special tables in the temples."[69]

Examples could be cited from both the ancient and modern world of mock combats, some expressly linked with the seasons or festivals, some not. In a Hittite ritual, a mock battle takes place between a group representing the men of Ḫatti and one representing the men of Māša. At the end of the struggle, the men of Ḫatti win and present one of their prisoners "to the god."[70] Among the most interesting ancient attestations is found in Herodotus:

> At Papremis there is a special ceremony in addition
> to the ordinary rites and sacrifices. . . . As the sun draws
> towards setting, only a few of the priests continue to
> employ themselves about the image of the god, while the
> majority, armed with wooden clubs, take their stand at
> the entrance of the temple; opposite there is another
> crowd of men, more than a thousand strong, also armed
> with clubs and consisting of men who have vows to per-
> form. The image of the god, in a little wooden gold-
> plated shrine, is conveyed to another sacred building on
> the day before the ceremony. The few priests who are left
> to attend to it, put it, together with the shrine which con-
> tains it, in a four-wheeled cart which they drag along
> towards the temple. The others, waiting at the temple
> gate, try to prevent it from coming in, while the votaries
> take the god's side and set upon them with their clubs.
> The assault is resisted, and a vigorous tussle ensues in
> which heads are broken and not a few actually die of the
> wounds they receive. That, at least, is what I believe,
> though the Egyptians told me that nobody is ever killed.[71]

Other ritual battles are attested to in ancient Egypt,
including one at Buto, associated with Min, that has similarities to the conflict described by Herodotus.[72] In ancient
Greece, ritual combats are recorded, notably for the *litho-
bolia* (ritual pelting with stones) and raillery connected with
Damia and Auxesia at Troezen.[73] Other examples include the
feast of Danlis in Argos, the Katagogia in Ephesus, and the
ballachiadai at Argos.[74] In communities throughout Europe,
and the world generally, there are numerous instances of ritual fights usually associated with a festival, though sometimes connected with none.[75] Thus, according to Jacob
Grimm, "in many places [in Germany] two persons, dis-
guised as Summer and Winter, make their appearance, the
one clothed with ivy or *singrün*, the other with straw or

moss, and they fight one another till Summer wins. The custom . . . belongs chiefly to districts in the middle Rhine."[76]

Ritual combats take place during the coronation ceremonies of Egypt, Africa, India, and England.[77] In a panel
depicting the Memphite Osirian rituals of the month of
Khoiakh (closely connected, as Sethe has shown, with kingship[78]), shows the raising of a _Dd_-pillar and a ritual combat
"between people representing the inhabitants of Buto, the
pre-dynastic capital of Lower Egypt, some of whom cried
out as they fought 'I choose the Horus N.'"[79] Thus, this day
included both rituals representing the resurrection and
burial of Osiris, "but also a ritual combat depicting the triumph of his son and successor, Horus, and what looks
remarkably like a triumphal royal procession."[80] There is
also a sham fight at Abydos in honor of Osiris,[81] and a ritual
combat at Letopolis connected with the worship of Horus
that appears to be associated with the royal rites of enthronement.[82] During the accession of Egyptian king
Senusert I, a "mock battle" was fought.[83]

We have an apparent survival of the ritual combat in
Christian Ethiopia, where it was customary at the enthronement festival in Aksum for a lion and an ox to be
chained. While the king felled the ox with his own hand,
his retinue would kill animals and birds.[84] During the older
English coronation rite (last performed at the accession of
George II), at the banquet in Westminster Hall that concluded the coronation, a person called "the King's Champion" appeared. He entered the hall with two trumpeters, a
"sergeant-at-arms," two attendants carrying his lance and
shield, and a herald. After the trumpeter sounded a signal,
the herald read a proclamation that the champion would
fight anyone disputing the king's title to the throne.[85] In
Ganda, in Africa, Irstram writes, "we found both a real

struggle for the throne and several sham fights. Immediately after Katikiro's solemn announcement of the name of
the elected king, he bade those who were dissatisfied with
the choice to fight for their candidate to the throne. He
even offered to provide the weapons. It then sometimes
happened that fighting actually took place, and this then
continued until only one of the rival princes was left
alive."[86]

But if conflict was often a part of the coronation, the
king was also granted the ability to overcome and repel
opposing powers. H. P. L'Orange observes in the ancient
world what he terms "the gesture of power." He shows
with numerous illustrations that this gesture was made by
raising the right hand, the palm facing forward, as is commonly done when taking an oath.[87] L'Orange notes that "the
outstretched right hand of the king" is endowed with
supernatural powers. The gesture could be used to bless or
to curse.[88] "From the outstretched divine hand supernatural
powers emanate, repelling all hostile and evil forces. . . . The
supernatural redeeming power in the emperor's outstretched right hand presupposes higher powers and abili-
ties dwelling in him. Through the emperor, manifesting his
power in this gesture, divine interference in human affairs
takes place."[89]

Procession

As part of many coronation ceremonies the king toured
his kingdom and received homage from his subjects, a procession that many times followed the course of the sun.[90] In
ancient Egypt from the time of Menes, each pharaoh paraded
ceremoniously around a fortified wall, and the ritual came to
be called "the procession round the wall."[91] Similarly, after
Solomon had been anointed as king of Israel, a procession

went with the new king from the sanctuary to the throne, whereupon he took his place on the throne and received the obeisance of the officials and the royal princes (see 1 Kings 1:40, 53). During the Babylonian *Akītu* festival (in which the king played a central role, although it was not a coronation rite per se) a procession took place, in which the statue of the god left the city temple, embarked on a ship, and made a journey to the *Akītu*-house, afterward returning to his temple on the same boat. The participation of the king in the ceremony was essential, and it is clear that the populace joined in and found it a period of great joy and feasting.[92] This element of the coronation rite is also found in the ceremonies of India, Cambodia, Siam, Japan, Fiji, and Africa.[93]

Garment

Kings are commonly clothed with special garments during their coronations. Some of our best evidence for this feature of accession rites is found in accounts of enthronement ceremonies in South and East Asia. In India the king is invested with two garments and a mantle at the time of his coming to the throne. Similarly, in Cambodia the king's ministers traditionally place a red mantle with gold embroidery on the king's shoulders during his coronation.[94] There was a similar ceremony for the Siamese king. The king was given a white robe symbolic of purity for his ceremonial bath of purification and anointment. Following this ceremonial bath the king withdrew, reappearing shortly thereafter in his full royal robes, including the gold-embroidered *pha-nun*, or Siamese national lower garment, and a gold-embroidered robe or long tunic.[95] During the enthronement ceremony for the Japanese emperor, clothing in a royal garment also plays an important part.[96]

In medieval and modern European accession rites,

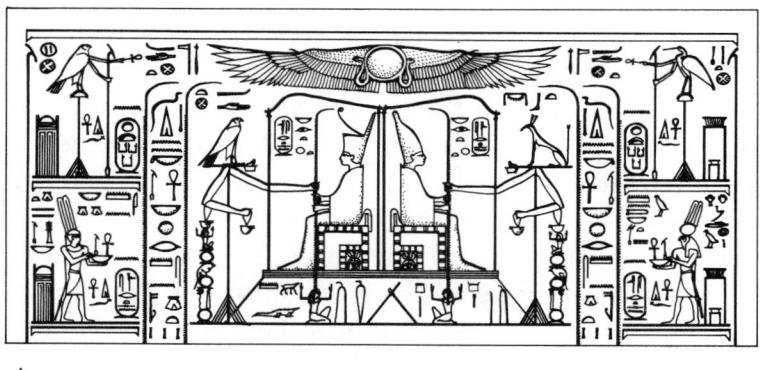

A.

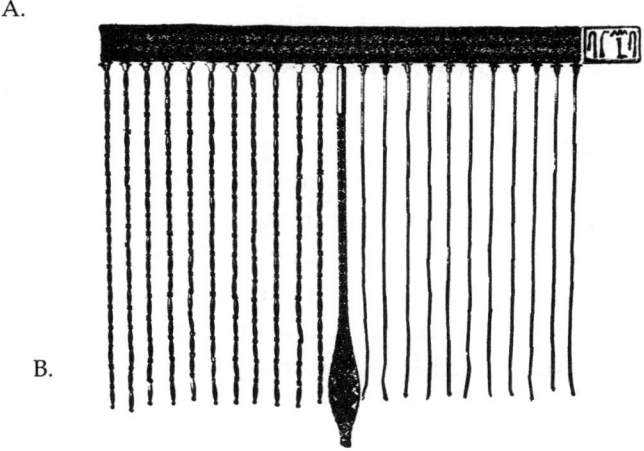

B.

Figure 35. The Sed festival of Senwsret III is shown on this stone lintel
(A) from his temple at Medamud (c. 1860 B.C.). He wears the archaic
white garment from which his hands emerge to receive the palm frond
of "millions of years" from Horus and Seth. The small divine figures at
either corner wear the bull's tail, from which the festival takes its name.
An actual example of this ritual girdle (B) was found in the tomb of the
lady Senebtisy (c. 1962 B.C.).

clothing in regal garments plays a central role. One of the oldest preserved Christian coronation ceremonies is the Spanish rite, during which the king "disrobes, and is arrayed in white vestments designed with special openings to admit of the anointing. The Archbishop of Pamplona proceeds to anoint him in front of the high altar according to the custom, but unfortunately what the custom is is not specified. The king after the anointing changes his raiment for precious vestments, and returns to the high altar. The archbishop then proceeds with the accustomed prayers."[97]

The evidence for clothing in royal robes at the coronation ceremonies in the ancient Near East is somewhat less certain. However, according to Bleeker, the ḥb sd (Sed festival), the main festival of the king in ancient Egypt, should be translated "the festival of the garment, in the sense of re-investiture. . . . This accords with what has already been established: one of the central rituals—if not the main one of the festival—is the king's donning and wearing the sd robe of archaic design."[98] "By donning the sd robe," Bleeker notes in another study, "the king renewed his office."[99]

Possibly there was a rite of investiture at the coronation of the Israelite king, similar to that at the Sed festival; and the royal robe may have looked like the garment of the high priest, which is described in great detail in Exodus 28.[100]

Crown

The root sense of coronation implies that the king is crowned, and, indeed, this is a central part of many, though by no means all, accession rites. In ancient Egypt the king was given the two crowns—of Upper and Lower Egypt. The red crown of Lower Egypt was a "flat cap, with spiral in front and tall projection at rear," while the white crown of Upper Egypt was "tall and conical with a knob at the top."[101] There is no direct evidence concerning the receipt of a crown by the Israelite king at the time of his enthronement, but the high priest's crown (described in Exodus 29) may reflect the type used by the king. The Persian king's dress also included a cap, described in detail by Dhalla: "The cap was made of stiffer material, and was higher than that worn by any of [his] subjects. It assumed a broader circular shape, as it reached the flat top, and a blue fillet [or band], spotted with white, encircled it at the bottom."[102]

In his study of coronation ceremonies among African tribes, Irstram found nineteen tribes where the king was crowned. These crowns included bands of cloth or cow-hide, caps, and actual metal crowns.[103] The Siamese crown was "a cone of several stages terminating in a spire,"[104] whereas in India it was a gold plate.[105] In Japan, on the other hand, it is not proper to speak of a "coronation," since the emperor received no crown. He did, however, wear the tallest form of the black lacquered headdress of standard court costume.

Conclusion

Some general observations concerning enthronement ceremonies are warranted: (1) Although the actual elements of the coronation ceremonies of the various cultures under study may differ substantially from each other, and although no one people has a coronation ceremony that reflects in all its particulars the pattern described above (much less the full complement of elements listed in Appendix A), there are still sufficient similarities in the rites to justify their comparison. (2) Much of what is contained in the ceremonies of enthronement seems distinctly foreign to the thought and forms of twentieth-century man, as indeed it should, since the pattern is widely attested in antiquity, and appears to derive from the ancient world.

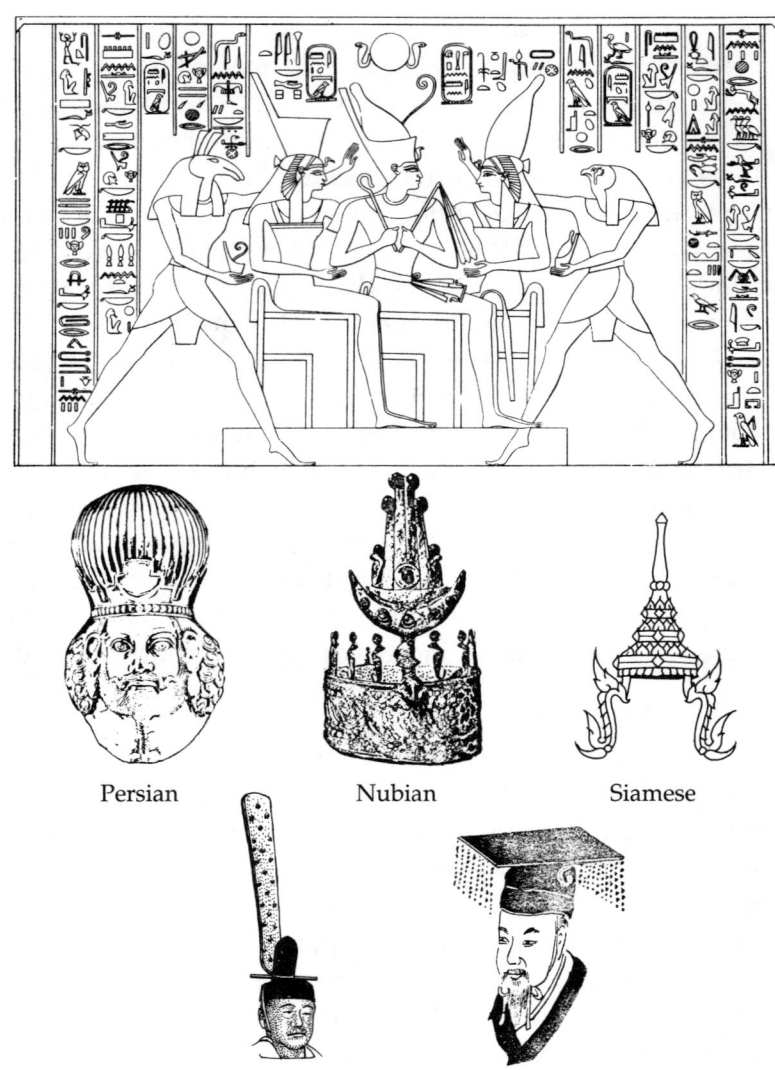

Persian   Nubian   Siamese

Japanese   Chinese

(3) The coronation rites are intimately linked with the priesthood. Those carrying out the coronation rites are nearly always of sacerdotal rank, and even the king himself is generally of priestly grade or is endowed with priestly power. (4) The site of the coronation ceremonies is nearly always sacred space. In many of the cultures where coronation ceremonies are attested, the temple serves as the site of the ceremony, given its position as sacred space par excellence. In others, a church or some other sanctuary was chosen, which strengthened considerably the association of the enthronement rites with the sacred. Access to this sacred space, be it temple, church, or other area, is generally restricted, at least during the time of the coronation liturgy.

Figure 36. In this bas-relief from Thebes (c. 1080 B.C.), upper left, the priest-king Heri-Hor is enthroned between the maternal embrace of the two goddesses, Wadjet with the red crown of Lower Egypt and Nekhbet with the white crown of Upper Egypt. Seth and Horus hasten forward offering miniature crowns as well. From the bulging eminence of the Persian crown to the mandala temple tower of the Siamese, the emphasis is on height, showing the preeminence of the king among men.

Appendix A:
Features of the Coronation Ceremony[106]

1. Austerities. Previous to their coronation, some kings prepared themselves for the ceremony through fasting, remaining in solitude, or some other act of discipline.

2. Secrecy. The coronation ceremony, which often contained religious secrets known only to the initiated, was frequently guarded in order to prevent the entrance of the uninitiated.

3. Reverence. During the coronation ceremony itself, those who were allowed to attend were expected to maintain a discrete silence.

4. Humiliation. During certain ceremonies, the king became the butt of practical jokes, sneers, derision, and "grotesque and fantastic puns" and was sometimes even the object of a severe beating.

5. Promises. In another important constituent of the coronation ceremony, "the king is admonished to rule justly and promises to do so."

6. Gods. A feature particularly evident in ancient coronation ceremonies but found less often in modern ones is the impersonation of the gods by priests or other officials.

7. Ablution. During this part of the coronation rite, the king was ceremonially washed.

8. Anointing. A feature of the ceremony that generally followed the ablution was an anointing of the king with oil.

9. Sacrifices. Animal sacrifice frequently attended the installation rituals of the king. Human sacrifice is also attested, but only rarely.

10. Jubilation. Numerous coronations end with ritual rejoicing that was frequently accompanied by acclamations such as "Long live the king!"

11. New Name. During the course of the coronation

ceremonies, the king generally acquired a new name, often either a title or the name of a predecessor.

12. Rebirth. During many coronation rituals, some act suggesting the rebirth process was performed: acting as one who is new to the world, going through a burial ceremony, being ritually reawakened, or acting like a newborn babe.

13. Creation. The coronation ceremony was thought of as a time of new creation, a day like the day on which the world was created. This intimate association of coronation and creation was often ritually expressed by the ceremonial repetition of the creation account.

14. Combat. This is often a ritual combat or "sham fight," a fight or battle enacted in a ritual in order to illustrate a battle told of in myth. The result of this battle is the (temporary) destruction of the cosmic order or of the life of the community.

15. Marriage. A "sacred marriage" between the king and his consort frequently accompanies the other rituals associated with the coronation, and in some rituals it is the final act.

16. Procession. The coronation ceremony generally included a ritual procession, either around the sacred site of the king's enthronement or through his realms, in order that the king might receive homage from his people.

17. Garment. In the course of the enthronement ceremony, the king was generally clothed with a garment endowed with special powers.

18. Crown. During the coronation rite, the king was frequently given a crown, cap, or some other head covering with sacred associations.

19. Shoes. In many coronations, the king puts on shoes or other footwear as a part of the rites.

20. Regalia. During the installation rites, the king

receives various symbols of his regal power: a sword, a scepter, or a ring.

21. Throne. The ritual enthronement of the king during the coronation ceremony is enacted even more frequently than the bestowal of the crown or the receipt of other regalia.

22. Masks. The use of masks by priests impersonating gods is evident in certain ancient royal rites.

23. Communion. In a number of coronation rites, the king received food or drink of a ceremonial or sacramental nature.

24. Feast. In the course of most coronation rituals, a feast was given for the king and all others attending the ceremony.

25. Dominion. In a number of cultures, the new king performed a rite, such as taking a set number of ceremonial steps, touring the kingdom, or shooting an arrow.

26. Officials. In many cultures, officials were consecrated either in the course of the coronation ceremony or shortly thereafter.

27. Progression. In most of the coronation ceremonies under study, the king was permitted to be consecrated several times, progressing each time in the scale of kingship.

Appendix B:
Features of the
Coronation Ceremony in Selected Cultures

	Fiji[107]	India[108]	England[109]	Siam[110]	Africa[111]	Japan[112]	Egypt[113]	Israel[114]
1. Austerities		x	x	x	x	x		
2. Secrecy	x	x		x	x	x	x	
3. Reverence	x				x	x		
4. Humiliation	x	x			x		x	
5. Promises	x	x	x	x	x	x		x
6. Gods					x		x	
7. Ablution	x	x		x	x	x	x	
8. Anointing		x	x		x		x	x
9. Sacrifice		x		x	x	x	x	x
10. Jubilation	x		x	x	x	x	x	x
11. New Name		x		x	x	x	x	x
12. Rebirth	x	x	x	x	x	x	x	x
13. Creation	x	x					x	
14. Combat	x	x	x	x	x		x	
15. Queen	x	x			x			
16. Procession	x	x		x	x	x	x	x
17. Garment	x	x	x	x	x	x	x	x
18. Crown	x	x	x	x	x		x	x
19. Shoes		x	x	x	x	x	x	
20. Regalia	x	x	x	x	x	x	x	x
21. Throne		x	x	x	x	x	x	x
22. Masks							x	
23. Communion	x	x	x		x	x		x
24. Feast	x			x	x	x	x	x
25. Dominion	x	x			x		x	x
26. Officials	x		x	x	x	x		
27. Progression	x	x	x	x				

Notes

1. See Henri Frankfort, *Ancient Egyptian Religion* (New York: Columbia University Press, 1949), 50.

2. See Cyril J. Gadd, *Ideas of Divine Rule in the Ancient Near East* (London: Oxford University Press, 1948), 21.

3. David N. Talbott, *The Saturn Myth* (New York: Doubleday, 1980), 20, 329; cf. John W. Perry, *Lord of the Four Quarters* (New York: George Braziller, 1966), 16, 18; Frederick H. Borsch, *The Son of Man in Myth and History* (Philadelphia: Westminster, 1967), 80, 87–88.

4. Arthur Hocart, *Kingship* (London: Oxford University Press, 1927).

5. See Tor Irstram, *The King of Ganda* (Lund: Ohlssons, 1944).

6. See J. C. Heesterman, *The Ancient Indian Royal Consecration* (Gravenhage: Mouton, 1957).

7. See D. C. Holtom, *The Japanese Enthronement Ceremonies* (Tokyo: Kyo Bun Kwan, 1928), and *FK*.

8. See *KG*, passim.

9. Roland de Vaux, *Ancient Israel*, 2 vols. (New York: McGraw Hill, 1965), 102.

10. See Alan Gardiner, "The Coronation of King Haremhab," *Journal of Egyptian Archaeology* 39 (1953): 25.

11. See *KG*, 245–47.

12. See M. N. Dhalla, *Zoroastrian Civilization* (New York: Oxford University Press, 1922), 227.

13. *FK*, 151.

14. See Hocart, *Kingship*, 78.

15. H. G. Quaritch Wales, *Siamese State Ceremonies: Their History and Function* (London: Bernard Quaritch, 1931), 124.

16. See Irstram, *The King of Ganda*, 72.

17. See Hocart, *Kingship*, 76.

18. "The Significance of Initiation," in *Initiation*, ed. C. J. Bleeker (Leiden: Brill, 1965), 15.

19. Mircea Eliade, *The Sacred and the Profane* (New York: Harcourt and Brace, 1959), 188.

20. See Samuel H. Hooke, *Babylonian and Assyrian Religion* (Norman: University of Oklahoma Press, 1963), 47; cf. Thorkild Jacobsen, *The Treasures of Darkness* (New Haven: Yale University Press, 1976), 16.

21. See C. J. Bleeker, "Initiation in Ancient Egypt," in *Initiation*, 55–56; H. W. Fairman, "Worship and Festivals in an Egyptian Temple," *Bulletin, John Rylands Library* 37 (1954–55), 174, 187, 201; cf.

M. V. Seton-Williams, *Ptolemaic Temples* (Cambridge: The Author, 1978), 38.

22. See Carl Kerenyi, *Eleusis* (New York: Bollingen Foundation, 1967), 118; George Mylonas, *Eleusis and the Eleusinian Mysteries* (Princeton: Princeton University Press, 1961), 225.

23. Mylonas, *Eleusis and the Eleusinian Mysteries*, 281.

24. Irach Taraporewala, "Mithraism," in *Forgotten Religions*, ed. Vergilius Ferm (New York: Philosophical Library, 1950), 205.

25. See Eliade, *The Sacred and the Profane*, 130; cf. also Mircea Eliade, *Patterns in Comparative Religion* (Cleveland: World, 1963), 188–89, 193–94; Maurice A. Canney, *Newness of Life* (Calcutta: University of Calcutta Press, 1928), 67; W. B. Kristensen, *The Meaning of Religion* (The Hague: Nijhoff, 1960), 447; A. J. Wensinck, "The Semitic New Year and the Origin of Eschatology," *Acta Orientalia* 1 (1923): 166, 186; Robert A. Wild, *Water in the Cultic Worship of Isis and Osiris* (Leiden: Brill, 1981), 125, 153.

26. See Samuel A. B. Mercer, *The Pyramid Texts*, 4 vols. (New York: Longmans and Green, 1952), 4:55; cf. Aylward M. Blackman, "An Ancient Egyptian Foretaste of the Doctrine of Baptismal Regeneration," *Theology* 1 (1920): 140–41.

27. See Blackman, "An Ancient Egyptian Foretaste," 135, 137–38; Aylward M. Blackman, "Some Notes on the Ancient Egyptian Practice of Washing the Dead," *Journal of Egyptian Archaeology* 5 (1918): 124; Samuel A. B. Mercer, *The Religion of Ancient Egypt* (London: Luzac, 1949), 348–50; Wild, *Water in the Cultic Worship*, 145.

28. See Aylward M. Blackman, "The House of the Morning," *The Journal of Egyptian Archaeology* 5 (1918): 155; *KG*, 83; Eva L. R. Meyerowitz, *The Divine Kingship in Ghana and Ancient Egypt* (London: Faber and Faber, 1960), 159.

29. Geo Widengren, "Royal Ideology and the Testament of the Twelve Patriarchs," in *Promise and Fulfilment*, ed. F. F. Bruce (Edinburgh: Clark, 1963), 207.

30. *Catachesis Mystagogica* III.6 (*Catachesis XXI*), in *PG*, 33:1093.

31. TB, *Horayoth* 12a.

32. See Geo Widengren, "Israelite-Jewish Religion," in *Historia Religionum*, 2 vols., ed. C. J. Bleeker and Geo Widengren (Leiden: Brill, 1969), 1:258–59.

33. Irstram, *The King of Ganda*, 64–65.

34. See Zoe Kincaid, "The Ceremonies of Accession," in *Enthronement of the One Hundred Twenty-fourth Emperor of Japan*, ed. Benjamin W. Fleisher (Tokyo: Japan Advertiser, 1928), 31, 34.

35. See E. S. Drower, *The Mandaeans of Iraq and Iran* (Oxford: Clarendon, 1937), 102–4.

36. See Helmer Ringgren, in "Initiation Ceremony of the Bektashis," in *Initiation*, 203–4.

37. Oliver R. Gurney, "Hittite Kingship," in *Myth, Ritual, and Kingship*, ed. Samuel H. Hooke (Oxford: Clarendon, 1953), 118.

38. See Ernst Kutsch, *Salbung als Rechtsakt im Alten Testament und im Alten Orient* (Berlin: Topelmann, 1963), 41–52; Mercer, *The Religion of Ancient Egypt*, 348.

39. See Kutsch, *Salbung als Rechtsakt*, 52–63; cf. also J. A. Soggin, *"maelaek,"* in *Theologisches Handwörterbuch zum Alten Testament*, 2 vols., ed. Ernst Jenni and Claus Westermann (Munich: Kaiser, 1971), 1:914.

40. *Apocalypsis Mosis* 9:3, cited in *The Apocrypha and Pseudepigrapha of the Old Testament in English*, 2 vols., ed. R. H. Charles (Oxford: Clarendon, 1976), 2:143.

41. See Hocart, *Kingship*, 79–96.

42. R. M. Woolley, *Coronation Rites* (Cambridge: Cambridge University Press, 1915), 29.

43. Arthur M. Hocart, "Initiation," *Folklore* 35 (1924): 312.

44. See *KG*, 46; cf. also John A. Wilson, *The Culture of Ancient Egypt* (Chicago: University of Chicago Press, 1962), 102.

45. *KG*, 246.

46. See Geo Widengren, "The Sacral Kingship of Iran," in *La regalita sacra/The Sacral Kingship*, vol. 4 in *Studies in the History of Religions* (Leiden: Brill, 1959), 255–56.

47. See de Vaux, *Ancient Israel*, 108.

48. Wales, *Siamese State Ceremonies*, 38, 85, 88, 102–3, 125.

49. See *FK*, 152.

50. On the use of new and hidden names, see Bruce H. Porter and Stephen D. Ricks, "Names in Antiquity: Old, New, and Hidden," in *BSAF*, 1:501–22.

51. Mercer, *The Religion of Ancient Egypt*, 350; cf. Blackman, "An Ancient Egyptian Foretaste," 138–41.

52. See Istram, *The King of Ganda*, 57–58; cf. Ivan Engnell, *Studies in Divine Kingship in the Ancient Near East*, 2d ed. (Oxford: Blackwell, 1967), 5.

53. See Aage Bentzen, *King and Messiah* (London: Lutterworth, 1955), 26.

54. *KG*, 320.

55. Midrash, *Rabbah, Samuel* 17; TB *Yoma* 22b, cited in Raphael

Patai, "Hebrew Installation Rites," *Hebrew Union College Annual* 20 (1947): 170.

56. C. J. Bleeker, *Egyptian Festivals* (Leiden: Brill, 1967), 95. It is also interesting to note the consistency with which the recitation of the creation account is found in temple rituals in the ancient Near East. Hugh Nibley, in his luminous study of the Egyptian background of the Joseph Smith papyri, *The Message of the Joseph Smith Papyri* (Salt Lake City: Deseret Book, 1975), 131, notes that the creation story constitutes a focal point in Egyptian religious literature and in the temple ritual. E. A. E. Reymond further shows that the creation account played a major role in the temple liturgy at Memphis (see *The Mythical Origin of the Egyptian Temple* [New York: Barnes and Noble, 1969], 273–85). Similarly, the *Enuma Elish*, the Babylonian creation account, was recited in the *Akītu*-house in Babylon in the course of the *Akītu* (New Year's) festival, and possibly on other occasions as well (see F. Thureau-Dangin, *Rituels Accadiens* [Paris: Leroux, 1921], 136, lines 279–84, and W. G. Lambert, "Myth and Ritual as Conceived by the Babylonians," *Journal of Semitic Studies* 13 [1968]: 106). While it is uncertain that the creation account of Genesis 1:1–2:4 was used in the temple ritual of Israel before the Babylonian exile, a reference in the M Taʿanit 4:2–3 clearly indicates that one of the responsibilities of the courses of laymen (*'anshe maʿamad*) in the postexilic temple was to read sections of the Genesis account while the Levites and priests performed the sacrifices (further see Stephen Ricks, "Liturgy and Cosmogony: The Ritual Use of Creation Accounts in the Ancient Near East," 118–25, in this volume, *Temples of the Ancient World*).

57. See Mircea Eliade, *Myth and Reality* (New York: Harper and Row, 1963), 39; cf. Heesterman, *The Ancient Indian Coronation*, 10.

58. Hocart, *Kingship*, 189–90; cf. Eliade, *Myth and Reality*, 39.

59. Helmer Ringgren, "Light and Darkness in Ancient Egyptian Religion," in *Liber Amicorum: Studies in Honour of Professor Dr. C. J. Bleeker* (Leiden: Brill, 1969), 144.

60. Ivan Engnell, *A Rigid Scrutiny* (Nashville: Vanderbilt University Press, 1969), 181, n. 4.

61. Jane E. Harrison, *Epilegomena to the Study of Greek Religion* (Cambridge: Cambridge University Press, 1921), 1.

62. H. J. Rose, "A Suggested Explanation of Ritual Combats," *Folk-Lore* 36 (1925): 331.

63. H. Gaster, *Thespis* (New York: Norton, 1977), 38, 62.

64. Irstram, *King of Ganda*, 165.

65. Paul Tillich, *The Dynamics of Faith* (New York: Harper, 1957), 54.

66. Geo Widengren, "The Sacral Kingship of Iran," 252.

67. See J. A. Black, "The New Year Ceremonies in Ancient Babylon: 'Taking Bel by the Hand' and a Cultic Picnic," *Religion* 11 (1981): 56, who describes "symbolic representations of certain episodes in the Epic of Creation" without saying that it is in the form of a sham fight; see also Erich Ebeling, *Tod und Leben nach den Vorstellungen der Babylonier* (Berlin: de Gruyter, 1931), 33; Engnell, *Studies in Divine Kingship*, 36; W. G. Lambert, "The Great Battle of the Mesopotamian Religious Year," *Iraq* 25 (1963): 189–90; Svend Aage Pallis, *The Babylonian Akītu-Festival* (Copenhagen: Høst, 1926), 215–16; Geo Widengren, *Religionsphänomenologie*, 378. According to Gaster, "A Canaanite Ritual Drama," in *Journal of the American Oriental Society* 66 (1946): 75, ritual combats represent "the struggle between summer and winter, rain and drought, fertility and blight, old year and new." In general, Gaster explains instances of ritual combats as seasonal (see Gaster, *Thespis*, 37–41).

68. See Plutarch, *De Iside et Osiride* 19; cf. Hugh W. Nibley, *The Message of the Joseph Smith Papyri: An Egyptian Endowment* (Salt Lake City: Deseret Book, 1975), 225. Horus and Seth were known as "the two fighters" (H. te Velde, *Seth, God of Confusion* [Leiden: Brill, 1967], 33). Significantly, combat may also have been an element connected with the primal origins of the Egyptian temple (cf. Eve A. E. Reymond, *The Mythical Origins of the Egyptian Temple* [New York: Barnes and Noble, 1969], 13, 25, 107, 209).

69. Johannes de Moor, *New Year with Canaanites and Israelites* (Kampen: Kok, 1972), 8.

70. Hans Ehelolf, "Wettlauf und szenisches Spiel im hethitischen Ritual," in *Sitzungsberichte der Preussischen Akademie der Wissenschaften, Philosophisch-historische Klasse* 21 (1925): 269–72. Albin Lasky, "Ein ritueller Scheinkampf bei den Hethitern," *Archiv für Religionswissenschaft* 24 (1926): 80–82, sees in this ritual a trace of human sacrifice and views it as a possible forerunner of drama.

71. Herodotus II, 63, in *The Histories*, tr. Aubrey de Sélincourt (Baltimore: Penguin Books, 1972), 153–54.

72. See Drioton, "Les fêtes de Bouto," *Bulletin de l'Institut d'Égypte* 25 (1942–43): 6; idem, *Les fêtes égyptiennes* (Cairo: Éditions de la Revue du Caire, 1944): 10–13.

73. See Pausanias II, 30, 5; II, 32, 2–3; cf. Herodotus V, 82–87; see Martin P. Nilsson, *Griechische Feste von religiöser Bedeutung mit Ausschluss des Attischen* (Leipzig: Teubner, 1906), 413–16; cf. Hermann Usener, "Heilige Handlung," *Archiv für Religionswissenschaft* 7 (1904):

300–301, also published in Hermann Usener, *Kleine Schriften* (Leipzig: Teubner, 1913), 4:439–40.

74. See Nilsson, *Griechische Feste*, 402–8, 416–17; Usener, "Heilige Handlung," 297–313. For examples from modern Greece, see Adolf Wilhelm, "Caterva," *Archiv für Religionswissenschaft* 16 (1913): 630; George Calderon,"Slavonic Elements in Greek Religion," *The Classical Review* 27 (1913): 79–81.

75. See Wilhelm Mannhardt, *Wald- und Feldkulte: Der Baumkultus der Germanen und Ihrer Nachbarstämme*, ed. W. Heuschkel, 2nd ed. (Berlin: Borntraeger, 1904), 549–52. Further examples from Europe are provided in Alb. Ostheide, "Zum Martinsfest," *Archiv für Religionswissenschaft* 10 (1907): 156, who cites an example from Siebenbürgen; Ludwig Radermacher, *Beiträge zur Volkskunde aus dem Gebiet der Antike*, in *Sitzungberichte der Akademie der Wissenschaften in Wien* 187, no. 3 (1918): 13–16; Paul Sartori, *Sitte und Brauch*, 3 vols. (Leipzig: Heims, 1914), 3:120–21, 124, 133–34, 165, 179, 195, 199, 202, 220, 234–35, 252, 271. In his discussion of the Damia and Auxesia passage in Pausanias II, 30, 4, James G. Frazer, *Pausanias's Description of Greece*, 6 vols. (New York: Biblo and Tannen, 1965), 3:267–68, gives examples of sham fights in Peru, Tonga, among Indians of the southeastern United States, in India, China, and Africa (cf. Frazer, *The Golden Bough*, 7:98, 9:173; idem, *Aftermath: A Supplement to The Golden Bough* [New York: Macmillan, 1937], 375–78).

76. Jacob Grimm, *Teutonic Mythology*, 4 vols. (Gloucester, Massachusetts: Peter Smith, 1976), 2:764–65.

77. See Hocart, *Kingship*, 78–95; Irstram, *King of Ganda*, 60–61; Pedersen, "Canaanite and Israelite Cultus," *Acta Orientalia* 18 (1940): 9–10; Engnell, *Rigid Scrutiny*, 183.

78. See Kurt Sethe, *Beiträge zur ältesten Geschichte Ägyptens* (Leipzig: Hinrichs, 1905), 134.

79. A. M. Blackman, "Myth and Ritual in Ancient Egypt," in *Myth and Ritual*, ed. S. H. Hooke (London: Oxford University Press, 1933), 22, 24; cf. 23, fig. 4, panel 3; cf. H. Brugsch, *Thesaurus Inscriptionum Aegytiacarum*, 6 vols. (Leipzig: Hinrichs, 1884), 5:1190.

80. Ibid., 24.

81. Cf. Kurt Sethe, *Aegyptische Lesestücke zum Gebrauch im akademischen Unterricht* (Leipzig: Hinrichs, 1924), 70–72.

82. See Kurt Sethe, *Die altaegytischen Pyramidentexte* (Leipzig: Hinrichs, 1922), PT 908d-e; idem, *Der dramatische Ramesseumpapyrus: Ein Spiel zur Thronbesteigung des Königs* (Leipzig: Hinrichs, 1928), 113–15; cf. also Alan B. Lloyd, *Herodotus Book II*, 2 vols. (Leiden: Brill,

1976), 257, for a listing and brief discussion of the various ritual battles attested in ancient Egypt.

83. *KG,* 128.

84. See August Dillmann, *Über die Regierung, insbesondere die Kirchenordnung des Königs Zarʿa-Jacob, Abhandlungen der Königlichen Akademie der Wissenschaften zu Berlin* 69:2 (1884): 75. Similarly, Bahrām Gōr kills a lion and is recognized as king, according to Tabarī (cf. Widengren, *Religionsphänomenologie,* 378).

85. E. O. James, *Christian Myth and Ritual* (London: Murray, 1937), 54–55; Hocart, *Kingship,* 94.

86. Irstram, *King of Ganda,* 61.

87. H. P. L'Orange, *Studies on the Iconography of Cosmic Kingship in the Ancient World* (Oslo: Aschehoug, 1953), 139, 142–69.

88. Ibid., 139–40; cf. L. W. King, *Babylonian Magic and Sorcery* (London: Luzac, 1896), xi–xii; Edward Yarnold, *The Awe-Inspiring Rites of Initiation* (Slough: St. Paul Publication, 1972), 68–69; R. T. Rundle Clark, *Myth and Symbol in Ancient Egypt* (London: Thames and Hudson, 1960), 231.

89. L'Orange, *Iconography of Cosmic Kingship,* 143–47.

90. See *Kingship,* 80, 85; Heesterman, *The Ancient Indian Coronation,* 55, 62, 137; Wales, *Siamese State Ceremonies,* 107.

91. Mercer, *The Religion of Ancient Egypt,* 351; cf. Theodor H. Gaster, *Thespis* (New York: Norton, 1977), 80.

92. See H. W. F. Saggs, *The Greatness That Was Babylon* (New York: Hawthorn Books, 1962), 384.

93. See Gaster, *Thespis,* 98; Irstram, *The King of Ganda,* 72; Hocart, *Kingship,* 77, 80, 82.

94. See Hocart, *Kingship,* 74, 77, 81–82.

95. See Wales, *Siamese State Ceremonies,* 74, 77.

96. See *FK,* 2.

97. Woolley, *Coronation Rites,* 135.

98. Bleeker, *Egyptian Festivals,* 120.

99. "Features of the Ancient Egyptian Religion," in *The Rainbow: A Collection of Studies in the Science of Religion* (Leiden: Brill, 1975), 125.

100. See Helmer Ringgren, *The Messiah in the Old Testament* (Chicago: Allenson, 1956), 13.

101. K. A. Kitchen, "Crown," in *New Bible Dictionary* (Wheaton, Illinois: Tyndale House, 1962), 280–81; cf. Alan H. Gardiner, *Egyptian Grammar* (London: Clarendon, 1927), 491, 571.

102. Dhalla, *Zoroastrian Civilization,* 259.

103. See Irstram, *The King of Ganda,* 56–57, 71–72.

104. Wales, *Siamese State Ceremonies,* 95.

105. See Hocart, *Kingship*, 80.

106. This list of features of the coronation ceremony is based on the list given in ibid., 70–71.

107. Information taken from ibid., 76–77. See also 104 (queen), 113 (officials), 188–90 (creation).

108. Information taken from ibid., 77–81. See also 101 (queen); Heesterman, *Ancient Indian Royal Consecration*, 156 (humiliation), 168 and 200 (sacrifice); Eliade, *Myth and Reality*, 39 (creation).

109. Information taken from Hocart, *Kingship*, 92–97. See also 116–17 (officials).

110. Information taken from Wales, *Siamese State Ceremonies*, 124–25. See also 72–73 (sacrifice).

111. Information taken from Irstram, *The King of Ganda*, 56. See also 26 (feast), 39 (officials), 74 (jubilation), 165 (reverence).

112. Information taken from *FK*, 151–52. See also Fleisher, *Enthronement*, 2 (sacrifice), 4 (procession), 24 (throne), 36 (procession), 55 (promises).

113. Information taken from Hocart, *Kingship*, 83–85. See also C. J. Bleeker, *Hathor and Thoth* (Leiden: Brill, 1973), 86 (secrecy); *Egyptian Festivals*, 94–95 (creation); Gasper, *Thesis*, 81 (humiliation); Mercer, *The Religion of Ancient Egypt*, 359–60 (sacrifice), 364–65 (feast); M. A. E. Ibrahim, *The Chapel of the Throne of Re of Edfu* (Brussels: Fondation Egyptologique Reine Elisabeth, 1975), 16 (jubilation); *KG*, 128 (combat); R. O. Faulkner, *The Ancient Egyptian Pyramid Texts* (Oxford: Clarendon, 1969), 91 (shoes).

114. Information taken from Hocart, *Kingship*, 86. See also 1 Samuel 11:15 (sacrifice); 2 Kings 13:15–17 (dominion); 1 Chronicles 29:21–23 (sacrifice, feast); de Vaux, *Ancient Israel*, 108 (new name); S. Skikszai, "King," in *The Interpreter's Dictionary of the Bible*, 4 vols. (Nashville: Abingdon, 1962), 3:14 (procession); Helmer Ringgren, *The Messiah in the Old Testament*, 13 (garment); *Israelite Religion* (Philadelphia: Fortress, 1966), 226 (regalia); Widengren, "Royal Ideology," 208, 211 (communion).

11

Temple, Covenant, and Law in the Ancient Near East and in the Old Testament

John M. Lundquist

The following is an attempt to extend our understanding of the role of covenant and law in ancient Israel and to show their intimate relationship to the temple. To begin, I will review the historical process of temple restoration. A victorious king (or a prophet) builds or restores a temple. The building or restoration of the temple legitimizes the state or the society (in cases that do not deal with the political state in the formal sense). The act of legitimization is ritually celebrated in and through the covenant process. The content of the covenant ceremony is law. Thus it is my contention that the building or restoration of temples served as the impetus in the ancient Near East for the "codification" of customary law. Let me put it more succinctly: The temple founds (legitimizes) the state; covenant binds the foundation; law underlies the covenant. Just as this ideological/ritual complex flourished—and in its ideal form was supported by Israel's prophets—so in prophetic constructions of restoration, the same complex is found to be central.

This chapter originally appeared in Israel's Apostasy and Restoration: Essays in Honor of Roland K. Harrison, *ed. Avraham Gileadi (Grand Rapids, Michigan: Baker, 1988), 293–305.*

Definitions

Temple

Let me first define the main terms of the argument. By *temple* I mean an association of symbols and practices that we find connected in the ancient world with both natural mountains/high places[1] (the *temple* par excellence) and edifices. The set of symbols and practices include, but are not exhausted by, the following: the cosmic mountain, the primordial mound, waters of life, the tree of life, sacral space, and the celestial prototype of the earthly. These emphasize spatial orientation and the ritual calendar; the height of the mountain/building; revelation of the divine prototype to the king or prophet by deity; the concept of "center," according to which the temple is the ideological, and in many cases the physical, center of the community; the dependency of the well-being of society on the proper attention to the temple and to its rituals; initiation, including dramatic portrayal of the cosmogonic myth; extensive concern for death and the afterlife, including the practice of burial within the temple precincts; sacral (covenant-associated) meals; revelation in the Holy of Holies through the means of the tablets of destiny; formal covenant ceremonies in connection with the promulgation of law; animal sacrifice; secrecy; and the extensive economic and political impact of the temple in society.[2]

State

By *state* I mean a highly centralized and socially stratified polity that exercises a monopoly of force, has the power to enforce its own laws, and possesses an ideology that legitimizes a ruling hierarchy around a temple/covenant religious system. At its most succinct, as far as the ancient

Near East is concerned, the state, I believe, can be defined
as a king (invested with kingship by the gods in a temple)
plus a capital city.[3] I am here distinguishing between the
formal state and the nonstate polities in the ancient Near
East. I firmly believe that the previously outlined "temple
ideology"[4] is found, with appropriate and predictable
exceptions, in each stage of the social/evolutionary process—
tribe, chiefdom, and state[5]—and throughout Israelite history. What I call the "primordial" ancient Near Eastern conception of the temple, and what is called the "chaos-cosmos
ideology" by Folker Willesen,[6] is in fact present both at the
Sinai experience, as recorded in Exodus 19–25, and in the
Solomonic temple construction. In terms of biblical scholarship, we may say that a pre-deuteronomistic temple ideology influences both Sinai and Jerusalem. For our purposes,
let us distinguish between the temple as the dwelling place
of deity (see Isaiah 6) and as a house of prayer (see Isaiah
56).[7] But note that both an exilic prophet, Ezekiel, and a postexilic prophet, Zechariah, reflect the older, common ancient
Near Eastern temple ideology.[8]

The central difference between Mosaic and Solomonic
Israel is that the former was not a state polity, while the
latter was. To use George E. Mendenhall's terminology, we
are dealing with the difference between a "community" and
a "political monopoly of force."[9] Even though the common
ancient Near Eastern temple symbolism underlaid both
societies, the "political" element was missing in the Mosaic,
while it was central in the Solomonic. The temple experience legitimized both societies through a covenant ceremony: at the mountain in the Mosaic, and at the temple of
Solomon in the Solomonic. As I have written elsewhere,
"the ideology of kingship in the archaic state is indelibly
and incontrovertibly connected with temple building and

with temple ideology."[10] "The ideology of kingship" is present at both Sinai and Jerusalem. In Sinai, YHWH is the king; in Jerusalem, Solomon is the king. This kind of formal distinction, I feel, is very important in understanding the central differences and similarities in ancient Israel at various stages of her development.

Covenant

By the term *covenant* I mean a formal, ritually enacted ceremony mediated by a prophet or king in (more exactly "in front of," or "on," in the case of a mountain) the temple, a ceremony in which the community is founded through the people's "indexical" acceptance of the revealed law. The term *indexical* comes from Roy Rappaport and refers to both verbal and physical responses during a ritual ceremony in which a participant signals to a coparticipant "that he accepts whatever is encoded in the canons of the liturgical order in which he is participating." Rappaport further writes, "Physical acts (such as kneeling, raising the hands, etc.) carry indexical messages more convincingly than does language."[11] For evidence of indexicality in biblical covenant ceremonies, see Exodus 19:8; Joshua 24:16; 1 Kings 8:22; 2 Chronicles 6:13; 2 Kings 23:3; Nehemiah 8:5–6.

Mendenhall's definition of the covenant process at Sinai bears an interesting resemblance to my definition: "The covenant at Sinai was the formal means by which the seminomadic clans, recently emerged from state slavery in Egypt, were bound together in a religious and political community. The text of that covenant is the Decalogue. Since a covenant is essentially a promissory oath, it is only in this way that a social group could be made responsible to new obligation."[12]

Law

By *law* I mean the existing body of customary judicial precedents—the so-called "just laws" in the Mesopotamian tradition—that reflect "what might be called the sense of justice in a community,"[13] along with the community's traditions of law court procedures that state that the ideals of justice enshrined by the community are actually applied in specific situations. This latter, Mendenhall calls "techniques."[14] I am speaking, in other words, of the combination of the "constitution" and the "case law." By *codification* I mean the promulgation by a king or prophet of the "policy and techniques"—the laws—of restoring and building temples as part of a covenant ceremony.[15]

State Formations and Law Code Origins

In each ancient tradition a first promulgation typically occurs early in the history of that particular society. Subsequent "state renewal" covenant ceremonies at the temple will promulgate new laws but will also repromulgate the old, hallowed, canonical tradition. This is brought out most clearly in the Israelite tradition through a consideration of the first promulgation at the mountain through Moses, with subsequent renewals recorded under Joshua, Solomon, and Josiah, and during the time of Ezra. We are dealing in these instances with very different polities, in the technical sense, and can thus see that the temple ideology persists over time at different stages of political development/evolution.

> The central position of temple building/rebuilding/restoring in the royal inscriptions of the kings of ancient Western Asia is well known. In general, the pattern for these kingdoms would seem to be similar, a pattern that would also fit the Israelite state under Solomon:

the state is not necessarily fully formed immediately upon the accession to kingship of a given charismatic figure. As with Israel in the time of David, state formation began in that time, but it was not finalized until the reign of his successor. Further, the process of temple building/rebuilding/restoring does not necessarily take up the king's main attention in the first year or two of his reign. If we may take the Babylonian year names as an example of this, in most cases the first few years were taken up with building/rebuilding walls, defeating remaining enemies, and in general solidifying control over the kingdom. Then, in the case of Sumuabum, the first king of the First Dynasty of Babylon, for example, it is the fourth year that bears a name connected with temple building; in the case of his successor, Sumulael, it is the seventh; in the case of his successor Sabium, the eighth; in the case of Hammurapi, it is the third.[16]

Law Codes and Temples

In connecting the promulgation of the law codes with the building of temples, we should consider the ancient Near Eastern king's or prophet's role as a "righter of wrongs." The core of social legislation in the ancient Near East is expressed by Hammurapi in the Epilogue: help the widow, right wrongs, etc. Indeed, this pattern goes back in attested form to Urukagina, who gives us "our first evidence of the king's right, at the beginning of his reign, to issue a set of decrees—often abrogating existing traditional law—aimed at righting social wrongs."[17] It was this that the king (or the prophet, in the case of Moses, but recall that "Moses is to a great extent depicted in royal categories"[18]) decreed in the temple, or it was this that he received as a result of incubation, visitation, revelation, etc.[19] The "law codes" are an elaboration of this motif.

The true nature of the codes is spelled out at the

moment of revelatory expression following the exit of the king/prophet from the temple: do justice, protect the widow and orphan. It would be after this that royal scribes would elaborate the revelatory utterances, along with the central core of the received tradition, into a full-fledged code. The king's essential role can be understood by the phrase "righter of wrongs." Law, or the "royal judgments," as F. R. Kraus characterizes the Code of Hammurapi, is a natural extension of this essential role;[20] law comes into being at its implementation.

I suggest the following as the succession of events early in the history of a society that gives us what we commonly designate *law*. The king/prophet ascends to leadership over a community that is at one of the well-defined stages of political development; he issues a decree (the *mišarum* in Babylonia, the *yāšar* in Israel), an interim legislation showing him to be a "king of justice," having "done justice in the eyes of *YHWH*." Of course, in the meantime society continues much as before on the basis of law already decreed by earlier kings and on the basis of the jurisprudence built on common law. Next, the king builds, renovates, or rededicates the main temple of his city, at which time the fuller version of the laws is decreed and elaborated into a stele by royal scribes. In the case of Hammurapi's code, we must distinguish between the prologue and epilogue and the laws themselves, both of which might have been constructed by different sets of scribes, working under different stylistic and religious/political directives.[21] Again, the issuance of the *mišarum* decree (usually in the first full year of the Babylonian king)[22] and the building of the temple do not occur in the same year. But, as I have stated, we are dealing with a process that sees the gradual development of the community into a full-fledged formation during the first several years of its existence.

Even though it is not possible to associate explicitly the promulgation of law with the building of a temple, the two are definitely closely associated in the Gudea Cylinders, the Code of Urukagina, and the Code of Hammurapi.[23] The origin of law and of legal traditions must be sought in a ritual setting. More importantly, *law is introduced and mediated ritually* in a temple setting. Failure to understand the full implications of this fact has led occidental scholarship into the trap of animosity toward the temple.[24] A glance at the scene illustrating the stele on which the Code of Hammurapi is inscribed, and at statements in its prologue, clearly illustrates this point. Certainly, this association of law and temple is the message the majority of the ancient Near Eastern community that actually saw the stele would have received. According to J. Klima, because the majority of the population were illiterate, what they would have taken away from a view of the stele could have been the scene showing Hammurapi receiving the sceptre of authority from Šamaš.[25]

Of course, it is also necessary to point out here another important fact learned from the stele of the Code of Hammurapi: the temple legitimizes authority. This is also the case with Moses and with other Israelite leaders, such as Solomon and Josiah. As Mendenhall has expressed it, the temple is "the ritual functioning system that establishes the connection between deity and king."[26]

The Sinai Experience

The primary example of what I am trying to demonstrate comes from the Sinai experience (see Exodus 19–25). Even though there is no political state at Sinai, we nevertheless find that what I call the temple ideology is central to that society's functioning. While I will not go into the problem of dating per se, I will focus on seven motifs found in the Sinai narratives, motifs that I think can justifiably be shown to be early, probably dating back to the time of Moses himself and to the Sinai experience.[27] It does not matter that the Sinai covenant lacks treaty curses, or even that it possibly lacks the historical prologue.[28] We are not dealing here with the treaty covenant at all, but with the temple covenant system that founds and legitimizes the state.[29]

I would even predict that the treaty-covenant form is secondary to and derived from the temple covenant system. The motifs are the mountain, law, covenant, pillars, sacrifice, covenant meal, and cosmic sanctuary. The evidence produced here from the ritual/belief systems of Israel's neighbors is not introduced to "prove" that any one of such customs or their totality provides us with an "origin" of a similar practice in the Sinai narratives or elsewhere in the Hebrew Bible. I have attempted elsewhere to delineate a common ancient Near Eastern temple ideology[30] and here simply attempt to further demonstrate ancient Israel's participation in that ideology.

Mountains

To begin with, natural mountains serve as symbols of, and in fact are, sacred places to which kings and prophets go to receive instruction from deities. According to Kurt Bittel, "Mountains . . . were considered, from early Hittite times onwards, to be the place where the deities were believed to be present, and where special ceremonies devoted to their worship were performed."[31] It did not particularly matter whether there were actual structures built on the mountains. In some cases the Hittite inscriptions specifically state that once the king arrived at the location, a tent was constructed in which the king would carry out a ritual in front of a *ḫuwaši*-stone.[32] Thus the king or prophet ascends the mountain to carry out ritual obligations and, in the thesis developed here, to commune with deity. What is the content of the communication? It is law.

That the content of the revelation received on the mountain is law is shown in several sources. The clearest expression of this concept appears in the Code of Hammurapi. The prologue to the Code is virtually one continuous litany of Hammurapi's temple-related bequests, cleansings, rebuildings, and rededications. The Hammurapi stele depicts Hammurapi standing before Šamaš in a clearly ritual setting, receiving the tokens of authority; this indicates that the Babylonian scribes compiled the laws of the Code, as well as the prologue and epilogue, in the chief temple complex of Babylon, Esagila.

Law and Sacred Mountains

The chief evidence for the proposition that law originates in the temple or on the sacred mountain is the Sinai account itself. Moses ascends the mountain amid extensive ritual preparations by the people waiting below. The content of the revelation received by Moses on the mountain is law. These laws serve as the foundation pattern by which the society will live for many generations. Even though that society undergoes political transformations, the original promulgation of revealed law in the temple serves as the basis for future developments. Let us consider four well-attested instances of recovenanting in a temple setting in Israelite society: Joshua 24, Solomon's prayer of dedication of the Jerusalem temple, Josiah's covenant at the conclusion of the reform, and the recovenanting of Jews returned from

Babylonian exile in the time of Ezra. In each of these cases, the people were recovenanted in a temple setting, but no new law was promulgated. Why? Because the code of Sinai, which had been revealed by deity in a temple setting, was still the religious and social basis of the society.

As part of the system I call state renewal, covenant ceremonies were carried out yearly at the New Year's festival when the temple was cleansed and rededicated. The state would be renewed during this time, and a new covenant would be enacted. The king would go into the temple, but a new set of laws would not be revealed; the old set would be repromulgated. The juristic content of each covenant ceremony is generally evident, but in some cases, as in 1 Kings 8:55–66, the legal content is very ambiguous.

Codification and the Temple

Codification, by which I mean the promulgation of the ideals of justice of a given society within the context of temple building, refurbishing, or dedication, cannot be properly understood outside of this ritual setting. Law itself, of course, encompassing customary law, simply exists, with no identifiable origin in historical times. But the ancient community's concept of justice is formally enthroned within that community through a temple covenant ceremony. It is in this sense that law cannot be said to exist outside of an ordered, cosmic community. A community is made cosmic through the foundation of the temple. The elaborate ritual, architectural, and building traditions that lie behind temple construction and dedication are what allow the authoritative, validating transformation of a set of customary laws into a code.[33]

The temple creates law and makes law possible. It allows for the transformation of a chaotic universe into a

Figure 37. In this detail of an eighteenth-century Tibetan painting of the birth of the Buddha, he is shown, after having emerged from his mother's side, pointing to heaven above and the earth beneath. The small lotus flowers at his feet indicate his first footsteps to the four cardinal directions, confirming that he is the sacred center and that his influence extends everywhere. The gods Indra and Brahman wait to wash, anoint, and wrap him in white cloth.

cosmos. It is the very capstone of universal order and by logic and definition creates the conditions under which law is possible. This connection is brought out most dramatically in a tradition that may turn out to be not far removed from that of the ancient Near Eastern states, namely Hinduism.[34] According to Hindu traditions, the most important ritual action performed at the temple building site just before the metaphysical plan is laid out on the ground is the levelling of the ground. The process of levelling the ground by the king—repeated by each new temple

Figure 38. A bronze relief from the Balawat gates shows Shalmeneser III making a pilgrimage to the source of the Tigris in the midst of the mountains and erecting a stele to commemorate his accomplishment.

builder—is seen as establishing order itself in the world. According to one tradition, the Buddha, "as soon as born, stepped forth upon the earth and beneath his steps [seen as achieving the process of levelling], the earth lay smooth and even, for by his footfalls the Law (*dharma*) was carried throughout the world and became universal. The leveled earth became its substratum."[35] In this instance, the ritual preparation of the temple site is seen as the means of cosmicizing the world, at which point law immediately comes into existence.

Covenant and Pillars

The concept of covenant, as it exists in the Sinai narratives and in many other ancient settings, must be expanded to include the pillar. Covenant ceremonies are carried out at

Figure 39. In this mural from Mari, Ishtar-of-the-Palace gives the rod and ring to King Zimri-Lin in the innermost Holy of Holies, below which is depicted the outer chamber with water goddesses purifying the participants. These rooms are flanked by sacred trees and cherubim.

temples in front of stone or wooden pillars. "Covenants are sealed in temples or near pillars standing near temples, and thus they derive their binding efficacy on the ancient society from the temple's authoritative, legitimizing position within the society."[36]

One important type of pillar, the previously mentioned *ḫuwaši*-stone, played a significant role in Hittite religion. One instance, for example, records that after arriving at the mountain and setting up his tent the king, "attended by his servants," performed "a ritual in an ordinary way, culminating in a libation in front of a *ḫuwaši*-stone."[37] According to O. R. Gurney, "In most cult-centers the deity had a stela or *ḫuwaši*-stone set up not only in his temple but also in a locality outside the town, in the open country, usually by a grove or a spring, or on a mountain."[38] Numerous texts

depict the sacrifice of animals and the sharing of a communal meal at these stones.[39]

Pillars are known to have been associated with temples
in Mesopotamia and Palestine since at least Chalcolithic
times.[40] It is probable that the practice of erecting bronze
pillars, as in Jerusalem, developed from the practice of
erecting wooden pillars that were sheathed with bronze.
We have examples of this practice in the Gudea inscriptions and at Khorsabad.[41] The bronze pillars thus represent the ubiquitous trees of life that flank temple entrances
and that border scenes of temple ritual (Khorsabad in the
former case, Mari in the latter).[42] Like the *djed* pillar in
Egyptian architecture,[43] the pillar symbolizes strength,
solidity, binding efficacy, endurance, continuity, and cosmic
order.

The pillar must play the same legitimizing role that I
have described for the temple itself. The process of state
renewal in Israel, which is, after all, what the covenant-
making process is in the period of the Monarchy, derived its
power from the temple. The pillar symbolizes the sanctity within which the state envelops itself. The king or the
prophet enters the temple (or ascends the mountain);
the law is revealed to him there; he is given the tablets of
the law (or the "tablets of the decrees" in Mesopotamia—
see the expositions of this point, as it relates to Mesopotamian and Israelite traditions, by Widengren and Jacobsen[44]); he then returns to a ritually prepared community and
writes the law in some form. In the case of historical
temples, the pillars would already stand as part of the
temple construction. In the case of the "primordial" experience at Sinai, Moses erected pillars in front of which he
brought the people under covenant.[45]

Animal Sacrifice

The next point that is central to the Sinai experience (Exodus 24:5–8), and to temple ritual in general, is animal sacrifice. Animals are as ubiquitous a feature of temple symbolism as trees of life and waters of life.[46] Animals flank the trees of life not only in the famous Mari temple reliefs but also on the facades of the Khorsabad temples. The bloody sacrifice of animals in connection with temples/ shrines is so ancient and so widespread that it requires little further documentation here. In the great inner Asian hiero-centric states, people would come from all over the empire to the great yearly rites, driving herds of tribute animals before them.[47] A visit to a temple, as the facades on the Khorsabad temples imply, means bringing, or having supplied, animals for sacrifice. The purpose of the sacrifice is to seal and to sanctify the covenant. Gurney translates a most interesting Hittite text, roughly contemporary with the historically attested aspects of the Sinai narratives, in which the themes of blood sacrifice, covenant, and covenant meal are conjoined:

> They lead in a goat and the master of the house consecrates the goat in front of the table to Sanda with wine. Then he holds out a bronze axe and says: "Come, Sanda, and let the Violent Gods come with you, who are clothed in blood-stained garments and girt with the cords (?) of Lulahhi men, who have a dagger in the belt, draw bows and hold arrows. Come and eat! And we will take the oath." When he has finished speaking he puts the bronze axe down on the table and they slaughter the goat. He takes the blood and smears the drinking tube which is inserted into the tankard with the blood. They bring the raw liver and the heart and the master of the house offers them to the god and takes a bite. They do an imitation (?).

Then he puts his lip to the tube and sips and says:
"Behold, Sanda and Violent Gods, we have taken oath.
Since we have bitten the raw liver and drunk from one (?)
tube, therefore Sanda and Violent Ones, do not again
approach my gate." Then they cook the liver and the
heart with fire and cut up all the rest of the goat. . . . He
takes the shoulder and breast. . . . Then they surround the
table and eat up the shoulder and breast. Then [just as
they wish (?)] to eat and drink, so he brings, and they eat
[up (?) . . .] and they drink [. . .] the tankard.[48]

Gurney states that this text "is the clearest expression of
the belief in the efficacy of this solemn rite" (that is, "killing
an animal to sanctify a covenant or treaty").[49] The conjunction of animal sacrifice and temple for the Akkad period is
found at the north Syrian site of Tel Chuera and, in strikingly similar pictorial fashion, on the White Obelisk of
Assurnasirpal I. In the former case, the excavations uncovered, from in front of the Akkad period Nord-Tempel, evidence of an offertory stairway at the east entrance. Found
near the stairway were what appear to be an offering table
and an adjacent *Wanne*, which would have received the
blood of the offerings.[50] The White Obelisk, from a time
period much closer to that of Moses, shows an elaborate
cult installation in front of a pillared temple before which a
lowing bovine is being led to the slaughter. This latter sacrifice was performed by Assurbanipal at the *bīt Naṭḥi* of the
temple of Ishtar in Niniveh.[51]

It has sometimes been the practice among scholars to
look at recent Bedouin customs to explain the origins and
meaning of animal sacrifice in connection with covenant
making in the Hebrew Bible. However, the practice of sacrificing animals in front of temples as part of covenant ceremonies is extremely ancient, as my examples show.

The Covenant Meal

The covenant meal of Exodus 24:9–11, seen by many scholars as an alternative and editorially distinct mode of covenant sealing, is seen by E. W. Nicholson as an integral part of the entire ceremony of Exodus 24:3–8.[52] And indeed, as the previously quoted Hittite text shows, communal meals are an integral part of temple-related covenant ceremonies, being the final installment in the whole process. Again, one need not look to recent Bedouin customs for an explanation of this practice. It is extremely ancient and widespread. The temple ritual described in the Gudea Cylinders ends with a festive meal and the fixing of the destinies for the coming year. The *Akītu* festival in Babylon was concluded by an extraordinary sacrificial meal attended by both gods and people. The annual temple rededicatory festival in Egypt during the Greco-Roman period was concluded by a communal meal, as was the dedicatory festival at the New Year in Jerusalem in the time of Solomon.

Given the inherent aspect of secrecy in the ancient world in relation to temple ceremony, the covenant meal was the one instance, in many cases, in which common people could be present and actually partake of the blessings of renewal that the temple ceremonies promised.[53] In the context of Exodus 24, we have a people, formerly unsanctified (Exodus 19) and unqualified to enter the presence of deity, now ritually sanctified and covenanted on the basis of the revealed law and permitted to attend a sacral meal in the deity's presence.

The Cosmic Sanctuary

Finally, the concept of the cosmic sanctuary, of which the earthly sanctuary is but a patterning (Exodus 25:8), is central to the thesis presented here. Only such a sanctuary, built after the cosmic model, can properly serve as the locus of a legitimizing covenant system. Central to temple covenant systems all over the ancient Near East is the idea that the temple plan is revealed to the king or the prophet by deity. Again, many examples could be enumerated. Gudea of Lagash was visited in a dream in a temple of Lagash and shown the plan of the temple by a goddess, who gave him a lapis lazuli tablet on which the plan of the temple was written. Perhaps the best example of this aspect of temple building is the Sinai episode itself, in which, according to D. N. Freedman, "this heavenly temple or sanctuary with its throne room or holy of holies where the deity was seated on his cherubim throne constituted the *tabnīt* or structure seen by Moses during his sojourn on the same mountain, cf. Exodus 25:8."[54] Likewise at Ras Shamra, where, according to F. M. Cross, "Ba'l founded his temple on Mount Ṣapon in order to make manifest his establishment of order, especially kingship among the gods. The earthly temple of Ba'l manifested not only Ba'l's creation of order, but at the same time established the rule of the earthly king."[55]

Thus order cannot exist, the earth cannot be made cosmic, society cannot function properly, law cannot be decreed, except in a temple established on earth that is the authentic and divinely revealed counterpart of a heavenly prototype. As J. Z. Smith has written so cogently for the *Enuma Elish*, it is "not so much a cosmogony as it is a myth of the creation of a temple."[56] It is the creation of the temple, with its cosmic overtones, that founds and legitimizes the state or the society, which, in turn, makes possible the formal promulgation of law. Once promulgated in the ritual manner described, the law serves as the text of a covenant process carried out in front of the temple's pillars, accompanied by animal sacrifice and a communal meal. All these features, so characteristic of ancient Near Eastern temple practice from earliest times, are embedded within the earliest traditions of Late Bronze Age community formation in biblical Israel.

The Temple and the Prophetic Future

Given the sanctity and the authority of the temple and its legal system, which were revealed by YHWH to Moses on Sinai, we should not be surprised to find that the temple system is an integral part of prophetic Israel's view of the future. This is revealed most clearly in Ezekiel's temple vision of Ezekiel 40–48. Moshe Greenberg, in his recent study of this section of Ezekiel, sees the importance of its temple centeredness in, among other things, his "lofty conception of a prophet's responsibility in an age of ruin."[57] At the moment of greatest ruin, of deepest despair, "the hand of the Lord came upon me and brought me in divine visions to the land of Israel, where he sat me down on a very high mountain" (Ezekiel 40:1–2, New American Bible). And thus we enter again the realm of the temple ideology that I have attempted to explicate.

Similarly, Qumran, a community that viewed itself as authoritative Israel, held at its communal heart a divinely revealed, temple-centered legal system, complete with the plan of an idealized future temple.[58]

Notes

1. See David Noel Freedman, "Temple without Hands," in *THPBT*, 21–30.

2. See my articles "The Legitimizing Role of the Temple in the Origin of State," in this volume, *Temples of the Ancient World*, 151–206; "What Is a Temple? A Preliminary Typology," in this volume, 76–97; and "The Common Temple Ideology of the Ancient Near East," in Truman G. Madsen, ed., *The Temple in Antiquity* (Provo: BYU Religious Studies Center, 1984), 53–76.

3. See Lundquist, "Legitimizing Role of the Temple," 153–55.

4. See Lundquist, "What Is a Temple?" 76–97.

5. Kent V. Flannery, "The Cultural Evolution of Civilizations," *Annual Review of Ecology and Systematics* 3 (1972): 399–426.

6. Folker Willesen, "The Cultic Situation of Psalm LXXIV," *Vetus Testamentum* 2 (1952): 289–306.

7. See Jon D. Levenson, "From Temple to Synagogue: I Kings 8," in *Traditions in Transformation, Turning Points in Biblical Faith,* ed. Baruch Halpern and Jon D. Levenson (Winona Lake, Indiana: Eisenbrauns, 1981), 146–66.

8. See Baruch Halpern, "The Ritual Background of Zechariah's Temple Song," *Catholic Biblical Quarterly* 40 (1978): 167–90.

9. George E. Mendenhall, "The Monarchy," *Interpretation* 29 (1975): 159.

10. Lundquist, "Legitimizing Role of the Temple," 153.

11. Roy Rappaport, "The Obvious Aspects of Ritual," in *Ecology, Meaning and Religion* (Richmond, Virginia: North Atlantic Books, 1979), 193, 199.

12. George E. Mendenhall, "Ancient Oriental and Biblical Law," *Biblical Archaeologist* 17, no. 2 (May 1954): 28.

13. See F. R. Kraus, "Ein zentrales Problem des altmesopotamischen Rechtes: Was ist der Codex Hammu-rabi?" *Genava* 8 (1960): 283–96.

14. Mendenhall, "Ancient Oriental and Biblical Law," 26.

15. See ibid., 32–38; Kraus, "Ein zentrales Problem des altmesopotamischen Rechtes," 283–96; J. Klima, "Gesetze," *Reallexikon der Assyriologie* 3 (1966): 243–55; Jorgen Laessoe, "On the Fragments of the Hammurapi Code," *Journal of Cuneiform Studies* 4 (1950): 173–87; J. J. Finkelstein, "Ammisaduqa's Edict and the Babylonian Law Codes," *Journal of Cuneiform Studies* 15 (1961): 91–104.

16. Lundquist, "Legitimizing Role of the Temple," 175–76.

17. Thorkild Jacobsen, *Toward the Image of Tammuz and Other Essays on Mesopotamian History and Culture,* ed. William L. Moran (Cambridge: Harvard University Press, 1970), 150–51.

18. Ivan Engnell, *Studies in Divine Kingship in the Ancient Near East* (Uppsala: 1943), 174, as quoted in Arvid S. Kapelrud, "Temple Building, a Task for Gods and Kings," *Orientalia* 32 (1963): 61.

19. Note Gudea in Cylinder A.XII–XIII, following the revelation to him in a dream; Hammurapi in Esagila, as expressed in the prologue and the epilogue to the Code of Hammurapi; Moses on Sinai; Solomon in his dedicatory prayer. In Gudea Cylinder B.XVIII, we read that his work was carried out "according to the decrees of Nana and Ningirsu."

20. Kraus, "Ein zentrales Problem des altmesopotamischen Rechtes."

21. See D. J. Wiseman, "The Laws of Hammurapi Again," *Journal of Semitic Studies* 7 (1962): 162, 168; Klima, "Gesetze"; Jacobsen, *Toward the Image of Tammuz*.

22. See Finkelstein, "Ammisaduqa's Edict and the Babylonian Law Codes," 91–104.

23. See Lundquist, "What Is a Temple?" 87–88; Samuel N. Kramer, *The Sumerians: Their History, Culture and Character* (Chicago: University of Chicago Press, 1963); *ANET*, 165, 178.

24. See Mendenhall, "Monarchy," 155–70; Hugh W. Nibley, "Christian Envy of the Temple," *Jewish Quarterly Reviews* 50 (1959–60): 97–123, 229–40, reprinted in *Mormonism and Early Christianity*, in *CWHN*, 4:391–434.

25. See Klima, "Gesetze," 244.

26. Quoted in Lundquist, "Legitimizing Role of the Temple," 160.

27. See E. W. Nicholson, "Covenant Ritual in Exodus 24:3–8," *Vetus Testamentum* 32 (1982): 74–86; Frank Moore Cross, "The Priestly Tabernacle in the Light of Recent Research," in *THPBT*, 169–80; James P. Hyatt, *Exodus, New Century Bible Commentary* (Grand Rapids, Michigan: Eerdmans, 1980); Mendenhall, "Ancient Oriental and Biblical Law."

28. See George E. Mendenhall, "Covenant Forms in Israelite Tradition," *Biblical Archaeologist* 17, no. 3 (September 1954): 59–61; Dennis J. McCarthy, *Treaty and Covenant*, rev. ed. (Rome: Biblical Institute, 1978), 248–50.

29. See Moshe Weinfeld, "Berîth," in G. Johannes Botterweck and Helmer Ringgren, eds., *Theological Dictionary of the Old Testament* (Grand Rapids: Eerdmans, 1974–), 2:266.

30. See Lundquist, "Common Temple Ideology," 53–76.

31. "Hittite Temples and High Places," in *THPBT*, 66.

32. See ibid.

33. See Lundquist, "Legitimizing Role of the Temple," 151–206.

34. See Karl-Heinz Golzio, *Der Tempel im alten Mesopotamien und seine Parallelen in Indien* (Leiden: Brill, 1983).

35. Stella Kramrisch, *The Hindu Temple* (Delhi: Motilal Banarsidass, 1976), 1:16–17.

36. See Lundquist, "Legitimizing Role of the Temple," 190–91.

37. Bittel, "Hittite Temples and High Places," 66.

38. *Some Aspects of Hittite Religion* (Oxford: Oxford University Press, 1977), 27.

39. See ibid., 27–28, 36–38.

40. See Claire Epstein, "Aspects of Symbolism in Chalcolithic Palestine," in Roger Moorey and Peter Parr, eds., *Archaeology in the Levant, Essays for Kathleen Kenyon* (Warminster, England: Aris and Phillips, 1978), 29.

41. See Lundquist, "Legitimizing Role of the Temple," 31 n. 112, 32 n. 139, 32 n. 144; H. York, "Heiliger Baum," *Reallexikon der Assyriologie* 4 (1975): 274.

42. See Lundquist, "Common Temple Ideology"; Yasin M. Al-Khalesi, *The Court of the Palms: A Functional Interpretation of the Mari Palace,* ed. Giorgio Buccellati (Malibu, California: Undena, 1978); York, "Heiliger Baum," 274.

43. See William F. Albright, *Archaeology and the Religion of Israel,* 5th ed. (Garden City, New York: Doubleday, 1968), 143.

44. See *AAHB,* 7–21; Thorkild Jacobsen, *The Treasures of Darkness* (New Haven: Yale University Press, 1976), 178–79.

45. See Carol L. Meyers, "Jachin and Boaz in Religious and Political Perspective," *Catholic Biblical Quarterly* 45 (1983): 167–78.

46. See Lundquist, "What Is a Temple?" 88; Lundquist, "Common Temple Ideology."

47. See Hugh Nibley, "The Hierocentric State," *Western Polistical Quarterly* 4 (1951): 226–53, reprinted in *The Ancient State,* in *CWHN,* 10:99–147.

48. As quoted in Gurney, *Some Aspects of Hittite Religion,* 29–30.

49. Ibid., 30.

50. See Anton Moortgat, *Tell Chuera in Nordost Syrien* (Köln: Westdeutscher Verlag, 1962).

51. See J. E. Reade, "Assurnasirpal I and the White Obelisk," *Iraq* 37 (1975): 129–50.

52. See "Covenant Ritual in Exodus 24:3–8," 85.

53. See Lundquist, "What Is a Temple?" 86.

54. Freedman, "Temple without Hands," 174.

55. Cross,"Priestly Tabernacle in the Light of Recent Research," 174.

56. J. Z. Smith, *Map Is Not Territory* (Leiden: Brill, 1978), 99.

57. Moshe Greenberg, "The Design and Themes of Ezekiel's Program of Restoration," *Interpretation* 38 (1984): 208.

58. See Ben Zion Wacholder, "The Dawn of Qumran: 11Q Temple and the Teacher of Righteousness," *Society of Biblical Literature 1980 Abstracts,* ed. Charles E. Winquist and Paul J. Achtemeier (Chico, California: Scholars, 1980), #S111; Daniel R. Schwartz, "The Three Temples of 4Q Florilegium," *Revue de Qumran* 37 (1979): 83–91.

PART 4

The Temple in the Book of Mormon and Ancient America

12

The Temple in the Book of Mormon: The Temples at the Cities of Nephi, Zarahemla, and Bountiful

John W. Welch

Temples were important throughout the ancient world, more so than most people realize. When wandering through the archaeological remains and perusing written records of those often spectacular sacred buildings, modern secular people are disadvantaged in trying to comprehend the devotion and awe that ancient people must have felt toward their temples, whether in Mesopotamia, the Mediterranean, or Mesoamerica. Ancient civilizations dedicated their scarcest public resources to the extensive tasks of building, furnishing, and operating the beautiful temples that dominated the central precincts of so many of their lands and cities. Those buildings were not only viewed as "the one point on earth at which men and women could establish contact with higher spheres,"[1] but they also "represented stability and cohesiveness in the community, and their rites and ceremonies were viewed as essential to the proper functioning of the society."[2] Public veneration at every holy place was freely offered by the faithful, who gathered often at the temple for religious instruction, coronations, sacrifices, and other sacred rites and crucial functions. Meanwhile, death threats were posted to protect the sanctity of ancient temples against improper intruders.[3]

Evidence in the Book of Mormon indicates that temples were equally important among the Nephites, both in their religion and in their society. Prominent on the landscape of each of the three successive Nephite capital cities of Nephi, Zarahemla, and Bountiful was a temple, probably one of the most important structures in town. These temples functioned as meeting places; there the domain of the king met the sphere of the priest, and worshipers assembled, made contact with divine powers, and learned the mysteries of God. Although we have little direct information about the design of temples in the Book of Mormon or the rituals performed in them, the scriptures give strong clues about those teachings and ordinances, leaving little doubt that temples were the site of many key events in Nephite civilization and in their worship of the Lord Jesus Christ. In or at the temple, Nephite kings were crowned, religious teachings were dispensed, and the plan of salvation was taught; there the people were exhorted to proper behavior, sacrifices symbolizing the atonement of Christ were performed, and religious and legal covenants were made and renewed. Fittingly, the Book of Mormon story culminates as the resurrected Jesus appeared at the temple.

Besides culturally binding the Nephites together, the temple also shaped and unified their outlook on the world. The sacred activities performed at the temple preserved, embodied, and perpetuated the historical roots of Nephite beliefs and practices in ancient Israel's past. At the same time, they symbolized and looked forward to the presence of Jesus Christ, the Son of God. Thus the temple unified past, present, and future.

Ancient temples also combined the realms of God and

man, the immortal and the mortal, the eternal and the temporal, the reign of God and the rules of society. Modern observers should remember that the separation of church and state is largely an artificial boundary that is predominantly a modern construct. In the ancient Near East, the concepts of king and prophet, palace and temple, secular law and divine commandment were close companions, if not synonymous concepts;[4] and the same condition appears to have existed among the early Nephites (see, for example, Omni 1:19–20; Words of Mormon 1:17; Mosiah 2:31; 5:5; 11:9–10).

In an effort to better understand the role of such temples in the Book of Mormon, this article employs a variety of tools, procedures, and resources, both ancient and modern, historical and revealed. It assumes that temples were as important to the Nephites as they were to most advanced societies in antiquity, and it rejects modern tendencies that marginalize sacred things in general and temples in particular. This article attempts to examine every reference to temples in the Book of Mormon, in order to glean subtle information from those verses and their contexts. In doing this, I have tried especially to understand words and motifs as a Nephite might have understood them, staying alert to the possibility that temple allusions may be found even in simple words and phrases.

This quest has necessarily led me into the study of many parts of the law of Moses. As difficult as it may be for casual modern readers to see, many Jews consider Leviticus to be the most sacred book in scripture—and for good reason when one looks below the surface to its underlying religious themes. But comparing and relating biblical information about the law of Moses to the temple in the Book of Mormon raises many questions: What do we know about the temple under the law of Moses, particularly as it existed during Lehi's day in 600 B.C.? How did the Nephites understand and apply the provisions in the law of Moses relating to the temple? Did they keep all of that law, or only some of it? What changes occurred in the law and the temple during various stages in the history of the Nephites—changes not in the eternal aspects of the gospel, but changes in certain practices, priestly and ecclesiastical organization, and emphasis?

In this research, I have also attempted to relate each reference to the temple in the Book of Mormon to its primary mission, namely the convincing of Jew and Gentile that Jesus is the Christ. Well is the Book of Mormon subtitled "Another Testament of Jesus Christ," for on its pages are the covenants and teachings of Christ. Significantly, the most sacred presentations of those doctrines in the Book of Mormon are often associated with the temple.

To shed further light on these topics, my analysis turns ultimately to the doctrinal texts that typically surround references to the temple in the Book of Mormon. I call these texts "temple texts," and I find that they hold important clues to understanding the temple in the Book of Mormon as well as the gospel of Jesus Christ.

I define a "temple text" as one that contains the most sacred teachings of the plan of salvation that are not to be shared indiscriminately, and that ordains or otherwise conveys divine powers through ceremonial or symbolic means, together with commandments received by sacred oaths that allow the recipient to stand ritually in the presence of God. Several such texts are found in the Book of Mormon. In addition to the text of Ether 1–4 regarding the brother of Jared,[5] the most notable are Jacob's speech in 2 Nephi 6–10,

Benjamin's speech in Mosiah 1–6, Alma's words in Alma 12–13, and Jesus' teachings in 3 Nephi 11–18.

In this study, I have tried to remain open to the possibility of making connections, in both directions, between ancient and modern Latter-day Saint temple experiences. Several things in the temple texts of the Book of Mormon bear far more than an accidental similarity to the Latter-day Saint temple experience.

The discussion below is organized chronologically. It begins with a consideration of the religious setting out of which Lehi and Nephi came, particularly the law of Moses, sacrifice, and certain Israelite concepts that Lehi and Nephi would have understood and embraced in terms of their prophetic knowledge of the plan of redemption through the atonement of Jesus Christ. It then discusses the temple built by Nephi in the city of Nephi around 570 B.C. and compares it with other ancient Near Eastern temples and their functions. The concluding sections then examine the Nephite temples at Zarahemla and Bountiful. While it is possible to confidently draw several conclusions about temples in the Book of Mormon, we still yearn for greater knowledge about these sacred places of Christian worship among the Nephites.

The Nephites, the Temple, and the Law of Moses

Part of the legacy brought by Lehi and Nephi to the New World was the law of Moses as contained on the plates of brass (see 1 Nephi 4:15; 5:11). Because many provisions in the law of Moses, as preserved in the Bible, pertain directly to the performance of certain sacrifices, observances, and ordinances in the house of the Lord, any study of the temple in the Book of Mormon must begin by saying something about the meanings of the law of Moses among the Nephites. This, however, is a difficult task, inviting further research and thought. To echo the sentiment of Robert Millet in this regard, we can "only wish that there were more and greater evidences"[6] to help us answer even a few of the many questions that surface when one tries to step back into the dispensation of Moses—who was one of the Lord's greatest spokesmen,[7] but also one of the most misunderstood.

The extent to which we may surmise that the Nephites observed the temple-related provisions of the law of Moses turns largely on how we understand Nephite attitudes toward the law of Moses in general. Since many factors and perspectives must be kept in mind in reaching even tentative conclusions, the following preliminaries are rather lengthy. But addressing the perennial question of how the Nephites understood the law of Moses sets the stage for any discussion of Nephite temples.

Strict Observance of the Law of Moses

Three Nephite statements explicitly attest that the Nephites were strict in keeping the law of Moses, and each of these statements sheds light on Nephite temple practices. Spanning the times of Nephi (sixth century B.C.), Jarom (fourth century B.C.), and Alma (first century B.C.), these statements connect the strict observance of the law of Moses with the building of the temple of Nephi, the observance of holy days, and the performance of the outward ordinances of the law of Moses.

As Nephi founded the city of Nephi and laid plans for building the temple there, he first affirmed that he and his people "did observe to keep the judgments, and the statutes, and the commandments of the Lord in all things, according to the law of Moses" (2 Nephi 5:10). Nephi's use of the traditional list *judgments, statutes, commandments,* and *law* recalls the words of King David's royal charge to his temple-building son Solomon: "Keep the charge of the Lord thy God, to walk in his ways, to keep his statutes, and his commandments, and his judgments, and his testimonies, as it is written in the law of Moses" (1 Kings 2:3).[8] Both Solomon and Nephi fulfilled this charge by keeping all the law of the Lord, which would have included its provisions regarding the building and operating of a temple of God (see Exodus 25–27; Deuteronomy 12:5–7; 1 Kings 5:3–5).

Second, two hundred years after Lehi left Jerusalem, Jarom similarly recorded that the Nephites still "observed to keep the law of Moses and the sabbath day holy unto the Lord. And they profaned not; neither did they blaspheme. And the laws of the land were exceedingly strict" (Jarom 1:5). Here we learn again that the Nephites were very diligent in keeping the law of Moses. They did not profane or blaspheme; that is, they did not speak or act in any way that would desecrate or make profane (worldly) anything that was holy, especially the name of God, the law, the temple, or its sacred space.[9]

Moreover, they observed the laws of the sabbath. While Jarom may have had in mind only the weekly sabbath, he may also have been speaking of the holy days such as Passover, Pentecost, and the Day of Atonement, for those days were also holy days under the law of Moses.[10] For example, assuming that a version of Leviticus 16 was found on the plates of brass, then the Nephites celebrated the Day of Atonement with its respective temple ordinances, for the law defined that day as "a sabbath of rest unto you" (Leviticus 16:31). The Day of Atonement was a sabbath no matter on what day of the week it fell. Although we cannot know for sure which holy days were considered sabbaths by Lehi or his posterity or how they observed them, Jarom's statement puts us on notice that the Nephites were strict in some way to observe each day that was a sabbath under their law, which most likely would have required the observance of certain temple-related holy days.

Third, more than three hundred years later, the Nephites were still living the law of Moses strictly. The account of the trial of Korihor in Alma 30 begins by mentioning two years of peace that were disrupted by his agitation. The record attributes that peace to the strict observance of the law: "There began to be continual peace throughout all the land. Yea, and the people did observe to keep the commandments of the Lord; and they were strict in observing the ordinances of God, according to the law of Moses; for they were taught to keep the law of Moses until it should be fulfilled" (Alma 30:2–3). This statement draws special attention to the fact that the Nephites kept not only the commandments (the general ethical portions of the law, such as the Ten Commandments), but that they also observed "the ordinances of God." Most likely those "ordinances" were the "outward performances" of the law of Moses, for on several occasions the writers of the Book of Mormon coupled the words "performances and ordinances" (2 Nephi 25:30; Mosiah 13:30; Alma 30:23; 4 Nephi 1:12), and those authors used these two words together to mean the "outward performances" of the law of Moses (Alma 25:15). Those ordinances were evidently the sacrifices and offerings that looked forward to and were fulfilled by and in the atoning sacrifice of Jesus Christ, for after the coming of Christ, the record states that the Nephites "did not walk any more after the performances and ordinances of the law of Moses; but they did walk after the commandments" given by the Lord (4 Nephi 1:12). Thus, I conclude that the word *ordinances*[11] in Alma 30:3 refers principally to the rules of blood sacrifices and burnt offerings that were expressly overruled by Jesus when he spoke from heaven in 3 Nephi 9:19.

The idea that the Nephites continued to observe the ritual ordinances and ceremonial performances of the law of Moses down to the coming of Christ is supported further by one of Korihor's allegations. Alma 30 tells how Korihor accused the Nephite church of teaching (and presumably observing) what he considered to be "foolish ordinances and performances which are laid down by ancient priests, to usurp power and authority over them" (v. 23). Korihor's derision is evidence that the Nephites observed the full range of ancient ordinances taught from the time of Adam to Moses, along with the priestly sacrificial portions of the law of Moses, which Korihor would have considered to be among the most "foolish" parts of Alma's ancient traditions. Korihor's words were probably critical of the higher mysteries taught by Alma according to the holy order of the Son of God (see Alma 12:9; 13:1–13), as well as of the performances of the sacrificial laws of the Pentateuch.

Details and Daily Sacrifice

In reading these texts from Nephi, Jarom, and Alma, we can easily see that the Nephites lived the ethical and eternal portions of the law of Moses. What remains uncertain, but crucial to our understanding of the Nephite temple, is the extent to which they followed the preexilic biblical laws regarding daily sacrifice and temple holy days.[12] Without speaking conclusively, Elder Bruce R. McConkie once wrote, "There is, at least, no intimation in the Book of Mormon that the Nephites offered the daily sacrifices required by the law or that they held the various feasts that were part of the religious life of their Old World kinsmen."[13] Because the Book of Mormon offers little evidence on this point, it is understandable how one might infer that the righteous Nephites did not use their temples in making daily sacrifices. However, four Book of Mormon passages link the Nephite observance of the law of Moses with the performance of sacrifice, one even implying daily sacrifice, all of which they understood as symbolizing the atoning sacrifice of Jesus Christ. Those four texts are as follows:

1. In describing the performances and ordinances of the law of Moses, Abinadi called it "a law which they were to observe strictly *from day to day*, to keep them in remembrance of God and their duty towards him" and as "types of things to come" (Mosiah 13:30–31; italics added). The phrase "from day to day" strongly suggests that the Nephites respected daily reminders and performances of the law of Moses. Nowhere does Abinadi hint that such daily performances were inappropriate, so long as they were correctly understood as symbols of Christ, of his support and mercy from day to day (cf. 2 Nephi 28:32; Mosiah 2:21; 4:24), of mankind's need to remember him from day to day (Alma 58:40), and of offering daily prayer (Psalms 86:3; 88:9; Mosiah 4:11; 21:10; Alma 31:10; 34:38). Abinadi accused Noah and his priests of many things. If the priests of Noah had not been attending to the appropriate daily requirements of the law, it is reasonable to assume that Abinadi would have raised that point against them, because he specifically acknowledged the need to observe the law daily, and the priests told Abinadi that they taught and lived that law (see Mosiah 12:28). Instead, Abinadi accused Noah and his priests of material excesses, idolatry, drunkenness, whoredom, and misunderstanding the spirit of the law of Moses, and he quoted the Ten Commandments to

them because they had violated those laws. As far as we know, however, Abinadi did not accuse wicked Noah of violating any other laws, and this suggests that Noah and his priests were at least going through the outward motions of observing those performances and ordinances.

2. King Benjamin's people brought the firstlings of their flocks to the temple to make sacrifices and burnt offerings (see Mosiah 2:3). That these were *firstlings* (i.e., firstborn male animals) further shows that these people took the details of the law of Moses seriously, for the law required the people to take their firstlings to the temple to be sacrificed (see Deuteronomy 12:5–6, 19–20). Since the days of Adam, such sacrifices symbolized the sacrifice of God's first and only begotten son (see Moses 5:5–8).

3. Amulek taught that the great and last sacrifice of Jesus would not be a sacrifice performed by man, "neither of *beast,* neither of any manner of *fowl*" (Alma 34:10; italics added). By mentioning beasts and fowl, Amulek encompassed the two legally acceptable categories of blood sacrifices designated in Leviticus 1, namely beasts taken from the herds of cattle or the flocks of sheep or goats of the person offering the sacrifice, and birds, specifically turtledoves or pigeons (see vv. 3–17). Grain offerings were allowed, but only as a substitute, "as the poor man's burnt offering . . . to duplicate the manifold purposes of the burnt offering for the benefit of those who cannot afford a burnt offering of a quadruped or bird."[14] Given Amulek's higher understanding of the infinite and eternal sacrifice that would be made by Jesus Christ, he obviously knew that the ultimate sacrifice yet to come would not be the kind prescribed by the law of Moses. But his words about animal sacrifice do not deprecate such offerings or indicate that the Nephites no longer made such sacrifices. Indeed, on the contrary, if the

Nephites no longer offered such sacrifices, it is unlikely that Amulek would have brought up this detail in speaking to his Zoramite audience who, only a short time earlier, had split from the Nephites precisely because the Zoramites refused to keep all the law of Moses (see Alma 31:9–10). Thus, if the Nephites themselves had abandoned the sacrifices just mentioned by Amulek, it is hard to imagine that his Zoramite opponents would not have used that point against him.

4. When the voice of Jesus spoke out of the darkness in 3 Nephi 9, he told the people, "*Ye* shall offer up unto me *no more* the shedding of blood; yea, *your* sacrifices and *your* burnt offerings shall be done away, for I will accept none of *your* sacrifices and *your* burnt offerings" (3 Nephi 9:19; italics added). These words imply that the surviving righteous Nephites had themselves offered such sacrifices, which had been fully accepted until the law of Moses was fulfilled in Christ.

Taken together with several other general facts (for example, Ammon's converts were taught to understand and keep the law of Moses in Alma 25:15–16; Nephi's Lamanite converts were likewise taught in Helaman 13:1; and the law was kept by the Nephites who believed the prophecies of Samuel in 3 Nephi 1:25), these references strongly indicate that the Nephites continued to observe the law of Moses in fine detail, including the performance of sacrifices at their temples.

Against this evidence, I find only Sherem's accusation. He claimed that Jacob had led the Nephites astray, so that they "keep not the law of Moses" (Jacob 7:7). How is this accusation to be understood in light of the testimonies of Nephi and Jarom that they did keep that law? Was Sherem telling the whole truth when he said that the Nephites did not keep the law? Probably not, since Sherem's stock in trade was misrepresentation and distortion. Moreover, if Sherem could have accused Jacob of neglecting any specific parts of the law of Moses, surely he would have pinpointed them; instead, he based his indictments on the vaguer allegations of blasphemy, false prophecy, and causing apostasy (see Jacob 7:7). So we may assume that Sherem's point was somewhat more subtle. Indeed, Sherem's objection arose not from the claim that Jacob had altered the outward practices or legal requirements of the law of Moses, but from the fact that Jacob had reinterpreted the law as pointing to Christ. That doctrine "convert[ed] the law of Moses into the worship of [Christ]" (Jacob 7:7). Clearly, the meaning and the object of Nephite worship had been changed, and Sherem objected to this, but there is no evidence that the rules or practices themselves had been altered. Ultimately we learn that Sherem's problem stemmed from his failure to understand that all prophets have spoken concerning Christ (see Jacob 7:11), which means that he would have raised the same objection against Isaiah, Hosea, or Jeremiah as he leveled against Jacob. Accordingly, Sherem's objections were based on theological, interpretative, or hermeneutical mistakes, not complaints about altered ceremonies or performances.

Law and Gospel

This is not the place to discuss many other features of the law of Moses that can be found behind the scenes in the Book of Mormon, but many such factors show that the Book of Mormon should be understood as both Jewish and Christian, not one or the other. The prophets of the Book of Mormon present a thoroughly Christian theology and religion against a background of ancient Israelite law and culture. In this regard, the following points are helpful in approaching Book of Mormon texts, which meld the law of Moses with the eternal gospel of Jesus Christ, as unnatural as that combination might appear to some.

First, we must cautiously and frequently remind ourselves that the law of Moses is not easy to understand. The moral rules and holy principles taught in Deuteronomy, for example, are extremely demanding and sanctifying. As Hugh Nibley concludes in his discussion of the profound demands of humility, generosity, and consecration required by Deuteronomy, "They are very special laws given to very special people. They are simply fantastic as far as the world is concerned. But that is just the point, says the Lord."[15]

Various branches of Judaism, ancient and modern, have struggled mightily and in good faith, between themselves and within themselves, to interpret and apply this extensive and detailed law. Their inquiries have generated thousands of books and articles, and still their quest goes on. The priests of Noah misunderstood it. Even the people of ancient Jerusalem, "did they understand the law?" (Mosiah 13:32). Abinadi says they did not, and many other ancient prophets like Abinadi tried to explain and teach the law. How much less should Gentiles expect to understand all the legal and religious significance of the law of Moses? Modern minds steeped in Western thought have a hard time understanding many sections in the law of Moses—a law that regulated virtually all aspects of life, from personal affairs to public interests, from commercial transactions to sacred religious duties. Having the fullness of the restored gospel helps in the most important respects, in that it reveals the broad purposes and ultimate meanings of the law as a whole; but having that kind of broad prophetic perspective can obscure the former significance of many details that are now obsolete and irrelevant in modern times. Caution should be exercised in this area of study.

Above all else, the Nephites clearly understood the gospel of Jesus Christ and the doctrines of the Messiah, but that understanding was superimposed on their observance of the law of Moses to give even further meaning to this already profoundly rich system of symbolism and religious devotion to the Holy One of Israel. Instead of abrogating the Israelite system, the Nephite understanding infused it with joy that brought its commandments more to life. Accordingly, it is important to allow room for all the ordinances of the law of Moses as well as the ceremonies of Christ's eternal gospel to operate concurrently in Nephite temples down to the coming of Christ.

Like the Nephites, many prophets in ancient Israel understood the gospel and correctly anticipated the coming atonement of Jesus Christ. Most leaders in Jerusalem and probably a substantial portion of the Israelite population around the time of Lehi, however, rejected or misunderstood those teachings. While they made the mistake of looking beyond the mark and missing the point of the law (see Jacob 4:14), readers today should not look short of the mark by underestimating the value of the law to the righteous souls who lived under it. Even something as seemingly mundane as the biblical dietary laws, when properly understood, comprise a powerful ethical and religious system that features consecration, fosters holiness, reverences life, eschews violence, and is viewed by Jews as making every home a temple.[16]

Those ancient Israelites who understood the gospel of Jesus Christ and who embraced and lived the higher order of the priesthood after the Son of God understood the performances and ordinances of the law of Moses in light of their knowledge of Christ. They realized that eternal salvation did not come through the sprinkling of the altar or walls of the temple with blood (which in the biblical world was believed to contain the spirit or life and thus was consecrated to God),[17] and like Abinadi they knew that salvation did not come "by the law alone" (Mosiah 13:28; see also 2 Nephi 25:23–27). They realized that the true covenant with the Holy One of Israel had to be written, not on tablets of stone, but in the hearts and lives of faithful, obedient people (see Jeremiah 31:33).

I see no reason, however, why such an ancient person should have been relieved of the duty to obey the law of Moses simply by realizing the ends of the law or by knowing the final goal of eternal life. It is not inconsistent for one who holds the higher priesthood to live concurrently the higher and the lower laws. Today, in the Church, the Aaronic Priesthood is bestowed on young men and on recent converts so that they may learn the principles of the gospel pertaining to the lower order of the priesthood, and Church leaders holding the highest keys of the holy priesthood teach and supervise the work of those holding the lower priesthood. Similarly, Nephite prophets holding the rights and powers of the higher priesthood would not act inconsistently or in a manner unbecoming to their higher spiritual standing if they were to fulfill both the higher and the lower orders of the priesthood that were in effect in their time. Nephi speaks clearly of the deadness of the law, but at the same time reaffirms the necessity of living and teaching the law (see 2 Nephi 25:25–27), and there is no evidence that this presented any awkwardness for the Nephites. They respected God's laws and obeyed them. They believed that only a wicked person like King Noah would change the law (see Mosiah 29:22–23). They rejoiced in the law, especially those portions of the law that most clearly typified Christ. Of all the provisions in the law of Moses, those dealing with the laws of sacrifice and the symbolic rituals of the temple, such as the scapegoat rite (see Leviticus 16) and the required eating of the passover lamb (see Exodus 12:3–10; 24:15; 34:18; Numbers 9:1–5), had the greatest potential for filling the minds and spirits of Nephite believers with meaningful conviction and certain testimony of the Messiah who was soon to come. The Nephites knew that obedience and remembrance were among the indelible principles of the gospel. Ample evidence likewise indicates that prophets such as Isaiah, Micah, Jeremiah,[18] and Ezekiel continued to observe and to honor the law of Moses without exception,[19] notwithstanding their clear prophetic knowledge of Jesus Christ.

It also appears that Jesus himself continued to observe the law of Moses until it was fulfilled. He was circumcised and presented at the temple of Jerusalem eight days after his birth; he was present in the temple at the age of twelve; he withstood the temptations of Satan by affirming that he would live by "every word that proceedeth out of the mouth of God" (Matthew 4:4), and nothing indicates that he excluded any of the laws of the Pentateuch from this statement (indeed, he quotes from Deuteronomy in rebuffing Satan).[20] Jesus traveled frequently with his disciples long distances to be present in Jerusalem at the time of such holy days as the Feast of Tabernacles (see John 7:2–3); he approved the observance of the minutiae of the law but reminded people not to neglect the "weightier matters of the law" (Matthew 23:23); he not only healed the leper in Mark 1:40–44, but purified and sent him to the temple to make sacrifices according to the law of Moses;[21] Jesus did not deny the laws of impurity, but considered them "of less gravity than moral impurity."[22] At his Last Supper, he and his disciples ate a lamb (presumably one that had been prepared for the Passover meal by the sacrificial rites in the temple); and he selected the Passover, with all its symbolism, as the season in which to finish his infinite atoning sacrifice. He did not eat unclean foods or transgress any of the food law provisions of the law of Moses (as required by Deuteronomy 12:20–28). If he had eaten such foods, Peter would not have needed the revelation he received in Acts 10:11–16. And if Jesus had committed any serious infractions of the law, his accusers would have held those against him.

Of course, we do not know the manner in which Jesus observed every provision of the law, and it is clear that he disagreed with some interpretations of the law advocated by the Pharisees and other Jewish groups around him. But, however he understood those provisions, Jesus (even with his eternally superior knowledge of all things) observed and then fulfilled every provision of the law down to its last jot and tittle, as scholars interested in Jesus' Jewishness have only recently begun to fully appreciate.[23] By suggesting that the Nephites were true to their word and were strict to observe the law of Moses and its statutes, ordinances, judgments, and commandments, I mean to imply that the Nephites were no more or less Jewish than Jesus himself.

Shadows of Shadows

Another difficulty in attempting to ascertain what the Nephites meant when they said they were strict to observe the law of Moses is that we cannot always be sure about the state of the law in Jerusalem around 600 B.C. Not only was that law composed of types and shadows of things to come, but much of it now remains hidden from our view by the intervening passage of hundreds of years.

The law consisted, at least, of five books of Moses. The Nephites cherished those books as one of their religious treasures inscribed on the plates of brass. Nevertheless, we cannot know for certain what version of those writings was on the plates. Since Leviticus, for example, may have been edited somewhat after 600 B.C., all of the technicalities and formalities found especially in some of its so-called priestly sources may have been unknown to Lehi and his posterity. While I reject the extreme conclusions of the higher critics of the Bible regarding the documentary hypothesis,[24] it seems to me that Latter-day Saint doctrine teaches that all of the words in the first five books of the Bible have not been preserved exactly as Moses originally gave them; from the book of Moses, we know this especially to have been the case with the first chapters of Genesis. Textual changes, additions, and deletions (some inspired, some not) evidently occurred during the six (often apostate) centuries between Moses and the end of the biblical period.

Even if we could accurately reconstruct the law of Moses as it existed in the seventh century B.C., we would still wonder how much Lehi knew about the entire law and its applications. How much of the written law would he have technically understood? How much of the oral law or the practices of the priests inside the temple would he have known? How much culture did Lehi take with him, either intentionally or inadvertently? He probably knew a lot. He would have witnessed public events such as coronations, and he undoubtedly attended many convocations of men, women and children at the temple and elsewhere. Of the religious, political, and literary activities in and around the

city of Jerusalem, and perhaps in other lands as well, Lehi
was probably an astute observer. He knew the ways of that
world well enough to be critical of them and to be a forceful
advocate of the messages of the Lord in the streets of
Jerusalem. He would have been about forty or fifty years
old when he left Jerusalem,[25] and so he was a mature, lifetime participant in many of the events that transpired in
Jerusalem from the days of Josiah's temple reforms down to
the first year of the reign of King Zedekiah. While Lehi
would not have known or accepted everything in the
ancient world, he would have known many things about
which we no longer have the faintest clue.

Biblical Law or Jewish Law?

While we cannot reconstruct Lehi's cultural and textual
backgrounds with precision, we can be certain that one
should not confuse the law of Moses written on the brass
plates with the later varieties of Jewish law that proliferated
among various Jewish communities several centuries after
Lehi left Jerusalem. The Sadducees came to promote one
understanding of the law, the Samaritans another; the
Pharisees accepted numerous oral sources of religious law,
and these were eventually embodied in the Mishnah, the
Talmuds of Babylonia and Palestine, and other rabbinic
writings. The records from Dead Sea Scrolls preserve yet
another very different legal system based on the law of
Moses, and the works of Philo of Alexandria show that
Hellenistic Jews understood the law in yet another way.
Thus, in saying that the Nephites observed the law of
Moses, one must be careful to understand that this does not
mean that Lehi was a Rabbinic Jew of the fourth century
after Christ.

Failing to keep this historical framework in mind can

lead to confusion. For example, regarding the Nephite observance of "Jewish festivals," there is no question that they did not observe the postexilic festivals and memorials such as Purim, Nikanor (Fast of Esther), the Fast of Tammuz, Hanukkah, or aspects of the older holy days that were introduced into Judaism only after Lehi left Jerusalem.[26] But to the extent that holy days were part of the preexilic law of Moses, it is logical to assume that the Nephites were committed to observing those holy days in one way or other, although we do not know how they understood each provision of the law, or how the Spirit inspired their prophets to interpret each statute or ordinance. For example, if Exodus 29:38–42 and Numbers 28:3–8 were part of the Pentateuch in Lehi's time, then it follows that he offered sacrifice in *some* fashion "day by day," likely reminding them of their need to thank God daily and to acknowledge his sustenance of life from day to day. Again, we do not know how the Nephite priests understood the phrase "day by day"; perhaps they interpreted it to mean "from time to time" or "daily during a certain period." Several Old Testament scriptures regarding daily sacrifice use "day by day" or "daily" only in reference to the seven days of certain festival periods (see Numbers 28:24; 2 Chronicles 30:21; Ezra 3:4; Nehemiah 8:18; Ezekiel 45:23); thus, the Nephites may have understood Exodus 29 and Numbers 28 to require daily sacrifice only within certain time periods. In any event, "day by day" need not mean every day; Alma speaks of miracles happening "day by day" (Alma 37:40), probably meaning often, or from time to time. But in whatever way they understood this rule, they would have observed it accordingly.

We are not at liberty to assume, however, that the Nephites could freely ignore certain provisions of the law

of Moses as they had it, on the grounds that those requirements were beneath their religious dignity or station. While
they rejected the wicked elements of the culture in
Jerusalem, they did not reject the sanctity of their written
religious law. In time, a careful study of each provision
of the law of Moses with respect to the Book of Mormon
will be completed. Already, much has been written about
numerous elements in the law of Moses among the Nephites,[27] and more will hopefully be forthcoming soon.
Although many questions will undoubtedly always remain
beyond our understanding, evidence is already sufficient to
conclude that the Nephites took the words of the great
prophet and lawgiver Moses very literally and integrated
them thoroughly with their understanding of the gospel of
Jesus Christ.

Indeed, this blending of elements from both the Old and
New Testaments is one of the most distinctive characteristics of the Book of Mormon. The Nephite record bridges
both Jewish and Christian backgrounds. The world of the
Book of Mormon is neither Jewish nor Christian, but both, if
both those terms are properly understood. The ability of the
Book of Mormon to unify both testaments of the Bible (the
Old and the New) and its ability to speak to both Jew and
Gentile are perhaps two of its most important and yet most
often overlooked strengths. Its Title Page declares that it is
to serve "to the convincing of the Jew and Gentile that Jesus
is the Christ." Seeing and appreciating its Jewish dimensions helps the book speak to its Jewish audience as well as
its Gentile adherents.

Accordingly, the study of the temple among the
Nephites requires an awareness of both Jewish and
Christian elements. It demands the understanding of many
scriptures, both ancient and modern. It calls for careful

research to locate and evaluate temple-related materials ranging from the ancient Near East and the Bible to the modern far west and continuing revelation.

Father Lehi's Temple Legacy

A part of Lehi's spiritual legacy to his children was a reverence for the temple as the house of Jehovah. It appears that Lehi observed temple practices and precepts as best he could, even though he had no physical temple to utilize after he left Jerusalem. That devotion appears to have cultivated in his righteous children a longing for the temple that encouraged Nephi to seek divine approval to marshal the resources to build a temple patterned after the one they had left behind in Jerusalem.

Although Lehi condemned the wickedness of the Jews in Jerusalem, he was not critical of the temple. Instead, he looked forward to the restoration of the dispersed Jews to the land of Israel (see 1 Nephi 10:3) and to the proper worship of the Holy One of Israel that would then be possible. In his first recorded vision, Lehi saw a pillar of fire dwelling upon a rock and learned that the city of Jerusalem had become an "abomination" and would be destroyed (1 Nephi 1:6, 13). Although Lehi understood from that vision that the Lord no longer dwelt in the temple at Jerusalem (the word *abomination* implies the defilement of something sacred, i.e., the temple), there is no reason to believe that he became anti-temple. He testified against the people because of their wickedness (see 1 Nephi 1:19) and laid blame at the feet of "the pastors of [the] people" (1 Nephi 21:1), but never does he suggest that these problems called for an elimination of temple worship as such.

Leaving Jerusalem, Lehi fled into the desert, returning to the ways of Israel under the patriarchs and Moses in the wilderness. Passing allusions give us only a few glimpses of the religious life of Lehi and his family during their migration. For example, at his first camp site he built an altar of stones on which he gave thanks to the Lord by offering sacrifice (see 1 Nephi 2:7). One may infer that this was Lehi's regular practice as he moved from camp to camp.[28] This conduct was normal for an Israelite. The right to offer a sacrifice was not limited to any selected class of priests: "At solitary altars . . . any Israelite could serve. The solitary altars were numerous and scattered throughout the country; there was probably no settlement without its altar, and altars could even be found outside cities, in the countryside."[29]

By building his altar out of natural stones, Lehi was expressly observing the law of Moses, which required uncut rocks to be used for altars: "An altar of earth thou shalt make unto me . . . in all places where I record my name I will come unto thee, and I will bless thee. . . . Thou shalt not build it of hewn stone: for if thou lift up thy tool upon it, thou hast polluted it" (Exodus 20:24–25).[30]

By offering such sacrifices, Father Lehi was also following patterns set by the patriarchs of old: Abraham built altars in the open on which he offered sacrifice, as he did to commemorate God's appearance at Moreh (see Genesis 12:6–7) and to prepare for the offering of his only son Isaac (see Genesis 22:9); likewise the patriarch Jacob built an altar at El-elohe-Israel (see Genesis 33:20).[31] Undoubtedly, sacrifices of thanksgiving were also made when Lehi's party "exceedingly rejoiced" as they reached the sea (1 Nephi 17:6) and when Lehi declared upon arrival that their new promised land was "consecrated" only to those who serve the Lord (2 Nephi 1:7).

Moreover, the temple was viewed throughout the

ancient Near East as an artificial mountain on which the Lord dwelt.[32] During his sojourn in the wilderness, Nephi used mountains in lieu of a temple as places to commune with God. When Nephi received the same vision of the tree of life as his father had seen, he was "caught away in the Spirit of the Lord, yea, into an exceedingly high mountain" (1 Nephi 11:1). Later the Lord told Nephi to "arise, and get . . . into *the* mountain" (1 Nephi 17:7; italics added), indicating that praying on top of a mountain had become a regular practice for Nephi (see 1 Nephi 18:3). This natural setting may have led Nephi to speak of the entire cosmos as a heavenly temple: "He ruleth high in the heavens, for it is his throne, and this earth is his footstool" (1 Nephi 17:39; cf. Isaiah 66:1).[33]

The Book of Mormon repeatedly states that Lehi dwelt in a tent (1 Nephi 2:6, 15; 3:1; 4:38; 5:7; 7:5, 21, 22; 9:1; 10:16; 15:1; 16:6). God's tent was associated with the temple in Israelite thought. As Hugh Nibley has pointed out, "the cult of the tent was as important to the Hebrews" as it was to the Arabs.[34] Nephi's statements may also allude to the fact that God "dwelt in a tent" (the portable tabernacle, a precursor of the temple) during Moses' exodus from Egypt.[35]

On several occasions Lehi used ordinary language that may reflect temple ideas. For example, when he told his children that God had said that "inasmuch as ye will not keep my commandments ye shall be cut off *from my presence*" (2 Nephi 1:20; italics added), Lehi may have meant that they would not be allowed to enter into a holy temple, for phrases such as "before the Lord" or in the "presence of the Lord" can be "considered an indication of the existence of a temple."[36] Likewise, when Lehi dedicated his son Jacob to spend all his days "in the *service* of thy God" (2 Nephi 2:3; italics added), it seems likely that he was prophesying of Jacob's consecration as a priest (see 2 Nephi 5:26) and of his future temple service, for the Hebrew words for service *(avodah, sharat)* often appear in phrases such as "the service of the tabernacle" (Exodus 30:16), "service in the holy place" (Exodus 39:1), and the "work of the service of the house of God" (1 Chronicles 9:13). In addition, by calling Jacob his "firstborn" in the wilderness (2 Nephi 2:1–2, 11), Lehi appears to allude to another aspect of the law of Moses: "The firstborn of thy sons shalt thou give unto me" (Exodus 22:29).

Several of the main doctrines taught by Lehi seem to echo and presage temple types and teachings. He emphasized covenant making and keeping the commandments (see 2 Nephi 1; 4), the creation and fall of Adam and Eve (see 2 Nephi 2), the tree of life (see 1 Nephi 8), Satan and opposition (see 2 Nephi 2:11, 26–27), the promised Messiah (see 1 Nephi 1), and the redemption (see 1 Nephi 10:5; 2 Nephi 2:6). These themes are readily at home in the context of the ancient temple typologies known to Latter-day Saints today that would have been familiar to Lehi through the writings found on the plates of brass.

In light of such factors and Lehi's knowledge of the temple of God in Jerusalem, one may well surmise that Lehi held the temple in high esteem and provided much of the inspiration that assured the establishment and functioning of temples among the Nephites for generations to come.

The Temple of Nephi

Only a few years after the death of Lehi, the Nephites built a temple. Their written history as a separate group begins with the temple. After separating from his brothers Laman and Lemuel, Nephi led this group of faithful followers to a land they called Nephi. With only a small population facing the rigorous challenges of establishing themselves in a new land, Nephi nevertheless soon laid plans to construct a temple. Having grown up in and around Jerusalem, Nephi had witnessed firsthand the splendor and significance of the temple of Solomon that dominated the skyline of that city. In an effort to strengthen his fledgling colony with the same kind of spiritual and political cohesiveness that was symbolized by that temple once commissioned in Jerusalem by God, Nephi spared no available resource in providing a similar temple for his new city.

During the first few years, crops flourished and the people began to multiply (see 2 Nephi 5:13). Wood, ores, gold, silver, and precious stones were found; construction and metal working began (see 2 Nephi 5:15). These successes provided the materials and skilled craftsmen necessary for this small community to commence building a temple.

Of its design and structure Nephi states, "The manner of the construction was like unto the temple of Solomon" (2 Nephi 5:16). In saying this, Nephi "could only have meant that the general pattern was similar."[37] From this, one may understand that the basic physical conception of the temple of Nephi was essentially comparable to that of the distinctive temple of Solomon, which divided its sacred space into three areas on a straight-line axis with the innermost being the most holy. In the opinion of some scholars, Solomon's temple was distinctive in that it "consisted of three rooms one behind the other, with a narrow front. . . . What is characteristic of the Jerusalem Temple is rather that the three rooms stand one behind the other in a straight line, and that the building is the same width all along its length" with the middle room being the largest."[38] Apparently, Nephi built his temple in this same fashion so that it could be used for functions similar to those performed in the temple of Solomon.

It may be completely coincidental, and while there are obvious differences between all varieties of temples, it is interesting to observe that sanctuaries at the center of the top of certain Mayan temples (for example, at Tikal) are divided into three small areas arranged in a straight row, each one being a step higher than the other. Although little is known about Mesoamerican temples, ethnohistorians have surmised that, in cases of two- and three-roomed temples in Mesoamerica, "worshippers could enter only the outer room of the temple, while the slightly raised, more sacred, inner chamber was restricted to priests," with altars along the back wall.[39] Expanding on similar ideas, John Sorenson has drawn the following further comparisons between the prototypical Israelite temple and Mesoamerican temple structures:

> The temple of Solomon was built on a platform, so people literally went "up" to it. Inside were distinct rooms of differing sacredness. Outside the building itself was a courtyard or plaza surrounded by a wall. Sacrifices were made in that space, atop altars of stepped or terraced form. The levels of the altar structure represented the layered universe as Israelites and other Near Eastern peoples conceived of it. The temple building was oriented so that the rising of the sun on equinoctial day (either March 21 or September 21) sent the earliest rays—considered "the glory of the Lord"—to shine through the temple doors, which were opened for the occasion, directly into the holiest part. The same features generally characterized Mesoamerican temple complexes. The holy building that was the temple proper was of modest size, while the courtyard area received greater attention. Torquemada, an early Spanish priest in the New World, compared the plan of Mexican temples with that of the

temple of Solomon, and a modern scholar [Laurette Sejourne] agrees.[40]

Some critics have stumbled over an alleged contradiction between the fact that 2 Nephi 5:15 says that abundant supplies of wood and precious ores were found by the Nephites when they arrived in the land of Nephi, while the next verse states that the Nephite temple lacked some of the precious things of Solomon's temple because "they were not to be found upon the land."[41] Nephi, however, does not claim that his temple was "just like" Solomon's; only that it was built "after the manner" of Solomon's. Inasmuch as Israelite temples were built at Tel Arad, Beer-Sheba, Leontopolis, Elephantine, and probably elsewhere as well, Nephi's temple was not unique.[42] While similar in several important respects, none of these Israelite temples were like Solomon's, however, in size or splendor.

Moreover, when Nephi says his temple was "not built of so many *precious things*," he probably is not speaking of gold or silver, which were found in the land of Nephi. The common Book of Mormon phrase "gold, silver, and precious things" appears to parallel the Near Eastern formulaic expression in which "precious things" commonly referred to precious *gems*. Thus, while Nephi mentions an abundance of metallic ores (gold, silver, and copper) in his description of the new promised land (see 1 Nephi 18:25), he conspicuously fails to mention gems or "precious things," such as carbuncle, emerald, sapphire, and diamond, which Solomon used extensively in constructing his temple (see 2 Chronicles 3:6; also Exodus 39:10–13).[43] Accordingly, the Book of Mormon is consistent; Nephi could not decorate his temple with the same kinds of precious things as were used in Solomon's temple. Nevertheless, Nephi consciously used Solomon's temple as far as possible as a pattern for the temple in the city of Nephi, and he was proud to report that "the workmanship thereof was exceedingly fine" (2 Nephi 5:16).

The Temple and the Founding of the Nephite State

Why was Nephi so concerned about building such a costly temple? Many reasons come to mind. Some reasons were strictly religious. Nephi had risked his life to obtain the plates of brass so that the Nephites could obey the commandments of God contained in the law of Moses (see 1 Nephi 4:15), and they kept the law of Moses, "look[ing] forward with steadfastness unto Christ, until the law shall be fulfilled" (2 Nephi 25:24). It would have been impossible for the Nephites to obey the commandments of the law of Moses without a temple. At the temple, the law required them to assemble three times a year to be taught (see Deuteronomy 31:11), to redeem their firstborns (see Exodus 13:2), to offer atoning sacrifices for their transgressions (see Exodus 20:24–25; Leviticus 16:3), to consult Jehovah for oracles (see Exodus 18:15; Deuteronomy 33:8–10), to enter symbolically into the presence of the Lord, and to conduct many other ordinances and performances required as their prophets and leaders directed them in preparation for the coming of Christ.

Other reasons were political. The temple served vital functions in the development of the Nephite state, and at various stages in Nephite history temples were crucial in transmitting power from one regime to the next, in promulgating law, and in maintaining public order. The common ancient practice of constructing a temple to legitimize a new state is distinctly observable in 2 Nephi 5–10, at the formation of the Nephite kingship.[44]

When Nephi and those who believed him separated

themselves from the main body of Lehi's clan soon after Lehi's death, they faced the task of founding a political and religious regime that could withstand the inevitable attacks that soon descended on them, both verbally and physically (see 5:34). The prophet's followers called their new land Nephi and themselves the people of Nephi (see 2 Nephi 5:8–9). They recognized Nephi as their founding ruler, king, prophet, and teacher. His first known decree confirmed the continuation of the law of Moses in this society: "And we did observe to keep the judgments, and the statutes, and the commandments of the Lord in all things, according to the law of Moses" (2 Nephi 5:10), thus giving the group religious authority.

Nephi's little community, however, also needed to establish political legitimacy. They were a splinter group. For centuries the Lamanites would continue to accuse them of illegitimate beginnings, with their grievances originating at the time when Nephi took "the ruling of the people out of their hands" (Mosiah 10:15). And there was uncertainty about Nephi's position. His people wanted him to be king, but he objected at first, knowing that Christ was the true king and that nothing should detract from one's loyalty and obedience to the heavenly king. While initially resisting the title of king, Nephi proceeded to do as much as he could for his people in establishing and leading this infant state. As he says, he did everything that "was in [his] power" (2 Nephi 5:18).

One of the things that would have been within Nephi's power was to invoke powerful symbols to enhance the stability and legitimacy of his people. The construction of a temple was an important sign in the ancient world that a new society was soundly based and that the leader had been divinely authorized. The fact that Nephi recorded the building of this temple in the same text in which he discusses law, kingship, and the prohibition of marriage between his people and the Lamanites (see 2 Nephi 5:8–10, 18–25) shows that the temple was probably perceived by Nephi and his people as having important political as well as religious significance.

The prophecies and rules issued by Nephi in 2 Nephi 5:19–25 and the "covenant speech" given by Jacob under the direction of Nephi (see 2 Nephi 6–10) were, in my opinion, most likely all delivered at the temple. They were probably proclaimed at or around Nephi's coronation and the temple's dedication. Indeed, the text in 2 Nephi 5–10 makes good sense as a temple text and features several themes of constitutional force among the Nephites.

Research has supplied ample evidence for the thesis that the building or restoration of temples was an integral part in the formation and legitimization of the typical ancient Near Eastern state or society,[45] and that evidence correlates with the elements present in 2 Nephi 5–10. In fact, the formation of an ancient Near Eastern state could scarcely be legitimated without a temple, covenant making, and the promulgation of law. From the time of David and Solomon (see 2 Samuel 7), it is impossible to understand kingship in Israel without temples or to comprehend temples without kingship. The two are "inseparably bound up with each other."[46] Only with an enduring house of God could the king establish a royal house that was lasting—firmly grounded forever (see 2 Samuel 7:13, 16, 25, 29). Ahlström explains how this principle operated in the ancient Near East generally:

> In the case of administrative centers it was necessary to build a house for the prefect or governor and a house for the god, i.e., a temple. These two buildings were the

physical expressions of the national government representing king and god. Temples built by the king were state administrative places which often became the financial centers and the large land holders of the country. . . . This is the political reality behind the idea of the king as temple builder. By constructing cities and temples the king acted as the protector and organizer of the country and its people.[47]

Lundquist asserts further that "the act of legitimization is ritually celebrated [at the temple] in and through the covenant process. The content of the covenant ceremony is law."[48] Such construction projects and the attendant promulgations of law at ancient temples through covenant ceremonies were essential to the successful creation of ancient states, for the mere accession to the throne by a charismatic figure did not assure the perpetuation of the state.

A new king would typically trace his authority to God and announce interim legislation establishing himself as a king of justice; but as soon as possible in the first decade of his rule, like Nephi, "the king builds, renovates, or rededicates the main temple of his city, at which time the fuller version of the laws is decreed and elaborated into a stele by royal scribes."[49] The Babylonian kings used stone monuments, sometimes represented by pillars but also described as "tablets of the law,"[50] reminiscent of the tablets containing the Ten Commandments that according to tradition were kept in the Holy of Holies in the temple of Solomon (see Exodus 25:16; Hebrews 9:4).

At the commencement of the covenant convocation at which the law was promulgated or reestablished, the community was first ritually prepared to receive the law; they then offered sacrifices of animals and ate a sacred meal. Those involved in the sacrifices sometimes noted their bloodstained garments and drank the blood and ate parts of the sacrificial animal as they made their oath to keep the law. All this was performed in the ritual presence of the deity.[51]

So important was the role of temple builder or restorer for legitimate kings in Israel that, after the destruction of Jerusalem (see 2 Nephi 1:4; 6:8), it became a prominent matter of messianic expectation that the temple would be rebuilt.[52] Beyond the political sphere and into the prophetic, it is evident that Ezekiel and the Qumran community both employed these practices typologically, expressly envisioning the construction of a temple of cosmic proportions in order to usher in the restoration of Israel and the true reign of God, the divine king, in the last days.[53]

Lundquist adduces evidence that all the main details of establishing a temple in connection with legitimizing a new political kingship were persistent not only in the ancient Near East generally, but specifically in ancient Israel.[54] Thus one might expect Nephi to observe similar formalities, at least to a certain extent. In order to determine whether or not Nephi followed a similar pattern, the ancient Near Eastern practices can be compared with the text of 2 Nephi 5–10. The following discussion shows that all of the main traditional elements connect the construction of Nephi's temple with the commencement and establishment of his kingship:

Divine calling of the king. Following the basic patterns and practices "according to the reigns of the kings" of Israel (Jacob 1:9, 14), Nephi established his legitimacy as ruler by recalling the fact that Jehovah had selected him to be the leader of his people. The first recorded promise given to Nephi by God was "Thou shalt be made a ruler and a teacher over thy brethren" (1 Nephi 2:22). Significantly, this divine commission is mentioned by Nephi in 2 Nephi 5, for it legitimized Nephi as a ruler and justified the existence of his people as a separate society (see vv. 19–22). Although Nephi may have wondered if the Lord's promise authorized him to be a *king* (since God only said that Nephi would become a *ruler*) or to be a ruler over anyone other than his brothers (an aspect of the promise that Nephi insisted had been already fulfilled—see v. 19), God's investiture gave Nephi sufficient authority to institute a kingship among the Nephites, and it assured that the Nephite government would be sacral. At the end of Nephi's reign, using language that took its form from God's original promise to him, Nephi in turn "anointed a man to be a king and a ruler over his people" (Jacob 1:9), an ordinance that one may safely assume occurred at the temple.

Promulgation of law. After affirming the continued validity of the old law (see 2 Nephi 5:10), Nephi (like most ancient kings) issued a new law at the time of his coronation. Nephi's law prohibited any Nephite from marrying a Lamanite (see 2 Nephi 5:23). Those who would break this law were afflicted with a severe curse. The formula "and the Lord spake it, and it was done" (2 Nephi 5:23) confirms that the people accepted this rule as law, effectively codifying it.

Consecration of priests. Nephi next consecrated Jacob and Joseph to be priests and teachers (2 Nephi 5:26).[55] An essential part of the temple ascension of new potentates in the ancient world was to install temple priests and administrators who would rule under the new king. This consecration usually occurred at the temple. The same pattern was repeated later in the Book of Mormon when King Mosiah II became king and when priests were appointed as the first official act of the new coregency (see Mosiah 6:3).

Of course, these Nephite priests were not priests or Levites by birth. They were ordained "after the manner of

[God's] holy order" (2 Nephi 6:2). The persistence of that phrase in the Nephite record (Alma 6:8; 13:1, 8, 10–11) shows that the Nephites consciously based their priesthood authority on principles lodged in God's holy order, rather than in tribal rights or inheritances.[56] Indeed, they looked to Melchizedek as the paragon of priesthood (see Alma 13:14–19), probably in large part because Melchizedek was the most conspicuous priest in the Pentateuch who was not a Levite.[57] But Melchizedek lived before the time of Moses, and so one might well wonder how Lehi could rightly purport to live the law of Moses without having Levites to officiate in the sanctuary. If Lehi or Nephi ever struggled with this issue, they gave no indication to that effect; and we can easily imagine several reasons why they did not.

First, revelation guided Nephi in deciding whom to ordain; if there were to be sacrifices as God required, then there had to be priests to perform those sacrifices, and if there were no Levites in the colony, then the priests had to be ordained from among the available people. (Actually, the Nephites faced and overcame a similar conceptual difficulty when they accepted Nephi as a king, for the rights of kingship in Jerusalem presumptively belonged exclusively to the tribe of Judah and the house of David, whereas the Nephites were of the tribe of Manasseh.)

Second, the Nephites may have viewed the priestly inheritance of the Levites as belonging only to the temple in Jerusalem; the centralization of temple worship that was accomplished by the reforms of Josiah in 625 B.C. gave the Levites increased, if not exclusive, control over the temple in Jerusalem,[58] but that does not imply that Levites officiated in Israelite temples outside of the capital, such as that at Elephantine in Egypt during the Babylonian captivity.[59] Under Josiah's reforms, Levites had special rights only in the "chosen place" in Jerusalem; elsewhere, however, it has been argued, the Levite was "an ordinary layman."[60]

Third, by returning to the typology of the exodus from Egypt, Lehi's colony assumed a posture that had previously recognized all of Israel as "a kingdom of priests, and an holy nation" (Exodus 19:6). As historian John Bright observes, "The later theory that all cultic personnel must be Levites, all priests of the house of Aaron, did not obtain in early Israel."[61] The theology of the Exodus took precedence over the Levitical limitations on priesthood.

Fourth, although the history of the priesthood in ancient Israel is complicated and obscure, it is clear that certain priests, such as Zadokites and Gibeonites, officiated in the temple of Solomon in addition to Levites. Aelred Cody notes that "if Ezek. 44:6–10 condemns the practice of having uncircumcised foreigners serving in the Temple, it is because the practice existed."[62]

Fifth, Nephi may simply have viewed the appointment of priests as a rightful prerogative of the king.[63] King David appointed priests, including his sons (see 2 Samuel 8:15–18; 20:25–26), and—although it was viewed by some as a sin—Jeroboam "made priests of the lowest of the people, which were not of the sons of Levi" (1 Kings 12:31; 13:33).

Sixth, the term *Levite* may well have been a functional title in addition to a genealogical one. In other words, when Nephi consecrated Jacob and Joseph as priests, in a sense they actually became Levites. As Bright explains: "'Levite' was also a functional designation meaning 'one pledged by vow'; men of any clan thus dedicated to Yahweh could become Levites. In the course of time, many priestly families and individuals not of Levitic lineage were so reckoned because of their function—as was Samuel (1 Chron. 6:28)."[64] Thus, it is clear that the genealogical tribe of Levi did not have an exclusive monopoly on all temple priesthood in ancient Israel, especially among the Nephites.

Memorial established. At the time when the temple of Nephi was built, God also instructed Nephi to make a new set of plates. This suggests that the small plates of Nephi were made in connection with the temple dedication and political formation of the Nephites as a people.[65] Those plates accordingly served the traditional function of the new "tablets of the law" or the pillar or stele often set up in the ancient Near East as a monument to the creation of new political orders. Nephi indicated at the time of his coronation that he was commanded to write on those plates things "which are good in [God's] sight, for the profit of thy people" (2 Nephi 5:30). Among those things that would be considered "good in God's sight" were God's laws and commandments as well as prophecies (cf. 1 Nephi 5:10–12; Jacob 1:4). The historical record, however, was kept on the large plates of Nephi.

Acceptance by the people. Each new law or political order in the ancient Near East was traditionally submitted to a "ritually prepared community"[66] for their acceptance. Jacob's speech (2 Nephi 6–10) is a covenant speech (see 9:1), and one may surmise that it was delivered at the newly completed temple of Nephi. It certainly emphasizes several temple themes.

Jacob's purpose was to motivate the people "to act for [themselves]—to choose the way of everlasting death or the way of eternal life" and thereby to become "reconciled unto God" (2 Nephi 10:23–24). This can be profitably compared with the text of the covenant renewal of Joshua 24, where the people of Israel were given essentially the same choice in connection with the establishment of the social and religious order of Israel implemented by Joshua in the promised land of Israel. In his speech, Jacob instructed the people so that they might "glorify the name of [their] God" (2 Nephi 6:4). Such glorifying may have involved ceremonies, prayers, hymns, and sacrifices at the temple. Jacob then quoted Isaiah's prophecy that kings and queens shall bow down and lick the dust of the Lord's people (see 2 Nephi 6:6–7). He also promised that the Lord would deliver his covenant people (see 2 Nephi 6:17). These promises would have been powerful as a coronation text.

Jacob then called to the people: "Hearken unto me, my people; and give ear unto me, O my nation; for *a law* shall proceed from me, and I will make my judgment to rest for a light for the people. My righteousness is near; my salvation is gone forth, and mine arm shall judge the people. The isles shall wait upon me, and on mine arm shall they trust" (2 Nephi 8:4–5; italics added). Jacob addressed his people as a new community "in whose heart I have written *my law*" (2 Nephi 8:7; italics added). Reciting these texts religiously reinforced the new law and the establishment of Nephi's new political regime.

Further temple themes in Jacob's speech. Just as the covenant making at Mount Sinai involved the issuance of the Ten Commandments, Jacob ends his speech by rehearsing ten "woes" (see 2 Nephi 9:28–38). These curses and the Ten Commandments are similar in both content and covenantal functions,[67] and the close connection between the temple and the Ten Commandments, especially as a type of entrance requirement, has been noted by Moshe Weinfeld and Klaus Koch.[68]

Much of Jacob's speech revolved around a discussion of the day of judgment, when people will be resurrected to stand before God "clothed with purity, yea, even with the robe of righteousness" (2 Nephi 9:14). Perhaps ritual vestments representing these robes of righteousness were worn by the priests at the temple of Nephi. Jacob finally proclaimed that the day of judgment will culminate with the exclamation: "Holy, holy are thy judgments, O Lord God Almighty—but I know my guilt; I transgressed thy law, and my transgressions are mine; and the devil hath obtained me, that I am a prey to his awful misery" (2 Nephi 9:46). Seen in connection with the making of covenants at the formation of the fledgling Nephite state, such a declaration could well have been repeated by the people of Nephi as part of their temple ceremonies, both at the time of Nephi's coronation and as a regular matter thereafter.

The Temple of Nephi from Jacob to Limhi

After the coronation and reign of Nephi, the temple of Nephi continued to serve the people of that land for almost four hundred years. Nephi's younger brothers Jacob and Joseph served as its first priests and teachers (see 2 Nephi 5:26; Jacob 1:18), having been "ordained after the manner of [God's] holy order" (2 Nephi 6:2). It appears that Jacob's posterity not only remained responsible for keeping records on the small plates of Nephi, but also served as the principal line of priests associated with this temple.

What transpired inside or around the temple of Nephi? Although we have only scant evidence dating from the times of Jacob, Enos, Omni, and others in this lineage, one may assume that these priests performed the main sacrifices required of them by the law of Moses. On the Day of Atonement, for example, the high priest in Israel performed important sacrificial ceremonies to purify himself, his garments, the temple, and all the people "from the uncleanness of the children of Israel" (Leviticus 16:19).[69] This seems to be closely related to Jacob's profound desires that the blood of his people "might not come upon [his] garments" (Jacob 1:19; see also Mosiah 2:28) and also connected with his concern that God might rid from his people the defilements and pollutions of "iniquity and abomination" (Jacob 2:16). At one point Jacob took off his garments and shook them before the people at the temple to rid them of impurity (see 2 Nephi 9:44). Jacob spoke often of "holiness" (e.g., 2 Nephi 8:11; 9:15, 20, 46, 48), purity (2 Nephi 9:47), and uncleanness (2 Nephi 8:24; 9:14, 40), which in the ancient Israelite mind would have been states closely associated with the Mosaic concepts of holiness and purification that came through sacrifice by the shedding of blood at their temple.

Holding these holy places in reverence and respect surely helped the Nephites also to approach and develop faith in their promised savior Jesus Christ. Accordingly, it was no accident that Lehi, Nephi, and Jacob spoke frequently of their Lord Jesus Christ as the Holy One of Israel and mentioned the "holiness which is in him" (2 Nephi 2:10). It was likewise no accident that Mormon, Moroni, and other Book of Mormon writers spoke often about "the holiness which is in Christ" (3 Nephi 26:5) and the "glory of God, and the holiness of Jesus Christ" (Mormon 9:5). Their sensitivity to the holiness of the Lord was undoubtedly enhanced by their reverence for and worship at the temple, his holy house.

Most certainly the temple of Nephi was used as a place of instruction, as were all typical temples of the ancient Near East.[70] When all Israel gathered at the temple, the law was read to them "in their hearing . . . that they may hear, and that they may learn, and fear the Lord" (Deuteronomy 31:11–12). Likewise, Jacob taught his people "in the temple" (Jacob 1:17) after the death of Nephi (see Jacob 2:1), that they might hear "the word of God" (Jacob 2:11, 23) and "fear" for their eternal welfare (Jacob 3:8–11). In that speech Jacob revealed to the people their innermost thoughts and the wickedness of their hearts (see Jacob 2:5–6), and he chastened them especially concerning their violation of God's law of chastity and their growing obsession with riches (see Jacob 2:16–35). If these themes were selected by Jacob for his temple sermon to remind the Nephites of covenants they had previously made to eschew adultery and to consecrate the riches of the promised land back to the Lord of that land, then Jacob's words may offer clues about the nature of the early Nephite temple covenants and ordinances. This would also explain why Jacob says that the Nephites who violated these commandments were worse off than the Lamanites (see Jacob 3:7), for, to those who are under solemn covenants, behavior to the contrary is a more serious matter.

The temple was also the place where the early Nephites would have gathered for their annual religious celebrations and holy days. Jarom accurately reflects the vital importance of observing these holy days (each of which was considered to be a sabbath) when he reports that his people "observed to keep the law of Moses and the sabbath day holy unto the Lord. And they profaned not" (Jarom 1:5). As discussed above, all this points to functions involving the temple, especially during the three main sabbaths of Passover, Pentecost, and Ingathering (or Day of Atonement and Tabernacles). Because of their social and symbolic functions, the observance of these holy days appears to have been very important in ancient Israel. Indeed, in the opinion of one historian, in early Israel (and by implication, among the Nephites) worship "did not center in a sacrificial system, but in [the three] great annual feasts . . . at which the worshiper was expected to present himself before Yahweh [at the temple]."[71]

Other Nephite gatherings and instruction occurred during this period, but one can only surmise that they occurred at the temple: The temple would have been the logical place for Jacob's farewell speech (see Jacob 4–6). The temple would also have been the most arresting place for Sherem to have confronted Jacob with his accusations of blasphemy, false prophecy, and leading people into apostasy (see Jacob 7:7), and to have submitted himself to the divine ordeal of asking for a sign from God. But no further mention of the temple is found in the small plates of Nephi down to the time of the first King Mosiah.

The evident decline of Jacob's family during the time of Omni, Amaron, Chemish, and Abinadom (see Omni 1:1–11) probably signals a concurrent decline in the importance attributed to the temple of Nephi during these years. John Sorenson found archaeological evidence in Kaminaljuyu that might correspond with a decline in importance of temples in the city of Nephi during this same era:

> The central sacred area at that time seems to have consisted of rows of large burial mounds. These were probably where the elders of the kin groups were buried and honored. This custom basically agrees with the treatment of honored leaders of Israelite kin groups in Palestine when they died. Perhaps during the centuries of warfare and "stiff-neckedness" after Nephi and Jacob died (Enos 1:22–24), the original temple fell into disuse as a center for religious practices, while burial rites for the group's patriarchs were emphasized. At least we hear nothing about the temple between Jacob's day and the time when the Zeniffites reoccupied the land, over 400 years later.[72]

Following that period of decline, the righteous Nephites

were warned by God during the reign of Mosiah I to flee northward out of the land of Nephi. It must have been a difficult personal loss for each member of that group to have left the sacred sites in the city of Nephi. People today can perhaps empathize by imagining those Nephites, like the Saints leaving Nauvoo, treasuring one last view of their temple as they left it behind. How much more poignant the Nephite departure must have been, since the Nephite temple had served its people for centuries longer.

Not all of the Nephites, however, accepted this as a permanent separation. Zeniff and his group were driven almost irrationally and at enormous expense to reinherit the land of Nephi (see Omni 1:27–29; Mosiah 9:1–4), and most likely their motivation was significantly connected with the temple there. Land was plentiful elsewhere, and Lehi's blessings extended to all the land including "those who should be led out of other countries by the hand of the Lord" (2 Nephi 1:5); but only in the land of Nephi stood the temple of Nephi. Perhaps the Zeniffites were uncomfortable living in the city of Zarahemla without a temple, or perhaps they considered the temples there, built by people whose religion had seriously degenerated, to be defilements and an intolerable abomination. In any event, they soon left the city of Zarahemla and returned to the city of Nephi where they reclaimed their former temple city, having to endure heavy tribute and suffer loss of life to maintain their position.

With great excess, Zeniff's son, King Noah, conducted an extensive construction program in the city of Nephi, especially refurbishing and outfitting the temple of Nephi and his palace, along with added towers and fortifications that were closely associated with the main temple precinct (see Mosiah 11:9–12). His projects are reminiscent of typical ancient Near Eastern kings who built and maintained magnificent administrative complexes, complete with a temple, palace, and fortifications, to enhance and solidify their political power over their territory.[73] As was the case during the monarchy in Israel, where "priests were civil servants appointed by the king,"[74] the priests who served in the temple of Nephi under King Noah were likewise his appointees (see Mosiah 11:5).

This temple would have been the likely place where Abinadi delivered his prophetic denunciations of Noah and his priests. The citizenry of that city would have normally congregated there, and so Abinadi would have found a ready audience at the temple. Since it was often a place for swearing of judicial oaths, the temple would also have been a most appropriate place for the prophet to deliver his curses of divine judgment in the name of God. If Abinadi indeed spoke at the temple, his simile curse that Noah's life "shall be valued even as a garment in a hot furnace" (Mosiah 12:3) can meaningfully be understood as sacral imagery: in other words, he is essentially saying that Noah and his priestly garments will be consumed before the face of the Lord should he attempt to enter into the holy presence of the Lord in that temple, just as God's consuming presence on Mount Sinai "ascended as the smoke of a furnace" (Exodus 19:18) and threatened to consume any unworthy person who set foot on that mount (see v. 12). Especially in light of the strong connections between the story of Abinadi and the celebration of the Feast of Pentecost (the Israelite holy day that celebrated the giving of the law on Sinai),[75] Abinadi's reference to a "furnace" seems to be more than a casual allusion to the distinctive description of Mount Sinai in Exodus 19 and, by extension, to any temple where one symbolically entered into the presence of the Lord.[76]

After the death of King Noah, the temple of Nephi continued to serve the people of that city as its religious and political center. When Ammon and his party from Zarahemla arrived in the city of Nephi, King Limhi sent out a proclamation that all his people should "gather themselves together to the temple, to hear the words which he should speak unto them." Limhi then spoke to them as "witnesses this day" that "iniquities and abominations" had brought them into bondage. He promised them deliverance if they would "turn to the Lord with full purpose of heart, and put [their] trust in him, and serve him with all diligence of mind" (Mosiah 7:18–33). In other words, he reviewed their adverse political circumstances, caused his people to acknowledge or confess their guilt in the presence of temple witnesses, and he offered them an opportunity to reestablish their broken covenant with the Lord. Ammon then followed Limhi by delivering to the people the final covenant speech that King Benjamin had given at the temple in Zarahemla (see Mosiah 2:9–5:15), and Ammon carefully explained all its words and requirements "so that they might understand all the words which he spake" (Mosiah 8:3). Those words revealed to the people at their temple the all-important name of Jesus Christ and the doctrine of his atonement, which is the only way by which salvation comes, and led them in the making of a covenant to do God's will, to be obedient to his commandments, and to take upon them the name of Christ.

Thus, from the time of Jacob to the end of the second century B.C., the temple of Nephi served in the land of Nephi primarily as a center of teaching, but also of covenant making and of political and religious administration. Although much remains unknown about that holy place, enough can be said about its essential features to define and reconstruct its basic characteristics.

Holy Places in the Lands of Zarahemla and Bountiful

The Book of Mormon contains little information about the construction of temples north of Nephi. The only direct reference to the temple in Zarahemla is found in connection with King Benjamin's covenant renewal and coronation speech (see Mosiah 1:18–2:7), while several unnamed temples in the land of Zarahemla are mentioned in Alma 16:13 as places where Alma and Amulek preached repentance. The only reference to the temple in the land of Bountiful is in 3 Nephi 11:1, where the resurrected Lord Jesus Christ appeared to a group of two thousand five hundred righteous people who had gathered there.

Why does the Book of Mormon say so little about these temples? Perhaps because of the sanctity of these buildings and their ordinances. On several occasions, Book of Mormon writers were told not to record certain sacred teachings and experiences (see, for example, Alma 8:1; 3 Nephi 17:15; 19:34; Ether 4:1), and on such occasions it appears to be more than a lack of room on the plates that deterred them from writing. In addition, in abridging these records, Mormon and Moroni probably assumed that references to the temple prior to the coming of Christ had become obsolete and irrelevant once the fulfillment of the law of Moses was announced (see 3 Nephi 9:19). The fact that little information about the temple of Nephi is found on the small plates does not disprove the thesis that Mormon minimized pre-Easter temple material as he abridged the large plates, for the contents of the small plates were expressly limited to "preaching," "revelation," and "prophesying" (Jacob 1:4), none of which would have included an extensive discussion of temple ordinances or practices. Those topics may have been recorded on other Nephite records. To the extent that modern readers might need more information about the role of the temple under the law of Moses (which the Nephites and their converts continued to observe strictly until the sign of the death of Christ—see Alma 25:15; 30:3; Helaman 13:1; 3 Nephi 1:24–25), the abridgers may have assumed that the Bible and other records would be available to supply the basic background information (see Mormon 7:8–9; Ether 1:4).

Nevertheless, despite the lack of overt comments in the Book of Mormon about these temples, contextual details surround each reference to temples in the books of Mosiah, Alma, Helaman, and 3 Nephi. These pieces of information yield substantial information about these important religious Nephite buildings.

For the Nephites in the land of Zarahemla, the temple was a paragon of holiness where God dwelt. Given the frequency of statements in the Book of Mormon that God does not live in unholy temples (Mosiah 2:37; Alma 7:21; 34:36; Helaman 4:24), surely the Nephites carefully guarded the holiness of these houses of God. The holiness of righteous temples is never discussed in the Book of Mormon, but by examining the passages that refer to "unholy temples," it is possible to extract several details that seem to have characterized the holy nature of temples among the Nephites. Nephite prophets regularly admonished the people to be righteous by reminding them that God does not dwell in unholy temples. This language assumes that some temples were holy, where God dwelt, while others were unholy, which God shunned. For example, speaking from his tower beside a holy temple, King Benjamin associated unholy temples with God's enemies:

> I say unto you, that the man that doeth this, the same cometh out in open rebellion against God; therefore he listeth to obey the evil spirit, and becometh an enemy to all righteousness; therefore, the Lord has no place in him, for he dwelleth not in unholy temples. Therefore if that man repenteth not, and remaineth and dieth an enemy to God, the demands of divine justice do awaken his immortal soul to a lively sense of his own guilt, which doth cause him to shrink from the presence of the Lord, and doth fill his breast with guilt, and pain, and anguish, which is like an unquenchable fire, whose flame ascendeth up forever and ever (Mosiah 2:37–38).

This text yields several clues about the ideal Nephite temple. First, God resides in the temple, and he will not take up residence in a hostile place. Second, righteous people come into the presence of the Lord in the temple; in saying that the unrepentant sinner will "shrink from the presence of the Lord," Benjamin alludes to the standard Israelite concept that the righteous appear before the face of the Lord in his holy temple. Finally, burnt offerings were sacrificed at or in the temple; the image of "an unquenchable fire, whose flame ascendeth up forever and ever" should have reminded Benjamin's audience of the holocaust offerings (cf. Mosiah 2:3) consumed completely by fire unto the Lord in the temple according to the law of Moses.

In speaking to the righteous people of the city of Gideon, Alma similarly testifies that God does not dwell in unholy temples, supplying the following explanation:

> He doth not dwell in unholy temples; neither can filthiness or anything which is unclean be received into the kingdom of God; . . . I have said these things unto you that I might awaken you to a sense of your duty to God,

that ye may walk blameless before him, that ye may walk
after the holy order of God, after which ye have been
received. And now I would that ye should be humble,
and be submissive and gentle; easy to be entreated; full
of patience and long-suffering; being temperate in all
things; being diligent in keeping the commandments of
God at all times; asking for whatsoever things ye stand in
need, both spiritual and temporal; always returning
thanks unto God for whatsoever things ye do receive
(Alma 7:21–23).

Building upon the temple imagery used by Benjamin,
this text associates the holiness of the temple with further
elements: namely, becoming clean; awakening a sense of
duty to God; walking blameless before God after his holy
order; acquiring the attributes of humility, submissiveness,
gentleness, teachability, patience, long-suffering, temper-
ance, and diligence in keeping the commandments; praying; and giving thanks. From this list it is reasonable to infer
that the Nephite temple featured ordinances of purification,
covenants that created duties or obligations to God, admission into the holy order of God, sacred teachings that promoted humility and gentleness and the submission of one's
will to God's plan, the issuance of commandments that one
promised to keep diligently, petitions to God for temporal
and spiritual blessings, and the return of thank offerings
and prayers of gratitude to God.

Amulek also draws upon temple imagery in his concluding comments to the Zoramite poor, who had been
refused entry to the synagogue in Antionum to offer prayer
on the Rameumptom. In contrast to that unholy place of
worship, the holy temple fosters individual hearts of righteousness: "The Lord hath said he dwelleth not in unholy
temples, but in the hearts of the righteous doth he dwell;
yea, and he has also said that the righteous shall sit down

in his kingdom, to go no more out; but their garments should be made white through the blood of the Lamb" (Alma 34:36). In this text, Amulek associates with the temple the concept of God's dwelling place, the reception of the righteous into God's kingdom, and the purification of one's garments. Having one's garments washed white through the blood of the Lamb was an important religious concept for the Nephites (see 2 Nephi 9:44; Jacob 2:2; Mosiah 2:28; Alma 5:21; 13:11; 34:36; 3 Nephi 27:19). It may well have had something to do with their temple ceremony, vividly typifying the purifying and cleansing power of the atoning blood of Jesus Christ. Likewise, from Amulek's words it appears that entering into God's presence and symbolically sitting down in his kingdom may have been a part of the Nephite temple experience.

During the days of Nephi, the son of Helaman, the Book of Mormon turns again to the concept of unholy temples to describe the weakened spiritual condition of the Nephites: "They saw that they had become weak, like unto their brethren, the Lamanites, and that the Spirit of the Lord did no more preserve them; yea, it had withdrawn from them because the Spirit of the Lord doth not dwell in unholy temples—Therefore the Lord did cease to preserve them by his miraculous and matchless power, for they had fallen into a state of unbelief and awful wickedness" (Helaman 4:24–25). This text associates the withdrawal of the spirit of God from the people with the loss of his powers of preservation. From this linkage, one can infer that the underlying idea of a holy temple among the Nephites embraced the belief that God's presence there afforded protection and strength, both individually and collectively.

Thus, the temples of Zarahemla and Bountiful were probably known primarily as sacred places, more holy than ordinary synagogues and sanctuaries. Although we have no information about who could be admitted inside these temples, synagogues and other sanctuaries figure prominently as common places of ordinary worship or as general gathering places,[77] whether among the Nephites (see Alma 16:13; 3 Nephi 18:31–32; Moroni 7:1), Lamanites (see Alma 21:9–16, 19–20; 23:2–3; 26:29), Nehorites (see Alma 4–5), Amalekites (see Alma 21:16), or Zoramites (see Alma 31:12; 32:1–12). Temples, on the other hand, are rarely mentioned, which seems to give them special status. Lamanite temples in the land southward are referred to in Alma 23:2 and 26:29. The cement construction of temples, synagogues, and sanctuaries in the land northward is briefly noted in Helaman 3:9, 14. Temples are never mentioned in the book of Ether, so it is unclear what use, if any, the Jaredites made of temples. In contrast to temples, Nephite synagogues were characteristically open to all people (see 2 Nephi 26:26), even to excommunicants (see 3 Nephi 18:32). Only Lamanites and Zoramites restricted access to their synagogues, based on political prejudice (see Alma 23:2) or social class distinction (the Zoramites judged the poor to be "filthiness" and therefore unworthy to enter their sacred space—Alma 32:3).

The Temple of Zarahemla around the Time of Benjamin

The second capital city to be occupied by the Nephites was the city of Zarahemla. Its temple served the land of Zarahemla during the first two centuries before Christ. Once again, very little is known about the architecture of the temple in Zarahemla: No information is given about when, how, why, or by whom it was built. It may have been constructed from scratch by the first Mosiah and his son Benjamin, or (following ample Mesoamerican and ancient

Near Eastern precedents) it could have been a remodeled temple built on top of an old temple that had been used by the people of Zarahemla prior to the arrival of the Nephites in that land about 200 B.C.

The main text that involves the temple of Zarahemla is found at the beginning of the book of Mosiah. It names the temple as the site of King Benjamin's monumental covenant renewal speech delivered at the time of his son's coronation. All the people in the land of Zarahemla were commanded to "gather themselves together, to go up to the temple to hear the words" that Benjamin would speak (Mosiah 1:18). They came in "great number, even so many that they did not number them" (Mosiah 2:2); and they brought

> the firstlings of their flocks, that they might offer sacrifice and burnt offerings according to the law of Moses; and also that they might give thanks to the Lord their God, who had brought them out of the land of Jerusalem, and who had delivered them out of the hands of their enemies, and had appointed just men to be their teachers, and also a just man to be their king, who had established peace in the land of Zarahemla, and who had taught them to keep the commandments of God, that they might rejoice and be filled with love towards God and all men (Mosiah 2:4).

When they came up to the temple, they pitched their tents family by family around the temple, with the tent door open to the temple, so that they could remain in their tents and listen to the words of the king as he spoke from a tower he had built near the temple (see Mosiah 2:5–7). From information found in this significant introduction and Benjamin's ensuing speech, a few basic facts about the temple in Zarahemla can be gleaned.

This temple was thought of as a high place. The people in the land of Zarahemla are said to "go up" to this temple.

Since a river ran near the city of Zarahemla, most people, however, would have come geographically "down" to this location. Obviously the image that was prevalent in the ancient Near East and in Jerusalem of the temple as a mountain ("let us go up to the mountain of the Lord"— Isaiah 2:3) still held sway among the Nephites.[78] The connection between the temple and mountain imagery surfaces once again in the Book of Mormon when the later Nephi was given the binding power to "say unto this temple it shall be rent in twain . . . and unto this mountain, be thou cast down" (Helaman 10:8–9); whether or not a physical rending and toppling was envisioned here, what Nephi was ultimately given in this regard was the power to strike down the legitimacy of unrighteous temples.

The temple of Zarahemla, like the tabernacle in Israel, was a place for numbering the people (compare Numbers 1–2). When the people of Benjamin gathered, they had become too numerous to number at the outset of the ceremony (see Mosiah 2:2); but before the people dispersed, priests were appointed and "the names of all those who had entered into a covenant with God" were taken (Mosiah 6:1–3). The size of this crowd stretched the capacity of the temple at Zarahemla to the limits. Not only did Benjamin need to build a tower from which to speak, but the normal procedures for numbering the people had to be altered.[79]

This temple was a place of sacrifice. The people brought firstlings of their flocks that they might offer sacrifice and burnt offerings according to the law of Moses. With these sacrifices, the Nephites gave thanks and rejoiced at the temple, especially for deliverance from their enemies, and expressed thanks for their good leaders and for peace.

It has been questioned whether firstlings were ever used for burnt offerings or sacrifices under the law of Moses.[80]

Clearly they were. Under that law, the firstlings (i.e., first-born male animals) were dedicated to the Lord (see Exodus 13:12, 15). Israelites were forbidden to use them for work or gain (see Deuteronomy 15:19–20). They were to take the firstlings to the temple to be sacrificed (see Deuteronomy 12:5–6, 11–14). Their blood was sprinkled upon the altar and their fat was burnt (see Numbers 18:17–18), and what was left was given to the individual and his household, to be eaten at the temple (see Deuteronomy 15:19–20). This symbolized the shedding of Christ's blood and was a type of his giving to his disciples ("Take, eat; this is my body"—Matthew 26:26). Since the days of Adam and Eve, the offering of firstlings at open altars has symbolized the sacrifice of God's first and only begotten son (see Moses 5:5). By bringing their firstlings to the temple, Benjamin and his people observed not only the ancient principles of sacrifice in general, but at the same time the specific provisions of the law of Moses with respect to the sacrifice of firstlings.

The temple of Zarahemla served as a gathering place where solemn official business was transacted. As mentioned previously, gathering at the temple was mandatory under the law of Moses: "Three times in the year all thy males shall appear before the Lord God" (Exodus 23:17), especially so that they could "hear" the word of the Lord.

> Moses commanded them, saying, At the end of every seven years, in the solemnity of the year of release, in the feast of tabernacles, when all Israel is come to appear before the Lord thy God in the place which he shall choose, thou shalt read this law before all Israel in their hearing. Gather the people together, men, women, and children, and thy stranger that is within thy gates, that they may hear, and that they may learn, and fear the Lord your God, and observe to do all the words of this law (Deuteronomy 31:10–12).

Benjamin's people likewise came to the temple to hear the word of the Lord, so that "the mysteries of God [could] be unfolded to [their] view" (Mosiah 2:9). In addition, other Nephite gatherings at this time occurred at temples (see, for example, Mosiah 7:17).

In Benjamin's case, every man in the land of Zarahemla, with his wife and children, pitched his tent near this temple. The presence of tents and families at Benjamin's convocation indicates that this was a traditional temple observance. Since Benjamin could have avoided the tedious task of having his speech copied and distributed to his people simply by having them leave their tents outside the temple precinct so that they could gather more closely around him to hear his words, these tents probably had some religious significance to the Nephites. Tents or booths were important in Israelite worship, since the Israelites remembered how they dwelt in tents during their forty years in the wilderness after the exodus from Egypt. Even God dwelt in a tent (the Tabernacle) until a permanent temple could be built in Jerusalem. This history was especially remembered in Jewish observances at the time of the Feast of Tabernacles, as John Tvedtnes and others have discussed, and many connections between that festival and Benjamin's speech have been noted elsewhere.[81]

In relation to understanding the temple in the Book of Mormon, attention should also be paid to further connections that exist between King Benjamin's speech and the Israelite Day of Atonement,[82] a holy day that was particularly laden with symbols of Christ and the day on which the temple figured more prominently than on any other pre-exilic Israelite celebration.[83] Since the Day of Atonement and the Feast of Tabernacles fell at or around the same time in ancient Israel,[84] it is possible to see influences from both of these holy days upon Benjamin's speech. While we cannot conclude absolutely that Benjamin's speech was given on or around the Day of Atonement, it appears that Benjamin has taken the main themes of that holy day, worked them into his discourse, and overlaid them with his Christian perspectives, revelations, and insights. In reading Benjamin's speech, one must be constantly alert to its crowning Christian superstructure as well as its persistent Mosaic underpinnings.

The hypothesis that Benjamin's speech embraces the themes of the Day of Atonement is initially suggested by the fact that Benjamin refers so often to the Atonement; he does so seven times (Mosiah 3:11, 15, 16, 18, 19; 4:6, 7). The number may be purely accidental, but doing something "seven times" is saliently characteristic of rituals performed on the Day of Atonement and other purification ceremonies prescribed in the book of Leviticus.[85] The priest's finger is dipped in the blood seven times; the blood is sprinkled seven times on the house, on the altar, and on the mercy seat (see Leviticus 4:6, 17; 8:11; 14:7, 16, 27, 51; 16:14, 19). Milgrom asks, "Is it an accident that the sevenfold sprinkling is the seventh rite [in Leviticus 4:3–12] as well as in the purification of the scale-diseased person [Leviticus 14:24–25]?" Given "the frequency of the number seven" in the rituals of the law of Moses, Milgrom doubts that its occurrence is inadvertent or insignificant in the Bible.[86] The same assumption applies in Benjamin's case.

Many salient features of the Day of Atonement are present in Mosiah 1–6. On that day, all were required to "afflict" their souls (see Leviticus 16:29–31; 23:27–32). It is not clear what is meant by "afflicting" one's soul, but if Benjamin was speaking on or near a day when the people were afflicting themselves, his deprecating descriptions of humans as being not even "as much as the dust of the earth" (Mosiah 2:25) and being an "enemy to God" (Mosiah 3:19), whose "nothingness" makes them "unworthy creatures" (Mosiah 4:11), fit powerfully into that context. Israelites who did not afflict their souls on this day were "cut off" from among the people (Leviticus 23:29), and similarly Benjamin speaks of blotting out the person who transgresses the covenant (see Mosiah 5:11) and of "cast[ing] him out" (Mosiah 5:14).

On that day, a special atonement was made to purify the temple by sprinkling blood on it and its altar (see Leviticus 16:14–19). If such a temple purification had just taken place in Zarahemla—or was about to take place—this would have given concrete contextual impact to Benjamin's emphatic point that God "dwelleth not in unholy temples" (Mosiah 2:37). Under the law of Moses, the temple priest on that day would also cleanse the people from certain kinds of iniquities and transgressions (see Leviticus 16:21–33), particularly sins against God (see Mosiah 4:2–3). Of primary concern were the sins of inadvertence (see Numbers 15:27) and sins of rebelliousness.[87] Those who "brazenly rebel"[88] were not eligible to have their transgression forgiven through the sacrifices of atonement (see Numbers 15:30–31). Benjamin has similar concerns with regard to sin. He explains in detail that the atoning blood of Christ covers the inadvertent sins of those "who have died not knowing the will of God concerning them, or who have ignorantly sinned" (Mosiah 3:11); and he who sins "contrary to his own knowledge" (Mosiah 2:33) receives Benjamin's harshest condemnation (see Mosiah 2:38–40): "Wo unto him who knoweth that he rebelleth against God!" (Mosiah 3:12); "the Lord has no place in him" (Mosiah 2:37).

The importance of the Day of Atonement was to be impressed upon all, even the little children. All who had passed puberty were required to observe the requirements of this day. Similarly, Benjamin stresses the application of his ceremony to all except "little children" (Mosiah 3:21) and "the infant" (Mosiah 3:18).

Leviticus 16:7–10 prescribes the well-known Day of Atonement scapegoat ritual, one of the strongest symbols in the Old Testament of the expiation of sin through the atonement of Jesus Christ. In this ritual, the high priest took two goats, one for Jehovah and the other for Azazel (apparently the name for the prince of the devils). The goat for Jehovah was sacrificed, but upon the other the high priest placed his hands and symbolically transferred to it all the sins of Israel. That scapegoat was then taken into the desert to remove sin from the covenant people of Israel. Perhaps Benjamin had a similar consequence in mind when he said that anyone who did not make and keep God's covenant would be driven away and cast out, as a man would drive out an intruding ass from among his flocks. Perhaps an ass was actually driven out of the temple precinct by one of the priests as Benjamin said, "Even so shall it be among you if ye know not the name by which ye are called" (Mosiah 5:14). Benjamin might have preferred the ass over the goat for several reasons: availability, for the symbolic value of its fabled stubbornness, from connections between the ass and the Nephites' ancestors Lehi (whose name means "jawbone [of an ass]"—cf. Judges 15:15–17) and Joseph (Speiser's translation of Genesis 49:22 sees Joseph as a wild ass colt), and because the ass was uniquely redeemable by the slaying of a lamb (see Exodus 13:13; 34:20).[89] The difference between an ass and goat is not critical; among Israel's neighbors it made little difference what kind of animal was used. Hittite expiatory rituals, for example, drove bulls, rams, mice, and vermin out of the ground.[90]

The Rabbis taught that the scapegoat's atonement was effective only when accompanied by repentance.[91] From this developed a tradition of "asking forgiveness of one another on the eve of the Day of Atonement."[92] Benjamin likewise implores his people to settle up with their neighbors: to "live peaceably, and to render to every man according to that which is his due," and to "return [any]thing that he borroweth" (Mosiah 4:13, 28).

From this came the importance of confession on the Day of Atonement. Forms of confession varied. The priest's confession would cover all the iniquities of the people, and then it had to "be matched by the remorse of the people," generally saying something like "we have trespassed, we have dealt treacherously" or "for the sin wherein we have sinned."[93] This is to be compared with confession of the people of King Benjamin of their carnal and sinful state (see Mosiah 4:2, 5), specifically echoing the king's acknowledgment of his own "worthless and fallen state" (Mosiah 4:5): "I am also of the dust" (Mosiah 2:26).[94] For those who thus confess and repent, this becomes the one day in the year when forgiveness is granted to all (see Leviticus 16:29–34).[95]

Giving gifts to the poor was also an important part of the Day of Atonement. "It is customary to send gifts to the poor, and a duty to ask forgiveness from one another and to appease each other."[96] Benjamin's exhortations about giving liberally to the poor, reconciling with your neighbor, and realizing that we are "all beggars" (Mosiah 4:13–28) would be especially pertinent messages at a Day of Atonement celebration, where "restitution to man must precede sacrificial expiation from God."[97] This, along with prayer, was a necessary condition of obtaining remission of sins ("calling on the name of the Lord daily," and imparting of your substance, "for the sake of retaining a remission of your sins from day to day"—Mosiah 4:11, 26).

The Day of Atonement for all Israel thus became a time of "true joy."[98] Similarly, Benjamin and his people experienced "exceedingly great joy" (Mosiah 4:11) and they "rejoiced" (Mosiah 2:4; 4:12) abundantly. This was a time of feeling the nearness of God to all his creatures,[99] just as Benjamin exulted in the "goodness of God, and his matchless power, and his wisdom, and his patience, and his long-suffering towards the children of men" (Mosiah 4:6).

This true joy was rooted in the sublime and profound holiness of the day. So holy was the Day of Atonement that on this day—but on this day alone—could the unspeakable name of God, *YHWH*, be pronounced; ten times in all during the Day of Atonement service would the priest say this name out loud, and each time the people would fall prostrate on the ground (according to rabbinic sources).[100] Just as hearing and receiving the name of God had profound impact on the people in Jerusalem, so it did on the people in Zarahemla, where this giving of "a name" was accorded extraordinary prominence and held in great reverence and holiness. Benjamin states that one of the main purposes of the assembly was to "give this people a name" (Mosiah 1:11–12). In great solemnity and emphasis,[101] he reveals the name of "Jesus Christ, the Son of God, the Father of heaven and earth, the Creator of all things," along with the name of his mother Mary (Mosiah 3:8). Finally, he gives the people the name and tells them that "this is the name that I said I should give unto you" (Mosiah 5:11).

The ineffable name of God, *YHWH*, was never to be spoken lightly in ancient Israel. Just as the Jewish traditions allowed the priest to utter this name ten times during the Day of Atonement liturgy, it is interesting that in Benjamin's speech, the expanded name of God as "Lord God" (five times), "Lord God Omnipotent" (twice) and "Lord Omnipotent" (three times), appears a total of ten times.[102] Seven of these utterances are in the words spoken by the angel to Benjamin (Mosiah 3:5, 13, 14, 17, 18, 21, 23). It seems more than coincidental because the number seven reflects "spiritual" perfection, and thus it is the spirit or angel that uses the name seven times, as well as the name "Christ" exactly seven times, and the root "atone" appears seven times in this seven-part speech.

The other three utterances of the expanded name of God are in Benjamin's own words (see Mosiah 2:30, 41; 5:15). Three is the number of "real" completeness; thus Benjamin himself, a mortal, pronounces the name three times. Moreover, it is significant that these three utterances come at important ceremonial breaking points in the speech, not merely at random or in inconsequential places. The holy name is given at the end points of three of the chiastic sections of Benjamin's speech. Mosiah 2:30 is the breaking point between the first two sections of the speech. It is quite plausible that the people would have fallen down at this point as they heard Benjamin pronounce the holy name of God as well as while he announced his son Mosiah to be their new king (see Mosiah 2:29–30).

Mosiah 2:41 is another clear breaking point in the speech. I think it likely that the people would have fallen down as they heard Benjamin pronounce the holy name on this occasion and as he imposed the judgment of God upon the people. In Mosiah 4:1, Benjamin observes that the people "had fallen to the earth," but the text does not say when they had done so. Since the sacred name is mentioned seven times in rapid succession in Mosiah 3:5–23, it is possible that the people remained in a fallen state throughout

Benjamin's words about the fall of Adam (vv. 11, 16, 19) and the atonement of Christ (vv. 13, 17–21). The final utterance of the holy name is in Mosiah 5:15, the final verse of the speech. Although the text is silent on this point, the people may have fallen down again as they heard Benjamin praise God and as he "sealed" the people to God.

For such a great day, sacred preparations were in order, especially those made by the high priest. Rabbinic writings report special efforts taken to keep the high priest awake during the night of the Day of Atonement, and pious men followed this example.[103] Benjamin's preparations, also, were substantial. He was awakened at night—"Awake; and I awoke. . . . Awake, and hear"—Mosiah 3:2–3)—by the visitation of an angel from God. He met with his sons (see Mosiah 1:10–18) and carefully wrote his speech in advance (see Mosiah 2:7).

If these dozen factors build a plausible case for concluding that Benjamin's speech was, among other things, a thoroughly Christianized observance of the basic requirements of the Day of Atonement under the law of Moses, then we may fairly safely assume that the Nephites observed at the temple of Zarahemla the essence of the rituals of that very holy day and the other holy festivals as ordained by Jehovah. Most of all, we may appreciate in some detail how the Nephites likely understood the ceremonies of that temple—most dramatically the practices of the Day of Atonement—as looking forward to the ultimate day of Christ's atonement: to the purifying power of his atoning blood and to the need for his faithful followers to repent and be charitable in response to his infinite and eternal sacrifice. This has great significance in corroborating the assertions of Nephi, Jarom, and Alma that the Nephites were indeed strict in observing the law of Moses.

In addition, we may note two further functions served by the temple in Zarahemla. First, it was the traditional place for the coronation of kings. As Stephen Ricks has documented, this is consistent with ancient practices.[104] At the temple in Zarahemla, Benjamin announced that his son would become king (see Mosiah 2:30), after which Mosiah was consecrated to be a ruler and king over the people; assuredly that anointing took place in or at the temple (see Mosiah 6:3).

And last, this temple was a place of covenant making and renewing for all the people.[105] By their king's covenant speech, Benjamin's people were taught the principles of the atonement of Jesus Christ. In response, they all cried out in unison for forgiveness. As a result, they received forgiveness of their sins (see Mosiah 4:2–3), they were born again (see Mosiah 5:2–4), and Benjamin was able to rid his garments of their blood (see Mosiah 2:28). By covenant they agreed to promote social justice (see Mosiah 4:13–28) and to obey God's commandments (see Mosiah 5:5), and in return they were given the new name of Christ (see Mosiah 5:7)[106] and were sealed up as sons and daughters of God to receive everlasting salvation and eternal life (see Mosiah 5:7, 15). Although this gives us only a sketchy outline of this particular covenant ceremony performed at the temple in Zarahemla, its broad outlines are distinct and recognizably familiar, including the precepts of obedience, sacrifice, atonement, purification, consecration, putting on the attributes of Christ, and being sealed up unto God.

Soon after Benjamin's death, Nephite society outgrew its central temple in the city of Zarahemla. When the Nephites gathered a few years later (presumably at the temple of Zarahemla) to hear the official reading of Limhi's record upon his return to Zarahemla, the people had to be divided into two bodies (see Mosiah 25:1, 4). This may have been one of the last such assemblies at the temple of Zarahemla. Thirty years later, when King Mosiah delivered his resolution to abandon the kingship and to institute the reign of Judges, he did not call the people together, but communicated to them in writing (see Mosiah 29:4), while they assembled in separate groups around the land to cast their voice pursuant to the new law of Mosiah (see Mosiah 29:39). With the institution of kingship abandoned, and with the population becoming large and diverse, the temple would no longer function as a single civic and religious center for the growing and fragmenting Nephite population.

Church and Temple in Zarahemla at the Time of Alma the Younger

Reconstructing an adequate picture of life in Zarahemla around 100 B.C. is even more complicated than for other periods of Nephite history. During the reign of Benjamin (died c. 119 B.C.), it seems that there was only one temple in the land of Zarahemla. At least the religion was closely supervised by Benjamin and the "holy prophets" who assisted him in seeing that false preachers and teachers were silenced and punished (Words of Mormon 1:16–17). That world of unanimity changed dramatically during the reign of Mosiah.

First, Limhi and his people escaped from the city of Nephi, arriving in Zarahemla shortly after Mosiah took the throne. It is unknown what became of these people, but it could not have been easy for them to have been integrated into Nephite society: They came without possessions; their average level of education would have been different, and probably inferior, to that of the Nephites; and they probably spoke a different dialect. The extent to which they accepted and adopted the religious practices observed at the temple in Zarahemla is unknown.

Second, Alma and his covenant group also arrived in the land of Zarahemla during Mosiah's reign. This group did not merge into mainstream Nephite society, but it remained separate, probably due to the covenant they had made "to bear one another's burdens" and to live as "the fold of God" (Mosiah 18:8). Alma's group had lived for over thirty years away from any temple; his priests functioned exclusively as teachers (see Mosiah 18:18), and Alma "commanded them that they should preach nothing save it were repentance and faith on the Lord" (Mosiah 18:20). From this it appears that they placed little emphasis on sacrifice. Moreover, unlike Nephi, Alma the Elder refused to become a king over his people (see Mosiah 23:6–12), but he became "their high priest . . . the founder of their church" (Mosiah 18:16).

Just as the later-arriving Ammonites were allowed by Alma the Younger to remain separate and encouraged to keep their covenant never to take up arms again (see Alma 27:28; 56:6–8), so Alma's group also was given considerable autonomy, being granted power by King Mosiah to organize and administer seven churches independent of royal supervision or review (see Mosiah 26:17). Since King Mosiah probably kept control over the temple, it seems likely that Alma's group continued to have little to do with that temple after they arrived in Zarahemla. Alma insisted that all the people in Zarahemla be baptized, presumably requiring them to take the same covenant as those who had been baptized at the Waters of Mormon. All who refused to join this new order became "a separate people" (Mosiah 26:4). Soon others in the church became high priests: there was a high priest over the people of Ammon (see Alma

30:20), and another high priest in the land of Gideon (see Mosiah 30:21). Apparently they officiated at their own local temples, for Alma and Amulek preached repentance "to the people in their temples, and in their sanctuaries, and also in their synagogues, which were built after the manner of the Jews" (Alma 16:13). At the same time, the followers of Nehor organized their own religious movement, complete with priests and synagogues. Soon the temple of Zarahemla was not the only temple in the land. In less than a generation, considerable religious pluralism emerged in the land of Zarahemla.

Alma the Younger was appointed the high priest over the land of Zarahemla when he became the first chief judge. In this capacity he probably supervised and officiated at the temple of Zarahemla, taking over that responsibility from the king when the kingship was abandoned. In the ninth year of his reign, Alma relinquished the judgment seat to Nephihah (see Alma 4:17, 20), but he "retained the office of high priest unto himself . . . and confined himself wholly to the high priesthood of the holy order of God" (Alma 4:18, 20). Given the needs of the people in his day, Alma focused all of his energies, as well as his doctrinal thinking, on "bearing down [on the people] in pure testimony against them" (Alma 4:19). This appears to have ushered in a new period in the religious history of the Nephites. Although they continued to observe the law of Moses, greater importance was placed on developing personal Christian virtues. National assemblies, group covenants, collective confessions, and organized ceremonies seem to have given way at this time to an almost exclusive emphasis on personal righteousness (see Alma 5, 7), individual repentance (see Alma 34, 36), and ubiquitous private prayer (see Alma 33–34). The temple of Zarahemla is never mentioned again in the Book of Mormon.

Alma 12–13 as a Temple Text

The best indication of how Alma understood the holy priesthood ordinances that were of central importance in his day is found in his sermon in Alma 12–13. Ironically, this speech was delivered to the wicked men of Ammonihah. Apparently Alma needed to warn them completely before sealing them to destruction, and thus he taught them the fullness of the gospel according to the most sacred pattern he knew. In those two chapters, Alma teaches that God will provide men access to certain "mysteries," but only according to the "heed and diligence" that they give (Alma 12:9–11). While we cannot be certain that Alma was alluding in this speech to specific elements of a Nephite temple ordinance, many factors support that idea.[107] For one thing, the word *mysteries* seems to refer to priesthood or temple ordinances. Benjamin unfolded the "mysteries of God" to his people by speaking to them at the temple (Mosiah 2:9). Likewise, in ancient religions, for example from the Hellenistic world, the word *mysteries* was often used to describe "cultic rites . . . portrayed before a circle of devotees," who "must undergo initiation" and who are promised "salvation by the dispensing of cosmic life," which is sometimes "enacted in cultic drama," accompanied by a strict "vow of silence."[108] Alma told the wicked Ammonihahites that many people knew the Nephite mysteries, but, like himself, they were laid under a strict condition of secrecy (see Alma 12:9). Nevertheless, the plan of life, as taught by Alma, provided all people a chance to know these mysteries in full, on conditions of humility (see Alma 12:10–11; 13:13–14) and through the administrations of righteous priests and teachers (see Alma 13:16; cf. Mosiah 2:9; Alma 26:22).

The first section of this sermon (Alma 12:12–27) describes the judgment of God and tells how mankind can avert a second death by obeying a new set of commandments. According to Alma's exposition, the fall of mankind was prefigured by Adam's violation of a first set of commandments (see Alma 12:22); and since all people must die in order to come to judgment (see Alma 12:24), messengers ("angels") were sent and God revealed to mankind the plan of mercy through the Son (see Alma 12:29–30). Mankind was then given a second set of commandments (see Alma 12:32), accompanied by an oath that whoever broke those commandments should not enter into the rest of the Lord but instead would die an ultimate, or last, spiritual death (see Alma 12:35–36).

After stating the fundamentals of the plan of salvation, Alma continued his discourse in words that apparently retrace the steps of a sacred Nephite rite that evidently involved an ordination to the priesthood (see Alma 13:1) and prepared the way for obedient people to "enter into the rest of the Lord" (Alma 13:16). This Nephite ordinance was evidently a symbolic ritual, since Alma says that it was performed "in a manner" that looked forward to the redemption of the Son of God (Alma 13:2). That manner, however, is mentioned by Alma only in veiled terms. At a minimum, it appears that the Nephite ceremony referred to a premortal existence, for the candidates were assured that they had been "called and prepared from the foundation of the world" with a "holy calling" (Alma 13:3; see also vv. 5, 8). That calling "was prepared with, and according to, a preparatory redemption for such," implying that it was provided by God before the world began (Alma 13:3); and it was patterned after, in, and through the preparation of the Son (see Alma 13:5). In this setting, the participants were "ordained with a holy ordinance," "taking upon them the high priesthood of the holy order" (Alma 13:6, 8). Thereby they became "high priests forever, after the order of the Son." After these preparatory ordinances, and after making a choice "to repent and work righteousness rather than to perish," the candidate was sanctified by the Holy Ghost, his garments were washed white, and he "entered into the rest of the Lord" (Alma 13:9–10, 12).

Judging by the limited and closely guarded clues that Alma gives in Alma 12–13, we can venture that Nephite religious practices included some form of priesthood ordination that called people to a life's work of repentance, peace, and righteousness. Based on the appearance of the following elements in Alma 12–13, the Nephite temple ceremony utilized familiar temple motifs, including abundant creation imagery regarding the fall of Adam and Eve (see 12:22–26), the redemption (see 12:25–33), the issuance of commandments (see 12:31–32), one's calling (see 13:3–8), clothing (see 13:11–12), the facing of judgment (see 12:14, 32–35), and symbolic entrance into the presence of God (see 12:36; 13:12). Alma 12–13 gives the best information about sacred Nephite ordinances during the time of the Nephite judges. Presumably these rites were administered primarily at the temple in Zarahemla but possibly also at other sanctuaries or sacred places under the direction of a high priest.

The temple themes in Alma 12–13 are found elsewhere in Alma's sermons and writings and throughout the Book of Mormon. Consistent with the fact, Nephite priests commonly reminded the people of the rites and ordinances they had experienced, "to stir them up in remembrance of the oath which they had made" (Mosiah 6:3). The appearance of those themes in the Book of Mormon, as well as in the apocryphal Jewish and Christian writings, has been discussed by Hugh Nibley, who focuses attention especially on the constancy of the common pattern comprised of such things as the plan of salvation, the promise of heavenly treasures, premortality, creation motifs, instructions given to Adam and Eve, the tree of life, ritual combat against the powers of evil, purification, the road back to God, apocalyptic and ritual imagery, ordinances, the right and left hand, the white garment, the strait way, covenant making, petition for admission, and entrance into God's presence.[109] Such themes are often embodied in the texts of the Book of Mormon, which may reflect the doctrines taught and the ordinances administered in the Nephite temples during the time of Alma.[110]

The Temple of Bountiful

The all-important fact known about the temple of Bountiful was that Jesus appeared to the Nephites there. The singularity of that epiphany transformed all things of the Nephites and put them all in an entirely new perspective, so that "all things had become new" (3 Nephi 15:3).

In the first century before Christ, the city of Bountiful was a relatively new, small, but important Nephite settlement (see Alma 22:29). Located near the narrow neck of land, it marked and guarded the northern boundary of Nephite territory and held an important military position preventing the Lamanites from completely encircling the Nephites and thereby blocking their escape into the land northward. Because this outpost was of vital interest to Nephite security (see Alma 50:32; Helaman 1:28; 3 Nephi 3:23) and Lamanite prisoners were held there (see Alma

52:39), it is reasonable to assume that once Moroni fortified this site (see Alma 52:9), no one was stationed or allowed to live there who was not fiercely and unquestionably loyal to the Nephite cause. The fact that these settlers built, operated, and maintained a temple in this remote and obscure site confirms their devotion to the most orthodox Nephite values and traditional practices.

The city of Bountiful must have been fairly small. Even one hundred years after its settlement, the town's entire population was able to gather at the temple. The entire crowd, consisting of men, women, and children, totaled only two thousand five hundred people (see 3 Nephi 17:25). If the average family size was four or five, this amounts to only 500 to 625 families. Nevertheless, included in that crowd were several men of great spiritual stature led by Nephi, the prophet to whom Jesus announced his birth the day before he was born in Bethlehem, and who raised his brother from the dead. Eleven other very worthy Nephite men lived in this community, and together with Nephi they were called to serve as Jesus' twelve disciples in the New World.

These people epitomized the law of obedience. When the sign of the birth of Jesus had been given, some among the Nephites had argued that it was no longer necessary to live the law of Moses because the Messiah had come, and therefore the old law was finally abrogated. Nephi, however, corrected this error, explaining that the law of Moses would not be put into abeyance until it had been entirely fulfilled (see 3 Nephi 1:25). Accordingly, Nephi's righteous followers in Bountiful continued to observe each and every provision of the law of Moses, as they understood it, until such time as they should be instructed otherwise. Among these obedient people undoubtedly also were many people who had risked their lives by refusing to disavow the prophecies of Samuel the Lamanite, even in the face of death threats should his five-year prophecy go unfulfilled. Their old religious system could not yet have been entirely the same as a full and exclusively Christian worship, for these righteous people, who remained strict in living the law of Moses even in anticipation of the immediate coming of Christ, were still confused and amazed by the teachings of Jesus (see 3 Nephi 15:2) when he appeared to them and taught them how "all things had become new" (3 Nephi 15:3).

3 Nephi 11–18 as a Temple Text

I have explored elsewhere in detail the prospect that the words and events reported in 3 Nephi 11–18 can and should be understood as reflecting a sacred temple experience.[111] I will not repeat all of that analysis here; but to complete the present discussion of temples in the Book of Mormon, I will briefly summarize that interpretation to identify some of its main features and clarify its significance.

It is important that Jesus appeared at the temple (see 3 Nephi 11:1–12). Since he could have chosen to appear anywhere he wanted, his appearance at the temple communicated to his followers that the temple would continue to have a central role in their religious life. Given the long history of the Nephites relative to the temple, it would not have surprised them that the Lord would choose to teach them at the temple. For six centuries, temples had been important religious and political centers for teaching, preaching, imparting the mysteries, making royal proclamations, and for various gatherings and sacrifices. What might have been surprising to the Nephites, however, was that Jesus continued to associate so closely with the temple.

By appearing at the temple, Jesus demonstrated that all things would become new, not that the old things would simply be cast off.

It is also significant that a crowd of men, women, and children had gathered at the temple in Bountiful, not knowing that Jesus would appear to them that day. Because there is no mention of destructions in the land Bountiful at the crucifixion of Christ, and because this gathering probably occurred several weeks, if not months, after the signs of Christ's death, one must wonder if these Nephites had assembled themselves on one of their traditional holy days to appear before the Lord and to hear the word of God. It seems that they gathered early in the morning, for the events in 3 Nephi 11–18 certainly filled an entire day. The fact that they came with women and children proves that the meeting was not simply an emergency session of city elders or some other meeting to consider mundane political affairs.

While we do not know why they gathered on that occasion, it is obvious that sooner or later the Nephites would have wondered what they should do next. They knew that the law of Moses had been fulfilled, and they knew that they should no longer offer blood sacrifices or burnt offerings, but they had not yet received instructions as to how they should proceed. It would not have been obvious to them how to separate out the fulfilled elements of the law of Moses from the eternal elements of the gospel of Jesus Christ, for even Adam had offered sacrifice by the shedding of blood. So without further instruction, they would not have known God's will concerning the order to be observed after the coming of Jesus Christ. They received that further light and knowledge as they entered into a new covenant with God, received the laws and commandments of that covenant, and were endowed with power and authority to baptize, to teach, and to bestow the gift of the Holy Ghost. All of this was done to prepare the people to pass through the final judgment, to enter into God's presence (see 14:21–23), and to be "raise[d] up at the last day" (see 3 Nephi 15:1).

I refer to 3 Nephi 11–18 as the Sermon at the Temple. Enumerated and discussed elsewhere are many factors that demonstrate the ritual context of this text. Some of these factors are clear and strong, while others are simply supporting, contributing, or faint. Nevertheless the cumulative effect of all of these elements is to construct a picture that, to my mind, makes the best sense of this entire day's experience. This interpretation is not the only way to view this material,[112] and my interpretation cannot be proved beyond all reasonable doubt, but in terms of illuminating individual details as well as accounting for all parts of the picture, no other model I know makes as much sense of the entire text as does the interpretation that sees it as a temple text.

That view is confirmed to a large extent by the fact that the Nephites enshrined the words of Jesus in formal language that they used in praying (see 3 Nephi 13:9–13), performing baptisms (see 3 Nephi 11:25), administering the sacrament (see 3 Nephi 18:5–11; Moroni 4–5), bestowing the gift of the Holy Ghost (see Moroni 2), and ordaining priests and teachers (see Moroni 3). From such reverence, it is evident that the Nephites did not view the words of Jesus as a casual extemporaneous moral discourse or informal personal conversation. His words had eternal significance that endowed these people with divine knowledge and power. To perpetuate the memory of formative experiences like these, sacred ceremonies might well have been instituted, helping the people remember and reenact the events that they had witnessed.

Several elements in the Sermon at the Temple strongly suggest its ceremonial nature. Altogether, the people fell down (see 3 Nephi 11:12), they all shouted Hosanna (see 3 Nephi 11:17), and others bowed themselves (see 3 Nephi 11:19), indicating a sacred environment and ritual actions. Ordinations were performed (see 3 Nephi 11:21–22; 12:1; 18:37), the absence of evil was assured (see 3 Nephi 11:28–30), witnesses were called (see 3 Nephi 11:35–36; 17:25), and Jesus instructed the people to give strict heed to the words of his newly ordained disciples (see 3 Nephi 12:2). The people received instruction concerning the making of oaths (see 3 Nephi 12:33–37), the offering of group prayers (see 3 Nephi 13:9–13), the wearing of true sacred clothing (see 3 Nephi 13:25, 28–31), and the entering into the presence of God through a narrow entrance (see 3 Nephi 14:13–14).

In addition, several other factors can be identified that bear more than a casual or accidental similarity to the Latter-day Saint temple experience. The people identified Jesus as a divine heavenly being by experiencing the marks on his hands and in his side (see 3 Nephi 11:14–15). The commandments issued in the Sermon at the Temple in 3 Nephi 12–13 are not only the same as the main commandments always issued at the temple, but they appear largely in the same order: obedience and sacrifice (see 12:19), evil speaking of the brethren (see 12:22), chastity and a higher understanding of marriage and divorce (see 12:28–32), love for one's enemies and obedience to the law of love or the law of the gospel (see 12:39, 41–45), and alms to the poor and consecration of one's life to the worship and service of God (see 13:1, 20, 24). Before advancing further into his presentation, Jesus instructed the people that before they might come to him they should first be reconciled with their brothers and sisters (see 12:23–24). He exhorted them to become "perfect" (12:48), a word that implies not only ethical perfection but also the full initiation into the covenants of the religion and the achievement of full harmony with God.[113]

The Sermon at the Temple conveyed to people knowledge and power that was so holy it could not be given to other people; the threatened penalty was death, "lest they . . . turn again and rend you" (3 Nephi 14:6). In the end, the people were invited to make a three-fold petition (ask, seek, and knock) so that the Father might open and allow the righteous to "enter into the kingdom of heaven" (3 Nephi 14:21). Before the Sermon at the Temple ended, Jesus prayed unspeakable things on behalf of the parents and in turn blessed their children; this great blessing of the Nephite families occurred in the midst of fire, God, angels, and witnesses (see 3 Nephi 17:17, 21, 24–25). He also gave them a new name (see 3 Nephi 18:5, 11). None of these elements are unfamiliar or inconsequential to the temple as far as Latter-day Saints are concerned.

A number of weaker factors also can be brought into this picture—not that they prove the picture, but that they make sense in this context. For example, the Beatitudes promise the ultimate blessings of eternal life, similar to promises made in the temple. My interpretation does not turn upon these additional suggestions, but they are worth noting.

Jesus' Sermon and Temple Texts in Exodus and Leviticus

Finally, it must have been particularly impressive to the Nephites to see the new law fulfill so many elements of their old law. In addition to the long list of Old Testament elements that have previously been found in the Sermon on the Mount,[114] consider the temple legacy of Exodus 19–24 and its connections with 3 Nephi 11–18. The chapters from Exodus contain the biblical account of God's appearance to Moses on Mount Sinai (equated with the temple—see Exodus 15:17), when the law of Moses was given and the people covenanted to keep it. That revelation took place on a mountain, in a space that had been set apart as sacred and holy (see Exodus 19:21). The Israelites washed their clothing and for three days prepared to meet God (see Exodus 19:14). Laws were given, including rules regarding sacrifice, worship of God, obedience, adultery, and covetousness. These commandments became the stipulations of Jehovah's covenant with Israel, who was promised, "He shall bless thy bread, and thy water; and I will take sickness away from the midst of thee" and "the number of thy days I will fulfil" (Exodus 23:25–26). In return, the Israelites promised their exclusive dedication to the God of Israel (see Exodus 23:32–33). The people all answered with one voice, "All the words which the Lord hath said will we do" (Exodus 24:3). Moses wrote the words of the covenant, built an altar (see Exodus 23:4), and sprinkled blood on the people, "the blood of the covenant, which the Lord hath made with you concerning all these words" (Exodus 23:8). As the Nephites looked back on the divine and ritual-laden origins of the law of Moses, they could easily see its fulfillment in the new revelation that they received from Jesus at the temple in Bountiful, at a symbolic mount, with laws concerning sacrifice, obedience, adultery, and consecration, down to the healing of the sick, the blessing of bread, and the drinking of the cup of the blood of the new testament.

In broad terms, the main themes of the Sermon at the

Temple are also the topics treated in the book of Leviticus, regarded by Jews as the most sacred of the five books of Moses. Its main concerns are implementing the law of sacrifice (chs. 1–7, 17), bestowing the priesthood (chs. 8–10), assuring purity (chs. 11–16), holy living and loving one's neighbor (ch. 19), defining chastity (ch. 20), hallowing the sabbath days (ch. 23), eschewing blasphemy (ch. 24), and caring for the poor and consecrating property to the Lord (chs. 25–27). Not being steeped in the ethical and spiritual dimensions of the law of Moses, modern LDS readers tend to overlook the profound religious legacy of these underlying purposes of the law that have enduring relevance to the temple.[115]

Jesus identified himself as the prophet-like-Moses and said, "I am he that gave the law, and I am he who covenanted with my people Israel" (3 Nephi 15:5). The continuity from the law of Moses to the law of Christ is nowhere more visible than it was at the temple in Bountiful, as Christ gave the Nephites laws, covenanted with them, and made all their old things new.

Conclusion

The temple in the Book of Mormon is a complex subject. Some facts about Nephite temples are obvious and clear; others are subtle, obscure, and inferential. Drawing general conclusions is difficult and challenging. Nevertheless, although most readers probably assume that the Book of Mormon contains very little information about temples, dozens of precious pieces of information can be coaxed out of the text with little or no coercion.

The Nephite record bridges both Jewish and Christian backgrounds. The world of the Book of Mormon is neither Jewish nor Christian, but both, if properly understood.

Nephite temples were infused with both the strict observance of the law of Moses and the prophetic comprehension
of the gospel of Jesus Christ. The Book of Mormon's invitation to harmonize the word of God in all of its dispensations
and manifestations and its ability to unify both testaments
of the Bible are perhaps two of its most important, and yet
most often overlooked, strengths in today's world of often-
strained Jewish and Christian relationships. No other text
better shows a religious group valuing both the strict observance of the law of Moses and its fulfillment in Jesus Christ.

From the time of Lehi, to the temple period of Nephi
and Jacob, to the temple convocations in Zarahemla and
Bountiful, changes occurred among the Nephites with
respect to the temple—not changes in the eternal aspects of
the gospel, but changes in practice, priestly and ecclesiastical organization, and emphasis. In the earlier periods, the
temple played a greater political role, especially in conjunction with the establishment and enhancement of king-
ships. Later, King Benjamin's speech was filled with specific
Israelite themes and terms, particularly those characteristic
of the holy celebrations of the Day of Atonement and Feast
of Tabernacles, which he infused with Christian knowledge
and perspectives. By the time of Alma the Younger, following the abandonment of kingship in the land of Zarahemla,
the political function of the temple diminished, and the
Israelite elements become far less obvious. Alma's emphasis
was on teaching the plan of salvation, cultivating personal
righteousness, and regularizing local church worship. With
the coming of Christ in 3 Nephi, blood sacrifice and burnt
offerings came to an end, and a new sacred order was established. The differences between that new order and the
prior Nephite ritual order were great enough that the
people saw the continuity between the two and yet were

amazed and astonished at how all of the old had become new, evidently down to minute details.

In light of all that can be said about temples in the Book of Mormon, it is finally well to remember that in 1829, when the Book of Mormon was translated, Joseph Smith had scarcely thought or dreamed of a temple. Two years later he and the Church would move to Kirtland, where a temple was dedicated in 1836. The ordinances of washing, anointing, and the washing of feet were performed in that temple, but the full endowment was not given until 1843 in Nauvoo. Joseph Smith did not live to see the completion of the Nauvoo Temple, but he completed the task of revealing its essential architectural and ceremonial components that epitomize the gospel of Jesus Christ and its eternal laws and ordinances. In retrospect, we can see today that the blueprint of the Restoration for worshiping the Lord Jesus Christ in his holy house was already largely embedded in the texts of the Book of Mormon.

Notes

1. Hugh W. Nibley, "Temples: Meaning and Functions of Temples," in *EM*, 4:1459.

2. Stephen D. Ricks, "Temples through the Ages," in *EM*, 4:1463.

3. The temple of Jerusalem, for example, featured warnings inscribed in stone, notifying foreigners that they were not allowed to enter the temple. The temple inscription found in 1871 reads, "No man of another nation to enter within the fence and enclosure round the temple. And whoever is caught will have himself to blame that his death ensues" (C. K. Barrett, *The New Testament Background: Selected Documents* [New York: Harper and Row, 1961], 50). For an inscription on a temple in Philadelphia in Asia Minor, see Moshe Weinfeld, "The Decalogue: Its Significance, Uniqueness, and place in Israel's Tradition," in *Religion and Law: Biblical-Judaic and Islamic Perspectives,* ed. Edwin Firmage, Bernard Weiss, and John Welch (Winona Lake, Indiana: Eisenbrauns, 1990), 35.

4. In ancient Israel, and in the ancient Near East generally, "religion and state could not be separated" (G. W. Ahlström, *Royal*

Administration and National Religion in Ancient Palestine [Leiden: Brill, 1982], 18).

5. For the temple symbolism in Ether 1–4, see "The Brother of Jared at the Veil," by Catherine M. Thomas, following this chapter.

6. Robert L. Millet, "The Cultural and Religious Background of the Nephites: Was It Jewish or Christian?" unpublished preliminary paper, presented at Brigham Young University, 22 January 1993. As I discuss further below, I believe that this paper sets up a problematic, or at least inadequately defined, dichotomy: the terms *Jewish* and *Christian* in their proper sense are not mutually exclusive in the Book of Mormon's view.

7. Moses appeared at the transfiguration of Jesus (see Matthew 17:3) and in the Kirtland Temple (see D&C 110:11), and he was also a type of the Savior himself (see 3 Nephi 20:23).

8. For a brief discussion of the meanings of these important Hebrew terms, see my 1988 F.A.R.M.S. Update entitled "Statutes, Judgments, Ordinances, and Commandments," reprinted in *Reexploring the Book of Mormon*, ed. John W. Welch (Salt Lake City: Deseret Book and F.A.R.M.S., 1992), 62–65.

9. The word *profane* derives from Latin, *pro* (in place of) and *fanum* (a temple, including the land around it), i.e., *profano*, I desecrate. In Webster's 1828 dictionary of the American language, the word's main meanings include "irreverent to any thing sacred," "proceeding from a contempt of sacred things," "polluted, not pure"; its last meaning is "obscene."

10. For one scholar's assessment of this complex issue, see Israel Knohl, "The Priestly Torah versus the Holiness School: Sabbath and the Festivals," *Hebrew Union College Annual* 58 (1987): 65–117.

11. Using the word *ordinance* to mean a particular law, as in *municipal ordinance*.

12. Evidence for the Nephite observance of preexilic Israelite holy days, especially the Day of Atonement, appears further below in connection with King Benjamin's speech, pages 346–53.

13. Bruce R. McConkie, *The Promised Messiah* (Salt Lake City: Deseret Book, 1978), 427. Elder McConkie was deliberately cautious in his approach, prefacing the statement quoted above as follows: "We *suppose* their sacrifices were those that antedated the ministry of Moses and that, since they had the fulness of the gospel itself, they kept the law of Moses in the sense that they conformed to its myriad moral principles and its endless ethical restrictions. We *suppose* this would be one of the reasons Nephi was able to say, 'The law hath become dead unto us'" (italics added).

14. Jacob Milgrom, *Leviticus 1–16* (New York: Doubleday, 1991), 195.

15. Hugh Nibley, "How to Get Rich," in *Approaching Zion*, in *CWHN*, 9:195.

16. See Jacob Milgrom, "The Biblical Diet Laws as an Ethical System," in *Studies in Cultic Theology and Terminology* (Leiden: Brill, 1983), 104–18.

17. See, for example, Milgrom, *Leviticus 1–16*, 533–34; "The Biblical Diet Laws," 106–7.

18. Jeremiah urged the people to cease their voluntary free-will offerings until such time as their hearts were pure, but he "has nothing to say whatsoever concerning the fixed Temple sacrifices" (Milgrom, "The Biblical Diet Laws," 120).

19. Milgrom considers it to have been "conclusively demonstrated that the prophets did not object to the cult per se but only to its abuse" (Milgrom, *Leviticus 1–16*, 482).

20. For an overview of scholarship concerning Jesus' relationship to the law during his lifetime in Palestine, see Donald A. Hagner, *The Jewish Reclamation of Jesus* (Grand Rapids: Academie Books, 1984), 87–132.

21. For a discussion of the legal and religious implications of this passage, see J. Duncan M. Derrett, *Studies in the New Testament*, 5 vols. (Leiden: Brill, 1986), 4:1–8.

22. So concludes Roger P. Booth in his book-length study entitled *Jesus and the Laws of Purity: Tradition History and Legal History in Mark 7* (Sheffield: JSOT Press, 1986), 219.

23. Several scholars, in different ways, have argued that Jesus' view on the law did not lead to disobedience. For discussions of Jesus and Judaism in general, see James H. Charlesworth, *Jesus within Judaism* (New York: Doubleday, 1988); E. P. Sanders, *Jesus and Judaism* (Philadelphia: Fortress, 1985); Geza Vermes, *Jesus and the World of Judaism* (London: SCM, 1983).

24. The Documentary Hypothesis asserts that the five books of Moses as we know them today are an amalgamation mainly of four written or oral sources: the Jahwist source, which used the name *YHWH* throughout; the Elohist source, which began using the name *YHWH* only after it was revealed to Moses on Sinai; the Priestly source, written by priests who used the name of Jehovah only after the generation of Moses; and the Deuteronomist source. The five main pillars of this theory, according to which these four sources allegedly can be segregated from each other, are "(a) the use of different names for the Deity; (b) variations of language and style; (c)

contradictions and divergences of view; (d) duplications and repetitions; (e) signs of composite structure in the sections" (U. Cassuto, *The Documentary Hypothesis* [Jerusalem: Magnes, 1983], 14). Cassuto discusses the limitations and shortcomings of the Documentary Hypothesis and finds each of its pillars to be without adequate foundation. Nevertheless, some of the distinctive textual tendencies that have made the Hypothesis seem plausible still offer valuable, though not always conclusive, insights.

25. See John L. Sorenson, "The Composition of Lehi's Family," in *BSAF*, 2:176.

26. See, generally, Abraham P. Bloch, *The Biblical and Historical Background of the Jewish Holy Days* (New York: KTAV, 1978); and *The Biblical and Historical Background of Jewish Customs and Ceremonies* (New York: KTAV, 1980).

27. On the Nephite understanding of the law of homicide in the law of Moses, see John W. Welch, "Nephi's Slaying of Laban: A Legal Perspective," *Journal of Book of Mormon Studies* 1 (1992): 119–41. For numerous legal materials in the Book of Mormon, see various chapters in Welch, *Reexploring the Book of Mormon*: on terms for law (ch. 16), the Ten Commandments (ch. 18), inheritance and tribal structure (ch. 24), the festival of Weeks or Pentecost (ch. 38), the festival of the Fifteenth of Av (ch. 39), slavery laws and legal reform (ch. 44), the law of apostate cities in Deuteronomy 13 (ch. 50), legal exemptions from military duty (ch. 54), the remembrance of the Exodus and the feast of Passover (ch. 56), the law of witnesses in the case of an unobserved murder (ch. 70), theft and robbery (ch. 72), and the execution of an infamous robber (ch. 73). See also Welch, "Law and War in the Book of Mormon," in *Warfare in the Book of Mormon*, ed. Stephen D. Ricks and William J. Hamblin (Salt Lake City: Deseret Book and F.A.R.M.S., 1990), 46–102; "Lehi's Last Will and Testament: A Legal Approach," in *The Book of Mormon: Second Nephi, The Doctrinal Structure*, ed. Monte Nyman (Provo: Religious Studies Center, 1989), 61–82; "Series of Laws in the Book of Mormon," F.A.R.M.S. Preliminary Report (Provo: F.A.R.M.S., 1987); "If a man . . . The Casuistic Law Form in the Book of Mormon," F.A.R.M.S. Preliminary Report (Provo: F.A.R.M.S., 1987); "Theft and Robbery in the Book of Mormon and Ancient Near Eastern Law," F.A.R.M.S. Preliminary Report (Provo: F.A.R.M.S., 1985); "King Benjamin's Speech in the Context of Ancient Israelite Festivals," F.A.R.M.S. Preliminary Report (Provo: F.A.R.M.S., 1985).

28. See Hugh W. Nibley, *An Approach to the Book of Mormon*, in *CWHN*, 6:245–46.

29. *TTS*, 16.

30. On the distinction between a "stone altar" and an "altar of stones," see Nibley, *An Approach to the Book of Mormon*, 246.

31. See, generally, *TTS*, 48–57.

32. See, for example, Thomas B. Dozeman, *God on the Mountain* (Atlanta: Scholars, 1989); see also the section on mountains and high places as symbols of the temple and other sacred space in Donald W. Parry, Stephen D. Ricks, and John W. Welch, *A Bibliography on Temples of the Ancient Near East and Mediterranean World* (Lewiston, New York: Mellen, 1991), 120–24.

33. For a discussion of the throne and footstool as two of the symbols of the inner sanctum of the temple of Solomon, see *TTS*, 251–57.

34. *Lehi in the Desert, The World of the Jaredites, and There Were Jaredites*, in *CWHN*, 5:51.

35. See Frank Moore Cross, Jr., "The Priestly Tabernacle in the Light of Recent Research," in Truman G. Madsen, ed., *The Temple in Antiquity* (Provo: BYU Religious Studies Center, 1984), 91–105.

36. *TTS*, 26.

37. See John L. Sorenson, *An Ancient American Setting for the Book of Mormon* (Salt Lake City: Deseret Book and F.A.R.M.S., 1985), 143.

38. Roland de Vaux, *Ancient Israel*, 2 vols. (New York: McGraw Hill, 1965), 2:317; for a general description of the temple of Solomon, see pages 312–30. For a discussion of the architectural uniqueness of the temple of Solomon as compared with other temples in Palestine, Syria, and Egypt, see Ahlström, *Royal Administration*, 34–36. He concludes that no exact parallel for the temple of Solomon has been found. Thus, the idea of building a temple "after the manner of the temple of Solomon" probably had specific reference to its distinctive layout and design, not its splendor or some other feature. After all, the Nephite temple was built by a small group that included only a few men at that time.

39. Gary M. Feinman, "Mesoamerican Temples," in *Temple in Society*, ed. Michael V. Fox (Winona Lake, Indiana: Eisenbrauns, 1988), 69; see also Laurette Sejourne, "El Templo Prehispanico," *Cuadernos Americanos* 149, no. 6 (November-December 1966): 129–67.

40. Sorenson, *Ancient American Setting*, 143 (fn. omitted). Sorenson has noted similarities between their temple typologies in "The Significance of an Apparent Relationship between the Ancient Near East and Mesoamerica," in *Man across the Sea*, ed. Carroll Riley, Charles Kelley, Campbell Pennington, and Robert Rands (Austin: University of Texas Press, 1971), 227, and between blood sacrifice in the Semitic world and in Mesoamerica (unpublished paper [1951]. He noted also

that Padre Torquemada compared the Aztec temple plan to the Temple of Solomon (see Sejourne, "El Templo Prehispanico," 143). See also Gregory M. Taylor, "Temple Ritual and Tradition in Mesoamerica and the Book of Mormon," unpublished paper, F.A.R.M.S. Archive, 1986. But adequate treatment of Mesoamerican temples, their similarities to, and differences from Israelite and other ancient temples must await further exploration and research.

41. See E. D. Howe, *Mormonism Unvailed* (Painesville, Ohio: By the author, 1834), 45–46; Marvin W. Cowan, *Mormon Claims Answered* (Salt Lake City: n.p., 1977), 36; G. T. Harrison, *That Mormon Book: Mormonism's Keystone Exposed—or the Hoax Book* (By the author, 1981), 26; B. H. Roberts, *Studies of the Book of Mormon*, ed. Brigham D. Madsen (Urbana, Illinois: University of Illinois, 1985), 14, 17, 259–61.

42. Solomon Zeitlin traces the Jewish law prohibiting the building of temples outside Judea to the time, long after Lehi, when the high priest Onias III fled to Egypt and Ptolemy VI gave him permission to build a temple there (see "The Offspring of Intermarriage," *Jewish Quarterly Review* 51 [1960]: 139).

43. See B. H. Roberts, *New Witnesses for God* (Salt Lake City: Deseret News Press, 1909), 3:522–23; Welch, "Finding Answers to B. H. Roberts' Questions and 'An Unparallel'" (Provo: F.A.R.M.S., 1985), 13–14.

44. For a previous report of this material, see my F.A.R.M.S. Update, based in part on research by John Lundquist, in the F.A.R.M.S. Newsletter for November 1991, "Kingship and Temple in 2 Nephi 5–10," also in Welch, *Reexploring the Book of Mormon*, 66–68.

45. See Hugh W. Nibley, "The Hierocentric State," in *The Ancient State*, in *CWHN*, 10:99–147; John M. Lundquist, "Temple, Covenant, and Law in the Ancient Near East and in the Old Testament," in this volume, 265–87.

46. See Eckhard von Nordheim, "König und Tempel," *Vetus Testamentum* 27 (1977): 443. Niek Paulssen, *König und Tempel im Glaubenszeugnis des Alten Testamentes* (Stuttgart: Katholisches Bibelwerk, 1967) also discusses the various manifestations of the relationship between king and temple in the courtly, deuteronomic, priestly, and chronicler's records in the Old Testament.

47. Ahlström, *Royal Administration*, 1–2.

48. Lundquist, "Temple, Covenant, and Law," 265.

49. Ibid., 271.

50. Ibid., 279.

51. See ibid., 280–81.

52. Donna Runnalls, "The King as Temple Builder: A Messianic

Typology," in *Spirit within Structure,* ed. E. J. Furcha (Allison Park, Pennsylvania: Pickwick, 1983), 23–25.

53. See Lundquist, "Temple, Covenant, and Law," 303; W. J. Dumbrell, "Kingship and Temple in the Post-Exilic Period," *Reformed Theological Review* 37, no. 2 (1978): 35–36.

54. Lundquist, "Temple, Covenant, and Law," 265, 267–68.

55. On the priests' duty to teach (Deuteronomy 33:10), see de Vaux, *Ancient Israel,* 2:353–55.

56. For further details, see Robert L. Millet, "The Holy Order of God," in *Book of Mormon: Alma, the Testimony of the Word,* ed. Monte S. Nyman and Charles D. Tate, Jr. (Provo: Religious Studies Center, 1992), 61–88.

57. See John W. Welch, "The Melchizedek Material in Alma 13:13–19," in *BSAF,* 2:259.

58. See Aelred Cody, *A History of Old Testament Priesthood* (Rome: Pontifical Biblical Institute, 1969), 129–41.

59. Little is known of the operation of the temple at Elephantine, but apparently it was established by Jews who practiced a syncretist religion and gave no heed to Josiah's reforms centralizing temple worship in Jerusalem (see de Vaux, *Ancient Israel,* 2:340–41).

60. *TTS,* 61–62, 70.

61. John Bright, *A History of Israel,* 2nd ed. (Philadelphia: Westminster, 1972), 162.

62. Cody, *A History of Old Testament Priesthood,* 12; see also *TTS,* 72, 80; de Vaux, *Ancient Israel,* 2:372–86.

63. See de Vaux, *Ancient Israel,* 2:376.

64. Bright, *A History of Israel,* 163.

65. For an extended analysis of the political aspect of these plates, see Noel B. Reynolds, "The Political Dimension of Nephi's Small Plates," *Brigham Young University Studies* 27, no. 4 (1987): 15–37.

66. Lundquist, "Temple, Covenant, and Law," 279.

67. See John W. Welch, "Jacob's Ten Commandments," *F.A.R.M.S. Update* (March 1985), reprinted in Welch, *Reexploring the Book of Mormon,* 69–72.

68. See Weinfeld, "The Decalogue," 32–47; Klaus Koch, "Tempeleinlassliturgien und Dekaloge," in *Studien zur Theologie der alttestamentlichen Überlieferungen,* ed. Rolf Rendtorff and Klaus Koch (Neukirchen: Neukirchener Verlag, 1961), 45–60.

69. The Day of Atonement is discussed further in connection with King Benjamin's speech (Mosiah 2–5).

70. See Ahlström, *Royal Administration,* 47, 55.

71. Bright, *A History of Israel,* 164.

72. Sorenson, *Ancient American Setting*, 145 (footnotes omitted).

73. Ahlström, *Royal Administration*, 10–18, gives several examples of royal complexes with temples, palaces, and fortifications built by Egyptians, Hittites, Canaanites, and others, sounding very similar to the building projects of King Noah.

74. de Vaux, *Ancient Israel*, 2:376.

75. See Welch, *Reexploring the Book of Mormon*, 135–38.

76. Regarding the temple as "the seat of the divine presence," see de Vaux, *Ancient Israel*, 2:325–27.

77. See John W. Welch, "Synagogues in the Book of Mormon," in Welch, *Reexploring the Book of Mormon*, 193–95.

78. For the temple as a cosmic mountain, see John M. Lundquist, "What Is a Temple? A Preliminary Typology," in this volume, *Temples of the Ancient World*, 83–117; Donald W. Parry, "Garden of Eden: Prototype Sanctuary," in this volume, 126–51.

79. Note the ironic comparison between Benjamin's tower, used for righteous peaceful purposes, and King Noah's tower near the temple in Nephi, which he used as a military lookout (see Mosiah 11:10–12).

80. It is argued that firstlings belonged to the Lord and therefore could not be counted as personal property, whereas all sacrifices and burnt offerings had to be selected from a man's own personal property (see, for example, M. T. Lamb, *The Golden Bible* [New York: Ward and Drummond, 1887], 109–10; Jerald and Sandra Tanner, *Covering Up the Black Hole in the Book of Mormon* [Salt Lake City: Utah Lighthouse Ministry, 1990], 62).

81. See John A. Tvedtnes, "King Benjamin and the Feast of Tabernacles," in *BSAF*, 2:197–221; Hugh Nibley, "Tenting, Toll, and Taxing," in *The Ancient State*, in *CWHN*, 10:33–98; "Old World Ritual in the New World," in *An Approach to the Book of Mormon*, in *CWHN*, 6:295–310; Welch, "King Benjamin's Speech in the Context of Ancient Israelite Festivals."

82. I am grateful to Gordon Thomasson, Robert Smith, John Tvedtnes, and others, who collaborated in identifying many elements of Israelite holy days in the Book of Mormon.

83. On the preexilic dating of this festival, see Milgrom, *Leviticus 1–16*, 1070–71.

84. See Welch, "King Benjamin's Speech in the Context of Ancient Israelite Festivals," 3–5.

85. Almost half of all scriptural occurrences in the Old Testament of the precise instruction "seven times" are found in Leviticus (see Milgrom, *Leviticus 1–16*, 233, 273, 516–17, 532–34, 1031–33, 1037–39).

86. Ibid., 234.

87. See M *Yoma* 8:8–9. The Hebrew word translated "transgressions" in Leviticus 16:21 comes from *pasha'*, "to rebel" (*Encyclopedia Judaica*, 5:1384).

88. Ibid., 1385.

89. I thank Gordon C. Thomasson for contributing to these ideas on the possible ritual use of the ass in the ancient Near East and in the Book of Mormon.

90. David G. Wright, in his presentation to a Regional SBL meeting, Provo, 1985, cites examples of this from the Hittite rituals of Pulisa, Ashella, Uhhamuwa, and the Shurpu Series.

91. See M *Yoma* 8:8–9; Maimonides, *Yad* (*Mishneh Torah*), *Teshuvah* 1:2–4.

92. *Encyclopedia Judaica*, 5:1378; see also Hayyim Schauss, *The Jewish Festivals* (Cincinnati: Union of American Hebrew Congregations, 1938), 132.

93. *Encyclopedia Judaica*, 5:1379.

94. Kings also recited negative confessions on the annual year renewal festival: e.g., from the Babylonia Year-rite texts, cited in J. Black, "The New Year Ceremonies in Ancient Babylon: Taking Bel by the Hand and a Cultic Picnic," *Religion* 11 (1981): 44: "I have not sinned, Lord of the lands; I have not been negligent of your godhead, etc." This compares closely with the negative confessions of Benjamin in Mosiah 2:13. Negative confessions are found in Book 125 of the Egyptian *Book of the Dead*.

95. Compare *Jubilees* 34:17–18.

96. *Encyclopedia Judaica*, 5:1381.

97. Ibid., 1386.

98. Ibid., 1382, especially citing Philo.

99. Ibid., 1383.

100. See Schauss, *The Jewish Festivals*, 135. The number ten is a symbolic number, representing completeness and perfection.

101. This revelation comes at the chiastic center of the third section of Benjamin's speech.

102. The ten places are Mosiah 2:30, "Lord God doth support me"; 2:41, "Lord God hath spoken it"; 3:5, "Lord Omnipotent who reigneth"; 3:13, "Lord God hath sent his holy prophets"; 3:14, "Lord God saw that his people were . . . stiffnecked"; 3:17, "Lord Omnipotent [only means of salvation]"; 3:18, "Lord Omnipotent [atoning blood of]"; 3:21, "Lord God Omnipotent [name of]"; 3:23, "Lord God hath commanded me"; 5:15, "Lord God Omnipotent, may seal you his." It is reasonable to believe that the tetragrammaton *YHWH* stood

behind these ten intensified references to deity. Moreover, only in Benjamin's speech do the expressions "Lord God Omnipotent" or "Lord Omnipotent" ever appear in the Book of Mormon, possibly indicating the ceremonial or sacred character of these names, given the temple context of Benjamin's speech.

103. See Bloch, *The Biblical and Historical Background of the Jewish Holy Days*, 33, citing M *Yoma* 19b; Schauss, *The Jewish Festivals*, 133.

104. See "King, Coronation, and Covenant in Mosiah 1–6," in *Rediscovering the Book of Mormon*, ed. John L. Sorenson and Melvin J. Thorne (Salt Lake City: Deseret Book and F.A.R.M.S., 1991), 213.

105. See Stephen D. Ricks, "The Ideology of Kingship in Mosiah 1–6," in Welch, *Reexploring the Book of Mormon*, 116.

106. See Truman G. Madsen, " 'Putting on the Names': A Jewish-Christian Legacy," in *BSAF*, 1:458–81; M. Catherine Thomas, "Taking the Name of Christ in King Benjamin's Speech," unpublished paper, presented at BYU Book of Mormon Symposium, 1989.

107. For further discussion of Alma 12–13, including other temple-related observations, see my article entitled "The Melchizedek Material in Alma 13:13–19," 2:238–72; and Millet, "The Holy Order of God," 61–88.

108. Gerhard Kittel, *Theological Dictionary of the New Testament*, 10 vols. (Grand Rapids, Michigan: Eerdmans, 1967), 4:803–7. For a discussion of a narrower use of the word *mysteries*, see my article "The Calling of a Prophet," in *First Nephi, The Doctrinal Foundation*, ed. Monte S. Nyman and Charles D. Tate, Jr. (Provo: BYU Religious Studies Center, 1988), 45–46 and n. 51.

109. See Hugh W. Nibley, *Temple and Cosmos*, in *CWHN*, 12:212–319; *The Message of the Joseph Smith Papyri: An Egyptian Endowment* (Salt Lake City: Deseret Book, 1975), especially pages 255–86; on the occurrence of these themes in the Dead Sea Scrolls, see the *Odes of Solomon*, the *Hymn of the Pearl*, the *Pistis Sophia*, Cyril's *Lectures on the Ordinances*, and the *Gospel of Philip*.

110. For a survey of the sacred teachings of the Nephites that may have been contained in their temple ceremonies, see Charles B. Grosso, "The Book of Mormon and Temple Worship," unpublished paper, F.A.R.M.S. archives, 1982, 25–32.

111. See John W. Welch, *The Sermon at the Temple and the Sermon on the Mount* (Salt Lake City: Deseret Book and F.A.R.M.S., 1990).

112. Robert A. Cloward emphasized at the BYU Book of Mormon Symposium, February 1993, the fact that the Sermon on the Mount in the Joseph Smith Translation of the Bible was given to Jesus' apostles as they departed on missions. Noel B. Reynolds has expressed a pref-

erence to see the Sermon on the Mount as a preparation for baptism. Neither of these positions is excluded by my interpretation, but neither do they account for all that is going on in the text of 3 Nephi 11–18. The Sermon at the Temple is more than missionary training and more than prebaptismal gospel essentials.

113. See Welch, *Sermon at the Temple,* 57–62.

114. See ibid., 116–21.

115. Similarly, for a greater appreciation of the exalted character of the law of Moses in the book of Deuteronomy, see Nibley, "How to Get Rich," 178–201.

13

THE BROTHER OF JARED AT THE VEIL

M. Catherine Thomas

The temple is the narrow channel through which one must pass to reenter the Lord's presence. A mighty power pulls us through that channel, and it is the sealing power of the at-one-ment of the Lord Jesus Christ. The Savior's *at-one-ment* is another word for the sealing power. By the power of the at-one-ment, the Lord draws and seals his children to himself in the holy temples.

In scripture we can study how the ancient great ones were drawn through that narrow channel to find their heart's desire: we find, for example, Adam, cast out, bereft of his Lord's presence, searching relentlessly in the lonely world until he finds the keys to that passage to the Lord. Abraham searches for his priesthood privileges (see Abraham 1:1) and after a diligent quest exclaims, "Thy servant has sought thee earnestly; now I have found thee" (Abraham 2:12). Moses on Horeb, Lehi at the tree, Nephi on the mountain top—all these men conducted that search which is outlined and empowered in the temple endowment, gradually increasing the hold, the seal, between themselves and their Lord.

This was the very search for which they were put on earth: to rend the veil of unbelief, to yield to the pull of the Savior's sealing power, to stand in the Lord's presence, encircled about in the arms of his love (see D&C 6:20; 2 Nephi 1:15). This then is the temple endowment: having been cast out, to search diligently according to the revealed path, and at last to be clasped in the arms of Jesus (see Mormon 5:11).

In particular, I wish to focus briefly on some of the temple elements in the experience of the brother of Jared: (1) the tower of Babel, (2) his period of probation, (3) his experience at the cloud-veil, and (4) some observations on faith and knowledge as revealed in the brother of Jared's search for the heavenly gift. One can see that these four elements follow a temple pattern: a false religion is offered; a period of probation or trial of faith is provided; and upon obedience, light and knowledge are granted.

Part 1: The Tower of Babel

The brother of Jared's rejection of the spiritual chaos at the tower of Babel was a critical part of his ultimate endowment. By ancient tradition the tower of Babel was inspired by Nimrod, the grandson of Ham, who sought to dethrone God by bringing men into constant dependence on his, Nimrod's, power. A multitude followed Nimrod, persuaded that it was cowardice to submit to God. The people began to build the tower, apparently some type of temple, as their objective was to reach heaven by means of the tower.[1] God's response was to break up their evil combination by scrambling their languages, thus depriving them of the powerful Adamic language.[2] The name *babel* means, in Akkadian, "gate of God" and is a play on the Hebrew *balal*, meaning "to mix or confound." It is apparent then that the tower of Babel was a counterfeit gate of God, or temple, that Ham's priesthood-deprived descendants built in rebellion against God.

Part 2: Probation

Jared and his family and friends rejected this temple and were spared the Lord's punishments. The Jaredite community enjoyed both the spirit of at-one-ment and the Adamic language and wanted to enlarge their privileges of righteousness, not diminish them. Thus they set out on the quest that is initiated by a period of stringent testing and training (gathering of animals and plants, trekking through wilderness, building two sets of barges, and enduring strong chastening). As their obedience and sacrifice increased, so did their privileges with the Lord, for "the Lord did go before them, and did talk with them as he stood in a cloud, and gave directions whither they should travel" (Ether 2:5). Successful navigation of their tests brought the brother of Jared to the need for more light and thus to the mount Shelem.

Part 3: The Brother of Jared at the Cloud-Veil

The word *shelem* has three main Hebrew consonants forming a root word that spans a wide spectrum of meanings: peace, tranquility, contentment, safety, completeness, being sound, finished, full, or perfect. *Shelem* (and *shalom*) signify peace with God, especially in the covenant relationship. It also connotes submission to God, which we see in the Arabic words *muslim* and *islam.* In particular, *shelem* has reference to the peace offering of the law of sacrifice, which corresponds to the seeking of fellowship with God,[3] and thereby has a relationship to the meanings of the at-one-ment; that is, *shelem,* fellowship, sealing, and at-one-ment have an obvious relationship. When the brother of Jared carried the stones in his hands to the top of the mount, whether or not a temple peace offering is implied, he sought a closer fellowship or at-one-ment with the Lord.

Therefore, the mount is called *shelem* because of its exceeding height (see Ether 3:1), not because *shelem* means great height, but rather that it suggests a place that is suitably high for temple activity.

The small stones themselves suggest meanings beyond their practical use in the barges. Note that he did *molten* the stones, or extract them from the rock of the mount itself and shape them by fire: white, clear, and glasslike, they evoke the Urim and Thummim (Hebrew, "lights and perfections"). What is the relationship between these sixteen small stones and the two Urim and Thummim stones that the Lord gives the brother of Jared later on? It seems that the brother of Jared was led to fashion that which would give his community not only practical light, but spiritual light as well; indeed, they were the very instrument of his calling as prophet, seer, and revelator. The small stones evoke the white stone mentioned in Revelation 2:17 and explained in Doctrine and Covenants 130:10–11, which stone becomes a Urim and Thummim to those who come into the celestial kingdom, "whereon is a new name written, which no man knoweth save he that receiveth it. The new name is the key word."

At the top of the mount, the brother of Jared seems to be operating under the influence of forces of which he is not fully conscious, but which his spirit seems to understand. He says that he is there for light, but his words reveal that his greatest concern is his unredeemed nature. He even appears to be afraid of the Lord's anger here and is so overcome with his inadequacy that he seems to be fighting the temptation to withdraw. It is with deliberate courage that he presses on past this fear, taking heart in the knowledge that the Lord has commanded him to ask and receive what he needs in spite of his fallen nature.

The fear he manifests suggests similar scenes in at least two other places in scripture when people have a close encounter with the Lord: the first example is King Benjamin's people who fall to the earth "for the *fear* of the Lord had come upon them. And they had viewed themselves in their own carnal state. . . . And they all cried aloud with one voice, saying: O have mercy, and apply the atoning blood of Christ that we may receive forgiveness of our sins, and our hearts may be purified; for we believe in Jesus Christ" (Mosiah 4:1–2; italics added). They experience pain and fear at their spiritually induced awareness of their fallenness in contrast to God's perfection. They plead for and receive a cleansing response from the Lord.

The second example comes from Isaiah's vision of the Lord. "Woe is me! for I am undone; because I am a man of unclean lips, and I dwell in the midst of a people of unclean lips: for mine eyes have seen the King, the Lord of hosts" (Isaiah 6:5). The Lord responds by cleansing him in his presence.

As the unredeemed soul, even a guiltless one, closes the gap between himself and his Maker, he perceives the contrast as so overwhelmingly great that he is sorely tempted to shrink back, to give up the quest. Those who will not be redeemed do shrink, overcome by fear of this encounter (e.g., the Israelites in Exodus 20:18–21); but those who are determined to be redeemed press boldly on, and, exercising mighty faith, penetrate the veil, and receive the transformation they so desire.

Standing now before this cloud-veil, having asked for light, the brother of Jared is stunned to see a finger appearing through the cloud-veil. He falls to the ground, struck with fear, because he *knows* what he sees. What he had held for so long in his "eye of faith" has just been visually con-

firmed. He has, to use Moroni's language, "ren[t] that veil
of unbelief" (Ether 4:15) with his persistent believing-as-
though-he-were-seeing, and has in some marvelous way
operated the law that quickens and focuses his spiritual
eyes. He had asked for the finger to touch the stones, and
that is what he saw—what he asked for and believed. As
Elder Packer observes, the world says, "seeing is believing:
show me!" "When," he says, "will we learn that in spiritual
things . . . *believing is seeing*? Spiritual belief precedes spiritual knowledge."[4]

The Lord says to the brother of Jared: "Because of thy
faith thou hast seen . . . for were it not so ye could not have
seen my finger. Sawest thou more than this?" (Ether 3:9;
italics added). It must have been with pounding heart that
the brother of Jared said: "Nay; Lord, show thyself unto
me" (3:10). A further dialogue takes place at the cloud-veil,
the Lord testing the brother of Jared's desire and preparation, after which he says, "Ye are redeemed from the fall;
therefore ye are brought back into my presence; therefore I
show myself unto you" (3:13). The brother of Jared receives
the heavenly gift, described by Moroni in Ether 12: "For it
was by faith that Christ showed himself unto our fathers
. . . and prepared a way that thereby others might be partakers of the heavenly gift. . . . Wherefore, ye may also have
hope, and be partakers of the gift, if ye will but have faith.
Behold it was by faith that they of old were called after the
holy order of God. . . . Wherefore, he showed not himself
until after their faith" (vv. 7–12; italics added). President
Ezra Taft Benson explained the holy order of God: "To enter
into the order of the Son of God is the equivalent today of
entering into the fulness of the Melchizedek Priesthood,
which is only received in the house of the Lord."[5]

Part 4: Faith and Knowledge

The brother of Jared's experience dramatizes the difference between *faith* and *knowledge*. We can see that the brother of Jared did not have a perfect knowledge before he went through the veil because he expressed fear and surprise at what he saw and learned. The Lord says that it was not the brother of Jared's perfect knowledge that dissolved the veil; rather, it was his exceeding faith (see Ether 3:6–9). It seems that Moroni means to say that once the brother of Jared had seen the Lord, he *then* had perfect knowledge of the Lord, and the Lord could not then withhold anything from him. Moroni says: "And after the brother of Jared had beheld the finger of the Lord, because of the promise which the brother of Jared had obtained by faith, the Lord could not withhold anything from his sight; wherefore he showed him all things, for he could no longer be kept without the veil" (Ether 12:21).

The knowledge given by the Holy Ghost, the first comforter, is not a perfect knowledge, though it prepares and draws the seeker to that perfect knowledge. Faith, produced by the revelations of the Holy Ghost, is an assurance or *pre-knowledge* that what the Lord says is true (see Alma 32:34). But faith is designed to proceed along and become perfect knowledge, which is seeing something for ourselves after we have believed in, and been obedient to, the assurances of the Holy Ghost.

Faith is not an end in itself, it is a means to an end, and that end is to be like and to be with the Lord. When we say in our testimony meetings, "I know that the Lord Jesus lives," without having actually seen him, we mean that the Holy Ghost has given that assurance to our souls. But we do not have a perfect knowledge until, after an extended period of probation, we see for ourselves as the brother of

Jared did. Joseph Smith observed, "Men at the present time testify of heaven and of hell, and have never *seen* either—and I will say that no man *knows* these things without this."[6] Faith in the Lord Jesus Christ leads in one direction and that is into the Lord's presence.

Moroni teaches this principle when he says, "And he [the brother of Jared] *saw* . . . and he had faith no longer, for he *knew*, nothing doubting" (Ether 3:19; italics added). A small sampling of several pertinent scriptures will show that the Lord often uses the word *know* with the word *see* when referring to spiritual knowledge.

> 1 Nephi 5:4: "If I had not *seen* the things of God in a vision I should not have *known* the goodness of God."

> 3 Nephi 11:15: "The multitude . . . did *see* with their eyes and did *feel* with their hands, and did *know* of a surety." [The Prophet Joseph said, "No one can truly say he knows God until he has handled something and this can only be in the Holiest of Holies."[7]]

> Alma 36:26: "Many have been born of God, and have tasted as I have tasted, and have *seen* eye to eye as I have *seen*; therefore they do *know* of these things . . . as I do *know*."

> D&C 45:46: "You now *behold* me and *know* that I am."

> D&C 50:45: "And the day cometh that you shall hear my voice and *see* me, and *know* that I am."

> D&C 93:1: "Every soul who forsaketh his sins and cometh unto me, and calleth on my name, and obeyeth my voice, and keepeth my commandments, shall *see* my face and *know* that I am."

The *Lectures on Faith* make it clear that seeing the Lord is a pivotal point in a comment on 1 Peter 1:3–5:

> [Peter] says that all things that pertain to life and

godliness were given unto them through the *knowledge* of God and our Savior Jesus Christ. And if the question is asked, how were they to obtain the knowledge of God? (for there is a great difference between believing in God and knowing him. . . . And notice, that all things that pertain to life and godliness were given through the *knowledge* of God) the answer is given—through faith they were to obtain this knowledge; and, having power by faith to obtain the knowledge of God, *they could with it obtain all other things which pertain to life and godliness.*[8]

Joseph Smith says similarly in another place: "The Lord will teach him [the receiver of the second comforter] face to face and he may have a *perfect knowledge* of the mysteries of the kingdom of God, and this is the state and place the ancient saints arrived at."[9] And the Prophet Joseph again: "Then Knowledge through our Lord and Savior Jesus Christ is the grand key that unlocks the glories and mysteries of the Kingdom of Heaven."[10] Joseph speaks of the kind of experience that the brother of Jared had and makes a connection to temple ordinances:

God hath not revealed anything to Joseph, but what He will make known unto the Twelve, and even the least Saint may know all things as fast as he is able to bear them, for the day must come when no man need say to his neighbor, Know ye the Lord; for all shall know Him . . . from the least to the greatest. How is this to be done? It is to be done by this *sealing power*, and the other comforter spoken of, which will be manifest by revelation.[11]

Moroni says that "there never were greater things made manifest than those which were made manifest unto the brother of Jared" (Ether 4:4), but he says that they will not go forth to us, the Gentiles, until the day that we repent and become clean and sanctified and exercise faith like the brother of Jared. Then he says that the Lord will manifest unto the Gentiles the things the brother of Jared saw, even to the unfolding all his revelations (see Ether 4:6–7):

> Come unto me, O ye Gentiles, and I will show unto you the greater things, the knowledge which is hid up because of unbelief. Come unto me, O ye house of Israel, and it shall be made manifest unto you how great things the Father hath laid up for you, from the foundation of the world; and it hath not come unto you, because of unbelief. Behold, when ye shall rend that veil of unbelief . . . then shall ye *know* (Ether 4:13–15; italics added).

These possibilities pertain perhaps to this life, perhaps to the life to come, but the pattern of the brother of Jared points the way. Having rejected all counterfeit worship, having pushed on past all comfortable way-stations, having sacrificed to come up to the full measure of obedience to the Lord, the brother of Jared received his endowment on the top of mount Shelem, where the Savior of the world sealed him his. President Benson taught: "God bless us to receive all the blessings revealed by Elijah the prophet so that our callings and election will be made sure. I testify with all my soul to the truth of this message and pray that the God of Abraham, Isaac, and Jacob will bless modern Israel with the compelling desire to seek all the blessings of the fathers in the House of our Heavenly Father."[12]

Notes

1. See Josephus, *Antiquities*, 1.4.

2. See Joseph Fielding Smith, *The Way to Perfection* (Salt Lake City: Genealogical Society of Utah, 1935), 69.

3. See Francis Brown, S. R. Driver, Charles A. Briggs, *The New Brown, Driver, and Briggs Hebrew and English Lexicon of the Old Testament* (Boston: Houghton, Mifflin and Co., 1907), 1022–24; also LDS Bible Dictionary, s.v. "Sacrifices," 767.

4. Boyd K. Packer, "What Is Faith?" in *Faith* (Salt Lake City, Deseret Book, 1983), 43; italics added.

5. Ezra Taft Benson, "What I Hope You Will Teach Your Children about the Temple," *Ensign* 15 (August 1985): 6.

6. *WJS*, 10.

7. Ibid., 120.

8. *Lectures on Faith* (Salt Lake City: Deseret Book, 1985), 7:18; italics added.

9. *WJS*, 5; italics added.

10. Ibid., 201.

11. *TPJS*, 149.

12. Ezra Taft Benson, "What I Hope," 10.

14

Ancient Temples:
What Do They Signify?

Hugh W. Nibley

What most impressed me last summer on my first and only expedition to Central America was the complete lack of definite information about anything. We knew ahead of time that of the knowledge of the ancient cultures there wasn't much to be expected, but we were quite unprepared for the poverty of information that confronted us in the guided tours of ruins, museums, and lecture halls. It was not that our gracious guides knew less than they should. It is just a fact of life that no one knows much at all about these oft-photographed and much-talked-about ruins.

In the almost complete absence of written records, one must be permitted to guess, because there is nothing else to do; and when guessing is the only method of determination, one man's skill is almost as good as another's. An informed guess is a contradiction of terms, so our initial shock of nondiscovery was tempered by a warm glow of complacency, on finding that the rankest amateur in our party was able to pontificate on the identity and nature of most objects as well as anybody else.

One would suppose it to be a relatively easy thing to

This article first appeared in the Ensign *(September 1972), 46–49. It was reprinted in* CWHN, 8:265–73.

decide whether a given structure had served as a hospital, a monastery, a palace, a storeroom, a barracks, a temple, a tomb, or an office. But it is not easy at all, with everything looking just alike. Usually, we do not even know who the builders were or what their names were or where they came from.

Stock phrases, such as "We know as little about the history of the Mixtecs as we do about the Zapotecs," may confirm a scientist's integrity, but they hardly establish him as an authority. Admission of ignorance, though a constant refrain in guidebooks and articles, is really no substitute for knowledge. This writer is as ill-equipped as any ten-year-old to write about the people of ancient America, because he has never seen their records—but then who has?

The vast archives of the Old World civilizations that bring their identities and their histories to life simply do not exist for the New World, and so all we can do as we sit drinking lemonade in the shade is gaze and emote and speculate and rest our weary feet.

There are two things, however, about ancient American ruins upon which everyone seems to agree: (1) the reliefs that adorn the walls of some of these structures with ritual games, sacrifices, processions, audiences, and well-known religious symbols leave little doubt that they were designed to be the scenes of religious activities, and (2) some of these religious structures were laid out to harmonize with the structure and motion of the cosmos itself, as witness the perfectly straight axial ways that point directly to the place of the rising and setting sun at solstices and equinoxes, or the total of 364 steps and 52 slabs to a side that adorns the great pyramid of Chichen Itza.

It is an eloquent commentary on the bankruptcy of the modern mind, as Giorgio de Santillana points out, that we can find so little purpose or meaning in the magnificent and peculiar structures erected by the ancients with such immense skill and obvious zeal and dedication.[1] These great edifices are found throughout the entire world and seem to represent a common tradition; and if they do, then we have surely lost our way.

Counterparts to the great ritual complexes of Central America once dotted the entire eastern United States, the most notable being the Hopewell culture centering in Ohio and spreading out for hundreds of miles along the entire length of the Mississippi River. These are now believed to be definitely related to corresponding centers in Meso-america.[2]

Ranging further abroad, we see a convincing resemblance when we visit the famous ritual complex sites of the Old World and find the same combination of oddities on the same awesome scale. Pyramids and towers first catch our eye whether in Asia or America, and closer inspection reveals the familiar processional ways, stone alignments and colonnades, ceremonial gates, labyrinthine subterranean passages and chambers with their massive sarcophagi for priests and kings, reliefs depicting processions and combats, images of kings, gods, priests, and dangerous carnivores and serpents in stone.

While those who dig in the ruins of both hemispheres discover many similarities in the use of gold, turquoise, seashells, feathers, cotton textiles, and abstract designs, such as key patterns, spirals, and swastikas, the Western experts doggedly defend their domain as New World specialists. They are unencumbered by extensive knowledge of the Old World and still insist that there was absolutely no similarity in the details of development in America and the Mediterranean countries. Then they mention similarity after

Medicine Wheel,
Plains Indian
1 | 1500 A.D.

Monk's Mound,
Hopewell
2 | 800 A.D.

High Banks Works,
Hopewell
3 | 400 A.D.

La Venta,
Olmec
4 | 800 B.C.

Tenochtitlan,
Aztec
5 | 1400 A.D.

Sacsahuaman,
Inca
6 | 1450 A.D.

Figure 40. In an endless search for the cosmic order, mankind has built huge, astronomically oriented structures.

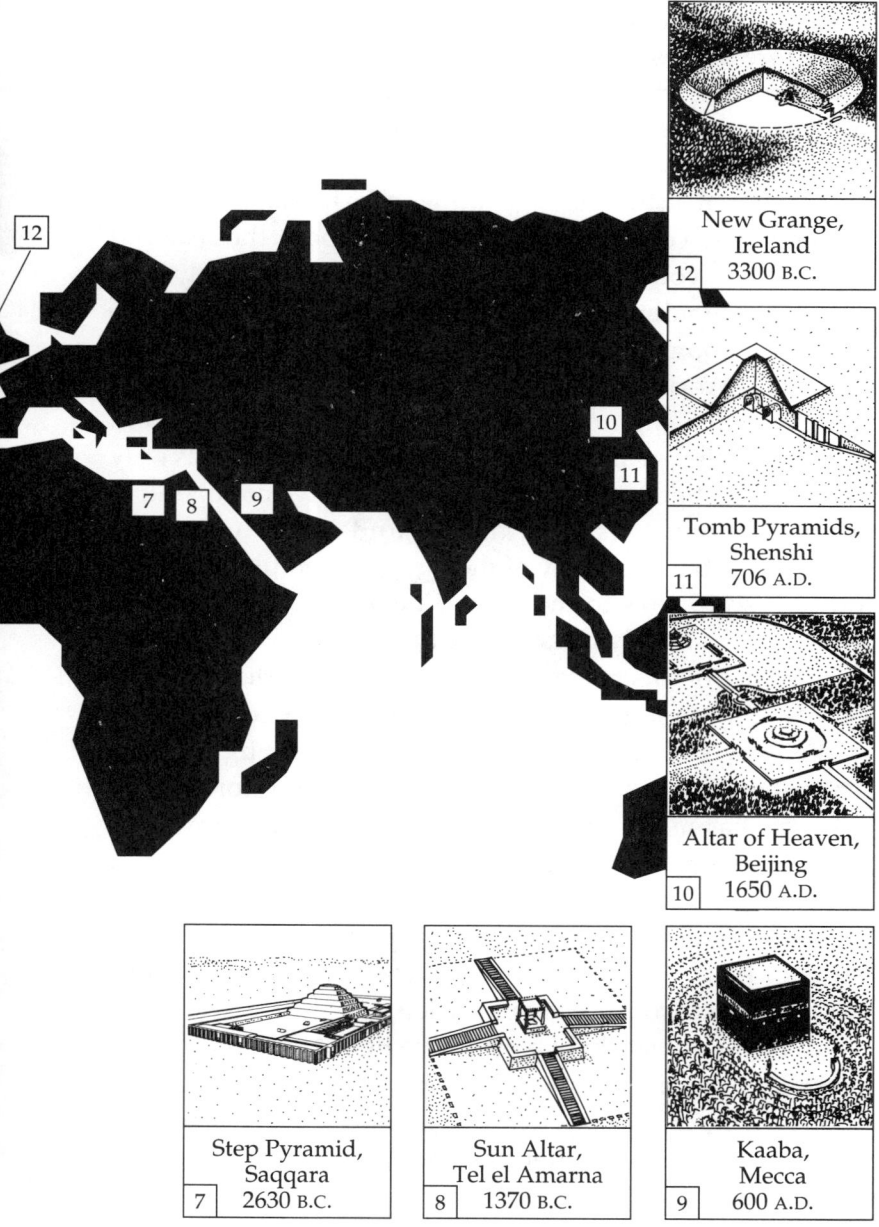

New Grange,
Ireland
12   3300 B.C.

Tomb Pyramids,
Shenshi
11   706 A.D.

Altar of Heaven,
Beijing
10   1650 A.D.

Step Pyramid,
Saqqara
7   2630 B.C.

Sun Altar,
Tel el Amarna
8   1370 B.C.

Kaaba,
Mecca
9   600 A.D.

similarity with, of course, the understanding that such likenesses are the result of mere coincidence.

As for the idea of possible contact between the hemispheres, a magisterial gesture toward the map has always
been thought sufficient to explain everything, obviating the
necessity of reading the rich and wonderful libraries of the
ancients who could tell us a great deal about the real and
possible intercourse over the waters if we would only give
them our attention.

Whole rooms full of ancient writings have been found
in the Old World at actual ruin sites with which they were
contemporary, and from such we may learn the nature and
purpose of the great buildings. Strangely enough, it is only
in the present generation that really extensive comparative
studies among these documents and ruins have been
undertaken. Serious study of the Egyptian temples, with the
aid of inscriptions found in and near them, is only now
being systematically pursued for the first time.

Because of this neglect, it is not surprising that comparison of Old World ritual complexes with their counterparts
in the New World has hardly even begun, though resemblances between the two have never failed to impress even
the most casual observer of the past 150 years. However,
such studies as have been undertaken invariably suggest
emerging patterns common to both worlds. Without com-
mitting ourselves to any dogmatic position (it is still too
early for that), we can still indulge like stout Cortez in a few
wild surmises from a peak in Darien.

In his recent study of a primitive Egyptian temple complex, Egyptologist Philippe Derchain declares that "one can
almost compare the ancient Egyptian temple to a power-
house where diverse energies are converted into electric
current or to a control room where, by the application of

very little effort, . . . one can safely produce and distribute energy as needed along the proper power lines."[3] Such powerhouses were not confined to Egypt; we find them everywhere, in the Old World and the New.

The ruins of such centers of power and control still comprise by far the most impressive remnants of the human past. Today the great plants are broken down and deserted; the power has been shut off. They mean nothing to us anymore, because we don't understand how they worked.

The most sophisticated electronic gadget in perfect working order is nothing in the hands of one who has never heard of electricity, and it would only frustrate even an expert if he found no power outlet to plug into. Perhaps the old powerhouses were something like that. And did they ever really work?

A great many people went to a lot of trouble for an unusually long time to set up these mysterious dynamos all over the world. What could they possibly have derived from all this effort? They must have gotten something, to have kept at it so long and so enthusiastically. For that matter, some of the holy places still carry on: pilgrims still travel in vast numbers to Mecca, Jerusalem, Rome, and Benares, hoping to experience manifestations of supernatural power.

Countless reports are on record at those famous sites of ingenious attempts to duplicate by fraud certain miraculous displays during the pilgrimages, attesting the fading or fictive nature of the vaunted powers from on high.

It is remarkable that some principal centers of world power are still located at the ancient sites where the corporate life of the race was thought to be renewed in the great New Year rites presided over by the king as god on earth. These sacred centers flourished in the heart of Rome, at the Altar of the Sun in Peking, in the Kremlin, in Jerusalem, in

Cairo (the ancient Memphis), in Mexico City, and else-where. Such pouring of new forces into fossil molds is what the philosopher Oswald Spengler calls "pseudomorphs," endowing a new power structure with a specious authority in which no one any longer believes.[4]

The idea that divine power can be conveyed to men and used by them through the implementation of tangible earthly contrivances and that these become mere antique oddities once the power is shut off is surprisingly con-firmed and illustrated by the Book of Mormon. Thus the Liahona and the Urim and Thummim were kept among the national treasures of the Nephites long after they had ceased their miraculous functions.

Before the finger of the Lord touched the sixteen stones of the brother of Jared, they were mere pieces of glass, and they probably became so after they had fulfilled their pur-pose. And the gold plates had no message to deliver until a special line of communication was opened by supernatural power.

In themselves these objects were nothing; they did not work by magic, by a power that resided *in the objects them-selves* so that a person has only to get hold of the magical staff, seal, ring, robe, book of Moses or Solomon or Peter in order to become master of the world. The aids and imple-ments that God gives to men work on no magic or auto-matic or mechanical principle, but only "according to the faith and diligence and heed which we . . . give unto them" (1 Nephi 16:28) and cease to work because of wickedness (1 Nephi 18:12).

Some have thought it strange that God should use any earthly implements and agents at all, when he could do all things himself just as easily. But even the Moslems, who protest that Christianity places needless intermediaries, notably Jesus and the Holy Ghost, between God and man, declare in their creed that they believe "in God and his Angels and his Prophets and his Books."[5] Does God need all these to do his work with men? However we may rationalize, the fact is that he does make use of them.

But what about all these ancient powerhouses—what would happen if they were restored? Nothing, in my opinion. They might be repaired and put in working order, but that would no more make them work than setting up a Liahona or Urim and Thummim, with all of the working parts in order, would enable us to use them. Without power from above, nothing will happen, for this is not magic.

It is doubtful if any of the known powerhouses ever really worked, except for the temple at Jerusalem (of which duplicates were made all over the Christian world as centers of pilgrimage in the Middle Ages), where the key manifestations in the life of the Savior took place. But what of the others? If they enjoyed no real dispensations of heavenly power, they really did not need to justify their existence, with all the trouble and expense of building them or keeping them in operation as the focal centers of the world's religious life.

The gesture of faith was not without its reward, however, and the by-products of the ancient temple were easily worth the time and effort that went into constructing and operating it, since the result was nothing less than civilization itself.

Ancient civilization was hierocentric, so that everything came from the temple. The Egyptians carried on for centuries like "a people searching in the dark for a key to truth," as I. E. S. Edwards put it.[6]

Abraham, while he pitied the futility of Pharaoh's zeal, respected his sincerity: though "cursed . . . as pertaining to the Priesthood," Pharaoh was nonetheless "a righteous man, . . . seeking earnestly to imitate that order . . . of the first patriarchal reign." In return he was blessed "with the blessings of the earth, and with the blessings of wisdom" (Abraham 1:26), and with the most stable, humane, and enlightened of civilizations.

If the Egyptian religion fed on its hopes, so do all the others; the Jews ever hoping for Jerusalem, the temple, and the Messiah; the Latter-day Saints still hoping for the fulfillment of the promises of the tenth Article of Faith.

One thing that leads us to suspect that most of the great powerhouses whose traces still remain were never anything more than pompous imitations or replicas is their sheer magnificence. The archaeologist finds virtually nothing of the remains of the primitive Christian church until the fourth century, because the true church was not interested in buildings and deliberately avoided the acquisition of lands and edifices that might bind it and its interests to this world.

The Book of Mormon is a history of a related primitive church, and one may well ask what kind of remains the Nephites would leave us from their more virtuous days. A closer approximation to the Book of Mormon picture of Nephite culture is seen in the earth and palisade structures of the Hopewell and Adena culture areas than in the later stately piles of stone in Mesoamerica.

C. Northcote Parkinson has demonstrated with withering insight how throughout history really ornate, tasteless, and pompous building programs have tended to come as the aftermath of civilization.[7] After the vital powers are spent, then is the time for the super-buildings, the piling of stone upon stone for monuments of staggering mass and proportion. It was after the disciples of the early church decided to give up waiting for the Messiah and to go out for satisfaction here and now that the Christians of the fourth century took to staging festivals and erecting monuments in the grand manner, covering the whole Near East with structures of theatrical magnificence and questionable taste.

How unlike the building program of the Church today, which can barely erect enough of our very functional, almost plain chapels to keep abreast of the growing needs of the Latter-day Saints.

Though such piles as the great pyramid-temple of Chichen Itza are surpassed by few buildings in the world in beauty of proportion and grandeur of conception, there is something disturbing about most of these overpowering ruins. Writers describing them through the years have ever confessed to feelings of sadness and oppression as they contemplate the moldy magnificence—the futility of it all: "They have all gone away from the house on the hill," and today we don't even know who they were.

Amid the ruins of the New World, as in Rome, we feel something of both the greatness and the misery, the genuine aspiration and the dull oppression, the idealism and the arrogance imposed by the heavy hand of priestcraft and kingcraft, and we wonder how the ruins of our own super buildings will look someday.

The great monuments do not represent what the Nephites stood for; rather, they stand for what their descendants, mixed with the blood of their brethren, descended to. But seen in the newer and wider perspective of comparative religious studies, they suggest to us not only the vanity of mankind and the futility of man's unaided efforts, but also something nobler: the constant search of men to recapture a time when the powers of heaven were truly at the disposal of a righteous people.

Notes

1. Giorgio de Santillana, *Hamlet's Mill* (Boston: Gambit, 1969), 3–5.

2. James B. Griffin, "Mesoamerica and the Eastern United States in Prehistoric Times," in *Handbook of Middle American Indians*, ed. Robert Wauchope (Austin: University of Texas, 1966), 4:111–31; D. S. Brose and N. Greber, *Hopewell Archaeology* (Kent: Kent State University, 1979).

3. Philippe Derchain, *Le Papyrus Salt 825*, in *Academie royale de Belgique* 58 (1965): 14.

4. Oswald Spengler, *The Decline of the West*, 2 vols. (New York: Knopf, 1928), 2:189, speaks of "historic pseudomorphosis."

5. George Sale, *The Koran* (London: Warne, n.d.), 55, 105, 109.

6. Iorwerth E. S. Edwards, *The Pyramids of Egypt* (Maryland: Penguin, 1964), 29.

7. Cyril Northcote Parkinson, *Parkinson's Law or the Pursuit of Progress* (Boston: Houghton Mifflin, 1957), 59–69.

Part 5

The Temple
according to Judaism

15

Demarcation between Sacred Space and Profane Space: The Temple of Herod Model

Donald W. Parry

To illustrate the pure condition of the temple of Jerusalem, the city of Jerusalem, and the land of Israel, ancient Jewish *midrashim* tended to exaggerate with the intent of showing the antithetical relationship between sacred and profane space. For instance, *Sifre on Deuteronomy Pisqa 37* states that "the refuse of the land of Israel, is superior to the best place in Egypt."[1] Other accounts produced by the same author(s) relate that four kingdoms of the world argued for possession of the least significant mountains of Israel because even the most inferior areas of the land of Israel were superior to the remaining parts of the world.[2] Why is the land of Israel superior to neighboring Egypt, and why are the least significant areas of Israel superior to the remaining parts of the world? The answer to this question lies in the fact that the temple of the Lord existed in the land of Israel, causing all parts of Israel to possess a degree of holiness.

The fact that a temple existed in the land of Israel forced the Jewish rabbinic authorities to develop an interesting and unique theology concerning sacred space. According to several rabbinic documents, the land of Israel was divided

413

into ten concentric zones of holiness. The premier rabbinic record that identifies the various gradations of holiness is M *Kelim* 1:6–9. It states:

> There are ten degrees of holiness:
> The land of Israel is holier than all the [other] lands. . . .
> The cities that are surrounded with walls are holier than it. . . .
> Within the wall of Jerusalem is holier than they [the foregoing]. . . .
> The Temple Mount is holier than it. . . .
> The rampart is holier than it. . . .
> The Court of the Women is holier than it. . . .
> The Court of Israel is holier than it. . . .
> The Court of the Priests is holier than it. . . .
> [The space] between the porch and the altar is holier than it. . . .
> The sanctuary is holier than it. . . .
> The Holy of Holies is holier than them all.[3]

While each of the zones possessed a certain degree of holiness, the outer zone (the land of Israel) possessed a lesser degree of holiness than the innermost zone (the Holy of Holies), which possessed the greatest degree of holiness.

In what manner did the rabbis demarcate between the various zones of holiness? How, for example, did the rabbis delimit between the holiness of the Court of the Priests and the Court of Israel, which possessed a lesser degree of holiness? The purpose of this paper is to examine the demarcations found within the Temple of Herod system, especially with regard to the careful separation of sacred from profane space. The investigation will first review the antithetical relationship that exists between sacred and profane space. This review will be followed by a detailed discussion of the rabbinic method of demarcating between sacred and profane space. Furthermore, the sacral/nonsacral constitution of the subterranean areas below the temple and aerial space above the temple will be considered. We will limit our discussion to the period of the Temple of Herod (18 B.C.–A.D. 70).

The Nonconterminous Nature of Sacred and Profane Space

Definition of Sacred Space: In order to better understand the essence of sacred space,[4] one must juxtapose the concepts of the sacred and profane and provide a comparison of the two. Although the two concepts are contradictory and "mutually exclusive,"[5] one cannot be defined completely without the other, for one gains definition from the other.

Otto's definition of holiness summarily describes the nature of the sacred, for holiness is something "wholly other" than the profane world.[6] In terms of categorization, sacred space belongs to a category far removed from the profane. The sacred contains elements of mystery, the supernatural, and inviolability. It is an item of the intellect and is said to exist perceptually.[7] Only those who perceive that sacred space exists will acknowledge its existence. Brevard Childs's work on the holy explains the manner in which sacred space is viewed perceptually or emotionally. He calls one's relationship with sacred space an emotional "experience" that "fills that particular space with its unique character."[8] Those who experience sacral space and its corresponding sacral architecture generate a unique religious response, a response far different from one's reaction to empirical space. That is not to say that empirical space and secular architecture do not create their own emotional content,[9] but religious geography with its religious architecture has at its very foundation a set of beliefs that points to the origins or primary fundamentals of a particular religious system. Hans J. Klimkeit's language is not unlike that of Childs. He refers to sacral space as having a "value of its own" due to "an emotional accent" held by those who perceive it to be sacred space.[10]

Sacred space is intimately connected with temple space—they are often one and the same. The very meaning of the term *temple* in the Hebrew language demonstrates this idea. In the Hebrew Bible[11] one of the principal roots from which the English words *sanctuary* and *temple* originate is *QDŠ, which has the basic meaning of "separation" or "withdrawal" of sacred entities from profane things.[12] Specifically, the Qal verbal form of *QDŠ denotes something that is "holy" or "withheld from profane use." The Niphal form of the same root refers to showing or proving "oneself holy." The Piel verbal form speaks of placing a thing or person "into the state of holiness" or declaring something holy. In the Hiphil verbal form, the root letters *QDŠ have reference to the dedication or sanctification of a person or thing to sacredness.[13] In all instances, the meaning of the Hebrew root *QDŠ pertains to separation from the profane.

Definition of Profane Space: Sacred and profane are not conterminous but represent "two antithetical entities."[14] Sacred space is temple space, and profane space is chaos. However, as mentioned above, we can appreciate sacred space fully only when we understand its relationship to the profane. The Latin word *profanum* (English "profane") literally means "before" or "outside" the temple, formed from *pro* (meaning "outside") and *fanum* (meaning "temple").[15] The equivalent Hebrew word is ḥôl, which, according to Marcus Jastrow, has the meaning of "outside of the sanctuary, foreign, profane, common."[16] If the temple is the consecrated place created "by marking it out, by cutting it off from the profane space around it,"[17] then the profane space represents unconsecrated space, the peripheral area that remains after the sacred has been removed.

In his work *Images and Symbols*, Mircea Eliade speaks of profane space as being "objective," "abstract," and "non-essential."[18] Human beings gather upon profane space and celebrate human actions. It is temporal, nonreligious geography, which is centered around the mundane events of humanity. Profane space deals with physical geography, or "empirical geography," and its field is "empirical space."[19] Caillois's studies in *Man and the Sacred* have aptly shown that the two concepts—sacred and profane—can never be united, but must be separated, lest confusion come.[20]

The Jews that belonged to the Second Temple period were well aware that sacred space was set amidst profane space. In what manner could the rabbinic authorities develop well-defined borders that would serve to delimit the two antithetical entities—sacred and profane space? How could the Jews create a dividing line between the orderliness of sacral space and the anomalous condition of profane space? The authorities were well aware of the rigid lines needed to separate the sacred from the profane. We will now deal with those rigid lines.

The Careful Delimitation between Sacred and Profane Space according to the Rabbis

This section deals with sacred space and sacral architecture as ordered, well-defined, and nonhomogeneous topos. We will look at the preciseness with which the Jews of the Second Temple era carefully delimited the temple's various zones and created borders between the sacred and the profane. Walls and gateways created borders and divided sacred from profane space. Both the subterranean areas of

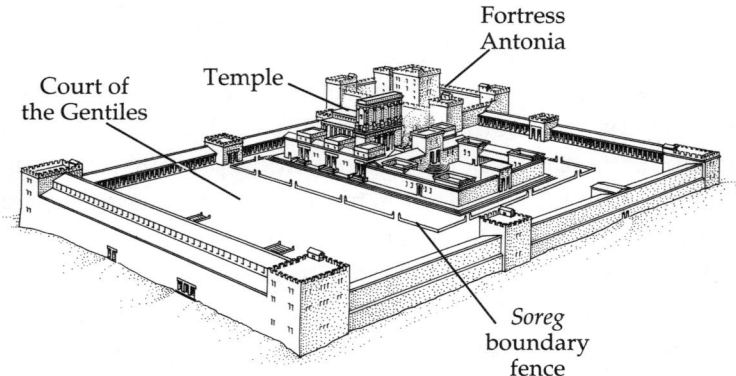

Figure 41. The Temple of Herod possessed various grades of holiness, including zones or courts for the Gentiles, Israelite Women, Israelite men, and members of the priesthood.

the temple and the aerial space above the sanctuary were momentous considerations for the Jewish sages. The demarcation of zones of holiness outside of the immediate temple area, such as the city of Jerusalem and the land of Israel, were also the subjects of rabbinic deliberations.

The architectural boundaries of the sacred precinct needed to be well defined, visible, and obstructive. Borders had to be established that identified grades of space, and regulations had to exist that enforced the segregation. Architecturally, the borders of the temple (speaking of the Israelite temple paradigms) were most easily represented by the wall. The same wall that retained the sacred aura inside also barred the profane to the outside. At the same time a breach in the wall needed to exist that would allow the profane to be transcended, or would offer an opening into the sacred. Such breaches in the walls were represented by the temple doors, gates, and veils. The Jews during the Second Temple period were well aware of the various chal-

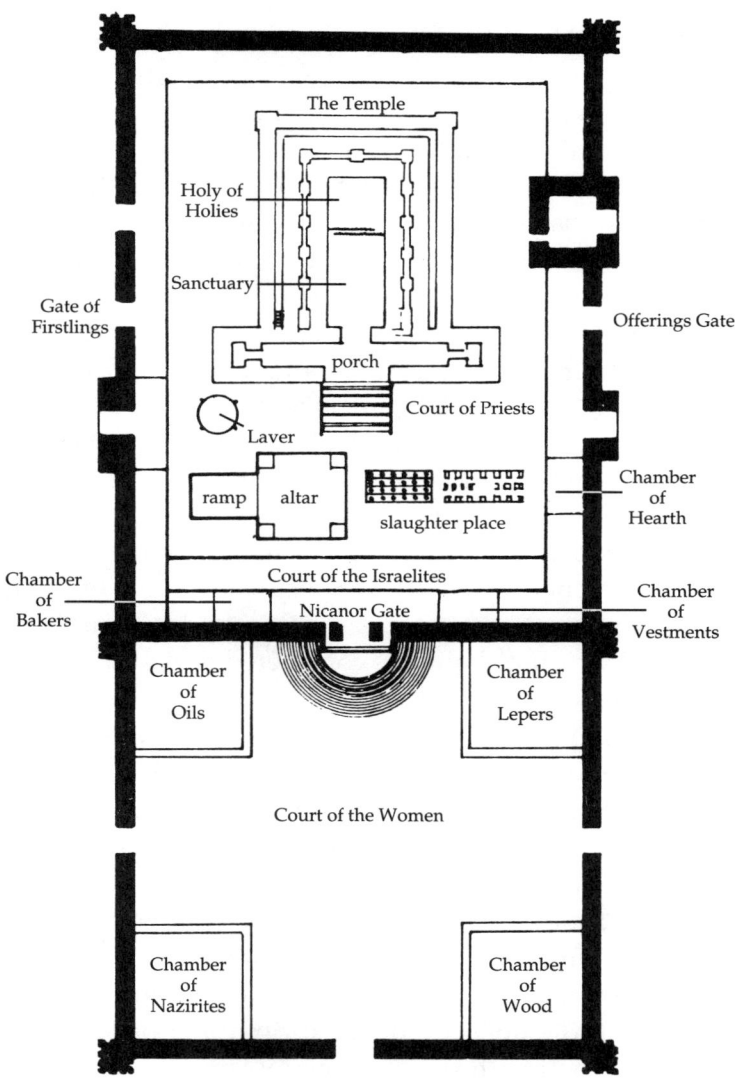

lenges involved in delimiting a precise area of space that would be called holy and segregating that area from secular space. To carry the challenge a step further, the Jews needed to demarcate every zone of sanctity in relation to other zones of the temple precinct.

With regard to the many gates that existed in the temple precinct, the sages determined with great care and deliberation precisely what fraction of the gates belonged to the interior, as opposed to the exterior, of a given zone. According to M *Pesahim* 7:12, the interior parts of the door stop (or jamb) were considered to belong to the interior of the enclosure, while the outside parts of the door stop belonged to the exterior: "From the stop of the door inwards counts as inside, and from the stop of the door outwards counts as outside."

The earliest known commentary on M *Pesahim* 7:12 adds additional information. Specifically speaking of the gates belonging to the court of the Priests, the *Gemara* states that the door jamb should be considered part of the interior of that court. Nothing is said about the other gates that belong to the other courtyards. With regard to the gates of the city of Jerusalem, however, the door jamb belongs to the outside of the wall.[21] We learn from this that the sages considered that the exact point of separation between two juxtaposed temple zones existed at the door jamb. In most instances the door jamb was considered to be part of the interior, but in one interpretation the door jamb belonged to the exterior. It is possible, and the texts are unclear in this regard, that the determining factor of inner or outer door jamb was whether the gate swung inward or outward.

Another related discussion centered upon the actual moveable gate itself. Did it contain the quality of holiness that belonged to the inner territory, or did it possess the

sanctity of the outer zone? The answer to the question had
relevance to at least one gate within the temple precinct, as
well as to the gates of the city of Jerusalem. It is written in
the Talmud that the gates of Jerusalem were not sanctified
because the lepers sheltered themselves near the gates from
the atmospheric elements, e.g., from the winter rains and
the summer sun. In other words, the presence of ritually
impure lepers caused the gates to lose any sanctity that may
have once been attached to them. Similarly, the Nicanor
Gate, which existed between the court of the Women and
the court of Israel, did not possess the sanctity of the court
of Israel. "Why was the gate of Nicanor not sanctified?
Because lepers stand there and insert the thumbs of their
hands [into the Court]."[22] The extension of the leper's
thumbs into the court of Israel has reference to the leper
who has completed the days of purification. According to
rabbinic law, the leper presented himself at the Nicanor
Gate, extended his thumb and big toe into the sanctuary,
where the priest then applied sacrificial blood.[23]

For practical purposes the architects built cells or chambers into the great thick outer wall of the temple precinct.
At times, the cells were designed so that persons could pass
back and forth through the building between the rampart
and the court. This type of construction raised several questions concerning the exact demarcation between sacred and
profane space. What about chambers built into a wall that
had a door opening outward into the rampart—is the area
sacred within the chamber? To this question the sages
responded with a negative answer. However, if the chamber's roof is level with the pavement of the court, then the
roof is considered to be holy. As is the case in many
instances, an exception to the ruling existed. The exception
to this concept is cited by the sages—if the doors open into

the courtyard, the rooms of the chamber are deemed to possess sanctity, but the roofs are not sacred. The cellars of the temple provide an exception to this, however, for they are not sanctified at any time.[24]

What about a chamber that had a door on each end of the building, one opening onto holy ground and the other onto unholy ground? Where is the dividing line that separates sacred from profane space? Talmudic sources make reference to two chambers that fit this description—the Chamber of Hewn Stone and the Chamber of the Fireplace. The Chamber of Hewn Stone, built into the great temple wall, was located on the border between the court of the Priests and the rampart. The sages determined that the building itself was situated half on holy ground and half on nonholy ground. It had two doors, one opened to holy ground (the court of the Priests) and the other to unholy ground (the rampart).[25] The Chamber of Hewn Stone served as the gathering place for the Sanhedrin. Maimonides writes that the Sanhedrin would sit in the half of the Chamber of Hewn Stone that stood upon nonholy ground.[26]

The Chamber of the Fireplace was situated within the same wall as the Chamber of Hewn Stone but lay westward several cubits. Although larger than the Chamber of Hewn Stone, the Chamber of the Fireplace possessed similar architectural features. It was divided into four rooms; two were located on holy ground and two on profane ground. Flagstones were set into the ground to mark the division between the two.[27] "There were four cells in the Chamber of the Hearth, like small rooms opening into a hall, two within holy space and two outside of holy space, and the ends of marked pavement separated between the holy and the profane."[28]

While no flagstones are mentioned with reference to the

Chamber of Hewn Stone, it is possible that they were utilized in demarcating space in this chamber, given their usefulness in demarcating space. Flagstones were also used to separate the Court of the Priests from the Court of Israel,[29] and in the chamber above the tripartite temple building, flagstones separated the Holy of Holies from the Holy Place.[30]

Another architectural component, which is mentioned in connection with Solomon's Temple, was found in the Temple of Herod. A two-part cedar partition was used in Solomon's Temple to divide the Holy Place from the Holy of Holies (see 1 Kings 6:16). During the period of the Second Temple, two curtains were employed between the two zones rather than the wooden partition. Between the two curtains was a space that measured one cubit. The veils were designed so that the outer curtain was fastened to the northern wall and the inner curtain was fastened to the southern wall. As the high priest would enter the Holy of Holies on the Day of Atonement, he would enter from the south, travel northward between the two veils until he reached the entrance of the inner veil at the north end, and then enter the sanctum. Evidently, the purpose of the two veils was to protect the sanctity of the Holy of Holies from the view, either accidental or purposeful, of proximal ministering priests. Given the sages' preoccupation with determining exact spatial borders throughout the temple precinct, the question naturally arose whether the cubit of space between the two veils held the sanctity of the sanctum or the Holy Place. While the text of TB *Yoma* 51b–52b presents the discussion of the rabbis with regard to this issue, the text does not reveal a clear-cut decision.

Preliminarily, one may guess that the walls of the temple were simple demarcating lines that acted as visual and physical barriers between gradational zones. In a sense they were just that, with the side of the wall representing the sanctity of the zone that it faced. But the rabbis, desiring to be more precise in their demarcations, addressed the matter of the thickness of the walls. In a mishnaic statement in M *Pesahim* 7:12, it was declared that the thickness of the walls counted as the inside of that respective zone. Maimonides, commenting on that statement, adds that the thickness of the walls was considered part of the interior with regard to both uncleanness and the consumption of offerings.[31] Windows also, which were set in various walls, were to be considered as part of and possessing the sanctity of the interior.[32] Practical situations of cultic life required rabbinic response. Jewish law dictated that the paschal lamb was to be eaten within the walls of Jerusalem, and if removed, then the food was declared unclean for consumption. It was possible that, while preparing the passover offering, one of its limbs would accidently project outside of the wall of Jerusalem. If this situation were to occur, then special prescriptions provided for the removal of that defective limb from the remainder of the passover lamb. This was accomplished by first scraping the flesh of the limb off the bone up to the first joint. After this exercise the limb might be cut off at the joint. All the while the person performing this activity had to take care not to break the bone of the limb (see Exodus 12:46).[33]

Another Talmudic illustration demonstrates that the walls of the court of Priests represented a border between two temple zones. Rabbi Ammi, speaking in Rabbi Eleazar's name, presented the illustration. What is the ritual status of an animal whose legs are unintentionally extended outside of the court? Is the animal still fit for the altar? Rabbi Ammi's response to this situation was, "If he [the priest] cut off its legs and then slaughtered it, it is fit; if he slaughtered and then cut off [the legs] it is unfit."[34] Yet another Talmudic example lists a concern for spatial demarcation. Rabbi Abba b. Mammel noted that the gateway of the wall of the Court of the Priests carefully divided the purity of certain priesthood officiants. He stated that if certain temple workers carry the flesh of the Passover sacrifice to another company and the front bearers go "outside the walls of the temple court while the rear ones had not yet gone out, those in front defile their garments while those behind do not defile their garments."[35]

A similar case study deals with the level of purity of a member of the priesthood who causes a portion of his body to leave the court of Priests while the remainder remains within the court. The rabbis ruled that if the priest's hands only were projected out of the court of the Priests, the person would yet be considered cultically pure. Similarly, if the person extended both his hands and his feet outside of the court, but his torso remained within the court, the person would yet retain his sanctity. The response toward the entire body or person was different. The authorities concluded that if a temple officiant left the court's premises with the intention of tarrying outside of the court, he would then be required to immerse himself in the cleansing pool. If it was his intention, however, to briefly leave the premises and shortly return, he would then be required to wash his hands and feet only. The text raises the issue of one who leaves the court due to "nature's call." It states that "he who eases himself needs immersion, and he who answers nature's call requires sanctification of hands and feet."[36]

The Temple Mount was known to have a number of tunnels that aided members of the priesthood in their cultic duties. According to Maimonides, entrances of tunnels opening into the courts are holy, while those opening up outside of the courts are profane.[37] Tunnels opening outward into the Temple Mount (*Har ha-Bayit*) that originate outside of the courtyards are not as holy as the Temple Mount, but if the tunnel begins in the court and opens outside of the court into the Temple Mount, it is equal in holiness to the Temple Mount.[38]

Aerial and Subterranean Space

To this point we have seen the manner in which the Jewish sages, using architectural components, determined precisely where profane space ended and sacred space began. Two other dimensions of sacred space should be treated here—aerial and subterranean space.

Aerial Space: The rabbinic sources build a case for the sanctity of the airspace above the temple precinct.[39] A simple statement attested in TB *Zevahim* 26a provides a summary on the matter—"the airspace of within is as within." That is to say, the sanctity of the airspace within a defined area is to be considered equal to the sanctity of that area. A modern commentator has paraphrased this statement by writing that "the airspace of a place is as the place itself."[40] Hence, the airspace that exists within the walls of a given zone of the temple carries the same sanctity as the area's surface and its appurtenances. By way of extension, the airspace of a court is governed by the same regulations as the zone itself.[41]

Having established these facts, the sages were able to treat various circumstances that had relevancy to sanctuary airspace. For instance, when a priest projected his hands into the court of Priests, but his body remained outside of the court, it was as if full entry had been made by that person.[42] This ruling produced grave results for the unclean person who projected his hand into the court. According to Maimonides, if a ritually impure person stretched forth his hand into the sanctuary, he would be flogged.[43]

Outside of the tripartite temple building itself, the most sacred area of the temple precinct was north of the sacrificial altar. Lesser sacrifices may be slaughtered in any part of the court, but the sacrifices of a higher sanctity must be offered on the north side.[44] If, however, a priest stood in the southern portion of the court, extended his hands into the northern area, and in this manner slaughtered the sacrifice, then "his slaughtering is valid." Apparently the sanctity of the area did not magically draw its powers from the pavement, but the very airspace of the north territory was seen to be equal to the pavement itself. The Talmud continues by explaining that if the greater portion of a priest's upper body, including his head, is extended into the northern portion of the court, then it is as if his entire person had entered that zone.[45]

Under the same regulations that stated "the airspace of within is as within," the sages ruled that the airspace above the altar was equal in sanctity to the altar itself.[46] The point is significant, for the altar was a prominent focal point of the entire precinct, second only to the Holy of Holies. Similarly, the airspace above the altar's ramp, ledge, and foundation possessed the same degree of sanctity as the airspace above the altar.[47] For evidence of this, the rabbis refer to Leviticus 1. According to verse 15, when the sacrificial bird is offered, its head must be pinched in a prescribed manner while upon the altar. The body of the bird rests upon the altar, while its head is found in the airspace above the altar. Can the head of the bird lose its sanctity because it does not touch the altar? According to the sages, the answer is no.

The sages are in agreement that the holiness of the airspace above the altar is equal to the holiness of the altar itself.

The question was raised concerning the vessels of the temple—when a utensil or vessel is suspended in the air between the altar and a sacrificial offering, does it not act as a barrier between the altar and sacrifice, thereby blocking the sanctity of the airspace? The rabbis ruled that the vessel does not create a barrier, for it too is holy.[48] In fact, the concept dealing with the pavement's airspace and the altar's airspace is identical to the airspace of the utensil. The airspace of the utensil is equal to the sanctity of the utensil itself. It is necessary for the operations of the temple cult that this be the case. It has been ruled by the sages that both the vessel and the blood of the sacrificial animal are equally holy. When the priest pours the blood of the jugular veins straight into the vessel, the blood remains sanctified as it travels through the air. From the cultically clean animal, through cultically clean airspace, to the cultically pure vessel, the blood remains unblemished. Hence, the holiness of the airspace above a vessel is equal to the holiness of the vessel itself.[49]

According to the scheme found in M *Kelim* 1:6–9 and elsewhere, Jerusalem was also considered a zone of holiness. Therefore, similar to the courtyard zones of the temple precinct, the airspace of the city of Jerusalem, too, was equal in sanctity to the city itself. *Encyclopedia Talmudica* cites the example of a person standing in a tree, that "as a person stands upon the branches of a tree, he is regarded as standing in the airspace above the ground."[50] The Mishnah equates Jerusalem's airspace with its pavement: "If a man says to his children, 'Behold, I slaughter the Passover-offering on behalf of whichever of you goes up first to Jerusalem,' as soon as the first has inserted his head and the greater part of his body [in Jerusalem] he has acquired his portion (M *Pesahim* 8:3)."[51]

Moving outward beyond all the zones of holiness as listed in M *Kelim* 1:6–9, we discover that the aerial space belonging to heathen lands is equal to the soil of the area. Maimonides' tutelage concerning the airspace of heathen lands is instructive. He compares the soil of heathen lands to an area where graves are found.[52] Similarly the airspace of heathen lands is unclean. If a Jew walks upon heathen land, or even thrusts his head or the greater portion of his body into heathen airspace, that person will become unclean.[53] In this regard there existed a metonymical relationship—part of the body represented the entire person. Sacred vessels, also, if extended into heathen airspace would become unclean.[54]

Although both heathen soil and airspace is unclean, the uncleannness of the heathen soil is greater than the uncleanness of the airspace, says Maimonides.[55] The reason for this is direct contact of heathen soil conveys uncleanness, but not so much uncleanness is conveyed by overshadowing.[56] Hence, one who becomes unclean by virtue of heathen soil is required to be cleansed the third and seventh days, while one who becomes unclean by virtue of the airspace above heathen soil has need of immersion only. Furthermore, if one travels through heathen land, he will incur seven-day uncleanness, but if he travels by sea through heathen countries, it is as if he had become unclean because of heathen airspace, and not its soil. Syria stands as an exception to this ruling: its soil is unclean like any other heathen country, but its airspace is clean like the land of Israel.[57] A second exception concerns a person who walks along an area over which the ocean may swell during a storm, for the person remains clean in such a place.[58] T. *Ahilot* 18:5 adds the following concepts: If a person enters heathen lands in a box, the person is clean. If, however, a person enters heathen land in a carriage or boat, he is unclean. Finally, if more than one-half of a chair is extended into a heathen land, then it is unclean.

Subterranean Space: We have addressed the issue of the sanctity of aerial space; now we must look at the subterranean areas of the temple. It was understood by the sages that the surface of the courts and buildings located within the temple precinct was sacred. It was taught by the School of Ishmael that "the pavement sanctifies." For this reason, nothing must exist upon the ground which would "interpose" between the priest and the pavement. Questionable, however, was the area below the paved surface—the depths. Two contradictory views existed. The first considered the soil and area below the surface to be sacred. According to this view the ground was first sanctified by David "to the nethermost soil." A note in the Epstein version of the Talmud states that the expression "nethermost soil" should read literally "the soil of the deep."[59]

A second and more popular view of the temple's subterrane held the area to be profane. According to M *Tamid* 1:1, a priest who suffered an accident, such as a seminal issue, would descend below the surface of the temple through a passageway until he reached the ritual baths. The unclean priest would immerse himself, dry himself by the fire, and take his place by other priests who awaited the opening of the gates. Jewish law prevented the priests from returning to the sacred ground of the temple, for those who immersed themselves in the ritual baths were required to wait for sunset.[60] Rather, at the opening of the gates of the temple, the priests would depart. The *Gemara* cites M *Tamid* 1:1 as evidence that the temple's subterrane was profane. In a statement attributed to Rabbi Johanan, the Talmud states

"[M *Tamid* 1:1] supports the view . . . that the subterranean passage possessed no sanctity."[61]

Although it is clear that the subterranean areas of the temple became a location for unclean priests, the temple depths were also unclean by virtue of a second reason. A natural but profane act[62] was conducted under the surface area of the temple, for it was there that a privy was located.[63] A door was found on the privy, and a locked door signaled to a potential occupant that the privy was occupied; an unlocked door allowed a person entrance.

The rabbis held other concerns about the subterrane. M *Parah* relates the preventive measures that the authorities took to ensure that a corpse would not desecrate any area of the Temple Mount. One prescription dealt with the rabbinic ruling with regard to the "tent" (or shadowing). According to the law, the tent of a corpse was able to defile in three separate but similar ways: (1) If the corpse is found above or overshadows a person or utensil, that person or utensil becomes unclean. (2) If the corpse is found under the same covering as a person or utensil, that person or utensil becomes unclean. (3) If the corpse is found beneath a person or utensil, that person becomes unclean.[64] In the context of the depths below the ground surface of the temple, the third case has the greatest relevance. The Jews needed assurance that no graves existed below the surface of the temple, so they hollowed out the depths.[65] A further measure added additional confidence to the temple community when a causeway was constructed extending from the Temple Mount to the Mount of Olives "for fear of any grave in the depths below."[66] This causeway may have shared a purpose similar to the bridge connecting the upper city with the Temple Mount. The bridge was constructed to allow the high priest and other temple workers to reach the temple without passing through the lower marketplace.[67]

The Demarcation of Space outside of the Temple Precinct

A broader picture regarding the demarcation of space should be examined here. Rabbinic literature illustrates the sages' attempts to carefully delimit space outside of the temple area, including the city of Jerusalem, the land of Israel, and the lands of the Gentiles.

The city of Jerusalem metonymically was an extension of the temple and its holiness. The three camps or gradations that existed at the time of the Israelites' sojourn in the wilderness were, during the period of the Second Temple, superimposed upon Jerusalem and the temple. "The Temple and Jerusalem were the direct continuation of the camp and Tabernacle of the wilderness. The rabbis . . . divided Jerusalem into three sections: the priestly camp (temple), the Levitic camp (the Temple Mount), and the Israelite camp (the city)."[68] The Tabernacle was replaced with the temple, the camp of Levites became equated with the Temple Mount, and Jerusalem replaced what was known as the camp of Israel.[69] *Numbers Rabbah* 7:8 grades persons within the three camps. The city of Jerusalem, like the temple, possessed precise boundaries. Within the city a high degree of sanctity was found; without the city existed a lesser degree. Space outside of the city was called the "border,"[70] having the connotation of peripherality or marginality.

The walls of Jerusalem were vital in separating the sacred from the profane. They became physical verticalities, retaining inside themselves the mystical power of holiness. The walls represented border configurations par excellence, symbolizing linear divisions between zones. "Space, however, consists not only of localities, but is determined as well by directions, and finally by its borders, or boundaries."[71] J. G. Davies believes that sacred space has a distinct identity and must have "pronounced borders."[72] Standing in antithesis to sacred space is profane space, which has no borders and is largely unidentifiable.

Jerusalem's walls served as precise borders that defined and demarcated space. Many examples from the Second Temple period can be cited. A practical problem existed within the borders of Israel concerning the ownership of trees. Throughout the land of Israel, with the exception of the cities of refuge and the city of Jerusalem, when disputations arose affecting the ownership of trees, the location of the roots became the factor of determination. The tract of land that possessed the tree's roots (or, at least, the majority of the roots), also possessed the tree. In this matter, though, Jerusalem and the cities of refuge were exceptions. The tree's roots were not a factor in determining ownership, but the tree's branches were. If the roots of the tree were located outside of the walls, but its branches extended over the wall into the city, then the branches (i.e., its fruits) belonged to the city.[73]

The term *wall* is frequently used by the Talmudic authors who demonstrated particular interest in the sacred tithes and offerings. Jerusalem's wall played a role in the complex laws governing the second tithe.[74] The second tithes were to be eaten within the walls of Jerusalem; if they were eaten outside of the walls, the offender would incur stripes and flogging.[75] Similarly, whoever encouraged others to eat consecrated animals outside of the walls was subject to excommunication.[76] According to the Mishnah, if a person unintentionally removed sacred flesh outside of

Jerusalem's walls, he was given two options: If he had already passed beyond Mount Scopus (the hill northeast of Jerusalem, which is the last elevated area from which Jerusalem is visible), then he was instructed to burn the flesh on the spot. If, however, the person could yet see the city, he was to return to the temple and burn the flesh there.[77]

Conclusion

We first viewed the manner in which physical geography and hiero-geography are not conterminous but represent antithetical situations. Sacred space and sacral architecture are carefully delimited and possess precise borders that serve to separate the holy from the profane. Several examples from rabbinic literature demonstrated the manner in which the Jews utilized the walls and gateways to divide and demarcate various planes of holiness, both within and without the temple precinct. With regard to spatial delimitation, both the subterranean areas of the temple and the aerial space above the sanctuary received due consideration by the Jewish sages—the subterrane was considered to be profane; aerial space was seen to be holy.

What was the significance of meticulous demarcations between sacred and profane space? Sacred space, of course, was holy because of its connection to God—his divine appearance to a particular site or his selection of the site. R. D. Martienssen explains that the very first step towards "arranged and controlled space"[78] is the selection of the site. Site designation promptly suggests a delimitation between a sacred "inside" centered area and a chaotic homogeneous "outside" area, or a perceptible division between holy and profane space. Hence, sacred space is divided from the profane in order to protect the interests of the temple community, whose desire it is to approach God within the boundaries of the temple.

Notes

1. Reuvan Hammer, *Sifre, A Tannaitic Commentary on the Book of Deuteronomy* (New Haven: Yale University Press, 1986), 70.

2. See ibid. In a related set of circumstances, the rabbinic authorities demonstrate that the Israelites themselves desired to have the temple located within their territory (cf. *Genesis Rabbah* 22:8 and 26:3). *Genesis Rabbah* 99:1 contradicts a statement listed in TB *Megillah* 16b that states that the temple was built in the territory of Benjamin. The rabbis deal with this problem by dividing the temple into different parts. The portion of temple located in the territory of Benjamin included the vestibule, the Holy Place, and the Holy of Holies; and the section of the temple that belonged to the territory of Judah included the chambers of the priest, the courts, and the Temple Mount (see TB *Megillah* 26a; cf. *Sifre on Deuteronomy Pisqa* 62).

TB *Yoma* 12a presents a slightly different picture. "What lay in the lot of Judah? The Temple Mount, the cells, the courts. And what lay in the lot of Benjamin? The Hall, the Temple, and the Holy of Holies. And a strip of land went forth from Judah's lot and went into Benjamin's territory, and on this the temple was built." *Sifre on Deuteronomy Pisqa* 352 explains that the sanctuary was built in the "portion of Benjamin, and a triangular section extended from that portion to that of Judah" (quoted in Hammer, *Sifre,* 366). This text continues by quoting Genesis 49:10, "The scepter shall not depart from Judah," and explains, "That refers to the Hall of Hewn Stones which was situated in the portion of Judah, as it is said"; then Psalms 78:67–68 is quoted (Hammer, *Sifre,* 366). Here we are not interested in attempting to solve the apparent contradictions that exist in the literature. The sources are pointed out because they demonstrate the careful interest held by the rabbis in producing tribal borders, especially with regard to the temple.

3. All translations are the author's unless otherwise indicated.

4. Incidentally, the Latin word *sacrum* ("sacred") coincides with the Hebrew QDŠ, meaning "consecrated" (*The Concise Oxford Dictionary of English Etymology,* ed. T. F. Hoad [Oxford: Clarendon, 1986], 413).

5. So says Roger Caillois, *Man and the Sacred,* trans. Meyer Barash (Westport: Greenwood, 1980), 20. Davies writes that "any attempt, outside the prescribed limits, to unite sacred and profane brings confusion and disaster" ("Architecture," in *Encyclopedia of Religion,* ed. Mircea Eliade, 16 vols. [New York: Macmillan, 1987], 1:385). Also, the

sacred and the profane cannot "approach one another without losing their proper nature: either the sacred will consume the profane or the profane will contaminate and enfeeble the sacred" (384).

6. Rudolf Otto, *The Idea of the Holy*, trans. John W. Harvey (London: Oxford University Press, 1936), 25–30.

7. This helps explain why so many foreign invaders have, at different periods in the history of the Israelites, chosen to tread unauthorized within the sacred precincts of the temple. Perhaps the sanctity of the area had very little religious impact upon them.

8. Brevard Childs, *Myth and Reality in the Old Testament* (London: SCM, 1960), 83.

9. "By attaching his experience to certain limited areas, he makes the qualitative distinctions within space of sacred and profane, each bearing its emotional character. This scheme is extended beyond the individual experience as cosmic events are also given spatial qualities" (ibid).

10. Hans J. Klimkeit, "Spatial Orientation in Mythical Thinking as Exemplified in Ancient Egypt: Considerations toward a Geography of Religions," *History of Religions* 14 (May 1975): 274.

11. See Yehoshua M. Grintz, "*Bēt ha-Miqdāš*" (in Hebrew), *Encyclopedia Hebraica*, ed. B. Natanyahu, 20 vols. (Jerusalem: Encyclopaedia Printing, 1957), 8:555, where the different names of the temple as they appear in the Hebrew Bible are listed: *bēt Yhwh*, *bēt E'lôhîm*, *hēkāl qôdeš* (Jonah 2:5[4]); *hēkāl Yhwh* (2 Kings 24:13); and *miqdāš*. The usual name in the Mishnah and related literature, i.e., the Tosephta, is *Bēt ha-Miqdāš*. Of this name the encyclopedia states, "this name is found only one time in the Bible" (555). The *Targum of Jeremiah* calls the temple the "house of the Shekinah" (2:7; 3:17; 7:15; 14:10; 15:1).

12. Francis Brown, S. R. Driver, and Charles A. Briggs, *A Hebrew and English Lexicon of the Old Testament* (Oxford: Clarendon, 1977), 871.

13. See Ludwig Koehler and Walter Baumgartner, eds., *Lexicon in Veteris Testamenti Libros* (Leiden: Brill, 1953), 825–26.

14. Davies, "Architecture," 1:384.

15. *Concise Oxford Dictionary of English Etymology*, 372.

16. Marcus Jastrow, *Dictionary of the Targumim, Talmud Babli, Yerushalmi and Midrashic Literature* (New York: Judaica, 1975), 433.

17. Mircea Eliade, *Patterns of Comparative Religion* (New York: Sheed and Ward, 1958), 368.

18. Mircea Eliade, *Images and Symbols*, tr. Philip Mairet (New York: Sheed and Ward, 1961), 39–40.

19. Here it is helpful to note Klimkeit's definition of empirical

space: "Empirical space . . . is in practice the particular space we see and record photographically. . . . It is always filled with objects meeting our eye. We can here draw a parallel with empirical time. Just as early man could not conceive of abstract and empty time as such in his 'historical' thinking, but only time filled by events—'gefullte Zeit,' as Gerhard von Rad says—his concept of space is seldom purely abstract and vacuous" ("Spatial Orientation in Mythical Thinking," 274).

20. Caillois recognizes the "reciprocal relationships" that exist between the sacred and profane and therefore suggests that they "have to be strictly regulated" (Man and the Sacred, 23).

21. TB Pesahim 85b.

22. Ibid.

23. Compare n. 16 of the Soncino edition of the Talmud, TB Yevamot 7b; see also TB Nazir 45a.

24. See TB Pesahim 86a; cf. TB Yoma 25a.

25. See TB Yoma 25a.

26. See Maimonides, Yad VIII, 1, 5, 17.

27. See M Middot 1:6; TB Yoma 15b-16a.

28. M Middot 1:6.

29. See ibid. 2:6.

30. See ibid. 4:5.

31. See Yad VIII, 1, 6, 9.

32. See M Pesahim 7:12.

33. Ibid.

34. TB Zevahim 25a-26a.

35. TB Pesahim 85b.

36. TB Zevahim 20b.

37. Ibid. For a treatment of tunnels opening into holy or unholy ground, see A. Kimelman, "The Area of the Temple Mount and the Ḥel (Rampart), and the Laws Pertaining Thereto" (in Hebrew), Ha-Maayan 8, no. 3 (1968): 10.

38. See Kimelman, "The Area of the Temple Mount," 11.

39. Was the airspace intrinsically holy? ET, 1:336–37, comments on the topic of intrinsic airspace. For the airspace above an individual's courtyard, or the airspace of a mikveh (ritual pool of immersion), a field, and other areas, see ET, 1:332–35.

40. Ibid., 336.

41. See ibid., 338.

42. See TB Zevahim 32a; cf. Zevahim 20b.

43. See Maimonides, Yad VIII, 3, 3, 18.

44. See TB Menahot 3a; TB Zevahim 55a.

45. See TB *Zevahim* 26a.

46. The author of TB *Shevuʿot* 17a speaks concerning an unclean person who is suspended in the airspace of the temple, but concludes that no rules are made with regard to that person. The text, while difficult, demonstrates that the creators of the Talmud were giving consideration to the problem of temple airspace.

47. See TB *Zevahim* 87b; *ET*, 1:337.

48. See *ET*, 1:337.

49. See TB *Zevahim* 25b; cf. *Zevahim* 97b.

50. *ET*, 1:339.

51. Herbert Danby, tr., *The Mishnah* (Oxford: Oxford University Press, 1983), 147.

52. The Jewish doctrine that depicts heathen soil as unclean probably predates the reign of Herod, perhaps to the early period of the Second Temple (Gedalyahu Alon, "The Levitical Uncleanness of Gentiles," in Alon, *Jews, Judaism and the Classical World*, trans. Israel Abrahams [Jerusalem: Magnes, 1977], 187). Alon rejects the idea that political maneuvers and situations extant at the time of the Second Temple period resulted in the Jewish doctrine (see ibid). Rather, the space is unclean because the gentiles worshiped idols, and their houses were unclean because abortions possibly took place within them (see ibid., 186, n. 75).

53. Cf. T *Ahilot* 18:5.

54. See Maimonides, *Yad* X, 1, 11, 1–6.

55. See ibid.

56. See M *Oholoth* 2:3; cf. T *Ahilot* 18:1, 5.

57. See Maimonides, *Yad* X, 1, 11, 1–6. Why the land of Syria stands as an exception in this instance is unknown. Perhaps Maimonides had in mind M *Oholoth* 18:7, which states that fields lying adjacent to the land of Israel are clean and are subject to the laws of tithes. Unfortunately, the connection between clean fields and clean airspace is not direct.

58. See M *Oholoth* 18:6.

59. TB *Zevahim* 24a.

60. On the laws pertaining to the ritual baths, see M *Tevul Yom*, passim.

61. TB *Tamid* 27b.

62. Jacob Milgrom, citing Deuteronomy 23:13–14, deduces that "urination, by implication, does not defile" ("Further Studies in the Temple Scroll," *Jewish Quarterly Review* 71, nos. 1–2 [1980]: 97).

63. See M *Tamid* 1:1; also Saul Lieberman, "Palestine in the Third and Fourth Centuries," *Jewish Quarterly Review* 36 (1946): 45, n. 33.

Milgrom, citing 11QTemple col. 46:13–16, points out that lavatories were not found in the Temple City ("Further Studies in the Temple Scroll," 97).

64. For a discussion of various aspects of the tent, see *ET*, 1:288–91.

65. See M *Parah* 3:2–3.

66. Ibid., 3:6.

67. See Michael Avi-Yonah, "Jerusalem in the Hellenistic and Roman Periods," in *The World History of the Jewish People: The Herodian Period*, ed. Michael Avi-Yonah (New Brunswick: Rutgers University Press, 1975), 249.

68. Jacob Milgrom, "Temple Scroll," *Biblical Archaeologist*, 41, no. 3 (1978): 117.

69. See TB *Zevahim* 55a. On the tripartite division of Jerusalem, see further the remarks of Maimonides in *Yad* VIII, 1, 7, 11; and in his *Commentary on* M *Kelim* 1:8.

70. TB *Kiddushin* 80a.

71. Klimkeit, "Spatial Orientation in Mythical Thinking," 277.

72. Davies, "Architecture," 391; see also J. G. Davies, *Temples, Churches, and Mosques—Religious Architecture* (New York: Pilgrim, 1982), 240.

73. See M *Maᶜserot* 3:10; TB *Makkot* 12a.

74. See M *Kelim* 1:8; TB *Yevamot* 86b; TB *Makkot* 12a.

75. See TB *Makkot* 18a-18b; TB *Menahot* 70b.

76. See TB *Bezah* 23a.

77. See M *Pesahim* 3:8.

78. R. D. Martienssen, *The Idea of Space in Greek Architecture* (Johannesburg: Witwatersrand University Press, 1956), 1. Site selection is an essential aspect of having ordered space. As Martienssen has written, "the notion of architecture . . . implies a pre-determined end, a conceptual origin, of which the material expression is only the completing process" (ibid., 2).

16

Temple Motifs in Jewish Mysticism

William J. Hamblin

The Destruction of the Second Temple

When a temple is the center of the spiritual life of a people, what do they do if it is destroyed? Jews and Christians faced this dilemma in A.D. 70 when Titus sacked Jerusalem and destroyed the Second Temple.[1] Thereafter, despite two abortive attempts to rebuild their temple,[2] Jews were left without a central focus for their ritual worship. Indeed, without a temple, they could not fulfill all of the requirements of the Mosaic law of sacrifice.[3] They thus became a people eternally condemned to fail to keep the commandments of God that were connected to the temple.

Three possible solutions developed in response to this intolerable situation. The Pharisees created an ideology focusing on the minute obedience to all of God's nontemple-related commandments as expounded in the Bible, Talmud, and other Rabbinic literature.[4] When God was ready, he would send his Messiah and the temple could be rebuilt.[5] Until then, the Jews had to be content with fulfilling those portions of the law that could be obeyed without a temple. This response became normative for Rabbinic Judaism.

For the Christians, on the other hand, the destruction of the temple at Jerusalem was seen as a fulfillment of Christ's prophecy (found in Matthew 24:1–2; Mark 13:1–2; Luke 21:5–6). With the spread of the authority of the Imperial Church following the conversion of Constantine (A.D. 312), teachings concerning the temple were increasingly allegorized. Inasmuch as Christ's atonement had fulfilled the requirement of Mosaic temple sacrifices, such sacrifices were no longer necessary.[6] Nonetheless, as Hugh Nibley has pointed out, medieval Christians retained an ambivalent attitude toward the Jewish temple, claiming that it was no longer important, but still recognizing its vast spiritual power.[7]

Finally, there was a third response, that righteous humans could ascend into heaven and worship at the celestial temple. This paper will focus on the nature of the ascent to the celestial temple in Jewish thought during and after the Second Temple period.[8]

The Heavenly Ascent in the Ancient Near East

The idea of the celestial ascent is one of the most widespread and long-lasting religious concepts in history.[9] Archaic, nonbiblical ascension myths from Mesopotamia and Egypt date back to the early third millennium B.C.[10] Within the Jewish tradition, this idea can be seen in the writings of Isaiah (eighth century B.C.) and Ezekiel (sixth century B.C.). Related and expanded versions of the ascent to the celestial temple are found in pseudepigraphic Enoch materials dating in their current form to at least the second century B.C., Qumran documents (second century B.C. to first century A.D.), Philo (c. 20 B.C. to A.D. 50),[11] and in numerous other Jewish and Christian apocalyptic and pseudepigraphic writings.

I would argue, following James Tabor and others,[12] that the heavenly ascent of the Jewish mystics cannot be understood in isolation. The parallels between Jewish, early Christian, Hellenistic, Gnostic, and Egyptian ascension texts and rituals are too numerous and exact to be explained by random chance.

Tabor has developed a typology for ascension into heaven in the eastern Mediterranean world during the first centuries before and after Christ. Although there are many variations in detail, there nonetheless emerges a basic common pattern. Most ascension texts include most of the following elements:

1. A mortal is taken up to the highest heaven.

2. The ascent is an extraordinary privilege.

3. The way is fraught with danger and can be successfully undertaken only through divine permission and power.

4. There is great distance between the earthly and heavenly realms, with increasing beauty and splendor (or danger for the uninvited) as one moves up, and an increasing sense of alienation from the world below.

5. The ascent itself is a transforming experience in which the candidate is progressively glorified.

6. The climax of the journey is an encounter with the highest god.

7. One is given secret revelations, or shown mysteries.

8. The ascent is followed by a return to the world below to continue life as a mortal.

9. What is seen and heard can be selectively passed on by the recipient of the celestial ascension.

10. The one who has ascended faces the opposition of lower spiritual powers upon his return.[13]

Although many characteristics of the Judeo-Christian ascent literature parallel these broader characteristics of the ancient Near East, there are also other elements unique to the Judeo-Christian versions of the celestial ascent and vision of God. Ithamar Gruenwald, one of the leading figures in the study of these ascension visions, adds six additional specific elements that are characteristic of the celestial vision of God in biblical accounts.[14]

1. God is sitting on a throne, often called a *merkavah* (Eng. "chariot").
2. God possesses anthropomorphic qualities and features.
3. God's throne is in the Holy of Holies in the celestial temple (Heb. *hēkhāl*).[15]
4. The temple is filled with fire, light, gold, crystal, and gems, symbolizing the brilliant glory of God.
5. God is surrounded by angels who minister to him. (These angels fulfill the role of priests in the heavenly temple, paralleling the Levite priests in the earthly temple.)[16]
6. The angels are singing hymns, paralleling the earthly temple hymns, rituals, and liturgies.[17]

Thus, for many Jews and Christians in the early Christian period, the heavenly residence of God was conceived of as a vast celestial temple.[18] Martha Himmelfarb, a leading scholar of this subject, informs us that "with the single exception of the Testament of Abraham, all the later ascent apocalypses . . . understand heaven as a temple either explicitly or implicitly."[19] Thus, many ascents into heaven contain an important element of the entry into the celestial temple; indeed, in many ways the two are essentially synonymous.

The earthly temple was simply a pale shadow and imitation of the glories of its celestial prototype.[20] Although the earthly temple had been destroyed because of the sins of Israel, the original celestial prototype continued to exist in heaven. Following the example of the ascents and visions of ancient prophets such as Enoch, Abraham, Moses, Isaiah, and Ezekiel,[21] many Jews came to believe that they too could ascend to the celestial temple. If properly prepared, a person could ascend into heaven, visit the celestial temple, perform the proper rituals there, and even enter into the presence of God and receive a revelation of the celestial mysteries. The Jewish practices and literature related to these ideas are known to modern scholars as *Merkavah* and *Hekhalot* mysticism.

Ascension to the Heavenly Temple in Hekhalot and Merkavah Literature

Gruenwald summarizes the historical origins of the post-Second Temple Jewish ascension literature (first through the seventh centuries A.D.) as follows:

> The very rise of Merkavah mysticism was connected with the name of Rabbi Yohanan ben Zakkai, who was himself an eyewitness to the events that led to the destruction of Jerusalem. Thus, in a sense, the preoccupation with mystical problems could well be interpreted as being one of the ways in which people reacted to the disasters which befell them. When the cultic centre of the nation was no longer available, some people adapted beliefs and cultivated experiences which in some sense could replace experiences which had once been connected with the now destroyed Temple.[22]

Merkavah and Hekhalot literature focuses on three fundamental themes: the celestial *hekhalot*, meaning "temples or palaces"; the divine *merkavah*, or "chariot/throne" of God; and *be-reshit*, meaning literally "in the beginning," but referring to esoteric interpretations of the creation. All of these concepts form interrelated parts of the secret revelation obtained during the ascent to the celestial temple.

In a general sense the term *hekhal* means "palace or mansion," but in its technical usage it refers to the Temple of Solomon.[23] Within the context of the Hekhalot mysticism, it seems best conceived of as a series of concentric courts, palaces, halls, chambers, shrines, or levels of the great celestial temple of God. Generally speaking, God himself dwells within the highest, most sacred, and innermost sanctuary—the Holy of Holies of the celestial temple.

An interesting possible parallel to this concept can be found in the Gospel of John. "In the House of my Father [*oikia tou patros mou*]," Jesus tells us, "there are many dwelling places [*monai*]" (John 14:2).[24] The use of the phrase "House of my Father" occurs only twice in John's Gospel: here, referring to heaven, and in John 2:16 which states, "Do not make the House of my Father a house of trade." In John 2:16 the Father's House is clearly the Temple of Jerusalem, which was frequently called the "House of God" or the "House of Yahweh."[25] By extension, then, the use of the phrase "Father's House" in John 14:2 could be seen as describing heaven as a celestial temple. The "many rooms" in God's heavenly temple might therefore refer to the conceptual equivalent of the *hekhalot* of the celestial temple in the Jewish ascension texts. Indeed, this is precisely how the term was interpreted by some of the earliest Christian exegetes such as Origen, Clement of Alexandria, and Irenaeus.[26] As will be noted later, each of the *hekhalot* in the ascension texts represents a different degree of glory, increasing as one nears the throne of God in the highest *hekhal*.

Ezekiel's experience following the destruction of Solomon's temple served as an important prototype for the ascent to the celestial temple of the later Merkavah mystics. *Merkavah* in Jewish mysticism refers to the celestial chariot of fire that Ezekiel saw in vision (see Ezekiel 1, 10). This celestial chariot has two roles in Merkavah mysticism: it can be both the mechanism by which the visionary ascends into heaven (this is based on Elijah's ascent into heaven in a chariot of fire—2 Kings 2:11), and it is the divine throne in the celestial Holy of Holies from which God rules the universe. "The mystical tradition of the Jews during the talmudic period is called *Ma'aseh Merkavah* [the work of the divine chariot] and together with the so-called *Ma'aseh Bereshit* [the work of the creation of the world] it forms the two branches of the so-called esoteric teachings in Judaism at that period."[27] *Ma'aseh be-reshit,* the "work of the creation" has reference to a wide range of Jewish esoteric speculations on the meaning of creation and the nature of the universe.

These three aspects of esoteric Jewish speculation—*hekhalot*/temples, *merkavah*/chariot-throne, and *be-reshit*/creation—are closely connected, and can be seen as representing different phases or elements of the celestial ascent. The mystic ascends into heaven by means of the celestial chariot or *merkavah*. In the heavens, the initiate passes through a series of *hekhalot*—palaces, temples, or levels—until he enters into the presence of God. God is seated on a throne, which is also described as a *merkavah,* in the highest level of heaven. There, the mysteries of God are revealed to the visionary, centered around the secrets of Creation, called the *ma'aseh be-reshit.* These mysteries include cosmogony (the creation of the universe), cosmology (description of the universe), and eschatology (the last days and ultimate destiny of mankind).

Nature of the Ascent

What were the actual experiences, if any, behind these ascension texts? There are at least five possible interpretations. First, the Hekhalot visionaries may simply have been charlatans who falsely claimed to ascend into heaven in order to gain power and influence over their followers.

Second, accounts of the visions may be allegorical, designed to teach moral principles and spiritual truths along the lines of Dante's *Divine Comedy*. Third, the visionary experiences may have been a type of ritual initiation where the mysteries of heaven were revealed to the initiate through ritual, drama, or secret teachings.[28] Fourth, the visions may have derived from some type of psychologically altered state of consciousness—trances, dreams, hallucinations, psychosis, hypnosis, or intoxication—which were interpreted by the visionary as representing an actual ascent into heaven. Finally, the visions may represent real experiences of visionaries who did indeed actually ascend into heaven.

The fact that many visionaries may have been charlatans or psychotics does not necessarily imply that all of them were. Some may have seen actual visions of heaven.[29] Others may have used accounts of the experiences of real visionaries as literary motifs. Be that as it may, it is remarkable that nearly all of the visionary ascents to the celestial temple—whether from Jewish, pagan, or Christian sources—exhibit many parallels, indicating that all of these ideas and documents were somehow conceptually and historically linked together.[30]

A Typology of the Ascent to the Celestial Temple

I would now like to present a typology of some of the basic elements of the celestial ascent as found in the Hekhalot, Merkavah, and related ascension literature.[31] This typology draws from a large number of texts that differ in date, author, and place of origin. But whatever differences may be found in detail, Peter Schaffer's synopsis has demonstrated that the parallels between these texts are numerous and often quite exact.[32] Thus, whatever the historical relationships between these texts, it is quite clear that they all shared a related view of the celestial ascent.[33]

The Ascension Mysteries Are Reserved for the Elect

Initiates into the celestial mysteries had to be of the highest moral and intellectual character, leading sinless lives.[34] The *Hekhalot Rabbati* tells us that "only those can go down to the vision of the Merkabah who fulfill two qualifications: '. . . he who reads the Bible and studies Mishnah, Midrash, Halakhoth, and Aggadoth . . . and he who fulfills all which is written in the Torah and keeps all the prohibitions of statutes and judgments and laws which were declared to Moses on Sinai.' "[35] According to *Hekhalot Rabbati* 13, the initiate must be "pure of idolatry, sexual offenses, bloodshed, slander, vain oaths, profanation of the Name [of God], impertinence, and unjustified enmity, and who keeps every positive and negative commandment."[36] Thus, intellectual maturity, knowledge of scripture, and personal righteousness were the major qualifying factors for those wishing to be initiated into the ritual ascent into heaven.

Ritual Purification before Ascent

Candidates possessing these moral characteristics were often required to further prepare for their ascent through fasting and ritual purifications.[37] "Even the slightest possible suspicion of impurity, defined according to the strictest rabbinic law, is enough to have the ecstatic dismissed from before the [celestial] throne [of God]."[38]

Secrecy

As will be discussed below, a major purpose of the ascent was to gain a revelation of the celestial mysteries. Because of the extreme importance of this revelation, both the mechanism of the ascent, and the teachings and revelations learned during the ascent were kept strictly secret.[39] This information was generally transmitted only orally, and then to no more than three students at a time.[40] Indeed, "the *Mishnah* . . . forbids the study of the *Ma'aseh Merkavah* in public."[41] As with other mystery religions found in the classical Mediterranean world,[42] the secrets of the Jewish and Christian celestial mysteries were well kept, making it often difficult to know exactly what the texts are discussing. It was usually assumed that the student would have a teacher present to explain the obscure meaning of the texts. This makes it "very difficult to guess what the Merkavah speculations of the circle of Rabban Yohanan ben Zakkai [one of the founders of Merkavah mysticism] were like."[43]

Physical Mechanism of the Ascent

According to the most important Hekhalot document, the *Hekhalot Rabbati*, an important mechanism for making the ascent into heaven was trances, which were taught and practiced at the earthly temple in Jerusalem. The document tells us that "R. Nehunya ordered an assembly of all the leading scholars, that he might declare to them the secrets of the ascent. R. Ishmael assembled every Sanhedrin [council], great or small, at the third gate of the temple and R. Nehunya sat and instructed the chosen few who sat before him, while the rest of the scholars stood at a distance separated from them by globes of fire and torches of light."[44] Thereafter Rabbi Nehunya entered into a trance, describing his visionary ascent to his followers.

The actual process of the ascent into heaven is described in a number of different ways.[45] Some climb ladders or stairways into heaven (based on Jacob's vision at Beth-el near Beer-sheba of a ladder or stairway into heaven—Genesis 28:10–22). For others a great wind carries them away; for instance, a whirlwind is mentioned in the ascent of Elijah (see 2 Kings 2:11). Some are enveloped by a cloud;[46] while others are carried to heaven by a bird.[47] The ascent into heaven is frequently associated with the ascent of a sacred mountain.[48] For instance, on Mount Sinai Moses sees God (see Exodus 24:9–11; 33:11, 20–23), receives the law (see Exodus 20–23), and has a vision of the heavenly tabernacle/temple (see Exodus 25:9, 40; 26:30; 27:8). Abraham is said to have ascended Mount Horeb to offer sacrifice preliminary to his ascent into Heaven.[49] The transfiguration of Christ also occurs on a "high mountain" (Matthew 17:1–2; Mark 9:2; Luke 9:28). At the top of the mountain might be a temple,[50] throne, a paradisiacal garden,[51] or the Tree of Life.[52]

Based on the stories of Elijah and Ezekiel in the Bible (for Elijah, see 2 Kings 2:11; for Ezekiel, see Ezekiel 1, 10; cf. Psalm 104:3; Isaiah 66:15; Jeremiah 4:13), ascension into heaven by means of a celestial chariot became a common metaphor. Indeed, in Jewish mystical circles the phrase "entering or descending into the chariot" ultimately became synonymous with ascending into heaven. Jewish ascension mysticism as a whole became known as *ma'aseh merkavah*, meaning "the work of the [celestial] chariot."

Number of Heavens

By whatever mechanism our initiate entered into the celestial realm, he usually passed through a number of different "heavens," often called *hekhalot* in the Jewish ascension literature.[53] The exact number of heavens differs in the texts, varying from one to ten.[54] However, there are generally seven heavens, each associated with one of the seven moving celestial bodies seen in the visible sky.[55]

It is worth noting that in ascension literature heaven is not the equivalent of "paradise." Rather, the celestial paradise is simply one place or *hekhal* within the various levels of the celestial realm. Paradise, as a specific location within the celestial realm, is most frequently located in the third heaven.[56] The highest heaven, or "heaven of heavens"—the conceptual equivalent of the Holy of Holies in the earthly temple—is where God resides on his throne.[57]

Gradation in Glory between the Different Levels of Heaven

The nearly universal belief that there were multiple heavens concentrically surrounding the celestial Holy of Holies and throne of God was naturally linked to a belief in gradations of glory in each level or *hekhal*. The higher the heaven and the closer to the residence of God, the greater the glory.[58] Each of the levels or *hekhalot* of Heaven were inhabited by angels possessing different degrees of glory.[59] Some of the earliest Christian fathers saw this as reflecting the degrees of glory for the righteous dead.[60]

The Angelic Host

These heavens are inhabited by both the righteous dead and by endless concourses of angels who are sometimes called the "holy sons of God."[61] It is a common notion that these heavenly angels are constantly singing praises to God. This is not just pleasant music making, however. The angels are in fact performing the celestial prototype of the earthly temple liturgy, as partially preserved in the book of Psalms in the Bible. According to Himmelfarb, "certain liturgical formulae taken from the [earthly] temple service were introduced into these doxologies [of the angels in heaven]."[62]

The angels are the priests of the celestial temple.[63] Since the visionary is permitted, and even required, to participate in the singing of this celestial liturgy to God, there is a strong implication that the visionary is also given some type of priesthood authority as part of his heavenly ascent.[64] Indeed, in the *Testament of Levi,* Levi is given his priesthood during his ascent to the heavenly temple.[65] This authority—the Levitical or Aaronic priesthood—is then eventually passed to Levi's descendants, who form the exclusive Jewish temple priesthood for the earthly temple.

Passing the Guardians

As noted above, the heavens were conceived of as a vast palatial temple-complex, composed of a series of concentric courts, halls, chambers, and shrines. The heavens are enclosed by "a wall which was built of white marble (or crystal) and surrounded by tongues of fire."[66] To move between the various sections or *hekhalot* of the celestial temple, the visionary initiate must pass through a series of doors or gates, each guarded by angels.[67]

As the visionary ascends into heaven, he is often paralyzed with terror and confusion.[68] He is able to progress from level to level only through the assistance of angelic guides who protect the visitor and explain what he is seeing.[69] The assistance of the angels is not guaranteed, however. Some of the angels encountered in the ascent to the celestial temple oppose the admission of a mortal into the heavenly sanctuary.[70] They will allow the visionary to pass only if he knows the proper passwords—often secret names of the angels[71]—and has the proper tokens or seals. "All the different versions of the Hekhaloth lay great emphasis upon the knowledge of various seals (*khotemoth*) described as magical names either of the angels or of aspects of the godhead, that must be shown as passports to the gate-keepers at the entrances to the seven palaces."[72] In summary, the visionary can enter into the celestial temple only if he has authorization from an archangel or God himself.

The dangers for the unworthy in the celestial ascent are well illustrated by the famous Rabbinic story of the "four who entered paradise."[73]

> Four men entered a garden [*pardes* = paradise]. Ben Azzai, Ben Zoma, Aher and R. Akiba. One looked and died; One looked and was struck [mad]; One looked and cut the plants. One went up in peace and came down in peace. Ben Azzai looked and died. . . . Ben Zoma looked and was stuck [mad]. . . . Elisha [Aher] looked and cut the plants. . . . R. Akiba went up in peace and came down in peace. [The TB version adds:] The ministering angels attempted to push R. Akiba away also. The Holy One, blessed be He, said to them, Leave this elder alone, for he is worthy to avail himself of my glory.[74]

This cautionary tale demonstrates the dangers for the unprepared or unworthy who attempt the celestial ascent.

Celestial Initiation: Anointing and the Celestial Robe

As the visionary approaches closer to the celestial Holy of Holies and the throne of God, he undergoes a process of ritual initiation and transformation into a being of celestial glory, becoming a member of the heavenly angelic host. Since the angels are frequently described as forming the celestial temple priesthood, initiation into their ranks is closely connected with the reception of priesthood authority, authorizing the visionary to participate in the celestial liturgy and sacrifices. Two main elements are involved in this transformation: anointing and receiving a celestial robe or garment.

Purification and anointing are the preliminary parts of the initiation. For example, during the ascension of Enoch—a fundamental prototype of all later Hekhalot visionaries—God said to his angels, "extract Enoch from [his] earthly clothing, and anoint him with my delightful oil, and put him into the clothes of my glory."[75] This passage indicates that before entering the celestial temple, the initiate is required to shed his earthly clothes and don celestial robes.[76] These robes are similar to those worn by the angels and God himself.[77] Morton Smith has argued convincingly that the donning of such new garments is symbolic of ritual initiation throughout the Ancient Near East.[78]

Likewise, Isaiah is allowed to enter into the presence of God in the innermost sanctuary of the seventh Heaven only because he has the proper celestial robe or garment: "The Holy Isaiah is permitted to come up here [to the throne of God], for his robe is here."[79]

Gruenwald believes there are two types of celestial garments. There "are the white garments of the righteous . . . [which] are eschatological garments; but we do have another type of heavenly garments: . . . mystical garments. These garments most likely are to protect the mystical visionary from all kinds of dangers [during the ascent]."[80] This suggests that there may have been an actual physical garment that the visionaries wore as part of their ascension rituals, as well as a celestial garment reserved for the righteous in heaven. This interpretation is partially confirmed by the story of Rabbi Yohanan b. Zakkai wrapping himself in his *tallith* garment when studying the mysteries of the chariot,[81] and by the robe used when Christ taught an unnamed initiate the "Mysteries of the Kingdom" according to the *Secret Gospel of Mark*.[82]

The Secret Names of God

The need for secrecy concerning the celestial ascent is in part because a key concept of the celestial mystery is the revelation of the most secret and sacred names of God and the angels.[83] Pronouncing the tetragrammaton *Yod-He-Waw-He* (often vocalized today as Yahweh or Jehovah) was restricted to the High Priest in the Holy of Holies in the earthly temple on Yom Kippur, the most sacred day of the Jewish year.[84] "The secret name, or names, of God played a great role in some of the ancient Jewish concepts of creation," which "might be connected with certain speculations concerning the uttering of the tetragrammaton during the [earthly] temple service."[85] Likewise, the rituals and mysteries of the celestial temple are closely associated with the knowledge of the tetragrammaton. Since the visionary often learned the secrets of the Holy Name, which could be pronounced only by the High Priest, the celestial ascent seems to imply an initiation into the highest Israelite priesthood.

The ritual use of names is widespread in the celestial ascent. When Abraham is called to ascend into heaven, God sends to him the angel Yahweh-el (Iaoel) "through the mediation of my [God's] ineffable name."[86] Likewise, Rashi's commentary on the famous ascent of the four Rabbis into paradise[87] claims that "they ascended to heaven by means of a Name."[88] Those who misuse their knowledge of these sacred names receive eternal condemnation.[89] Thus, the sacred names of the angels and God are to be kept secret and only revealed to those who are worthy to ascend to the celestial temple.[90]

Altar

As the visionary approaches the inner sections of the celestial temple, he frequently passes by the celestial altar, where one of the leading angels—often Michael or Metatron—is offering the daily sacrifices in heaven paralleling the daily sacrifices in the earthly temple.[91]

Veil

Paralleling the curtain or veil in front of the Ark of the Covenant in the Holy of Holies of the earthly temple (described in Exodus 26:31–33; 30:6; Numbers 18:7; Leviticus 16:2; 2 Chronicles 3:14; Matthew 27:51; Mark 15:38; Luke 23:45)[92] is a veil or curtain (Heb. *pargod*) separating the throne of God in the Holy of Holies of the celestial temple from the rest of heaven.[93] Whereas most of the angels are not allowed to pass through the veil and view the face of God,[94] some visionary initiates, such as Enoch, who "enjoys a qualitative superiority over the angels," are permitted to do so.[95]

Led by Right Hand

Having learned the secret names of God and the angels and having been purified, anointed, and clothed in a celestial robe, the initiate is now prepared for the ultimate goal of his ascent to the celestial temple—the vision and revelation of God. He is introduced into the celestial Holy of Holies[96] by one of the archangels, who sometimes takes him by the right hand, and guides him into God's presence.[97] Metatron/Enoch shows R. Ismael "the Right Hand of MAQOM [the Omnipresent One], laid behind (Him) because of the destruction of the Holy Temple. . . . And I [Ismael] went by his side and he took me by his hand and showed me (the Right Hand of MAQOM)."[98] Likewise, Enoch claims that "Michael, one of the archangels, seizing me by my right hand and lifting me up, led me out into all the secrets of mercy."[99]

The Throne of God

Having passed through the veil, the visionary is now allowed to see God seated upon his throne in the innermost Holy of Holies of the celestial temple.[100] The throne is frequently described as being made of crystal,[101] having wheels, and being surrounded by cherubim and other *hayyot*—strange celestial creatures such as those found in the books of Ezekiel and Revelation (see Ezekiel 1; 10; Revelation 4–5). Descriptions of the celestial throne in the Hekhalot literature are frequently dependent upon Ezekiel's vision of the *merkavah*, the chariot-throne of God (see Ezekiel 1:16; 10).[102]

Revelation of the Secrets of God

One of the fundamental purposes of the ascent to the heavenly temple is to learn the secret mysteries of God. These mysteries are described by the Rabbis as "what is above [the earth], what is beneath [the earth], what was before time, and what will be hereafter."[103] The mysteries that are revealed center on the mystery of the creation of the universe (cosmogony), the nature of the universe (cosmography), and the ultimate destiny of mankind (eschatology). "Where a revelation of the ways of God with man is given," Gruenwald informs us, "it is simultaneous with a revelation of the secrets of nature."[104]

According to the *Hekhalot Rabbati*, creation was brought about by a "wondrous and strange and great secret; the name through which the heaven and the earth were created, and all the orders of creation of the world (*sedrei bereshit*) . . . were sealed by it."[105] All creation is also bound together by an great cosmic oath formulated at the foundation of the world.[106]

When these mysteries are revealed to the visionary, he is frequently ordered to write and preserve the secrets. "The secrets [of God] had been disclosed to the legendary sages of antiquity [such as Enoch] who in turn put them into books which were sealed away, and in that condition they were preserved till the eschatological time came to open them."[107]

Salvation through the Heavenly Mysteries

The mysteries of heaven are not revealed to the visionary merely to satisfy his idle curiosity. Rather, "apocalyptic
revelation is one of the first, and necessary, stages in the
process of salvation."[108] The secret knowledge revealed to
humans during their ascent to the celestial temple is fundamental to their salvation.[109] An intregal part of the knowledge learned through the celestial mysteries was often a
revelation of the correct principles of scriptural interpretation. "They [the sectaries at Qumran] claimed that among
the revelations given them were the correct explications of
Scripture. Some of their writings in fact were eschatological
commentaries to Scripture, and in them they believed to
have uncovered the exclusive inner meaning and terms of
reference of the biblical text."[110]

Rebellious Angels and Occult Secrets

The importance of maintaining the secrecy of the revelations received in the celestial ascent is reflected in the legends
concerning the unauthorized revelation of celestial secrets by
the rebellious angels.[111] Rebellious angels were said to have
overheard some of the celestial mysteries, and thereafter they
taught mankind the secrets of heaven, which were passed
down to wizards and magicians in an apostate version of the
authentic revelations from God.[112] Thus, occult sciences such
as astrology and magic, as well as many elements of pagan
mystery religions and philosophy, were often seen as unauthorized forms of the true celestial mysteries.[113]

Exaltation

The culminating event of the celestial ascent is the exaltation of the visionary. The vision of God and the revelation of the mysteries of heaven are frequently equated with

the glorification and exaltation of the visionary. The visionary is clothed in the "clothes of [God's] glory,"[114] he is crowned,[115] seated on a throne beside God.[116] The visionary is raised in glory and authority above the angels of heaven, having received a revelation of the celestial mysteries and secret knowledge of God.

An interesting example of this idea comes from a Christian ascension text known as the *Ascension of Isaiah*: "But they [the righteous dead] were not sitting on their thrones, nor were their crowns of glory on them. And I asked the angel who (was) with me, 'How is it that they have received these robes, but are not on thrones nor in crowns?' And he said to me, . . . 'They will receive their robes and their thrones and their crowns when he [Christ] has ascended into the seventh heaven.'"[117] In other words, in Christian versions of the celestial ascent, the full exaltation of the righteous dead can only be obtained through the atonement, resurrection, and ascension of Christ.

Divinization

The visionary has now become immortal, glorified, and privy to the secret knowledge of God. He is given authority over the angels and power over the forces of nature. Is it legitimate to say that the visionary has become deified?[118] In fact, there are a number of elements in Jewish and Christian Ascension literature indicating that in some traditions the ultimate purpose of the ascent is the divinization of the visionary.

The prototype of all visionary ascents into heaven in the Hekhalot literature is Enoch. Enoch is said to have put on the robes of the glory of God, which transformed him into a celestial being: "I [Enoch] had become like one of his [God's] glorious ones, there was no observable difference."[119] But this is not all, for Enoch also received a secret celestial name, Metatron, and was enthroned in Heaven. As a glorified celestial being, Enoch/Metatron figures prominently throughout all Hekhalot and later Kabbalistic (late medieval Jewish mystical) literature as the most important celestial personage after God himself, superior even to the archangel Michael.[120]

Indeed, Enoch/Metatron is referred to by a number of titles and descriptions that point to his deification. Most importantly, he is called "lesser YHWH (*Yahweh qatan*)."[121] He is said to be "little less than God," whose "name is like the name of his master (God)"; indeed, he is specifically called *"elohim"* and *"shadday,"* two of the names of God in the Old Testament.[122] Enoch/Metatron is "seated on a Throne like the Throne of Glory," and "all keys [powers of God] are committed to Metatron." Because of the vast celestial authority he holds, "it was Metatron (rather than God) who showed himself to Moses and to the prophets."[123]

Although Metatron is the most well-known example of divinization, other mortals are also said to have become deified through their celestial ascent, including Moses,[124] Melchizedek,[125] and an unknown visionary from Qumran, who claimed that

> El Elyon gave me a seat among those perfect forever
> a mighty throne in the congregation of the gods . . .
> I shall be reckoned with gods
> and established in the holy congregation.[126]

The idea that the visionary ascent conferred divine powers upon the Merkavah mystic is manifest in later Kabbalistic texts. The celestial ascent was said to give the visionary incredible powers. "If the righteous wished, they could create a world . . . For Rava created a man (*golem*)."[127] This refers to the Kabbalistic legend of the Golem, or artificial man, which the Kabbalistic masters were said to be able to create because of their mastery of the secrets of creation.[128]

Thus, when the Merkavah visionaries ascend into heaven, they are provided with robes, crowns, and thrones, given the secret knowledge of God, the power to create worlds, human beings, and the title of "Lesser Yahweh." A reasonable conclusion from this is that they have become gods. The implication is that divinization was sometimes seen as the ultimate goal of the visionary ascent to the celestial temple.

Ascension Motifs in Late Medieval Times

The practice of the Hekhalot and Merkavah ascension rites seems to have declined after the seventh century. Jewish mystical impulses became increasingly dominated by neoplatonic emanationism and obsessed with gematria. Although the actual practice of the ascension rituals and visions seems to have declined, many of the ideas, texts, and practices of the Hekhalot and Merkavah visionaries were transmitted to later medieval Jewish mystics. The most important late medieval manifestation of ascension mysticism is found in Kabbalism. Though the subject of the transmission of ascension motifs from antiquity through the Middle Ages requires a full study, the developments of motifs can only be briefly summarized here. The following comments represent a preliminary analysis.

Kabbala

Kabbalism—a form of late medieval Jewish mysticism—developed in southern France in the twelfth century.[129] The most important center of Kabbalism emerged in Spain, where the greatest Kabbalistic text, the *Zohar*, or *Book of Splendor*, was compiled.[130] Although some elements of the earlier Hekhalot ascent were discarded or reinterpreted by the Kabbalists, much of the ancient ascent tradition survived.[131]

Christian Kabbalists

Beginning in the late fifteenth century, Christian Renaissance sages, in their endless quest to recover the lost secrets of antiquity, began the serious study of Hebrew, not only to help them understand the Old Testament in the original language, but also to gain access to the "secret knowledge" of the Jewish Kabbalists.[132] Many Kabbalistic works were translated from Hebrew into Latin and in the process were reinterpreted to fit the Renaissance magical Christian worldviews.[133]

One of the most important early figures in the history of the transmission of Kabbalistic lore from Rabbinic to Christian circles was the famous Renaissance philosopher Pico della Mirandola. He believed that Kabbala contained one of the most important proofs of the divinity of Christ.[134] Other important Renaissance works on Christian Kabbalism include the *Kabbala Denudata* of Knorr von Rosenroth and *De Arte Cabalistica* of Johann Reuchlin, which exerted a tremendous influence on later European esoteric thought.[135] Thus many esoteric concepts about the celestial ascents and temples were transmitted from Jewish Kabbalistic circles of the twelfth through sixteenth centuries A.D. to Western European Christian esoteric speculation in the fifteenth through nineteenth centuries.[136]

Freemasons and Christian Kabbalists

A final phase in the history of these ideas came in the late sixteenth century and early seventeenth centuries with the origins of Speculative Freemasonry in Scotland.[137] Freemasonry served as an esoteric sponge, absorbing and synthesizing a wide array of religious and occult ideas.[138]

Christian Kabbalism thus also came to play a role in the development of the esoteric ideas and practices of Freemasonry.

Summary

In summary, the discovery of new evidence from Qumran and the reevaluation of the long-ignored pseude-pigrapha and Jewish Hekhalot and Merkavah ascension lore has revealed a forgotten aspect of Judaism and Christianity at the time of the destruction of Herod's temple. An emerging consensus among many scholars is that during the first two centuries before and after Christ, a wide range of Jews, Christians, Gnostics, and pagans practiced a group of interrelated visionary ascension rituals. These rituals included the following concepts, ideas, or practices: limitation of the ascension to the elect; the necessity of ritual and moral purity; secrecy concerning the nature of the ascent and the knowledge learned during the ascent; ascension into various levels of heaven representing different degrees of celestial glory; encounters with a priestly angelic host, guardians, and guides; a heavenly initiation including anointing and receiving celestial robes; the knowledge and use of the secret names and tokens of God and angels; participation in celestial priesthood sacrifices and other rituals; passing through the veil of the celestial temple into the presence of God; a revelation of the secrets of creation; and the exaltation and even deification of the visionary.

These ritual practices and ideas were transmitted secretly among both Jewish and Christian esoteric elites but were finally rejected and condemned as heretical by the emerging orthodoxies of both Rabbinic Judaism and the imperial Christian church. Thereafter, these mysteries were suppressed, with elements surviving in the metaphysical speculations of the Jewish Kabbalists, Christian Hermeists, and medieval magicians. Although the full range of these rituals does not seem to have been preserved, late medieval Jewish Kabbalists did retain a wide array of ideas and practices that derived from these archaic mysteries. Ultimately, in the fifteenth and sixteenth centuries, these Kabbalistic speculations were adopted by Renaissance scholars and magicians in the form of Christian Kabbalism. By the seventeenth century, vague reflections of these archaic mysteries were making their way into the ideology and practices of early Speculative Freemasonry.

Notes

1. See Josephus, *The Jewish Wars,* VI, 230–VII, 175; David M. Rhoads, *Israel in Revolution: 6–74 c.e. A Political History Based on the Writings of Josephus* (Philadelphia: Fortress, 1976).

2. Sozomen, *Church History,* V, 52, discusses plans to rebuild the temple under Julian the Apostate, c. A.D. 361–64. Michael Avi-Yonah, *The Jews of Palestine: A Political History from the Bar Kokhba War to the Arab Conquest* (Oxford: Basil Blackwell, 1976), 266–67, discusses the attempt by the Jews to rebuild the temple and begin sacrifices from A.D. 614–17 during the Sasanid Persian occupation of Jerusalem.

3. On the nature of Israelite sacrifice, see Gary Anderson, "Sacrifice and Sacrificial Offerings," in *Anchor Bible Dictionary,* ed. David Noel Freedman (New York: Doubleday, 1992), 5:870–86.

4. For a general background on the Pharisees, see Anthony J. Saldarini, "Pharisees," ibid., 5:289–303, with extensive bibliography.

5. For background on the building of the eschatological temple, see Ezekiel 40–48 and the *Temple Scroll* from Qumran (11QT) in *The Dead Sea Scrolls in English,* trans. Geza Vermes, 3rd ed. (New York: Penguin, 1987), 128–58, with full edition by Yigael Yadin, *The Temple Scroll,* 3 vols. (Jerusalem: Israel Exploration Society, 1983). The description of New Jerusalem in Revelation 21:9–27 contains many similarities to the temple of Ezekiel (48:31–35) and the Qumran *Temple Scroll.* However, the New Jerusalem is explicitly said to have "no temple therein: for the Lord God Almighty and the Lamb are the temple of it" (Revelation 21:22). It may be that the entire city of New Jerusalem was conceived of as a temple.

6. This is a major theme of the letter to the Hebrews, especially chapters 8–10; see also George Buchanan, *To the Hebrews* (New York: Doubleday, 1972), 132–53.

7. See Hugh Nibley, "The Christian Envy of the Temple," in *Mormonism and Early Christianity*, in *CWHN*, 4:391–434; see also Isaiah Tishby, *The Wisdom of the Zohar: An Anthology of Texts*, 3 vols., tr. David Goldstein (Oxford: Oxford University Press, 1989), 3:867. Tishby cites Nibley's article (p. 900, n. 4) as definitive on this subject. It is worth emphasizing that although the early Christians abandoned the Mosaic temple sacrifices, which they saw as being superseded by the cosmic atonement of Christ, some Christian mystics were nonetheless active participants in Christian versions of the celestial ascension rituals and literature.

8. I would like to thank Janet Carpenter for her research assistance on this paper.

9. See Ioan Petru Colianu, "Ascension," in *Encyclopedia of Religion*, ed. Mircea Eliade (New York: Macmillan, 1987), 1:435–41.

10. Raymond O. Faulkner, "The King and the Star-Religion in the Pyramid Texts," *Journal of Near Eastern Studies* 25, no. 3 (1966): 153–61, discusses the ascent of the Pharaoh in the Pyramid Texts. In Mesopotamian myth, Etana ascends into heaven on the back of an eagle (see Stephanie Dalley, *Myths from Mesopotamia* [Oxford: Oxford University Press, 1991], 189–202). The idea of the heavenly ascent can be found in numerous religions, as outlined by Mircea Eliade, *Shamanism* (Princeton: Princeton University Press, 1964).

11. See Erwin R. Goodenough, *By Light, Light: The Mystic Gospel of Hellenistic Judaism* (New Haven: Yale University Press, 1935), on the mystical vision of God in Philo's thought.

12. See James Tabor, *Things Unutterable: Paul's Ascent to Paradise in its Greco-Roman, Judaic, and Early Christian Contexts* (Lanham, Maryland: University Press of America, 1986).

13. See Tabor, *Things Unutterable*, 87.

14. See *AMM*, 31. My list is based directly on Gruenwald's but expanded with material from other sources as indicated.

15. *Hekhal* is frequently translated as "palace," but in context, it seems clearly to be either the earthly or celestial temple (see Martha Himmelfarb, "Apocalyptic Ascent and the Heavenly Temple," *Society for Biblical Literature 1987 Seminar Papers*, ed. Kent H. Tichards (Atlanta: Scholars, 1987), 210–17; Morton Smith, "Observations on Hekhalot Rabbati," in *Biblical and Other Studies*, ed. Alexander Altmann [Cambridge: Harvard University Press, 1963], 144.

16. See Himmelfarb, "Apocalyptic Ascent and the Heavenly Temple," 212–14, on equating angels with priests.

17. See ibid., on the angelic hymns as celestial temple liturgies.

18. See Jay A. Parry and Donald W. Parry, "The Temple in Heaven: Its Description and Significance," in this volume; Himmelfarb, "Apocalyptic Ascent and the Heavenly Temple"; Victor Aptowitzer, *The Celestial Temple as Viewed in the Aggadah* (Jerusalem: The International Center for University Teaching of Jewish Civilization, 1980); William Riley, "Temple Imagery and the Book of Revelation: Ancient Near Eastern Temple Ideology and Cultic Resonances in the Apocalypse," *Proceedings of the Irish Biblical Association* 6 (1982): 81–102. The post-Second Temple Hekhalot visionaries based their understanding of the heavenly ascent to the celestial temple on four important revelations of God in the Hebrew Bible: 1 Kings 22:19; Isaiah 6; Ezekiel 1; 3:22–24; 8; and Daniel 7:9–10 (cf. Exodus 19:16–18; 20:15–18; 24:16–18; Deuteronomy 5:19–24; see J. Lindblom, "Theophanies in Holy Places in Hebrew Religion," *Hebrew Union College Annual* 32 [1961]: 91–106; also Buchanan, *To the Hebrews*, 132–37; cf. Revelation 7:15; 14:17; 15:5; 16:7). The earliest references to a celestial prototype for the Hebrew temple can be found in the descriptions of the building of the tabernacle, where Moses is told to build it based on the pattern of the celestial temple or tabernacle he was shown in vision on the mountain (see Exodus 25:9, 40; 26:30; 27:8).

19. See Himmelfarb, "Apocalyptic Ascent and the Heavenly Temple," 212. Himmelfarb mentions specifically *2 Enoch, The Similitudes of Enoch (1 Enoch)*, the *Apocalypse of Abraham*, the *Testament of Levi* (5:1), the *Ascension of Isaiah, 3 Baruch*, and the *Apocalypse of Zephaniah*. There is sometimes ambiguity between the structure of heaven as a whole symbolizing a temple, and a celestial temple being somewhere within one of the levels of heaven. In the *Testament of Levi* 5:1 the temple in the third heaven contains God's throne; TB *Haggigah* 12b has the temple in the fourth heaven; *Re'uyot Yehezkel* in the fifth heaven. For general studies of Judeo-Christian ascent literature, see Martha Himmelfarb, *Ascent to Heaven in Jewish and Christian Apocalypses* (New York: Oxford University Press, 1993); Mary Dean-Otting, *Heavenly Journeys: A Study of the Motif in Hellenistic Jewish Literature* (New York: P. Lang, 1984); and Martha Himmelfarb, *Tours of Hell: An Apocalyptic Form in Jewish and Christian Literature* (Philadelphia: University of Pennsylvania Press, 1983).

20. See Martha Himmelfarb, "From Prophecy to Apocalypse: The *Book of the Watchers* and Tours of Heaven," in *Jewish Spirituality: From*

the Bible to the Middle Ages, ed. A. Green (New York: Crossroads, 1986), 149–53.

21. See *1 Enoch; 3 Enoch; Apocalypse of Abraham; Ascension of Moses;* Isaiah 6; Ezekiel 1; 10; 40–48.

22. *AMM,* 47.

23. M. Ottosson, *"Hēkhāl,"* in *Theological Dictionary of the Old Testament* (Grand Rapids, Michigan: Eerdmans, 1978), 3:382–88.

24. Author's translation. See Otto Michel, *"Monē,"* in *Theological Dictionary of the New Testament,* 10 vols., ed. Gerhard Kittel (Grand Rapids: Eerdmans, 1967), 4:579–81. The KJV translation for the word *monai* is "mansions," deriving from the Latin Vulgate *mansio,* meaning not splendid palatial home in the modern sense, but a "stopping place" on a journey.

25. Author's translation. See Michel, *"Oikos,"* in ibid., 5:119–58. For the Old Testament usage, see Michel, *"Oikos,"* 120–21; also *"Bayt,"* *Theological Dictionary of the Old Testament.*

26. See Origen, *On First Principles (Peri Archon),* II, 11, 6; Clement of Alexandria, *Miscellanies (Stromateis),* IV, 6, 36, 3; VI, 14, 114, 1; VI, 107, 2; Irenaeus, *Against Heresies (Adversus Haereses),* V, 36. See also Hugh W. Nibley, "Baptism for the Dead in Ancient Times," in *Mormonism and Christianity,* 4:112–13, 116–17.

27. *AMM,* 74.

28. Jesus' revelation of the "Great Mystery" in the *Secret Gospel of Mark* could fit into this category (see William Hamblin, "Aspects of an Early Christian Initiation Ritual," in *BSAF,* 1:202–21). For a full discussion of the *Secret Gospel of Mark,* see Morton Smith, *Clement of Alexandria and a Secret Gospel of Mark* (Cambridge, Massachusetts: Harvard University Press, 1973).

29. It is interesting to note that Paul's vision as recounted in 2 Corinthians 12:2–4 is widely regarded as the only first-person account of a celestial ascent from this period (see Tabor, *Things Unutterable,* 1). For a general study of esoteric ideas in Paul's writings, see Alan F. Segal, *Paul the Convert: The Apostolate and Apostasy of Saul the Pharisee* (New Haven: Yale University Press, 1990).

30. See Tabor, *Things Unutterable,* 57–111.

31. For lists, descriptions, and sources of the major Hekhalot documents that will be quoted throughout this paper, see Gershom Scholem, *Major Trends in Jewish Mysticism* (New York: Schocken Books, 1961); *AMM,* 127–234; and most recently Peter Schaefer, *Synopse zur Hekhalot Literatur* (Tubingen: Mohr, 1983). The thorny problems of determining the exact date and provenance can probably

never be fully resolved and are irrelevant for the purposes of this paper.

32. See Schaefer, *Synopse zur Hekhalot Literatur*, passim.

33. It should be emphasized that there are many elements in Jewish ascension mysticism that we today would find very strange, including various magical incantations and practices and a strong emphasis on gematria. Gematria is a complex system of mystical interpretation of numbers, letters, and words. The most well-known example is found in Revelation 13:18, where the number of the "beast" is given as 666, which is frequently thought to represent a gematria on a name (see Gershom Scholem, "Gematria," in *Encyclopedia of Judaism* [Jerusalem: Keter, 1972], 7:369–74). Although I want to emphasize that these Jewish mystics were not "closet" Latter-day Saints, there are nonetheless some remarkable features of their ascension rituals and literature.

34. See TB *Haggigah* 14b; TY *Haggigah* 77a; TB *Kiddushin* 71a; 1QS 6:13–22; 1QS 5:24; *Hekhalot Zutreti* (*AMM* 142–43); *Hekhalot Rabbati* (*AMM*, 172); *Merkavah Rabbah* (*AMM*, 174); *Sefer Hekhalot* (*AMM*, 194). Emphasis is also sometimes placed on physiognomy (special physical characteristics denoting special spiritual power) and astrology (see *AMM*, 79–80, n. 21).

35. *Hekhalot Rabbati* 20:1, translated by Gershom Scholem, in *Jewish Gnosticism, Merkabah Mysticism, and Talmudic Tradition* (New York: Jewish Theological Seminary, 1965), 12, n. 5.

36. Translated by Smith, "Observations on Hekhalot Rabbati," 144.

37. See *1 Enoch* 41:10–11; *Testament of Levi* 3:6; Revelation 1:5–6; 4:8–11; 8:2–5; 15:1–8.

38. Scholem, *Jewish Gnosticism*, 12, discussing *Hekhalot Rabbati* 18. In the Book of Mormon we learn that "there cannot any unclean thing enter into the Kingdom of Heaven" (1 Nephi 15:34), a concept that would have been fully endorsed by the Merkavah visionaries.

39. See M *Haggigah* 2:1; TB *Haggigah* 2:1, 11b, 14b; TY *Haggigah* 77a; *Hekhalot Zutreti* (*AMM*, 142–44); *Merkavah Rabbah* (*AMM*, 178).

40. See *AMM*, 77–79, for a full discussion of the sources.

41. *AMM*, viii; see M *Haggigah* 2.1; cf. *1 Enoch* 93:11–12; *Hekhalot Zutreti* (*AMM*, 13). The New Testament describes several similar examples of secret teachings: Matthew 13:11; 16:21; 17:9; John 16:12; 1 Corinthians 3:1–2; 2 Corinthians 12:1–4. For numerous examples of secret teachings in early Christianity, see Hugh Nibley, "*Evangelium Quadraginta Dierum:* The Forty-day Mission of Christ—the Forgotten Heritage," in *Mormonism and Christianity*, in *CWHN*, 4:10–44, and Hamblin, "Aspects of an Early Christian Initiation Ritual."

42. See Marvin W. Meyer, ed., *The Ancient Mysteries: A Sourcebook* (San Francisco: Harper & Row, 1987); Walter Burkert, *Ancient Mystery Cults* (Cambridge, Massachusetts: Harvard University Press, 1987).

43. *AMM*, 85.

44. *Hekhalot Rabbati* 13, translated by Smith, "Observations," 144.

45. For a general discussion of these various mechanisms of the ascent into heaven, with numerous references to primary and secondary sources, see *AMM*, 119–23.

46. See *1 Enoch* 14:8; 39:3; 52:1; 70:2; 2 Kings 2:11. Moses ascended to heaven in a cloud according to *Pesikta Rabbati*, in A. Jellinek, *Bet ha-Midrash* (Jerusalem: Wahrmann, 1967), 1:59. Notice Christ's "ascent" into the presence of God is associated with a cloud during the transfiguration on the Mount (see Matthew 17:5; Mark 9:7; Luke 9:34–35). God also appears to Israel in a cloud (Exodus 16:10, 19:9).

47. See *Apocalypse of Abraham* 12:10; the Etana legend, cited in n. 9.

48. John M. Lundquist, "Studies on the Temple in the Ancient Near East," Ph.D. diss., University of Michigan, 1983, discusses several of these motifs.

49. See *Apocalypse of Abraham* 12; cf. Genesis 15; note the possible relationship of setting between Genesis 15:5 and JS Abraham 3:2 (in order to distinguish between the LDS book of Abraham and pseudepigraphical writings attributed to Abraham and Moses, I will designate the LDS scripture as JS [for Joseph Smith] Abraham or Moses).

50. Temples are often associated with mountains (see *1 Enoch* 24–25 translated in *OTP*; J. Maier, *Vom Kultus zur Gnosis* [Salzburg: Otto Muller Verlag, 1964]; *AMM*, 38).

51. See extensive bibliography in *AMM*, 38, n. 44. Dante, in his *Purgatorio*, also ascends a cosmic mountain to discover a sacred tree (see Canto 22.130–41) and paradise (see Cantos 28–33).

52. See *1 Enoch* 24:4–6 (*OTP* 1:26). Note the extensive parallels between Enoch's vision of the Tree of Life and Nephi's vision in the Book of Mormon: The tree is most beautiful (*1 Enoch* 24:5 = 1 Nephi 8:10–11; 11:8); its fruit brings eternal life for the righteous (*1 Enoch* 25:5 = 1 Nephi 8:10–12); an angelic figure guides and explains the vision (*2 Enoch* 24:6 = 1 Nephi 11:2–3); and there is a valley near the tree representing hell (*1 Enoch* 26:3–6, 27:1–2 = 1 Nephi 8:13, 26; 12:16–17). On the Tree of Life in Paradise, see *2 Enoch* 8:3; *3 Enoch* 5. Gruenwald adds that "the Tree of Life could be the place on which God rests, and God's theophany on the Tree of Life is, thus, a counterpart to his theophanies in the Temple and on His Throne of Glory" (*AMM*, 50–51). There is also a possible relationship between Lehi's

vision of the throne of God (see 1 Nephi 1:8, 14) and the tree of life (see 1 Nephi 8–14).

53. See *Masekhet Hekhalot* (*AMM*, 210); Michael A. Morgan, tr., *Sefer ha-Razim: The Book of Mysteries* (Chico, California: Scholars, 1983).

54. There appears to be only one heaven in the book of Revelation, or perhaps John's vision includes only the highest heaven. Three: 2 Corinthians 12:2; *Testament of Levi* 3. Five: *Apocalypse of Zephaniah* cited by Clement of Alexandria; Greek Baruch. Eight: *Re'uyot Yehezkel* (*AMM*, 134, n. 2, 136, 139). Ten: 2 *Enoch* 20:3 (*OTP*, 1:134). In 2 *Enoch* 22:6, the ninth heaven is called "Kukhavim" or "stars" (cf. JS Abraham 3:13). This may support the interpretation that the astronomy in the Book of Abraham reflects an ancient geocentric world view similar to that found in the ascension literature (see William J. Hamblin, John Gee, and Daniel C. Peterson, "And I Saw the Stars: the Book of Abraham and Ancient Geocentric Astronomy," unpublished manuscript; cf. Revelation 4:1; *Testament of Reuben* 1:6; 5:7; 6:9; *Testament of Judah* 21:4; *Testament of Levi* 14:3; 18:3–4).

55. See 2 *Enoch*; *Apocalypse of Abraham* 19; *Ascension of Isaiah*.

56. See 2 *Enoch* 8:1; *Apocalypse of Moses* 38:4; cf. discussion by Tabor, *Things Unutterable*, 113–19, and *AMM*, 90–92. This may be related to Paul's account of his celestial ascent in 2 Corinthians 12:2–4.

57. Note that in JS Abraham 3:3, 9, God resides on his throne in the highest part of heaven. For a discussion see Hamblin, Gee, and Peterson, "And I Saw the Stars." It is interesting to speculate that from this perspective, Christ's promise to the thieves with whom he was crucified, "today you will be with me in paradise" (Luke 23:43), is not a necessarily a promise of eternal exaltation as some Christians understand it, but simply a promise that they will enter into one of the levels ("mansions") or *hekhalot* of heaven, or one of the lower degrees of glory in LDS understanding.

58. Cf. similar concepts in JS Abraham 3:3–6, 16–19.

59. See *Ascension of Isaiah* 7–8; *Hekhalot Rabbati* 17.

60. See Origen, *On First Principles*, 1.6.2; see also further references in note 25.

61. 1 *Enoch* 71:1; the original reads "sons of the holy angels," which R. H. Charles equates with the *bene elohim* of the Old Testament (*The Apocrypha and Pseudepigrapha of the Old Testament in English* [Oxford: Clarendon, 1913], 2:233, 235). Cf. *Hekhalot Rabbati* (*AMM*, 159–60); *Ma'aseh Merkavah* (*AMM*, 183); *Masekhet Hekhalot* (*AMM*, 210); Morgan, *Sefer ha-Razim*.

62. Himmelfarb, "Apocalyptic Ascent and the Heavenly Temple," 210–12; cf. *Apocalypse of Abraham* 8:3; *Ascension of Isaiah* 9:40 (*AMM*, 40, n. 52); I. Elbogen, *Der judische Gottesdienst in seiner geschichtlichen Entwicklung* (Hildesheim: Georg Olms, 1962), 61 ff., 521–22. This idea is also found at Qumran, according to J. Strugnell, "The Angelic Liturgy at Qumran 4Q400," *Vetus Testamentum Supplement* 7 (1960): 318–45 (4Q400–407 = Vermes, *Dead Sea Scrolls in English*, 221–30; 2 *Enoch* 8:8). The Christian *Apocalypse of Paul* tells us that Hebrew—the liturgical language of the earthly temple—is also the language of the angels. When not singing, the angels are said to speak only in a reverent whisper (see *Hekhalot Rabbati* 3:1, 7:5).

63. See Himmelfarb, "Apocalyptic Ascent and the Heavenly Temple," 211.

64. See *1 Enoch* 71:11–12 (= *OTP*, 1:50), *Apocalypse of Abraham* 17:6–21 (= *OTP*, 1:697); Revelation 4:10; 5:9; 7:12; 11:17; 19:4.

65. See *Testament of Levi* 5:1.

66. *1 Enoch* 14:9 (= *OTP*, 1:20); *Hekhalot Zutreti* (*AMM*, 33 n. 13); TB *Haggigah* 14b; cf. Ezekiel 1:22; *1 Enoch* 71:5.

67. See *Ascension of Isaiah* 6:6 (= *OTP*, 2:164); cf. Isaiah 6:6; Revelation 4:1. This idea is perhaps related to idea of the "opening of heaven" in Ezekiel 1:1 and Syrian Baruch 22:1. *3 Baruch* (Greek) has doors separating each heaven. For related texts see, Revelation 4:1; *1 Enoch* 14:9; *Testament of Levi* 5:1; *3 Maccabees* 6:18. The ascension motifs in the Mithras Liturgy describe a series of doors leading into heaven (see *Papyri Graecae Magicae*, 4.475–829, translated in Hans Dieter Betz, *The Greek Magical Papyri in Translation* [Chicago: University of Chicago Press, 1986], 48–54).

68. See *2 Enoch* 21:2; *Apocalypse of Abraham* 10:1–2; a similar reaction is found in JS Moses 1:20.

69. See *2 Enoch* 21:3; *Hekhalot Rabbati* 17; cf. Nephi's angelic guide, 1 Nephi 11.

70. See TB *Haggigah* 15b; J. P. Schultz, "Angelic Opposition to the Ascension of Moses and the Revelation of the Law," *Jewish Quarterly Review* 61, no. 1 (1970): 282–307.

71. The obsession with angelic names is most pronounced in *Sepher ha-Razim*, see Morgan, *Sepher ha-Razim; Hekhalot Rabbati* 15; see also Betz, *The Greek Magical Papyri in Translation*, passim.

72. Scholem, *Jewish Gnosticism*, 32; see *Hekalot Rabbati* 17–18. The books of *Jeu* are filled with celestial seals (see Carl Schmidt, *The Books of Jeu, The Coptic Gnostic Library* 13, trans. Violet Macdermot [Leiden: Brill, 1978]).

73. *Toseftah Haggigah* 2:3; TY *Haggigah* 77b; *Midrash Rabba to Shir*

ha-Shiram 7d–8a. See discussion of the tale in *AMM*, 85–87, and Christopher Rowland, *The Open Heaven* (New York: Crossroad, 1982), 306–48.

74. *Toseftah Haggigah* 2:3, translated in Rowland, *The Open Heaven*, 310–12.

75. *2 Enoch* 22:9 (recension J) (= *OTP*, 1:138); cf. Chaldean Oracles; Acts 6:15; Origen, *On First Principles*, II, 3, 7; 2 Corinthians 5:3. In Revelation 6:11; 7:9–14, the saints in heaven wear splendid white robes.

76. See *2 Enoch* 22; *Pistis Sophia;* cf. *AMM*, 33–34.

77. See *1 Enoch* 71:1; Revelation 4:4; 6:11; 15:16; 1 Maccabees 10:89; 11:58; *Ascension of Isaiah* 9:6; 46:5.

78. *Clement of Alexandria and a Secret Gospel of Mark*, 243–44; note that the transfiguration of Jesus can be seen in this light, where Christ's clothes are transformed (see Matthew 17:2; Mark 9:3; Luke 9:29; see also Hugh Nibley, "Sacred Vestments," in *Temple and Cosmos*, in *CWHN*, 12:91–138).

79. *Ascension of Isaiah* 9:2 = *OTP* 2:169.

80. *AMM*, 61, n. 116. Gruenwald references Revelation 4:4 and the *Life of Adam* 40 on eschatological garments (cf. Ascension of Isaiah 9.2; *2 Enoch* 22:3; *3 Enoch* 12; TB *Shabbat* 88b.

81. See TB *Haggigah* 14b.

82. See Smith, *Clement of Alexandria and a Secret Gospel of Mark*, 175–78; Hamblin, "Aspects of an Early Christian Initiation Ritual."

83. See *Hekhalot Zutreti* (*AMM*, 145); *Merkavah Rabbah* (*AMM*, 175–76); *Ma'aseh Merkavah* (*AMM*, 182, 185). Secret names of God and angels are found throughout the *Shi'ur Qomah* (see Martin Samuel Cohen, ed. and tr., *The Shi'ur Qomah: Texts and Recensions* [Tubingen: Mohr, 1985], and Morgan, *Sepher ha-Razim*).

84. See TB *Kiddushin* 71a.

85. *AMM*, 11.

86. *Apocalypse of Abraham* 10:3 (= *OTP* 1:693). Rubinkiewicz reads the Slavonic name of the angel as "Iaoel," which he equates with *yhwh'l* or Yahweh-el (cf. *Hekalot Rabbati* 14:4–5).

87. See TB *Haggigah* 14b.

88. Cited in *AMM*, 52, n. 81.

89. "It should be noticed that in M *'Avot* i,13, Hillel the Elder is reported to have said: 'He who uses the Crown [Aramaic: *Taga*] is to pass away.'" According to the explanation found in *Avot de-Rabbi Nathan* (ed. Schechter) version A, chapter xii, the meaning of Hillel's saying is: "He who uses the *Shem ha-Meforash* (= the Ineffable Name) has no share in the world to come" (*AMM*, 53). From this perspective

the commandment, "Thou shalt not take the name of the Lord thy God in vain" (Exodus 20:7, Deuteronomy 5:11) is a reference not only to profanity, but also to the ritual abuse of the power of the Name.

90. See *Ascension of Isaiah* 7:5. The Essenes had a tradition of secret names of angels which they would not reveal to outsiders (see Josephus, *Jewish Wars*, II, 8, 7.)

91. See *Testament of Levi* 3.5; 4:6; *Zohar* 2.159a; Revelation 4; 6:9; 8:3; 9:13.

92. See Josephus, *Jewish Wars*, V, 212–20.

93. *3 Enoch* 45 (Odeberg, *3 Enoch*, 141–48); *Apocalypse of Paul* 44; Scholem, *Major Trends in Jewish Mysticism*, 72, 367; O. Hofius, "Der Vorhang vor dem Thron Gottes," *Wissenschaftliche Untersuchungen zum Neuen Testament* 14 (Tubingen, 1972).

94. See *1 Enoch* 14:21 (= *OTP*, 1:21); *Hekhalot Rabbati* 3:4.

95. *AMM*, 37; cf. *1 Enoch* 71:10; see also *2 Enoch* 24:1 (= *OTP*, 1:140), where Enoch spoke with God "face to face."

96. See Himmelfarb, "Apocalyptic Ascent and the Heavenly Temple," 210.

97. See *3 Enoch* 1:5.

98. *3 Enoch* 48A:1–2 (= *OTP*, 1:300); this translation is based on Odeberg, *3 Enoch*, 154–55. *Maqom* literally means "place," but it is used in 3 Enoch as a euphemism for God.

99. *1 Enoch* 71:3; *Apocalypse of Abraham* 15:2 (= *OTP*, 606). An early Christian illustration of God extending his hand from the cloud/veil and taking Christ into heaven by the right hand can be found in a late fourth- or early fifth-century ivory panel called "The Maries at the Sepulchre and the Ascension," now in the Bayerisches Nationalmuseum in Munich (see John Beckwith, *Early Christian and Byzantine Art* [Harmondsworth: Penguin, 1971], 51, illustration #37).

100. See *Re'uyot Yehezkel* (*AMM*, 137); *Hekhalot Rabbati* (*AMM*, 153); *Masekhet Hekhalot* (*AMM*, 209); cf. Revelation 4; 7:9; 16:17.

101. See Isaiah 6:1; Ezekiel 1:26; TB *Hullin* 89a; *1 Enoch* 14:18 (= *OTP*, 1:21).

102. See Daniel 7:9; *1 Enoch* 14:18 (= *OTP*, 1:21). In some versions there is a throne in each of the heavens or *hekhalot*, but God is sitting only on the throne in the highest heaven (see *Ascension of Isaiah* 7:14–33; *Re'uyot Yehezkel* [*AMM*, 59, n. 106]). The Ark of the Covenant is also sometimes seen as an earthly throne of God (see C. L. Seow, "Ark of the Covenant," *Anchor Bible Dictionary*, 1:388–89).

103. M *Haggigah* 2:1, discussed by Rowland, *The Open Heaven*, 277; cf. D&C 88:79.

104. *AMM*, 8, cf. 9.

105. *Hekhalot Rabbati* 9:5 (*AMM,* 11). This concept may be related to the discussion of Christ as God's "Word" in John 1. On the role of Christ and his name in salvation and creation, see Acts 4:12; Ephesians 1:21; 3:9; Colossians 1:16; Hebrews 1:2.

106. See *1 Enoch* 41:5 (= *OTP,* 1:32); *AMM,* 10–11.

107. *AMM,* 12; *1 Enoch* 82:1–3 (= *OTP,* 1:60); *4 Ezra* 12:36–38 (= *OTP,* 1:550); 14:23–26, 45–48 (= *OTP,* 1:554–555); Daniel 12. Note the parallel to the breaking of the seals in Revelation 10; 22:10.

108. *AMM,* 15; cf. *AMM,* 16, Revelation 4:1; *Testament of Levi* 5:1; 11:6; *3 Maccabees* 6:18; *1 Enoch* 14.

109. The Christian Gnostic movement likewise was based on the belief that they possessed the true *gnosis,* or knowledge of the secret celestial mysteries that would bring them salvation (see Giovanni Filoramo, *A History of Gnosticism* [Oxford: Basil Blackwell, 1990]; Kurt Rudolph, *Gnosis: the Nature and History of Gnosticism* [San Francisco: Harper & Row, 1983]; Elaine Pagels, *The Gnostic Gospels* [New York: Random House, 1979]). The major writings of the Church Fathers on Gnosticism are collected and translated by Werner Foerster, *Gnosis: A Selection of Gnostic Texts* (Oxford: Clarendon, 1972). The Nag Hammadi texts are collected in James M. Robinson, *The Nag Hammadi Library in English,* 3rd ed. (San Francisco: Harper & Row, 1988); and Bentley Layton, *The Gnostic Scriptures* (Garden City: Doubleday, 1987).

110. *AMM,* 20.

111. See Neil Forsyth, *The Old Enemy: Satan and the Combat Myth* (Princeton: Princeton University Press, 1987), 172–81; cf. Qur'an 2:94–97.

112. See *1 Enoch* 8–9 (= *OTP,* 1:16–17); 69:1–2 (= *OTP,* 1:47); Forsyth, *The Old Enemy,* 172–81. There were, however, some celestial secrets that the rebellious angels did not learn, according to *2 Enoch* 24:3 (= *OTP,* 1:142–143).

113. See Forsyth, *The Old Enemy,* 172–81.

114. *2 Enoch* 22:10 (= *OTP,* 1:138); see also 1QS 4:6–8, 11–13; 1QM 12:1–7; Origen, *On First Principles,* I, 6, 2; Nibley, "Sacred Vestments."

115. See Revelation 2:10; 3:11; 4:4; 1 Corinthians 9:25; 2 Timothy 4:7–8; James 1:12; 1 Peter 5:4; *4 Ezra* 2:43–45; *Shepherd of Hermas, Similitudes* VIII, 2, 1; VIII, 3, 6; TB *Berakhot* 17a. The angel Syndalphon ties crowns on the head of God in TB *Haggigah* 13b (see also *Hekhalot Rabbati* 3:2; 9:1; 16:5).

116. See Revelation 3:21, 4:4; Matthew 19:28; Luke 22:30; *3 Enoch* passim.

117. *Ascension of Isaiah* 9:10–18. It is interesting to note that verse

sixteen claims that Christ will remain on the earth after his resurrection for 545 rather than the standard forty days (see Acts 1:3). One wonders what Christ was supposed to be doing during his extra 505 days (cf. 3 Nephi 11–28).

118. "In the magical papyri the purpose of ascent is often divinization, taking on the power of god. In the apocalypses the visionary usually achieves equality with the angels in the course of the ascent" (Himmelfarb, "Apocalyptic Ascent and the Heavenly Temple," 212). For general background on the idea of deification in early christianity, see Keith Edward Norman, "Deification: The Content of Athanasian Soteriology," Ph.D. Dissertation, Duke University, 1980.

119. 2 Enoch 22:8.

120. For general background on Metatron, see Odeberg, 3 Enoch, 79–146; AMM, 235–41, with bibliographic references to other studies.

121. 3 Enoch 12:5. Gruenwald speculates that Iaoel (see Apocalypse of Abraham 10:3) may be the equivalent of Metatron (see AMM, 54, n. 84).

122. Odeberg, 3 Enoch, 116.

123. Ibid., 115.

124. See Ascension of Moses. Although I do not agree with all of his conclusions, Carl H. Holladay, Theios Aner in Hellenistic-Judaism (Missoula, Minnesota: Scholars, 1977), contains a complete study of the idea of the "Divine Man" in Jewish thought around the time of Christ.

125. See 11QMelch = Vermes, Dead Sea Scrolls in English, 300–301.

126. 4Q491, Morton Smith, trans., "Two Ascended to Heaven," in Charlesworth, Jesus and the Dead Sea Scrolls (New York: Doubleday, 1992), 296.

127. TB Sanhedrin, 65b, Moshe Idel, tr., Golem (Albany, New York: State University of New York Press, 1990), 27.

128. Ibid.

129. See Gershom Scholem, Origins of the Kabbalah (Princeton: Princeton University Press, 1987). Kabbala is also sometimes spelled Qabbala, or Cabala.

130. See The Zohar, 2nd ed. (New York: Soncino, 1984). For a general introduction to the history and significance of the Zohar, see Tishby, The Wisdom of the Zohar, 1:1–126.

131. Many of the passages relevant to the celestial ascent and the heavenly temple have been collected by Tishby, The Wisdom of the Zohar, 2:550–652, 3:867–940.

132. See Jerome Friedman, The Most Ancient Testimony: Sixteenth-

Century Christian-Hebraica in the Age of Renaissance Nostalgia (Athens: Ohio University Press, 1983).

133. See J. L. Blau, *The Christian Interpretation of the Cabala in the Renaissance* (New York: Columbia University Press, 1944).

134. See Chaim Wirszubski, *Pico della Mirandola's Encounter with Jewish Mysticism* (Cambridge: Harvard University Press, 1989). Indeed, Pico maintained that Kabbalism provided proof of the divinity of Jesus (see Pico della Mirandola, *Conclusiones Cabalisticae*, 7; also Wirszubski, 161–69, for discussion).

135. See Johann Reuchlin, *On the Art of Kabbalah: De Arte Cabalistica*, tr. Martin and Sarah Goodman (Lincoln and London: University of Nebraska Press, 1993, rpt. of 1983 ed.).

136. For an example of the late nineteenth-century formulation of esoteric speculation on the Kabbala, see Arthur Edward Waite, *The Holy Kabbalah* (New Hyde Park, New York: University Books, 1960).

137. See David Stevenson, *The Origins of Freemasonry: Scotland's Century, 1590–1710* (Cambridge: Cambridge University Press, 1988).

138. On the influences of Renaissance neoplatonism, hermeticism, Rosicrucianism, and Christian Kabbala on early Masonry, see Stevenson, *The Origins of Freemasonry*, 77–104, 133–35. On the connections between alchemy, hermeticism, Rosicrucianism, and Christian Kabbala, see Francis A. Yates, *Giordano Bruno and the Hermetic Tradition* (London: Routledge and Kegan Paul, 1964); and Francis A. Yates, *The Rosicrucian Enlightenment* (London: Routledge and Kegan Paul, 1975).

PART 6

The Temple
in the New Testament

17

Hebrews:
To Ascend the Holy Mount
M. Catherine Thomas

Hebrews is, to use Paul's[1] words, "strong meat" (Hebrews 5:14). Paul wants to preach strong meat, but he addresses members who will not digest it (see Hebrews 5:12). Nevertheless, he broaches doctrines that deal with the upper reaches of spiritual experience and Melchizedek Priesthood temple ordinances. My purpose will be to identify several passages that have relevance to temple ordinances. Paul's letter might be divided into two main ideas: the *promise* of the temple and the *price* exacted to obtain the promise. At several points I will add the Prophet Joseph Smith's commentary, without which much of the temple significance of the apostle's remarks in Hebrews would elude us.

The Promise

Paul urges the Hebrews, "Let us go on unto *perfection*; not laying *again* the foundation of repentance . . . and of faith" (Hebrews 6:1–2; italics added). They had tarried too long in the foothills of spiritual experience. Having "tasted of the heavenly gift, . . . the good word of God, and the powers of the world to come" (Hebrews 6:4–6), they could no longer delay resuming the climb lest they lose the *promise*. Paul warns, "Be not slothful, but followers of them who through faith and patience inherit [or, *are* inheriting] the promises" (Hebrews 6:12).

The *promise* that Paul refers to repeatedly is that same promise explained in Doctrine and Covenants 88:68–69: "Therefore, sanctify yourselves that your minds become single to God, and the days will come that you shall see him; for he will unveil his face unto you, and it shall be in his own time, and in his own way, and according to his own will. Remember the great and last *promise* which I have made unto you" (italics added). Paul uses several different terms in Hebrews for the experiences associated with this promise: for example, *obtaining a good report* (11:39), *entering into the Lord's rest* (4:3, 10), *going on to perfection* (6:1), *entering into the holiest* (10:19), *being made a high priest forever* (7:17), *knowing the Lord* (8:11; D&C 84:98), *pleasing God* (Hebrews 11:5), *obtaining a witness of being righteous* (11:4), and *having the law written in the heart* (8:10; 10:16; Jeremiah 31:31–34).[2] He speaks of boldly pursuing the fulfillment of the promise: Grasp, he says, the hope that is set before you, which enters behind the veil, where Jesus, as a forerunner, has already entered (see Hebrews 6:18–20, NIV).

Paul compares these Israelites to their ancestors of twelve hundred years earlier. He refers to the early Israelites' rejection of God's invitation to enter into his rest as the "provocation"; that is, Israel provoked God by refusing to enter his presence. Paul quotes from Psalm 95:8–11: "Harden not your hearts, as in the *provocation*, in the day of temptation in the wilderness: When your fathers tempted me, proved me, and saw my works forty years. Wherefore I was grieved with that generation, and said . . . they have not known my ways. So I sware in my wrath, They shall not enter into my rest" (Hebrews 3:8–11; italics added).

In this Exodus account to which Paul alludes, the children of Israel gazed at the quaking, smoking, fiery mount and refused to exercise the faith to go up. The upper reaches of the mount are, to be sure, not for the faint-hearted. The frightened Israelites foolishly told Moses *to go on their behalf* (see Exodus 20:18–21). The Lord, referring to the Melchizedek Priesthood as the key to God's presence, explains in modern revelation what it was that Israel rejected: "For without this [priesthood] no man can see the face of God, even the Father, and live. Now this Moses plainly taught to the children of Israel in the wilderness, and sought diligently to sanctify his people that they might behold the face of God; but they hardened their hearts and could not endure his presence; therefore, the Lord . . . swore that they should not *enter into his rest* while in the wilderness, which rest is the fulness of his glory. Therefore, he took Moses out of their midst, and the Holy Priesthood also" (D&C 84:22–26; italics added).

We can't escape the insight here that it was unnecessary for the Israelites to wander in the wilderness for forty years. Had they exercised faith in Jehovah, who is mighty to deliver, they might have abbreviated those trials and entered speedily into the promised land and into a Zion, even a translated society like Enoch's or Melchizedek's (see D&C 105:2–6). But, Paul laments, the early Israelites refused to enter because of *unbelief* (see Hebrews 3:19). He says, "Let us therefore fear, lest, a promise . . . of entering into his rest, any of you should . . . come short of. . . . For we which have believed *do* enter into rest" (Hebrews 4:1, 3; italics added). Among Paul's fellows were those who were even then entering into the Lord's rest.

The Joseph Smith Translation of Exodus 34 increases our vocabulary for what it was that Israel rejected: "I will take away the priesthood out of their midst; therefore my *holy order,* and *the ordinances* thereof, shall not go before them; for *my presence* shall not go up in their midst" (JST Exodus 34:1–2; italics added). The Prophet Joseph remarked on Israel's rejection using yet another term for the loss, that is, the term *last law:*

> God cursed the children of Israel because they would not receive the *last law* from Moses. When God offers a blessing or knowledge to a man, and he refuses to receive it, he will be damned. The Israelites prayed that God would speak to Moses and not to them; in consequence of which he cursed them with a carnal law. . . . [But] the law revealed to Moses in Horeb never was revealed to the children of Israel as a nation.[3]

When God gives the Saints the Melchizedek Priesthood, which is the power and authority to ascend into the presence of God through temple ordinances, they must come or be damned.

The Aaronic Priesthood retained the keys to the ministry of angels but not to the presence of God (see D&C 84:26). Hebrews opens with a discussion of Christ's superiority over ministering angels. Paul's point is that even though Israel chose a law of intermediaries, that is, the ministering of angels, they must not value angels over the direct presence of God. They had chosen the keys to an anteroom but rejected those to the throne room itself.

The history of Israel is punctuated by their preference for intermediaries over God himself. One scholar notes, "Once the immediacy of early prophecy comes to an end, the angels serve to mediate the secrets of nature, the heavenly world and the last age."[4] Josephus reports that the Essenes had a preoccupation with the secret names of angels,[5] and the fascination of the mystical kabbalistic Jews with angelic hierarchies is well known. The early Christian interposition of saints between God and man is another form of substitution of intermediaries for God himself.

One may indeed receive keys to discern and control angelic visitations (see D&C 129). Joseph Smith taught that there were keys of the kingdom, "certain signs and words by which false spirits and personages may be detected from true, which cannot be revealed to the Elders till the Temple is completed. . . . There are signs . . . the Elders must know . . . to be endowed with the power, to finish their work and prevent imposition."[6] But the applicant for exaltation must *exceed* the right to the ministry of angels in order to regain the presence of God. The Lord said to the Church in this dispensation with respect to angels assisting in the redemption of Zion: "Let not your hearts faint, for I say not unto you as I said unto your fathers: Mine *angel* shall go up before you, but not my presence [Exodus 33:2–3]. But I say unto you: Mine angels shall go up before you, and also *my presence*" (D&C 103:19–20; italics added).

In attempting to persuade the Hebrew members of the superiority of the Melchizedek law over the Aaronic, Paul implies that an order of holy beings prevails in the eternal worlds that the Saints are called to enter. Christ belongs to this order as did Melchizedek. Paul deals in three places with Melchizedek: chapters 5, 7, and, without naming him, in chapter 11. Though man is created a little lower than the angels here on earth, yet his destiny is to put all in subjection under him, as Christ did, who brings "many sons unto glory" (Hebrews 2:7–10). "Salvation is nothing more or less than to triumph over all our enemies and put them under our feet and when we have power to put all enemies under our feet in this world and a knowledge to triumph over all evil spirits in the world to come, then we are saved, as in the case of Jesus."[7] Alma teaches that "many, exceedingly great many," have entered into this holy order, Melchizedek being prototypical of them (see Alma 13:12, 17).[8]

Paul maintains that the Levitical law never could have brought its adherents into the Holy of Holies (e.g., Hebrews 7:11). Under the Levitical law only the high priest entered there, and that once a year. Therefore, so long as the Levitical or Mosaic law still stood, the way into the sanctuary necessarily remained veiled (see Hebrews 9:8). Christ rent the veil to the Holy of Holies to make entrance behind the veil possible, not for just one high priest, but for a whole kingdom of high priests (see Hebrews 10:20; Exodus 19:6).

Paul alludes to three levels of priesthood power. The Levitical, which could never make anyone perfect; Abraham's patriarchal power, which embraces eternal marriage; and Melchizedek's, which was a power greater still than Abraham's, "even power of an endless life, of which [order] was our Lord Jesus Christ, which [order] also Abraham [later] obtained by the offering of his son Isaac. [Abraham's] power [was not that] of a prophet nor apostle nor patriarch only, but of king and priest to God, to open the windows of Heaven and pour out the peace and law of endless life to man, and no man can attain to the joint heirship with Jesus Christ without being administered to by one having the same power and authority of Melchizedek"[9] (see JST Genesis 14:40; also Hebrews 7:6, 17). "If a man gets the fulness of God he has to get it in the same way that Jesus Christ obtained it and that was by keeping all the ordinances of the house of the Lord."[10] Thus, through obedience to Melchizedek Priesthood temple ordinances, fallen man and woman may develop into the order of Melchizedek, Abraham, and Christ.

But Paul perceives that his flock could not digest the full truth about Melchizedek's priesthood power (see Hebrews

5:11), so he alludes obliquely to him in Hebrews 11:33–34. That the allusion is to Melchizedek is clear from the Joseph Smith Translation of Genesis 14, which describes Melchizedek in nearly identical wording, saying that Melchizedek had the priesthood power of translation by which many of the citizens of his city obtained translation. Paul mentioned earlier in this chapter (see Hebrews 11:8–10) that Abraham, Isaac, and Jacob also sought an inheritance in this heavenly city of translated beings; that is, they sought to be translated and to join the city of Enoch, as had those who became Saints "during the nearly 700 years from the translation of Enoch to the flood of Noah."[11]

The Price

Paul refers repeatedly to suffering and sacrifice. It is at this point that we sense why the Saints of any day would tremble at ascending the holy mount. Temple covenants of sacrifice are quite comprehensive. Paul defines *high priest* as one who makes sacrifices for others (see Hebrews 5:1), referring to the function of the high priest in the Mosaic temple, but perhaps more broadly to all high priests. After all, the veil that Christ, the great high priest, rent for us was the veil of his own flesh, not only opening the way for us into the holiest, but showing how comprehensive is the sacrifice required to follow him and obtain his order (see Hebrews 10:19–20).

We have the ambiguous passage in Hebrews 5:7–9 that seems to refer at the same time both to Christ and Melchizedek: "Though he were a Son, yet learned he obedience by the things which he suffered." Sometimes this passage is misinterpreted to mean that Christ or Melchizedek had to suffer the consequences of not obeying before they learned to obey. Rather, the sense is that they were willing to submit to *suffering anything necessary* in order to come up to the full measure of obedience to God, and by so sacrificing, achieved perfection. Spencer Kimball says similarly: "To each person is given a pattern—obedience through suffering, and perfection through obedience."[12]

It is not just any sacrifice or suffering that suffices, but that which is necessary to fulfill what God requires (see 2 Nephi 31:9; 1 Samuel 15:22, obedience is "better than sacrifice"). Nevertheless, the sufferings and sacrifices of the Saints become, as Peter says, more precious than fine gold (see 1 Peter 1:7, 4:13). John Taylor wrote that Joseph Smith spoke in a similar vein to the twelve apostles: "You will have all kinds of trials to pass through. And it is quite as necessary that you be tried as it was for Abraham and other men of God. . . . God will feel after you and he will take hold of you, and wrench your heart strings, and if you cannot stand it you will not be fit for an inheritance in the celestial kingdom of God"[13] (see D&C 97:8).

How can one press forward in the midst of sacrificing and suffering? The Prophet Joseph answers in the *Lectures on Faith:*

> They are enabled by faith to lay hold on the promises which are set before them, and wade through all the tribulations and afflictions to which they are subjected by reason of the persecution from those who know not God, and obey not the gospel of our Lord Jesus Christ . . . believing that the mercy of God will be poured out upon them in the midst of their afflictions, and that he will compassionate them in their sufferings, and that the mercy of God will lay hold of them and secure them in the arms of his love.[14]
>
> Let us here observe, that a religion that does not require the sacrifice of all things never has power sufficient to produce the faith necessary unto life and salvation. . . . It was through this sacrifice [of all earthly

things], and this only, that God has ordained that men should enjoy eternal life; and it is through the medium of the sacrifice of all earthly things that men do actually know that they are doing the things that are well pleasing in the sight of God. When a man has offered in sacrifice all that he has for the truth's sake, not even withholding his life, and believing before God that he has been called to make this sacrifice because he seeks to do his will, he does know, most assuredly, that God does and will accept his sacrifice and offering, and that he has not, nor will not seek his face in vain. Under these circumstances, then, he can obtain the faith necessary for him to lay hold on eternal life.[15]

Referring to Paul's well-known quote about our fathers not being able to be perfect without us, nor we without them, I quote the Joseph Smith Translation rewording: "God having provided [Greek *provided beforehand*] some better things for them through their sufferings, *for without sufferings* they could not be made perfect" (JST Hebrews 11:40; italics added). The Prophet Joseph stated this idea in another place: "Men have to suffer that they may come upon Mount Zion and be exalted above the heavens."[16]

The Prophet Joseph used this same verse as a proof text for temple work for the dead. Scripture is susceptible of multiple interpretations, and, in this case, the ideas of suffering, of sacrifice, and of sealing are part of the larger picture of sanctification. In fact, the sacrifice that the sons of Levi will offer up is identified with the book of remembrance of the dead in Doctrine and Covenants 128:24, the section in which the prophet teaches the welding link necessary with ancestors and makes reference to Hebrews 11:40.

This much is clear then: life is not granted to us to *please* us or to *satisfy* our telestial ideas of what life should be, but rather it is to *develop and refine* us. In addition, the acquiring of godly light and knowledge requires an all-encompassing sacrifice, made perhaps over time, similar in our own limited sphere to the Savior's sacrifice in his greater sphere. As he drank the cup his Father gave him, so the Saints drink what the Lord Jesus gives them. The Savior's cup was not to be ministered to but to minister and to give his life a ransom for many (see Matthew 20:28).

Still on the subject of suffering, Paul remarks, "Others were tortured, not accepting deliverance [from trials and sufferings]; that they might obtain a better resurrection" (Hebrews 11:35). The Prophet Joseph defines *deliverance* as translation and identifies the place of habitation of those translated as "that of the terrestrial order and a place prepared for such characters; . . . [these who were translated] he held in reserve to be ministering angels unto many planets, and who as yet have not entered into so great a fulness as those who are resurrected from the dead."[17]

The Prophet Joseph explains, however, that some who were worthy to receive deliverance from their trials and sufferings by translation chose rather to prolong the labors of their ministries, understanding the refining power of sacrifice, so as to obtain the highest possible resurrection. But those who became translated beings or angels minister to the heirs of salvation (see Hebrews 1:14). Heirs of salvation are those who have been called and elected, but who still dwell in the telestial world (see D&C 7:6–7; 76:88; 77:11).

At the end of Hebrews Paul returns to the mighty promises associated with the ascent of the holy mount: He says the mount that Israel in his day confronts is not physical or earthly like the one their fathers refused to ascend; rather, the Saints' privileges are to "come unto mount Sion, and unto the city of the living God, the heavenly Jerusalem, and to an innumerable company of angels, to the general assembly and church of the firstborn, which are written in heaven, and to God the Judge of all, and to the spirits of just men made perfect, and to Jesus" (Hebrews 12:22–24). Then soberly, "*See that ye refuse not him that speaketh*" (Hebrews 12:25; italics added). Joseph said in further commentary on this passage:

> [The Hebrew church] came unto the spirits of just men made perfect, . . . to angels, . . . to God, and to Jesus Christ . . . ; but what they learned, has not been, and could not have been written. What object was gained by this communication with the spirits of the just, etc.? It was the established order of the kingdom of God—the keys of power and knowledge were with them [the angels] to communicate to the Saints—What did they learn by coming to the spirits of just men made perfect? Is it written? No! [It can't be written.] The spirits of just men are made ministering servants to those who are sealed unto life eternal and it is through them that the sealing power comes down.[18]

The urge to know the mysteries of godliness is no idle curiosity; rather, it is a divine drive to acquire that level of godly power modeled by Christ and others of his holy order. It is in addition the means of increasing one's power to bring others to Christ: "And if thou wilt inquire, thou shalt know mysteries which are great and marvelous . . . that thou mayest bring many to the knowledge of the truth" (D&C 6:11; see also Alma 26:22).

The insight lying interlinearly in Hebrews and in the Prophet Joseph's remarks suggests that men and women may do what Christ did by learning and applying eternal law, entering by conscious knowledge and power into their exaltation. This life, Paul seems to say, as does Amulek, is the time for men to prepare to meet God (see Alma 34:32). We may have "*boldness* to enter into the holiest by the blood of Jesus" (Hebrews 10:19). This achievement requires a faith that seems to border on audacity. But he reassures his readers that, as the Savior is so abundantly able to succor his people, we may "therefore come *boldly* unto the throne of grace, that we may obtain mercy, and find grace to help in time of need" (Hebrews 4:16).

The Prophet Joseph wrote an impassioned letter to his uncle about these stirring possibilities, quoting Hebrews 6:

> [Paul said,] "We have as an anchor of the soul, both sure and steadfast and which entereth into that within the veil" [Hebrews 6:18–19]. Yet [Paul] was careful to press upon them the necessity of continuing on until they . . . might have the assurance of their salvation confirmed to them by an oath from the mouth of him who could not lie. For that seemed to be the example anciently, and Paul holds it out to his brethren as an object attainable in his day. And why not? . . . If the Saints in the days of the apostles were privileged to take the [earlier] Saints for example and lay hold of the same promises . . . [that is] that they were sealed there . . . will not the same faithfulness, the same purity of heart, and the same faith bring the same assurance of eternal life—and that in the same manner—to the children of men now in this age of the world? . . . And have I not an equal privilege with the ancient saints? And will not the Lord hear my prayers, and listen to my cries, as soon as he ever did to theirs if I come to him in the manner they did?[19]

Many Saints in the Church hunger and thirst after greater righteousness and spiritual experience, just as our father Abraham did (see Abraham 1:2). The hunger is our birthright. Nevertheless, it is common to discourage such people out of fear that they will go off the track somehow in their pursuit, and of course that danger continuously presents itself. Old Scratch, as one of my friends calls the adversary, is always lurking behind a tree.

But the opposite risk is that members will straggle in the foothills of spiritual experience as Israel has repeatedly done. So Paul says, "Exhorting one another: and so much the more, as ye see the day approaching" (Hebrews 10:25); "for ye have need of patience, that, after ye have done the will of God, ye might receive the promise. For yet a little while, and he that shall come will come, and will not tarry" (Hebrews 10:36–37). Paul's letter is a powerful call to pay the price, to obtain the promise in spite of earth or hell, and to come all the way up the holy mount to the Lord Jesus Christ.

Notes

1. The basic premise in this paper is that the apostle Paul is the author of Hebrews, a fact that the Prophet Joseph Smith acknowledged on several occasions.

2. Joseph Smith says that the law written in the heart will be fulfilled when the Saints' callings and elections are made sure and when they receive the Second Comforter (see *WJS*, 19, n. 9).

3. *WJS*, 244; italics added.

4. *Theological Dictionary of the New Testament*, 1:80–81.

5. Ibid.

6. *WJS*, 20–21.

7. Ibid., 200.

8. See Robert Millet, "The Holy Order of God (Alma 13)," in *The Book of Mormon: Alma, the Testimony of the Word*, ed. Monte S. Nyman and Charles D. Tate, Jr. (Provo: BYU Religious Studies Center, 1992).

9. *WJS*, 245.

10. Ibid., 213.

11. Bruce R. McConkie, *Doctrinal New Testament Commentary*, 3 vols. (Salt Lake City: Bookcraft, 1974), 3:202.

12. Edward L. Kimball, ed., *Teachings of Spencer W. Kimball* (Salt Lake City: Bookcraft, 1982), 168.

13. As quoted by John Taylor, *JD*, 24:197.

14. *Lectures on Faith* (Salt Lake City: Deseret Book, 1985), 4:14–15.

15. Ibid., 6:7.

16. *WJS*, 244, 247.

17. Ibid., 41–42.

18. Ibid., 254 (cf. D&C 77:11).

19. Letter to Silas Smith, 26 September 1833, in *PWJS*, 299–301.

18

Temple Imagery
in the Epistles of Peter

Daniel B. McKinlay

Studies of the books of the New Testament have been in process for many centuries and have been especially intense during the last two. Also, in the past several decades considerable effort has been expended in trying to reconstruct, insofar as it is possible, the rites of ancient temples and to ascertain the various features that belonged to the total complex of the temple as a conveyer of reality. The purpose of this paper is to offer some seminal suggestions and examples of how these two areas of study may intercept, or, more specifically, how temple imagery may be recognized in two writings in the New Testament, 1 and 2 Peter. Although it is common in current biblical scholarship to label these two sections of the New Testament "pseudepigraphical" (meaning that they were written by others postdating Peter), his authorship or at least profound influence will be presupposed in this essay.[1]

An in-depth study of ancient temples reveals a wide spectrum of interrelated concepts. Some scholars, such as John Lundquist, have devised formal models or typologies to bring into focus a coherent picture of the temple.[2] For the purposes of this paper, temple imagery will be defined as selected practices and views that found expression in sacred space of some kind, not always limited to the inside of the temple building. Temples were sometimes regarded as artificial mountains, representing the symbolic center of the universe, the location where gods and humans could communicate.[3] The earthly temple was understood to be between two other temples: one below it and the other above, forming a three-level sacred conduit.[4] In these set-apart regions ancient peoples sought the stable direction afforded by the celestial spheres, as well as in the modes of existence in *Sheol* or *Hades*, the underworld. They were sites where important rites, including the offering of sacrifices, were enacted.[5] Integral to many of these rites was a celebration of the creation and founding of the universe, as well as the particular locale where the rites were performed. This occurred during the period known as the new year festival. Typically, the rites took place within or near the temple precincts.[6] The new year rites were associated with the crowning of a new king[7] or the reaffirmation of his rule through mimetic rituals of death and resurrection. The enthronement of the king entailed such notions as adoption ("Thou art my Son; this day have I begotten thee"—Psalm 2:7) and its consequence, heirship.

Related to the enthronement rites, hints of which can be discerned in the Old Testament, were the initiatory rites in the mystery religions. The enthronement rites belonged to royalty exclusively (although there were in some senses counterpart rites among the priestly caste), where the mystery initiatory rites were available to a larger privileged group. Although many of the later mystery religions bypassed the obligations usually inherent in covenants (except secrecy) as their brand of gnosis (divine knowledge) was imparted to them, some of the rites of earlier days, both royal rites and those dealt to a more inclusive group (such as the congregation of Israel), required integrity to agreements made. The entering into covenants is thus considered a part of temple imagery, even though not all covenants may have been entered into while inside a temple structure.

One element of sacred space and sacred buildings especially important in this essay is the use of consecrated stones, either for the building of altars or for building a temple. There are several places in the New Testament that make special mention of such stones, and these may very well relate to the rock with which Peter is identified in Matthew 16:18.[8]

Many of the motifs mentioned above are alluded to in 1 and 2 Peter, as should be expected if Peter is accepted as the genuine author of the two epistles, for his apostolic vocation was thoroughly immersed in the temple ethos. The foundation of this assertion lies in the recognition that Christians ascribe to him an especially solemn commission. In the pericope on the confession of Peter at Caesarea Philippi in Matthew (omitted in Mark and Luke, perhaps due to their sensitivity to the revealing of matters deemed by them to be particularly sacred), Peter is told that he will hold the keys of the kingdom, with the result that whatever he binds on earth will be commensurately bound, or we may say, sealed, in heaven. He is also told that the "gates of *hades*" will not overcome the "rock" with which he is identified in some way. It is noteworthy that the transfiguration occurred about a week later, and it was at this time, according to several Latter-day Saint leaders, that Jesus' promise to Peter began its fulfillment. Moses and Elijah were present, and each bestowed upon Peter the keys of the priesthood of his respective dispensation, including those of gathering and sealing.[9] Having received these keys, Peter likely pondered his role and the implications the keys had for every person who accepted Christ, and indeed for the cosmos insofar as it related to the three-tiered temples mentioned above. This, in some measure, he communicated in his epistles.

In the greeting in 1 Peter, the Apostle acknowledges his audience, the "elect," as having been symbolically initiated by the "sprinkling of the blood of Jesus Christ" (1:2). Several verses later, he identifies the source of their redemption "with the precious blood of Christ, as of a lamb without blemish and without spot" (v. 19). Sacrifice, a sacred act, took place (if it was done correctly) in sacred space, often within the precincts of a temple. When Peter likens the blood of Christ to the Paschal Lamb (which was without blemish), he calls to mind the Passover lambs sacrificed in the temple, commemorating the deliverance of Israel from Egypt. For the Jews the Exodus was the pivotal event in their salvific history. For the Christians the shedding of Christ's blood was the pivotal event in the cosmos. Both had salvific significance.

Along with the shedding and sprinkling of animal blood at the temple, another vital feature was involved, that of covenants. Or, as Paul E. Deterding puts it, "the reference [in 1 Peter] to sprinkling with the blood of Jesus Christ recalls the fact that the Old Covenant was sealed by the sprinkling of blood."[10] Jesus' atonement was the New Covenant, which superceded the Old. While not all covenants were necessarily made in the temple, their association with sacrificial blood merits claim to temple imagery in some contexts. One case in point is the record found in Exodus 24:3–8, where Moses teaches the Israelites the instructions of the Lord, and they covenant to obey all the directives. This event is followed the next day by the performance of burnt and peace offerings, and then the sprinkling of the blood of the oxen on the altar and on the people. Deterding refers to the latter act as the sealing of the covenant.[11] Note the presence of an altar in the Exodus pericope.

In his instructions to the members of the church, Peter admonishes them that inasmuch "as he which hath called you is holy, so be ye holy in all manner of conversation; Because it is written, Be ye holy; for I am holy" (1 Peter 1:15–16). Commenting on this, Oscar S. Brooks avers that "much of the material adapted in the instructions of the early Christians . . . goes back through the Synagogue to the holiness code of Leviticus 17–18."[12] While the code of Leviticus was cherished in the synagogue, certainly it would have stronger affinities with a consecrated temple. Peter's quotation of Leviticus 19:2 sounds similar to Jesus' injunction to be perfect, as God is perfect (see Matthew 5:48). In 3 Nephi 12:48 Jesus is added as a model, or exemplar, to that of the Father. This correlates significantly with the proposition that Christ is the epitome of the temple, the incarnate manifestation of what it stands for. Brooks's insight is therefore most vital, as he interprets Peter's conception of the convert's relationship with his Lord: "For Christ is on the one hand the ground of his salvation and at the same time the model of his conduct."[13] The ordinances (baptism figures predominantly in 1 Peter), the holiness code, and covenants in the temple reflect Christ's atonement. One identifies intimately with Christ by participating in the gestures of the ordinances that symbolize aspects of the Atonement: the preparation for burial and enthronement (which includes ablution and anointing), the crucifixion, death, and resurrection. These representational enactments and keeping of covenants entitled the convert to belong to the community of his temple-centered and perfect Master, the prototypal Anointed One.

The consecrated stone motif is found in 1 Peter 2:4–8, and, as scholars have noted, those verses contain temple imagery. This passage deals with the relationship between master and disciples. Jesus is the greatest living stone, as well as the chief cornerstone. Or, as Eduard Lohse states it, "the Church knows that Christ is the cornerstone on Mount Zion that supports her."[14] First Peter 2:6 quotes the first part of Isaiah 28:16, wherein the Lord says that he lays in Zion a foundation stone. Christian disciples are also "lively stones," which together, form a "spiritual house" (1 Peter 2:5).[15] "This house is spiritual," says Paul S. Minear, "because [it is] indwelt by the Holy Spirit. . . . As God builds this house out of the cornerstone and lively stones, the Spirit is at work in the construction."[16] Temples were built with stones, including a chief cornerstone.[17] David Hill explains further: "The true Israel is formed of those who belong to the 'spiritual temple' which is built upon Christ, the living stone."[18] Jerome H. Neyrey seems to notice the same line of thinking: "Tracing down the first catchword ('stone,' the other being 'chosen'), we find Jesus described as the cornerstone of a new temple (2:6), as a stone rejected by builders but still a headstone (2:7). . . . This story of Jesus is also the story of each Christian. As Jesus is the cornerstone of a new temple, so Christians are called to be 'living stones . . . built into a spiritual house' (2:5)."[19]

As "lively stones" that compose a spiritual house, members of the Christian community have a priesthood by which they offer up sacrifices (see 1 Peter 2:5). Along this line, Peter informs his audience in 1 Peter 2:9 what their identity is as Christians: "Ye are a chosen generation, a royal priesthood, an holy nation, a peculiar [or purchased] people." The people he describes here correspond in a certain way to a major characteristic of most temples: they are set apart from the realm of the profane. Lohse compares the recipients of 1 Peter to the writers of the Dead Sea Scrolls: "While the Palestinian community identifies itself as 'thy holy people,' the Christians understand themselves to be *ethnos hagion* (holy people, 2:9) that forms the new priesthood and is to perform priestly functions."[20] Indeed, it is the function of the priesthood to officiate or otherwise participate in cultic matters, and the royal priesthood implies that kings and queens, whose authority stems in part from rites in the temple cult, blend in with priests and priestesses.

This joint status of the royal and priestly, which often was transmitted from generation to generation, calls to mind a blessing to which the Christian aspired: to be an heir of "the grace of life" together with one's spouse (see 1 Peter 3:7). This evokes a salient feature of the new year rites: that of sacred marriage, a covenantal binding of husband and wife in tandem with their relationship to deity. A major concern with the rite of sacred marriage was fertility, the continuation of the species. On a temporal basis the begetting and bearing of children made heirship meaningful. Spiritual heirship is the reason behind adoption, which is referred to in the thanksgiving portion of 1 Peter. There the Apostle cites the action of the Father of Jesus Christ, who "hath begotten us again unto a lively hope by the resurrection of Jesus Christ from the dead, to an inheritance incorruptible, and undefiled, and that fadeth not away, reserved in heaven for you" (1 Peter 1:3–4). The law of adoption is exemplified in the Old Testament where, through an oracle of Nathan, the Lord says of David, "I will be his father, and he shall be my son" (2 Samuel 7:14; this oracle also speaks of the interrelationship of the Lord's house or temple with the kingly throne). It was understood that a line of inheritance would be established from David's house. Many scholars believe that several of the Old Testament psalms were both royal and cultic, and that they were recited in the temple. One such example is Psalm 2, of which verse seven reads: "I will declare the decree: the Lord hath said unto me, Thou art my Son; this day have I begotten thee." This verse wielded considerable influence as a guiding proof text in the early Church. It is quoted or paraphrased at Jesus' baptism and transfiguration; Paul alludes to it in the beginning of the most complex of his extant epistles (see Romans 1:4), and in Hebrews he quotes it outright (see 1:5; 5:5). This principle of adoption seems to have been applied to Christ by the Father, and then, by derivation, from Christ to his disciples. Though in the Christian milieu one experiences the initial blessing of adoption through baptism and the reception of the Holy Spirit, it is in the temple that the more mature or advanced ordinances pertaining to a royal priesthood and its anticipation of inheritance take place. The sacred marriage leading couples to become "heirs together" with Jesus Christ implies that heirship is not intended to be attained singly; men and women who become one flesh under the divine sanction of marriage fill the measure of their creation by being unified or reconciled in Christ, thus becoming as a unified pair joint heirs with the primal heir of the earth.

Speaking further on this point, J. N. D. Kelly comments that the word *inheritance* (*kleronomia*) "had rich associations for readers of the Old Testament, according to which the Jews as physical descendants of Abraham inherited the promises made to him."[21] The promises to Abraham were twofold: a large posterity and an inheritance in the land. Although Peter does not explicitly state it, Christian heirship likely had a significant liaison with the Abrahamic covenant, as Paul taught in Romans 8 and Galatians 3–4.[22]

Peter does associate inheritance with the sprinkling of blood, possibly recognizing the Abrahamic rite of circumcision as a token of the Abrahamic covenant portending the spilling of blood in the ultimate act of atonement.

In speaking of heirship and inheritance, then, Peter is dealing with a theme that can be traced at least as far back as Solomon's temple, perhaps as far as the tabernacle or even the time of Abraham (see Abraham 2:9–11). And as the prerogatives of the Spirit had once descended only upon a select few (i.e., prophets, judges, and the kings, ideally) but in the irruption of the Christian era became available to the whole body of Christ in the form of *charismata* or spiritual gifts, so the advantages and privileges of heirship in a ruling and sacerdotal sense were at first reserved only to kings and priestly families of the era of the law of Moses, but subsequently were common possessions of the Saints in the meridian of time.

A particularly challenging passage in 1 Peter is found in 3:18–20. Peter begins by discussing the suffering Christ as the righteous or just expiatory proxy for the unrighteous or unjust populace, one who closes the gap of estrangement they have with God. He refers to Christ's fleshly death followed by his quickening by the Spirit, and then proceeds to discourse on Jesus' mission to preach to the detained spirits in *Hades* who had been disobedient at the time of Noah. These verses have vexed quite a number of scholars, and varied opinions have been expressed. Serious students of early Christian history will recognize the account as a reference to the Christianized notion of *descensus ad inferos*. This is the case, for example, for Brooks, who states that "the idea that Jesus spent the interval between his death in *Sheol* or *Hades* was a very early part of the Christian belief. It was the natural implication of Judeo-Christian theology to assume that Christ like all departed ones had descended into *Sheol*."[23] But in the twentieth century not all scholars make that connection. John H. Elliott, apparently with approval, quotes W. J. Dalton as saying that 1 Peter 3:19 "has nothing to do with the *descensus*."[24] Most scholars discern and acknowledge the allusion but disdain it or want to deliteralize it. Wolfhart Pannenberg sees it as having kerygmatic value, but he places it in the mythological sphere, concluding that it was "not, like the crucifixion, a historical event."[25] John S. Feinberg notes that extrabiblical literature preceding the inception of the Christian era (in Greco-Roman mythology), as well as intertestamental and apocryphal writings, affirms the existence of an underworld.[26] This would accord with the view of the three-level universe, with an earthly temple in the middle—it being the naval of the universe—and counterpart structures being above the earth and below it. After going through an exegetical exercise, Feinberg concludes that "the idea of Christ's preaching anything to anyone is so improbable that it does not seem worthy of further consideration."[27] He concludes that what the passage really means is that "Christ preach[ed] by the Holy Spirit through Noah to the people of Noah's day."[28]

Some observers, beginning with Wilhelm Boussett, see the depiction of Christ going to the underworld as the tailoring of an old myth of a redeemer figure asserting his authority and subduing demons, to fit a story about Jesus.[29] There are similarities between the myth and the ritual dramatizations that were enacted during the new year festivals. The temple and ritual motifs may have seemed similar to myths, yet no doubt to the early Christians the *descensus* of Christ was the real event and was not perceived merely as the recasting of prevailing lore.

Curiously, some have concluded that these scriptures

describe someone other than Jesus preaching in *Hades*. On the basis of textual and other suggestions, some claim that the patriarch Enoch was originally the person who taught the disobedient spirits of Noah's time, and it has also been claimed that the deceased apostles were the preachers.[30] There have likewise been different views on who the spirits were to whom the message was given. The following possibilities have been submitted: the righteous spirits to whom the gospel was preached, with the happy announcement that they were to be released to heaven; nonbelievers, with the hope of converting them; and fallen angels such as those identified in Genesis 6:1–2.[31]

Traditionally 1 Peter 4:6 has been associated with 1 Peter 3:18–20. However, Martin H. Scharlemann thinks that this connection is the result of "beautifully executed somersaults."[32] He rejects combining the two on the grounds that they are separated by several verses and have different contexts. Thus: "The 'dead' of verse 6 are to be distinguished from 'the spirits in prison' of 3:19. They are the saints who have died in the Lord, having belonged to the first generation of believers under the covenant."[33]

If one takes seriously the proposition that Peter was acquainted with the cosmic function of the temple, a straightforward reading of the text makes sense: after the crucifixion Jesus' spirit (a tangible entity within its sphere) went to "paradise" to unlock the prison doors for the release of the spirits who would accept his gospel. His visit to the spirit world was intended to inaugurate the preaching of the kerygma in the bottom level of the three-part universe. Apparently those spirits who were unresponsive at the time of Noah and who had been detained for so many centuries were given some degree of relief.

Anthony Hanson notes: "The earliest Christian preachers

soon found themselves with the question: can those who have never known Christ be saved?"[34] The assertion that Jesus went to preach to the spirits in prison yields a positive answer to that query, which incidentally has also occurred to current scholars. Early Christians responded in the affirmative. In other words, the descent of Christ to the netherworld to open up the preaching of the gospel made universal salvation a possibility.[35]

This comprehensive plan also figures into a cognate and similarly mystifying scripture, 1 Corinthians 15:29. Jerome Murphy-O'Connor wrote in 1981 that contemporary commentaries were acknowledging, albeit reluctantly, the "custom" of vicarious baptisms for the dead at Corinth. They felt compelled to accept this view because of "the plain wording of the text," although they preferred to reject "the existence of such a bizarre practice" on the grounds of "dogma or other reasons."[36] Murphy-O'Connor likewise finds the practice distasteful. He determines that *baptizomenoi* means "to destroy or perish." He reasons: "If *hoi baptizomenoi* means 'those being destroyed,' in and through their apostolic labours, it seems most natural to interpret *hoi nekroi* as a reference to these who were 'dead' in an existential sense (cf., Colossians 2:13), because it was to these that Paul and others directed their preaching."[37] The author continues with an elaborate exegesis. But if the passage is interpreted in a direct, unconvoluted sense within the framework of universal salvation, it is perfectly consistent with the Petrine statements regarding the preaching of the gospel to the dead; the two concepts complement each other, contributing consistently to a major theme. Another scripture that fits in this context is Ephesians 4:8–10, which refers to Christ's ascent to heaven and his descent into the lower parts of the earth.

In this is seen again an allusion to a three-structured universe (heaven, earth, and spirit or underworld).

An important Christian application of an ancient royal
motif is brought out by Peter in 1 Peter 5:4, where he
promises the addressed elders that if they feed the flock
conscientiously, they will receive "a crown of glory," which,
like inheritance, "fadeth not away" (cf., 1:4). In fact, a crown
(*stephanos*) is a symbol of regal status. To be anointed and
crowned a king in a palace or temple was to follow the pattern of God, the heavenly king.

2 Peter is somewhat shorter than 1 Peter, but it is no less
rich in temple motifs. Peter calls attention in 2 Peter 1:4 to
"exceeding great and precious promises" that potentially
lead the Christians to become what the King James Version
translates "partakers of the divine nature."[38] Several scholars
in the West consider this concept (as they read it) utterly
extraneous to the overall spirit and content of the New
Testament. In some quarters it is looked upon with contempt; those who feel this way would prefer to see 2 Peter
deleted from the canon.[39] On the other extreme, scholars in
the Eastern Church look at the phrase as a support of their
view that *theōsis* or the divinization or deification of
humankind is really the ultimate object of the Christian commitment, as it relates to their ultimate destiny.[40] If being partakers of the divine nature is understood as blending in with
divine *ousios*, or substance, as defined in the Nicene Creed,
the Latter-day Saints will be as repelled by the notion as any
Protestant or Catholic. In a thoughtful essay Al Wolters challenges the common translation, "partakers of the divine
nature." He points out that *koinōnoi*, which is normally translated "partakers," is not an adjective but a noun, which can
better be translated "partner," "companion," or "fellow."[41] In
mulling through the possible meanings of *theia physis*,

usually rendered as "divine nature," Wolters proposes that it read "a divine being." He concludes that the phrase in 2 Peter 1:4 is "a reference to covenantal partnership."[42] While Kelly notes that verse four concurs with Greek mystical philosophy and with aspirations in mystery cults,[43] Wolters's construct has possibilities. It calls to mind the joint inheritance in 1 Peter as well as Galatians 3–4 and Romans 8. And, as Kelly brings out, the passage has an affinity with 1 John 1:3 and 2:29–4:1, in relation to the fellowship the children of God have with their Father.[44] The Christian, then, through covenantal partnership, becomes a candidate for salvation; that is to say, he or she becomes an heir.

After listing a catalog of recommended moral acquisitions and character traits (see 2 Peter 1:5–7), Peter advises that the Christians who obtain these "shall neither be barren nor unfruitful in the knowledge of [their] Lord Jesus Christ" (2 Peter 1:8). The image of fruitfulness recalls the expectation of prosperity emanating from the temple. Here that fruitfulness is tied in with the knowledge or gnosis of Jesus Christ, to which he refers in the following verses, especially verses 16–18.

Peter urges his readers: "Give diligence to make your calling and election sure: for if ye do these things [i.e., cultivate those attributes listed in verses 5–7], ye shall never fall" (2 Peter 1:10). The word *bebaios* ("sure") carries the notion of firmness and assurity, and in this regard it coheres conceptually with the temple stones spoken of in 1 Peter 2:4–8. On this point Neyrey says, "As regards legal matters, *bebaios* may refer to matters with legally guaranteed security."[45] The sureness or absolute reliability in realizing one's election is consistent with the idea of the pole star, with which the temple in heaven is associated, in that it is an immovable and steadfast symbol. That is why ancient people felt confident that in the temple they could get their bearings on the universe. Covenants, which were sometimes temple related, had a complete sense of dependability so far as the Lord's part of the agreement was concerned. As one studies the meanings of legal and other kinds of words in Hebrew (for example, *amen*), especially as they relate to God, one recognizes a sense of reassurance and trust in a world otherwise frought with insecurity and uncertainty. In the same vein, language expressed in the mystery religions could convey unmitigated confidence in one's outcome. (Unfortunately, faith in the mystery religions could lead sooner or later to a shattering disappointment. Peter's admonition leads to no such disillusionment.)

An intriguing, veiled reference to a temple theme is found in 2 Peter 1:14. There the Apostle says that he must soon "put off" this tabernacle, or in other words, die. (A similar image is used concerning the incarnation of Christ in John 1:14, where it says that "the Word was made flesh and dwelt among us.") The phenomenon of separating the spirit from the body as conveyed in this language is redolent of the putting off of a garment. As Brooks has it, "'Removal,' or putting off is found . . . in the New Testament writings in reference to putting off, as one does clothing, an evil disposition in preparation for receiving exhortations and teachings, usually about worship."[46] Kelly observes that "putting off" is found also in Romans 13:12; Ephesians 4:22, 25; Colossians 3:8; and James 1:21. They are "all passages summarizing forms of conduct characteristic of the readers' pre-Christian past—and therefore seems to have been a technical term."[47] One "puts off" a garment with the intention eventually of "putting on" another, so the two acts go together. In Galatians 3:27, Paul says that those who "have been baptized into Christ have put on Christ."

Hans Dieter Betz unveils this insight: "This concept, which has a powerful and long tradition in ancient religions, describes the Christian incorporation into the 'body of Christ' as an act of 'clothing,' whereby Christ is understood as the garment." He explains further: "This phrase presupposes the christological-soteriological concept that Christ is the heavenly garment by which the Christian is enwrapped and transformed into a new being. The language is certainly figurative, but it goes beyond the social and ethical inclusion of a religious community; it suggests an event of divine transformation."[48]

Without divulging too much detail, Peter in 2 Peter 1:16–18 refers to his experience at the Transfiguration. The language here has been identified with the mystery religions. It is the contention of this paper that when terminology of the mystery religions was used, the meaning that the New Testament authors accepted was not necessarily precisely the same as those religions accepted, for early Christianity was a revealed religion and did not need to borrow its teachings from partially true but defective cults. It is plausible that the early Christian devotees used terminology familiar to them and their audiences that was suitable in conveying the Christian proclamation to be delivered. The application was placed entirely within a Christian context.

That the Transfiguration was a templelike experience is suggested by the Apostle's reference to the location as "the holy mount" (2 Peter 1:18), inasmuch as manmade temples are artificial sacred mountains. Temples and mountains were places where humans received oracles, and that certainly is what happened during the Transfiguration.[49] Moreover, in the synoptic accounts of the Transfiguration, Peter makes the enigmatic offer to build three booths, perhaps in commemoration of the Festival of Booths or Tabernacles. Friedrich M. Borsch ties in "the association of the booths with the New Year festival and of both with the enthronement of kings."[50]

What Peter (as well as James and John) saw on the mount might well be called a "Christophany," that is, an appearance of Christ in his glory. It was a crucial event in redemptive history, sacred to the point that the four accounts in the New Testament that deal with it impart only meager information. The figure of the radiant Christ, according to Neyrey, "has alternately been understood, not as fulfillment, but as a prophesy of the *parousia* (the coming of Jesus in glory)."[51] He quotes a fuller statement by G. H. Boobyer: "The transfiguration prophesies the *parousia* in the sense that it is a portrayal of what Christ will be at that day, and in some degree a miniature picture of the whole second advent scene."[52] Peter, then, while on the mount, received a foretaste of the climactic event in salvation history. Thus he is a party to firsthand information of who Christ is and what his role is in the salvation of the human race. One might say that here as well as after the resurrection, he experienced the zenith of the apocalyptic vision.

Peter tries to impress upon his audience the vividness and reality of his message, which was not dependent on "cunningly devised fables." Rather, when he "made known" to them concerning the powerful coming (*parousia*) of the Lord, it was by virtue of his being an eyewitness of his majesty (2 Peter 1:16). Two words should be discussed here. Kelly states that "the verb 'make known' (*gnoizein*) is almost technical in the New Testament for imparting a divine mystery."[53] Although the word for "eyewitness" (*epoptēs*) can refer to an ordinary observer, it also designates one who has been initiated into a higher grade in the mystery religions.[54] This terminology related to the mysteries gives some support to the view, dealt with earlier in this paper, that it was during the transfiguration that Peter received the keys of the kingdom (Moses and Elijah appeared to bestow them upon him), the event taking place just a week after Peter was informed that he would be entrusted with important religious prerogatives related to eternal reality in the cosmos. This was an extraordinary thing for Peter; it placed a very real burden on him. It was a sacred exchange, and that probably accounts for the paucity of detail and the charges to secrecy better than the theory that is often referred to as the "messianic secret," whereby Mark (usually considered the first evangelist) claimed ignorance of Jesus' full role in his lifetime, both by himself as well as his disciples, by causing Jesus to swear the disciples to secrecy concerning his identity until the resurrection. It was not a matter of the early Church finding a creative way to attribute to the historical Jesus what he did not attribute to himself; it was a matter of keeping sacred things sacred.

One final word should be given. In an essay in a truly exhilarating book, Hugh Nibley discusses the themes in the early apocryphal writings, whose setting was largely the forty-day ministry, and whose subject matter was secret. By drawing a composite picture, Nibley makes it clear that the *descensus* was real to the Saints in Peter's day and that aspects relating to temples were prominent.[55] If we grant that Peter genuinely was present at the Transfiguration and was privy to the instructions of the forty-day ministry, it is only natural that he would have a comprehensive understanding of Christocentric salvation as it is embedded and expressed in the temple, and that he would with caution allude to selected features here and there. It is our privilege to benefit from his informed direction.

Notes

1. Norman Perrin and Dennis C. Duling, *The New Testament: An Introduction* (San Diego: Harcourt, Brace, Jovanovich, 1982), 375–79, 381–84, consider the fine Greek, the consistent quotations and allusions from the Septuagint, and "the most probable date for the circumstances envisaged in 4:12–5:11 [as] the reign of the emperor Trajan, 98–117," to be the decisive arguments against Petrine authorship. Their views on 2 Peter are even more skeptical.

2. See Truman G. Madsen, ed., *The Temple in Antiquity* (Provo: BYU Religious Studies Center, 1984), 53–76.

3. This view was prevalent all over the world, as noted by Ichiro Hori, "Mountains and Their Importance for the Idea of the Other World in Japanese Folk Religion," *History of Religions* 6 (August 1966): 3. After listing several examples, Hori states, "In each case, the mountains were believed to be the center of the world, the cosmic mountain, the pillar supporting and linking heaven and earth, or the residence of a god or gods."

4. In this regard, too, the temple took on the same function as the sacred mountain. Hori points out: "The mountain is believed to be the world of the dead; or the meeting place of the living and the dead; or a passageway from this world to the next, from the profane to the sacred and from earth to heaven. The mountain is also believed to be the world of the spirits and the world of the deities" (ibid., 22).

5. Hori observes that mountains "were the sites of religious services, in which sacrifices and prayers were offered and divine revelations and oracles received" (ibid., 3).

6. The closeness of the new year rites to the temple tends to strengthen claims of temple imagery found in ancient sources, such as those considered in this paper. Geo Widengren, "King and Covenant," *Journal of Semitic Studies* 2 (January 1957): 7–8, confirmed that Solomon's dedication of the Jerusalem temple took place during the new year festival. Similarly, E. O. James, "The Religions of Antiquity," *Numen* 7 (1960): 141, notes the same connection at a later date: "When the temple worship was restored at Jerusalem after the Exile under the control of the high-priest, the autumnal Annual Festival at the end of the agricultural year in the seventh month (Tishri) when the rains were due to begin and the vintage was completed, preserved the salient features of the traditional New Year ritual."

7. The act of enthroning a king, according to Frederick H. Borsch, *The Son of Man in Myth and History* (Philadelphia: Westminister, 1967), 95, consisted in "emulating the enthronement of the king-god

in heaven. (Usually this was performed in the temple of the city-state either built like or actually set upon a mountain or hill)."

8. Sherman E. Johnson, "The Dead Sea Manual of Discipline and the Jerusalem Church of Acts," in *The Scrolls and the New Testament*, ed. Krister Stendahl (New York: Harper and Brothers, 1957), 136, refers to the stones, cornerstones, and the rock associated with Peter as "rich Christian midrashic material." The richness is enhanced if understood within a temple context. See note 9 below.

9. See *WJS*, 9; Heber C. Kimball, *JD* 9:327; John Taylor, *JD* 21:162; Joseph Fielding Smith, *Doctrines of Salvation* (Salt Lake City: Bookcraft, 1955), 2:109–12.

10. Peter E. Deterding, "Exodus Motifs in First Peter," *Concordia Journal* 7 (March 1981): 60.

11. Ibid.

12. Oscar S. Brooks, "I Peter 3:21—The Clue to the Literary Structure of the Epistle," *Novum Testamentum* 16 (1974): 300.

13. Ibid., 302.

14. Eduard Lohse, "Parenesis and Kerygma in 1 Peter," trans. John Steeley, *Perspectives on First Peter*, ed. Charles H. Talbert (Macon, Georgia: Mercer University Press, 1986), 50.

15. There is a phrase in the Isaiah verse that Peter does not quote, yet Matthew Black, "The Christological Use of the Old Testament in the New Testament," *New Testament Studies* 18 (1971–72): 11, feels it is implied by Peter: "a sure foundation" (cf. Helaman 5:12).

16. Paul S. Minear, "The House of Living Stones: A Study of 1 Peter 2:4–12," *Ecumenical Review* 34 (1982): 242.

17. As a sidelight it is worth mentioning that the officiating priest wore precious stones in his regalia.

18. David Hill, " 'To Offer Spiritual Sacrifices . . .' (1 Peter 2:5): Liturgical Formulations and Christian Parenesis in 1 Peter," *Journal for the Study of the New Testament* 16 (1982): 59. A. R. C. Leaney, "1 Peter and the Passover: An Interpretation," *New Testament Studies* 10 (1963–64): 246, also sees the stones in these verses as comprising a "spiritual temple."

19. Jerome H. Neyrey, "First Peter and Converts," *The Bible Today* 22 (January 1984): 15.

20. Lohse, "Parenesis," 48. Aside from Paul's epistles, J. C. Coppens, "The Spiritual Temple in the Pauline Letters and its Backgound," in *Studia Evangelica*, ed. Elizabeth A. Livingstone (Berlin: Akademie-Verlag, 1973), 6:58–59, notes that, aside from Paul's epistles, "we have to go to I Peter, II, 4–10, to find again the temple-image. This is really the only passage of the New Testament

where the image is logically constructed on the basis of a building and where the three cultic elements, the temple, the priesthood, the sacrifices, are mentioned together. Here therefore the cultic context and intention are evident."

21. J. N. D. Kelly, *The Epistles of Peter and Jude* (London: Adam and Charles Black, 1969), 50.

22. An observation by David Flusser concerning inheritance is enlightening. He notes that the Dead Sea sectarians applied Psalms 37:22 (that the blessed would inherit the earth) to themselves, meaning in part that they would "inherit 'the mountain of the height of Israel', the Temple of Jerusalem" ("Blessed Are the Poor in Spirit," *Israel Exploration Journal* 10 (1960): 8).

23. Brooks, "I Peter 3:21—The Clue," 303.

24. John H. Elliott, "The Rehabilitation of an Exegetical Step-Child: 1 Peter in Recent Research," *Journal of Biblical Literature* 95 (1976): 249.

25. Wolfhart Pannenberg, *Jesus—God and Man*, tr. Lewis L. Wilkins and Duane A. Priebe (Philadelphia: Westminister, 1977), 272. By "historical" Pannenberg may mean that which is palpably verifiable. Still, he implies that Jesus' descent was not a concrete event. Similarly, Anthony Hanson, "Salvation Proclaimed: 1 Peter 3:18–22," *Expository Times* 93 (1982): 101, is comfortable in proposing that "we must demythologize the notion of *descensus ad inferos*."

26. John S. Feinberg, "1 Peter 3:18–20, Ancient Mythology and the Intermediate State," *Westminister Theological Journal* 48 (1986): 303.

27. Ibid., 328.

28. Ibid., 304.

29. See Joseph Hoffman, "Confluence in Early Christian and Gnostic Literature: The Descensus Christi ad Inferos," *Journal for the Study of the New Testament* 10 (1981): 42. Hoffman details how the myth coincides and deviates from the Christian story.

30. See Feinberg, "Ancient Mythology," 307, 320.

31. Ibid.; see also Hanson, "Salvation," 102.

32. Martin H. Scharlemann, " 'He Descended into Hell:' An Interpretation of 1 Peter 3:18–20," *Concordia Journal* 15 (1989): 313.

33. Ibid., 321.

34. Hanson, "Salvation Proclaimed," 103.

35. For Hoffman, "Confluence," 48–49, this is a distinctive aspect of the Christian descensus.

36. Jerome Murphy-O'Connor, " 'Baptizing for the Dead' (I Cor., XV, 29): A Corinthian Slogan?" *Revue Biblique* 88 (1981): 532.

37. Ibid., 534–35.

38. Robert M. Grant, *A Historical Introduction to the New Testament*

(New York: Simon & Schuster, 1972), 231, sees problems in the phrase, considering it to be bad Greek grammar.

39. Those scholars who feel this way also tend to be offended by what they regard as polemic toward those perceived as apostates, as indicated in chapter 2.

40. These two views are summarized in Al Wolters, "'Partners of the Deity': A Covenantal Reading of 2 Peter 1:4," *Calvin Theological Journal* 25 (1990): 28–29.

41. Ibid., 32–33.

42. Ibid., 35, 41.

43. Kelly, *The Epistles*, 303.

44. Ibid., 304.

45. Jerome H. Neyrey, "The Apologetic Use of the Transfiguration in 2 Peter 1:16–21," *Catholic Biblical Quarterly* 42 (1980): 515.

46. Brooks, "1 Peter 3:21—The Clue," 292.

47. Kelly, *The Epistles*, 83.

48. Hans Dieter Betz, *Galatians* (Philadelphia: Fortress Press, 1979), 187.

49. Sigmund Mowinckel, *He That Cometh*, tr. G. W. Anderson (Nashville: Abingdon Press, 1955), 299, 305, comments with interest on the idea that Justin Martyr understood that Elijah would anoint the Messiah. This notion may have been prevalent generally at the time.

50. Borsch, *Son of Man*, 385. Neyrey, "Apologetic Use," 509, believes that Peter's account is inconsistent with the picture given in the synoptic Gospels. In 2 Peter the Apostle is an eyewitness of the event, implying alertness and awareness, "whereas in the Synoptics Peter is first confused (Mark 9:6), falling asleep (Luke 9:32), frightened (Matthew 17:6–8) and then ignorant of the import of the event (Mark 9:9–10)." These synoptic descriptions of Peter do not necessarily obviate his involvement as an eyewitness. He could have been confused before and after the event, he could have been asleep during a part of the episode (as he was in the Garden of Gethsemane), and he very well could have been frightened, given the supernatural circumstances. But that does not mean that he could not have received divine knowledge and keys, the fuller significance of which could have occurred to him later.

51. Neyrey, "Apologetic Use," 510. Charles H. Talbert, "2 Peter and the Delay of the Parousia," *Vigiliae Christianae* 20 (1966): 138, likewise sees the Transfiguration as "a foreshadowing of the second advent."

52. Neyrey, "Apologetic Use," 510.

53. Kelly, *The Epistles,* 316–17.

54. Ibid. Kelly opts for the banal definition.

55. Hugh Nibley, "*Evangelium Quadraginta Dierum:* The Forty-day Ministry of Christ—The Forgotten Heritage," in *Mormonism and Early Christianity,* in *CWHN,* 4:16.

19

The Temple in Heaven:
Its Description and Significance
Jay A. Parry and Donald W. Parry

According to several old Jewish traditions, the earthly temple was a copy, counterpart, or mirror image of the heavenly temple. Victor Aptowitzer summarizes the Jewish point of view by writing that

> [Jewish] literature avers that in heaven there is a temple that is the counterpart of the temple on earth. The same sacrifices are said to be offered there and the same hymns sung as in the earthly temple. Just as the temple below is located in terrestrial Jerusalem so the temple above is located in celestial Jerusalem.[1]

Various collections of writings mention the existence of a heavenly temple, including the Old and New Testaments, the Apocrypha, Pseudepigrapha, Talmud, and a host of midrashic[2] materials. Some of the sources provide only a brief description of the temple, while others explain its significance. The goals of this chapter are twofold: First, we will attempt to provide a brief description of the temple in heaven. In this regard, the Revelation of John will prove to be of great assistance, but a number of roughly contemporary canonical and noncanonical sources will also be helpful. Second, and perhaps more importantly, we will attempt to determine what significance the heavenly temple holds for us.

515

Extracanonical References to the Temple in Heaven

A number of pseudepigraphic sources make reference to the celestial sanctuary. An explicit reference appears in *1 Enoch*, wherein the prophet Enoch ascends to heaven in a vision. The prophet views the magnificent heavenly temple made of crystal. He is permitted to approach an inner chamber of the temple (i.e., the Holy of Holies), where he beholds God seated upon his throne. Enoch's description of the heavenly Holy of Holies reveals the magnificence of the heavenly temple:

> In every respect it so excelled in . . . glory and great honor—to the extent that it is impossible for me to recount to you concerning its glory and greatness. As for its floor, it was of fire and above it was lightning and the path of the stars; and as for the ceiling, it was flaming fire. And I observed and saw inside it a lofty throne—its appearance was like crystal and its wheels like the shining sun; and [I heard?] the voice of the cherubim; and from beneath the throne were issuing streams of flaming fire. It was difficult to look at it. And the Great Glory was sitting upon it—as for his gown, which was shining more brightly than the sun, it was whiter than any snow.[3]

In the *Testament of Levi* 5:1, an angel of heaven opens the gates and permits Levi to enter the celestial temple. Once inside, Levi sees the Most High seated upon a throne of glory. The *Testament of Levi* 18:6 continues the idea: "The heavens will be opened up, and from the temple of glory sanctification will come upon him."[4]

Rabbinic literature[5] contains a host of implicit and explicit statements regarding the heavenly sanctuary. TB *Sanhedrin* 94 declares the earthly temple the "earthly dwelling" of God, and the celestial temple he calls the "heavenly dwelling." The author of *Genesis Rabbah* 69:7 calls the two dwellings the "terrestrial temple" and the "celestial temple" and believes that the two temples are separated by a mere eighteen miles. A number of references indicate that the earthly temple was a replica or duplication of the heavenly temple. One midrash states that the Lord "created the earthly temple, and over against it the heavenly temple, the one being the counterpart of the other,"[6] and another reads, "The earthly holy of holies is a counterpart of the heavenly holy of holies."[7] Similarly, it is written that "the earthly throne is a counterpart of the heavenly throne."[8] In connection with this, an old Jewish legend claims that as Moses and the Israelites were erecting the tabernacle upon the earth, ministering angels were erecting a second tabernacle in heaven.[9] This recalls numerous claims in Jewish literature that the temple rituals of the earthly high priest coincided with the ritual performances of Michael the great prince, who presented his offerings in the heavenly temple.[10] One major difference, however, existed between the two temple systems. Animal sacrifices were offered in the earthly temple, but in the celestial temple Michael offered up "the souls of the righteous."[11]

Similar to the earthly temple, the heavenly sanctuary possesses implements, fixtures, and zones necessary for the temple officiants to perform their ordinance work. The Jewish *haggadah,* or nonlegal, homiletic texts, mention the "heavenly altar,"[12] "the heavenly throne,"[13] the "heavenly holy of holies,"[14] and heavenly priestly officiants.[15] Yet in some important respects the earthly sanctuary was dissimilar to the heavenly temple. The earthly temple was built by the hands of man (although the measurements and plans for the temple were revealed by God), while the celestial temple was said to have been built by God himself (see Hebrews 8:2; Exodus 15:17).[16] Furthermore, the earthly temple was built for the temporal world, while the heavenly temple was built for the eternal world. It even possesses preexistent qualities. One haggadic source says of the preexistent nature of the heavenly temple: "Even before the world was created my temple existed on high."[17] Similarly, in the Pseudepigrapha, 2 *Baruch* declares that the temple was "prepared from the moment that [God] decided to create Paradise."[18]

The Heavenly Temple in the Bible

Intimations of a heavenly temple are scattered throughout the Bible. At least three Psalms hint at the idea of a heavenly temple. Psalm 11:4 states that "the Lord is in his holy temple, the Lord's throne is in heaven." Also, a chiastic verse in Psalm 102:19 states, "For he hath looked down from the height of his sanctuary; from heaven did the Lord behold the earth" (cf. Psalm 150:1). Victor Aptowitzer believes that Isaiah's vision of the Lord upon the high and lofty throne (see ch. 6) took place in the heavenly temple. His hypothesis is based upon a number of Jewish haggadic texts.[19] It is also possible that Micaiah (see 1 Kings 22:19), Ezekiel (see Ezekiel 1, 10), and Lehi (see 1 Nephi 1:8) were permitted a view of the temple of heaven. John the Revelator also saw the temple in heaven in his great vision. We will examine his description shortly.

In the New Testament, the heavenly temple is spoken of by the Apostle Paul. Writing to the Hebrews, Paul contrasted the service in the earthly temple by an earthly high priest with the ministrations in the heavenly temple by the great high priest, Jesus Christ. Paul identifies the earthly temple as "a worldly sanctuary. . . . A tabernacle, . . . wherein was the candlestick, and the table, and the shewbread" (Hebrews 9:1–2). The earthly temple possessed a Holy of Holies that housed "the golden censer, and the ark of the covenant" (9:3–4). The earthly priests, writes Paul, "serve unto the example and shadow of heavenly things" (8:5). The complement and fulfillment of the earthly temple is the heavenly temple, the "true tabernacle, which the Lord pitched and not man." Jesus himself served as "a minister" of the heavenly temple (8:2). Under the Mosaic law, the priests went into the "first tabernacle" to accomplish "the service of God. But into the second [tabernacle, i.e., the heavenly temple] went the high priest [Jesus] alone once every year, not without blood, which he offered for himself, and for the errors of the people" (9:6–7). Paul explains, "Christ being come an high priest of good things to come, by a greater and more perfect tabernacle, not made with hands, . . . by his own blood he entered in once into the holy place, having obtained eternal redemption for us. . . . For Christ is not entered into the holy places made with hands, which are the figures of the true, but into heaven itself, now to appear in the presence of God for us" (9:11–12, 24).

The Temple in Heaven according to the Book of Revelation

Our most definitive single source on the heavenly temple is recorded in the Revelation of John, where the backdrop for much of John's apocalyptic vision was the temple in heaven.[20] John's experience with the heavenly temple began with an ablutionary rite of approach (see Revelation 1:5–6), wherein the apostle was washed in the blood of Jesus and made a king and a priest. Then, while John was "in the Spirit on the Lord's day" (1:10), he found himself standing before the seven-branched lampstand (see 1:12), which in the days of the Mosaic tabernacle was located in the "holy place" of the tabernacle (Exodus 26:33–35). John's observation of the seven-branched lampstand shifted into a divine vision of the glorified Jesus (see Revelation

1:13–18), and the symbol of the Lord (the lampstand) actually became that which was symbolized (the Lord).

In Revelation 4:1, John beholds an open door in heaven that led from the Holy Place to the celestial Holy of Holies, or the throne room of God. The temple in heaven, like its earthly counterpart, required an ascension from one sacral zone to another zone possessing a higher degree of sanctity. Hence the voice instructed John to "come up hither." Once situated inside the temple's Holy of Holies, John viewed a number of elements unique to the temple, which he refers to throughout the book of Revelation. For instance, John identified the glories of the celestial throne room, with God the Father sitting upon the throne (the throne is the center of activities in the book of Revelation, being mentioned forty times). He sees the heavenly beings (cherubim), the incense altar, the seven-branched lampstand, the altar of sacrifice, worshipers wearing sacred vestments, the four horns of the altar, the ark of the covenant, incense bowls, and the sacrificed Lamb of God (Jesus). These temple items, also found in the earthly temple, must have been familiar to the Seer, who was familiar with the Temple of Herod.

At times John is explicit in his mention of the heavenly temple,[21] employing such phraseology as "another angel came out of the *temple which is in heaven*" (14:17; italics added), and "there came a great voice out of the *temple of heaven*" (16:17; italics added; cf. 7:15; 14:15; 15:5–8). Additional references in Revelation describe various aspects of the heavenly temple (see 4:1–11; 5:1–14; 8:1–5; 11:16–19; 15:1–8; 19:1–6; etc.), and the letters addressed to the seven churches contain temple esoterica (see 2:7, 10, 11, 17, 26; 3:5, 12, 21), or words intended to be understood only by the initiated, the inner group of religious persuasion. Esoterica may include passwords or special religious expressions.

Table 1:
Elements common to the earthly and heavenly temples

Earthly Temple		Temple in Heaven	
Description	References	Description	References
called "worldly sanctuary"	Heb. 9:1–2	called "temple in heaven" or "true tabernacle"	Rev. 7:15; 14:17; 15:5; 16:17, Heb. 8:2
seven-branched lampstand	Ex. 26:35	seven-branched lampstand	Rev. 1:12
trumpet	Ex. 19:13, 16, 19	trumpet	Rev. 8:2, 6
altar of sacrifice	Ex. 27:1–2; 39:39	altar of sacrifice	Rev. 6:9
sacral vestments	Ex. 29, 39	sacral vestments	Rev. 4:4; 6:11; 15:6
altar of incense	Ex. 30:1–6; 39:38	altar of incense	Rev. 8:3–5
four horns of the altar	Ex. 30:10	four horns of the altar	Rev. 9:13
ark of the covenant	Ex. 25	ark of the covenant	Rev. 11:19
golden censer	1 Kgs. 7:50	golden censer	Rev. 8:3–5
incense	Ex. 30:34–36	incense	Rev. 5:8; 8:3–4
incense bowls	1 Kgs. 7:50; Num. 7:13, 19, 25, 31, 37	incense bowls	Rev. 5:8
throne (mercy seat)	Ex. 25:22; Lev. 16:2	throne	Ps. 11:4; Rev. 7:9; 16:17
Holy Place	1 Kgs. 7:50	Holy Place	Heb. 9:11–12, 24
Holy of Holies	Ex. 26:25–33	Holy of Holies	Rev. 4:1–10
high priest	Heb. 4:14	high priest	Heb. 9:6–7
priestly officiants	Ps. 110:4; Heb. 7:17	priestly officiants[22]	Rev. 8:2–5
rites	passim	rites[23]	Rev. 4:8–11; 8:2–5; 15:1–8
24 priestly courses	1 Chr. 23:3–6	24 elders[24]	Rev. 4:4, 10; 5:8 D&C 77:5
cherubim	Ex. 25:18, 22; 1 Kgs. 6:23–28	four living creatures	Rev. 4:6–8; D&C 77: 2–3 (cf. Ezek. 1, 10)
worshipers	passim	worshipers[25]	Rev. 5:11; 7:9; 19:6
sacrifice of lambs	Ex. 29:39	slain Lamb of God	Rev. 5:6

Differences between the Earthly and the Heavenly Temple

While the above table demonstrates a number of similarities between the earthly and heavenly temples, it should be noted that several differences existed between the two temple systems. For instance, the earthly temple possessed man-made, lifeless cherubim. These were replicas of the real living creatures that exist in the temple of heaven (see Revelation 4:6–8; D&C 77:2–3; cf. Ezekiel 1, 10). The earthly temple was built by the hands of man, but the heavenly temple was erected through the workmanship of God himself (see Hebrews 8:2; Exodus 15:17). God visits his earthly temples (Hebrew *mishkānôt̲*, "tents," "tabernacles") for a time or a season, but he dwells eternally in his heavenly temple. The saints visit the earthly temple and worship God, having a hope for eternal life; but in the heavenly temple, exalted saints worship God forever. These are only a few of the differences, and others could also be listed. But the key is this: the heavenly temple is an eternal reality, while the earthly temple is temporary, designed to take us to the heavenly.

What Is the Significance of the Temple in Heaven?

Now that we have described the heavenly temple, it is appropriate to ask why it is significant. The following five categories help provide answers to this question: (1) The heavenly temple is the place of holiness par excellence, (2) the heavenly temple is the quintessential place of mediation, (3) the heavenly temple is the ultimate goal of the saints, (4) the heavenly temple is the place of ratification, and (5) the heavenly temple is the place from which revelation goes forth. Each of these categories will now be examined.

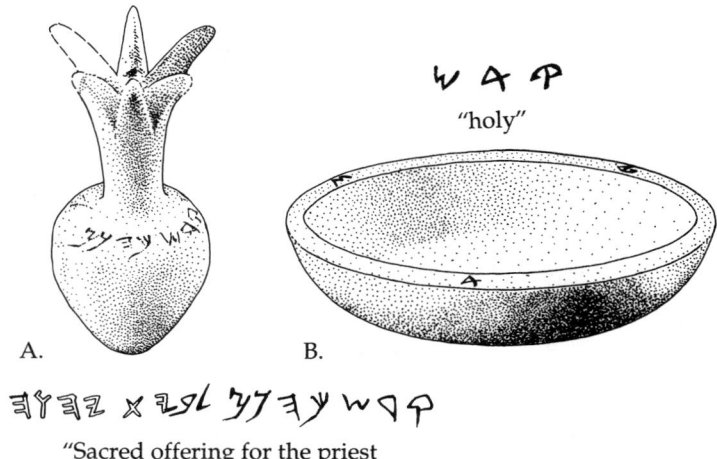

𐤔 𐤒 𐤒
"holy"

A.   B.

𐤄𐤅𐤄𐤆 𐤗 𐤶𐤉𐤋 𐤛𐤉 𐤣 𐤩 𐤔𐤒𐤒

"Sacred offering for the priest
of the House of the Lord"

Figure 42. This small ivory pomegranate (A) from the time of Solomon's Temple ornamented the top of a priest's staff, possibly serving as a sign of office. The inscription proclaimed it as set apart for sacred use. The simple clay bowl (B) from Megiddo is also set apart by its inscription. Bowls of various materials were used in temple service (see Isaiah 22:24).

1. The heavenly temple is the place of holiness par excellence.

This is clearly seen in one of the principal roots from the Hebrew Bible that is translated with the English words *sanctuary* and *temple*—the word *QDŠ, which has the basic meaning of "separation" or "withdrawal" of sacred entities from profane things.[26] In its different verbal forms, *QDŠ denotes something that is "holy" or "withheld from profane use"; the idea of showing or proving "oneself holy"; the placing of a thing or person "into the state of holiness"; and the dedication or sanctification of a person or thing, making it sacred.[27] A nominal derivation of *QDŠ is the masculine singular noun qōdeš. This labyrinthine term has reference to many aspects of the sacred,[28] all of which can be directly connected to its root meaning, the separation of the sacred from the profane.

A second biblical noun derived from *QDŠ* is *miqdāš*, commonly translated in English as "sanctuary" or "temple." The word is found seventy-three times in the Hebrew Bible.

The biblical scriptures leave no question that God requires his earthly dwelling places to possess a high degree of holiness, to be consecrated and set apart from the profanities of the world. If the earthly temple is holy, the heavenly temple serves as the very definition of holiness. Since God will not dwell in an unholy place (see Alma 7:21; 34:36; Helaman 4:24), one central purpose for a heavenly temple would be to serve as a holy place in which God and the saints will dwell forever.

2. The heavenly temple is the quintessential place of mediation.

The focus of the gospel of Jesus Christ is the Atonement, and the purpose of the Atonement is mediation between God and man. Many different aspects of the gospel in ancient times represented that Atonement—and the eventual oneness the saints would have with God in heaven—without actually being the Atonement. Thus, the law of Moses represented "a shadow of good things to come, and not the very image of the things" (Hebrews 10:1); the Israelite high priest, who on the Day of Atonement administered the Mosaic law, served as a "shadow of heavenly things" (8:5); the earthly temple, as discussed above, represented a copy, image, or "figure" (9:9) of the true or real[29] temple in heaven. These three earthly elements of the gospel—the law of Moses, the high priest, and the temple— each pointed to the atonement of Jesus Christ and his subsequent ministry in the temple in heaven. The sacrificial ordinances of the law of Moses prefigured the sacrifice and crucifixion of Jesus, the office and ministries of the priestly minister typified the atonement of Jesus Christ, and the earthly temple signified the heavenly temple.

As the earthly high priest entered the temple to make atonement for "the iniquities of the children of Israel, and all their transgressions in all their sins" (Leviticus 16:21; see also Hebrews 9:7), even so Jesus Christ, who is called the "high priest" (Hebrews 9:11), offered himself up for the sins of the world. Paul wrote, "For Christ is not entered into the holy places made with hands, which are the figures of the true; but into heaven itself, now to appear in the presence of God for us: nor yet that he should offer himself often, as the high priest entereth into the holy place every year with blood of others. . . . So Christ was once offered to bear the sins of many" (Hebrews 9:24–25, 28).

In a unique and special sense, the Israelite high priest, while performing his duties on the Day of Atonement, acted as a mediator between God and Israel. Similarly, but in a complete sense, Christ the high priest entered heaven and made intercession for all of mankind (see Hebrews 7:25). Paul, in his lengthy comparison of the earthly and heavenly temples, declared that Jesus is the "mediator of a better covenant" (Hebrews 8:6), and "the mediator of the new covenant" (JST, Hebrews 9:15). Hence, when the earthly high priest acted as mediator, the earthly temple served as a place of mediation between God and man, while the heavenly temple serves as the true mediation place, with Jesus the high priest serving as mediator.

3. The heavenly temple represents the ultimate goal of the Saints.

The earthly temple is a microcosmic representation of the celestial temple. It is a miniature model, a preparatory edifice where worshipers practice and rehearse rites, looking forward to the moment when they will be permitted entrance into the heavenly temple. In a most wonderful way, the spirit felt in the earthly temple—with its harmony and unity, its joy and peace, its purity and power—will be magnified a thousandfold in the celestial realms, where the throne of God is found. The Utopian setting of the earthly temple, where persons make consummate efforts to see eye to eye and to consecrate their lives unto a Godlike life, anticipates or prefigures the heavenly environment, where harmony and integrity are the rule.

4. The heavenly temple is the place of ratification.

The fact that earthly temples provide a sacred place for holy ordinances is well known. Conceivably, the rites and ordinances performed in the earthly temple will be ratified and sealed in the heavenly temple. Several scriptures suggest this possibility (see Matthew 16:19; 18:18; Helaman 10:7; D&C 1:8; 124:93). The following example illustrates the connection between heaven and earth. Note the relationship between the terms *earth* and *heaven:*

> And verily, verily, I say unto you,
> that whatsoever you seal on *earth*
>   shall be sealed in *heaven;*
> and whatsoever you bind on *earth,*
> in my name and by my word, saith the Lord,
>   it shall be eternally bound in the *heavens;*
> and whosoever sins you remit on *earth*
>   shall be remitted eternally in the *heavens;*
> and whosoever sins you retain on *earth*
>   shall be retained in *heaven.*
> (D&C 132:46; italics added.)

5. The heavenly temple is the place from which revelation goes forth.

The scriptures make clear that the earthly temple is a

place where revelation is received. "Let this house [Nauvoo Temple] be built unto my name," the Lord said, "that I may reveal mine ordinances therein unto my people; for I deign to reveal unto my church things which have been kept hid from before the foundation of the world" (D&C 124:40–41). The Lord's people have typically received the word of the Lord while in the temple. Joseph Smith and Oliver Cowdery were the recipients of manifold revelations while in the Kirtland Temple (see D&C 110). King David's song of praise included a testimony of having a prayer answered in the temple: "In my distress I called upon the LORD, and cried unto my God: he heard my voice out of his temple" (Psalm 18:6, cf. 3:4; D&C 109:77; 1 Kings 8:49). Directly related to this, the prophet Jeremiah revealed God's word unto the cities of Judah while standing in the temple courtyard (see Jeremiah 26:2).

Other prophets received important instructions from the Lord while in the temple. As mentioned above, the lengthy vision received by John the Revelator was received in the heavenly temple. Other examples include the experiences of Isaiah (Isaiah 6), Micaiah (1 Kings 22:19), Ezekiel (Ezekiel 1, 10), Lehi (1 Nephi 1:8), and the seventy elders (Exodus 24:9). In addition, the so-called biblical incubation texts, or texts in which an individual makes ritual preparation in a sanctuary setting with the intent of receiving revelation,[30] disclose additional revelatory experiences in a temple setting. The texts include Jacob (Genesis 28:10–19; 46:1–4), Samuel (1 Samuel 3), Solomon (1 Kings 3), and Moses (Exodus 24:18; 34:28; Deuteronomy 9:9, 18).

It is clear that revelation is often received in the earthly temple—and it is equally clear that the revelation originates in the heavenly temple, since that is the dwelling place of God. Once again we have the imperfection of the earthly temple (where only some revelations are received) standing against the perfection of the heavenly temple (where all revelations originate).

God as a Temple

The heavenly sanctuary, like its earthly counterpart, possesses a number of significant features. It is a place of holiness par excellence, it is a place of mediation, it represents the ultimate goal of those who worship at the earthly temple, it is the place of ratification, and it is the place from which revelation goes forth. More important than this list of significant features, however, is the fact that God himself is a temple. A number of scriptures so testify. The Lord told Ezekiel that Jehovah would be "as a little sanctuary" to the scattered tribes of Israel (Ezekiel 11:16). The Psalmist wrote, "Lord, thou hast been our dwelling place in all generations" (Psalm 90:1; cf. Psalm 91:2). Isaiah stated that the Lord was as a "sanctuary" unto the righteous, "a stone of stumbling and . . . a rock of offence" unto the wicked (Isaiah 8:14). Similarly, in the New Testament, Jesus told the Jews, "Destroy this temple, and in three days I will raise it up. Then said the Jews, Forty and six years was this temple in building, and wilt thou rear it up in three days? But he spake of the temple of his body" (John 2:19–21). John, after describing the New Jerusalem, declared, "And I saw no temple therein: for the Lord God Almighty and the Lamb are the temple of it" (Revelation 21:22).

How is it that God is a temple? As the temple of heaven is a place that serves the divine and eternal purposes of God, so does God himself have the attributes of that temple—his body and presence represent the ultimate place of holiness, he is the mediator, his godly status represents the ultimate goal of temple worshipers, he is the divine ratifier, and finally, he represents the embodiment of truth and revelation.

We also are temples when we yield ourselves to the Holy Ghost and let him dwell within us (cf. 1 Corinthians 3:16–17; 6:19; 2 Corinthians 6:16; D&C 93:35). As we become pure and holy through Christ, we eventually join with the Godhead in a blissful union in the celestial world. There, dwelling in the heavenly temple, we join with God as a temple in perfect oneness. We then will receive unto ourselves the attributes of the heavenly temple: We will be holy through the mediation of Christ; we will be at one with God; we will have reached our goal of dwelling with God; all our righteous acts will have been ratified; and, as we live on a great Urim and Thummim (see D&C 130:8–9), we will have access to all light and truth. When we become inhabitants of God's heavenly temple we will more completely fulfill Christ's great intercessory prayer, wherein he asked the Father, "that they all may be one; as thou, Father, art in me, and I in thee, that they also may be one in us" (John 17:21). Surely that is the final great purpose of a temple in heaven.

Notes

1. Victor Aptowitzer, *The Celestial Temple as Viewed in the Aggadah* (Jerusalem: International Center for University Teaching of Jewish Civilization, 1980), 1.

2. A *midrash* is an ancient Jewish exposition of a scriptural passage.

3. *1 Enoch* 14:16–18, 20, in E. Isaac, "1 (Ethiopic Apocalypse of) Enoch," in *Old Testament Pseudepigrapha*, 2 vols., ed. James H. Charlesworth (Garden City: Doubleday, 1983), 1:21.

4. H. C. Kee, "Testament of Levi," in *Old Testament Pseudepigrapha*, 1:795.

5. The belief in a celestial temple was widespread among the Jews. Aptowitzer, *Celestial Temple*, 1, states, "We find the concept among the ancient Babylonians and later among Christians and Moslems. The aggadic legends on the theme are scattered far and wide; they are found in both early and later sources."

6. *Tanhuma Vayakehel* 7, in Aptowitzer, *Celestial Temple,* 10.

7. TY *Berakhot* 4.

8. *Mekhilta, Song at the Sea,* 10:26–27, in Aptowitzer, *Celestial Temple,* 10.

9. See *Numbers Rabbah* 112:12.

10. See *The Lord by Wisdom,* quoted in Aptowitzer, *Celestial Temple,* 23 (additional references, pp. 21–22).

11. *Ein Ya'akov on Hagiga* 12b, in Aptowitzer, *Celestial Temple,* 21.

12. *Pesikta Rabbati* 33:150.

13. *Mekhilta, Song at the Sea,* 10:26–27, in Aptowitzer, *Celestial Temple,* 10.

14. TY *Berakhot* 4.

15. See TB *Hagigah* 12b; TB *Menahot* 110a.

16. See *Genesis Rabbati* 9.

17. *Tanhuma Naso* 19, commenting upon Jeremiah 17:12; Habakkuk 2:20; Isaiah 6:1; and Exodus 25:8.

18. *2 Baruch* 4:3–4.

19. See Aptowitzer, *Celestial Temple,* 4–6.

20. "That the Book of Revelation is especially concerned with the Temple can be observed from a brief vocabulary count: John the Seer gives *naos* no less than a third of its forty-five New Testament uses; *hieron,* restricted in its New Testament use to the physical edifice, does not occur in the Apocalypse" (William Riley, "Temple Imagery and the Book of Revelation," *Proceedings of the Irish Biblical Association* 6 [1982]: 88).

21. George B. Gray also believes that John plainly identifies the heavenly temple. He states that "the belief in a temple within heaven is expressed with all clearness" in the Revelation of John (*Sacrifice in the Old Testament: Its Theory and Practice* [New York: KTAV, 1971], 164).

22. R. J. McKelvey, *The New Temple: The Church in the New Testament* (Oxford: Oxford University Press, 1969), 164–65, discusses the priesthood in the setting of the heavenly temple:

The heavenly priesthood is an interesting feature of the Apocalypse. We have met the conception already in Revelation 7:14–15. That is to say, the faithful in heaven are in the posture of priests; compare the statement in v. 9 that they are "standing." Although John is thinking primarily of the martyrs (7:14a), it is clear that he thinks of the new priesthood as including all Christians (1:5–6; cf. 5:9). This priestly service begun on earth is continued in heaven, and, as we shall see presently, in a profounder way. Its basis is the priestly work of Christ on the cross; it is this that makes the faithful priests (1:5–6; 7:14). Ideally all Israelites were priests. . . . Those represented as priests in the heavenly temple are "from every nation" (7:9; cf. 5:9). Admission to the new priesthood depends no longer upon racial descent, but upon the blood of the Lamb (7:14f). Furthermore, those who comprise it are not simply priests, but high priests: they stand before the throne of God (7:9, 15), i.e., inside the holy of holies (cf. 22:3–4). In a similar vein possibly is the description of the faithful as dressed in white robes: white was the colour worn by the high priest when serving in the holy of holies (M. Yoma 3:6; 7:4), and John's priest-angels are similarly dressed (15:6).

23. On ritual in the heavenly temple, see Gray, *Sacrifice in the Old Testament*, 160–64.

24. Regarding the connection between the twenty-four priestly courses and the twenty-four elders, Riley has written that the "number [24] especially is reminiscent of the twenty-four courses of priests who rotated Temple service and whose presence in the Temple had a certain representative dimension" ("Temple Imagery and the Book of Revelation," 92).

25. The temple worshipers in John's Revelation number in the millions. This is similar to an old Jewish work which states, "1,018 camps stand before the Shekinah in the temple in heaven to chant before him 'Holy, Holy, Holy' each day. In each camp there are 10,180,000 ministering angels, for they stand before the Shekinah in the temple in heaven" (*Sefer Raziel* 24a; cited in Aptowitzer, *Celestial Temple*, 28).

26. See Francis Brown, S. R. Driver, and Charles A. Briggs, *A Hebrew and English Lexicon of the Old Testament*, trans. Edward Robinson (Oxford: Clarendon, 1977), 871. Compare also the definitions of *temple* provided by Menahem Haran, *Temples and Temple Service in Ancient Israel* (Oxford: Clarendon, 1977), 13–15; and G. R. H. Wright, *Ancient Building in South Syria and Palestine* (Leiden: Brill, 1985), 1:225–26.

27. Ludwig Koehler and Walter Baumgartner, eds., *Lexicon in Veteris Testamenti Libros* (Leiden: Brill, 1953), 825–26.

28. In addition to the temple, other aspects of the sacred connected with the Hebrew *QDŠ include God, his name, and his divine actions (see Exodus 15:11; Leviticus 20:3); holy places outside of the temple, including the city of Jerusalem (see Isaiah 48:2) and the land of Israel (see Zechariah 2:12); things directly associated with sacred places, such as the temple furniture (see Exodus 30:29; 2 Chronicles 35:3), the

altar (see Exodus 29:37; Deuteronomy 9:24), anointing oil (see Exodus 30:25), incense (see Exodus 30:35), priestly vestments (see Leviticus 16:4), and the bread of the presence (see 1 Samuel 21:5); persons directly associated with sacred places, such as the priests (see Leviticus 21:6) and the people of Israel (see Jeremiah 2:3; Psalms 114:2); and holy days and festivals (see Isaiah 58:13; Exodus 35:2). Of course, Deity is always the ultimate source of holiness in a temple setting—"The holy or the Holy One are simultaneously that which awakens fear and that which draws to itself"—as Sigmund Mowinckel has shown, *Religion and Cult*, trans. John F. X. Sheehan (Milwaukee: Marquette University, 1981), 54–55. The work was originally written under the title *Religion og Kultus* (Oslo: Land og Kirke, 1950). For a scholarly definition and treatment of the concept of holy, see Rudolph Otto's classic work, *The Idea of the Holy*, trans. John W. Harvey (London: Oxford University Press, 1958); and Roger Caillois, *Man and the Sacred*, trans. Meyer Barash (Westport: Greenwood, 1980), 20.

29. On the definition of *real* in a temple setting, see John Lundquist, "What Is Reality?" in this volume.

30. For instance, "Moses, as an incubant, spent the night in the sanctuary (Exodus 24:18), offered sacrifices (Exodus 24:4–8), purified himself (Exodus 19:10–15), and washed his clothing (Exodus 19:10–15), thus fulfilling the four 'constitutive parts of the procedure' of incubation. In return, Yahweh revealed his law to the prophet" (Donald W. Parry, "Sinai as Sanctuary and Mountain of God," in *BSAF*, 1:493). For an extensive study of dream incubation in the ancient Near East, see Robert K. Gnuse, *The Dream Theophany of Samuel* (Nashville: n.p., 1980).

PART 7

The Real and the Symbolic

20

On the Sacred and the Symbolic

Hugh W. Nibley

The "Terrible Questions"

What are the "terrible questions"? When Clement, the earliest authentic Christian writer after the New Testament, was a student in Rome, he nearly went crazy trying to find the answers to the terrible questions. Not a professor in Rome could help him as he pestered them by asking "Do I have a life after death? Won't I exist at all? Couldn't I have existed before I was born? Won't we remember anything after this life, or is the whole vast stretch of time simply to be oblivion and silence, in which we would not only not be there, but there would be no memory of our ever having been?" Such thoughts led naturally to others: "When was the world made, what was there before it was made, or was it always there? It seemed clear to me that if it was created, it would have to pass away [dissolve], and if it passed away, what then? Would it be a matter of total oblivion and silence, or something else that we can't even imagine?"[1]

It was not until he met Peter at a general conference in Caesarea that Clement could get some straight answers, as Peter began telling him about the premortal existence and the Council in Heaven,[2] telling of the fall and redemption and other things related to the gospel plan. When Clement, thinking of his dead father and mother, asks, "Will those be excluded from Christ's kingdom who died before his ministry?" Peter answers: "Now, Clement, you are pressing me to talk about some things that cannot be openly discussed, but I will tell you as much as I am allowed to." He then assures Clement that his parents are not in hell, although they never were baptized, and that ample provisions have been made for their salvation, which Clement may be qualified to learn of later.[3] Plainly, the early Christians had something close to what we would call an endowment, that is, a confidential discipline which dealt head-on with those terrible questions.

Has modern science put the questions to rest or come up with satisfying answers? Consider the conclusion of a recent book entitled *Black Holes* by an eminent nuclear physicist:

> We have come to the end of our story about the universe. It is full of violent actions and grim forebodings, of horrors unfolded and mysteries still to be explored. . . . The natural reaction to such a tale is that . . . each of us can continue to live our lives untouched by these immensities and by the catastrophes to come. The satisfaction gained from the simple round of life need be unaltered even when seen against this vast backdrop of the universe. We may live and die without raising up our eyes to the heavens, secure in the safety of our cotton-wool globe. Yet that is false. We cannot divorce our lives from . . . the basic problems . . . of the universe. It is the answers, or lack of them, which determine our actions, even from day to day. For whatever we do, we must somehow come to terms with the infinite before we can act [one act has another for a goal, but the highest-level goals are always there]. . . . The highest-level goals . . . are based on the wish to survive and for loved ones to survive. This is the highest-level goal of all. . . . The wish for survival, in one form or another, is absolutely essential for our continued existence.[4]

The conclusion then is that we, for all our modern sophistry, cannot escape the terrible questions. But "survival in one form or another," leaving everything up in the air, is hardly a scientific solution. That carries us only as far as the cemetery at best, and C. P. Snow reflects pointedly on the plight of the greatest scientists of his generation: "Does anyone really imagine that Bertrand Russell, G. H. Hardy, Rutherford, Blackett, and the rest were bemused by cheerfulness as they faced their own individual state? In the crowd, they were the leaders; they were worshipped. But, by themselves, they believed with the same certainty that they believed in Rutherford's atom that they were going after this life into annihilation. Against this, they only had to offer the nature of scientific activity; its complete success on its own terms. But it is whistling in the dark when they are all alone."

The word *endowment* is well chosen in both its forms—*endowment* and *enduement*—which Joseph Smith uses interchangeably. To endow is to bestow a gift on one, to furnish or enrich with something in the nature of a gift; it is to enrich, clothe, invest, furnish. The last named is nearer to *endue,* suggesting the Greek *endyō,* "take upon oneself, clothe, to put on."[5] The Latter-day Saints' endowment is in the nature of endowment insurance, in which the policy provides for the payment of an endowment at the expiration of a fixed term of years, and only when the recipient has fulfilled certain stipulations. Such ideas were new to many of the Saints. "Be assured, brethren," said Brigham Young,

> there are but few, *very few* of the Elders of Israel . . . who know the *meaning* of the word *endowment.* To know, they must experience; and to experience, a temple must be built. Let me give you the definition in brief. Your

endowment is, to receive all those ordinances in the House of the Lord, which are necessary for you, after you have departed this life, to enable you to walk back to the presence of the Father, passing the angels who stand as sentinels, being enabled to give them the key words, the signs and tokens, pertaining to the Holy Priesthood, and gain your eternal exaltation in spite of earth and hell.[6]

"We come into this world weak and frail mortals," as Charles C. Rich explained it. "We have an agency given us, with an opportunity of doing good and evil. We are invited to obey the gospel, which embraces principles that will *endow* the willing and obedient with exaltation and eternal life." It is that opportunity to direct our actions toward the eternities that makes this "a glorious world, for it is here we are enabled to obtain our blessings and endowments."[7]

The endowment was not only necessary to the exaltation of the individual, but to the spreading of the gospel in its fullness, a spreading of light to the nations.[8] Joseph Smith said, "A man of God should be endowed with all wisdom knowledge & understanding to teach & lead people,"[9] and that not only in the Church, but throughout the world: they were first "to be endued" in Kirtland, "and then the Elders would go forth and each must stand for himself,"[10] that individually and collectively the Saints might have the satisfaction of "seeing the blessings of the endowment rolling on and the kingdom increasing and spreading from sea to sea."[11] In order to spread the light and knowledge effectively, God has gathered "the people of God in any age of the world . . . to build unto the Lord an house" in which to receive the ordinances. "This was purposed in the mind of God before the world was, . . . to prepare them for the ordinances & endowment, washings & anointings, . . .

administered in a house prepared for the purpose" in every dispensation of the gospel.[12]

Something of the richness and scope of the endowment is indicated in Joseph Smith's record of the first time it was "administered in its fullness" on May 4, 1842:

> I spent the day . . . instructing them in the principles and order of the Priesthood, attending to washings, anointings, endowments and the communication of keys pertaining to the Aaronic Priesthood, and so on to the highest order of the Melchizedek Priesthood, setting forth the order pertaining to the Ancient of Days, and all those plans and principles by which any one is enabled to secure the fullness of those blessings which have been prepared for the Church of the Firstborn, and come up and abide in the presence of Eloheim in the eternal worlds. In this council was instituted the ancient order of things for the first time in these last days, . . . things spiritual, and to be received only by the spiritual[ly] minded.[13]

Naturally, great knowledge can only be received by degrees; it is not all a single package. "Abraham's endowment . . . was greater than that which his descendants Aaron and Levi would be allowed," for "Abraham's patriarchal power . . . [was] the greatest yet experienced in [the] church."[14] The Prophet gave the nine Brethren "the Endowment ordinances in their fullness for the first time" on the above date.[15]

The endowment itself is eternal and essentially unchanging, and hence there is only one: "God purposed . . . that there should not be an eternal fullness until every dispensation should be fulfilled and gathered together in one . . . unto the same fullness and eternal glory; . . . therefore He set the ordinances to be the same forever and ever, and set Adam to watch over them, to reveal them from heaven to man, or to send angels to reveal them."[16] It is an "ancient order of things" restored "for the first time in these last days,"[17] "after the order of the covenant which God made with Enoch, it being after the order of the Son of God; which order came, not by man, . . . but of God."[18] "The gospel has always been the same; . . . Noah was a preacher of righteousnes. He must have been baptized and ordained to the priesthood by the laying on of hands, etc."[19] The mysteries of godliness are "the ordinances of the temple preparing us for life in the eternities," and the whole thing is endless (see D&C 19:10–12), prepared from the foundations of the world (see D&C 128:5). "It is necessary in the ushering in of the dispensation of the fulness of times . . . that a whole and complete and perfect union, and welding together of dispensations, and keys, and powers, and glories . . . be revealed from the days of Adam even to the present time" (D&C 128:18). "Whenever men can find out the will of God and find an administrator legally authorized by God, there is the kingdom of God."[20] To be endless is to be divine, "then shall they be gods, because they have no end, . . . because they continue" (D&C 132:20).

The Temple

The Prophet insisted emphatically that there could be no proper endowments until a house was built for them: "Finish that temple and God will fill it with power."[21] The idea of the temple is a compelling one, not just spiritual, but supremely practical. If people are to come together and act in union, a specific time and place must be stipulated with the proper appointments for the planned activities. A recent collection of studies, *The Temple in Antiquity*, notes that all temples have in common a specific "place, cult, and personnel."[22] At all times, the temple was, as it was for ancient Israel, "the place which the Lord your God shall choose out of all your tribes to put his name there, even unto his

habitation shall ye seek, and thither thou shalt come"
(Deuteronomy 12:5). It is still the place where all things are
gathered in one, "appointed by the finger of the Lord, . . .
even the place of the temple" (D&C 84:3–4).

The mystique of the temple lies in its extension to other
worlds; it is the reflection on earth of the heavenly order,
and the power that fills it comes from above. That is why all
the *middot,* or sacred measurements, of the building have to
be so carefully observed (see 1 Kings 6:2–36). So in modern
times, all is "according to the pattern . . . given . . . hereafter"
(D&C 94:5). How the temple is put into phase with the cosmos itself appears in the dedication. The description of the
surveying of the foundation of the great temple at Edfu, still
preserved on the walls there, vividly recalls a like event in
St. George: "Precisely at 12 m., President Brigham Young, at
whose side stood Presidents John W. Young and Daniel H.
Wells, broke ground at the south-east corner, and, kneeling
on that particular spot, he offered the dedicatory prayer."[23]
The southeast corner, Brigham Young explained, because
that is where the light comes from. Coordination of time
and place by the stars and the compass set the earthly
temple into the framework of the cosmos. The word *temple*
itself expresses the idea most clearly.[24]

The temple is a multipurpose structure with but one
object, just as the endowment is a series of ordinances all
having the same end. For the Jews, there and there only
"you shall bring your sacrifices. . . . And there ye shall eat
before the Lord your God, and ye shall rejoice in all that ye
put your hand to, ye and your households"; all great public events and celebrations were centered there (Deuteronomy 12:6–7). For the Latter-day Saint, it was to be a house of
prayer, of fasting, of faith, of learning, of glory, of order (see
D&C 88:119; 109:8). It is a school, "that all those who shall

worship in this house may be taught words of wisdom out of the best books, and that they may seek learning even by study, and also by faith" (D&C 109:14). The Saints are to "prepare . . . for that which is to come" (D&C 1:12), "that they may be perfected in the understanding of their ministry, in theory, in principle, and in doctrine" (D&C 97:14). It is a place of refuge in a hostile world (see D&C 97:27–28), and the center from which the Brethren go forth into that world to "proclaim thy word[,] . . . seal up the law, and prepare the hearts of thy saints for all those judgments thou art about to send, in thy wrath, . . . that thy people may not faint in the day of trouble . . . that they may gather out . . . [and] come forth to Zion" (D&C 109:38–39).

Concerning the temple in the last times: "And for the fulness of times . . . I will gather together in one all things, both which are in heaven, and which are on earth; and also with all those whom my Father hath given me out of the world" (D&C 27:13–14). The messengers came in quick succession: Moroni, Elias, John, Elijah, who bring all generations together; the patriarchs, who bring the covenants together; and finally Adam, or Michael, who brings all things together as "the father of all, the prince of all, the ancient of days" (D&C 27:11; cf. 27:5–14). Surprisingly, Peter, James, and John come next as we go back in time, for it was they who brought the gospel to Adam in the first place, "By whom I have ordained you and confirmed you to be apostles" (D&C 27:12). Thus the endowment, including the offices of Peter, James, and John, is already anticipated in August of the year 1830.

The Great Gap

The first step in preparing "a more gifted people" is to set them apart, to get them out of an environment in which everything exercises a downward drag in the relentless manner of gravitation. "This world is a very wicked world," said the Prophet Joseph, ". . . The world grows more wicked and corrupt. In the earlier ages of the world a righteous man . . . had a better chance to do good, to be believed, . . . than at the present day."[25] In our world, says the Lord, "all flesh is corrupted before me, and the powers of darkness prevail upon the earth" (D&C 38:11). This is no place to realize the blessings of one whose "design . . . in making man . . . was to exalt him to be as God. . . . The mystery, power and glory of the pr[ie]sthood is so great and glorious that the angels desired to understand it and cannot."[26] Those who wish to "come unto Mount Zion, and unto the city of the living God, the heavenly place, the holiest of all" (D&C 76:66), must be "strangers and pilgrims on the earth," as "all holy men" have been (D&C 45:12–13).

The first order God gave to his people was to remove themselves utterly from the world, to be completely different, holy, set apart, chosen, special, peculiar ('am sǝgullāh—sealed), not like any other people on the face of the earth (see Deuteronomy 7:6). If "glory, and salvation, and honor, and immortality, and eternal life; kingdoms, principalities, and powers" are to be theirs (D&C 128:23), they must be sanc-tified, con-sacr-ated, hagios, qadōsh, all of which mean set off or cut off by a fence, an insurmountable wall, an unbridgeable gap. "Assemble yourselves together, and organize yourselves, . . . sanctify yourselves; yea, purify your hearts, and cleanse your hands and your feet before me, that I may make you clean" (D&C 88:74). The almost fanatical insistence of the Jewish laws on distinction between the clean and the unclean in all things has the purpose of keeping Israel from backsliding into the ways of the world. Nay, the earth itself must "be sanctified from all unrighteousness, that it may be prepared for the celestial glory," which was meant to be its permanent and proper condition (D&C 88:18, 20). Any who are not sanctified must needs "inherit another kingdom" (D&C 88:21). When "Moses . . . sought diligently to sanctify his people," he first had to lead them into the wilderness, completely apart and by themselves (D&C 84:23). The Passover was their escape from the fleshpots of Egypt and the corruption of a world that would destroy them; it was to be eaten even with your loins girt, shoes on your feet, staves in your hands, in a hurry; and after it was finished with not a scrap left behind, the people were to hit the road and never look back (see Exodus 12:10–11). As soon as they were clear of their enemies, Moses was commanded, "Go unto the people and sanctify them to day and to morrow, and let them wash their clothes" (Exodus 19:10). In a like circumstance, the Nephites were all to be rebaptized (see 3 Nephi 11:21; 19:10–13). The exercises of the priesthood cannot begin until the whole operation is removed from ordinary things by making the sharpest possible distinction (ləhaḇdîl) between two worlds. The elaborate instructions of Leviticus (chapters 10 and 11), telling what the people may eat and not eat, wear and not wear, who is clean and who is not, etc., are no mere priestly officiousness, but the strenuous insistence on the difference between being in the covenant and out— there is no middle ground; nothing is more important than preserving the sanitary gap between what is holy and what is ḥillal in every aspect of life (see Leviticus 20, 24, 26).

The proximity of a world in which we do not belong is a constant threat; and, preceding the endowment, Adam receives the garment that is to protect him as he goes forth into the world, not only against it, but against himself, i.e., from the temptations and enticements in which he will find himself.[27] It is a strict arrangement, but could one ask less of a race of priests and kings (see Exodus 19:6; Revelation 1:6), "Priests and Kings, who have received . . . fulness and . . . glory, . . . after the order of Melchizedek, . . . Enoch, . . . [and the] Son" (D&C 76:56–57)?

The Creation Drama

The great epics of literature begin with the poet asking the Muse the epic questions—How did it all begin? and What is it all about? The answer here takes us back to the story of the creation, beginning with the Council in Heaven.[28] Throughout the world, the creation story has been traditionally presented in dramatic form, beginning with the *Prologue in Heaven* and the triumphant *Hymn of the Creation*.[29] Ever since the "indescribable, . . . unimaginable" conditions of the "'zeroth' moment," according to a recent study from the Harvard Observatory, the whole life of the universe has been one continual evocation of "Order from Chaos," in which the less organized matter takes the form of ever more organized particles and forces: from chaos, to hadrons, to photons, to leptons, to atoms and on to galaxies, stars, and, finally, to living organisms and intelligent life; how it all happened is a complete and total mystery.[30]

The Creation is not the "instantaneous and simultaneous" appearance of everything *ex nihilo,* to use Aquinas's expression, nor is it an infinitely long but random series of mindless accidents: it is both a process and a planned and directed operation. The prologue is timeless; in fact, our time was not measured unto man until Adam left the garden and started counting the hours in this dreary world (cf. Abraham 5:13). For the rest, "all things . . . are manifest, past, present, and future, and are continually before the Lord" (D&C 130:7). This world is to have its own time for its inhabitants, but that is all—"Is not the reckoning of God's time, angel's time, prophet's time, and man's time, according to the planet on which they reside?" (D&C 130:4). Time has been a great stumbling block in imagining these things, but the important thing is to recognize that the whole drama of the universe is a single epic, yet it is divided, as all great sagas are (for example, the Greek dramas), into distinct episodes such as a trilogy of plays, each of them consisting of three acts, each act divided into scenes. Any one of these segments could be presented as a play in itself, yet each one is tied to all the others; and from beginning to end, they are all just parts of one story. So we must understand that a creation drama is not the absolute beginning of all things; rather we break into the action which has been going on for ages, all as part of the same mighty cycle.

Thus we need not begin the story of the earth in the era of radiation or with the first atoms or molecules; neither do we begin with creatures of the primordial ooze. What concerns us is what concerns our parent, Adam. His world begins to take form when the waters which cover the earth are divided and the dry land appears (see Genesis 1:9–10; Abraham 4:9–10). The process continues, forming mountains and hills on which the forces of erosion go to work as torrential rains, making great rivers and their tributaries. So between them, mountain building and erosion are basically responsible for that variety which gives beauty to an otherwise flat and uninteresting terrain. Then comes the breakup of the cloud-cover as first the sun and then the moon appear, miraculously occupying exactly the same amount of space in the sky as seen from the earth—a phenomenon which astronomers show to be inconceivable by mere laws of probability.

Since our focus is on the story of man, we skip over ages belonging to lower orders of things which have, in fact, according to the latest report, been almost totally exterminated, as one general ambience upon the earth has given way to another one. We come in on the show just as the great plant revolution takes place, when the angiosperms appear on the earth with revolutionary suddenness, a violent explosion of new life, as grass, flowers, shrubs, and trees appear, in that order. This new type of plant life, appearing so suddenly, made it possible for new types of animals to appear, beginning with the elephant and followed by the great grazing and browsing herds feeding upon the new cereals. These, in turn, gave rise to a thriving population of great carnivores, which preyed upon and depended upon the herds for their existence. Today, we are told that a layer of iridium deposited around the world, perhaps by meteors, marks the abrupt extinction of almost every life form at the end of the age of dinosaurs and the equally sudden appearance of totally new life forms in the tertiary, which is actually labeled the "new world," in which man last appears.[31]

It would seem that man at first was something of a primitive, like a small child, living happily with the animals in a timeless world, which only receives passing notice, since his real career does not begin until he marries into the covenant (see Moses 3:21–24).[32] Having been properly wed to Eve, with her he takes the great step forward by accepting God's law, after which they enter another world, the Garden of Eden.

Most Glorious and Beautiful

At a very early time, mountains, hills, rivers, and streams were expressly intended to provide variety and beauty to the scene. When the earth was finally in a proper state to receive man, the makers agreed that it was good and beautiful (see Genesis 1:25, Moses 2:25). It was meant to remain so. When Adam entered the garden, it was like receiving a marvelous Christmas or birthday present: an earth provided with all sorts of vegetable and animal life—everything that Adam could possibly need in it. He was invited to enjoy an unlimited variety of exquisite fruits, to have a good time dressing the garden and taking good care of it; he was to be happy, and along with him all the other creatures as well: "And I, God, blessed them, and said unto them: Be fruitful, and multiply, and replenish the earth" (Moses 2:28; cf. 22). Adam, now knowing what the Lord's purpose is toward all his creatures, is put in charge of the whole project: "Have dominion . . . over every living thing that moveth upon the [face of the] earth" (Moses 2:28). This is seen throughout the ancient literature to be a charge of grave responsibility for Adam, to supervise the increase and prosperity of all creatures (though many Latter-day Saints have treated it as a license to exterminate!). When the time comes to restore that blessed state of the earth which the gospel anticipates, then "Zion must increase in beauty, and in holiness; . . . Zion must arise and put on her beautiful garments" (D&C 82:14).

The commandment to have joy in the garden was carried over into the world that followed, for when Adam grasped the situation, he said: "Blessed be the name of God, for because of my transgression my eyes are opened, and in this life I shall have joy. . . . And Eve, his wife, heard all these things and was glad" (Moses 5:10–11). Likewise, when the Israelites were driven out of the lush valley of the Nile, which was "like the garden of the Lord" (Isaiah 51:3), into the dry hill country, as Adam was from the garden, God reassured them that it would still be a beautiful world if they would listen to him: "I will give you the rain . . . in his due season. . . . And I will send grass," that is, as long as you "take heed to yourselves" (Deuteronomy 11:14–16). They are to have joy and revel in the two great commandments upon which "hang all the law and the prophets" (Matthew 22:40)—since, if they are fully observed, none of the other commandments are necessary: "and now, Israel, what doth the Lord thy God require of thee, but to fear the Lord thy God, to walk in all his ways, and to *love* him . . . with all thy heart and with all thy soul" (Deuteronomy 10:12; italics added). The second commandment is like unto it. Since God loves all his creatures, you must do the same— you must love the stranger, the widow and the orphan, because he loves them; you must be concerned for them, because he is concerned for them (see Deuteronomy 10:18–19). Whether in Eden or out of it, everything he has given you is his (see Deuteronomy 10:14); therefore, you should give it to all in the same spirit he does, imparting freely of your substance in joy and happiness (see Deuteronomy 15:8, 18).

Abiding by the commandments should fill us with the love of giving: "O that there were such an heart in them, that they would fear me, and keep all my commandments, . . . that it might be well with them, and with their children for ever!" (Deuteronomy 5:29). So the first commandment given is "Thou shalt love . . . with all thine heart, . . . soul, and . . . might" (Deuteronomy 6:5). "And these words, which I command thee this day, shall be in thine heart" (Deuteronomy 6:6), failing which nothing but destruction awaits Israel, "because thou servedst not the Lord thy God with joyfulness, and with gladness of heart, for the abundance of all things" (Deuteronomy 28:47).

When the Prophet Joseph feels to exult, he breaks into a
hymn on the beauties of the natural world (see D&C
128:23). How was he brought to the sacred grove for the
opening of this dispensation?

> I looked upon the sun the glorious luminary of the
> earth and also the moon rolling in their magesty through
> the heavens and also the stars shining in their courses
> and the earth also upon which I stood and the beast of the
> field and the fowls of heaven and the fish of the waters
> and also man walking forth upon the face of the earth in
> magesty and in the strength of beauty whose power and
> intiligence in governing the things . . . are so exceding
> great and marvilous even in the likeness of him who cre-
> ated <them> [sic].[33]

What set him to thinking was, by contrast, the world of
early nineteenth-century rural America, the world that men
had made, which to us seems like an Age of Innocence: "I
pondered many things in my heart concerning the sittua-
tion of the world of mankind the contentions and
divi[si]ons the wicke[d]ness and abominations and the
darkness which pervaded the minds of mankind [sic]."[34] At
the site of this tragic discrepancy, he reports, "my mind
became exceedingly distressed"—it raised one of the terrible questions: "Therefore I cried unto the Lord for mercy
for there was none else to whom I could go."[35]

The World

From his happy situation, Adam was cast out into the
world. *Sacrifice* became the order of the day. Adam built an
altar and sacrificed. The very essence of the temple in Israel
was sacrifice; every major ordinance performed there was
accompanied with sacrifice, and the altar was the center of
every sacred activity.[36] This is recounted in Moses 5:5–7,
where we find Adam offering sacrifice in obedience to

God's command "that they should worship the Lord their God." He explained to the angel that his only reason for making the sacrifice was to obey the Lord's command; and then it was explained to him that this was "a similitude of the sacrifice of the Only Begotten," whose sacrifice had redeemed him on condition that he "repent and call upon God in the name of the Son forevermore" (Moses 5:5–8). Repentance and sacrifice are the plan of life while we are on this earth: "the sacrifice required of Abraham in the offering up of Isaac, shows that if a man would attain to the keys of the kingdom of an endless life; he must sacrifice all things."[37] The Israelites were aware of this: "As Jehovah thy God has redeemed thee: therefore, I command thee this thing today" (Deuteronomy 15:15; author's translation). The first thing Moses taught the Israelites when they were alone in the desert was that each one must give something up, a freewill offering, every individual as his heart moves him. The freewill offering is absolutely required, it cannot be evaded; what makes it free is that the individual, though he *must make* the sacrifice, may decide for himself how much he will give, for the purpose of the sacrifice is to test *him* as it did Abraham (see Exodus 25:1–2; Deuteronomy 12:6–7).

The Gospel Law

The gospel was given to Adam and Eve when, "after many days" of sacrificing, "an angel of the Lord appeared unto Adam" and taught him the plan of salvation (Moses 5:6–9). Adam and Eve joyfully embraced it and taught it to their children (see Moses 5:10–12). But "Satan came among them, saying, . . . Believe it not; . . . and men began from that time forth to be carnal, sensual, and devilish" (Moses 5:13). The gospel entails a definite pattern or style of life best defined as the opposite of "carnal, sensual, and devilish."

One of the charges or responsibilities connected with adherence to the gospel is reiterated in the "Olive Leaf" revelation: "Organize yourselves; . . . establish a house, even a house of prayer. . . . Therefore, cease from all your light speeches, from all laughter, from all your lustful desires, from all your pride and light-mindedness, and from all your wicked doings" (D&C 88:119, 121).

As to *light-mindedness,* humor is not light-minded; it is insight into human foibles. There is nothing light-minded about the incisive use of satire often delivered with an undertone of sorrow for the foolishness of men and the absurdity of their pretenses. Such was the cutting humor of Abinadi addressing the priests of King Noah—there was nothing light-minded about it, though it might raise a chuckle. What *is* light-minded is *kitsch,* delight in shallow trivia; and the viewing of serious or tragic events with complacency or indifference. It is light-minded, as Brigham Young often observed, to take seriously and devote one's interest to modes, styles, fads, and manners of speech and deportment that are passing and trivial, without solid worth or intellectual appeal. There are times when nonsense is not light-minded, but insightful. Horace is the classic example: his good-natured and funny satire is a sad exposure of the evils and corruption of his times, so disturbingly like our own.

As to *laughter,* Joseph Smith had a hearty laugh that shook his whole frame; but it was a meaningful laugh, a good-humored laugh. Loud laughter is the hollow laugh, the bray, the meaningless laugh of the soundtrack or the audience responding to prompting cards, or routinely laughing at every remark made, no matter how banal, in a situation comedy. Note that "idle thoughts and . . . excess of laughter" go together in D&C 88:69.

As to *light speech* and speaking evil, my policy is to criticize only when asked to: nothing can be gained otherwise. But politicians are fair game—the Prophet Nathan soundly denounced David though he was "the Lord's anointed," but it was for his private and military hanky-panky, thinking only of his own appetites and interests. Since nearly all gossip is outside the constructive frame, it qualifies as speaking evil.

As to *lustful desires* and unholy practices, such need no definition, one would think. Yet historically, the issue is a real one that arises from aberrations and perversions of the endowment among various "Hermetic" societies which, professing higher knowledge from above, resort to witchcraft, necromancy, and divination, with a strong leaning toward sexual license, as sanctioned and ever required by their distorted mysteries. It is surprising to find such goings-on even in sober communities such as the Plymouth and Massachusetts Bay colonies, and in the lives of some of the greatest figures of the Renaissance and Reformation. It was part of the mystique to be riotously over-sexed, and Joseph Smith has been so accused without a shadow of justification.

The scriptural injunction to secrecy (see Psalm 25:14; Amos 3:7; Proverbs 3:32) follows from the stringent necessity of keeping a discrete distance from the world. "Pearls before swine" is not an expression of contempt, but a commentary on the uselessness of giving things to people who place no value on them, have no use for them, and could only spoil them.[38] The guarding of their secrets got the early Christians into a great deal of trouble. But if there is one thing all the "mysteries" have in common, it is the insistence on secrecy.[39] In many cases, the only capital some secret societies have is the capacity to mystify and excite curiosity in others—the classic instance being the Shrine of the Bottle in Rabelais's *Pantagruel*.[40] But for us, there is no appeal whatever in secrecy as such. Sacred things, if freely discussed in public, would invariably be distorted, vulgarized, misinterpreted beyond recognition, and so lost. "Remember that which cometh from above is sacred, and must be spoken with care, and by constraint of the Spirit," without which spirit it is a great "condemnation" (D&C 63:64). Why should not these things become the subject of frank discussion among the Saints? Because that would make them a subject of contention, and one of the first words of the Lord to the Nephites was that there should be no contention among the people (see 3 Nephi 11:29–30). Historically, religious issues becoming the subject of contention have brought endless misery and suffering; long, horrendous wars have been fought over the issues of ordinances—baptism, chrism, sacraments, consecration, tonsure, vestments; over doctrines of salvation, atonement, original sin, and so forth; and over the dates of sacred observances.

The Ritual Enactment of Curses

The ritual performance of a curse was anciently an imitation sacrifice. The priest shed his own blood either for the king, whom he originally represented, or for the people, whom the king also represented (see 1 Samuel 13:8–14). But as he can represent them by proxy, so he too may shed his blood by proxy by the sacrificial beast. All of this, of course, is "a similitude of the sacrifice of the Only Begotten" (Moses 5:7), which atoned for the sins of all, and thus redeems or saves from death.

In the old covenant, when the leper is declared clean and his life restored, two birds are taken: one is killed and the other is drenched with its blood (see Leviticus 14:1–6), and then allowed to fly away free, taking the leper's sins with it, while the patient is sprinkled with the same blood (see Leviticus 14:7). Being thus delivered from death, he washes his clothes, shaves his hair, and bathes. Then he brings two lambs, one for trespass, the price of sin (see Leviticus 14:8–12); its blood is placed upon the right ear of the one to be cleansed and upon the thumb of his right hand (see Leviticus 14:14). Then the priest takes the oil held in his left hand (see Leviticus 14:15), and after sprinkling it puts it on the right ear and right thumb of the healed person, where the blood had been, pouring the rest of the oil on his head (see Leviticus 14:17–18)—it is the oil of healing.[41] This is a private version of the public rite in which Aaron and his sons lay their hands on the head of a ram, transferring their guilt to it, slay it, and then put the blood on their own thumbs and ears (see Leviticus 8:22–24). The ram is burnt for a sin-offering as an atonement (see Leviticus 9:2–7). It is clear when one thinks back to the ram that was sacrificed in the place of Isaac, Abraham's offering of his only son, that this all looks forward to the great atoning sacrifice, the whole idea being to celebrate our redemption from death (see Exodus 13:8–10). We are told that a covenant must be made by the shedding of one's own blood unless a substitute can be found to *redeem* one (see Numbers 8:13–15). In ancient times, all the sacrifices were symbolic (see Leviticus 5), and Maimonides says that in the entire history of Israel only nine heifers were really sacrificed. Certainly one of the striking things about the newly discovered *Temple Scroll* is the avoidance of bloody sacrifice, which takes place only at a discrete distance from the temple.

The *ear* has a significance in ancient Israel. When a

servant in Israel, out of pure love, wished to be sealed to a master for the rest of his life, even though free to go his own way, his bond was made sure by fixing his ear to the door with a nail driven through it (see Deuteronomy 15:16–17). It was a relatively painless operation, since there are only three nerves in the lobe of the ear. But it would be hard to find a more convincing symbol of anything fixed in a sure place (Isaiah 22:23).

One penalty is particularly interesting, because of a very early Christian writing known as the *Discourse on Abbatôn*, which goes back to Apostolic times in Jerusalem. It was discovered in a chest preserved from the earliest days of the Church in the house of John Mark's mother. Timothy, the Bishop of Alexandria, while attending a conference at Jerusalem, persuaded the aged keeper of the old Church archives to show him the book. It tells how, when the council was held at the foundation of the world and Adam was chosen to preside over the project, Satan refused to recognize him, saying, "It is meet that this man Adam should come and worship me, for I existed before he came into being. And when my father [it is the Lord speaking to the apostles] saw his great pride and that his wickedness and evil doing had reached a fullness, he commanded the armies of heaven, saying remove the token [mark, document, authorization] which is in his right hand, remove his *panoply* [protective armor] and cast him down to earth, for his time has come."[42] With him go all his followers, for "he is the head over them and their names are written in his hand." The angels were reluctant to demote so great a one "and they did not wish to remove the writing from his hand. And my father commanded them to bring a sharp sickle and cut him at breast level from shoulder to shoulder, on this side and on that, right through his body to the vertebra of his shoulders." This cost him a third of his strength and rendered him forever incapable of prevailing by force. Henceforth, he gains his ends by deception and trickery, which makes him all the more dangerous.[43]

Names, Signs, and Seals

A *token*, according to the *Oxford English Dictionary*, is "something given as the symbol and evidence of a right or privilege, upon the presentation of which the right or privilege may be exercised."[44] To be more specific, a sign (*signum*) was both a pointing (related to *zeigen*, teach, didactic, etc.) and a touching (touch, take, tactile, *dactyl*). In particular, it was the *dexter*, the right hand or taking hand, and as such is universal in the *dexiosis* of the mysteries. For the Manichaeans, the right hand was used for bidding farewell to our heavenly parents upon leaving our primeval home and the greeting with which we shall be received when we return to it.[45] Tokens were used extensively in regulating ancient social and religious gatherings; they are all means of identification, whose main purpose is security.[46]

The free interchange of terms, each denoting items that may be themselves interchanged, is apparent in the law of Moses: "And thou shalt shew thy son in that day, saying, This is done because of that which the Lord did unto me when I came forth out of Egypt. And it shall be for a sign (*lǝʾôṯ*) unto thee upon thine hand, and for a memorial (*lǝzikkārôn*) between thine eyes, that the Lord's law may be in thy mouth: for with a strong hand hath the Lord brought thee out of Egypt. . . . And it shall be for a token upon thine hand, and for frontlets between thine eyes: for by strength of hand the Lord brought us forth out of Egypt" (Exodus 13:8–9, 16).

As one approaches the camp of Israel, carefully guarded

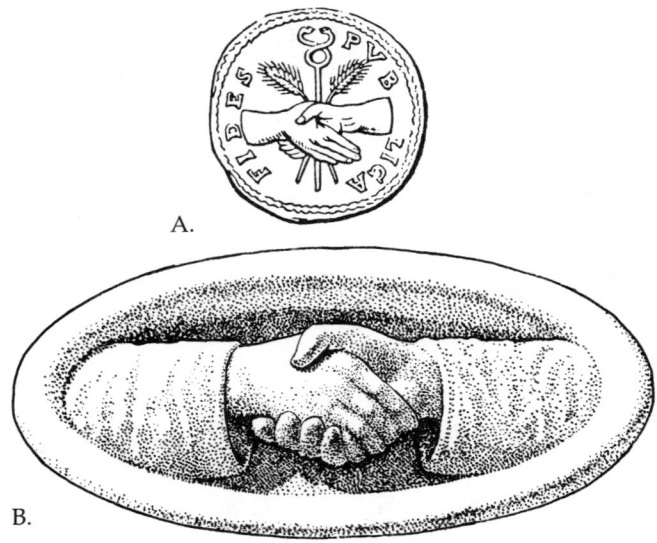

Figure 43. As illustrated on this brass coin (A) of Domitian (c. A.D. 100), the clasped hands have always represented the recognition and acceptance of those who were once apart, as well as the giving and receiving of knowledge. On the coin, the staff of Hermes and wheat stalks held between the palms represent initiation into the mysteries. The exterior of the Salt Lake Temple displays this symbol (B) under the all-seeing eye of God on its east and west center towers.

in a dangerous environment, one first gives a sign to be seen from afar. Then, being recognized, one approaches and at closer range gives his name. This establishes closer identity. *Nomen est omen:* every name is an epithet indicating exactly in the manner of a token above a distinguishing mark, indication, or characteristic trait, which distinguishes one from all other members of the society. To receive a new name (cf. Revelation 2:17) is to receive a new role or persona, to be identified with a particular situation or association, as is indicated by surname, family name, or nickname, each placing one in a particular relationship to society. Of great importance in the earliest tradition of the human race is the secret name by which the hero is known only to his parents; when the *femme fatale* wheedles the secret of this name from him, terrible things ensue (Re of the Sun's Eye, Lohengrin, the Fisherman). After the sign and the name comes the closest approach, an actual handclasp or embrace.

The word *seal,* which is so important, is simply the diminutive of *sign, sigillum* from *signum.* It is a word rendered *peculiar* in Deuteronomy. Like the other tokens, it can represent the individual who bears the king's seal, who bears the authority.[47] Its particular value, however, is as a time-binder. The seal secures the right of a person to the possession of something from which he or she may be separated by space and time; it guarantees that he shall not be deprived of his claim on an object by long or distant separation. The mark on the seal is the same as that which he carries with him. And when the two are compared, his claim is established, but only if neither of the tokens has been altered. This is the control anciently exercised by tally-sticks, such as the Stick of Joseph and the Stick of Judah.[48]

Let us recall again that a servant was forever bound to his master in love and devotion by his own free will when his ear was nailed to a doorpost—signifying that he would never walk out on his lord; he was now bound by a sure sign. The nail as a sure fixing of contracts is one of the most ancient of symbols. At the center of the Germanic world was the shrine of the *Irminsul,* the central column or tent pole around which the universe revolved. Into this at a great gathering of the new year, the "year nail" was driven to secure the order of the cosmos for another age. The *Irminsul* identifies *Weltnagel* with the cosmic tent pole of the the tabernacle—the "center stake" (*yatad*) that holds all in place with the aid of the stakes driven like nails around it.

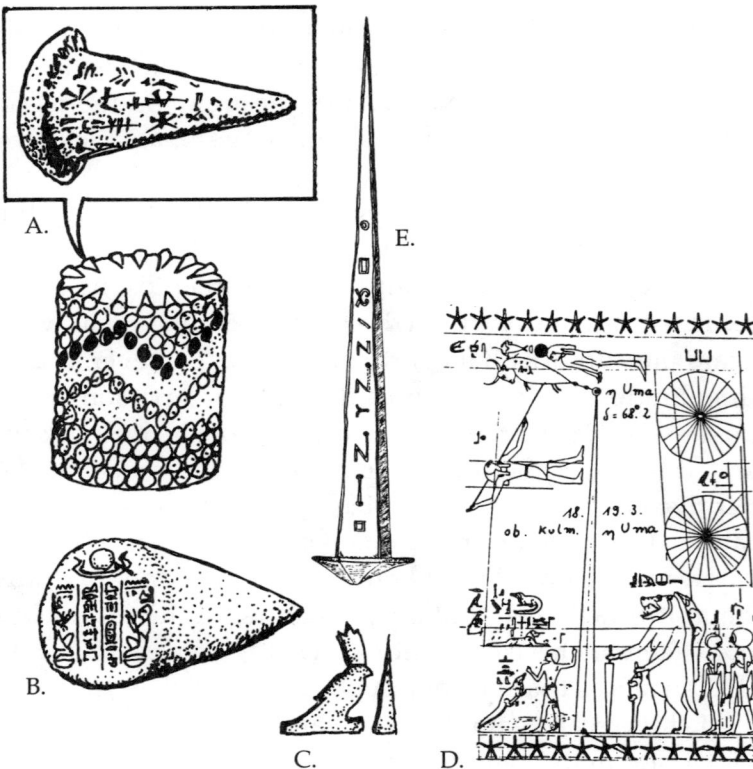

Figure 44. Symbolic clay nails inscribed with expressions of gratitude to the gods were set into the temple walls of Lagash in ornamental patterns (A) as well as in Egypt (B). The ancient god Sopdu is shown as a crowned falcon preceded by the pivot in the Pyramid Texts of Unas (C). On the Senmut astronomical ceiling (D), c. 1500 B.C., the nail symbol marks the still center around which the Bull, or Big Dipper, is fastened and revolves. Magical figures adorn this bronze nail (E) from Pergamum (c. A.D. 200).

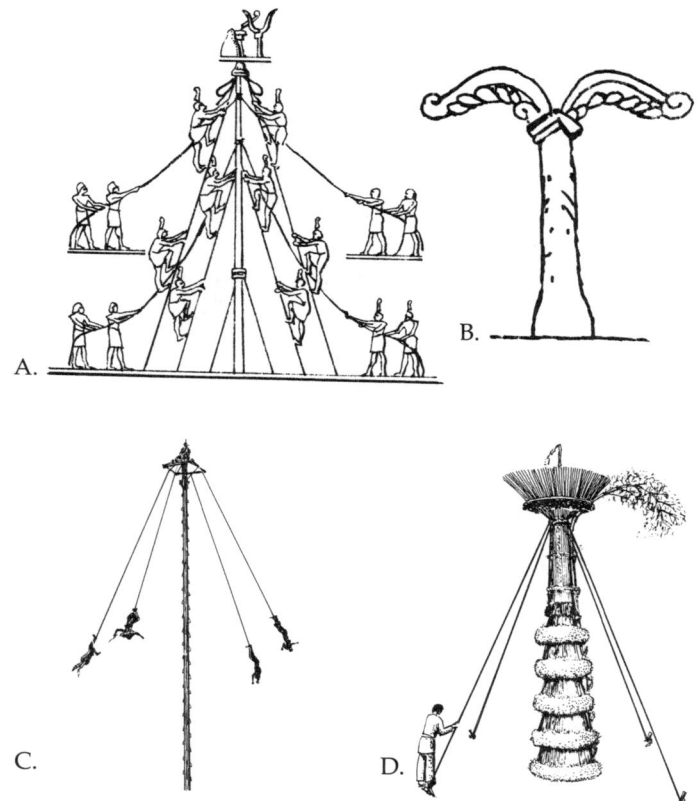

Figure 45. To celebrate the mystery of the world pillar, the ancient
Egyptians erected a pole (A) crowned with a miniature temple of the
god Min. The Irminsul (B) was a stylized tree pillar worshiped by the
Saxons at Marsberg. It was cut down by Charlemagne in A.D. 772.
The Totonac Indians of Mexico still perform a ceremony (C) in which
the *voladores*, revolving dancers hanging from ropes, symbolize the four
seasons of the circling year. In Japan, villagers still erect *ōtaimatsu* of
reed and bamboo (D) on their temple grounds. After the festival, these
symbolic pillars are burned, thus completing the cycle of creation to
dissolution.

The earliest temples of Mesopotamia have huge clay nails placed into their walls to ensure stability both architecturally and symbolically. In Egyptian, the archaic nail symbol stands for Sirius and the Sothic Cycle as well as Sopdu, the turning point of the cosmic cycle, the moment of the revival of life in the universe. In the royal tent or temple or Tabernacle of the camp of Israel, the central pole of the tent was commonly identified with the pole of the heavens, and the tent itself with the *Weltenmantel* or expanse of the firmament.[49] What kept the central stake or pole of Zion in place were the pegs, stakes, or nails driven around it to hold the ropes firmly in place.

The Law of Consecration

One important covenant that will someday govern life on earth is the law of consecration. "No covenant was ever given more easy to understand," said Brigham Young, so when the Saints ignore it, they do it consciously. Yet it is this law to which the related steps—the law of God, the law of sacrifice, and the law of the gospel—are meant to lead us. Reluctance to fulfill this promise, the hardest of all to observe, was foreseen from the first: "If you will that I give unto you a place in the celestial world, you must prepare yourselves by doing the things which I have commanded you and required of you" (D&C 78:7). And that for the purpose and intent "that you may be equal in the bonds of heavenly things, yea, and earthly things also, for the obtaining of heavenly things. For if ye are not equal in earthly things ye cannot be equal in obtaining heavenly things" (D&C 78:5–6).

The extreme importance of this law must be stressed, the more so since it is not well received: "And let every man deal honestly, and be alike among this people, and receive alike, that ye may be one, even as I have commanded you" (D&C 51:9). In return for this, the Lord guarantees the prosperity of the land in ancient as in modern times. And the command is to "organize my kingdom upon the consecrated land" (D&C 103:35). The land itself is consecrated for "an everlasting order for the benefit of my church, and for the salvation of men until I come" (D&C 104:1). The law will be an economic arrangement to tide us through—"in your temporal things you shall be equal" (D&C 70:14); it will be a perfectly safe undertaking, since it will have the Lord's guarantee that those who will be observing it "should be blessed with a multiplicity of blessings," even as in ancient Israel (D&C 104:2). One day we will be required to live the law: "It is contrary to the will and commandment of God that those who receive not their inheritance by consecration . . . should have their names enrolled with the people of God" (D&C 85:3). According to the Prophet Joseph: "When we consecrate our property to the Lord it is to administer to the wants of the poor and needy, for this is the law of God."[50]

The basic principles set forth are (1) insistence on absolute equality, and (2) the importance of receiving it by covenant, not as a suggestion or proposition, but as a binding contract that cannot be broken. As in Israel, when "a tribute of a freewill offering" was required of every man "as he is able" (Deuteronomy 16:10, 17), it was in recognition of blessings received. The spirit of the thing is all-important; in doing this, you and every single member of the community, including strangers, must join together and be happy as one big happy family (see Deuteronomy 16:10–11). Remembering Abraham, all are to "rejoice in every good thing which the Lord thy God hath given unto thee, and unto thine house . . . and [to] the Levite, and the stranger

that is among you . . . [that] the Levite, the stranger, the
fatherless, and the widow . . . may eat within thy gates, and
be filled" (Deuteronomy 26:11–12). At that time you will
say, "I have brought away the things of my house which
have been sanctified (consecrated), and also have given
them to the Levite, stranger, fatherless, widow, according to
all thy commandments" (cf. Deuteronomy 26:13). All must
share and share equally, and if they do this not grudgingly
but "with all your heart and soul, . . . as you have promised
and covenanted this day, you will be his peculiar [sealed]
people, set apart, the wonder of other nations, that you may
be a holy people, as he has said" (cf. Deuteronomy 26:16–19;
28:46). To preserve the spirit and letter of consecration at all
times, no Israelite might charge interest on a loan, and all
were bound by "the Lord's release" to cancel all debts every
seven years (Deuteronomy 15:1–3). And don't worry about
losing your capital, because God will guarantee it, "for the
Lord shall greatly bless thee" if you do it (Deuteronomy
15:4).

The Saints were "bound together by a bond and
covenant that cannot be broken by transgression " (D&C
82:11). "And it shall be done according to the laws of the
Lord"; it is "for your good" whatever you may think about
it (D&C 82:15–16), the basic rule will be that "you are to be
equal . . . to have equal claims on the properties, . . . every
man according to his wants and his needs, inasmuch as his
wants are just" (D&C 82:17; cf. 2 Timothy 5:6). No one can
deny the tenor and meaning of D&C 38: "The poor have
complained before me. . . . I am no respecter of persons.
And I have made the earth rich . . . and deign to give unto
you greater riches, even a land of promise, a land flowing
with milk and honey" (vv. 16–18). "Wherefore, hear my
voice and follow me, and you shall be a free people, and ye

shall have no laws but my laws, . . . and let every man esteem his brother as himself" (D&C 38:22, 24). "I say unto you, be one; and if ye are not one, ye are not mine" (D&C 38:27). D&C 42:31–32 is even stronger than this.

Following the great endowment bestowed by Christ himself on the Nephites (cf. 3 Nephi), the people enjoyed almost four generations of life on earth as it was meant to be: "And they had all things common among them; therefore there were not rich and poor, bond and free, but they were all made free, and partakers of the heavenly gift" (4 Nephi 1:3). So it was with the Saints in the days of the Apostles who had been instructed to ask God outright, "give us this day our daily bread" (Matthew 6:11), and rejoiced in having "all things common" (Acts 4:32).

Equality and humility are what the law of consecration requires and what it begets. "In order to receive the Endowment," said the Prophet in 1835, the brethren should "prepare the[i]r hearts in all humility for an endowment with power from on high."[51] Indeed, what later held up the giving of the endowment "concerning the Twelve" was that "they are under condemnation, because they have not been sufficiently humble in my sight, and in consequence of their covetous desires, in that they have not dealt equally with each other in the division of the moneys which came into their hands."[52] It had been a "grievous sin" that they should consider themselves unequal,[53] and they were told that there would be no endowment for those who make invidious comparison or "watch for iniquity."[54]

Jewish authorities, contemplating today the return of a temple to Jerusalem, are particularly worried that the old elitism of the priesthood will cause mischief and jealousy. But under the present order, there is no rank whatever in the temple. "Under the Levitical order," Joseph Smith

explained, "only the High Priest can enter the veil, but
through the Melchizedek order, all men who prove worthy
may be admitted into the presence of the Lord."[55] The difference is an enormous one; it is the magnanimous principle
behind our work for the dead: "In my Father's kingdom are
many kingdoms in order that ye may be heirs of God and
joint heirs with me. I do not believe the Methodist doctrine
of sending honest men, and noble minded men to hell, . . .
but I have an order of things to save the poor fellows at any
rate, and get them saved for I will send men to preach to
them in prison and save them if I can."[56] It is all in the spirit
of God's own work; his infinite work and glory is "to bring
to pass the immortality and eternal life of man," to share
everything he can with others (Moses 1:39).

"For I, the Lord, am not to be mocked in these things" (D&C 104:6)

The children of Israel were told that if they kept the law
of consecration, they would be a sign and a wonder to the
nations (see Deuteronomy 26:18–19; 28:1–14); but if they did
not keep it, they would be another kind of sign and wonder:
"They shall be upon thee for a sign and for a wonder, and
upon thy seed for ever. Because thou servedst not the Lord
thy God with joyfulness, and with gladness of heart, for the
abundance of all things" (Deuteronomy 28:46–47). Never
forget, they are warned, that all they have comes from one
source—they are never to get the idea that they have earned
it, "lest when thou hast eaten and art full, . . . and thy silver
and thy gold is multiplied, . . . and thou say in thine heart,
My power and the might of mine hand hath gotten me this
wealth" (Deuteronomy 8:12–13, 17). And no one is to think,
"for my righteousness the Lord hath brought me in to possess this land; . . . not for thy righteousness" (Deuteronomy

9:4–5, 13). When the Nephites fell from grace, they kept right on building and adorning their churches and prospering greatly, "and from that time forth they did have their goods and their substance no more common among them" (4 Nephi 1:25). Though one may prosper under other schools of economy, that is not the way the Lord wants it, and the Nephites were preparing themselves for the wars of extinction that lay ahead.

One may refuse to accept the law of consecration without offense, but having once accepted it, one must follow its principles or fall under the condemnation of God. "Inasmuch as some of my servants have not kept the commandment, but have broken the covenant, . . . I have cursed them with a very sore and grievous curse" (D&C 104:4). Their acceptance of the covenant was only with feigned words, while they followed the way of covetousness. It is vain to rationalize and make special cases, for "none are exempt from this law who belong to the church" (D&C 70:10). Much economic sophistry has gone into evading the terms of this agreement, and it was on this point that the Prophet said, "Those who limit the designs of God as concerted by the grand council [of heaven] cannot obtain the Knowledge of God & I do not know but I may say they will drink in the Damnation of their souls."[57] Satan concentrates his efforts on this particular objective, using covetousness as his infallible weapon. Sex runs a very poor second in the race with greed when it comes to corrupting the hearts of men and turning them away from God, as we learn in the Enoch literature. When the Saints were told "to prepare and organize [themselves] by a bond or everlasting covenant that cannot be broken," they were also told that "otherwise Satan seeketh to turn their hearts away from the truth, that they become blinded and understand not the things which are prepared for them" (D&C 78:10–11). And when the Brethren engaged in what they considered shrewd financial practices, the Lord spoke, "Let them repent of all their sins, and of all their covetous desires, . . . for what is property unto me? saith the Lord" (D&C 117:4). As to the properties in Kirtland—let them go! "Have I not made the earth? Do I not hold the destinies of all the armies of the nations of the earth? Therefore, will I not make solitary places . . . to bring forth in abundance? . . . Is there not room enough on the mountains . . . or the land where Adam dwelt, that you should covet that which is but the drop?" (D&C 117:6–8). The Lord ends this admonition with a stinging rebuke: Let them "be ashamed of . . . all their secret abominations, and of all [their] littleness of soul before me" (D&C 117:11).

Prayer

Prayer is designed to bring about a perfect union of minds and concentration of intelligence on a single object.[58] In the direst straits, the Saints are told they can overcome if they "remain steadfast in [their] minds in solemnity and [in] the spirit of prayer" (D&C 84:61). This steadfastness requires that intense concentration and unity of thought on which the Egyptians placed such store in their temples; indeed, they felt that the continued existence of the universe itself somehow depended on unflagging mental effort on the part of those whose awareness made it a reality.

Everyone is aware that the power of thought is important on solemn occasions; but it is also demanding and exhausting, and most of the cults have traditionally taken an easier way, urging the mind to go all out by mind-altering drugs—by peyote, mushrooms, opium, marijuana, etc.; by tantric spells, yoga, drums, incense, dancing, chanting to the heavy beat; and by even more dignified procedures like pageantry, lights, vestments, temple bells, incense, litanies, spectacles, and pomp and circumstance. These have, as John Chrysostom pointed out long ago, a definite narcotic effect, no matter how mild. He warns against even statuary and paintings in the churches as at best distractions. Edward Lytton's once-famous novel *Zanoni* gives a vivid picture of the extremes to which such shenanigans can be carried—he is writing particularly of the Masons.[59] But the spirit of the gospel is intelligence, and nothing is more important than the preservation of perfect sobriety throughout, so that any manifestations that should occur may not be attributed to tricks or narcotics.

There have been many manifestations in the temples, but one does not expect them as the order of the day. Heavenly visitors have always been few and far between, for the purpose of our being here is to test us when we are left on our own. The founders of the dispensations have a virtual monopoly on the major visitations. And that is as it should be. One comet in a hundred years is quite adequate to prove beyond a doubt that comets really exist; it is not necessary to repeat their visitations every month. So the Prophet can tell the people, "I testify that no man has power to reveal it, but myself, things in heaven, in earth and in hell—and all shut their mouths for the future."[60] Do we need more? Yes, the testimony of Jesus Christ, which is available to everyone on demand.

The Sanctity of Sacred Things

To reveal sacred things is to hold their true value in contempt, to despise and throw away the endowment, the only plan ever offered mankind for eternal happiness. "There is a superior intelligence bestowed upon such as obey the Gospel . . . which, if sinned against, the apostate is left naked and destitute of the Spirit of God, and he is, in truth, nigh unto cursing."[61] They who turn away from the covenants "become as much darkened as they were previously enlightened, and then, no marvel, if all their power should be enlisted *against* the truth."[62] "He that will not receive the greater light, must have taken away from him all the light which he hath; and if the light which is in you become darkness, behold, how great is that darkness!"[63]

This was exactly the situation of the infamous "Watchers"[64] in the time of Enoch. When "the works of darkness began to prevail among all the sons of men," a sort of crash-program was undertaken to stem the tide of apostasy, as "the Gospel began to be preached . . . by holy angels sent forth from the presence of God," as well as earthly ministers (Moses 5:55, 58). According to the very ancient, firmly established, and widely documented tradition, some of those angels who came down to call men to repentance as "Watchers"—to oversee and report conditions on earth—allowed themselves to be seduced by the daughters of men, forgot their calling, and fell from grace. Their unspeakable sin was to use the sacred in an unhallowed connection, even as Cain did, claiming that since they had all the ordinances, their activities were authorized of heaven. A general principle is stated in the *Zohar,* and with equal clarity by Joseph Smith, that "whenever the Holy One . . . allowed the deep mysteries of wisdom to be brought down into the world, mankind were corrupted by them and attempted to declare war on God."[65] Thus the Watchers "used the great knowledge entrusted to them to establish an order of things on earth in direct contradiction of what was intended by God: 'There will be false priesthoods in the days of Seth,' Adam prophesied, and 'God will be angry with their attempts to surpass his power.'"[66] "The angels and all the race of men will use His name falsely, for deception." "Woe unto you who . . . pervert the eternal covenant, and reckon yourselves sinless!" was said of them.[67] "Their ruin is accomplished because they have learnt all the secrets of the angels";[68] "they have received the ordinances, but have removed themselves from the way of life." "In the days of my fathers," says Enoch, "they transgressed . . . from the Covenant of Heaven, . . . sinned and betrayed the *ethos* [law of the gospel]; . . . they also married and bore children, not according to the spiritual order, but by the carnal order only."[69] "Woe unto you who . . . lead many astray by [your] lies, . . . who twist the true accounts and wrest the eternal covenant, and rationalize that you are without sin."[70] The punishment of the watchers, like that of Cain, was to be rejected by both heaven and earth, and there are many accounts of how their great leaders remained suspended, hanging between heaven and earth (in the Book of Mormon fashion; cf. Alma 1:15) until the day of judgment.

The endowment is either the real thing or it is nothing, and if it is real or if I accept the probability that it is, I cannot compromise in the least degree. *Inter finitum et infinitum non est proportio*—eternal life is an all-or-nothing proposition; one does not arrange to enjoy a brief stay in eternity or to bask in the transient glory of a special-effects heaven.

It has been a subject of wonder to students of ancient religion how well the secrets of the old mysteries were kept, though they were the heart of the religious experience and dominated thought and action, and though every important person in late antiquity was initiated into the mysteries, yet to this day the literature has given no certain account of what went on. There is constant reference to them in the drama, both tragic and comic, and in poetry (Pindar) and especially in Plato. But it is always discreetly veiled: "He who has ears to hear, let him hear!" In the celebrated cases when the doings of the mysteries were exposed in tipsy or playful carouse, as in the case of Alcibiades, the outcome was disastrous and the guilty parties discredited for life.[71] Actually, in revealing sacred things one gives away nothing but one's own integrity, though that is everything. It is significant that none of the "frightful disclosures" of the temple ordinances made in the sensational literature of the nineteenth century had the expected impact—they all fizzled, as indeed they must, since to one who does not understand their significance, these sacred things have no interest at all.

In those cases where secrecy and mystification are almost the whole stock and trade of a secret society or lodge, it is understandable that much should be made of it. In the Old Kingdom of Egypt during a revolution, "the King's Secret," which gave him his authority and power, was exposed to common view, whereupon the kingdom collapsed. For it turned out that the awesome king's secret was that there was no secret! It had been lost.

The Veil of the Temple

Throughout the ancient world, the veil of the temple is the barrier between ourselves and both the hidden mysteries of the temple and the boundless expanses of cosmic space beyond. An example of the former is "the veil of Isis," which no man has lifted,[72] and of the latter is the veil that hangs across the back of the last chamber in the Egyptian temple, beyond which lie eternity and the worlds beyond. The Jewish literature often mentions the veils between the worlds,[73] and the book of Moses clearly recalls the tradition of the book of *Enoch:* "Millions of earths like this . . . would

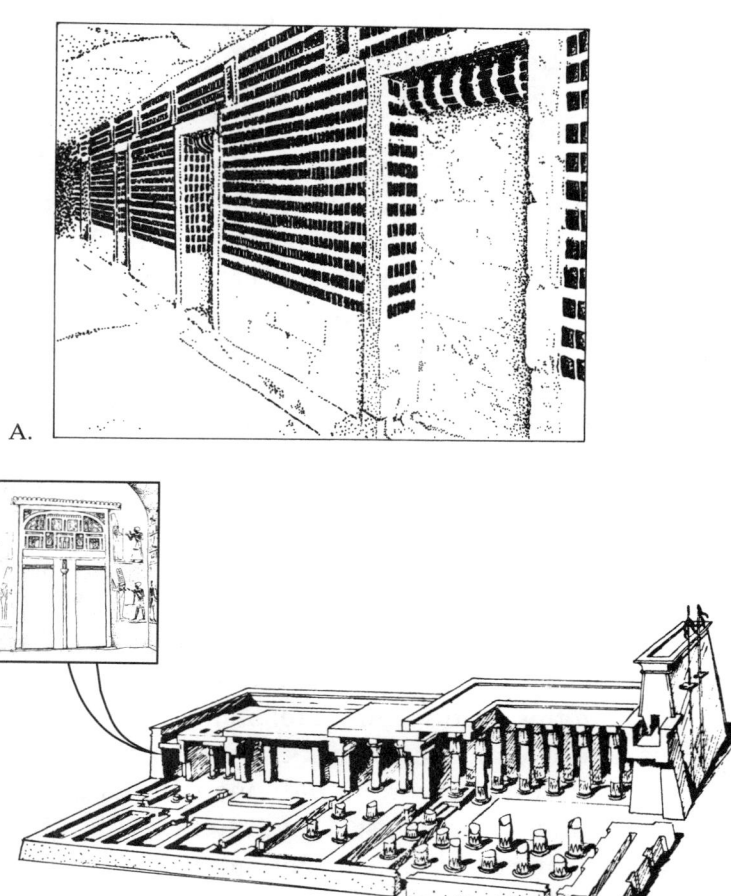

Figure 46. Deep under his southern tomb, Djoser had his artists create a replica of a rolled reed mat (A) used as a door covering in imperishable stone and glazed tile. This "spirit door" served as a symbolic entrance into the next world, such as this doubled version in the temple Seti I built for Osiris at Abydos (B). The most sacred of the temple ceremonies were performed in front of this so-called "spirit door," the rolled-up veil dividing this world from the next.

not be a beginning to the number of thy creations; and thy curtains are stretched out still" (Moses 7:30).

In the ancient temples, the partition is a veil rather than a wall, to show that it is not absolutely impenetrable and that messengers can pass through it, that dim sights and distant sounds might be detected, that we are not wholly cut off from our heavenly home unless we choose to be. The idea is set forth in a passage well known to Latter-day Saints: "The veil was taken from our minds, and the eyes of our understanding were opened" (D&C 110:1), and this while standing before the real veil.[74] It is the place of *signum et responsum* to establish the identity and *bona fides* of one who wishes to pass. We find it in the oldest Egyptian and Babylonian texts, and it plays an important part in the Egyptian funerary literature and especially in Facsimile 2 to the book of Abraham. In the Shabako text, the oldest of all religious writings, the hero in the first step of his progress passes through the veil after answering the questions and goes on to be received into the arms of his father and mount his throne.

Early in this century, Sir Aurel Stein discovered some graves in a seventh-century cemetery. In one of the tomb chambers, two veils were found, one still hanging suspended from wooden pegs;[75] they were near life size and showed the king and queen in a formal embrace at the veil, the king holding up the square on the right side and the queen holding the compass on the left. Located at the navel was the sun as the center of the system, from which twelve spokes extended to the white dots in the circle, indicating the twelve-month course of the year, or the life cycle. At the side of the two intertwined figures appears the Big Dipper. It was at once recognized that the scene represents the sacred marriage of the king and queen at the New Year, celebrating the new age and inaugurating the new life cycle

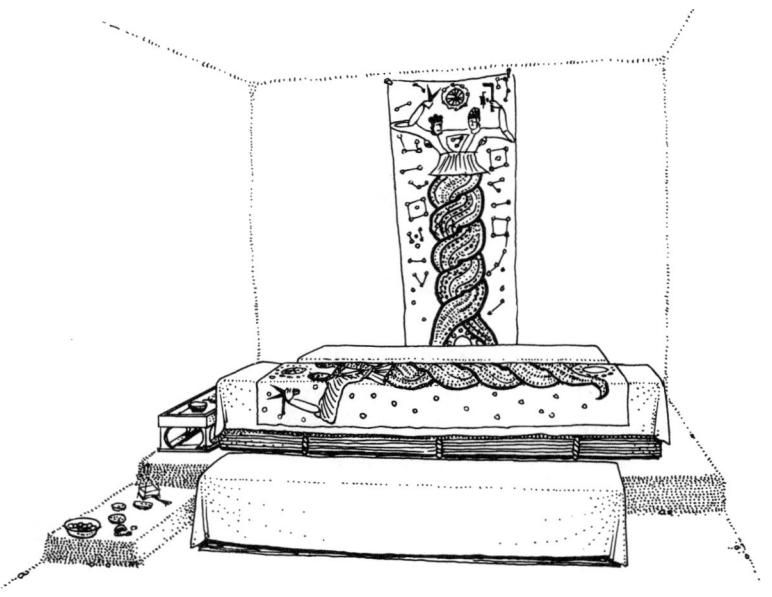

Figure 47. Though Fan Yen-Shih accepted a Buddhist name and was praised as a good Confucian bureaucrat, he also included Taoist paintings of the First Ancestors. Fu Hsi on the right holds a square, and his sister/wife Nü-wa holds up a compass. The encircling constellations place them at the time of creation when she drew the circle of Heaven and he ruled the four-cornered earth.

with the drama of creation. The compass and square are viewed as the instruments marking out both the pattern of the universe and the foundations of the earth.[76]

The Archaic Order

One can easily detect familiar echoes of the endowment in religious institutions and practices throughout the world. The phenomenon is readily explained by Joseph Smith; and students of comparative religion have now come around to the same conclusion, namely, that the real endowment has been on earth from time to time and has also been spread abroad in corrupted forms so that fragments from all parts of the world can be traced back to common beginnings. "It is reasonable to suppose," wrote Joseph Smith, "that man departed from the first teachings, or instructions which he received from heaven in the first age, and refused by his disobedience to be governed by them."[77] "But . . . man was not able himself to erect a system or plan with power sufficient to free him from a destruction which awaited him"; hence it was necessary to put him on the track again, as "from time to time these glad tidings were sounded in the ears of men in different ages of the world."[78] "Certainly God spoke to [Abel]: . . . and if He did, would He not . . . deliver to him the whole plan of the Gospel? . . . And if Abel was taught of the coming of the Son of God, was he not taught also of His ordinances?"[79] The cosmic connection is never missing from this archaic knowledge, as is well known today, and the Prophet wrote, "For our own part we cannot believe that the ancients in all ages were so ignorant of the system of heaven as many suppose."[80] He then went on to show how Abraham too had the endowment.[81] For the Prophet Joseph, the patriarchal priesthood was "this 'holy order' of parents and children back to Adam."[82] "The endowment you are so anxious about you cannot comprehend now, nor could Gabriel explain it to the understanding of your dark minds."[83]

Because of the inevitable tendency of men to stray "as the sparks fly upward" (Job 5:7), the tradition has been contaminated. Thus, according to Joseph Smith, "Free Masonry, as at present, [is] the apostate endowments, as sectarian religion [is] the apostate religion."[84] Some surviving institutions, including the "old Catholic Church,"[85] are deserving of respect, though without authority. "Bro Joseph ses

Masonry was taken from the Preasthood, but has become degenrated, but menny things are perfect [*sic*]."[86]

In view of all this, it is instructive to view particular cases in which the most impressive survivals of the old endowment shine through clearly; usually it is those things which appear to conventional religion and scholarship incongruous, meaningless, or absurd. The Old Testament itself is full of such things.

Traces in the Old Testament

There is no need to look hard in Genesis, for the story of Adam is the endowment. However, in recent years, a large corpus of early Adam texts has come forth in which the endowment theme is paramount. A better example to illustrate the pervasive nature of the theme is the case of Noah, which parallels that of Adam in a remarkable way.

The Case of Noah

In Genesis 7:7–9, Noah registered the animals two by two, even as Adam named them. From then on, like Adam (see Moses 3:19–20), Noah lived intimately with the animals (Genesis 7:16; 8:1). After the Flood, Noah found himself in a new world (see Genesis 7:23–8:19), even as Adam did before and after the Fall. In this new world, God commanded every form of life to "be fruitful, and multiply upon the earth," just as in Eden (Genesis 8:17). After the Flood, Noah found himself in a lone and desolate world (Genesis 7:23), and, like Adam, proceeded to build an altar, sacrificing every clean beast and fowl (see Genesis 8:20). God accepted the sacrifice and promised that the perennial cycle of life, like the course of the spheres, would continue henceforward (see Genesis 8:21–22). Like Adam's offspring, Noah's promptly departed from righteousness, "for the imagination of man's heart is evil from his youth; neither will I again smite . . . every thing living" (Genesis 8:21).

After having commanded the creatures to multiply, God gave the same order to Noah that he gave to Adam—to have dominion and be responsible for the felicity of those creatures (see Genesis 9:1–2). Meat was added to Noah's diet, as grain was to Adam's (who had been a fruit gatherer in the garden), but only to be used sparingly (see Genesis 9:3–4). There is to be no enmity between man and beast, or between man and man. For just as surely as one man sheds the blood of another, another man will shed his blood (cf. Genesis 9:6). This is not a commandment to avenge blood, but a warning against the cycle of blood and horror, the eternal vendetta with which Satan rules the world. The law of Moses sought to check it by cities of refuge and mandatory cooling-off periods (see Numbers 35:11). The shedding of blood is a mortal offense to the earth itself (see Genesis 9:4–5), for her purpose is to "bring forth abundantly"; and to take life is to reverse the order for which the earth was created (see Genesis 9:7; Moses 7:48). In making this covenant with Noah and his posterity (see Genesis 9:11), God set up a sign (oath), a sign visible in the distance (see Genesis 9:12–17), visible to both parties in the covenant and for the benefit of "every living creature" (Adam's "every form of life"; Genesis 9:15). For God is considerate of every living creature and of all living flesh that is upon the earth (see Genesis 9:13–17).

Even as Adam's "sons and daughters . . . began to divide two and two in the land" (Moses 5:3), so the sons of Noah spread across the earth to populate it while Noah, exactly like Adam, takes to gardening (see Genesis 9:20). He celebrated the most ancient of all recorded festivals, the wine feast of intoxication that celebrates the ending of the

Flood.[87] Noah, like Adam, enters his new world clothed with a special garment, which garment enjoys a conspicuous place in the ancient literature. Genesis 9:23 tells us that Shem and Japheth took the garment and both tried it on; then they returned and put it back on Noah, being careful to look away. In a wealth of very old texts, this is identified both as the garment of skins given to Adam upon leaving the garden and the garment which gave him priesthood and kingship over all creatures.[88] When Ham wore the garment, the animals, seeing it, did obeisance to him, thinking that his was the same priesthood and kingship as Adam. And thus he deceived them and introduced the false priesthood into the world.

The Case of Jacob

It was at Beth-el, the house of God, that Jacob had his vision, set up his stone circle and altar, and received the promise of progeny that was given to Abraham as well as a title to the promised land; he declared the place to be very special, "none other but the house of God, and this is the gate of heaven" (Genesis 28:17). There he made the covenant that his children thereafter made at the temple, that he would pay a tithe if God would give him this life's necessities and grant that he return again to the presence of his Father (see Genesis 28:20–22). According to the *Zohar*, Abraham had been through all this before at the same place, where later Jacob made a covenant with Laban in the same manner: Let us make a covenant between us, properly recorded and notarized (cf. Genesis 31:44). So Jacob took a stone and set it up as a pillar, while his brethren made a stone circle there and had a feast (cf. Genesis 31:45–46). The covenants and bonds were completed: This stone witnesses in the middle between you and me today, says Laban (cf.

Genesis 31:48), the middle being that of the circle in which each party claimed a half (see 2 Samuel 2:13–15). "Therefore was the name of it called Galeed" (*Gal-ed,* the circle of the sign or token—Genesis 31:48). Then Jacob made a sacrifice and held a feast on the mountain, and they spent all night in the camp (see Genesis 31:54)—anticipating Sinai. The next morning Laban went his way, but Jacob had a strange experience—his covenant was no longer to be with a man: Angels were in the place, and when he saw them he said, God's camp must be here (cf. Genesis 32:1–2). Next comes his wrestling with the Lord, which so perplexed the Doctors that they changed the Lord to an angel, but "when one considers that the word conventionally translated by 'wrestled' (*yeaveq*) can just as well mean 'embrace,' and that it was in this ritual embrace that Jacob received a new name and the bestowal of priestly and kingly power at sunrise"[89] (cf. Genesis 32:24–30), the dawn of a new day, there is plainly more here than the Doctors perceived.

Jacob represents here the figure of Adam, the primordial man, and "the place where the dream of Jacob occurred is the place where Adam was created, namely, the place of the future Temple and the centre of the earth."[90] "And Jacob called the place Peniel, because I have seen Eloheim face to face and my spirit [*nefesh,* soul] has been saved [survived]." At that moment, the sun rose as he crossed the water Penuel, limping on his thigh (cf. Genesis 32:30–31).

Later Jacob was instructed to resume operations on the site of the temple (Beth-el), settling there and making an altar to the God who had appeared to him and delivered him from the hand of Esau (see Genesis 35:1). He was to establish a holy society, a little Zion on the spot, instructing all his people to renounce the alien gods, wash themselves and change their garments (see Genesis 35:2). Then they were ready: "Let us arise and go up to the house of the Lord, and there I will make a sacrifice to the God who answered me in the day of my distress" (cf. Genesis 35:3). There seemed to be repetitions of this altar building and sacrificing, always for the same reason—at a place where God had appeared and saved Jacob; the same commandments are given to him as were to Adam and Abraham on like occasions (see Genesis 35:7, 9–12).

According to a study of Altmann, Jacob actually repeats the entire experience of Adam, being visited by heavenly messengers who instruct him in the ordinances. The sleeping Jacob is "Adam who has forgot his image," for "in his earthly existence, Jacob, who stands for Man, is sunk into sleep, which means he has become forgetful of his image and counterpart upon the Divine Throne." The visitation repeats the awakening of the preexistent Adam, "as it were, pushed out from the Chariot of the King. He is asleep here below."[91] This is the "Sem-sleep" of the Egyptian temple rites,[92] being pushed from the chariot and being thrust forth from the *Merkavah*, the presence of God or one's heavenly home.

The Case of Adam

In the noncanonical sources, Adam appears in a very different light from the one who ate the fruit—"whose mortal taste brought death into the world and all our woe."[93] A few passages from a large literature must suffice. A reluctant awakening came in our own generation with the discovery of the Dead Sea Scrolls, whose purpose is to prepare a community of pious sectaries for the return of "a true temple to Judah and Israel," and setting forth the nature of that temple and the ordinances and covenants that should go with it. The scrolls show us that the scribes and Pharisees had indeed taken over and changed things at Jerusalem. A new Adam emerges in the much older text, leading the Saints to the desert: "For unto you is the wisdom of the Sons of Heaven, to give the perfect way of understanding. For God has chosen them for the eternal covenant, so theirs is all the glory of Adam."[94] "As Adam brought his sacrifice," according to this tradition, "he put on the vestments of the high priest. . . . In the Holy Writ, it is said, 'God created man in his image,' it means [that very] Adam, who was anointed as a high priest, and designated to serve his Maker."[95] "When he [the High Priest, Simeon] put on his glorious robes and clothed himself in perfect splendor," says Ben Sirach, "(then) all flesh hasted together and fell upon their faces to the earth, to worship before the Most High, . . . for his was the glory of *Adam*."[96] The rabbis, on the other hand, insist that the glorification of Adam was "a tragic mistake," in spite of such passages as Psalms 8:6 and Ezekiel 28:12–14, which probably arose from *Christian* "deification of man."[97] It was this Adam of the Jews which appealed to the Christians, who got rid of it when their leaders got the Alexandrian fever. This we see in such transitional works as *2 Enoch*, which tells us that when Satan saw Adam in the Garden, "He understood that I was going to create another world, because Adam was the Lord of the earth to rule and control it; . . . so he attacked him through Eve and seduced her without further trying to tempt Adam."[98] "On the day that Adam went forth from the Garden, he made an offering to the Lord at sunrise, and from that day forth he covered his shame"—this from *Jubilees*, a book claimed by both Jews and Christians.[99]

In the earliest Christian writings, Peter discusses the case of Adam with Clement. "You said the first man was a prophet," says Clement, "but you didn't say that he was anointed. But if he was not anointed a prophet, he could not have been a prophet, could he?" To this Peter answered, smiling, "If the first man prophesied, it is certain that he was anointed, . . . though the scripture does not tell us about that; . . . what you should have asked is how, being the first man, he could have been anointed with the anointing of Aaron, who in this world was the first to receive the anointing of the special priesthood of Aaron after the pattern of the other anointing. . . . He was a leader of the people and as such a priest and a king [*rex primitiarum*]. This was a type of other things." Clement: "Don't try to fool me, Peter, for, of course, Adam was not anointed with *real* oil, but with some pure and eternal oil made by God," etc. Here he falls into the trap that caught all the Christians and Jews thereafter, the obsession with a purely "spiritual" temple. But Peter is not trying to fool him (this is in the playful style of a Platonic dialogue). "And Peter at this appeared indignant: Do you think, Clement, that we can know everything before the time? . . . I can give you the answer, but I shall tell you about these things only when you are ready to hear them!"[100] Among the questions thus postponed was how Clement's dead father and mother were to be saved without having embraced the gospel.

The Case of Enoch

Nothing better illustrates the hostility of the Doctors—Jewish and Christian—to the temple and the endowment than the case of Enoch, whose great prominence in the early scriptures was all but effaced by their efforts.[101] The Enoch literature has been discovered since the middle of the nineteenth century. A consideration of the name and office of Enoch should suffice to show his intimate ties with the endowment.

It is usual to derive the name of Enoch from the root *HNK, meaning basically to taste, hence to test, "to give attention to"; from this is derived, in turn, the idea of teaching or training, designating Enoch as "the first vehicle of . . . the genuine *gnosis*." A related meaning is "to consecrate," making Enoch "the consecrated one, from whom authentic solutions [are] to be expected touching the secrets of this world and the world beyond." This puts the figure of Enoch, A. Caquot avers, in the center of a study of matters dealing with initiation in the literature of Israel, notably the Dead Sea Scrolls. Enoch is a great Initiate who becomes the great Initiator. He is on another level of existence, and his work is to conduct others there. A recent study which declares the Hebrew meaning of the root "unknown" suggests the Canaanitish *khanaku*, "Follower" (*Gefolgsmann*), i.e., in the way of the initiate. The idea was strengthened by "the great role which Enoch plays in Qumran," with its impressive "prophetic initiation." The old Hebrew book of *Enoch* bore the title of *Hekhalot*, referring to the various chambers or stages of initiation in the temple. Enoch, having reached the final stage, becomes the Metatron to initiate and guide others. "I will not say but what Enoch had Temples and officiated therein," said Brigham Young, "but we have no account of it."[102] Today we have many such accounts.[103]

The Case of Abraham

Today Abraham is recognized as a pivotal figure in the ordinances of the temple.[104] The theme of Abraham's life is sacrifice (see D&C 132:49–50), and the motive and reward of the endowment is movingly set forth at the beginning of the book of Abraham, in which the desire of his life is to bestow blessings upon his fellowmen, even as God bestows them (see Abraham 1:2; Moses 1:39). Some Jewish scholars today attribute to Abraham rather than to Moses the founding of the ordinances of atonement in the temple.

Apostasy and Restoration

The book of 1 Samuel opens with a temple operating on a full schedule, but soon the indolent and corrupt priests cause a falling off and people stop coming to the temple. Through direct revelation to Samuel, the endowment is restored, but tension between priest and king continues. Another restoration was in order in the time of Josiah. It began with a great purging from the land of all the alien elements that had filtered into the religion of Israel (see 2 Chronicles 34:3). In the process of renovating the temple, the original book of the law was discovered by the High Priest Hilkiah, and from that it was possible to restore the ordinances in their purity, for the record made it clear that Israel had strayed alarmingly from the path (see 2 Chronicles 34:21). Even so, Abraham, after the falling away of his fathers, was able to make a new beginning, "but the records of the fathers . . . God preserved in mine own hands" (Abraham 1:31). It was not Hilkiah, but Josiah, the king, who took complete charge of the operation, as Saul had attempted, thereby incurring the rebuke of Samuel. But Josiah's complete command takes us by remarkable transition into a field of study which has proven most fruitful during the past fifty years, a study in which temple rites are central. The subject is "patternism," and the transition is provided by the Book of Mormon.

Josiah's name marks him as a sponsor of the "Yahwist" reform of the temple. As the Lachish Letters show, there was much opposition to the movement. Josiah was a contemporary of Lehi, who was also on the side of Yahvists at the time when there were "many prophets" in the land (1 Nephi 1:4), meeting with stiff opposition, as did Lehi himself when he took up the cause. When the Nephites went astray as the Jews had, they were fortunate in having a king who was an ardent student of the scriptures—the brass plates—as was Josiah, and who was determined to maintain the observances of the temple. He named his son and successor Mos-iah, thus neatly combining the memory of Josiah with that of the great model he followed, Moses. Lehi followed the Rekhabite example, now so vividly illustrated in the Dead Sea Scrolls, by going out into the desert to preserve the ancient faith and await further revelation; and, shortly after arriving in the new world, Nephi followed the same course, leading his own people away from his apostate brethren into the wilderness, there to build a modest replica of the temple at Jerusalem (see 2 Nephi 5:16). The Rekhabites, as a reward for their faithfulness, were put in charge of the ordinances of the temple (see Jeremiah 35).

King Benjamin not only gathered all the people at the temple for a full-fledged *qāhal* (assembly) in the ancient manner, but also to celebrate the great event in the history in any ancient state—a coronation—when the new king would be acclaimed, and the drama of the creation rehearsed to mark the beginning of a new age of the world and a new life cycle of vegetable life; the contest with the powers of darkness would establish the king as the victorious one worthy to rule the New Age. There are some thirty-six points in which Mosiah's coronation followed the pattern of the ancient year rite or coronation ceremony.[105]

The remarkable uniformity of the great *panegyris* (general or national assembly), as celebrated at many ceremonial complexes throughout the world and throughout history,[106] suggested a probable single point of origin for the institution. The word *patternism,* emerging in the 1930s, calls attention to the remarkable uniformity of the institution and has led to various theories explaining it. A common background is now universally conceded; however, many theories are put forth to explain how and where it originated and how it spread.

One of the striking confirmations of Mosiah's account which was overlooked in the list noted above was the erection of a special wooden tower from which the king addressed the people on the subject of divine kingship. Just such a tower and address are described in Nathan the Babylonian's eyewitness account from the ninth century of the installation of the Exilarch, or ruler of the Jews of the Captivity. Benjamin's great farewell address and the covenanting and feasting that go with it are a clear anticipation of the greatest celebration of all, when the Nephites met at the temple after the great destruction, there to be instructed and endowed by the Lord in person (see 3 Nephi 11–18). An unfailing episode of the year rite everywhere was the combat of the king or hero, representing him with the powers of death and darkness, a theme touched on in the Psalms of David. This combat recalls the Lamech story of bloody rivalry for the kingship and dire betrayals, and also supplies the clue to its universality; for with this ritual extravaganza, "their works were abominations, and began to spread among all the sons of men" (Moses 5:52); "and thus the works of darkness began to prevail among all the sons of men" (Moses 5:55). These are the very rites in which Abraham is entangled at the beginning of the book of Abraham, his own fathers having embraced that perverted version of the endowments. But as if that were not enough, the Prophet Joseph Smith has provided the most enlightening presentation of the drama to be found in literature, and that as early as 1830. Never has man's condition been set forth with greater economy and power than in the primal drama of "everyman" in the first chapter of the book of Moses.

After a magnificent prologue in heaven (see Moses 1:1–8), Moses is left on earth to his own resources; and, just as Satan finds Adam cast out of the garden and desperately calling upon God in a dark world, Satan seizes his foul advantage and strikes again when he finds Moses flat on his back in the dark. He introduces himself as the Only Begotten, the rightful ruler; and when Moses challenges and mocks him, a lively *stichomythia* ("conversation in alternate lines") ensues, ending when Satan drops all virtuous pretense and launches a frontal attack of such ferocity that Moses is quite overwhelmed and cast down; he knows the bitterness of hell (as the king always does in the year drama); crying from the depths with his last ounce of strength, he is delivered. Satan is cast out and Moses is again in the presence of God, who formally declares him the victor over many waters (a stock theme in the year rites), and appoints him the divine king: "For they shall obey thy command as if thou wert God, . . . for *thou* shalt deliver *my people*" (Moses 1:25–26).

The Egyptian Heritage

The Egyptian rites in which Abraham found himself involved are richly documented, but no other writing can compare in importance with the oldest known book in the world, a text prepared for the presentation of the endowment on the occasion of the founding of the First Dynasty in Egypt, that of Menes, a drama, staged in the temple of Memphis for its dedication and the king's coronation more than five thousand years ago. "The impact of the Memphite theology was so fundamental," writes Louis V. Žabkar,

> that its effect and influence on Egyptian religious thought remained constant until the end of the Egyptian religion. Unparalleled in the history of the ancient Orient as far as its *cosmogonic* signification is concerned, it traveled from century to century, from one theological system to another; its theme resounds from the first line of Genesis, and from there on through the Old Testament and to the latest period of Hebrew literature, it reaches the pages of the New Testament, witnessing to what extent this conception of the creative power of the Word of God persisted in the ancient Orient, becoming a universal theological theme.[107]

It begins (cols. 3–4) with the Council in Heaven at the foundation of the world and proceeds to tell of the choosing of the Only Begotten to inherit and preside; of the rejection of the counterclaims of Seth, who argues priority in age; and of the establishing of the ordinances of the temple, central to which is a baptism representing death and resurrection (cols. 7–19). The center part of the text has been destroyed, but the extensive latter part is a doctrinal treatment of the plan of creation and salvation. All hail the plan of the Most High God presented to the Council; he plans and executes as he conceives in his heart and utters with his tongue his plan to be approved by the assembled hosts of the gods and preexistent spirits (cols. 53–54, 57). Every living thing is invested with his divine power, shared by "gods, mortals, beasts, all creeping things and other forms of life" (col. 54). Man is spiritually begotten and physically formed, the future ruler of the earth, endowed with eyes to see, ears to hear, a nose to smell, etc. (col. 56). The earth being prepared with all good things to receive him, a law is given to implement and explain the purpose of the earth as a place of probation: "All who do good will be for eternal life, and all those who do evil for eternal bondage. This law is to be the measure of all things"—it is the purpose of all man's actions of earth (col. 57). "And God finished his work . . . and was pleased with it" (col. 59). The heavenly plan was then implemented and carried out on earth as messengers came down and men were instructed to build temples where they could rehearse this same creation story at the beginning of each year, and as fields and cities sprang up around these holy centers (cols. 59–61). Then comes the episode of Osiris, who nearly dies but is rescued from the depths at the last moment and revived as the resurrected one. Emerging (like Moses) triumphant over the waters, he proceeds to the veil and beyond "in the footsteps of his father, the Lord of Eternity, to the great throne," where he is received with happy homecoming and is embraced by the heavenly family; the Ancient of Days takes him into his embrace and conducts him to his throne (cols. 62–64).

One neglected source that richly deserves study and has been widely hailed as the greatest of all dramas is the two Oedipus plays of Sophocles, which the scholars also denounce as amoral and nonsensical, since they simply can't see the point of any of it. The second play, *Oedipus at Colonus*, is nothing less than an introduction to the mysteries to which the preceding play is a preparation. On request we would gladly pursue this noble work, but time and place will not allow it here.[108]

Loss of the Endowment

Man, forever falling short of the fullness of his promise, never completely lives up to the blessings of the endowment. Adam blessed his posterity, said Joseph Smith, because "he wanted to bring them into the presence of

God"; likewise "Moses sought to bring the children of Israel into the presence of God, through the power of the Priesthood, but he could not. In the first ages of the world they tried to establish the same thing; and there were Eliases raised up who tried to restore these very glories, but did not obtain them." For this glory is to be revealed only in "the dispensation of the fullness of times."[109] Apparently the endowment has been more than humanity can handle: "If the Church knew all the commandments, one-half they would condemn through prejudice and ignorance."[110]

The Perplexity of the Jews

The rabbis, who hold no priesthood but only certificates of learning, have always had an ambivalent attitude towards the temple. They cannot but echo the reverence and yearning of the prophets for it, yet the idea of the return of a real temple repels them as both dangerous and naive. E. Goodenough has found that among the Jews of the Graeco-Roman world "have survived a great number of archaeological remains covered with pagan symbols which quite amaze one familiar with the accepted traditions of Judaism." The rabbis like that as little as they do the disclosures of the Dead Sea Scrolls, and "no attempt has yet been made to analyze the material to see what sort of Judaism could have produced them."[111] Jacob Neusner has expressed the embarrassment of the rabbis in a recent study in which he reports that "in the case of early Rabbinic Judaism, . . . we have a considerable corpus of laws which prescribe the way things are done but make no effort to interpret what is done. These constitute ritual entirely lacking in mythic, let alone theological, explanation."[112] That is, no explanation whatever is offered for the ancient temple ordinances.

Though fully one-third of the Mishnah is taken up with

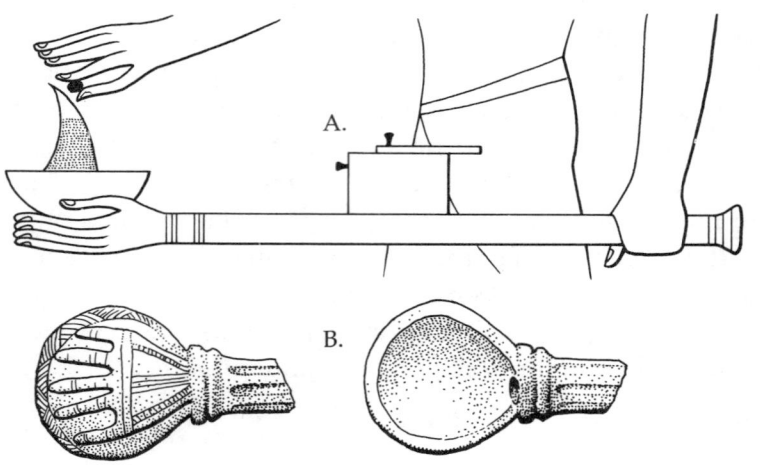

Figure 48. The "golden spoons" of Exodus 25:29 were used to burn incense. They frequently took the form of a cupped hand, such as this Egyptian example (A) of Beni Hasan (c. 1100 B.C.), and this Semitic example (B) from Megiddo.

temple ordinances, none of the rabbis who wrote it (third century B.C. to third century A.D.) ever participated in such a ritual. For them the acts performed in the temple "bore no more concrete relevance to everyday life than did the cultic laws"; they spent their days in a "most serious effort . . . to create a corpus of laws to describe a ritual life which did not exist."[113] "The ritual [itself] is myth," Neusner insists, "in the sense that it was not real, was not carried out"; therefore "the explanation of the ritual . . . is skipped. . . . We deal with laws made by people who never saw or performed the ritual described by those laws."[114] Neusner gives as an example the imitation killing of the red cow as if it were in the Temple; in this ordinance, "the effort is [made] to replicate the Temple's cult in every possible regard."[115] It is performed on the Mount of Olives facing the temple, so that everything that is done is a mirror image of the real thing with the right and left hands reversed. In the real temple, the priest, gird up with his robe, "slaughtered with his right hand, and received the blood in his left."[116] "The sprinkling of the blood . . . [thus] accomplishes atonement, or *kapporah*."[117] The hand is held in such a manner as to hold the blood, as it holds the oil in the anointing.

While everything is thought of as "converging upon, and emanating from, the Temple," it is now only "metaphysical reality; . . . the rabbis think about transcendent issues primarily through rite and form."[118] Likewise, "what people are told to do is what they are supposed to think"— think of themselves as performing the rite, but never trying to interpret it.[119] The teachers of an early day explained that in the temple, "attentiveness leads to ritual cleaning," which leads in turn to washing and anointing, which leads to holiness, hence to humility, hence to fear of sin, hence to piety, hence to the Holy Spirit, and finally to the resurrection of the dead, which culminates in the figure of Elijah. What does all this pointing to the resurrection and to Elijah have to do with the temple? Nothing at all, says Neusner, but such a sequence may suggest significant connections to a Latter-day Saint.

The Temple Scroll

The newly discovered *Temple Scroll,* one of the Dead Sea Scrolls, has focused the attention of the Jews on the temple from new and unfamiliar angles. Jacob Milgrom, who like Neusner has visited Brigham Young University from time to time, has studied this scroll exhaustively. He informs us that, according to its authors, "the entire Scroll was the speech of God."[120] It begins with the covenant with Moses on Mount Sinai, which is where the children of Israel are introduced to the endowment; "the Scroll affirms that a

Temple must exist in the land (Exodus 25:8–9) and that its blueprint . . . was known to David." Understandably, this is an embarrassment to the Jews of present-day Israel—what about the temple now? The *Temple Scroll* points out that the temple is placed on earth at various levels of perfection: The First House was not the Second House or, of course, "the messianic Temple which God Himself will build on 'the Day of Blessing.'" But in all temples at all times, the *ordinances* remain ever the same, though with the growing perfection of the Saints, features may be added, such as "the cherubim-*kapporet*, the Urim and Thummim, and the participation of the twelve tribes" in the temple of the last days.[121] Another change in the temple of the last days is the tendency to extend the priestly regimen to the entire people, so that they too become holy, each a priest (cf. Exodus 19:6). Naturally, the rabbis regard the shedding of blood as permanently done away with and attribute the lack of blood sacrifice in Christianity to the following of the Jewish tradition.[122]

The Christian Endowment and Its Loss

The restoration of the gospel in the meridian of times centered wholly around the temple and endowment. As reported in the Gospel of Luke 1:5–6, it begins with a righteous priest and his wife, both direct descendants of Aaron, "walking scrupulously (*amemptoi*) in all the commandments and fulfillment of the covenants (*dikaiomasis*) of the Lord" (author's translation). The language is right out of the Dead Sea Scrolls, where we also find righteous priestly families living the law in its purity and awaiting further revelation. An angel from on high breaks the long, long silence of four hundred years when he appears to the priest while he is ministering at the altar before the Holy of Holies, and tells him that he has come in answer to prayer—just as the angel appeared to Adam at the altar—and that his message is all one of joy and rejoicing. The priest's son will be filled with the Holy Ghost and turn much of Israel back again "to the Lord their God" (Luke 1:16)—it was a restoration of the gospel. The child is coming in the spirit of Elijah to turn the hearts of the fathers to the children, "and the minds of those who did not believe to righteousness," and in so doing, "prepare for the Lord a people properly endowed (*supplied, equipped*)" (Luke 1:17; author's translation). But the fathers and those who did not believe (note the significant use of the past tense), the disobedient spirits of old, are all dead. How can the expected prophet bring a great light "to those who sit in darkness?" How indeed! His office is to baptize, from which certain conclusions are obvious. Zacharias, the priest, was baffled and asked for a sign in the nature of a challenge: "Whereby shall I know this?" (Luke 1:18). In answer to this, the angel identifies himself by name and explains his mission: "I have come to preach the gospel to you" (cf. Luke 1:19). He gives him a sign—to be struck dumb until a certain time, because he did not take the words of the angel seriously.

Today, Roman Catholic scholars see in Matthew 16:18–19 a reference to the temple. It would appear now that the gates of "hell prevailing" has nothing to do with the forces of evil attacking the Church; the express statement is that "the gates of hades will not hold back those who belong to it," for the object [*autēs*] is in the genitive and the antecedent is the Church. Those who belong to the Church cannot be held back. Why so? Because Peter has the keys to the work that will release them—he is authorized to open the gate (see Matthew 16:19). That this deals, as is now recognized, with the mysteries is clear from the next verse, in which the disciples are commanded not to make a word of this known to the world, while from that time on, Jesus Christ [the name appeared in the preceding verse in full for the first time] began to show his disciples how he would be totally rejected by the temple authorities—elders, high priests, and scribes—and be put to death (see Matthew 16:21). When Peter protests and says this is going too far, the Lord rebukes him sharply for taking seriously the things of men rather than the things of God. We are now on a wholly different level.

A theme that runs all through the Gospel of John is the absolute refusal of the Jewish people and their leaders to take literally what Jesus tells them. It is customary to view John as the most "spiritual," philosophical, allegorical, and mystical book of the New Testament. Yet allegory and abstraction were the breath of life to the schools of the day; if Christ's teachings were of that nature, no one would have been in the least offended, yet in no other gospel are the Lord's hearers so puzzled, baffled, offended and angered as in the Gospel of John. What kind of a "Great Teacher" is this, who constantly perplexes and enrages his students?: "From that time many of his disciples went back, and walked no more with him" (John 6:66). For neither did his brethren believe in him (see John 7:5). "Then said the Jews among themselves, . . . what manner of saying is this that he said?" (John 7:35–36). "Have any of the rulers or of the Pharisees believed on him?" (John 7:48). "Why do ye not understand my speech? *even* because ye cannot hear my word. Ye are of your father the devil" (John 8:43–44). "This parable spake Jesus unto them: but they understood not what things they were which he spake unto them" (John 10:6). "And many of them said, He hath a devil, and is mad; why hear ye him?" (John 10:20). Plainly, he was speaking of things which neither the schoolmen of the times, nor the later schoolmen who produced conventional Christian theology, wanted to understand. In his last days with the disciples and his appearances after the resurrection, he taught them the mysteries of the endowment. The Last Supper was at the Passover, and Jesus associated his doings there with the rites of the temple. "Since I am going to prepare a place for you," he told the disciples, "it is proper for me to tell you about it. In my Father's house [the temple] are many *monai* [places where one stops on passing through, the *hekhalot* of the temple or chambers of the temple]. And having prepared a place for you, I will come back and be your *paralemptor* [the technical term for one who guides one through the mysteries], so that you can be where I am, you know the path I am taking" (cf. John 14:2–4). To this Thomas said, "No, we don't know!" (cf. John 14:5). "I am the way, the truth, and the life. You will not get to the Father any other way" (cf. John 14:6)—i.e., other than through the Son.

A large literature, beginning with Acts and including the many Coptic and Hebrew discoveries of recent years, reports that the Lord did return and for forty days instructed the disciples in the doctrine and in the ordinances, conspicuous among which was baptism for the dead.[123] Though the death of Jesus Christ ended sacrifice by the shedding of blood, the Christians were, if anything, more attached to the temple than the Jews.[124] What kind of a temple was it without a shedding of blood? The epistle to the Hebrews explains that Christ became a "merciful and faithful high priest . . . to make reconciliation for the sins of the people" (Hebrews 2:17). He was "faithful . . . as also Moses was faithful" (Hebrews 3:2). "Seeing then that we have as great high priest, that is passed into the heavens,

Jesus the Son of God, let us hold fast the things we have agreed to [or covenants we have taken—*homologias*]" (Hebrews 4:14; author's translation). Every high priest offers sacrifices for sins, and no man taketh this honor upon himself save he were called of God, as was Aaron (see Hebrews 5:1, 4), but Christ is "a priest for ever after the order of Melchisedec" (Hebrews 5:6). For as the Son learned obedience, he *is* to be obeyed (see Hebrews 5:8–9). Paul recognizes that these things are "very hard to teach because you are dull of hearing" (cf. Hebrews 5:11). He mentions baptisms, laying on of hands, resurrection of the dead, and judgment, which are initiatory rites (see Hebrews 6:2). He mentions the supreme penalty: "they crucify to themselves the Son of God afresh, and put him to an open shame," referring to the public divulgence of sacred things (Hebrews 6:6). Armed with hope, the soul is that "which entereth into that [which is] within the veil," where Jesus, "an high priest after the order of Melchizedek" is our *prodromos* (Hebrews 6:19–20). Paul is particularly concerned with making clear to the Jewish converts that there is no real conflict between the Aaronic and Melchizedek priesthoods. The lower priesthood is naturally succeeded by the higher one, the important difference being that the priest himself enters no *horkomosia* ("covenant"), while the higher priesthood is "with a making of covenants" to be a priest forever after the order of Melchizedek; this was "a [*diathēkē*, covenant]" (see Hebrews 7:20–22). This is a high priest "made higher than the heavens" (Hebrews 7:26). Though the "carnal ordinances" lasted only until the time of reformation (see Hebrews 9:10–13), yet the New Testament also requires the shedding of blood, "but where there is a testament, the one making it must necessarily be responsible unto death" (Hebrews 9:16; author's translation). "Almost all things are by the law purged [cleansed] with blood; and without shedding of blood is no remission" (Hebrews 9:22). "Having . . . [the] boldness to enter into the holiest by the blood of Jesus" (Hebrews 10:19), we pass "through the veil, that is to say, his flesh; . . . having our hearts sprinkled from an evil conscience, and our bodies washed with pure water" (Hebrews 10:20, 22). Naturally the theologians have said that this is a passage from a carnal to a purely spiritual order of things, but nothing in Christian tradition nor, in fact, down to the present time is more indisputable than that it was *real* blood and *real* water that were required for sanctification by the new covenant, just as the old was *real* blood and *real* water. This has always been an embarrassment to the churchmen.

The Gnostics

Because of the endowment, the Latter-day Saints have been labeled Gnostics by ministers who have little knowledge of the term. The so-called "Gnostics" are always distinguished in the early days from those possessing the real gnosis—mentioned twenty-seven times in the New Testament. The gnosis was that special "knowledge" which the Lord imparted to the disciples in their secret session. With the death of the last apostle, according to the earliest church historian, Hegesippus, when no one was left who could call them to account, a swarm of pretenders suddenly appeared on the scene, each claiming that he had the true gnosis, especially the ordinances, imparted by the Lord to his disciples after the resurrection.

The Gnostics could get away with that because the church no longer had knowledge of those things. In his great work the *First Principles,* Origen confesses that the church no longer has answers to the terrible questions, nor can one find in the scriptures any account of how such ordinances as baptism, sacrament, and marriage should be performed. Irenaeus, Augustine, and a host of others confirm his admission. The Gnostics enjoyed a brief but sensational advantage until the obvious inadequacy of their claims became apparent. Valentinius, one of the first and most important, got a huge following because he claimed that he could tell "what we were, what we became; where we were, whither we have been cast; whither we hasten, whence we are delivered; what birth is, what rebirth is."[125]

But the Gnostics could only answer the great questions by dematerializing everything, as is clear from *Papyrus Bodmer* LX. Geo Widengren says that the prime teaching of Gnosticism was that "the origin of the material world . . . [was] a result of activity of the evil power,"[126] and "that matter is evil in and of itself; . . . the spiritual, . . . as such is divine."[127] This is exactly what the later church taught. The appeal of the Gnostics lay in their exploitation of traditions and rumors from the Early Church dealing with ordinances. Those teachings and practices which the many Gnostic sects (Epiphanius lists eighty-eight of them) had in common can reasonably be taken as copies of a true original. Just so, the Egyptian ordinances of Pharaoh (which were in fact the main inspiration of the Gnostics) were earnest imitations of the real thing and may give us a very good idea of what the original was like. So the main practices of the Gnostics retain clear echoes of the endowment.

These, according to Widengren, are the soul's progress toward a heavenly home in which it must pass gates and challenges, but enjoys the help of a holy guide. The spirit is going back to his home where his throne, garment, crown (or wreath), and court all await him.[128] To all this light and glory is placed the opposition of Ahriman, of darkness and death, for an evil power created this physical world. There is one sent from heaven to rescue us from the prison of the world, the Savior, often identified with the Primal Man. The poem "The Pearl" brings these ideas together.[129] Typical is the Coptic *Apocryphon of John:* "Through the establishment of the perfect Temple [what the Qumran people were also looking for] Adam can return to God"; also, we learn that Jesus Christ brought all the signs which he taught the Apostles "from the Father out of the House of the Living."[130] Coptic writings such as *1 Jeu* and *2 Jeu* are particularly concerned with signs revealed in the temple in the process of preparing one for the next world. In the *Gospel of Philip*, the three levels of the temple represent three degrees of holiness. Baptism is the holy place, but the Holy of Holies is higher; the former signifies resurrection, but the latter is the marriage covenant, which goes beyond.[131] A time will come when the temple work will be universal;[132] meantime, the rending of the veil signified that the ordinances were now open to all and that no worthy one would be held back.[133]

There are two main centers of Gnostic teaching, the Iranian and the Syro-Egyptian, but in the end it all goes back to the popular traditions of Iran, Widengren concludes,[134] and from it we get the Buddha, Mani, the Imam, the Manichaeans, Bogomils, Cathari, Baptists, Rosicrucians, Bohemists, Masons, Swedenborgians, and others. It is plain that the Gnostic impostors picked up much of their material from the mysteries, and though the subject has been endlessly debated, the question "How do the mystery cults relate to the Gnostics?" remains to this day unanswered, "because there is no generally accepted concept of the Gnosis, while the fundamental features of the Mysteries are also debated."[135] M. P. Nilsson thought that Orphism was about as far back as one could trace the mysteries:

Orphism is the combination and the crown of the manifold religious movements of the archaic period. The development of the cosmogony in a speculative direction, with the addition of an anthropogony which laid the principal emphasis on the explanation of the mixture of good and evil in human nature; the legalism of ritual and life; the mysticism of cult and doctrine; the development of the other life into concrete visibility, and the transformation of the lower world into a place of punishment by the adaptation of the demand for retribution to the old idea that the hereafter is repetition of the present; the belief in the happier lot of the purified and initiated;—for all these things parallels, or at least suggestions, can be found in other quarters. The greatness of Orphism lies in having combined all this into a system, and in the incontestable originality which made the individual in his relationship to guilt and retribution the centre of its teaching.[136]

Hermeticism

Hermeticism was the doctrine that all the wisdom in the world was originally put into the thirty-six books of Thoth or Hermes.[137] The rites were based on these books, and the priest who conducted the Egyptian endowment had to know at least six books of Thoth by heart, those explaining the seals and the sacrifices.[138] Clement of Alexandria, in the most instructive work on the mysteries, calls the well-known Egyptian *Book of the Dead* "hermetic," and attributes it to Thoth.[139]

The idea of an "archaic wisdom," *prisca arcana,* or "primeval revelation," a knowledge of the ancients far in advance of later times, has always intrigued philosophers and theologians. But today it is the scientists who are taking it seriously. Joseph Smith was well acquainted with the idea: "From time to time these glad tidings were sounded in the ears of men in different ages; . . . certainly God spoke to

Figure 49. The ibis-headed Thoth, as god of writing, records the passage of years on the notched palm rib, the hieroglyph for a year, as also shown three times above him in the upper right corner. The palm rib rests on a young tailed frog, which crouches on the *shen* sign of eternity. These three symbols together refer to vast numbers of years—like the seemingly innumerable tadpoles in a pool of water.

[Abel], . . . and if He did, would He not . . . deliver to him the whole plan of the Gospel? . . . And . . . was he not taught also of His ordinances? . . . For our own part we cannot believe that the ancients in all ages were so ignorant of the system of heaven as many suppose."[140] It is interesting that, at the very time Joseph Smith was preparing the things of the endowment, he was most deeply interested in his Egyptian studies.[141] The field of hermetic writings is immense, and the instructions to which it has given rise are almost without number.

Asking Too Much?

The endowment, charged with meaning at every step, demands the closest attention and a brain and intellect that are clear and active. How easily it overloads the circuits as the tired mind takes refuge in dreamland! A School of the Prophets was necessary to prepare the Brethren for their endowments in the first place,[142] and the leaders began to understand only when the veil was taken from their minds. The eyes of their understandings were opened. Brain, intellect, mind, eyes, understanding—it is a strenuous intellectual exercise from first to last. "I advise all," said the Prophet, "to go on to perfection and search deeper and deeper into the mysteries of Godliness."[143] As for himself, "It has always been my province to dig up hidden mysteries, new things, for my hearers."[144] How much easier to relax and fall into a routine increasingly geared to efficiency and the reduction of time and effort.

When we enter the temple, we leave one world and step into another. Conversely, when we leave the temple, we leave one world, sometimes with a sigh of relief, and return to the other. If the Latter-day Saints are going to continue building temples, they must make up their minds as to which world they are going to live in. It should not be hard to decide if only we are willing.

Which Is the Real World?

We are about to learn that we have had it backwards. We do not need the temple experience to tell us what all sages, poets, saints, and everybody else have always known, namely that this world is "weary, stale, flat, and unprofitable," a vale of tears, etc.;[145] and all because everything in it is irrevocably headed for oblivion, as everyone finds out sooner or later. It is an outrage, but everybody accepts it because they have no other choice; but the Latter-day Saints do have another choice, and they may not evade it. Our present version of "the World" is particularly unreal. At present, the most discussed book on the condition of America today is Robert Bellah's *Habits of the Heart: Individualism and Commitment in American Life*.[146] Bellah and his wife gave some enlightening talks at Brigham Young University some years ago and appreciate our position better than most. Bellah's book has a number of contributors and is based on interviews with hundreds of Americans. It shows an almost complete absence of "transcendent purpose" in their lives: the enlightened minority differ from the bemused majority only in that "all of them would like to find some meaning to life beyond the next promotion or home improvement." The Harvard sociologist Daniel Bell concludes in the book that only religion can relieve the devastation of this "hedonistic consumerist civilization." "From the boardroom to the bedroom, strategy, technique, self-seeking and the notion of strict contractual obligation have supplanted decency and intimacy, respectively." The most admired writer of our time, Raymond Carver, "distills a bleak vacuity, . . . a sense of something—structure, meaning, purpose—missing." The contributors find only "deepening circles of desolation inscribed by our individualism, . . . our incorrigible self-centeredness." "We have lost our balance," writes one reviewer, "scuttled our cultural traditions that used to offset our individualism; community has atrophied among us and the self grown cancerous." "We do not argue with one another, we do not even share a discourse."

And that is the *real world?* Historically, a strong dose of temple work is the only thing to cure that myopia. Joseph Smith understood perfectly and described vividly the situation in his day in the great epistle to the Elders in Kirtland, emphasizing the immense gap between the two orders of existence:

> Consider for a moment, brethren, the fulfillment of the words of the prophet; for we behold that darkness covers the earth, and gross darkness the minds of the inhabitants thereof—that crimes of every description are increasing among men—vices of great enormity are practiced—the rising generation growing up in the fullness of pride and arrogance—the aged losing every sense of conviction, and seemingly banishing every thought of a day of retribution—the intemperance, immorality, extravagance, pride, blindness of heart, idolatry, the loss of natural affection; the love of this world, and indifference toward the things of eternity increasing among those who profess a belief in the religion of heaven, and infidelity spreading itself in consequence of the same—men giving themselves up to commit acts of the foulest kind, and deeds of the blackest dye, blaspheming, defrauding, blasting the reputation of neighbors, stealing, robbing, murdering; advocating error and opposing the truth, forsaking the covenant of heaven, and denying the faith of Jesus—and in the midst of all this, the day of the Lord fast approaching when none except those who have won the wedding garment will be permitted to eat and drink in the presence of the Bridegroom, the Prince of Peace![147]

What a picture he gives of those idyllic far-away times of our national innocence! "The inhumanity and murderous disposition of this people! It shocks all nature; it beggars and defies all description; . . . too much for human beings; it cannot be found among the heathens. . . . It cannot be found among the savages of the wilderness."[148]

What is more, he knows that things are only going to get worse;[149] back in 1835, he announced that "the Lord declared to His servants, some eighteen months since, that He was then withdrawing His Spirit from the earth; and we can see that such is the fact. . . . The governments of the earth are thrown into confusion and division; and *Destruction*, to the eye of the spiritual beholder, seems to be written by the finger of an invisible hand, in large capitals, upon almost every thing we behold."[150] The extremists take over[151] and the ambitious corporations prevail—for even they are not forgotten in the prophecies.[152] When "the whole earth groans," who is to be trusted in such a world? "The world always mistook false prophets for true ones," said Joseph;[153] and he noted that loyalty oaths and protestations are actually signals of desperation and mistrust.[154] There is no help in politics: "My feelings revolt at . . . having anything to do with politics."[155] In the end, any solution given "without revelation, without commandment, . . . would prove a curse."[156]

"A man's character is his fate," said Heraclitus—the tragedy is not what becomes of us, but what we become. Four major steps to success in public life today are things which Joseph Smith insists no one should ever indulge in under any circumstances, namely to (1) aspire, (2) accuse, (3) contend, and (4) coerce. It is striking how these very operations are brought into perspective in the person of Satan, who aspires (that was his undoing, according to Joseph Smith), who accuses (devil; Greek *diabolus* and Hebrew *satan* both mean "accuser")—he becomes an "accuser of his brethren" as he charges his heavenly visitors with trying to rob him of his kingdom and greatness. He contends even with the Lord, and even in the garden; indeed, "the spirit of contention is not of me, but is of the devil" (3 Nephi 11:29). As to coercion, his trump card is to buy up military might and rule the earth with shocking violence.

An Urgent Call

The Prophet foresees the total collapse of world order,[157] with a sore vexing of the nations,[158] as "the adversary spreadeth his dominions, and darkness reigneth; and the anger of God kindleth against the inhabitants of the earth; and none doeth good, for all have gone out of the way" (D&C 82:5–6). The Old Testament ends with the best-known passage of scripture about the endowment (Malachi 4:5–6) and on a note of grim foreboding: "Remember ye the law of Moses my servant, which I commanded unto him in Horeb for all Israel, with the statutes and judgments" (i.e., covenants, terms of endowment—Malachi 4:4). These are to be revived at a time of great crises: "Behold, I will send you Elijah the prophet before the coming of the great and dreadful day of the Lord: And he shall turn the heart of the fathers to the children, and the heart of the children to their fathers, lest I come and smite the earth with a curse" (Malachi 4:5–6). By the report that Elijah has already come, we now "may know that the great and dreadful day of the Lord is near, even at the doors."[159] Therein is also hope, for Elijah's coming makes it possible to forestall the curse: How shall God rescue you in this generation? By sending the Prophet Elijah.[160] To those who received their endowments to go forth from Kirtland into the world he said, "The destroying angel will follow close at your heels and . . . destroy the works of iniquity, while the saints will be gathered."[161] "The keys of this dispensation are committed into your hands; and by this ye may know that the great and dreadful day of the Lord is near, even at the doors" (D&C 110:16).

Is the presence of the temple in our midst a guarantee of safety? How often have the Jews made that mistake! For the greater the blessing promised, the greater the penalty and the risk. It was expressly of the endowment that the Lord said, "Of him unto whom much is given much is required; and he who sins against the greater light shall receive the greater condemnation. Ye call upon my name for revelations," but in not heeding them "ye become transgressors; and justice and judgment are the penalty . . . unto my law. . . . When ye do not what I say, ye have no promise" (D&C 82:3–4, 10). God was not pleased with the many Latter-day Saints who had "treated lightly His commands."[162] The discernment of spirits was of primary importance among the gifts and powers of the priesthood precisely because false spirits have been frequently found among the Latter-day Saints.[163] It was failure to live up to covenants made in the temple that got the Saints driven from Kirtland, Missouri, and Nauvoo, as Brigham Young pointedly observed. A week before the martyrdom of Joseph and Hyrum, Brigham wrote, "I preached in the Temple [Kirtland] in the morning, and brother F. D. Richards in the afternoon. . . . The Saints were dead and cold to the things of God."[164]

What is the result of failing to live up to our covenants? It is to be under Satan's influence; there is no other alternative, for you *cannot* "serve two masters" (Matthew 6:24). With the first slip, the sinner begins to put distance between himself and God. Satan instantly took advantage of Adam and Eve's delinquency to alienate them from God. It was he who excitedly called attention to their guilt and urged them to make coverings of fig leaves and to hide themselves. It was *not* to stir them to repentance, but to urge them to try a cover-up, hiding from God and thereby estranging themselves from him. It was the Lord who sought them out and spoiled Satan's game by offering and commanding perpetual repentance. Even so, one who fails to live up to his covenants tries to hide first by looking for loopholes in the language of the endowment. Brigham Young has commented on the futility and hypocrisy of this procedure; there is no way, he observes, by which one can possibly misunderstand or wrest the language of the covenants, no matter how determined one is to do it. We can rationalize with great zeal—and that is the next step—but never escape from our defensive position. Many have noted the strong tendency of Latter-day Saints to avoid making waves. They seem strangely touchy on controversial issues. This begets an extreme lack of candor among the Saints, which in turn is supported by a new doctrine, according to which we have a Prophet at our head who relieves us of all responsibility for seeking knowledge beyond a certain point, making decisions, or taking action on our own.

Adam did well to obey, but he was not to be guided through obedience alone, and heavenly teachers came to explain things to him and to discuss them with him, even as all the patriarchs, prophets, apostles, and people of Israel are invited by the Lord to come and reason with him. One way of seeking immunity from guilty feelings is to take the offensive behind the sanction in extreme conservatism, which is supposed to place one's loyalty beyond suspicion, while one piously denounces others.

Back to the Present World

Those who would discover "what has made this country great" must necessarily appeal to history. But even in the most extensive studies, such as Bellah's, the history examined is both brief and local, all too short and limited to get to the root of the problem. The one solid core of American culture is the Bible, and the theme there is "What will make Israel Great?" The answer is written in every chapter of the Old Testament. The Israelites were to understand that this was not to be viewed as mere tradition or custom. You and each of you are entering upon a solemn covenant this day, here and now: "The Lord made not [only] this covenant with our fathers, but with us, even us, who are all of us here alive this day" (Deuteronomy 5:3). Merely to acknowledge and agree to it is not enough. "O that there were such an heart in them, that they would fear me, and keep all my commandments always, that it might be well with them, with their children for ever!" (Deuteronomy 5:29). Every hour of the day, the covenant (endowment) makes demands upon the individual; it is never out of his mind, especially the first great commandments: "Thou shalt love the Lord thy God . . . with all thy might. And these words, which I command thee this day, shall be in thine heart" (Deuteronomy 6:5–6). And there is to be no cheating; you may not deviate to the right or left (see Deuteronomy 28:14). To hedge, however slightly, in fulfilling obligations under the covenant is an abomination—the one crime God will not tolerate is meanness of spirit (see Deuteronomy 17:1).

But it is worth it. If the people "observe . . . to do all his commandments, . . . the Lord thy God will set thee on high above all nations of the earth"; his people will be overwhelmed with blessings in every possible aspect of life (Deuteronomy 28:1–6). "Your enemies that rise up against you shall be smitten and scattered" (cf. Deuteronomy 28:7), "and your prosperity will be boundless" (cf. Deuteronomy 28:11). But "if thou wilt *not* hearken," curses await you exactly matching the blessings, all in reverse (Deuteronomy 28:15); and these curses will dog you in all your undertakings "until thou be destroyed, and until thou perish quickly" (Deuteronomy 28:20).

As Moses presents the propositions to them one by one to be received by covenant, after each one is given, "All the people shall say, Amen!" (Deuteronomy 27:14–26). And what will they be cursed for? Graven images, holding parents in contempt, removing a neighbor's landmark, taking advantage of a blind person or of strangers, orphans, or widows in court; incest and sexual perversions; striking a neighbor off guard; taking or giving a fee for killing; and finally, "Cursed be he that confirmeth not all the words of this law to *do* them. And all the people shall say, Amen" (Deuteronomy 27:26).

President Kimball, on a great and solemn occasion (the United States Bicentennial), declared himself "appalled and frightened" by the delinquency of the people in keeping just such laws of fairness and justness. He pointed to three grave derelictions: (1) the contempt for the environment, (2) the rule of money, and (3) trust in military might.[165]

And here is another list to match these pervasive evils. Both the older and the younger Nephi list four things that will bring a church or civilization to destruction: "All churches which are built up [1] to get gain, . . . [2] to get power over the flesh, . . . [3] to become popular in the eyes of the world, . . . [4] who seek the lusts of the flesh, . . . must be consumed as stubble" (1 Nephi 22:23). The younger Nephi is just as explicit: "Now the cause of this iniquity of the people was this—Satan had great power, . . . tempting them to seek for [1] power, and [2] authority, and [3] riches, and [4] the vain things of the world" (3 Nephi 6:15). Note that authority and popularity are interchangeable in the two lists, as they should be, for in our world in which the *image* is all, they are virtually indistinguishable. Need we note that these four vices are the things that spell success today, making "lives of the rich and famous" increasingly the envy and ideal of young and old?

Consecration, the Great Stumbling Block

It will be noted that almost all the crimes listed in Moses' catalogue are those of a mean-spirited nature, and this brings us to the acid test of the law of consecration. This embodies the one quality devoid of all meanness, the only thing, Moroni tells us, which can save a people from destruction by making them worthy of saving, and that is *charity* (see Ether 12:33–37). The gifts and promises dealing with the law of consecration are the center of world history. It is the "hierocentric principle." As far back as the record goes, the temple has been the center of world history, the heart and soul of every great nation and civilization, for good or evil. Ours is for good: "We have the revelation of Jesus, and the knowledge within us is sufficient to organize a righteous government upon the earth, and to give universal peace to all mankind."[166] But nowhere else will you find it. What could demand a greatness of soul, a generous hand, and a magnanimous heart more than this one instrument of salvation? Today, many declare with the poet Yeats, "Things fall apart, the center cannot hold, mere anarchy is loosed upon the world." That center, the only one of proven permanence, is the Covenant of Israel, to which our ancestors looked for strength before its restoration in its fullness.

It was when the Saints balked at keeping the law of consecration that the Lord said, "I, the Lord, am not to be mocked in these things. . . . Organize yourselves and appoint every man his stewardship . . . over earthly blessings, which I have made and prepared for my creatures [that means they must be shared!]" (D&C 104:6, 11, 13).

"And it is my purpose to provide for my saints, for all things are mine. But it must needs be done in my own way; and behold this is the way that I, the Lord, have decreed to provide for my saints, that the poor shall be exalted, in that the rich are made low" (D&C 104:15–16). Can there be any doubt that that last was meant to be jarring? It would be hard to find a declaration less calculated to soothe and delight the success-oriented person of today. Admittedly, one living by the law of consecration would be hopelessly out of place in our competitive and acquisitive society. But in the same way that a healthy person would be out of place in an isolation ward or asylum, an honest person would be out of place in a casino or jail, or a chaste person out of place at a sex orgy or porno festival. Should we recommend that they all adjust to their surroundings and not make waves?

"The ordinances must be kept in the very way God has appointed; otherwise their Priesthood will prove a curse instead of a blessing."[167] There is no margin for rationalization or manipulation: "The moment we revolt at anything which comes from God the Devil takes power."[168] One who wants it both ways, as Brigham Young said, must suffer the most excruciating torture on this earth.[169] Because of the basic contradiction, his plans go constantly awry, his projects fizzle, his big idea leads nowhere; no longer does his confidence wax strong in the presence of God.

But can one expect the impossible of ordinary people—to deny the world they live in? We do it every time we proclaim the truth of the First Vision. We used to sing a sentimental song about the First Vision, and then go home to Sunday dinner, back to the comfortable real world. But as Brigham Young kept reminding the Saints, the real world is Zion, the only enduring order of things, the Order of Enoch.[170] The Saints stubbornly refused to see it.[171] For that they were driven from Missouri, where they were to build the great temple of the last days,[172] and continued to be driven from Nauvoo; the Elders did not want to hear of it.[173] Today, as in Brigham's day, we focus our attention on the overthrow of the wicked rather than the sanctification of ourselves: "Do not be too anxious for the Lord to hasten his work. Let our anxiety be centered upon one thing, the sanctification of our own hearts, the purifying of our own affections."[174]

Notes

1. See *Clementine Recognitions* I, 1, in *PG* 1:1207. Cf. Hugh W. Nibley, "The Terrible Questions," in *Temple and Cosmos*, in *CWHN*, 12:336–78.

2. See *Clementine Recognitions* I, 24 and 28, in *PG* 1:1220, 1222.

3. See ibid., I, 52, in *PG* 1:1236; cf. *Mormonism and Early Christianity*, in *CWHN*, 4:103–4.

4. John G. Taylor, *Black Holes* (New York: Avon, 1973), 187–88.

5. *Webster's Third International Dictionary* (Springfield, Massachusetts: G&C Merriam, 1971), 750.

6. *JD*, 2:31; italics added.

7. Ibid., 19:251.

8. *PWJS*, 71, 82.

9. See *WJS*, 214.

10. *PWJS*, 183.

11. *WJS*, 131.

12. Ibid., 212–13.

13. *TPJS*, 237; cf. *HC* 5:1–2 (4 May 1842).

14. *WJS*, 303; cf. D&C 110:12.

15. *WJS*, 304.

16. *TPJS*, 168.

17. Ibid., 237.

18. JST Genesis 14:27–28.

19. *TPJS*, 264.

20. Ibid., 274.

21. *WJS*, 245.

22. See Shaye J. D. Cohen, "The Temple and the Synagogue," in Truman G. Madsen, ed., *The Temple in Antiquity* (Provo: BYU Religious Studies Center, 1984), 154.

23. *Deseret News*, 2 May 1877, 201.

24. See Hugh W. Nibley, "What Is a Temple," in Madsen, *Temple in Antiquity*, 19–37; in *Mormonism and Early Christianity*, in *CWHN*, 4:355–90.

25. *TPJS*, 196.

26. *WJS*, 85.

27. See Jonathan Z. Smith, "The Garments of Shame," *History of Religions* 5 (Winter 1966): 217–38.

28. Cf. Hugh W. Nibley, "The Expanding Gospel," *Brigham Young University Studies* 7 (1965): 3–27; reprinted in *Temple and Cosmos*, in *CWHN*, 12:177–211.

29. See Hugh Nibley, *The Message of the Joseph Smith Papyri, an Egyptian Endowment* (Salt Lake City: Deseret Book, 1975): 260–61, 264, 267–68, 275–76.

30. Eric Chaisson, "The Broadest View of the Biggest Picture," *Harvard Magazine* 84 (January–February 1982): 21–25.

31. See Kenneth Weaver, "Meteorites: Invaders from Space," *National Geographic* 170 (September 1986): 390–418.

32. See Joseph Fielding Smith, *Doctrines of Salvation*, 3 vols. (Salt Lake City: Bookcraft, 1961): 2:69–71.

33. *PWJS*, 5.

34. Ibid.

35. Ibid., 6; cf. Milton Backman, *The First Vision* (Salt Lake City: Bookcraft, 1980), 156.

36. Cf. Hugh Nibley, "The Meaning of the Atonement," in *Approaching Zion*, in *CWHN*, 9:554–614; Hugh W. Nibley, "A New Look at the Pearl of Great Price," *Improvement Era*, 73 (March 1970): 84–94.

37. *TPJS*, 322.

38. Cf. John W. Welch, *The Sermon at the Temple and The Sermon on the Mount* (Salt Lake City: Deseret Book and F.A.R.M.S., 1990), 70–72, 103–4.

39. Cf. Hugh W. Nibley, "Baptism for the Dead in Ancient Times," *Improvement Era*, 51 (1948): 836–38; reprinted in *Mormonism and Early Christianity*, in *CWHN*, 4:109–13.

40. See *The Works of Rabelais*, Book V, Chapters XXXIV–XLVII, 616–39.

41. See Nibley, *Message of the Joseph Smith Papyri*, 110.

42. *Discourse on Abbatôn*, 1a–b, 4a–6a, 9a–13b, in E. A. W. Budge, *Coptic Martyrdoms, etc., in the Dialect of Upper Egypt* (London: British Museum, 1914; reprint New York: AMS, 1977), 225–26, 228–29, 231–35, 474–75, 477–78, 480–83.

43. *Discourse on Abbatôn*, 14a–b, in Budge, *Coptic Martyrdoms*, 235, 483–84.

44. *Oxford English Dictionary*, 2nd ed., 20 vols. (Oxford: Clarendon, 1989), 18:196.

45. See Hans Jonas, *The Gnostic Religion* (Boston: Beacon, 1963), 222–23.

46. See Hugh W. Nibley, "Sparsiones," *Classical Journal* 40 (1945): 515–43; reprinted in *The Ancient State*, in *CWHN*, 10:148–94.

47. See Nibley, *Message of the Joseph Smith Papyri*, 174, 264, 274–75, 277, 281; cf. Nibley, *Mormonism and Early Christianity*, in *CWHN*, 4:37, n. 77.

48. See Hugh W. Nibley, "The Stick of Judah," *Improvement Era*, 56 (1953): 16–17, 38–41, 90–91, 123–27, 150–52, 191–95, 250, 266–67, 331–32, 334, 336, 338, 341, 343–44; reprinted in *Since Cumorah*, in *CWHN*, 8:1–48.

49. See Hugh W. Nibley, "Tenting, Toll, and Taxing," *Western Political Quarterly* 19 (1966): 604; reprinted in *The Ancient State*, in *CWHN*, 10:41; cf. especially nn. 27–28.

50. *TPJS*, 127.

51. *PWJS*, 61.

52. Ibid., 71.

53. Ibid., 72.

54. Ibid., 82.

55. Ibid., 205.

56. *WJS*, 368.

57. Ibid., 245–46.

58. See Hugh W. Nibley, "The Early Christian Prayer Circle," *Brigham Young University Studies* 19 (1978): 41–78; reprinted in *Mormonism and Early Christianity*, in *CWHN*, 4:45–99.

59. Edward B. Lytton, *Zanoni* (New York: Burt, 1885).

60. *WJS*, 369.

61. *TPJS*, 67.

62. Ibid.; italics added.

63. Ibid., 95.

64. Hugh Nibley, *Enoch the Prophet*, in *CWHN*, 2:178–83.

65. Harry Sperling and Maurice Simon, trans., *Zohar*, 5 vols. (New York: Soncino, 1984), 1:257.

66. *Apocryphon of John* 1:73–74.

67. *1 Enoch* 99:2.

68. *1 Enoch* 65:6.

69. *1Enoch* 106:13–17a.

70. *1Enoch* 98:15; 99:2.

71. See Fabio Mora, "I 'Silenzi erodotei,' " *Studi Storico Religiosi* 5 (1981): 209–11, citing Herodotus II, 170; Karl Albert, "Kult und Metaphysik bei Platon," *Studi Storico Religiosi* 5 (1981): 5–14.

72. Plutarch, *de Osiride et Iside*, 9.

73. See Nibley, *Message of the Joseph Smith Papyri*, 245–51.

74. See *PWJS*, 186.

75. See Sir Mark Aurel Stein, *Innermost Asia*, 3 vols. (Oxford: Clarendon, 1930), 2:707; see also Hugh Nibley, "Sacred Vestments," in *Temple and Cosmos*, in *CWHN*, 12:114–15, fig. 28.

76. See Giorgio de Santillana and Hertha von Dechend, *Hamlet's Mill* (Boston: Gambit, 1969), picture and caption facing 273; Nibley, "The Early Christian Prayer Circle," 66–67; in *Mormonism and Early Christianity*, in *CWHN*, 4:73–74.

77. *TPJS*, 57

78. Ibid., 58.

79. Ibid., 59.

80. Ibid., 59.

81. See ibid., 60–61.

82. *WJS*, 304; *TPJS*, 237.

83. *PWJS*, 82.

84. Benjamin F. Johnson, *My Life's Review* (Independence, Missouri: Zion's Printing, 1947): 96.

85. *WJS*, 381–82.

86. Heber C. Kimball to Parley P. Pratt, 17 June 1842, Church Archives.

87. See *Papyrus Leiden* T32; III, 10–20, in Bruno H. Stricker, "De Egyptische Mysterien: Pap. Leiden T32," *Ondheidkundige mededeelingen uit het Rijksmuseum van Oudheiden te Leiden* 34 (1953): 18–19; Hugh W. Nibley, *Abraham in Egypt* (Salt Lake City: Deseret Book, 1981), 154–56.

88. See Louis Ginzberg, *Legends of the Jews*, 7 vols. (Philadelphia: Jewish Publication Society of America, 1946–47), 1:177; *Book of Jasher* 7:24–30; "Nimrod," *Jewish Encylopedia*, 12 vols. (New York: Funk and Wagnalls, 1901–06), 9:309–11.

89. Nibley, *Message of the Joseph Smith Papyri*, 243.

90. Alexander Altmann, "The Gnostic Background of the Rabbinic Adam Legends," *Jewish Quarterly Review* 35 (1944–45): 390–91.

91. Ibid.

92. See Nibley, *Message of the Joseph Smith Papyri*, 146–48.

93. For example, see John Milton, *The Poetical Works of John Milton*, ed. David Masson, 3 vols. (London: Macmillan, 1874), 1:133.

94. 1QS 4:22–23.

95. Alexander Kohut, "Parsic and Jewish Legends of the First Man," *Jewish Quarterly Review* 3 (1891): 239.

96. Ben Sirach 50:11, 16; 49:16; see R. H. Charles, *The Apocrypha and Pseudepigrapha of the Old Testament* (Oxford: Clarendon, 1964), 506, 508, 510.

97. Altmann, "Gnostic Background of the Rabbinic Adam Legends," 387.

98. *Secrets of Enoch* 31:3–6.

99. *Jubilees* 3:27.

100. *Clementine Recognitions* I, 47–48, in *PG* 1:1235.

101. R. H. Charles, *Book of Enoch* (Oxford: Clarendon, 1912), ix.

102. *JD*, 18:303.

103. See the references in Hugh Nibley, "The Enoch Figure," in *Enoch the Prophet*, in *CWHN*, 2:19–20, 56.

104. See Nibley, "New Look at the Pearl of Great Price," 163–65.

105. See Hugh Nibley, "Old World Ritual in the New World," in *An Approach to the Book of Mormon*, in *CWHN*, 6:295–310.

106. See Hugh W. Nibley, "The Hierocentric State," *Western Political Quarterly* 4/2 (1951): 226–28; reprinted in *Ancient State*, in *CWHN*, 10:99–102.

107. Louis V. Žabkar, "The Theocracy of Amarna and the Doctrine of the BA," *Journal of Near Eastern Studies* 13 (1954): 87.

108. Cf. Hugh W. Nibley, "Three Shrines: Mantic, Sophic, and Sophistic," in *Ancient State*, in *CWHN*, 10:343–51.

109. *TPJS*, 159.

110. Ibid., 112.

111. Erwin Goodenough, *Jewish Symbols in the Greco-Roman Period*, 10 vols. (New York: Pantheon, 1953), 1:vii.

112. Jacob Neusner, "Ritual without Myth: The Use of Legal Materials for the Study of Religions," *Religion* 5 (1965): 91.

113. Ibid.

114. Ibid., 91–92.

115. Ibid., 95.

116. Ibid.

117. Ibid.

118. Ibid., 100.

119. Ibid.

120. "The Temple Scroll," *Biblical Archaeologist* 41 (September 1978): 109.

121. Ibid.

122. See ibid., 120.

123. See Nibley, "Baptism for the Dead in Ancient Times,"

Improvement Era, 51 (December 1948): 786–88, 836–38; *Improvement Era*, 52 (January 1949): 24–26, 60; *Improvement Era*, 52 (February 1949): 90–91, 109–10, 112; *Improvement Era*, 52 (March 1949): 146–48, 180–83; *Improvement Era*, 52 (April 1949): 212–14; cf. *Mormonism and Early Christianity*, in *CWHN*, 4:100–167.

124. Cf. Hugh W. Nibley, "The Christian Envy of the Temple," *Jewish Quarterly Review* 50 (1959–60): 97–123, 229–40; reprinted in *Mormonism and Early Christianity*, in *CWHN*, 4:391–434.

125. *Evangelium Veritatis (The Gospel of Truth)* (Zürich: Rascher, 1956), XXII, 13–14.

126. *The Gnostic Attitude*, ed. Birger A. Pearson (Santa Barbara, California: Institute of Religious Studies, 1973), 12.

127. Ibid., 18.

128. See ibid., 6, 8.

129. This is included in Appendix III of Nibley, *Message of the Joseph Smith Papyri*, 267–72.

130. Carl Schmidt, ed. and tr., *Kephalaia* (Stuttgart: Kohlhammer, 1940), 41.

131. See *Gospel of Philip* 69 (117).

132. Ibid., 85 (133).

133. Ibid., 70 (118).

134. See Widengren, *The Gnostic Attitude*, 12–20.

135. Karl-Wolfgang Tröger, *Mysterienglaube und Gnosis im Corpus Hermeticum XIII* (Berlin: Akademie-Verlag, 1971), 3–4.

136. Martin P. Nilsson, "Early Orphism and Kindred Religious Movements," *Harvard Theological Review* 28 (July 1935): 230.

137. See Plutarch, *De Iside et Osiride*, 3.

138. See Theodor Hopfner, *Plutarch, über Isis und Osiris* (Prague: Orientalisches Institut, 1940–41), 59–60.

139. Eduard Naville, *Das ägyptische Totenbuch der XVIII. bis XX. Dynastie* (Graz: Akademische Druck- und Verlagsanstalt, 1971).

140. *TPJS*, 58–59.

141. See *PWJS*, 60, 104.

142. *See PWJS*, 72.

143. *WJS*, 366.

144. Ibid.

145. William Shakespeare, *Hamlet*, act I, scene ii.

146. Robert N. Bellah et al., *Habits of the Heart: Individualism and Commitment in American Life* (Berkeley: University of California Press, 1985).

147. *TPJS*, 47.

148. Ibid., 131.

149. See ibid., 135.

150. Ibid., 16.

151. See ibid., 136.

152. See ibid., 144; cf. Ether 8:18–20.

153. *TPJS,* 206.

154. See ibid., 146.

155. Ibid., 275.

156. Ibid., 256.

157. See ibid., 248–50.

158. See ibid., 252–53.

159. *PWJS,* 187; cf. D&C 110:16.

160. See *WJS,* 318.

161. *PWJS,* 83.

162. *TPJS,* 253.

163. See ibid., 204; cf. 213.

164. Manuscript History of Brigham Young, 9 June 1844, compiled by Elden Jay Watson (Salt Lake City: Smith Secretarial Service, 1968), 169

165. See Spencer W. Kimball, "The False Gods We Worship," *Ensign* 6 (June 1976): 4, 6.

166. *TPJS,* 392.

167. Ibid., 169.

168. *WJS,* 60.

169. See *JD,* 16:123.

170. Ibid., 17:113–14.

171. Ibid., 15:3.

172. Ibid., 13:148.

173. Ibid., 18:244.

174. Ibid., 9:3.

21

What Is Reality?

John M. Lundquist

The Real, or Reality, I take to describe the place where God dwells, the state of mind that he possesses, and the way he acts. I take the world, in the state of mortality it has known since the beginning of human history, to be—in large part—the contravention of this reality, to be a place where God does not and cannot dwell, where his perceptions do not prevail, and where humankind acts in a way contrary to his desires. The primary question is and always has been: How does one discover the mind of God?

Throughout history God has mediated his knowledge about the Real to humankind through various means: through dreams, visitations, and revelations to private individuals and to prophets. The scriptures contain an account of God's dealings with humankind and are a historical record of his revelations to prophets, or, in other words, of his transmission to them of knowledge of the Real.

It is my contention that, throughout history, the temple[1] has been the means that God has used as the primary vehicle through which to pass on to humankind knowledge concerning Reality; that the temple is the paradigm par excellence, the pattern by and through which humankind

This article originally appeared in By Study and Also by Faith, *2 vols. (Salt Lake City: Deseret Book Company and F.A.R.M.S., 1990), 1:428–38.*

has learned (1) where God lives (represented in the temple by the innermost sanctuary, the most holy place); (2) how one arrives there (the ritual process—rites of passage—the ordinances); and (3) what life there is like (a paradisiacal existence without evil and death, represented in the temple by actual or artistically produced springs, lush gardens, trees of life, etc.).[2] It is in and through the temple that people have gained the greatest and most significant knowledge about Reality.[3]

In the biblical tradition, as well as in many—if not all— cultures of humankind that have known or still know the institution of the temple, a far-reaching commonality of architectural symbolism, ritual practices, and religious symbolism has been noted.[4] Two features of this common tradition particularly relevant to my thesis here are that temple practices are revealed to prophets by God (the absence of prophecy within a religious community is commonly taken to be a sufficient explanation for the absence of full temple practices in that community[5]) and that the central feature of the revelation is an architectural plan that is itself an imitation or a model of a temple existing in heaven.[6]

I have stated above that Reality consists in part of the place where God lives. The innermost sanctuary of the temple, the most holy place, is a model on earth of the place where God lives. He does not live in the earthly temple's most holy place—this is clear from the Hebrew text of Exodus 19:18, 20, where the Lord descends out of heaven onto the mountaintop. He lives in heaven, the Real, but offers a glimpse into heaven through the most holy place on earth, where his presence is experienced by the prophet or the king on special occasions.

In or near the most holy place are arranged architectural and natural features that symbolize what I have elsewhere called "the Primordial Landscape": the waters of life, the tree of life, and the cosmic mountain (the most holy place of the ancient Near Eastern temple was thought to be located directly over the primordial hillock, the "Rock of Foundation" in the biblical tradition, the first ground to appear after the waters of chaos had receded, where earthly creation first took place; this hillock became the mountain, the archetype of the built temple).[7] These features symbolize the beauty and pristine purity of creation and of God's dwelling, as well as the saving gifts of the temple. Ultimately, the temple and its symbolism represent the eternal life that is the main characteristic of Reality.

Heaven is, as it were, one vast "temple without walls," because God's presence fills that space, and the temple is, by definition, a model of the place where God dwells. But he doesn't dwell permanently in the earthly shrine. He reveals the knowledge of how it should be built (see Exodus 25:8–9), according to the pattern of heaven itself. The highly organized contact with this earthly temple throughout history thus gives God's people knowledge of heaven, of the Real, and instills within them the desire to live ultimately in that place. They realize that this world is for the most part far removed from the Real, from the place where God dwells, from his perceptions and actions.

But how is the Real, or heaven, to be reached? The answer to this is to be found in the mountain—the archetype and prototype of the built temple. Exodus 19 points us conveniently and profoundly in the right direction. The way up the mountain involves ritual, or rites of passage, through which the prophet mediates knowledge of the Real to the people who have been prepared by this ritual to approach the holy place.

Initiation ritual is to the initiate a journey to the center.

In many of the great religious traditions of humankind, the gods are thought to live on a mountain, or to descend from heaven to a mountain, there to meet those who have made the arduous journey to the center to be instructed. The mountain is the center because it was the first place of creation, the central place in the universe from the perspective of the adherents of that religious tradition. It is the vertical pole connecting the heavens with the earth, the navel of the earth. To become one with God, one must join him at the mountain. The journey to the mountain and the ascent of the mountain once one has reached its base are arduous, difficult, fraught with danger and obstacles. Here we are introduced to the labyrinthine nature of initiation.

The journey to the center involves three kinds of movement: around (the practice of ritual circumambulation possibly originates in the necessity to circle around a mountain, as a process of reconnoitering, as one attempts to climb it), up (obvious), and into (moving ever closer to the center as one moves toward the summit). Herein we have the rationale for such temple complexes as Borobudur in Java—the initiate moves around, into, and up. These movements all find their origins in the very practical requirements of mountain climbing, which has always carried mystical overtones, even when viewed solely as a sport. If the mountain one is being asked to climb, as in Exodus 19, is perceived as the place to which Deity actually descends in order to meet with people, then the kinds of movement required to climb the mountain will themselves be enshrined and canonized.

One sees this clearly in connection with Mount Kailash in Tibet, the holy mountain par excellence, thought to be the site of the sacred mountain of the Hindu and Buddhist traditions, and anciently known as Mount Meru.[8] The impetus to build sacred mountains, to erect structures that resemble holy mountains (the Old Testament Mount Zion in Jerusalem becomes likened to the mountain of God in the wilderness), will result in similar architectonic arrangements, imitating the topography of the mountain—this is so clear in the Hindu tradition of temple building—as well as the types of physical movement necessary to negotiate it: circumambulation, walking upward (the threshold of each successive section of an Egyptian temple rises in absolute level as one approaches the rear of the building), and walking into the building toward the rear to the most holy place.

The difficulty of mortality, with its pitfalls and plateaus, is compared to the difficulty of climbing mountains, where the gods are to be found. Certain high points along life's path are commemorated and memorialized, formally and ritually, at the mountain and in the temple. Life for the religious person is an arduous journey to the center, with certain high points along this journey commemorated ritually through rites of passage: the passage to adulthood, marriage, and introduction into the mysteries. The ultimate stage of one's journey, the ultimate rite of passage, is death. In the great formal canonical traditions—Hinduism, Buddhism, the ancient religions, many contemporary forms of culture (such as the American Indian), and to a lesser extent contemporary Christianity—this journey is commemorated in a physical way, in buildings with formal ritual. In the mystical variants of these traditions, the whole process is carried out in the mind of the traveler. The canonical traditions combine the physical with the metaphysical; the mystical traditions eliminate the physical.[9]

The temple is a visual representation of all the symbolism of the mountain, and thus the architecture reflects this symbolism in a thoroughgoing and repetitive way (e.g., the

Pagoda structures of Indian, Chinese, Southeast Asian, and Japanese temple architecture, with the multilevel hipped roofs present on every building and gateway in the complex) and is a constant visual reminder that the visitor/initiate is engaged in a journey up a mountain, to heaven.

It is this symbolism that we meet in Exodus 19–24: the difficult, arduous, highly charged, and dangerous (because of the sacredness of the place) preparations that must be gone through before reaching the point of readiness to receive knowledge about heaven, its ways and its requirements.

Thus the purpose of life is to return to heaven, to the Real. Knowledge of this place and its requirements are revealed periodically through prophets in temples. The laws, for example, are often revealed through a prophet or king in a temple setting.[10] This process reveals the pattern of life: a difficult, arduous journey to the Real, assisted at various times by rites of passage that strengthen the person, leading, ideally, to even higher plateaus until the ultimate initiation, death, which will eventually bring the person into heaven itself. And here the instructional nature of the temple should be emphasized. The journey to the mountain, the ritual process, is accompanied by instruction about Reality, which may take many forms: dramatic plays in which actors reenact the story of creation;[11] visual representations of the exemplary life and of life's course, as is the case of the sculptures representing the Buddha's life in the galleries at Borobudur;[12] verbal instruction, as was the case between Moses and the Israelites at Sinai (see Exodus 19–24); or some combination of these.

During the historical existence of the human race, the temple has offered a respite from the harshness and unreality of life, beckoning the devotee to partake of the waters of

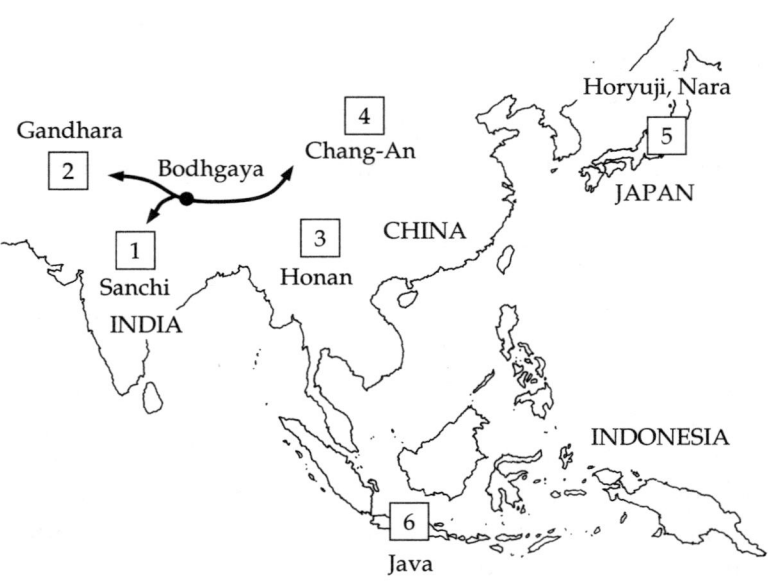

Figure 50. With the spread of Buddhism from its heartland in present-day Nepal, the formalized reliquary mound of the Indian *stupa* underwent many variations determined by the local culture. In spite of visual differences, there was a consistent emphasis on the radial symmetry of the mandala ground plan, a squared circle, and the ascent to a sacred center.

life that bubble up into the most holy place from the deep springs on which it is built (see Ezekiel 47:1; Joel 3:18; Zechariah 14:8; Psalm 46:4). Within a dark, misty, misleading world, the temple offers to the initiate a taste of paradise, so well exemplified by the formative dream, set in Liverpool,

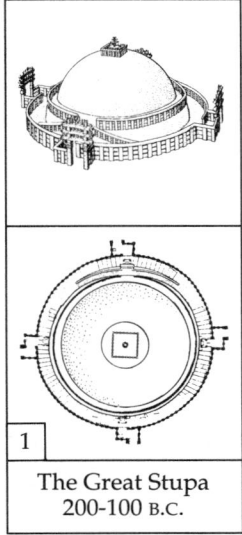

1

The Great Stupa
200-100 B.C.

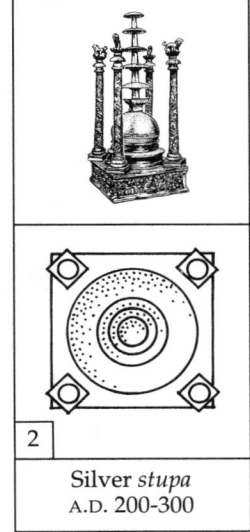

2

Silver *stupa*
A.D. 200-300

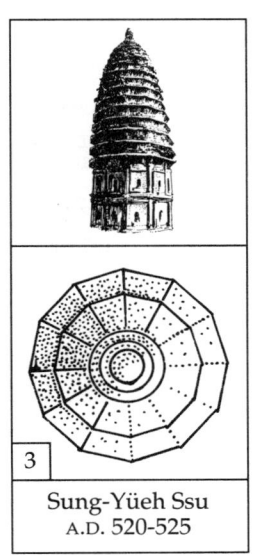

3

Sung-Yüeh Ssu
A.D. 520-525

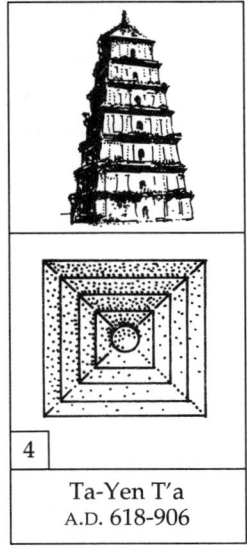

4

Ta-Yen T'a
A.D. 618-906

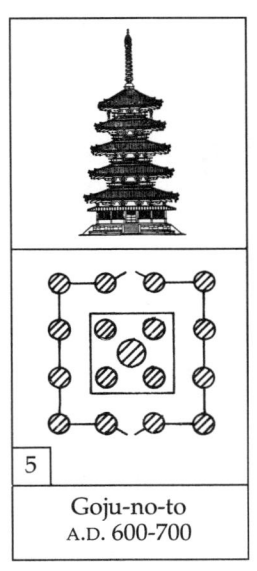

5

Goju-no-to
A.D. 600-700

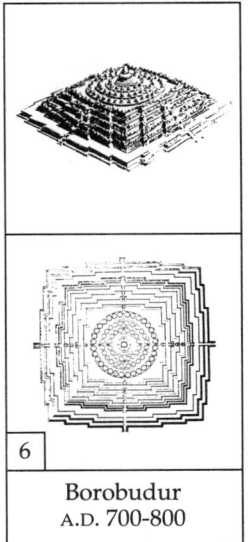

6

Borobudur
A.D. 700-800

experienced by the great psychologist Carl Gustav Jung in 1927: After a difficult ascent to the top of a hill in a dirty, sooty city (Liverpool), he encountered "a broad square dimly illuminated by street lights, into which many streets converged." The city's quarters were arranged radially around the square. A round pool stood in the center of the square, thus creating the squared circle, the mandala configuration, indicating the location of the temple in the topography of the dream. A small island stood in the center of the pool. On the brightly illuminated island, which stood out amidst the darkness that surrounded it, a magnolia tree stood. The tree seemed to be the source of light on the island. This combination of symbols, the "primordial landscape," provided for Jung the central message of his life, the central revelation: "Through this dream I understood that the self is the principle and archetype of orientation and meaning."[13] He had reached the Center, the Real, the Ultimate, which provided him with the insight and strength to continue his life's arduous journey after he was no longer under the influence of the temple setting of his dream. As a matter of fact, as I have pointed out elsewhere, the main formative insights of Jung's life were all mediated to him either as a result of profoundly moving visits to temple ruins, such as the stupas of Sanchi in India, or in dreams that were saturated with temple symbolism.[14]

And why do people seek out this path amidst the difficulties and complexities of life? Mircea Eliade answers: "The profound reason for all these symbols is clear: the temple is the image of the sanctified world. The holiness of the temple sanctifies both the cosmos and cosmic time. . . . Religious man wants to live in a cosmos that is similar in holiness to that of the temple."[15] The religious person wants to recover and return to heaven, the Real.

Figure 51. Jung admitted his frustration when he tried to paint the images of his dream. In spite of this limitation, this mandala was extremely significant to his spiritual development, and he observed, "The whole thing seemed like a window opening on to eternity."

The paradigmatic nature and purpose of the temple is made clear in Paul's discourses on Christ's atonement and the temple in Hebrews 7–10. Each part of the Mosaic tabernacle is seen as a precursor to, and a teacher about, the Savior. The ultimate holy place is clearly defined in Hebrews 9:12, 24, and 10:19—it is the place where God dwells: "by his own blood he entered in once into the holy place" (Hebrews 9:12). "But into heaven itself, now to appear in the presence of God for us" (Hebrews 9:24). Through his death the Savior passed into the presence of his Father, the real holy place of which the earthly is an imitation and a model.

That there is a temple in heaven is made clear in Revelation 11:19: "And the temple of God was opened in heaven, and there was seen in his temple the ark of his covenant." The temple on earth will continue to function during the Millennium, as is so dramatically demonstrated in Ezekiel 40–48, and in the chapters of Revelation that deal with the Millennium. The basic principle will still hold during the thousand-year reign of the Savior on the earth—the temple, with its most holy place, will serve as a reminder of the ultimate holy place, of the Real, of heaven where God dwells. But Revelation gives additional remarkable insight about heaven, the earth, and the temple. Following the resurrection and the judgment, "a new heaven and a new earth" are created, in which the heavenly Jerusalem descends from heaven to the earth, at which time God the Father himself will dwell on the earth with those worthy to be there with him (Revelation 21:1–3, 10). But now, in contradistinction to the historical plus millennial periods of the earth, when the temple existed as a copy on earth of the heavenly temple, a "piece of heaven on earth," there will no longer be any temple. The need for it will have disappeared with the presence on the renewed earth of the Father himself (see Revelation 21:22). Heaven, the Real, will have been brought down to earth in the form of the New Jerusalem, and the entire city is now suffused with the saving, paradisiacal symbols that in the period of earthly history were limited to the rather smallish temple itself.

> And I saw no temple in the city, for its temple is the Lord God the Almighty and the Lamb. And the city has no need of sun or moon to shine upon it, for the glory of God is its light, and its lamp is the Lamb (Revelation 21:22, RSV).

> Then he showed me the river of the water of life, bright as crystal, flowing from the throne of God and of the Lamb through the middle of the street of the city; also, on either side of the river, the tree of life with its twelve kinds of fruit, yielding fruit each month; and the leaves of the tree were for the healing of nations (Revelation 22:1–2, RSV).

Thus, from the perspective of the scriptures, the world is a poor substitute for Reality, which is to be found in heaven, where God lives. Life's purpose is to return to this heaven. The difficult journey is made lighter by access to the temple, which mirrors Reality. Access to the temple is gained by rites of passage and by observing the laws of God, which themselves were revealed in the temple and are sanctified by it. The ultimate initiation, death, will, following the resurrection and judgment, bring the worthy into the presence of God, on an earth made heavenly by being turned into one vast temple. The symbol and its referent will merge into one. Reality will reign supreme.

Notes

1. Anyone in the scholarly Latter-day Saint tradition who writes about the temple stands on the shoulders of Hugh Nibley, whose brilliance and personal example on this subject represent a beacon

light to those who would follow. This article is a struggling attempt to show my indebtedness to the man who introduced me to this subject, and to the lifelong joy that its study has given me.

2. See John M. Lundquist, "The Common Temple Ideology of the Ancient Near East," in Truman G. Madsen, ed., *The Temple in Antiquity* (Provo: BYU Religious Studies Center, 1984), 53–76.

3. I am taking an approach here that is remarkably close to, yet independent from, that of A. J. Bernet Kempers, "Barabudur: A Buddhist Mystery in Stone," in *Barabudur: History and Significance of a Buddhist Monument*, ed. Luis O. Gomez and Hiram W. Woodward, Jr. (Berkeley: Asian Humanities Press, 1981), 109–19. For example, Kempers writes, "I frequently use in connection with Barabudur other words such as Reality (as opposed to the phenomenal world, the "real" world of nonreligious people), Ultimate Reality, Absolute Reality, Totality" (109). "The meeting of Reality and Man is a central element in many religions, in which, consequently, the most essential sanctuaries provide a meeting place for the Holy and the worshipper"; and "The sanctuary establishes as a fact that there is—always—a relation between the world we live in and an Ultimate Reality which introduces meaning and certainty into our existance" (111). "The major mystery expressed in Barabudur—both in its general layout, construction, and symbolism, and in its additional decoration and reliefs—is the meeting of the Holy and Mankind, enacted by the descent of the Holy—of Ultimate Reality, Totality—and the ascent of Man" (112).

4. See Hugh W. Nibley, "What Is a Temple?" and "Looking Backward," in *Mormonism and Early Christianity*, in *CWHN*, 4:355–90; see Lundquist, "The Common Temple Ideology"; John M. Lundquist, "What Is a Temple? A Preliminary Typology," in this volume.

5. See Dennis J. McCarthy, "Covenant in Narratives from Late OT Times," in *The Quest for the Kingdom of God: Studies in Honor of George E. Mendenhall*, ed. Herbert Huffmon, Frank Spina, and Alberto Green (Winona Lake, Indiana: Eisenbrauns, 1983), 90–94; see also the comments by Yigael Yadin that were appended to David Noel Freedman, "Temple without Hands," in *THPBT*, 29.

6. See Freedman, "Temple without Hands," 21–29; Lundquist, "What Is a Temple?" in this volume, 83–117.

7. See Lundquist, "The Common Temple Ideology"; John M. Lundquist, "Temple Symbolism in Isaiah," in *Isaiah and the Prophets*, ed. Monte S. Nyman (Provo: BYU Religious Studies Center, 1984), 33–55.

8. See John Snelling, *The Sacred Mountain* (London: East West Publications, 1983).

9. For a good example of this latter point, see R. C. Zaehner, "Standing on the Peak," in *Studies in Mysticism and Religion Presented to Gershom G. Scholem* (Jerusalem: Magnes, 1967), 381–85.

10. See John M. Lundquist, "Temple, Covenant, and Law in the Ancient Near East and in the Old Testament," included in this volume, 272–94.

11. See Lundquist, "What Is a Temple?" 97–103.

12. See J. G. de Casparis, "The Dual Nature of Barabudur"; Kempers, "Barabudur: A Buddhist Mystery in Stone"; Hiram W. Woodward, Jr., "Barabudur as a Stupa"; Alex Wayman, "Reflections on the Theory of Barabudur as a Mandala," in *Barabudur: History and Significance of a Buddhist Monument*, 47–172. "The monument is only a framework for the sculpture" (Jacques Dumarcay, *Borobudur*, ed. and trans. Michael Smithies [Singapore: Oxford University Press, 1978], 31).

13. C. G. Jung, *Memories, Dreams, Reflections*, recorded and edited by Aniela Jaffe, trans. Richard and Clara Winston (New York: Vantage, 1965), 198–99.

14. See John M. Lundquist, "C. G. Jung and the Temple: Symbols of Wholeness," in *C. G. Jung and the Humanities: Toward a Hermeneutics of Culture*, ed. Karin Barnaby and Pellegrino D'Acierno (Princeton: Princeton University Press, 1990), 113–23.

15. Mircea Eliade, "The Prestige of the Cosmogonic Myth," *Diogenes* 23 (1958): 12.

22

Sacred Time and the Temple
Brian M. Hauglid

Mircea Eliade, the Romanian-born scholar of mythology and religion, examined cultures and civilizations through their myths[1] and fables and found a common religious link among them, concluding that there is a unity of spiritual history in humanity.[2] Interestingly, Eliade's findings were often connected to the idea of the temple.[3]

One significant concept developed throughout his writings is that of sacred time in the temple. Here, the idea of sacred time will be briefly examined to illustrate how and why the temple transcended chronological, or profane, time in the mind of ancient man. It is hoped that this brief investigation will benefit our own understanding of the function of time in relation to the temple.

Henry Corbin makes the significant observation that there are three temples: the celestial temple, the archetypal temple, and the temple of the soul. He characterizes the archetypal temple as the bridge between the other two:

> This Temple-archetype is itself a threshold, the communication Threshold between the celestial Temple and the Temple of the soul. Inasmuch as it is a material edifice, constructed in the image of the star or celestial Temple, it is the passage leading to the inner spiritual edifice. Because it leads back to the source, it is par excellence the figure and support of that mental activity designated in Arabic by the technical term *ta'wil*, that is to

say, an exegesis, a going-out of the soul towards the Soul.[4]

Anciently, to go back to the source meant going to the temple to experience sacred time. Before discussing what it meant to experience sacred time, it should be noted that sacred time is cyclical in nature and is distinctly different from our more modern conception of linear time. While cyclical time is best represented by an unbroken circle, linear time would be a horizontal line with definite beginnings and endings.

Linear time is a historical, chronological approach, in which what has happened has happened, and there is no going back. It is, in essence, irreversible. The Judeo-Christian tradition of time is also linear with definite historical occurrences and eschatological ramifications, wherein there was a beginning (creation) and there will be an end to the world as we know it, by virtue of the Second Coming, or as in the case with Judaism, a messianic figure. However, inherent even in this thinking is the idea that after death there will be a return to a higher state of existence. Perhaps this concept could best be portrayed by a circle with a horizontal line running through the middle, cutting the circle into two halves. This horizontal line would represent man's linear move through mortal time, with one end being birth and the other death. Before birth and after death, however, man exists in a cosmological eternal time represented by the circle. Doctrine and Covenants 3:2 and 1 Nephi 10:19 explain that God's work or time is one eternal round. Doctrine and Covenants 88:13 describes God as living in the "bosom of eternity" or "midst of all things."

In contrast, sacred time is reversible because the clock can move forward or backward. Why would one try to go backwards in time? Because "the experience of sacred time

will make it possible for religious man periodically to experience the cosmos as it was *in principio,* that is, at the mythical moment of creation."[5] In other words, in sacred time it
was possible, and to ancient man necessary, to go back to
the archetypal beginnings to relive those first moments of
creation.

Eliade calls this universal concept "the myth of the eternal return" and defines sacred time in terms of an eternal
return, or

> cyclical recurrence of what has been before, . . . the cycli-
> cal structure of time, which is regenerated at each new
> "birth" on whatever plane. The eternal return reveals an
> ontology uncontaminated by time. . . . Everything begins
> over again at its commencement every instant. The past
> is but a prefiguration of the future. No event is irre-
> versible and no transformation final. . . . In a certain
> sense, it is even possible to say that nothing new happens
> in the world, for everything is but the repetition of the
> same primordial archetypes; this repetition, by actualiz-
> ing the mythical moment when the archetypal gesture
> was revealed, constantly maintains the world in the same
> auroral instant in the beginnings.[6]

Sacred time is the *first* time, the archetypal time, the
time at which all things received meaning and life through
divine creation and decree. Its cyclical nature offered to man
a means whereby the actual activity that was evident in
those primordial moments could be reexperienced.
Significantly, ancient temple worship is replete with this
pattern of an eternal return to sacred time.

Much of our understanding of sacred time is due to
mythology, which served as a type of sanctuary in which
was housed the secrets of the universe. Myths contained the
creation stories as they took place *in illo tempore,* or at the
first instance, wherein primordial time was recovered into

a mythical present. Interestingly, archaic man returned to
sacred time through rites and ceremonies that reenacted primal myths of the creation. Accordingly, "for archaic man,
myth is a matter of primary importance. . . . Myth teaches
him the primordial 'stories' that have constituted him exis-
tentially."[7] It was an obligation on the part of the ancients
not only "to remember mythical history but also to reenact
a large part of it periodically."[8] "This faithful repetition of
divine models has a two-fold result: (1) by imitating the
gods, man remains in the sacred, hence in reality; (2) by the
continuous reactualization of the paradigmatic divine gestures, the world is sanctified. Men's religious behavior con-
tributes to the maintaining the sanctity of the world."[9]

Experiencing sacred time through these reenactment
rites projected man into the divine presence. Hence, ancient
man would, in essence, be contemporary with the gods.
Why? Being with the gods meant residing in the same place
as the gods in a cosmological purity untainted by the
coarser existence in which man then lived. And it was there
that the gods could be apprehended in a degree to actually
learn who they were and how they exercised their power of
creation, in order that it might be imitated. Once the knowledge of the origin of things was understood, one received
power to create at will. "Knowledge of the origin and exemplary history of things confers a sort of magical mastery
over them."[10]

Myth, like the temple, served as a means whereby man
could go back to the sacred time in which all things were
created and participate with the gods through rites and ceremonies depicting those creative acts. Thus, by being contemporary with these divine beings, archaic man learned
and received regenerative powers to control or renew his
environment to create order out of chaos. This power could

be manifested over plants, animals, and even time itself. Hence, the reenactment of ancient myths was a significant setting for the return to sacred time, whereby man could become more like the gods and secure divine powers.

Creation myths portrayed in temples fulfilled a longing of ancient man to experience divineness through contact with the time that existed in the first creative moments. (An important distinction is made between two Latin terms: the Latin term for temple, *templum,* and another that was found to have an etymological relationship, *tempus. Templum* designates the spatial, *tempus* connotes the temporal aspect of the motion of the horizon in space and time.[11]) Sacred time, for ancient man, evidenced a spiritual need to recapture the pureness and holiness that existed in the realm of the gods as embodied by temples. "Religious man's profound nostalgia is to inhabit a 'divine world,' [it] is his desire that his house shall be like the house of the gods, as it was later represented in temples and sanctuaries. In short, this religious nostalgia expresses *the desire to live in a pure and holy cosmos, as it was in the beginning, when it came fresh from the Creator's hands.*"[12] The temple, as a repository for sacred time, retains the original creative atmosphere first exhibited by the Creator and becomes at once a "divine world" innately infused with a sanctifying power to re-create and regenerate. This power of renewal is the ultimate aim of the eternal return to sacred time.

Ancient New Year festivals aptly illustrate three concepts that are associated with sacred time: the abolishing of past time, a return to a primordial chaos, and a repetition of the creative acts to recover order in the universe. In these festivals, the world was renewed annually, and even chronological time itself could be re-created through contact with the regenerative powers of the gods existing in sacred time. Note the direct correlation of this festival to the temple.

> The underlying meaning of all these facts seems to be the following: for religious man of the archaic cultures, *the world is renewed annually;* in other words, *with each new year it recovers* its original sanctity, the sanctity that it possessed when it came from the creator's hands. This symbolism is clearly indicated in the architectonic structure of sanctuaries. Since the temple is at once the holy place par excellence and the image of the world, it sanctifies cosmic life. This cosmic life was imagined in the form of a circular course; it was identified with the year. The year was a closed circle; it had a beginning and an end, but it also had the peculiarity that it could be reborn in the form of a *new* year. With each New Year, a time that was "new," "pure," "holy"—because not yet worn—came into existence.[13]

One example of how sacred time functioned in the ancient world is the Babylonian *akitu* festival, a New Year's ritual that took place in the temple of Marduk and lasted twelve days. Eliade discusses five parts of the ceremony that demonstrate the above-mentioned themes of an eternal return to sacred time:

1. *Regression into a mythical period before the creation.* According to the Babylonian creation myth *Enumah Elish,* before the earth was created all things were in a "marine abyss," a state of chaos and confusion represented by the god Tiamat, the sea monster. This regression to the mythical period abolished the past.

2. *A reactualization of the creation of the world.* Creation occurred when Marduk, a champion of the younger gods, defeated Tiamat in a major battle and used the torn pieces of Tiamat's body to create the cosmos. Marduk also defeated one of Tiamat's demons and from his blood

created man. This part of the ceremony was recited several times in the temple of Marduk.

3. *Participation of man through rites that make him contemporary with the creation.* Here man directly participated by performing the battle between Marduk and Tiamat, using two groups of actors. "This participation . . . projects him into mythical time, making him contemporary with the cosmogony."[14]

4. *A formula of creation in which the fate of each day and month is determined.* This is equivalent to re-creating the coming twelve months or, in other words, chronological time. Since there occurred an abolition of past time and a return to the original chaos, there also needed to be a repetition of the first act to create time anew. Also during this part of the ceremony occurred the "confession of sins and expulsion of the scapegoat,"[15] to ensure success in the coming year.

5. *The rebirth of the world and man.*[16] The result of the eternal return to sacred time in the *akitu* ceremony, finally, is to experience a rebirth or renewal of life and time. Inherent in these types of festivals is the supposition of a " 'death' and a 'resurrection,' a 'new birth,' a 'new man.' It would be impossible to find a more appropriate frame for the initiation rituals than the twelve nights when the past year vanishes to give place to another year, another era: that is, to the period when, through the reactualization of the Creation, the world in effect begins."[17]

As seen from the above discussion, sacred time was a significant part of ancient man's attempt to be with the gods and learn the power of renewal.

In summary, it should be evident that the concept of sacred time was a significant aspect of the ancient world. A return to the origins of things was essential to archaic man for two important reasons: man's desire to be in the presence of the gods and to relive their creative acts. The former implies a place unlike any other—the purest and holiest because it was closest to the original act of the Creator, who brought it into existence. Here the temple symbolized this primordial paradise in which the gods were manifested and to which man aspired. Yet implicit within the latter is man's desire to be like the gods by learning, in essence, how to become gods themselves, in order to imitate divine acts to create order out of chaos as it was done *in illo tempore*. This was accomplished through literal reenactments of creation stories, some actually played out by actors.[18] Also, to be in the presence of the gods, through this participatory activity, man was endowed with a regenerative power to create anew the life around him and to receive renewal himself. Even profane time was re-created through contact with the gods in sacred time. Sacred time was reversible and recoverable through these rites and ceremonies that projected man into a mythical present to reexperience rebirth and renewal, to again be in the presence of the gods and partake of their divine nature.

In conclusion, periodic recitations of the creation recovering the actual primeval time should be no surprise to Latter-day Saint temple worshipers. Though the ancient worldview of sacred time and the ancients' reenactments of the creative acts may differ in some respects to revealed truth, it is, perhaps, instructive to note some interesting parallels and insights to our own understanding of sacred time and the temple.

Notes

1. Mythology is generally treated as anything that is false, fiction or fable; however, anciently myths were used to transfer truth in the form of symbolic stories. We must be careful not to impose our modern definition of mythology upon the ancient world. Speaking of

Western scholarship in the past eighty years, Eliade says that "archaic societies" understood a myth to mean "a 'true story' and, beyond that, a story that is a most precious possession because it is sacred, exemplary, significant." This is unlike the scholars of the Western world who ofttimes see a myth to be a "fable," "invention," or "fiction" (*Myth and Reality* [New York: Harper and Row Publishers, 1963], 1).

2. For a thorough introduction to this idea, see Mircea Eliade, *A History of Religious Ideas*, 3 vols., tr. Willard R. Trask (Chicago: University of Chicago Press, 1978). In his preface to volume one, Eliade says "Consciousness of this unity of the spiritual history of humanity is a recent discovery, which has not yet been sufficiently assimilated" (xvi). See also Joseph Campbell, *The Hero with a Thousand Faces* (Princeton: Princeton University Press, 1949); and *The Masks of God*, 4 vols. (Arkana: Penguin Books, 1959). Campbell's studies show the universality of the human experience from a common denominator found in the subconscious mind of the human psyche. Though Campbell takes a psychological approach, he also uncovers an array of interesting data through the study of many different cultures and their myths. His work explores some of the foundations laid by C. G. Jung in "Archetypes of the Collective Unconscious," in *Twentieth Century Criticism: The Major Statements*, ed. William J. Handy and Max Westbrook (New York: The Free Press, 1974), 205–32.

3. According to Hugh Nibley, "the boldest and clearest recent statement embracing the world landscape of culture and religion is in the works of M. Eliade, and he brings it all back to the Temple." Nibley adds, "Before Eliade your humble informant was bringing out much of the picture in a doctoral thesis which disturbed and puzzled his committee in the 1930s" (Truman G. Madsen, ed., *The Temple in Antiquity* [Provo: BYU Religious Studies Center, 1984], 45).

4. Henry Corbin, *Temple and Contemplation*, tr. Philip Sherrard (London: Islamic Publications, 1986), 134. Corbin is here speaking of the *al-Batiniyya*, a medieval Islamic sect, who, though they did not build temples, took an approach of interiorization of the soul to reach God. (This is in deference to the Sunnis, who take a much more practical approach.) The root word *batn* means belly or stomach but also can be extended to include inner, interior, hidden or secret. Here the *al-Batiniyya* would be best translated as an esoteric sect.

5. Mircea Eliade, *The Sacred and the Profane: The Nature of Religion*, tr. Willard R. Trask (New York: Harcourt, Brace & World, 1959), 65.

6. Mircea Eliade, *The Myth of the Eternal Return* (Princeton: Princeton University Press, 1954), 88–90.

7. Eliade, *Myth and Reality*, 12. "Myth is essentially cosmological. As heaven in the cosmos is so vastly more important than our earth, it should not be surprising to find the main functions deriving from heaven" (Giorgio de Santillana and Hertha von Dechend, *Hamlet's Mill: An Essay Investigating the Origins of Human Knowledge and Its Transmission through Myth* (Boston: Godine, 1977), 50.

8. Eliade, *Myth and Reality*, 12–13.

9. Eliade, *The Sacred and the Profane*, 75–79.

10. Eliade, *Myth and Reality*, 90.

11. See Eliade, *The Sacred and the Profane*, 75–76.

12. Ibid., 65; italics in original.

13. Ibid., 75–76; italics in original.

14. Eliade, *Myth of the Eternal Return*, 58.

15. Ibid., 61.

16. See ibid., 55–58; James B. Pritchard, ed., *The Ancient Near East: An Anthology of Texts and Pictures* (Princeton: Princeton University Press, 1958), 31–39; and Robert Graves and Raphael Patai, *Hebrew Myths: The Book of Genesis* (New York: McGraw-Hill Paperbacks, 1966), 21–33, for an in-depth analysis of the *Enumah Elish* creation myth.

17. Eliade, *Myth of the Eternal Return*, 69; see also *KG*, 313–20, for an excellent discussion of the *akitu* ceremony in relation to the coronation of the king.

18. Creation drama is a widespread concept in archaic societies, particularly in the New Year festivals. See Eliade, *Myth of the Eternal Return*, 62–73, for an examination of several ancient societies that reenacted myths. For a discussion of ritual combat that was also acted out, see Hugh Nibley's brief, albeit insightful remarks in *Temple and Cosmos*, in *CWHN*, 10:73–77.

PART 8

The Temple and Sacred Vestments

23

Priestly Clothing in Bible Times

John A. Tvedtnes

The Bible and other early religious literature are replete with references to priestly clothing and its symbolism. Priestly garb from the time of Moses is described in sufficient detail to enable artists to depict it in various Bible encyclopedias and commentaries. This paper will examine the origin and meaning of priestly clothing in Bible times.

The Garments of Skin

According to Jewish tradition, the earliest priestly clothes were the garments of skin provided to Adam and Eve after the fall. "Unto Adam also and to his wife did the Lord God make coats of skins, and clothed them" (Genesis 3:21).

The first book of Adam and Eve, also called the *Conflict of Adam and Eve*,[1] reports a tradition whereby the clothing of the first couple was made by miraculous means. As Adam was praying, "the Word of God" came and told him to go to the seashore, where he would find the skins of sheep killed by lions.[2] "Take them and make raiment for yourselves, and clothe yourselves withal."[3]

Adam and Eve returned to the Cave of Treasures, in which they were living, and prayed that God would show them how to "make garments of those skins; for they had no skill for it." God sent an angel to make the garments for them. He placed palm-thorns through the skins, then stood and prayed God that the thorns in those skins would "be

Figure 52. The detailed instructions in Exodus 28 regarding the clothing for the high priest, priests, and Levites have guided many attempts by artists to reconstruct their appearance. Not surprisingly, they reflect the culture of the artist more than that of the time of Moses. The earliest depiction of the high priest (A) is at Dura Europos (c. A.D. 245), where the non-Jewish artist has dressed Aaron in typical royal Persian robes and trousers. In this miniature (B) from a thirteenth-century Hebrew manuscript, the high priest wears a crown and breastplate, with an inscription "breastplate of judgment" on it instead of the expected twelve jewels. In this eighteenth-century German engraving (C), the artist has given the high priest a decidedly Baroque appearance.

hidden, so as to be, as it were, sewn with one thread. And so it was, by God's order; they became garments for Adam and Eve, and he clothed them withal."[4]

Skin or Light?

The exact nature of the material from which the garments of Adam and Eve were made has long been in dispute. Some Jewish traditions have them made of the skin stripped from the serpent.[5] According to a midrash in *Minhat Yehukh* on Genesis 3:21, they were "garments of light," made of the hide of the female Leviathan, a gigantic sea monster.[6]

The idea that the garments were made of the skin of a reptile—specifically the serpent who had tempted Adam and Eve—is found in pseudepigraphal literature.[7] The Slavonic version of *3 Baruch* tells of "when the first-created Adam sinned, having listened to Satanael, when he covered himself with the serpent."[8] The Greek version reads, "And during the transgression of the first Adam, she (the moon) gave light to Samael when he took the serpent as a garment."[9]

The *Midrash Rabbah* informs us that Rabbi Meir's copy of the Torah or Law of Moses indicated that Adam and Eve received garments of light, not of skin.[10] The two Hebrew words for "light" (*ʾôr*) and "skin" (*ʿôr*) differ in but the initial letters, and are pronounced alike in modern Hebrew. This explains why some traditions have the garments of the first couple made of light, others of skin. An attempt to reconcile the two views is found in the Jewish tradition that the skin of the leviathan shone with a light brighter than the noonday sun. *Targum Onkelos*, Genesis 3:21, says that God "made garments of glory on the skin of their flesh."

Usually, however, tradition indicates that Adam and

Eve's garments of light had been given them before the fall.[11] When they sinned, God stripped them of the garment of light.[12] Abkir commented, "God made the high-priestly garments for Adam which were like those of the angels; but when he sinned, God took them away from him."[13]

Some traditions indicate that Adam and Eve had been clothed with a horny (reptilian?) skin that fell off, leaving them naked, whereupon the cloud of glory that surrounded them departed.[14] The garment of light, according to some accounts, was replaced by its earthly symbol, a garment of skin, after the fall.[15] By this reckoning, the garment of skin given to the first human couple was their own skin, not that of animals. This makes even more sense when one considers that the Hebrew root for "nakedness" (ʿrh) may be related to the word for "skin" (ʿôr). The *Book of the Rolls* explains it this way: "After the clothing of fig-leaves they put on clothing of skins, and that is the skin of which our bodies are made, being of the family of man, and it is a clothing of pain."[16]

Pseudepigraphal stories also reflect the idea of Adam and Eve being clothed in light prior to the fall. In the *Apocalypse of Adam*, the first man tells his son Seth:

> When God created me out of earth along with Eve your mother, I used to go about with her in a glory which she had seen in the aeon from which we had come. She taught me a word of knowledge of the eternal God. And we were like the great eternal angels, for we were loftier than the God who created us and the powers that were with him, whom we did not know.[17]

The *Conflict of Adam and Eve* also expresses this idea. En route to retrieve the skins used in the garments made by the angel, the first couple were stopped by Satan and then rescued by the Word of God, who told them that it had been the devil "who was hidden in the serpent, and who deceived you, and stripped you of the garment of light and glory in which you were."[18] Later, Adam says, "O God, when we transgressed Thy commandment at the sixth hour of Friday, we were stripped of the bright nature we had."[19] On another occasion, Satan, posing as an angel, tells Adam that God told him to take the first couple "and clothe them in a garment of light, and restore them to their former state of grace."[20]

The *Book of the Rolls* informs us that when Adam was created, "his body was bright and brilliant like the well-known stars in the crystal."[21] When Adam and Eve were placed on earth, "God clothed them with glory and splendour. They outvied one another in the glory with which they were clothed."[22] At the time of the fall, "they were bereft of their glory, and their splendour was taken from them, and they were stripped of the light with which they had been clothed . . . They were naked of the grace which they had worn . . . they made to themselves aprons of fig-leaves, and covered themselves therewith."[23]

If one follows the reasoning of these stories, the serpent was the cause of Adam and Eve's becoming naked,[24] and their "nakedness" was the loss of their premortal glory.[25] For example, in one account, Eve says: "And at that very moment my eyes were opened and I knew that I was naked of the righteousness with which I had been clothed. And I wept saying, "Why have you done this to me, that I have been estranged from my glory with which I was clothed?"[26]

From this account, the "nakedness" of Adam and Eve was spiritual in nature, that is, they lost their special covering of light (also termed "glory" and "righteousness"), which was subsequently replaced by the garments of skin.

This concept is found in the Coptic *Gospel of Philip,* where we read that "it is those who wear the [flesh] who are naked."[27]

The Koran also ties the nakedness of Adam and Eve to the loss of their primordial clothing:

> Children of Adam, We have created for you raiment which covers your nakedness and is a source of elegance; but the raiment of righteousness is the best. . . . Let not Satan seduce you, even as he turned your parents out of the garden, stripping them of their raiment that he might show them their nakedness.[28]

This idea is also reflected in the story of Zosimus. Arriving in a distant land to which he had been miraculously conveyed, Zosimus encounters a Rechabite and asks him, "Why are you naked?"[29] The man replies, "You are he [who is] naked, and you do not discern that your garment is corrupt, but my own garment is not corrupted."[30]

> But we are naked not as you suppose, for we are covered with a covering of glory; and we do not show each other the private parts of our bodies. But we are covered with a stole of glory [similar to that] which clothed Adam and Eve before they sinned.[31]

Origen, a second-century Christian scholar, expressed a view similar to those of early Jewish rabbis, explaining that the skin garments given to Adam and Eve contained a secret doctrine of the soul's losing its wings and coming to earth.[32]

The Stolen Garment

According to Jewish tradition, the skin garment given to Adam had an unearthly brilliance and supernatural qualities and was thus used by Adam and his descendants for priestly functions.[33]

Jewish tradition also provides us with some interesting stories concerning the fate of the original priesthood garment of Adam, along with some insights into the magical properties attributed to it two millennia ago. Perhaps the best-known is the one preserved in the *Book of Jasher:*[34]

> And Cush, the son of Ham, the son of Noah, took a wife in those days, in his old age, and she bare a son, and they called his name Nimrod, saying, At that time the sons of men again began to rebel and transgress against God, and the child grew up, and his father loved him exceedingly, for he was the son of his old age. And the garments of skin which God made for Adam and his wife, when they went out of the garden, were given to Cush. For after the death of Adam and his wife, the garments were given to Enoch, the son of Jared, and when Enoch was taken up to God, he gave them to Methuselah, his son. And at the death of Methuselah, Noah took them and brought them into the ark, and they were with him until he went out of the ark.[35] And in their going out, Ham stole those garments from Noah his father, and he took them and hid them from his brothers.[36] And when Ham begat his first-born Cush, he gave him the garments in secret, and they were with Cush many days. And Cush also concealed them from his sons and brothers, and when Cush had begotten Nimrod he gave him those garments through his love for him, and Nimrod grew up, and when he was twenty years old, he put on those garments. And Nimrod became strong when he put on the garments, and God gave him might and strength, and he was a mighty hunter in the field, and he hunted the animals and he built altars, and he offered upon them the animals before the Lord. And Nimrod strengthened himself, and he rose up from amongst his brethren against all their enemies round about. And the Lord delivered all the enemies of his brethren in his hands, and God prospered him from time to time in his battles, and he reigned upon earth.[37]

Among the earlier Jewish sources from which this story may have been drawn are *Pirqe de Rabbi Eliezer* 24 and TB *Pesahim* 44b. Several sources indicate that the wearer of the garment could not be slain and that wild animals prostrated themselves before him.[38] Esau, who took pride in being a great hunter, became jealous of Nimrod's prowess and sought to destroy him. According to one source, he challenged Esau to combat and, following Jacob's advice, got Nimrod to remove his protective garb so he could defeat him.[39] Here is the *Jasher* version, which is also known from earlier sources:[40]

> And Nimrod was observing Esau all the days, for a jealousy was formed in the heart of Nimrod against Esau all the days. And on a certain day Esau went in the field to hunt, and he found Nimrod walking in the wilderness with his two men. . . . And Nimrod and two of his men that were with him came to the place where they were, when Esau started suddenly from his lurking place, and drew his sword, and hastened and ran to Nimrod and cut off his head. And Esau fought a desperate fight with the two men that were with Nimrod, and when they called out to him, Esau turned to them and smote them to death with his sword. And all the mighty men of Nimrod, who had left him to go to the wilderness, heard the cry at a distance, and they knew the voices of those two men, and they ran to know the cause of it, when they found their king and the two men that were with him lying dead in the wilderness. And when Esau saw the mighty men of Nimrod coming at a distance, he fled, and thereby escaped; and Esau took the valuable garments of Nimrod, which Nimrod's father had bequeathed to Nimrod, and with which Nimrod prevailed over the whole land, and he ran and concealed them in his house. And Esau took the garments and ran into the city on account of Nimrod's men, and he came unto his father's house wearied and exhausted from flight, and he was

ready to die through grief when he approached his brother Jacob and sat before him. And he said unto his brother Jacob, Behold I shall die this day, and wherefore then do I want the birthright? And Jacob acted wisely with Esau in this matter, and Esau sold his birthright to Jacob, for it was so brought about by the Lord.[41]

Accordingly, Esau, like Nimrod before him, became a great hunter, ruling over men and animals.[42]

Jacob and Joseph

The stories of the preservation of the garments of Adam and Eve do not agree in the line through which they were transmitted. According to one tradition, the garments, though stolen by Ham, were recovered by Shem who, as Melchizedek, gave them to Abraham as his successor.[43]

Abraham passed the garments to his son Isaac and he to his eldest son Esau. When Jacob received from Isaac the blessing intended for Esau, "Rebecca took the favorite clothing of her elder son, Esau, which was with her in the house. And she put it on Jacob."[44] Isaac then blessed him, noting, among other things, "May nations serve you, and the people bow down to you. Become a lord to your brothers, and may your mother's sons bow down to you."[45] The blessing reminds us of the tradition that people bowed down to Nimrod when they saw him arrayed in the garments of Adam.

Early Jewish commentators saw evidence that Jacob was arrayed in the garment of Adam in Genesis 27:27, where we read that Isaac "smelled the smell of his raiment, and blessed him, and said, See, the smell of my son is as the smell of a field which the Lord hath blessed."[46] Origen reflected this view, when he cited the Genesis passage and used the term "divine garments."[47]

The concept of the divinely perfumed garment is also applied to Jacob's son Joseph who, when leaving prison to appear before Pharaoh, put on clean clothing brought from paradise by an angel.[48] Similarly, the angel Gabriel miraculously provided Joseph a garment to replace the "coat of many colors" taken from him by his brothers, so that he would not appear naked before the Midianites.[49]

Joseph's "coat of many colors" is said in *Keli Yaqar*, Genesis 37:3, to be the high priest's tunic,[50] while *Da'at* and *Hadar*, on Genesis 30:29–30, indicate that Jacob gave to Joseph the garment of Adam which Esau had taken from Nimrod. Ginzberg explained the reasoning behind this: "*Pargûd meṣuyyār* is a paraphrase of *passîm* which accordingly is not to be translated 'a coat of many colors,' but 'an upper garment in which figures are woven,' in accordance with Mishnaic *paspasîn* comp. *Nega'im* 11.6."[51]

Nibley has noted the Jewish tradition reported by the tenth-century Arab scholar Tha'labī that Joseph's garment, which was impregnated with the smell of paradise, had belonged to Adam and was passed down to Abraham and Joseph. According to one of Tha'labī's sources, the garment had miraculous powers by which Jacob regained his eyesight.[52]

Noah's Garment Again

At this point, we must return to the story of Noah:

> And Noah began to be an husbandman, and he planted a vineyard: And he drank of the wine, and was drunken; and he was uncovered within his tent. And Ham, the father of Canaan, saw the nakedness of his father, and told his two brethren without. And Shem and Japheth took a garment, and laid it upon both their shoulders, and went backward, and covered the nakedness of their father; and their faces were backward, and they saw

not their father's nakedness. And Noah awoke from his wine, and knew what his younger son had done unto him. And he said, Cursed be Canaan; a servant of servants shall he be unto his brethren. And he said, Blessed be the Lord God of Shem; and Canaan shall be his servant. God shall enlarge Japheth, and he shall dwell in the tents of Shem; and Canaan shall be his servant (Genesis 9:20–27).

The exact nature of Ham's sin is not clear from this passage. One Jewish tradition therefore adds that Ham, jealous of his position as the younger son, castrated his father in order to prevent Noah from having other children. What, indeed, was it that "his younger son had done unto him"? President Heber C. Kimball's answer was that Ham was cursed because he "pulled the clothing off from his father Noah, who had drank a little too much wine."[53]

According to Jewish tradition, the rewards given to Noah's other sons because of their good deed in covering their father were directly related to the kinds of garments they were given by God. Shem, who first set about to cover his father, received, as his reward, the *tallith*, while his brother Japheth, who joined him, was given the *toga*. Ham's descendants, by this account, were left naked.[54]

The *tallith* today is usually an undergarment covering the chest and upper back, worn by Orthodox Jewish men. For certain prayers, however, a larger version is worn draped over the head (hence the term "prayer shawl"). Anciently, it appears to have been a long garment.

Protection of the Garment

According to a number of early Jewish sources, the long garment worn by the Assyrians was the one allotted to Shem's descendants as a reward for his having covered his father Noah.[55] These garments are said to have remained

Figure 53. In this Dutch engraving of 1725, the worshiper wears the *tallith* over his three-corner hat. The "prayer shawl" has four embroidered corners from which hang the *tzitzith,* consisting of eight threads and five knots each. He wears *tefellin,* or phylacteries, on his left hand and forehead.

unsinged when the angel of the Lord burned the Assyrian army during Sennacherib's siege of Jerusalem.[56] Similarly, when Abraham was placed in the furnace by Nimrod, "his lower garments were not burned."[57]

When two of Aaron's sons offered "strange fire"[58] at the Tabernacle, a fire from the Lord came out and "devoured them." But their garments were apparently unharmed, for we read that their bodies were carried "in their coats out of the camp" (Leviticus 10:1–5). Of this, Ginzberg wrote, "Opinions differ as to whether the bodies of Nadab and Abihu were injured by the heavenly fire, which brought about their death, or not; but all agree that their garments remained intact."[59]

According to Jewish tradition, the Israelites who traveled in the wilderness with Moses were given special robes by angels. These robes grew with them but never wore out. Fire could not damage them, and they protected even the dead from worms.[60]

The garment was meant to be a protection, perhaps not from physical danger, but from spiritual. An early Christian document implores, "Clothe me in thy glorious robe and thy seal of light that ever shineth, until I have passed by all the rulers of the world and the evil dragon that opposeth us."[61]

The Garments of Wisdom

Just as early tradition attributes to the priesthood garments qualities which both protected the wearer and made animals and men subject themselves to him, so, too, we find accounts in which the garments are said to impart wisdom to the wearer. After the death of Moses:

> Then God said to Joshua the son of Nun, "Why do you mourn and why do you hope in vain that Moses yet lives? . . . Take his garments of wisdom and clothe yourself, and with his belt of knowledge gird your loins, and you will be changed and become another man. . . . And Joshua took the garments of wisdom and clothed himself and girded his loins with the belt of understanding. And when he clothed himself with it, his mind was afire and his spirit was moved.[62]

Perhaps Joshua inherited the very garments worn by Moses, just as the patriarchs are said to have passed Adam's original garments from father to son. Wearing the clothing of one's predecessor appears to denote succession to a position of authority. The expression concerning the "mantle (coat) of the prophet" passing to his successor comes from the story of Elijah and Elisha. When Elijah was taken into heaven,

> [Elisha] took up also the mantle of Elijah that fell from him, and went back, and stood by the bank of Jordan; And he took the mantle of Elijah that fell from him, and smote the waters, and said, Where is the Lord God of Elijah? and when he also had smitten the waters, they parted hither and thither: and Elisha went over. And when the sons of the prophets which were to view at Jericho saw him, they said, The spirit of Elijah doth rest on Elisha (2 Kings 2:13–15).

With this mantle, both Elisha and Elijah performed the miracle of dividing the waters of the Jordan (see 2 Kings 2:8, 14). In the pseudepigraphal *Lives of the Prophets*, we read that the garment was a sheepskin.

> With a sheepskin he [Elijah] struck the Jordan and it was divided, and they crossed over with dry feet, both he and Elisha.[63]

> He too [Elisha] struck the Jordan with Elijah's sheepskin, and the water was divided, and he too passed over with dry feet.[64]

Temple Clothing

Anciently, the priests, descendants of Aaron, wore special garments when serving in the tabernacle and later in the temple. Exodus 29:29 refers to "the holy garments of Aaron" in which he and his descendants were to be anointed and consecrated. In one of the books of the

Apocrypha, the priest Ezra refers to "the holy garment" he wore (1 Esdras 8:71).

Such was the sanctity of the priestly clothing that Ezekiel, after describing it, wrote that the priests should wear it only "when they enter in at the gates of the inner court," and that

> when they go forth into the utter court, even into the utter court to the people, they shall put off their garments wherein they ministered, and lay them in the holy chambers, and they shall put on other garments; and they shall not sanctify the people with their garments (Ezekiel 44:19).

The clothing of the anointed high priest was considered especially sacred (see Leviticus 21:10). According to Josephus, the punishment that came upon king Uzziah when he offered incense in the temple (see 2 Chronicles 26:16–21) resulted because he had "put on the holy garment," restricted for priestly use.[65]

Priestly Attire

The priesthood garments used in the tabernacle and temple in Old Testament times are described in Exodus 28 and 39 and in Ecclesiasticus (Ben Sirach) 45:6–15. The principal elements for the high priest's clothing were linen breeches, a coat, a robe, a bonnet with a gold mitre and a gold engraved frontlet attached, a girdle, and a garment called the ephod to which was attached a breastplate.

Pseudo-Philo 13:1 says that Moses set in order "all the vestments of the priests, the belt and the robe and the headdress and the golden plate and the holy crown. And the oil for anointing priests and the priests themselves he consecrated."[66]

Ezekiel wrote of the "linen garments," the "linen bonnets

upon their heads," and the "linen breeches upon their loins" to be worn by priests in the latter-day temple in Jerusalem (Ezekiel 44:17–18). He noted that linen was used instead of wool to prevent sweating.[67] The length of the garments was also intended to provide modest attire while serving in the house of the Lord. Speaking of the altar in the Jerusalem temple, Aristeas recorded: "The site had the ladder designed in a manner consistent with seemliness[68] for the ministering priests swathed up to the loins in 'leather garments.'"[69]

Another translation renders the latter part of this passage, "the ministering priests were robed in linen garments, down to their ankles."[70] This accords with an account in the Apocrypha that speaks of King Josiah "having set the priests according to their daily courses, being arrayed in long garments, in the temple of the Lord" (1 Esdras 1:1).

Aristeas described the garb of the high priest in glowing terms:

> It was an occasion of great amazement to us when we saw Eleazar engaged on his ministry, and all the glorious vestments, including the wearing of the "garment" with precious stones upon it in which he is vested; golden bells surround the hem (at his feet) and make a very special sound. Alongside each of them are "tassels" adorned with "flowers," and of marvelous colors. He was clad in an outstandingly magnificent "girdle," woven in the most beautiful colors. On his breast he wears what is called the "oracle," to which are attached "twelve stones" of different kinds, set in gold, giving the names of the patriarchs in what was the original order, each stone flashing its own natural distinctive color—quite indescribable. Upon his head he has what is called the "tiara," and upon this the inimitable "mitre," the hallowed diadem having in relief on the front in the middle in holy letters on a golden leaf the name of God, ineffable in glory. The wearer is considered worthy of such vest-

ments at the services. Their appearance makes one awe-struck and dumbfounded: A man would think he had come out of this world into another one. I emphatically assert that every man who comes near the spectacle of what I have described will experience astonishment and amazement beyond words, his very being transformed by the hallowed arrangement on every single detail.[71]

The other-worldly feeling at seeing the high priest thus arrayed was, of course, deliberate. The priestly clothing was intended to represent the garb of God and of the angels, as we shall see below. Aristeas supplemented his description of the priestly clothing with the following words of Eleazar, the high priest, to Aristobulus: "Further-more in our clothes he has given us a distinguishing mark as a reminder."[72]

The symbols of remembrance may be the fringes on the tallith, four in number.[73] The symbolism may be to the twelve tribes of Israel, which, in Old Testament times, were represented by four rows of three stones each set in the high priest's breastplate. The symbolism is explained in the apocryphal Wisdom of Solomon: "For in the long garment was the whole world, and in the four rows of the stones was the glory of the fathers graven, and thy Majesty upon the diadem of his [Aaron's] head" (Wisdom of Solomon 18:24).

The special sanctity of the priestly garments is indicated by the fact that when they wore out, rather than discard them, the Jews burned them in the temple during the feast of tabernacles.[74]

Investiture

The Bible describes the ceremony in which Aaron and his sons were ordained to the priesthood at the taber-nacle. They were washed with water, dressed in "the holy garments," anointed and consecrated (Exodus 28:40–41; 29:4–9; 40:12–15; Leviticus 8:12–13, 30; Psalm 133:2; Ben Sirach 45:8–15). This investiture was partially repeated each time the priests prepared for service, when they were required to wash and don the "holy garments" (Leviticus 16:3–4), which they then removed after completing the ordinances of the tabernacle or the temple (see Leviticus 16:23–24). Dressing in special clothing in the temple denotes a change in role, from that of mortal to immortal, from ordinary human to priest or priestess, king or queen. A number of ancient texts, both in the Bible and elsewhere, discuss temple clothing, its symbolism and some of its uses.

Perhaps the most impressive investiture account is the one ascribed to Levi, ancestor of Moses and Aaron, in a vision at Beth-El, where his father Jacob had experienced his dream of the ladder ascending into heaven.[75]

> And I saw seven men in white clothing, who were saying to me, "Arise, put on the vestments of the priesthood, the crown of righteousness, the oracle of understanding, the robe of truth, the breastplate of faith, the miter for the head, and the apron for prophetic power.[76] Each carried one of these and put them on me and said, "From now on be a priest, you and all your posterity." The first anointed me with holy oil and gave me a staff. The second washed me with pure water, fed me by hand with bread and holy wine, and put on me a holy and glorious vestment. The third put on me something made of linen, like an ephod. The fourth placed . . . around me a girdle which was like purple. The fifth gave me a branch of rich olive wood. The sixth placed a wreath on my head. The seventh placed the priestly diadem on me and filled my hands with incense, in order that I might serve as priest for the Lord God.[77]

The *Jubilees* version of this story also has the event taking place at Beth-El but has Jacob performing the ceremony for his son:

> And he [Jacob] abode that night at Bethel. And Levi dreamed that he had been appointed and ordained priest of the Most High God, he and his sons forever. And he awoke from his sleep and blessed the Lord . . . and [the lot of] Levi fell with the portion of the Lord. And his father put the garments of the priesthood upon him and he filled his hands.[78]

The pseudepigraphal *2 Enoch* also speaks of this kind of investiture:

> And the Lord said to Michael, "Go, and extract Enoch from [his] earthly clothing. And anoint him with my delightful oil, and put him into the clothes of my glory." And so Michael did, just as the Lord had said to him. He anointed me and he clothed me. And the appearance of that oil is greater than the greatest light, and its ointment is like sweet dew, and its fragrance like myrrh; and it is like rays of the glittering sun. And I looked at myself, and I had become like one of his glorious ones.[79]

The Hebrew version in *3 Enoch* has the angel Metatron, who is identified in Jewish tradition with Enoch, saying,

> The Holy One, blessed be he, fashioned for me a majestic robe, in which all kinds of luminaries were set, and he clothed me in it. He fashioned for me a glorious cloak in which brightness, brilliance, splendor, and luster of every kind were fixed, and he wrapped me in it.[80]

This story seems to be the same one recorded by Joseph Smith in Moses 7:2–4:

> From that time forth Enoch began to prophesy, saying unto the people, that: As I was journeying, and stood upon the place Mahujah, and cried unto the Lord, there

came a voice out of heaven, saying—Turn ye, and get ye upon the mount Simeon. And it came to pass that I turned and went up on the mount; and as I stood upon the mount, I beheld the heavens open, and I was clothed upon with glory; and I saw the Lord; and he stood before my face, and he talked with me, even as a man talketh one with another, face to face.

In the *Apocalypse of Abraham*, the archangel Jaoel takes Abraham by the right hand[81] and sets him on his feet (11:1), then takes him to heaven where the patriarch is given the garment formerly set aside for Satan (13:14). According to Jewish tradition, God gave Abraham the same kind of garment he himself wore when appearing to the prophets.[82]

Similar investiture stories appear in the Old Testament:

> The Spirit of the Lord God is upon me; because the Lord hath anointed me . . . to appoint unto them that mourn in Zion, to give unto them beauty for ashes, the oil of joy for mourning, the garment of praise for the spirit of heaviness. . . . I will greatly rejoice in the Lord, my soul shall be joyful in my God; for he hath clothed me with the garments of salvation, he hath covered me with the robe of righteousness, as a bridegroom decketh himself with ornaments, and as a bride adorneth herself with her jewels (Isaiah 61:1, 3, 10).[83]

> And [the angel] shewed me Joshua the high priest standing before the angel of the Lord, and Satan standing at his right hand to resist him. And the Lord said unto Satan, The Lord rebuke thee, O Satan; even the Lord that hath chosen Jerusalem rebuke thee: is not this a brand plucked out of the fire? Now Joshua was clothed with filthy garments, and stood before the angel. And he answered and spake unto those that stood before him, saying, Take away the filthy garments from him. And unto him he said, Behold, I have caused thine iniquity to pass from thee, and I will clothe thee with a change of

raiment. And I said, Let them set a fair mitre upon his head. So they set a fair mitre upon his head, and clothed him with garments (Zechariah 3:1–5).[84]

The Apron or Girdle

The Hebrew term translated "girdle" in the description of the priestly clothing (Exodus 28:8; 39:5) is rendered "apron" in the story of Adam and Eve: "And the eyes of them both were opened, and they knew that they were naked; and they sewed fig leaves together, and made themselves aprons" (Genesis 3:7).

Edersheim wrote that the priestly girdle was a type of sash/apron/robe combination, adding that it was quite long, reaching "below the feet, and required to be thrown over the shoulder during ministration. Hence its object must chiefly have been symbolical. In point of fact, it may be regarded as the most distinctive priestly vestment, since it was only put on during actual ministration, and put off immediately afterwards."[85]

That the girdle was considered to have supernatural qualities is asserted in the *Testament of Job*, where R. P. Spittler's translation in Charlesworth reads "cord" instead of "girdle." Job instructs one of his daughters, Hemera, to bring "three golden boxes" containing their inheritance, described as "multicolored cords" in most Greek manuscripts, as "multicolored objects" in a Greek manuscript of A.D. 1307/8 in Messina, Sicily, and as "three cordlike aprons" in Greek Manuscript 1238 (A.D. 1195) in the Vatican. Their "appearance was such that no man could describe, since they were not from earth but from heaven, shimmering with fiery sparks like the rays of the sun." Job instructed his daughters, "Place these about your breast, so it may go well with you all the days of your life."[86]

One of the daughters then asked what good the cords were, to which Job replied that "these cords will lead you into the better world, to live in the heavens."[87] He then told how the Lord used them to rid Job of his plagues and worms, telling him, "Arise, gird your loins like a man."[88] So Job put them on and the worms disappeared.[89] Job then continued his explanation: "Since you have these objects you will not have to face the enemy at all, but neither will you have worries of him in your mind, since it is a protective amulet of the Father. Rise then, gird yourselves with them before I die."[90]

So Hemera wrapped her girdle on, "And she took on another heart—no longer minded toward earthly things—but she spoke ecstatically in the angelic dialect. . . . And as she spoke ecstatically, she allowed 'The Spirit' to be inscribed on her garment."[91] Another of Job's daughters, "Amaltheia's Horn . . . bound on her cord. And her mouth spoke ecstatically in the dialect of those on high, since her heart also was changed, keeping aloof from worldly things."[92] When, after three days, Job became ill, it is said that he could not suffer pain "on account of the omen of the sash he wore."[93]

Removal of Shoes

Though special clothing was donned anciently before entering the temple, one piece of attire was always removed: the shoes or sandals. *Midrash Shemot Rabbah* indicates that one must stand barefoot in the presence of God, which is why the priests were barefoot while performing the service in the temple.[94]

Removal of street shoes enabled the temple to remain ritually pure from the ground, which was cursed because of the Fall of Adam (see Genesis 3:17–18). The practice of removing the shoes in sacred places is very ancient. The earliest biblical reference is to the time Moses first encountered the Lord:

> And when the Lord saw that he turned aside to see, God called unto him out of the midst of the bush, and said, Moses, Moses. And he said, Here am I. And he said, Draw not nigh hither: put off thy shoes from off thy feet, for the place whereon thou standest is holy ground (Exodus 3:4–5; also cited in Acts 7:33).

Similar words were addressed to Joshua, Moses' successor in the leadership of ancient Israel (see Joshua 5:15).

Shoes are necessary only on the earth because of the filth of the ground. By removing them, we symbolically leave the world outside the Lord's sanctuary. Muslims and others remove their shoes when entering mosques and other holy places (in Islam, one may not pray with one's feet shod). The Japanese and some other peoples even remove their shoes upon entering a house.

Shoes are not needed in the celestial world, where, according to pseudepigraphal works such as those attributed to Enoch, the angels walk on flames of fire, which is a purifying element, as in 1 Enoch 14:10–22 and 71:1. Therefore, in the presence of God, one goes barefoot. In this connection, we note that Joseph Smith described Moroni as being barefoot, while wearing an exquisite white robe that extended nearly to his ankles and wrists (see Joseph Smith–History 1:31).

Symbolism of Priestly Clothing

As with most things religious, there is a symbolism behind the priestly clothing used in biblical times. This symbolism, while multiple, ties to the ethical and moral values taught by the ancient prophets. Early Christians, during baptism, were also anointed and clothed in white garments,

in imitation of temple rites.[95] The Hellenistic synagogal
Prayer on Behalf of the Catechumens implores, "Grant them
[the] washing of regeneration, the garment of incorrup-
tion."[96] The white robe, along with the anointing, symbolized the Holy Ghost's protection against Satan.[97] In a pseudepigraphic text, the apostle Thomas anoints a group of
women who have changed their clothes, then baptizes them
and gives them bread and wine, saying, "let us receive the
dew of thy goodness." He compared their new clothing with
the linen cloth in which Christ's body was wrapped, asking
the Lord that they might be "girt about with thy power."[98]

Garments of Righteousness

In some scriptural and pseudepigraphal passages,
sacred clothing is equated with righteousness. Here are
some examples from the scriptures:

> O Lord, wilt thou encircle me around in the robe of
> thy righteousness! (2 Nephi 4:33).

> And the righteous shall have a perfect knowledge of
> their enjoyment, and their righteousness, being clothed
> with purity, yea, even with the robe of righteousness
> (2 Nephi 9:14).

> And righteousness shall be the girdle of his loins, and
> faithfulness the girdle of his reins (Isaiah 11:5; also cited
> in 2 Nephi 30:11).

> I put on righteousness, and it clothed me: my judg-
> ment was as a robe and a diadem (Job 29:14).

The same idea is found in a modern revelation: "Clothe
yourselves with the bond of charity, as with a mantle, which
is the bond of perfectness and peace" (D&C 88:125;
cf. 109:76, 80; 124:116). The Koran also compares the garments of Adam and Eve with the principle of righteousness

(Sura 7.27–28), as does *Apocalypse of Moses* 20:1–2, both of which were cited earlier. St. Ignatius wrote of being clothed with the grace of God.[99]

Paul wrote of putting on the "whole armor of God," and equated various virtuous qualities with armor such as would be worn by a soldier of his time, including "loins girt about with truth . . . the breastplate of righteousness . . . feet shod with the preparation of the gospel of peace . . . shield of faith . . . helmet of salvation, and the sword of the Spirit" (Ephesians 6:13–17; paraphrased in D&C 27:15; cf. D&C 63:37). To the Thessalonians he wrote of the "breastplate of faith and love; and for an helmet, the hope of salvation" (1 Thessalonians 5:8). He wrote to the Corinthians of the "armour of righteousness" (2 Corinthians 6:7 [see the list of virtues in verses 3–10]; cf. 2 Nephi 1:23). Of particular interest is his mention of the "armour of light" (Romans 13:12), which seems to tie the protective military clothing to the garment of light said to have been worn by Adam, discussed earlier.

The wearing of special clothing that symbolizes purity and righteousness is designed to impress these qualities on the mind of the person so clad. The use of clothing symbolism appears to be reflected in the following passage, where we note the use of such "temple-context" words as "seal" and "fellowship":

> For who shall put on your grace, and be rejected? Because your seal is known; and your creatures are known to it. And your [heavenly] hosts possess it, and the elect archangels are clothed with it. You have given us your fellowship.[100]

The use of sacred clothing to symbolize righteousness and purity is also found in a pseudepigraphic work entitled *The Shepherd of Hermas*. The text is attributed to Hermas, brother to Pius, bishop of Rome (A.D. 140–155), and comprises three books describing a vision in which an angel appeared to Hermas as a shepherd. The last of these books, the *Similitude,* speaks at length concerning the symbolism of the garment and of the temple. The Church, like the temple in D&C 101:43–64, is represented as a tower.[101] In the vision, an angel of the Lord crowns and sends into the tower those

> who had branches that were green and had offshoots, but no fruit, having given them seals. And all who went into the tower had the same clothing—white as snow. And those who returned their branches green, as they received them, he set free, giving them clothing and seals.[102]

Hermas then saw twelve virgins, four of them standing at the gate "clothed with linen tunics, and gracefully girded, having their right shoulders exposed,[103] as if about to bear some burden."[104] He was told by an angel that the tower represented the Church and that the virgins were

> holy spirits, and men cannot otherwise be found in the kingdom of God unless these have put their clothing upon them: for if you receive the name only, and do not receive from them the clothing, they are of no advantage to you. For these virgins are the powers of the Son of God. If you bear His name but possess not His power, it will be in vain that you bear his name.[105]

The angel then explained certain stones that had been removed from the tower, which "bore His name, but did not put on the clothing of the virgins. Their very names . . . are their clothing. Everyone who bears the name of the Son of God, ought to bear the names also of these; for the Son Himself bears the names of these virgins."[106] He went on to explain that all who hoped to remain in the building should wear the same garment and receive the name of God, and . . . also the strength of these virgins. Having received, then, these spirits, they were made strong, and were with the servants of God; and theirs was one spirit, and one body, and one clothing.[107]

The angel gave the names of the virgins standing at the gate as Faith, Continence, Power, and Patience. The other virgins or qualities of righteousness are Simplicity, Innocence, Purity, Cheerfulness, Truth, Understanding, Harmony, and Love. "He who bears these names and that of the Son of God will be able to enter into the kingdom of God."[108]

The symbolism found in the *Similitude* derives from the writings of Paul. The concept that the Saints are building blocks in the Church, with "Jesus Christ himself being the chief corner stone," is from Ephesians 2:19–22 (cf. 1 Peter 2:5–9, citing Isaiah 28:16). That the Saints are temples of God is also affirmed in 1 Corinthians 3:16–17 and 6:16, 19. St. Ignatius further compared Christians to stones in a temple.[109]

Wedding Garments

The virgins in the *Similitude* remind us that virgins are used in the New Testament to symbolize the righteous of the Church, the bride of Christ (see Matthew 25:1–11; D&C 45:56; 63:54). At the wedding feast of the Lamb, all who are invited must wear the appropriate garment or be cast out (see Matthew 22:11–13).

The Bible also mentions the special garments worn by the bride for her wedding (see Isaiah 49:18; 61:10; Jeremiah 2:32; Revelation 21:2). In one pseudepigraphal work, the daughter of Jephthah, knowing that she can never marry, lamented with these words:

> But I have not made good on my marriage chamber, and I have not retrieved my wedding garlands. For I

have not been clothed in splendor while sitting in my woman's chamber, and I have not used the sweet-smelling ointment, And my soul has not rejoiced in the oil of anointing that has been prepared for me.[110]

The pseudepigraphic story of Joseph and Aseneth has a number of references to special garments, particularly in association with Aseneth's preparations to become Joseph's bride. When she first heard that Joseph was coming, she "hurried into the chamber, where her robes lay, and dressed in a [white] linen robe interwoven with violet and gold, and girded herself [with] a golden girdle."[111] This was prior to Aseneth's conversion to the religion of Israel. Nevertheless, it reflects the importance that the ancient Egyptians—whose temple rites bore similarities to those of Israel—placed on ritual clothing.

Aseneth then went down to see Joseph and her parents, "and Pentephres and his wife rejoiced over her daughter Aseneth [with] great joy, because they saw her adorned like a bride of God."[112] Joseph began teaching Aseneth about his religious beliefs. Afterward, she fasted and prayed in sack-cloth and ashes, asking God to assist her in understanding the truth. The Lord sent his chief angel to earth, and he told the young woman, "Wash your face and your hands with living water, and dress in a new linen robe [as yet] untouched and distinguished and gird your waist [with] the new twin girdle of your virginity."[113]

Accordingly, Aseneth rushed to where she kept her garments "and dressed in her distinguished [and as yet] untouched linen robe, and girded herself with the twin girdle of her virginity, one girdle around her waist, and another girdle upon her breast. And she . . . washed her hands and her face with living water. And she took an [as yet] untouched and distinguished linen veil and covered her head."[114]

When she returned, the chief angel told her:

> And Joseph will come to you today . . . and you will be a bride for him for ever [and] ever. And now listen to me, Aseneth, chaste virgin, and dress in your wedding robe, the ancient and first robe which is laid up in your chamber since eternity, and put around you all your wedding ornaments, and adorn yourself as a good bride, and go meet Joseph.[115]

Later, when Joseph was coming to dinner at the house of Aseneth's parents, Aseneth removed her normal clothing,

> opened her big coffer and brought out her first robe, [the one] of wedding, like lightning in appearance, and dressed in it. And she girded a golden and royal girdle around [herself] which was [made] of precious stones.[116]

The bridal clothing, like the priestly clothing discussed earlier, was of white linen, symbolic of righteousness and purity. In the book of Revelation, John saw the Church as the bride of the Lamb. "And to her was granted that she should be arrayed in fine linen, clean and white: for the fine linen is the righteousness of saints" (Revelation 19:8). The heavenly woman "clothed with the sun, and the moon under her feet, and upon her head a crown of twelve stars" was evidently another representation of the Church (Revelation 12:1).

Heavenly Clothing

Priestly clothing, by its symbolic nature and pure whiteness, replaces the everyday garb which reminds us that we are in the world, thus bringing the wearer closer to heaven. A number of passages speak of removing one's corrupt earthly clothing and replacing it by the divine. Here is a sampling:

> And I was covered with the covering of your spirit, and I removed from me my garments of skin.[117]

> I raised my arms on high on account of the grace of the Lord: because he cast off my chains from me. And my Helper raised me according to his grace and his salvation. And I stripped off darkness and put on light. . . . And abundantly helpful to me was the thought of the Lord, and his incorruptible fellowship. And I was lifted up in the light, and I passed before his face.[118]

> Put off, O Jerusalem, the garment of thy mourning and affliction, and put on the comeliness of the glory that cometh from God for ever. Cast about thee a double garment of the righteousness which cometh from God; and set a diadem on thine head of the glory of the everlasting (1 Baruch 5:1–2).

Jesus, before ascending to heaven after a special visit to his apostles, reputedly declared, "From this moment on, I shall strip myself that I may clothe myself."[119]

The Garb of Angels

From numerous scriptural and pseudepigraphal descriptions (some of them noted above), we know that temple garments symbolize those worn in the celestial kingdom. Angels are frequently described as being clothed in special garments. We have, for example, the angels associated with the resurrection of Jesus. Matthew wrote of the angel, "his countenance was like lightning, and his raiment white as snow" (Matthew 28:3). Mark wrote of the angel seen at the tomb by the women, who was "clothed in a long white garment" (Mark 16:5), while Luke said there were two of them, "in shining garments" (Luke 24:4). John recorded that Mary Magdalene had seen "two angels in white" (John 20:12).

After Jesus ascended to heaven, two angels "in white apparel" appeared to the apostles (Acts 1:10). Later, an angel "in bright clothing" appeared to Cornelius to give him instructions (Acts 10:30). These descriptions are similar to the one given of the angel Moroni who, according to Joseph Smith, "had on a loose robe of most exquisite whiteness" (Joseph Smith–History 1:31).

In his vision, John saw a number of individuals dressed in marvelous clothing. "And I saw another mighty angel come down from heaven, clothed with a cloud . . . [who] lifted up his hand to heaven, And sware by him that liveth for ever and ever" (Revelation 10:1, 5–6). He also saw "seven angels [who] came out of the [heavenly] temple . . . clothed in pure and white linen, and having their breasts girded with golden girdles" (Revelation 15:6). The garb of angels is similarly described in *Apocalypse of Paul* 12.

Similar descriptions are found in various pseudepigraphic works. In *3 Maccabees* 6:18, two angels descend from heaven, "clothed in glory and of awe-inspiring appearance."[120] In fragments from the *Book of Jannes and Jambres*, we read that "two clad in white" were sent to accompany the Egyptian magician Jannes to Hades.[121]

Before appearing to Abraham, the angel Death "donned a most radiant robe and made his appearance sunlike and became more comely and beautiful than the sons of men, assuming the form of an archangel." As Death approached, Abraham detected "a sweet odor . . . and a radiance of light."[122] Abraham mistook him for Michael and greeted him with the words, "you who are sunlike in appearance and form, most glorious assistant, bearer of light, marvelous man."[123]

In another pseudepigraphic work, Abraham describes an angel who appeared to him:

> And I stood up and saw him who had taken my right hand and set me on my feet. The appearance of his body was like sapphire, and the aspect of his face was like chrysolite, and the hair of his head like snow. And a kidaris [headdress] (was) on his head, its look that of a rainbow, and the clothing of his garments (was) purple; and a golden staff/scepter [was] in his right hand.[124]

The "chief of the angels" who appeared to Aseneth prior to her marriage to Joseph also fits the pattern described in other passages:

> And Aseneth raised her head; and saw, and behold, (there was) a man in every respect similar to Joseph, by the robe and the crown and the royal staff, except that his face was like lightning, and his eyes like sunshine, and the hairs of his head like a flame of fire of a burning torch, and hands and feet like iron shining forth from a fire, and sparks shot forth from his hands and feet.[125]

Celestial Garments of the Righteous

"Thou standest clad in robes that grow old and desirest not those that are eternal?"[126]

That the righteous will wear splendid white clothing when received into the celestial kingdom was noted by John in the book of Revelation:

> And round about the throne were four and twenty seats: and upon the seats I saw four and twenty elders sitting, clothed in white raiment; and they had on their heads crowns of gold (Revelation 4:4).

> And white robes were given unto every one of them (Revelation 6:11).

> After this I beheld, and, lo, a great multitude, which

no man could number, of all nations, and kindreds, and people, and tongues, stood before the throne, and before the Lamb, clothed with white robes, and palms in their hands (Revelation 7:9).

The celestial garments given to the righteous at the time of the resurrection and judgment are a common motif in pseudepigraphic and kabbalistic literature. One of the more impressive descriptions is found in the book of 4 *Ezra:*

> I Ezra saw on Mount Zion a great multitude, which I could not number, and they were all praising the Lord with songs. In their midst was a young man of great stature, taller than any of the others, and on the heads of each of them he placed a crown, but he was more exalted than they. And I was held spellbound. Then I asked an angel, "Who are these, my lord?" He answered and said to me, "These are they who have put off mortal clothing and put on the immortal, and they have confessed the name of God: now they are being crowned, and receive palms." Then said I to the angel, "Who is that young man who places crowns on them and puts palms in their hands?" He answered and said to me, "He is the Son of God, whom they confessed in the world."[127]

The palms, crowns, and special clothing mentioned in this passage are motifs found in the temple anciently. The priests wore special garments, while the high priest wore a crown or plate of gold on his head. Palm fronds were carried to the Jerusalem temple during the Feast of Tabernacles. The wearing of the crowns implies that the righteous have become kings and queens, priests and priestesses, and have thus been anointed and invested with royal or priestly garb (see Exodus 19:5–11; 1 Peter 2:9; Hebrews 12:28–29, citing Deuteronomy 4:24; cf. Exodus 19:18).[128]

In some pseudepigraphic works, we read that the celestial garments of the righteous are laid up for them in heaven and will be made available to them after the resurrection.[129] For example, when Abraham was atop Mount Horeb, the archangel Iaoel declared of him to Azazel (Satan), "For behold, the garment which in heaven was formerly yours has been set aside for him, and the corruption which was on him has gone over to you."[130]

The *Martyrdom and Ascension of Isaiah* speaks of "the robes of the saints and their going out"[131] and states that "many will exchange the glory of the robes of the saints for the robes of those who love money."[132]

> But the saints will come with the LORD with their robes which are stored up in the seventh heaven above; with the LORD will come those whose spirits are clothed, they will descend and be present in the world, and the LORD will strengthen those who are found in the body, together with the saints in the robes of the saints, and will serve those who have kept watch in this world. And after this they will be turned in their robes upwards, and their body will be left in the world.[133]

The angel who shows Abraham the heavens speaks to him of the celestial clothing reserved for the patriarch:

> For above all the heavens and their angels is placed your throne, and also your robes and your crown which you are to see.[134]

> [When from the body by the will of God you have come up here], then you will receive the robe which you see, and also other numbered robes placed [there] you will see, and then you will be equal to the angels who [are] in the seventh heaven.[135]

The angel further spoke to Isaiah regarding the person who would be known on the earth as "the Son":[136]

> He who is to be in the corruptible world has not [yet] been revealed, nor the robes, nor the thrones, nor the

crowns which are placed [there] for the righteous, for those who believe in that LORD who will descend in your form. For the light which [is] there [is] great and wonderful.[137]

Arriving in the seventh heaven, the angel told Isaiah, "Behold! From there another voice which was sent out has come, and it says, 'The holy Isaiah is permitted to come up here, for his robe is here.'"[138] Of this visit to the seventh heaven, we read:

And there I saw Enoch and all who [were] with him, stripped of [their] robes of the flesh; and I saw them in their robes of above, and they were like the angels who stand there in great glory. But they were not sitting on their thrones, nor were their crowns of glory on them. And I asked the angel who [was] with me, "How is it that they have received these robes, but are not on [their] thrones nor in [their] crowns?" And he said to me, "They do not receive the crowns and thrones of glory—nevertheless they do see and know whose [will be] the thrones and whose the crowns—until the Beloved descends in the form in which you will see him descend."[139]

The angel then returned to the subject of Christ to come:

And then many of the righteous will ascend with him, whose spirits do not receive [their] robes until the LORD Christ ascends and they ascend with him. Then indeed they will receive their robes and their thrones and their crowns, when he has ascended into the seventh heaven.[140]

And I saw many robes placed there, and many thrones and many crowns, and I said to the angel who led me, "Whose [are] these robes and thrones and crowns?" And he said to me, "As for these robes, there are many from that world who will receive [them] through believing in the words of that one who will be named as I have told you, and they will keep them, and believe in them, and believe in his cross; [for they (are) these] placed [here]."[141]

The angel then told Isaiah, "And you shall return into your robe until your days are complete; then you shall come here."[142] By "robe," he evidently had reference to mortality, either the body itself or earthly clothing.

Based on these experiences, Isaiah later told King Hezekiah, "But as for you, be in the Holy Spirit that you may receive your robes, and the thrones and crowns of glory, which are placed in the seventh heaven."[143]

A number of early Christian texts note that the righteous will receive, in the resurrection, the garment which they shed in the heavenly realm in order to come to earth and take up the garment of corruption, the body. The Coptic *Gospel of Philip* notes that "those who wear the flesh" are naked. "In this world those who put on garments are better than the garments. In the kingdom of heaven the garments are better than those who have put them on."[144]

In the pseudepigraphal work known as the *Book of the Resurrection of Christ* by Bartholomew the Apostle, Thomas's son Siophanes dies, then returns to life to recount his experience. His soul was taken by Michael and wrapped in a fine linen cloth, then washed in the Acherusian lake.[145]

An early Christian document known as *The Hymn of the Soul* or *The Pearl* traces mankind's life in parable form. The soul of the protagonist removes his glorious royal garb before coming to "Egypt" (the earth) and replaces it with an earthly garment. After successfully accomplishing his purpose on earth, he returns to his (heavenly) parents and again dons the robe he had in the beginning.[146] Hugh Nibley has shown parallels to the story in the Coptic *Pistis Sophia*.[147]

The concept of celestial garments that are reserved for the righteous is also found in the Book of Mormon. Alma admonished the people to "keep your garments spotless," that they might "sit down with Abraham, Isaac, and Jacob, and the holy prophets . . . having your garments spotless even as their garments are spotless, in the kingdom of heaven" (Alma 7:25).

When righteous prophets are brought before God, they are allowed to don the special clothing reserved for them. Thus, when Nephi saw the apostle John in vision, John was "dressed in a white robe" (1 Nephi 14:19–20). A pseude-pigraphal work has the prophet Zephaniah writing of his visit to the celestial world, "I, myself, put on an angelic gar-ment."[148] One of the *Odes of Solomon* declares, "And I aban-doned the folly upon the earth, and stripped it off and cast it from me. And the Lord renewed me with his raiment, and possessed me by his light, and from above he gave me immortal rest."[149]

Ultimately, the righteous are received into the presence of God and allowed to wear the special clothing:

> The righteous and elect ones shall rise from the earth and shall cease being of downcast face. They shall wear the garments of glory. These garments of yours shall become the garments of life from the Lord of the Spirits. Neither shall your garments wear out, nor your glory come to an end before the Lord of the Spirits.[150]

> Receive what the Lord has entrusted to you and be joyful, giving thanks to him that has called you to heav-enly kingdoms. Rise and stand, and see at the feast of the Lord the number of those who have been sealed. Those who have departed from the shadow of this age have received glorious garments from the Lord. Take again your full number, O Zion, and conclude the list of your people who are clothed in white, who have fulfilled the law of the Lord.[151]

> Then Abraham, Isaac, and Jacob will rejoice, and I

shall be glad, and all the saints shall be clothed in righteousness.[152]

These passages are reminiscent of the wording of a modern revelation to Joseph Smith:

> Mine apostles, the Twelve which were with me in my ministry at Jerusalem, shall stand at my right hand at the day of my coming in a pillar of fire, being clothed with robes of righteousness, with crowns upon their heads, in glory even as I am . . . yea, even the dead which died in me, to receive a crown of righteousness, and to be clothed upon, even as I am (D&C 29:12–13).

That these heavenly garments resemble the clothing of earthly prophets or priests is implied in a story of Saul's visit to the witch of En-Dor. Samuel had appeared to her and she said to the king:

> "You are asking me about divine beings. For behold his appearance is not the appearance of a man. For he is clothed in a white robe with a mantle placed over it, and two angels are leading him." And Saul remembered the mantle that Samuel wore when he was alive.[153]

The *Manual of Discipline* says that the righteous will receive a garment of light (1QS 4), reminding us of the garment of light given to Adam and Eve. Satan has used his knowledge of celestial garb to deceive men, appearing in the emblems of his "priesthoods" as an angel of light. In *2 Adam and Eve* 17, Satan and his host appear to Jared in the guise of people from another country to lead the patriarch to the children of Cain. Along the way,

> Then said the elder to one of his companions, "We have forgotten something by the mouth of the cave, and that is the chosen garment we had brought to clothe Jared withal." He then said to one of them, "Go back, thou, some one; and we will wait for thee here, until thou come

back. Then will we clothe Jared and he shall be like us, good, handsome, and fit to come with us into our country."[154]

The one who returned, however, brought a "phantom" garment which, nevertheless, impressed Jared.[155]

Cleansing the Garments

Anciently, when one's person or clothing was defiled (e.g., by touching a dead body or by bodily issue), it was necessary to undergo ritual purification in water and change the clothes. Thus, we read that Kenaz, after a battle, "took off his clothes and threw himself into the river and washed himself. And he came up again, changed his clothes."[156]

Speaking of Jerusalem as his bride, the Lord declared through Ezekiel,

> Then washed I thee with water; yea, I throughly washed away thy blood from thee, and I anointed thee with oil. I clothed thee also with broidered work . . . and I girded thee about with fine linen (Ezekiel 16:9–13).

This cleansing was particularly important when entering the temple. We read, for example, that David washed, anointed himself, and changed his apparel before going into the house of the Lord (see 2 Samuel 12:20).

The cleansing of one's garments was ritually important in ancient Israel as a necessary preparation for appearing before God. Thus we read concerning the events in Sinai:

> And the Lord said unto Moses, Go unto the people, and sanctify them to day and to morrow, and let them wash their clothes, and be ready against the third day: for the third day the Lord will come down in the sight of all the people upon mount Sinai. . . . And Moses went down from the mount unto the people, and sanctified

the people; and they washed their clothes (Exodus 19:
10–11, 14).

This washing was to prepare the people for meeting the
Lord and becoming a "kingdom of priests" (Exodus
19:5–11). As such, it was an initiation into a new relationship with the God of their fathers, who had rescued them
from bondage in Egypt.

In ancient Israel, garments were cleansed before the performance of sacred functions (see Leviticus 16:23–24, 28). A
ritually unclean person was required to wash himself and
his clothes, sometimes following this practice by sacrifice
(see Leviticus 15:5–13, 16–27). The practice of cleansing
one's clothing seems to have applied to festival days as
well, such as the first day (the new moon) of the seventh
month, which was the most sacred month in the Israelite
calendar:

> And on the new moon of the month Jacob spake to
> all the people of his house, saying: "Purify yourselves
> and change your garments, and let us arise and go up to
> Bethel, where I vowed a vow to Him. . . . " And he went
> up on the new moon of the seventh month to Bethel. And
> he built an altar at the place where he had slept, and he
> set up a pillar there.[157]

Other passages indicate that ridding one's garments of
filth was symbolic of casting off sin:[158]

> Thou hast a few names even in Sardis which have not
> defiled their garments; and they shall walk with me in
> white: for they are worthy. He that overcometh, the same
> shall be clothed in white raiment; and I will not blot out
> his name out of the book of life, but I will confess his
> name before my Father, and before his angels (Revelation
> 3:4–5).

And may the Lord bless you, and keep your garments spotless, that ye may at last be brought to sit down with Abraham, Isaac, and Jacob, and the holy prophets who have been ever since the world began, having your garments spotless even as their garments are spotless, in the kingdom of heaven to go no more out (Alma 7:25).

Jude wrote of those who hate "even the garment spotted by the flesh" (Jude 1:23). His words were repeated in a modern revelation:

Save yourselves from this untoward generation, and come forth out of the fire, hating even the garments spotted with the flesh. . . . I am Jesus Christ, the Son of God; wherefore, gird up your loins and I will suddenly come to my temple (D&C 36:6, 8).[159]

We noted earlier that the wearing of proper raiment at the coming marriage supper of the Lamb is stressed in Matthew 22:11–13. In other passages, those who are not properly attired are said to be "naked":

Behold, I come as a thief. Blessed is he that watcheth, and keepeth his garments, lest he walk naked, and they see his shame (Revelation 16:15).

I counsel thee to buy of me . . . white raiment, that thou mayest be clothed, and that the shame of thy nakedness do not appear; and anoint thine eyes with eyesalve, that thou mayest see (Revelation 3:18).

The Blood of the Lamb

"Let thy garments be always white; and let thy head lack no ointment" (Ecclesiastes 9:8).

White clothing symbolizes purity. As such, it reminds the wearer that he should always conform his thoughts, his actions and his words to the righteous principles of heaven. The clothing of the righteous, in both the Bible and the Book of Mormon, is made white by being cleansed in the blood of the lamb.[160] John wrote:

> And one of the elders answered, saying unto me, What are these which are arrayed in white robes? and whence came they? And I said unto him, Sir, thou knowest. And he said to me, These are they which came out of great tribulation, and have washed their robes, and made them white in the blood of the Lamb. Therefore are they before the throne of God, and serve him day and night in his temple: and he that sitteth on the throne shall dwell among them (Revelation 7:13–15).[161]

In a similar vision, Nephi saw the twelve disciples Jesus would choose from among the Nephites, who would be "righteous forever; for because of their faith in the Lamb of God their garments are made white in his blood . . . and their garments were white even like unto the Lamb of God. And the angel said unto me: These are made white in the blood of the Lamb, because of their faith in him" (1 Nephi 12:10–11). Alma also explained this principle:

> For there can no man be saved except his garments are washed white; yea, his garments must be purified until they are cleansed from all stain, through the blood of him of whom it has been spoken by our fathers, who should come to redeem his people from their sins (Alma 5:21; see also Alma 13:11; 34:36; 3 Nephi 27:19; Ether 13:10–12; cf. D&C 76:69).[162]

It is by preaching repentance to the people that one's garments are made clean. Jacob shook his garment before the people assembled at the temple as a witness "that I shook your iniquities from my soul, and that I stand with brightness before him, and am rid of your blood" (2 Nephi 9:44; cf. Jacob 2:2 and see Acts 18:6). He later wrote:

> And we did magnify our office unto the Lord, taking

upon us the responsibility, answering the sins of the
people upon our own heads if we did not teach them the
word of God with all diligence; wherefore, by labor-
ing with our might their blood might not come upon
our garments; otherwise their blood would come upon
our garments, and we would not be found spotless at the
last day (Jacob 1:19).

King Benjamin likewise assembled the people at the
temple, "that I might be found blameless, and that your
blood should not come upon me, when I shall stand to be
judged of God of the things whereof he hath commanded
me concerning you . . . that I might rid my garments of your
blood" (Mosiah 2:27–28; cf. Mormon 9:35; Acts 20:26–27).[163]
Modern revelation has also made it clear that missionary
work is a means to free oneself from the "blood of this generation" (D&C 88:85–86; 112:33).[164] In another passage, after
exhorting early missionaries to preach, the Lord promised
them, "And inasmuch as they do this they shall rid their
garments, and they shall be spotless before me" (D&C
61:34).

The Savior's Vesture

"And I saw that a virgin was born from Judah wearing
a linen stole; and from her was born a spotless lamb."[165]

The Book of Mormon takes special note of the "white
robe" worn by Jesus when he appeared to the Nephites in
the city of Bountiful after his resurrection (3 Nephi 11:8). Its
"whiteness . . . did exceed all the whiteness, yea, even there
could be nothing upon earth so white as the whiteness
thereof" (3 Nephi 19:25). The celestial clothing worn by
Christ in John's vision is similarly described: "And in the
midst of the seven candlesticks one like unto the Son of
man, clothed with a garment down to the foot, and girt
about the paps with a golden girdle."[166]

Evidently, some of Jesus' contemporaries attributed miraculous powers to the clothing worn by the Savior during his mortal ministry. We read of a woman who touched the hem of Jesus' garment to be healed (see Matthew 9:20–22; Luke 8:44; Mark 5:27–28).[167] We read that the sick "besought him that they might only touch the hem of his garment: and as many as touched were made perfectly whole" (Matthew 14:36; Mark 6:56).

The robe of Jesus, like that of the high priest in ancient Israel (see Exodus 28:32) was woven as one piece (see John 19:23). Much has been written of this robe, some in popular fiction.[168] According to some of the legends, after the crucifixion (when the soldiers removed Jesus' clothing), the robe fell into Pilate's hands. Subsequently arrested, he was brought before the emperor at Rome, wearing the tunic of Christ. The emperor's rage calmed each time Pilate stood thus clothed in his presence, but returned as soon as Pilate departed. This cycle stopped when Pilate was either executed or accidentally slain.[169]

Matthew made a point of the symbolic importance of Jesus' robe being preserved intact: "And they crucified him, and parted his garments, casting lots: that it might be fulfilled which was spoken by the prophet, They parted my garments among them, and upon my vesture did they cast lots" (Matthew 27:35).

The prophecy cited by Matthew is from Psalm 22:18. Many of the Psalms, written by David, seem to be a prophetic view of his descendant and rightful successor, Jesus Christ.[170] The following may also be a prophecy of the Christ, though referring to actual historical characters.[171]

> And it shall come to pass in that day, that I will call my servant Eliakim the son of Hilkiah: And I will clothe him with thy robe, and strengthen him with thy girdle,

and I will commit thy government into his hand: and he shall be a father to the inhabitants of Jerusalem, and to the house of Judah. And the key of the house of David will I lay upon his shoulder; so he shall open, and none shall shut; and he shall shut, and none shall open.[172] And I will fasten him as a nail in a sure place; and he shall be for a glorious throne to his father's house. And they shall hang upon him all the glory of his father's house, the off-spring and the issue, all vessels of small quantity, from the vessels of cups, even to all the vessels of flagons. In that day, saith the Lord of hosts, shall the nail that is fastened in the sure place be removed, and be cut down, and fall (Isaiah 22:20–25).[173]

In Gethsemane, Jesus sweat great drops of blood (see Luke 22:44; D&C 19:18), which must have stained his garment red. The symbolic nature of the bloodstained garment is explained in a pseudepigraphal work that discusses the scapegoat which was cursed anciently with Israel's sins (see Leviticus 16:7–10):

And why [do you behold] the one that is accursed crowned? Because they shall see Him then in that day having a scarlet robe about his body down to his feet; and they shall say, Is not this He whom we once despised, and pierced, and mocked, and crucified? Truly this is He who then declared Himself to be the Son of God.[174]

Jewish tradition holds that the Messiah's garment will be red with blood, as from the winepress.[175] The same idea is found in several biblical passages (see Isaiah 63:1–8; Revelation 14:18–20; 19:13–15; Genesis 49:10–11; Lamentations 1:15). The apostle John wrote of his vision of the returning Christ:

And on his head were many crowns; and he had a name written, that no man knew, but he himself. And he was clothed with a vesture dipped in blood: and his

name is called The Word of God. And the armies which
were in heaven followed him . . . clothed in fine linen,
white and clean. . . . And he hath on his vesture and on
his thigh a name written, KING OF KINGS, AND LORD
OF LORDS (Revelation 19:12–14, 16).

Christ's celestial garb is therefore both royal and priestly in
nature.

Conclusions

The priestly garb of biblical times has traditionally been
associated with the celestial attire of God and of angels,
which is reserved for the righteous who will enter God's
presence. Because of its divine symbolism, miraculous powers (such as protection of the wearer's body) have been
attributed to priestly clothing. After the construction of the
tabernacle and later the temple, it was deemed inappropriate to wear the special outer garments outside the sanctuary. This changed in early Christianity. Hugh Nibley has
noted that Christians, longing to retain temple rites, transferred some of them to nontemple ceremonies. This
included the imitation of temple clothing in the celebration
of Christian sacraments or ordinances.[176] For example, the
wearing of the cossack (robe), the apron, the stole, and the
mitre by Roman Catholic clergy is a vestige of ancient
priestly dress used in the temple.

Investiture of kings and priests in much of Christianity
today also follows the ancient rite, with anointing and
clothing in special garments. Anciently, the investiture ceremony denoted a symbolic change from an earthly to a
heavenly status. Because the priestly clothing was considered to be divine in origin, it gave the wearer authority
to act as a representative of God among men. It was this

outward expression of an inner power that made priestly garb a fitting symbol of God's presence.

Notes

1. The document was composed in Arabic, probably in Egypt, in the eleventh century A.D. using earlier texts and was soon thereafter translated into Ethiopic. Charlesworth refers to the work as "The Conflict of Adam and Eve," though he does not include it in his *Old Testament Pseudepigrapha*. It was called *1 and 2 Adam and Eve* by S. C. Malan, whose translation appears in Rutherford H. Platt, Jr., ed., *The Forgotten Books of Eden* (Cleveland: World Publishing; copyrighted 1927 by Alpha House).

2. Theodoretus, in his commentary on Genesis 3:27 *(Quaestiones in Genesis)*, found it difficult to believe that God could have slain animals to provide clothing for Adam and Eve. The same concern may have given rise to the idea in TB *Sotah* 14a and *Midrash Bereshit Rabbah* 20:12 that these garments were made of wool or of linen. The priestly garments used by descendants of Aaron were made of linen.

3. *1 Adam and Eve* 50:6–7, in Platt, *The Forgotten Books of Eden*, 30.

4. *1 Adam and Eve* 52:3–9, in ibid., 34.

5. See *Pirqe de Rabbi Eliezer* 20; *Targum Yerushalmi* Genesis 3:21.

6. Cited in *LJ*, 1:80 and 5:103, n. 93. Ginzberg also refers us to Hizkuni on Genesis 3:21. For Leviathan, the "great serpent," see Job 41:1; Psalm 74:14; Isaiah 27:1.

7. We should note the very common belief that the serpent (and sometimes the lizard) does not die because it sheds its skin each year. Frazer noted the existence of this tradition among the ancient Phoenicians as well as among tribes of Africa, South America, and various islands of the South Pacific. Some legends indicate that God originally intended to tell humans to cast their skin as they grew old in order to become young again, but the message was somehow delivered to the serpent instead. The receiving of celestial garments in place of earthly garb is likewise thought in early Jewish and Christian lore to bestow eternal life and protection from earthly dangers. For a detailed study of the subject of the cast skin, see Sir James George Frazer, *Folk-Lore in the Old Testament* (New York: Tudor, 1923), 1:18, 26–32.

8. *3 Baruch* 9:7, Slavonic version, in *OTP*, 1:672.

9. Ibid., 1:673.

10. See *Midrash Bereshit Rabbah* 20:12.

11. E.g., *Midrash Bereshit Rabbah* 18:56; 20:12. According to this view, God and the angels are also clothed in light. In a Kabbalistic

text on the creation of the world, we read that the heavens were made from the light of God's garment (*Pirqe de Rabbi Eliezer* 3). For being clothed in light, see D&C 85:7. According to the *Book of the Rolls* f.93a, Adam's body, at the creation, was brighter than the sun.

12. See *Avot de Rabbi Nathan* 42:116–17; according to *3 Baruch* 4:16 (Greek), Adam and Eve lost the glory of God; cf. *3 Baruch* 13:4 (Slavonic).

13. *Yalkut Reubeni* I, 34, cited in *LJ*, 5:104, n. 93.

14. See *Pirqe de Rabbi Eliezer* 14; *Targum Yerushalmi* 3:7, 3:21; *Orehot Hayyim* I, 68c.

15. See *Zohar* I, 36b.

16. *Book of the Rolls* f.95b, in Margaret Dunlop Gibson, *Apocrypha Arabica* (London: Clay & Sons; Cambridge Univ. Warehouse, 1901), chapter on "Kitâb al Magâl, or The Book of the Rolls," 9.

17. *Apocalypse of Adam* 1:2–3, in *OTP*, 1:712.

18. *1 Adam and Eve* 51:5, in Platt, *The Forgotten Books of Eden*, 34.

19. *1 Adam and Eve* 37:4, in ibid., 26; see also *1 Adam and Eve* 8:2; 51:5.

20. *1 Adam and Eve* 60:16, in ibid., 41; cf. *1 Adam and Eve* 33:5–6.

21. *Book of the Rolls* f.93a, in Gibson, *Apocrypha Arabica*, 6.

22. *Book of the Rolls* f.94a, in ibid., 7.

23. *Book of the Rolls* f.95b, in ibid., 9.

24. When Satan rebelled, "God . . . deprived the Devil of the robe of praise and dignity" (*Book of the Rolls* f.93b, in ibid., 7). In view of the Book of Mormon teaching that Satan wants mankind to become like him (2 Nephi 2:18, 27), this may explain why he was so anxious that Adam and Eve be stripped of their heavenly clothing.

25. In some Bible and Book of Mormon passages, "nakedness" refers to mankind's sinful state (see 2 Chronicles 28:19; Lamentations 1:8; 2 Nephi 9:14; Mormon 9:5; cf. Revelation 16:15). This concept is reflected in the Jewish tradition that the fall caused Adam and Eve to become aware of their lack of good deeds (*Midrash Bereshit Rabbah* 19.6; *Pirqe de Rabbi Eliezer* 14; *Targum Yerushalmi* Genesis 3:10).

26. *Apocalypse of Moses* 20:1–2, in *OTP*, 2:281; the use of sacred clothing to denote righteousness is discussed later in this article.

27. *Gospel of Philip*, II, 3, 56, in Robinson, *The Nag Hammadi Library in English*, 134.

28. Koran 7:27, tr. Muhammad Zafrulla Khan (London: Curzon, 1975), 142.

29. *History of the Rechabites* 5:2, in *OTP*, 2:452.

30. *History of the Rechabites* 5:3, in ibid.

31. *History of the Rechabites* 12:2–3a, in ibid., 2:456–57.

32. See Origen, *Contra Celsum* IV, 40.

33. See *Sifre Divre ha-Yamim* 355; *Mekilta wa-Yassa^c* 5:51a; TB *Pesahim* 54b; *Avot de Rabbi Nathan* 57, 95; *Midrash Bereshit Rabbah* 20:12; Abkir in *Yalkut* I, 34; *Midrash Tanhuma ha-Qadosh weha-Yashan* 1:17–18, 33. Jerome, in his commentary on Genesis 27:16, mentioned the Jewish tradition that Adam's garment was worn anciently by the firstborn in the family, who performed priestly service before Aaron's time. Other early Christian sources also state that the garments of Adam and Eve were created before the world; for references, see *LJ*, 5:104, n. 93.

34. The *Book of Jasher* (from the Hebrew meaning "book of the righteous [one]") is not the book of that name mentioned in the Bible (see Joshua 10:13; 2 Samuel 1:18). Rather, it is a thirteenth-century A.D. document that imitates biblical Hebrew and was probably composed in Spain. It nevertheless preserves a number of early Jewish traditions known from midrashic and pseudepigraphal sources such as *Jubilees,* and is therefore valuable as a collection of Jewish lore. The English translation most familiar to us (and cited in this article) was published by J. H. Parry and Company of Salt Lake City in 1887.

35. Rabbi Bahya, in his commentary on Genesis 3:21, has the garment descending from Adam to Cain, then to Nimrod.

36. Regarding Ham's claim on the priesthood, see Abraham 1:25–27.

37. *Jasher* 7:23–32.

38. See Midrash ^c*Aseret Melakim* 38–39; *Zohar* I, 73b–74a, 142b; *Sabba, Toledot,* 28a; *Pirqe de Rabbi Eliezer* 24.

39. See *Hadar* and *Da^cat* on Genesis 25:29–32.

40. See *Targum Yerushalmi* Genesis 25:25; *Pirqe de Rabbi Eliezer* 32; *Yalkut Reubeni* I, 110; *Nur al-Zulm* 95; see also *LJ*, 5:276, n. 38.

41. *Jasher* 27:3–4, 7–12.

42. See *Midrash Bereshit Rabbah* 63:13.

43. See *Midrash Bereshit Rabbah*, 420–22; *Midrash Va-yiqra Rabbah* 25:6; *Midrash ba-Midbar Rabbah* 4:8; TB *Nedarim* 32b; *Tanhuma Buber* Genesis 76; *Pirqe de Rabbi Eliezer*. The *Book of the Rolls* f.110b (in Gibson, *Apocrypha Arabica*) notes that Melchizedek's priestly clothing was made of animal skins.

44. *Jubilees* 26:11, in *OTP*, 2:106. The same story is told in *Midrash Bereshit Rabbah* 63.13.

45. *Jubilees* 26:23–24, in *OTP*, 2:107.

46. *Midrash Tanhuma ha-Qadum weha-Yashan* I, 145, notes that the bodies of the pious emit a celestial fragrance of paradise; this fragrance was later identified with that of the incense used in the temple

(*Midrash Tanhuma ha-Qadum weha-Yashan* I, 145; *Midrash Bereshit Rabbah* 65:23; *Targum Yerushalmi* Genesis 27:27); see also *LJ*, 5:284, n. 92.

47. Origen, *Contra Celsum* I, 48.

48. See *Midrash Bereshit Rabbah* 89:9; *Zohar* I, 194b.

49. ʿAsarah ha-Ruge Malkut 20 (whence borrowed by *Hadar* and *Daʿat*); *Imre Noʿam* on Genesis 38:22–23, which has Raphael instead of Gabriel; cited in *LJ*, 5:330, n. 51.

50. In Alma 46:21–24 we read of a particular ceremony associated with the story of Joseph's garment. Because Jewish tradition indicates that Joseph's garment was the high priestly garment of Adam, this passage may have more meaning than previously supposed. In this passage, the desecration of the garment symbolizes being "ashamed to take upon them the name of Christ."

51. *LJ*, 5:329, n. 43.

52. Hugh Nibley, *An Approach to the Book of Mormon*, in *CWHN*, 6:219–22.

53. *JD*, 4:172.

54. *Midrash Bereshit Rabbah* 36:6; *Midrash Tanhuma ha-Qadum weha-Yashan* I, 48–50; cited in *LJ*, 5:192, n. 61.

55. TB *Shabbat* 113b; TB *Sanhedrin* 94a; *Midrash Tanhuma ha-Qadum weha-Yashan* I, 50; III, 13–14; *Tanhuma Noah* 15; *Tehillim* 11,100; cf. *Targum Yerushalmi* Numbers 11:26, cited in *LJ*, 6:363.4, n. 59.

56. TB *Shabbat* 113b; TB *Sanhedrin* 94a; Jerome on Isaiah 10:16; *Tosefta-Targum* 2 Kings 19:35; *Targum* 2 Chronicles 32:21; *2 Baruch* 63:8.

57. *Jasher* 12:33.

58. By this we are to understand that they did not use the incense prepared according to the formula mentioned in Exodus 30:34–38.

59. *LJ*, 6:75, n. 385, referring to Leviticus 10:1–2. His references are *Sifra* 10:2; TB *Sanhedrin* 52a; *Midrash Tanhuma ha-Qadum weha-Yashan* I, 50; III, 13–14; and *Tanhuma* Noah 15.

60. *Midrash Pesikta Rabbati*, 10, 92a–b; *Midrash Devarim Rabbah* 7:11; *Midrash Shir ha-Shirim Rabbah* 4:11; *Tehillim* 23, 199–200. The story was known to Justinian, *Dialogue*, 131.

61. *Acts of Philip* 144, in Montague Rhodes James, *The Apocryphal New Testament* (Oxford: Clarendon, 1955), 450.

62. *Pseudo-Philo* 20:2–3, in *OTP*, 2:329.

63. *The Lives of the Prophets* 21:14, in ibid., 2:397; this text follows the Greek Septuagint version of the Bible, while the Hebrew text has "mantle."

64. *The Lives of the Prophets* 22:5, in ibid., 2:397.

65. Flavius Josephus, *Antiquities of the Jews* ix, 10, 4.

66. *OTP*, 2:321.

67. According to *Midrash Bereshit Rabbah* 20:12, Rabbi Johanan said that the garments of Adam and Eve were like the fine linen garments from Beth-Shean.

68. As required by the law of Moses; see Exodus 20:26.

69. *Letter of Aristeas* 87, in *OTP*, 2:18.

70. *Letter of Aristeas* 4:10–11, in Platt, *The Forgotten Books of Eden*, 152.

71. *Letter of Aristeas* 96–99, in *OTP*, 2:19.

72. *Letter of Aristeas* 158, in ibid., 2:23.

73. In the verse that follows, Eleazar speaks of the *tephillin*, or phylacteries; one of the features of the phylactery box worn on the forehead is that it has four separate compartments, each containing a specific passage of scripture from the law of Moses.

74. See M *Sukkah* 5:2–3.

75. See *Testament of Levi* 7:4–8:1. The name Beth-El, given to the site by Jacob (Genesis 28:16–17), means "house of God," evidently because Jacob saw in vision the heavenly temple. Among other prophets who saw the heavenly temple are Isaiah, Ezekiel, Daniel, John the Revelator, Lehi, Nephi, and Enoch.

76. For virtues associated with garments, see the section Garments of Righteousness, later in this chapter.

77. *Testament of Levi* 8:2–10, in *OTP*, 1:791.

78. *Jubilees* 32:1, 3, in ibid., 2:116–17.

79. *2 Enoch* 22:8–10, in ibid., 1:138–39.

80. *3 Enoch* 12:1–3, in ibid., 1:265. He then speaks of having been given a new name. Charlesworth notes that in the Alphabet of Metatron, the angel wears eight garments, corresponding to the eight garments of the high priest (see note 12a, p. 265).

81. See *1 Enoch* 71:3, where the archangel Michael takes Enoch by the right hand to lead him into the mysteries; cf. Abraham 1:18.

82. See *Midrash Bereshit Rabbah* 58:9; *Midrash ha-Gadol, Sepher Bereshit* I, 362; *Mishle* 16, 38; *Tanuma Hayye* 4; *Aggadat Bereshit* 32, 68.

83. The passage is cited by Jesus in Luke 4:16–21.

84. The renunciation of the devil is also found in third-century A.D. Christian baptism, where the initiate is also anointed and dressed in white clothing. The practice, formerly confined to the temple, was ultimately moved to the more open ordinance because the temple had long since ceased to exist (see John A. Tvedtnes, "Olive Oil: Symbol of the Holy Ghost," in *The Allegory of the Olive Tree: The Olive,*

the Bible, and Jacob 5, ed. Stephen D. Ricks and John W. Welch [Salt Lake City: Deseret Book and F.A.R.M.S., 1994], 427–59).

85. Alfred Edersheim, *The Temple: Its Ministry & Services as They Were at the Time of Jesus Christ* (Grand Rapids: Eerdmans, 1965), 97.

86. *Testament of Job* 46:5–9, in *OTP,* 1:864.

87. *Testament of Job* 47:3, in ibid.

88. *Testament of Job* 47:5 (citing Job 38:3; 40:2), in ibid., 1:865.

89. See *Testament of Job* 47:6, in ibid.

90. *Testament of Job* 47:10–11, in ibid.

91. *Testament of Job* 48:2–3, in ibid., 1:865–66.

92. *Testament of Job* 50:1–2, in ibid., 1:866.

93. *Testament of Job* 52:1, in ibid., 1:867.

94. Theodoretus, commenting on Exodus 3:5 *(Quaestiones in Genesis),* makes the same inference; cf. TB *Rosh ha-Shanah* 31b and TB *Shekalim* 5:48d.

95. Johann Lorenz von Mosheim, *An Ecclesiastical History from the Birth of Christ to the Beginning of the Eighteenth Century,* 6 vols., tr. Archibald MacLaine (London: Tegg, 1842), 1:261–62. The ceremony is described by Cyril of Jerusalem, in his *Catechetical Lectures.*

96. *Apostolic Constitutions* viii, 6, 6; in *OTP,* 2:688.

97. For a more complete discussion of this subject, see my article "Olive Oil: Symbol of the Holy Ghost," 427–59.

98. *Acts of Thomas* 156–58, in James, *Apocryphal New Testament,* 432–33.

99. See *Ignatius to Polycarp* 1:3.

100. *Odes of Solomon* 4:7–9, in *OTP,* 2:736.

101. Cf. Ephesians 2:19–21; *Ignatius to the Ephesians* 2:10. The tower in the vineyard in Isaiah 5:1–7 (borrowed by Christ in Matthew 21:33–45) has sometimes been interpreted as the temple (see Ephrem in *Diatessaron Commentary* [Armenian] 16:19; Isaiah 5:2–5 in *Targum Jonathan;* TB *Sukkah* 49a).

102. Pastor of Hermas, *Similitude* 8:2, in A. Cleveland Coxe, *Fathers of the Second Century,* vol. 2 of *The Ante-Nicene Fathers,* ed. Alexander Roberts and James Donaldson (New York: Charles Scribner's Sons, 1913), 39–40.

103. This would imply that the robe was draped over the left shoulder.

104. Pastor of Hermas, *Similitude* 9:2, in Coxe, *Fathers of the Second Century,* 43.

105. *Similitude* 9:13, in ibid., 48.

106. Ibid.

107. Ibid.

108. *Similitude* 9:15, in ibid., 49.

109. See *Ignatius to the Ephesians* 2:10, cf. 3:23.

110. *Pseudo-Philo* 40:6, in *OTP*, 2:359.

111. *Joseph and Aseneth* 3:6, in ibid., 2:205–6.

112. *Joseph and Aseneth* 4:1, in ibid., 2:206.

113. *Joseph and Aseneth* 14:12, in ibid., 2:225.

114. *Joseph and Aseneth* 14:14–15, in ibid.

115. *Joseph and Aseneth* 15:9–10, in ibid., 2:227.

116. *Joseph and Aseneth* 18:5–6, in ibid., 2:232.

117. *Odes of Solomon* 25:8, in ibid., 2:758; note the earlier discussion about garments of skin and garments of light.

118. *Odes of Solomon* 21:3, 5–6, in ibid., 2:754.

119. *Apocryphon of James* 14, in Robinson, *The Nag Hammadi Library in English*, 35.

120. *OTP*, 2:528.

121. Papyrus Chester Beatty XVI.25a.

122. The sweet odor of garments from paradise was discussed above.

123. *Testament of Abraham* 16:6–10, in *OTP*, 1:892.

124. *Apocalypse of Abraham* 11:1–3, in ibid., 1:694.

125. *Joseph and Aseneth* 14:9, in ibid., 2:225.

126. *Hymn of the Soul*, the *Acts of Thomas*, in James, *Apocryphal New Testament*, 423.

127. *4 Ezra* 2:42–47, in *OTP*, 1:528. Cf. Revelation 7:13–15, cited below.

128. For crowns in the Bible, see 1 Corinthians 9:25; 2 Timothy 4:8; James 1:12; 1 Peter 5:4; Revelation 2:10; 3:11; 4:4, 10. The crown motif is also found in pseudepigraphal works, including *2 Baruch* 15:8; *Apocalypse of Elijah* 1:7–8; 4:29; *4 Ezra* 2:46; *Martyrdom and Ascension of Isaiah* 9:25.

129. *3 Enoch* 43:1–3 notes that when the souls of men return to God, they clothe themselves in his presence.

130. *Apocalypse of Abraham* 13:14, in *OTP*, 1:695.

131. *Martyrdom and Ascension of Isaiah* 1:5, in ibid., 2:157. The translator, M. A. Knibb, indicates that this expression typically relates, in pseudepigraphal literature, to the descent of the Beloved through the seven heavens (ibid., 2:157, note q).

132. *Martyrdom and Ascension of Isaiah* 3:25, in ibid., 2:161.

133. *Martyrdom and Ascension of Isaiah* 4:16–17, in ibid., 2:162.

134. *Martyrdom and Ascension of Isaiah* 7:22, in ibid., 2:167.

135. *Martyrdom and Ascension of Isaiah* 8:14–15, in ibid., 2:168.

136. *Martyrdom and Ascension of Isaiah* 8:25, in ibid., 2:169.

137. *Martyrdom and Ascension of Isaiah* 8:26, in ibid.

138. *Martyrdom and Ascension of Isaiah* 9:2, in ibid.

139. *Martyrdom and Ascension of Isaiah* 9:9–12, in ibid., 2:170.

140. *Martyrdom and Ascension of Isaiah* 9:17–18, in ibid.

141. *Martyrdom and Ascension of Isaiah* 9:24–26, in ibid., 2:171.

142. *Martyrdom and Ascension of Isaiah* 11:35, in ibid., 2:176.

143. *Martyrdom and Ascension of Isaiah* 11:40, in ibid.

144. *Gospel of Philip*, II, 3, 56–57, in Robinson, *Nag Hammadi Library in English*, 134–35.

145. See *Acts of Philip* 144, in James, *Apocryphal New Testament*, 185.

146. The hymn, though known independently, was incorporated into the *Acts of Thomas*, in James, *Apocryphal New Testament*, 412–13. See Nibley's treatment of the text in Hugh Nibley, *The Message of the Joseph Smith Papyri: An Egyptian Endowment* (Salt Lake City: Deseret Book, 1975), 267–72.

147. See Nibley, *The Message of the Joseph Smith Papyri*, 273–78.

148. *Apocalypse of Zephaniah* 8:3, in *OTP*, 1:514.

149. *Odes of Solomon* 11:10, in ibid., 2:745.

150. *1 Enoch* 62:15–16, in ibid., 1:44.

151. *4 Ezra* 2:37–40, in ibid., 1:527.

152. *Testament of Levi* 18:14, in ibid., 1:795.

153. *Pseudo-Philo* 64:6, in ibid., 2:377.

154. *2 Adam and Eve* 17:27–28, in Platt, *Forgotten Books of Eden*, 73.

155. *2 Adam and Eve* 17:32–33, in ibid.

156. *Pseudo-Philo* 27:12, in *OTP*, 2:340.

157. *Jubilees* 31:1, 3, in ibid., 2:114; the event took place at Beth-El, the site of Jacob's dream of the ladder and of Levi's vision of the men who washed, anointed, and clothed him to serve as a priest.

158. In the Ugaritic texts of the fourteenth century B.C., Anat, goddess of war, is bespattered by blood and gore as she slays men on the earth. She casts her filth into the sea and receives rain from her husband, the sky-god Baal, to wash her clean. The annual rains were seen by the Canaanites and related peoples to be Baal's means of cleansing the blood of the slain from the body of his wife, who was the earth. The idea of washing away "filthiness" is found in Proverbs 30:12 and Isaiah 4:4 (where the word parallels "blood"). In both passages, the Hebrew word for "filth" is cognate to the Ugaritic word used in the story of Anat. See the Ugaritic text and translation in Umberto Cassuto, *The Goddess Anath*, trans. Israel Abrahams (Jerusalem: The Magnes Press, The Hebrew University, 1971), 88–89.

159. In some passages of scripture, we read that the garments of the righteous shall be made clean (e.g., Ether 12:37–38 = D&C 135:5).

160. Cf. the following New Testament passages and note the use of temple terminology in each:

"But if we walk in the light, as he is in the light, we have fellowship one with another, and the blood of Jesus Christ his Son cleanseth us from all sin" (1 John 1:7).

"And from Jesus Christ, who is the faithful witness, and the first begotten of the dead, and the prince of the kings of the earth. Unto him that loved us, and washed us from our sins in his own blood, And hath made us kings and priests unto God and his Father; to him be glory and dominion for ever and ever. Amen" (Revelation 1:5–6).

161. This passages resembles *4 Ezra* 2:42–47, cited earlier in this article.

162. The "Lamb . . . slain from the foundation of the world" was seen by Enoch (Moses 7:47) and was later depicted by John the Baptist (John 1:29, 36) and the apostle John (Revelation 5:6; 13:8). Sanctification through his atoning blood is paramount in the plan of redemption. Some ancient religions practiced actual baptism in the blood of lambs and bulls.

163. This discourse was delivered by king Benjamin at the temple (Mosiah 1:18; 2:1, 5–7).

164. The passage from Doctrine and Covenants 88 is from the section denoted the "Olive Leaf" by Joseph Smith, which is a revelation specifically designed to prepare the Latter-day Saints for the temple that the Lord commanded them to build. In this connection, we note the Bible's most prominent temple hymn, Psalm 24, in which we read that those who are worthy to enter the sanctuary (the "hill of the Lord") are those who have "clean hands and a pure heart."

165. *Testament of Joseph* 19:8, in *OTP*, 1:824. This is the reading of the Greek ß text; the Armenian has "a multicolored stole."

166. Revelation 1:13; *Apocalypse of Zephaniah* 6:12 (in *OTP*, 1:513) similarly describes an angel: "And he was girded as if a golden girdle were upon his breast." We have seen the golden girdle in other passages cited earlier.

167. The "hem" is generally considered to be the tassel on the corner of the tallith worn by all Jewish men at the time, and called "the borders of their garments" by Jesus (Matthew 23:5; cf. Mark 12:38).

168. Note especially the novels of General Lew Wallace, *The Robe* and its sequel, *Demetrius and the Gladiators,* both of which later became major motion pictures.

169. See James, *Apocryphal New Testament,* 158, on "The Death of Pilate."

170. See and cf. Psalm 45:6–7; Hebrews 1:8; and note the comment by Peter in Acts 2:25–35.

171. Eliakim means "God will set up" and Hilkiah means "the portion of Jehovah"; both can be symbolic titles of Christ.

172. This seems to refer to the sealing power given by Jesus to his twelve apostles (see Matthew 16:19; 18:18).

173. Note that Jesus holds the "key of David" (Revelation 3:7). If this is a prophecy of Christ, the words "shall fall" perhaps refer to his death.

174. *Epistle of Barnabas 7*, in A. Cleveland Coxe, *The Apostolic Fathers,* vol. 1 of *The Ante-Nicene Fathers,* ed. Alexander Roberts and James Donaldson (New York: Charles Scribner's Sons, 1913), 141.

175. See *Tanhuma wa-Yehi* 10; *Targumim* 49:8–12; *Midrash ha-Gadol Bereshit* I, 735–9; *Yelammedenu* 35; cited in *LJ* 2:143, 5:367, n. 388.

176. See Hugh Nibley "Christian Envy of the Temple," in *Mormonism and Early Christianity,* in *CWHN,* 4:391–434.

24

The Garment of Adam in Jewish, Muslim, and Christian Tradition

Stephen D. Ricks

Although rarely occurring in any detail, the motif of Adam's garment appears with surprising frequency in ancient Jewish and Christian literature. (I am using the term "Adam's garment" as a cover term to include any garment bestowed by a divine being to one of the patriarchs that is preserved and passed on, in many instances, from one generation to another. I will thus also consider garments divinely granted to other patriarchal figures, including Noah, Abraham, and Joseph.) Although attested less often than in the Jewish and Christian sources, the motif also occurs in the literature of early Islam, especially in the *Isra'iliyyāt* literature in the Muslim authors al-Thaʿlabī and al-Kisā'ī as well as in the *Rasā'il Ikhwān al-Ṣafā (Epistles of the Brethren of Purity)*. Particularly when discussing the garment of Adam in the Jewish tradition, I will shatter chronological boundaries, ranging from the biblical, pseudepigraphic, and midrashic references to the garment of Adam to its medieval attestations.[1] In what follows, I wish to consider (1) the garment of Adam as a primordial creation; (2) the garment as a locus of power, a symbol of authority, and a high priestly garb; and (3) the garment of Adam and heavenly robes.[2]

1. The Garment of Adam as a Primordial Creation

The traditions of Adam's garment in the Hebrew Bible begin quite sparely, with a single verse in Genesis 3:21, where we are informed that "God made garments of skins for Adam and for his wife and clothed them." Probably the oldest rabbinic traditions include the view that God gave garments to Adam and Eve before the Fall but that these were not garments of skin (Hebrew *ʿôr*) but instead garments of light (Hebrew *'ôr*).[3] Rabbi Jacob of Kefar Ḥanan surmises that the section describing the investiture actually belongs after Genesis 2:25, which reads, "And they were both naked, the man and his wife, and were not ashamed," but was moved to 3:21 in order that the section "conclude not with the serpent but with a note of God's care."[4] *Genesis Rabbah* 3:21 runs as follows:

> In R. Meir's Torah it was found written, "Garments of light . . . refer to Adam's garments, which were like a torch [shedding radiance], broad at the bottom and narrow at the top. Isaac the Elder said: "They were as smooth as a finger-nail and as beautiful as a Jewel." R. Johanan said: "They were like the fine linen garments which come from Bethshean, garment of skin meaning those that are nearest to the skin."[5]

This passage continues with the names of other rabbis who said that the garments were made of goat's skin or wool. But divinely provided garb was not restricted to Adam at the time of creation. According to several rabbis, when God made woman (Genesis 2:22) he adorned her and decked her out with twenty-four pieces of finery (Isaiah 3:18–24). Muslim tradition, as seen in the *Rasā'il Ikhwān al-Ṣafā*, takes a different view—Adam was covered with hair until the expulsion from Paradise, at which time he lost it:

When God created Adam, first father of mankind, and his mate, He compensated for all their deficiencies by providing them with all they needed to survive and maintain their existence as individuals—provender, nourishment, cover, clothing, just as He did for all the other animals who were in that garden on top of that mountain in the East on the equator. For, since He had created them naked, He caused to grow, from the head of each, long hair which fell down along their bodies on all sides in thick profusion to their feet, black and soft as the most beautiful that graced any virgin maid. He raised them both as two beardless, adolescent youths of the finest form of any of the animals there. This hair, a garment to them both, covering their nakedness, served as their coat, carpet, cloak, and defense against cold and heat. They used to walk in that garden, plucking the various fruits, eating of them and living on them, strolling innocently in the lush meads and greenery, among the blooming flowers, peacefully, pleasantly, happy, content, and full of joy, without toil to the body or trouble to the soul. They were forbidden to overstep their station and take what was not theirs before the proper time, but they ignored the command of their Lord and were seduced by the words of their Foe. They took what had been forbidden, so they fell from their high rank, and their hair parted, revealing their nakedness. They were expelled thence, naked, banished, objects of contempt, punished by the imposition of new necessities for the sustenance of their lives in this world and new modes by which they must seek to secure their welfare.[6]

There is also a tradition that Adam's garment was made from the serpent or Leviathan. *Pirqe de Rabbi Eliezer* notes that "from the skin [of Leviathan] the Holy One, blessed be He, made garments of glory for Adam and for his helpmate."[7] According to Ginzberg, this tradition is intended to retain the sense of brightness for both *ʾôr* "light" and *ʿôr* "skin," since Leviathan's skin was believed to have a shining luster.[8] In another tradition in *3 Baruch,* Samael "took the serpent as a garment" in order to deceive Adam.[9] When God cursed the serpent, he caused it to lose its skin every year, just as Adam had lost the garment of light when he had transgressed.[10] *Pirqe de Rabbi Eliezer* also says that the garment of the first man was a "skin of nail" and he was covered with a "cloud of glory."[11] After he sinned Adam was deprived of both the skin of nail and the cloud of glory and saw that he was naked. In another version, after Adam and Eve sinned, the garment of light fell from them. When they repented, God made for them another garment. The first garment that Adam and Eve had worn fled to heaven, where it is now in the treasury of the heavens.[12] Thus, the writer of the *Odes of Solomon* exclaims, "I was covered with the covering of your spirit, and I removed from me my garments of skin."[13]

Erik Peterson observes that, according to the early Christian tradition, "Adam and Eve were stripped by the Fall, in such a way that they saw that they were naked. This means that formerly they were clothed."[14] Adam and Eve wore the "robe of light" or the "robe of sanctity" before their fall; thereafter, they assumed a "garment of humility."[15] Thus, the white robes[16] received by early Christians at the time of baptism—a practice that may go back to New Testament times and may be alluded to in Galatians 3:27: "For as many of you as have been baptized into Christ have put on Christ (Gk. *Christón enedúsasthe*)[17]—represents the garment worn by Adam before his fall, a return to that pre-transgression state of glory and grace.[18] Gregory of Nyssa places in sharp focus the contrast between skin vestments from the fallen world and garments of light from paradise: "As if Adam were still living in each of us, we see our nature covered with garments of skin and the fallen leaves of this earthly life, garments which we made for ourselves when we had been stripped of our robes of light, and we put on the vanities, the honors, the passing satisfactions of the flesh instead of our divine robes."[19] In a statement about baptism, Gregory explicitly connects the vestment given at the time of baptism and the paradisiacal garments of Adam and Eve: "Thou hast driven us out of Paradise and called us back. Thou hast taken away the fig-leaves,[20] that garment of our misery, and clad us once more with a robe of glory."[21] The nakedness that generally accompanied baptism during this period was widely understood to be a symbol of the return to Paradise.[22] Concerning the receipt of the garment at the time of baptism, Jerome states that "when ready for the garment of Christ, we have taken off the tunics of skin, then we shall be clothed with a garment of linen which has nothing of death in it,[23] but is wholly white so that, rising from baptism, we may gird our loins in truth and the entire shame of our past sins may be covered."[24] In other words, at the moment of baptism one removes clothes that represent death in the fallen world ("garments of skin"), and puts on white garments that symbolize life in Christ.[25] Roger Adams, in his study on iconographic evidence for baptism for the dead in antiquity, notes that a "parallel is made between the situation of Adam in the garden and that of the catechumen in the baptistry, and the candidate is to think of himself as if he were Adam in the garden."[26]

According to the *Genesis Rabbah*, when their eyes were opened after their disobedience later in the afternoon of that first Friday,[27] Adam and Eve began to sew, with great difficulty, the leaves of the fig tree, whose fruit had brought the occasion for death into the world, in order to make girdles, shirts, robes, and linen cloaks.[28] Muslim tradition portrays a somewhat similar scenario to that given in the Jewish sources: whereas, previous to his disobedience, Adam was covered with hair, afterwards this hair was taken away and he found himself naked. In the *Rasā'il Ikhwān al-Ṣafā* it states that angels taught Adam how to clothe himself from plant matter.[29] According to al-Thaꜥlabī, on the other hand, the first thing that Adam received following his disobedience was a makeshift apron, a garment of leaves that provided him covering against his nakedness.[30] Similarly, Jewish tradition stresses that the garments were for the purpose of hiding their nakedness, "covering their shame." Thus, *Jubilees* states that God clothed Adam and Eve "and sent them from the garden of Eden. And on that day when Adam went out from the garden of Eden, he offered a sweet-smelling sacrifice . . . in the morning with the rising of the sun from the day he covered his shame. . . . Therefore it is commanded in the heavenly tablets to all who will know the judgment of the Law that they should cover their shame and they should not be uncovered as the gentiles are uncovered."[31] There was a belief among the Jews that "the Patriarchs advanced to the spiritual stage where they assumed the garment of light," an idea depicted in the third-century A.D. synagogue at Dura.[32]

2. The Garment of Adam as a Locus of Power, a Symbol of Authority, and as Priestly Robes

The garment given by God to Adam represents not merely protection and repentance, but authority as well.[33] Of extraordinary brilliance and splendor and possessed of supernatural qualities,[34] Adam's garment was passed down from Adam to his descendants, who wore it as priestly robes. Thus the *Numbers Rabbah* states that "as Adam was about to sacrifice, he donned high priestly garments; as it says: 'God made for Adam and his wife coats of skin'

(Genesis 3:21). They were robes of honor which subsequent firstborn used."[35] The firstborn sons sacrificed while wearing the garment before priests took over the role of sacrificing the offerings.[36] Similarly, according to the *Midrash Tanhuma*, "the liturgy was performed by the firstborn in [Adam's garment]."[37] It was this garment, passed through the generations from Seth to Noah,[38] that was worn by Noah when he sacrificed on an altar.[39] It was one of the items that Noah saved and carried with him in the ark.

But the garment was also seen as having power that might be misused by those into whose hands the garment fell. It was stolen by Ham, who handed it down to his son Cush, who later gave it to Nimrod. Nimrod used this garment to obtain power and glory among men, and as a means to deceive man and to gain unconquerable strength.[40] Nimrod would also use the garment while hunting, which caused all the birds and other animals to fall down in honor and respect before him. As a result, the people made him king over them.[41] He first became king of Babylon, and "was soon able through skillful and subtle speeches to bring the whole of mankind to the point of accepting him as the absolute ruler of the earth."[42] Appropriately, it was the garment that finally cost Nimrod his life. Nimrod, according to one account, went forth with his people on a great hunt; at that time he was jealous of the great hunter Esau. As Nimrod approached with two attendants, Esau hid, cut off Nimrod's head, and killed the two attendants.[43]

Having obtained the garment, Esau either buried it[44] or sold it to Jacob along with his birthright. *Numbers Rabbah* relates that Jacob desired to offer sacrifice but could not because he was not the firstborn and did not have the birthright, part of which consisted of Adam's garment. It was for this reason that Jacob bought the birthright from

Esau, who said, "There is no afterlife, death ends every-thing, and the inheritance will do me no good," and will-ingly let Jacob have the garment, along with his birthright. Immediately Jacob built an altar and offered sacrifice.[45] Here, again, Muslim and Jewish traditions overlap. In the *Rasā'il Ikhwān al-Ṣafā*, Esau's sale of the birthright to Jacob was symbolized by the transfer of the sacred garment. Again, according to bin Gorion, "Esau's garment in which Rebekah clothed him, namely those made by God for Adam and Eve, had now rightfully become Jacob's, and Isaac rec-ognized their paradisiacal fragrance."[46] In a parallel tradi-tion, the early Church Father Hippolytus says that when Isaac laid his hands on Jacob, at the same time feeling Esau's skin garment, he knew that it was the legitimate heir to the blessing—the garment proved that, for Esau would hardly have parted with the garment if he had been worthy of it.[47] Similarly, according to al-Thaʿlabī, Jacob recognized the same fragrance in the garment of Joseph when it was brought to him by Joseph's brothers, and at the same time knew by the marks in it that it was the identical garment that he had received from his father and that Adam had received from God in the Garden.[48] When the jealous broth-ers took the garment away and lowered Joseph into the cis-tern, immediately Gabriel appeared and brought him a gar-ment to protect him, so that he was never without protection.[49] The *Testament of Zebulon* says that Joseph's brothers took from Joseph his garment of honor and put on him the garment of the slave, a reminder of traditions—also found in al-Thaʿlabī—of two portions of Joseph's garment, one that decayed and the other which was miraculously preserved.[50] It is Joseph's preserved garment that is men-tioned by Moroni in Alma 46:24: "Jacob . . . saw that a part of the remnant of the coat of Joseph was preserved and had

not decayed. And he said—Even as this remnant of garment of my son hath been preserved, so shall a remnant of
the seed of my son be preserved by the hand of God, and be
taken unto himself, while the remainder of the seed of
Joseph shall perish, even as the remnant of his garment."

The Talmudic tractate *Arakhin* explains the various parts
of the priestly garments:

> R. ʿAnani b. Sason said: Why is the portion about the
> priestly garments placed next to the portion about the
> sacrifices? It is to tell you that just as sacrifices procure
> atonement, so do the priestly garments. The tunic pro-
> cures atonement for bloodshed, as it is written: And they
> dipped the coat in the blood. The breeches procure atone-
> ment for incest, as it is written: And thou shalt make
> them linen breeches to cover the flesh of their nakedness.
> The mitre procures atonement for those of arrogant mind,
> in accord with what R. Hanina taught; for he said: Let
> that which is [placed] high procure atonement for acts of
> haughtiness. The girdle procures atonement for sinful
> thoughts of the heart, [for it atones] where it is [worn].
> The breastplate procures atonement for [error in] legal
> decisions, as it is written: And thou shalt make a breast-
> plate of judgment. The ephod procures atonement for
> idolatry, as it is written: And without ephod or teraphim.
> The robe procures atonement for slander, for the Holy
> One, blessed be He, said: Let that which emits a sound
> procure atonement for an act of sound [the voice]. The
> [golden] plate procures atonement for impudent deeds,
> for there it is written: And it shall be upon Aaron's fore-
> head.[51]

In Ezekiel 28:13, we have what may be the only canonical mention of Adam's garment outside of Genesis.[52] Ezekiel
says that in the Garden of Eden, the sardius, topaz, diamond, beryl, onyx, jasper, sapphire, emerald, carbuncle,
and gold were the covering that was to be found on those

who dwelled there. These stones are also found on the high priest's garment, as we see in Exodus 28:17–20. This passage in Ezekiel may be seen as an early attempt to connect Adam's clothing with that of the high priest. As in Revelation 4:3, precious gems are used as an indication of the glory of the divine presence.[53] The *Ezekiel Targum* states that the garments were covered with various stones, and the stones in turn were inlaid in gold. This fits the description of the high priest's garment found in Exodus 28 more closely than the description given of the clothing in Ezekiel 28.[54]

3. Garments of Adam as Heavenly Robes

Louis Ginzberg, in his *Legends of the Jews*, says that "we shall not go astray if we identify them [Adam's garments] with the celestial robes of the pious, frequently mentioned in pseudepigraphic literature, and in early Christian as well as kabbalistic writings."[55] The heavenly garment is described as a "shining garment" or "garments of light." "Garment of light" is the same imagery that we find in the description of Adam's garment.[56]

According to Rabbi Akiba, when Michael and Gabriel lead all the sinners up out of hell, "they will wash and anoint them, healing them of their wounds of hell, and clothe them with beautiful, pure garments and lead them into the presence of God."[57] Washing, anointing, and clothing are mentioned as a preparation for marriage in ancient Israel. "Then washed I thee with water; yea, I throughly washed away thy blood from thee, and I anointed thee with oil. I clothed thee also with broidered work, and shod thee with badgers' skin, and I girded thee about with fine linen, and I covered thee with silk" (Ezekiel 16:9–10). Similar ceremonies are mentioned elsewhere in the Old Testament (see Ruth 3:3) and in other parts of the ancient Near East as well.[58] Aaron and his sons participated in a complex ritual of washing, anointing, and clothing in priestly garments that qualified them for temple service. The ritual, outlined in Exodus 29, comprised a multipart ceremony, including: (1) ritual ablutions, or the washing with water (Exodus 29:4); (2) the vesting rite, wherein Aaron was given eight sacred garments (Exodus 29:5–6; the sons of Aaron were also vested); (3) the ceremony with "the anointing oil," which was first poured upon the recipient's head and then smeared (Exodus 29:7). The ordination of Aaron, recorded in Leviticus 8, runs along similar lines. First, Moses "washed [Aaron and his sons] with water" (Leviticus 8:6); "He put upon" Aaron the priestly garment (Leviticus 8:7–9); thereafter Moses anointed Aaron after he "took the anointing oil, and anointed the tabernacle" and all of its vessels and appurtenances, including the altar (Leviticus 8:10–11).[59]

The pseudepigraphic *Testament of Levi* contains an outstanding example of washing, anointing, and clothing:

> And the first man anointed me with holy oil, and gave me a staff of judgment. The second washed me with pure water, fed me with bread and wine, the holiest things, and clad me with a holy and glorious robe. The third clothed me with a linen vestment like an ephod. The fourth put round me a girdle like unto purple. . . . The sixth placed a crown on my head. The seventh placed on my head a priestly diadem and filled my hands with incense, that I might serve as a priest to the Lord God.[60]

The process of washing, anointing, and clothing in this and other priestly (and nonpriestly) settings is, according to Widengren and Jensen, strongly reminiscent of coronation ceremonies in the ancient Near East.[61]

In the ancient baptismal ceremonies of the early

Christian church, those baptized received an anointing, a white robe, and a ritual meal.[62] These garments were "commonly worn for eight days and were metaphorically called the garments of Christ or the mystical garments."[63]

Both the heavenly robe and Adam's garment were seen, in ancient times, to be a sign of honor and a reward for the righteous. In the *Targum Onkelos* to Genesis we read, "And the Lord God made for Adam and his wife garments of honor (to be worn) upon the skin of their flesh, and He clothed them."[64] In the Dead Sea Scrolls *Community Rule*, the faithful were to receive "life everlasting, and a crown of glory and a robe of honor, amid light perpetual."[65] In *4 Ezra*, Ezra sees in a vision the pious in heaven, and the angel explains that "these are they who have put off mortal clothing and put on the immortal, and they have confessed the name of God; now they are being crowned, and receive palms."[66] In another passage in *4 Ezra*, the writer calls for the people Israel to make up their minds about who is righteous and who is not, again using the imagery of the reward of the heavenly garment: "Those who have departed from the shadow of this age have received glorious garments from the Lord. Take again your full number, O Zion, and conclude the list of your people who are clothed in white, who have fulfilled the law of the Lord."[67] A similar picture is portrayed in *1 Enoch*, where it also emphasizes the agelessness of the garments: the righteous "shall have been clothed with garments of glory, and these shall be the garments of life from the Lord of Spirits; and your garments shall not grow old."[68] Philo, not uncharacteristically, spiritualizes the garment: "The heavenly garment of light is the garment of the priesthood,"[69] and "putting on the garment of light is another way of saying that God reveals the Logos by the light which radiated from it."[70]

Jewish sources show how the heavenly garment is held up as a "prize" for the righteous upon their return to the Father. In the *Martyrdom and Ascension of Isaiah*, Isaiah receives a vision in which the Lord says to him, "He who is to be in the corruptible world has not (yet) been revealed, nor the robed, nor the thrones, nor the crowns which are placed (there) for the righteous, for those who believe that Lord who will descend in your form."[71] Isaiah is later told by the Lord that "the holy Isaiah is permitted to come up here, for his robe is here."[72] Strikingly, the process is reversed when Isaiah returns to the earth: "And you shall return into your robe until your days are complete; then you shall come here."[73]

In the Christian tradition, the garment, besides being a symbol of the paradisiacal robes of Adam and Eve, is connected with the glory of the martyrs and the resurrection of the body. Tertullian, commenting on Revelation 7:13–14, writes: "We find in scripture an allusion to garments as being the symbol of the hope of the flesh . . . this symbolism also furnishes us with an argument for bodily resurrection."[74] Further, the heavenly garment itself plays an important role as a reward for the righteous upon their death: "It was a widespread belief in Christian Antiquity that the dead who went forth to eternal life were clothed with a white garment."[75] In his message to the church at Sardis, John writes, "He that overcometh, the same shall be clothed in white raiment; and I will not blot out his name out of the book of life" (Revelation 3:5). Under the altar John also saw the souls of those who were killed for the word of God, and he saw that "white robes were given unto every one of them" (Revelation 6:9, 11). In a vision of the heavens, he saw "a great multitude, which no man could number, of all nations, and kindreds, and people, and tongues," standing "before the throne, and before the Lamb, clothed with white robes, and palms in their hands" (Revelation 7:9). Describing a vision of heaven, Perpetua says in the early Christian *Passion of Perpetua and Felicitas:* "And I went up, and saw a vast expanse of garden, and in the midst a man sitting with white hair, in the dress of a shepherd, a tall man, milking sheep; and round about were many thousand clad in white."[76]

In both the Jewish and Christian traditions are accounts of righteous souls borne to heaven on, or wrapped in, sacred vestments. According to the *Testament of Abraham,* immediately after Abraham's death, "Michael the archangel stood beside him with multitudes of angels, and they bore his precious soul in their hands in divinely woven linen."[77] In the *Apocalypse of Moses,* after Adam sinned he immediately knew that he was deprived of the righteousness with which he had been clothed.[78] When near death, however, Adam received the assurance that God would not forget him. After he died, his spirit was taken to the third heaven, while his body was covered with three linen cloths brought by angels from the third heaven.[79] In the early Christian *Narrative of Zosimus,* the angels "rejoice at the spotless soul coming forth, and unfold their garments to receive it."[80] In the Coptic *Life of Pachomius* we read that at the point of death, an angel wraps the soul in a large spiritual garment and two angels bear him to heaven, one holding the ends of the garment behind, the other holding the ends of the garment in front of the soul.[81] Strikingly, in one of these accounts—the *Encomium of Eustathius*—the phrase "garment of light" is used to describe the robe in which the soul of the righteous departed is carried to heaven: "We saw [Michael] standing and spreading out his garment of light to invite the soul of that blessed woman."[82] Even the angels are sometimes described as being clad in white. Enoch describes the "sons of the holy angels walking upon the flame of fire; their garments were white—and their overcoats—and the light of their faces was like snow."[83]

Just as the garment of Adam is associated with the priestly garb, so the priest's garment can be seen as a type of the heavenly garment that the pious are to receive as a reward in the afterlife. *3 Enoch* has possibly the best example of the parallels between the rewards of the righteous and the clothing of the high priest:

> Out of the love which he had for me, more than for all the denizens of the heights, the Holy One, blessed be he, fashioned for me a majestic robe, in which all kinds of luminaries were set, and he clothed me in it. He fashioned for me a glorious cloak in which brightness, brilliance, splendor, and luster of every kind were fixed, and he wrapped me in it. He fashioned for me a kingly crown in which 49 refulgent stones were placed each like the sun's orb, and its brilliance shone into the four quarters of the heaven of Arabot, into the seven heavens, and into the four quarters of the world. He set it upon my head and he called me, "The lesser YHWH" in the presence of his whole household of the height, as it is written, My name is in him.[84]

Note here that the Lord clothes Enoch with a robe covered by precious stones, like the high priest's robe, and then places a kingly crown upon his head and calls Enoch "The lesser YHWH," in effect crowning him to become a vassal king. In a previous chapter we also find:

> The Holy One, blessed be he, made for me a throne like the throne of glory, and he spread over it a coverlet of splendor, brilliance, brightness, beauty, loveliness, and grace, like the coverlet of the throne of glory, in which all the varied splendor of the luminaries that are in the

world is set. He placed it at the door of the seventh heaven and sat me down upon it.[85]

Just as the garments of the priest are made "after the pattern" of the garment of God, we see here the throne being after the pattern of the throne of the Lord. In the *Martyrdom and Ascension of Isaiah,* for example, we find that "above all the heavens and their angels is placed your throne, and also your robes and your crown which you are to see."[86]

At the same time, the high priest's garment is "after the pattern of the holy garment of the Lord." The garment of the high priest was seen as being identical to those of the Lord. *Exodus Rabbah* says, "For this reason did God give unto him [the high priest] a garment after the pattern of the holy garment [of the Lord]."[87] The *History of the Rechabites* holds that the primary duty of angels who come to meet the soul immediately after death is to tell the soul that the Lord wants the soul to come to him immediately, after which they give the soul its garment.

> As the bride rejoices over her betrothed bridegroom, so the soul rejoices at the good news of holy angels. For they (the angels) say to it nothing except this alone: "O pure soul, your Lord is calling you to come to him." Then the soul with great rejoicing leaves the body to meet the angel. And seeing that pure soul, which has (just) left the body, all the holy angels unfold (for it) their shining stoles. And they receive it with joy, saying, "Blessed are you, O pure soul, the blest; for you have thoroughly done the will of God your Lord."[88]

Conclusion

In summary, the source of our knowledge of the garment of Adam is Genesis. But where the account in Genesis is strikingly spare, later Jewish and Muslim traditions are unswerving in describing its sacredness: it was divinely bestowed; it was originally a garment of skin; the skin itself may have been of some extraordinary origin such as Leviathan; it was a primordial creation, created on Friday evening; its celestial origins justify its use as priestly garb; its sacred nature and force as a symbol of authority was recognized by others who could either use or abuse them (Nimrod is a prime example of this); and the garment of Adam is seen as the type of the heavenly garb that would be acquired by the righteous.

These traditions show Adam, the first man, "in communion with God and clothed with righteousness, glory, and honor."[89] But Adam—and, by extension, all mankind—had "sinned and fallen short of the glory of God" (Romans 3:23, NIV).[90] The vestments given to Adam symbolize the dignity of fallen man and the possibility of restoring to him the glory of God that he had originally enjoyed.[91] Just as the old spiritual says, "All God's chillun got robes" as a sign of reward and honor, those who fear God will receive a share of his glory.[92]

Notes

1. I wish to thank F. V. Greifenhagen, Hugh W. Nibley, Arthur Pollard, and Darell D. Thorpe for sharing with me unpublished work they have done on the subject of the garment of Adam. It has proven immensely useful to me in the preparation of this paper.

2. While in the text of this essay I shall focus on the Jewish, Christian, and Islamic traditions, in the footnotes I shall allow myself to range somewhat more widely, exploring the motif of sacred garments in other ancient traditions as well.

3. Philo, in *Quaestiones in Genesim* I, 53, says that "the coat of skin simply means the human body," an idea shared by some rabbis since the Hebrew word ʿôr may either have the sense "skin of an animal" or "human skin"; cf. J. Harris, *Odes of Solomon* (Cambridge: University Press, 1911), 66–70, and J. M. Evans, *Paradise Lost and the Genesis Tradition* (Oxford: Clarendon, 1968), 70, 84–85, where he refers

to this notion as "semi-Gnostic." According to Jonathan Z. Smith, "The Garments of Shame," in *Map Is Not Territory* (Leiden: Brill, 1978), 16–17, "before their expulsion from Eden, Adam and Eve had bodies or garments of light, but that after the expulsion, they received bodies of flesh or a covering of skin." On this there is a "similar tradition regarding the bodies of light and skin in Samaritan, Christian, and Gnostic sources"; Irenaeus, *Refutatio Omnium Heresium*, I, 5, 5, in *PG*, 7:500–501; according to Tertullian, *Adversus Valentinianos* 24, in *PL*, 2:614, this is a Valentinian idea (the same is suggested in Tertullian, *De Resurrectione Carnis* 7, in *PL*, 2:849, where he also explains that this cannot be correct since, from the creation of Eve from himself, Adam had been aware of his flesh). Perhaps basing his statement on Philo, Origen, in *Contra Celsum* IV, 40, in *PG*, 11:1093, says that "They received garments of skin at the time of the fall," which Louis Ginzberg, in *LJ*, 5:103, understands to be "bodies, since before the fall they were spiritual beings." The notion of the garment as a "splendid robe" is also to be found in early Christianity, *The Pearl* 9: "And they took off from me the spendid robe/Which in their love they had wrought for me," in Edgar Hennecke and Wilhelm Schneemelcher, *New Testament Apocrypha*, tr. R. M. Wilson, 2 vols. (Philadelphia: Westminster, 1965), 2:498.

4. *Genesis Rabbah* 18:6 on Genesis 2:25; cf. S. David Garber, "Symbolism of Heavenly Robes in the New Testament in Comparison with Gnostic Thought," Ph.D. dissertation, Princeton University, 1974, 48.

5. *Genesis Rabbah* 20:12 on Genesis 3:21; cf. Smith, "The Garments of Shame," 16–17. According to *Pirqe de Rabbi Eliezer* 14 and *Genesis Rabbah* 196, when Eve partook of the fruit, "her glorious outer skin, a sheet of light smooth as a fingernail, had fallen away." Similarly, Samael, according to *3 Baruch* 9:7, took the form of a serpent "as a garment" in order to deceive Adam. When God cursed the serpent, he caused it to lose its skin every year, even as Adam lost his skin of light when he became naked; cf. Micha Joseph bin Gorion, *Die Sagen der Juden*, 5 vols. (Frankfurt: Rütten & Loening, 1913–27), 1:96.

6. This section of the *Rasā'il Ikhwān al-Ṣafā* can be found in Friedrich Dieterici, *Thier und Mensch vor dem König der Genien* (Leipzig: Hinrichs, 1879), 97; English translation in *The Case of the Animals versus Man Before the King of the Jinn*, tr. Lenn E. Goodman (Boston: Twayne, 1978), 161.

7. *Pirqe de Rabbi Eliezer* 20 on Genesis 3:21.

8. See *LJ*, 5:103.

9. *3 Baruch* (Greek) 9:7; in the Slavonic version of the same verse, it reads "he covered himself with the serpent."

10. See bin Gorion, *Sagen der Juden*, 1:96.

11. *Pirqe de Rabbi Eliezer* 10 on Genesis 3:10.

12. See bin Gorion, *Sagen der Juden*, 1:290–91.

13. *Odes of Solomon* 25:8; cf. 11:9–10, 13:2, 20:7, 21:2, 33:10; *Gospel of Truth* 20:30–34.

14. Cited in Daniélou, *Bible and Liturgy*, 51.

15. Gregory of Nyssa, *De Oratione Dominica*, Oratio 5, in *PG*, 44:1184 B.C.; *Refutatio Omnium Heresium* III, 23, 5, in *PG*, 7:963–64. In the Armenian *Book of Adam* 28–29, in Erwin Preuschen, *Die apokryphischen gnostischen Adamschriften* (Giessen: Ricker, 1900), 52–53, cited in Robert Graves and Raphael Patai, *The Hebrew Myths: The Book of Genesis* (New York: McGraw-Hill, 1964), 77–78, Adam responded to Eve's transformation by saying, " 'Eve, I would rather die than outlive you. If Death were to claim your spirit, God could never console me with another woman equaling your loveliness!' So saying, he tasted the fruit, and the outer skin of light fell away from him also." The same tradition is also to be found among the Samaritans; cf. John MacDonald, *The Theology of the Samaritans* (London: SCM, 1964), 138.

16. Garments of white linen are already prescribed for the priests in ancient Israel (see Exodus 39:27); the twenty-four elders in the Revelation of John who celebrate the heavenly rites are clothed in white (see Revelation 4:1) as are the martyrs who have triumphed over Satan (see Revelation 3:5, 18). Hugh Nibley points out in *The Message of the Joseph Smith Papyri: An Egyptian Endowment* (Salt Lake City: Deseret Book, 1975), 247, that "the classic robe of the initiate throughout the East has always been and still is the pure white (Plutarch, *de Isid.*, 77) wrap thrown over the shoulder, which also represents an embrace; . . . everything should be white." The white color of the garment is also mentioned by Gregory of Nyssa, *De Vita Moysis*, in *PG*, 44:409B; *In Canticum Canticorum*, Homilia 1, in *PG*, 44:764D, Homilia 11, in *PG*, 44:1005B-D; *De Oratione Dominica*, Orationes 2 and 5, in *PG*, 46:600; Theodore of Mopsuestia, *On Baptism* 4, A. Mingana, ed. (Cambridge: University Press, 1933), 68, 202; Paulus Warnfridus, *De Gestis Lungobardorum* VI, 15; Venantius Fortunatus, sixth-century bishop of Poitiers, in one of his poems, cited in Cote, *Archaeology of Baptism*, 54; see also Proclus, *Codex Sinaiticus Graecus* 491, f. 138 v-139, cited in Thomas M. Finn, *The Liturgy of Baptism in the Baptismal Instructions of St. John Chrysostom* (Washington, D.C.: Catholic University of America Press, 1967), 189, 191, where the phrase is *lamprón tó ésthēta*, "the shining garment"; W. Burghardt, "Cyril of Alexandria on 'Wool and Linen,' " *Traditio* 2

(1944): 484–86; Jean Daniélou, *The Bible and the Liturgy* (South Bend: University of Notre Dame Press, 1956), 50–51; John Edward Farrell, "The Garment of Immortality: A Concept and Symbol in Christian Baptism," S.T.D. thesis, Catholic University of America, 1974, 227–81; Finn, *The Liturgy of Baptism*, 191–97; Leonel Mitchell, *Baptismal Anointing* (Notre Dame: University of Notre Dame Press, 1966), 41, 75, 98, 127, 129, 178; J. Ohleyer, *The Pauline Formula 'Induere Christum': With Special Reference to the Works of St. John Chrysostom* (Washington, D.C.: Catholic University of America, 1921), 33–52; Johannes Quasten, "A Pythagorean Idea in St. Jerome," *American Journal of Philology* 63 (1942): 206–15; Leo Spitzer, "Additional Note on 'Wool and Linen' in Jerome," *American Journal of Philology* 64 (1943): 98–99, who cites a passage from Augustine to further corroborate Quasten's point and stresses the contrast between the interior and exterior.

White garments were also regularly employed in the worship of the heavenly deities—indeed, on ceremonial occasions generally— among the Romans; cf. Cicero, *De Legibus* II, 45; Horace, *Satirae* II, 2, 60–61; Ovid, *Amores* II, 13, 23; *Fasti* II, 654; IV, 619–20; *Metamorphoses* X, 431–35; *Tristia* III, 13, 13–14; V, 5, 7–8; Persius II, 39–40; Servius, *Commentarius in Aeneidem* X, 539; Tibullus II, 1, 16; Propertius IV, 6, 71. Similarly, white garments are used in ancient Greece; see Aeschines, *Against Ctesiphon* 77; Quintus Curtius Rufus, *Historia Alexandri* IV, 15, 27; and in the cult of the Syrian goddess; cf. Lucian, *De Syria Dea* 42; Apuleius, *Metamorphoses* VIII, 27. For modern discussions, see Mary Emma Armstrong, *The Significance of Certain Colors in Roman Ritual* (Menasha, WI: Banta, 1917), 35; Hans Berkusky, "Zur Symbolik der Farben," *Zeitschrift des Vereins für Volkskunde* 23 (1913): 153–63; Karl Mayer, *Die Bedeutung der weissen Farbe im Kultus der Griechen und Römer* (Freiburg im Breisgau, 1927), 19–28; Julius von Negelein, "Die volkstümliche Bedeutung der weissen Farbe," *Zeitschrift für Ethnologie* 33 (1901): 53–85; Gerhard Radke, *Die Bedeutung der weißen und der schwarzen Farbe in Kult und Brauch der Griechen und Römer* (Jena: Neuenhahn, 1936), 58–63. There is also substantial archaeological evidence for white baptismal robes; cf. Marion Ireland, *Textile Art in the Church* (Nashville: Abingdon, 1971), 73.

17. As Richard N. Longenecker, *Galatians* (Waco: Word Books, 1990), 156, notes, the Greek verb *enduō* "with a personal object means to take on the characteristics, virtues, and/or intentions of the one referred to, and so to become like that person." Thus, in this instance, the phrase means "you took on yourselves Christ's characteristics, virtues, and intentions, and so became like him," a phrase that may

have been "suggested to early Christian by baptismal candidates divesting themselves of clothing before baptism and then being reclothed afterwards"; cf. G. R. Beasley-Murray, *Baptism in the New Testament* (London: Macmillan, 1963), 148–49; James D. G. Dunn, *Baptism in the Holy Spirit* (London: SCM, 1970), 110; C. F. D. Moule, *Worship in the New Testament* (London: Lutterworth, 1961), 52–53. E. C. Ratcliff, "The Relation of Confirmation to Baptism in the Early Roman and Byzantine Liturgies—I," *Theology* 49 (1946): 263, states further that Galatians 3:27 probably "refers to the clothing of the company of the baptized with white robes"; see also Tertullian, *De Baptismo* 13, in PL, 1:1323.

18. See Erik Peterson, *Pour une théologie du vêtement*, trans. M.-J. Congar (Lyon: Edition de l'Abeille, 1943), 6–13. Various iconographic sources of the baptismal garment are to be found in Hanns Swarzenski, *Monuments of Romanesque Art* (Chicago: University of Chicago Press, 1967), pl. 20, fig. 45; pl. 173, figs. 380 and 381. Roger Adams, "The Iconography of Early Christian Initiation: Evidence for Baptism for the Dead," unpublished Final Project Report, Third Annual Commissioner's Research Fellowship, Church Educational System, The Church of Jesus Christ of Latter-day Saints, 1977, 51, is not reflecting the full range of the early Christian tradition when he states that "the garment that will be placed upon the catechumen at baptism is equated to the garment of skin placed upon Adam at the time of the fall." The range of symbolic and mystagogical meanings given to the garment is very wide, including "a symbol of union with the risen Christ," "a symbol for purity of life," "a symbol of forgiveness of sins"; see Hugh M. Riley, *Christian Initiation: A Comparative Study of the Interpretation of the Baptismal Liturgy in the Mystagogical Writings of Cyril of Jerusalem, John Chrysostom, Theodore of Mopsuestia, and Ambrose of Milan* (Washington, D.C.: Catholic University of America Press, 1974), 413–55, esp. 413–15.

19. *De Oratione Dominica*, Oratio 5, in *PG*, 44:1184 B-C.

20. In Jewish tradition, the fig tree is frequently associated with the Tree of Knowledge of Good and Evil, *Genesis Rabbah* 15:7, cf. TB *Berakhot* 40a; TB *Sanhedrin* 70a-b; Rashi, *On Genesis* III, 7, and see J. M. Evans, *Paradise Lost and the Genesis Tradition* (Oxford: Clarendon, 1968), 45–46. In *The Book of the Bee*, tr. E. A. Wallis Budge (Oxford: Clarendon, 1886), 23, the garments that Adam and Eve were clothed in after their transgression was neither the skin of animals (since they only came in pairs), nor their own flesh, but the "skin of trees," i.e., their bark. In the view of Theodore of Mopsuestia, *Fragmenta in Genesim* 3:22, in *PG*, 66:641, however, the garments of skin given to

Adam and Eve were not the skins of animals, since there was no sacrifice at that time, nor were they created *ex nihilo*, hence "they must have been made of the skin or inner bark of trees."

21. Gregory of Nyssa, *In Baptismum Christi*, in *PG*, 46:600A; cf. Gregory's statement about the father of the Prodigal Son clothing him with a robe: "not with some other garment, but with the first, that of which he was stripped by his disobedience" (*De Oratione Dominica*, in *PG*, 44:1144 B; *In Canticum Canticorum*, Homilia 11, in *PG*, 44:1005 D); see also Daniélou, *Bible and Liturgy*, 50–51.

22. See Finn, *Liturgy of Baptism*, 147–49; Daniélou, *Bible and Liturgy*, 39–40, who cites Cyril of Jerusalem, in *PG*, 33:1080A: "How wonderful! You were naked before the eyes of all without feeling any shame. This is because you truly carry within you the image of the first Adam, who was naked in Paradise without feeling any shame"; cf. Theodore of Mopsuestia, *On Baptism* XIV, 8, in Mingana, ed., *Commentary of Theodore of Mopsuestia*, 54; Gregory of Nyssa, *De Virginitate* 12, in *PG*, 46:374D; *In Baptismum Christi*, in *PG*, 46:600A; John Chrysostom, *Baptismal Instructions* XI, 28–29; Hippolytus, *Apostolic Tradition* XXI, 3; *Didascalia Apostolorum* 16; Germanus, Oratio 2 in *Dominici Corporis Sepulturam*, in *PG*, 98:289. Margaret R. Miles, *Carnal Knowing: Female Nakedness and Religious Meaning in the Christian West* (Boston: Beacon, 1989), 24–52, esp. 35–36, provides a number of other meanings for baptismal nakedness in the orthodox and heterodox traditions, including "stripping off the 'old man with his deeds,'" "imitation of Christ," "leaving the world," "death and rebirth," "new life," "quasi-martyrdom," and "bridal chamber." Cultic nakedness is well attested in the ancient world (cf. Smith, "Garments of Shame," 2–6). Eckstein, "nackt, Nacktheit," in E. Hoffmann-Krayer and Hanns Bächtold-Stäubli, ed., *Handwörterbuch des deutschen Aberglaubens*, 10 vols. (Berlin: De Gruyter, 1927), 5:823–916, provides an excellent introduction to the topic of nakedness in religion and folklore; see also Gustav Anrich, *Das antike Mysterienwesen in seinem Einfluss auf das Christentum* (Göttingen: Vandenhoeck & Ruprecht, 1894), 200–205; E. A. S. Butterworth, *The Tree at the Navel of the Earth* (Berlin: De Gruyter, 1970), 71–78; Farrell, "Garment of Immortality," 60–127; J. Heckenbach, *De Nuditate Sacra Sacrisque Vinculis* (Gießen: Topelmann, 1911), 8–34; Heuser, "Nacktheit," F. X. Kraus, ed., *Real-Encyklopädie der christlichen Altertümer*, 2 vols. (Freiburg im Breisgau: Herder, 1886), 2:465–67; Hans Leisegang, "The Mystery of the Serpent," in *The Mysteries*, ed. Joseph Campbell (Princeton: Princeton University Press, 1978), 236–41; Walter A. Müller, *Nacktheit und Entblößung in der*

altorientalischen und älteren griechischen Kunst (Leipzig: Teubner, 1906); Peter Nagel, *Die Motivierung der Askese in der alten Kirche und der Ursprung des Mönchtums* (Berlin: Akademie-Verlag, 1966), 91–94; Friedrich Pfister, "Nacktheit," in *Paulys Realencyclopädie der classischen Altertumswissenschaft*, ed. Georg Wissowa (Stuttgart: Metzler, 1935), 16:1541–49; Karl Weinhold, *Zur Geschichte des heidnischen Ritus*, in *Abhandlungen der Königlichen Akademie der Wissenschaften zu Berlin* (1896), 1:1–50.

23. Cf. Quasten, "A Pythagorean Idea in St. Jerome," 212, who observes that "the garment of linen is the garment of immortality according to religious and philosophic considerations of antiquity. There is one line going from Jerome to Apuleius, Plutarch, and Herodotus." Burghardt, "Cyril of Alexandria on 'Wool and Linen,' " 485, sees in Cyril of Alexandria's *De Adoratione et Cultu in Spiritu et Veritate* XI, 390, in *PG*, 68:749, a melding of an ancient Pythagorean principle with a Neo-Platonist, spiritualizing one: "With the Pythagoreans Cyril enunciates the general principle that wool is the symbol of death, since its origin is an animal destined to die. The implication is, of course, that the contrasted linen is a symbol of life and immortality. With the Neo-Platonists he refines the general principle, so as to see in the garments of wool dead works, that is, the works of passion and sin that bring spiritual death. To don garments of linen, therefore, is to renounce the works that lead to spiritual death, and by implication, to embrace those that lead to life and immortality. The new element is the interpretation that sees in the coolness of linen the chilling of passion"; see also Philip Oppenheim, *Das Mönchskleid im christlichen Altertum* (Freiburg im Breisgau: Herder, 1931), 57–65, on linen and wool garments.

24. Jerome, *Epistle LXIV*, 19, in *PL*, 22:613.

25. In the Christian tradition, the white garment of the baptizand, besides being a symbol of the paradisiacal robes of Adam and Eve, is connected with the glory of the martyrs and the resurrection of the body; see below.

26. See Finn, *Liturgy of Baptism*, 146–49; Daniélou, *Bible and Liturgy*, 39–40, who cites Cyril of Jerusalem, *Catechesis XX. Mystagogica II. De Baptismi Caeremoniis*, in *PG*, 33:1080A: "How wonderful! You were naked before the eyes of all without feeling any shame. This is because you truly carry within you the image of the first Adam, who was naked in Paradise without feeling any shame"; cf. Thedore of Mopsuestia, *On Baptism* XIV, 8, in *Commentary of Theodore of Mopsuestia*, ed. Mingana, 54; Gregory of Nyssa, *De Virginitate* 12, in *PG*, 46:374D; *In Baptismum Christi*, in *PG*, 46:600A; Adams, "Icon-

ography of Early Christian Initiation," 51, where he cites Jean
Daniélou, *Bible and Liturgy*, 13, on Theodore's commentary on baptism. In a ritual described in the Gnostic *2 Jeu* 47, Christ performs a
ritual in which "all his disciples were clothed in linen garment and
crowned with myrtle."

27. See *Genesis Rabbah* 18:6 on Genesis 2:25.

28. See *Genesis Rabbah* 19:6 on Genesis 3:7. The fourth-century
Church Father Hilary gave an allegorizing turn to the story of Jesus
cursing the fig tree, which he said was the same tree as that from
which Adam made his clothes, "for which reason the branch of the
fig tree is the Antichrist, while its blossoms that blossom in the sum-
mertime signify sin" (*Commentarius in Matthaeum* 26, in PL, 9:
1056–57).

29. Cf. Yves Marquet, *La philosophie des Iḫwān al-Ṣafā'* (Algiers:
Etudes et Documents, 1973), 217.

30. See Al-Thaʿlabī, *Qiṣaṣ al-Anbiyā* (Cairo: Mustafā al-Bābī al-
Ḥalabī wa-Awlāduhu, A.H. 1345), 21.

31. *Jubilees* 3:26–27, 31; cf. 7:20.

32. Erwin Goodenough, *Jewish Symbols in the Greco-Roman Period*,
13 vols. (New York: Pantheon Books, 1953–68), 1:28.

33. The garment as a sign of authority is found in the Gnostic
Gospel of Philip 57, which says, "In this world those who put on the
garment are better than the garment. In the kingdom of heaven the
garments are better than those who have put them on." This may
mean that the garment of the person in heaven have more power
than the person alone. We find an even more convincing passage in
Pistis Sophia 1:9, where Jesus is given authority immediately after (or
through) his putting on his garment after his death: "It happened
now when Jesus finished these words to his disciples, He continued
again with the discourse, and he said to them, 'Behold, I have put on
my garment and all authority is given to me through the first mystery.'"

34. See *LJ*, 5:103. During the Middle Ages the traditions of Adam's
garments of light and his priestly garments were combined in the
Yalquṭ 1:34 in ibid., 5:104: "God made high-priestly garments for
Adam which were like those of the angels; but when he sinned, God
took them away from him." According to Garber, "Symbolism of
Heavenly Robes," 50, "This was an attempt to retain 'skin' (ʿôr) in
Genesis 3:21 without losing the sense of "light" (ʾôr)." Similarly, *Zohar*
1:36b starts, "at first they had coats of light, which procured them in
the service of the highest of the high, for the celestial angels used to
come to enjoy that light. . . . After their sins they had only coats of

skin good for the body but not for the soul." Here we see that the garment of skin (temporal) mirrors the garment of light (spiritual). According to Smith, "Garments of Shame," 16, "before their expulsion from Eden, Adam and Eve had bodies or garments of light, but that after the expulsion, they received bodies of flesh or a covering of skin"; cf. Sverre Aalen, *Die Begriffe "Licht" und "Finsternis" im alten Testament, im Spätjudentum und Rabbinismus* (Oslo: Dwybad, 1951), 198–99, 265–66, 282–85.

35. *Numbers Rabbah* 4:8 on Numbers 3:45.

36. See *Genesis Rabbah* 20:12.

37. *Midrash Tanḥuma* 1:24.

38. In the Mandaean religion, there is a similar belief that the garment of Adam was inherited by Noah, *Das Johannesbuch der Mandäer*, ed. and trans. Mark Lidzbarski (Giessen: Töpelmann, 1905–15), 83; see Hans Schoeps, *Urgemeinde, Judenchristentum, Gnosis* (Tübingen: Mohr, 1956), 53. Cain, it appears, may have had this garment before Seth, but cast it off when he chose to follow evil, *Ginzā: Der Schatz oder das große Buch der Mandäer*, trans. Mark Lidzbarski (Göttingen: Vandenhoeck & Ruprecht, 1925), 128.

39. See bin Gorion, *Sagen der Juden*, 2:370.

40. See *LJ*, 1:177; bin Gorion, *Sagen der Juden*, 2:19. The supernatural power of the garment can be seen in the *Testament of Job* 46:7–53:8. The garment protects Job, and enables his daughters to speak in tongues and to proclaim the glory of God when they put it on.

41. See *Pirqe de Rabbi Eliezer* 24; cf. *LJ*, 1:177; M. Sel, "Nimrod," in *The Jewish Encyclopedia*, 12 vols. (New York: Funk and Wagnalls, 1905), 9:309. According to another source, recounted in bin Gorion, *Sagen der Juden*, 2:19–20, Cush loved Nimrod, the child, "and gave him a skin garment, which God had made for Adam as he went out of the Garden of Eden." From Adam the garment passed by descent to Enoch, Methusaleh, and Noah, from whom Ham stole it as they were coming out of the Ark. Ham gave it to his firstborn Cush, who gave it to Nimrod. Interestingly, according to Jacob of Serug, *nimrah* means "tiger, "crown," and "striped garment," B. Vandenhoff, "Die Götterliste des Mar Jakob von Sarug in seiner Homilie über den Fall der Götzenbilder,"*Oriens Christianus* 5 (1915): 240–41. According to *Jasher* 7:29, "Cush was concealed then from his sons and brothers and when Cush had begotten Nimrod, he gave him those garments through his love for him, and Nimrod grew up, and when he was twenty years old he put on those garments, and Nimrod became

strong when he put on the garments . . . and he hunted the animals and he built altars, and he offered the animals before the Lord."

42. Bernhard Beer, *Das Leben Abraham's nach Auffassung der jüdischen Sage* (Leipzig: Leiner, 1859), 7.

43. See bin Gorion, *Sagen der Juden*, 2:365–66; cf. *Pirqe de Rabbi Eliezer* 24; *Jasher* 27:7. In the *Apocalypse of Abraham* 13, the garment is passed on to Abraham: when Satan was rebuked for taunting Adam and Eve after their transgression, God tells him that the garment that had belonged to him in heaven would be given to Abraham.

44. See *Pirqe de Rabbi Eliezer* 24.

45. *Numbers Rabbah* 4:8; cf. bin Gorion, *Sagen der Juden*, 2:371. In other sources, Jacob is said to have stolen the garment from Esau, *Pirqe de Rabbi Eliezer* 24. However, as *Jasher* 26:17 indicates, Esau deserved to lose the garment: "Esau was a designing and a deceitful man, and an expert hunter in the field, and Jacob was a man perfect and wise." When Nimrod, king of Babel "went to hunt in the field . . . Nimrod was watching Esau all the days, for a jealousy was formed in the heart of Nimrod against Esau" (*Jasher* 27:2–3). But Esau lay in ambush, cut off Nimrod's head, and "took the garments of Nimrod . . . with which Nimrod prevailed over the whole land, and he ran and concealed them in his house," and this was the birthright he sold to Jacob (*Jasher* 27:7, 10).

46. Bin Gorion, *Sagen der Juden*, 2:371.

47. See Hippolytus, *Fragmenta in Genesin* 3, in *PG,* 10:604.

48. See al-Thaʿlabī, *Qiṣaṣ al-Anbiyā*, 79.

49. See ibid; according to Marc Philonenko, "Les interpolations chrétiennes des Testaments des Douze Patriarches et les manuscrits de Qoumrân," *Revue d'Histoire et Philosophie Religieuse* 39 (1959): 30, the author of the *Testament of the Twelve Patriarchs* "places peculiar emphasis on the stealing of Joseph's garment by his brothers. . . .They envied him because of it—apparently it was the mark of singular superiority."

50. See *Testament of Zebulon* 4:11; al-Thaʿlabī, *Qiṣaṣ al-Anbiyā*, 80.

51. TB *Arakhin* 16a.

52. There is considerable discussion on the meaning of this passage, as well as its proper referents. See Leslie C. Allen, *Ezekiel 20–48* (Dallas: Word Books, 1990), 89–95; P.-M. Bogaert, "Montaigne sainte, jardin d'Eden et sanctuaire (hiérosolymitain) dans un oracle d'Ezéchiel contre le prince de Tyre (Ez. 28:11–19)," *Homo Religiosus* 9 (1983): 131–53; N. C. Habel, "Ezekiel 28 and the Fall of the First Man," *Concordia Theological Monthly* 38 (1967): 516–24; Herbert May, "The King in the Garden of Eden: A Study of Ezekiel 28:12–19," in *Israel's*

Prophetic Heritage, ed. B. W. Anderson and W. Harrelson (New York: Harper and Row, 1962), 166–76; J. L. McKenzie, "Mythological Allusion in Ezekiel 28:12–28," *Journal of Biblical Literature* 75 (1956): 322–27; A. J. Williams, "The Mythological Background of Ezekiel 28:12–19?" *Biblical Theology Bulletin* 6 (1976): 49–61; Kalman Yaron, "The Dirge over the King of Tyre," *Annual of the Swedish Theological Institute* 3 (1964): 28–57; Frederick L. Moriarty, "The Lament over Tyre (Ez. 27)," *Gregorianum* 46 (1965): 83–88.

53. The High Priest's robe as a cosmic garment (*Weltenmantel*) may be seen in the *Wisdom of Solomon* 18:24: "On Aaron's long high-priestly robe was the whole world pictured, and the glories of the fathers were upon the graving of the four rows of precious stones and thy Majesty was upon the diadem of his head." In *Ben Sirach* 45:6–8, God permitted Aaron to be garbed in the robes of his majesty and glory, since Aaron was "one holy like unto him"; cf. Philo *De Vita Mosis* II, 117, 122, and see F. H. Colson, "Appendix to *De Vita Mosis* II," in *Philo*, 10 vols. (Cambridge: Harvard University Press, 1966), 6:609; Philo, *De Somniis* I, 215, 251; Josephus, *Jewish Antiquities* III, 7, 7 (184–85). On the cosmic garment in the ancient and medieval world, see Robert Eisler, *Weltenmantel und Himmelszelt: Religionsgeschichtliche Untersuchungen zur Urgeschichte des antiken Weltbildes*, 2 vols. (Munich: Beck, 1910), esp. 1:19, 25.

54. *Targum Ezekiel* 28:13. According to Jerome, *Epistola* 64 (ad Fabiolam) in PL, 22:613–15, the garment of the Christian priest is copied after that of the High Priest. Gregory the Great, *Epistolae* I, 9, 25, in PL, 77:470–71, makes a somewhat similar observation, though he gives it an allegorical interpretation. Eisler, *Weltenmantel und Himmelszelt*, 1:19, citing Durandus, notes that the "*cappa*" of the pope was an imitation of the high priest's tunic.

55. *LJ*, 5:103. The tradition of celestial garments is also present in Mandaeism and Manichaeism. In the Mandaean *The Canonical Prayerbook of the Mandaeans*, trans. E. S. Drower (Leiden: Brill, 1959), 30, n. 31, instructions are given concerning Adam: "Let him come and go down to the jordan [sic], be baptised, receive the pure sign, put on robes of radiant light and set a fresh wreath on his head," which Garber, in "Symbolism of the Heavenly Garments," 217, suggests may indicate that the baptismal ritual "included being clothed in a baptismal robe to signify the present imperishable soul and the clothing in glory after death" and that "there was investiture with a special white robe after one's first baptism," although he also notes Kurt Rudolph's judgment that "the symbolic style of the liturgical speeches probably means primarily that the baptism itself is the

clothing with light and eschatological existence, without any definite indication of an investment following the rite (as in the early Christian Church)." References to garments—the garment of Adam, garments for obedience and protection, heavenly garments, and baptismal robes—are frequent in Mandaean literature (cf. Lidz-barski, *Ginzā*, 13, 96, 128–29, 131, 191–92, 194, 243, 252–53, 259, 263, 348–49, 363, 430–31, 435, 488, 576–77; Lidzbarski, *Johannesbuch der Mandäer*, 83, 206). E. S. Drower, "ADAMAS—Humankind: ADAM—Mankind," *Theologische Literaturzeitung* 86 (1961): 177, notes that the Semitic *mānā* is "garment, vessel, robe," i.e., the secrecy of the teach-ing, and that "it is the head of the Cosmos from which manas origi-nate" for the initiate.

In Manichaeism, Garber notes in "Symbolism of Heavenly Robes," 223, "the believer longed to put on a shining robe of light." The Manichaean *Psalm of Thomas concerning the Coming of the Soul* states that "I await my robe until it comes and clothes him that shall wear it. . . . When therefore my shining robe comes and clothes him that shall wear it; when my pleasant fragrance strips itself of their stink and returns to its place . . . then I will sink their Darkness, . . . uproot their Darkness." The robe is the enlightening Light, the redemption of the Soul" (ibid., 225). The section "On the Five Elements" in the Manichaean *Book of the Giants* (from the *Book of Enoch*), mentions "The crown, the diadem, [the garland, and] the garment (of Light)" (Walter B. Henning, "The Book of the Giants," *Bulletin of the School of Oriental and African Studies* 11 [1943–46]: 62). The term *nalbaš šame* (*Himmelskleid*) is widely attested with reference to the gods in the lit-erature of the Mesopotamians (Ernst F. Weidner, "Das Himmelskleid," *Archiv für Orientforschung* 7 [1931–32]: 115–16). On the use of "golden garments" as sacred vestments for the gods and, in Assyria, as royal vestments, see A. Leo Oppenheim, "The Golden Garments of the Gods," *Journal of Near Eastern Studies* 8 (1949): 172–93.

56. In an interesting turn on the motif of the heavenly garment, Severus of Antioch, who frequently mentions the garment, believes that clothes will be unnecessary in the celestial realms: "If we crave for and need sensual food in the future painless life, it is then time to desire also clothes made of wool, . . . but it is very certain that the expected life is free from all such things," *Epistle (to Solon)* 96, in E. W. Brooks, "A Collection of Letters of Severus of Antioch," in *Patrologia Orientalis*, ed. François Graffin (Paris: Firmin-didot, 1920), 14:188. Then he quotes Basil as teaching that when Adam sinned "it was not fitting that he should have clothes; but there were others

prepared for man if he displayed virtues, clothes such as by God's grace glistened . . . shining garments, as of the angels also" *(Epistle [to Solon]* 96, in ibid., 14:190). He notes the garments of Jesus left behind in the tomb as proof that when we are beyond the need for food and drink we will also be beyond need of clothing *(Homily* 77, in ibid., 16:820). That the Lord left his clothes behind demonstrates, in his view, that he was like Adam in the Garden, "and that as God, even though clothed upon, it could only be with a most glorious garment of light" *(Epistle [to Solon]* 96, in ibid., 14:190).

57. Rabbi Akiba and Samuel Aba Horodezky, "Michael und Gabriel," *Monatsschrift für die Geschichte und Wissenschaft des Judentums* 72 (1928): 505.

58. Cf. Ruth 3:3, and see Jack M. Sasson, *Ruth: A New Translation with a Philological Commentary and a Formalist-Folklorist Interpretation* (Baltimore: Johns Hopkins University Press, 1979), 67–68; cf. *Joseph and Aseneth* 2:4, 3:6, 4:1, 14:12–14, 15:10, 18:5–6; *The Assumption: Narrative by Joseph of Arimathaea* 5, in *ANT*, 216; *Acts of Andrew* (Flamion Text) 121, in *ANT*, 418. Samuel Greengus, "Old Babylonian Marriage Ceremonies and Rites," *Journal of Cuneiform Studies* 20 (1966): 55–72, includes details from cuneiform sources that parallel the biblical passages. Other ceremonies that include washing, anointing, and clothing are unconnected with marriage; cf. the *Epic of Gilgamesh* II, 3, 14–27, where Enkidu eats breads, drinks wine, anoints himself with oil, and puts on a garment "and is like a man" in Heidel, Gilgamesh, Geo Widengren, "Heavenly Enthronement and Baptism: Studies in Mandaean Baptism," in *Religions in Antiquity: Essays in Memory of Ramsdell Goodenough*, ed. Jacob Neusner (Leiden: Brill, 1970), 578, who cites the passage in CT XV, 47:47–48: "Tammuz, the husband of her youth, bathe with pure water, anoint with fine oil, clothe him in a bright red garment!" These three actions, according to Widengren, are "precisely three of the central actions" in the Mandaean *massiqtā* (baptism) ceremony; see also Kurt Rudolph, *Die Mandäer*, 2 vols. (Göttingen: Vandenhoeck & Ruprecht, 1961), 2:105–12, 155–74, 181–88, 262–63, 264–81, for extended discussion of the *massiqtā* and of washing, anointing, and clothing. Washing, anointing, and clothing is also mentioned in the *Odyssey*, where new guests at the house of a great lord are washed, anointed, and clothed before joining the banquet table, III, 464–69; IV, 47–51; see John Gee and Daniel C. Peterson, "Graft and Corruption: On Olives and Olive Culture in Pre-Modern Mediterranean," in *The Allegory of the Olive Tree: The Olive, the Bible, and Jacob 5*, ed. Stephen D. Ricks and John W.

Welch (Salt Lake City: Deseret Book and F.A.R.M.S., 1994), 244, n. 252.

59. For an important discussion of this topic, see Donald W. Parry, "Ritual Anointing with Olive Oil in Ancient Israelite Religion," in *The Allegory of the Olive Tree,* esp. 268–71; Ernst Kutsch, *Salbung als Rechtsakt im Alten Testament und im alten Orient* (Berlin: Töpelmann, 1963), 22–27.

60. *Testament of Levi* 8:6–12; cf. *2 Enoch* 69:8, 70:4, 70:13, 71:16, 71:21–22. Geo Widengren, "Royal Ideology and the Testaments of the Twelve Patriarchs," in *Promise and Fulfillment,* ed. F. F. Bruce (Edinburgh: Clark, 1965), 204–5; Ludin Jensen, "The Consecration in the Eighth Chapter of Testament Levi," in *La regalità/The Sacral Kingship* (Leiden: Brill, 1959), 358–62.

61. See Jensen, "Consecration," 359; Widengren, "Royal Ideology," 202–3, 205–12; see also Stephen D. Ricks and John J. Sroka, "King, Coronation, and Temple: Enthronement Ceremonies in History," in this volume, for an overview of characteristic features of royal coronations. In the view of many in the ancient Near East, it is the receipt of the royal garment (and other insignia of the king) that is both symbol and substance of becoming a king, as Herodotus VII, 15, implies; see also A. Szabo, "Herodotea," *Acta Antiqua* 1 (1951): 85.

62. See Edwin O. James, *Christian Myth and Ritual* (London: Murray, 1937), 103. Baptismal anointings occurred either before or after the baptism; according to Mitchell, *Baptismal Anointing,* 10–11, the earliest unambiguous witness to baptismal anointing, Tertullian, mentions both pre- and postbaptismal anointing (*De Baptismo* 7–8, in *PL,* 1:13; *De Corona* 3, in *PL,* 2:98–99); Bernhard Welte, *Die postbaptismale Salbung: Ihr symbolischer Gehalt und Ihre sakramentale Zugehörigkeit nach den Zeugnissen der alten Kirche* (Freiburg im Breisgau: Herder, 1939), 22–41.

63. Cote, *Archaeology of Baptism,* also states:

> That Sunday folowing [the baptismal day] was called *dominica in albis depositis,* because those who had been baptized took off their white robes, which were laid by in the church as evidence against them if they broke their baptismal vows. Whitsunday (White Sunday), the English name for Pentecost, is supposed to have been so called from the white garments worn by the newly-baptized catechumens when it was the custom to administer that ordinance on the Vigil of Pentecost. The white garment was made to fit the body rightly, and was bound round the middle with a

girdle sash. The sleeves were either plain, like those of a cas-
sock, or else full, and gathered close on the wrists, like the
sleeve of a shirt, resembling the tunic worn by the ancients.

With this may be compared Geoffrey Wainwright, "Images of
Baptism," *Reformed Liturgy & Music* 19 (1985): 173, who also observes
that "christening gowns" may represent a Protestant relic of the old
practice of receiving garments at the time of baptism; cf. also Henry
John Feasey, *Old English Holy Week Ceremonial* (London: Baker, 1897),
239–40; Hugh W. Nibley, "Evangelium Quadraginta Dierum: The
Forty-day Mission of Christ—The Forgotten Legacy," in *Mormonism
and Early Christianity*, in *CWHN*, 4:17, 37–39.

64. *Targum Onkelos* to Genesis 3:21; cf. *Apocalypse of Elijah* 5:6;
Testament of Levi 18:14; *Vision of Isaiah* 9:17, 24–26; *Book of John the
Evangelist*, in *ANT*, 189, 193; Acts of Andrew (Flamion Text) 142–44,
in *ANT*, 450.

65. See *Community Rule* (1QS) 4:9; cf. 4Q161: "God will uphold him
with [the spirit of might, and will give him] a throne of glory and a
crown of [holiness] and many-colored garments." Josephus, in *Jewish
Wars* II, 123, states that the Essenes (probably to be connected with
the Dead Sea Scrolls, or at least some of them) make a point of always
being dressed in white. In *Jewish Wars* II, 137, Josephus observes that
a white garment is one of three items (along with a hatchet and loin-
cloth) given to the candidate upon entering the community at
Qumran. Todd S. Beall, *Josephus' Description of the Essenes Illustrated
by the Dead Sea Scrolls* (New York: Cambridge University Press, 1988),
46, suggests that 1QM (*War Scroll*) 7:9–10 may indicate a preference
for white at Qumran: "seven priests of the sons of Aaron, clothed in
garments of fine white linen: a linen tunic and linen trousers, and
girded with a linen girdle"; cf. Yigael Yadin, *The Scroll of the War of
the Sons of Light against the Sons of Darkness* (Oxford: Oxford
University Press, 1962), 219; Goodenough, *Jewish Symbols*, 9:168–69.
Perhaps on the basis of the latter statement by Josephus that Jean
Daniélou observes, in *The Dead Sea Scrolls and Primitive Christianity*
(Baltimore: Helicon, 1958), 42, that "the practice of dressing the newly
baptized in a white robe inevitably recalls the description in Josephus
of the white garments worn by those who were newly admitted to
the Essenian community"; cf. Beall, *Josephus' Description of the Essenes*,
155.

66. *4 Ezra* 2:44–45.
67. Ibid., 2:39–40.
68. *1 Enoch* 62:16.

69. Philo, *De Fuga* 110. On the spiritualization of religious values, see Robert J. Daly, *The Origins of the Christian Doctrine of Sacrifice* (Philadelphia: Fortress, 1978), 6–8, who notes that the word *spiritualization* needs to be understood in a larger sense than simply "antimaterialistic," including "those movements and tendencies within Judaism and Christianity" that attempted to emphasize "the inner, spiritual, or ethical significance of the cult over against the merely material" aspects of it; see also David Dawson, *Allegorical Readers and Cultural Revision in Ancient Alexandria* (Berkeley: University of California Press, 1992); Han-Jürgen Hermisson, *Sprache und Ritus im altisraelitischen Kult: "Zur 'Spiritualisierung' der Kultbegriffe im Alten Testament"* (Neukirchen-Vluyn; Neukirchener-Verlag, 1965); Daniel R. Schwartz, "Priesthoood, Temple, Sacrifices: Opposition and Spiritualization in the Late Second Temple Period," Ph.D. dissertation, Hebrew University, Jerusalem, 1979, 191–92; H. Wenschkewitz, "Die Spiritualisierung der Kultusbegriffe: Tempel, Priester, und Opfer im Neuen Testament," *Angelos* 4 (1932): 70–230.

70. Alexander Altmann, "A Note on the Rabbinic Doctrine of Creation," *Journal of Jewish Studies* 7 (1956): 201–2.

71. *Martyrdom and Ascension of Isaiah* 8:26; cf. 1:6; 4:16–17; 8:14; 9:2, 9–11, 17–18, 24–26; 11:40; in 3:25 we read: "And many will exchange the glory of the robes of the saints for the robes of those who love money," where Michael A. Knibb, translator and editor of the *Martyrdom in Old Testament Pseudepigrapha*, 2 vols., ed. James H. Charlesworth (Garden City, NY: Doubleday, 1985), 2:161, says that this is "perhaps an indication that Christians adopted a special form of dress."

72. *Martyrdom and Ascension of Isaiah* 9:2; cf. 9:17, 24–26; 11:40. In other instances, the garment of glory is given to one on a heavenly journey; cf. *2 Enoch* 22:8: "And the LORD said to Michael, 'Go, and extract Enoch from [his] earthly clothing. And anoint him with my delightful oil, and put him into the clothes of my glory'"; cf. Geo Widengren, "Royal Ideology," 210–11. The exchange of earthly for heavenly garments may be reflected in Paul's belief that the body of the resurrection is a glorified body that is put on, see 2 Corinthians 5:1–5; 1 Corinthians 15:35–44; see also *Acts of Thomas* 6–7, 146, in *ANT*, 367–68, 428–29.

73. *Martyrdom and Ascension of Isaiah* 11:35.

74. Tertullian, *De Resurrectione Carnis* 27, in PL, 2:834A-B; cf. Apocalypse of Peter (Ethiopic Text), in *ANT*, 520; Papyrus Bodmer X, 55:8, where the resurrection is compared with being clothed again; see also Daniélou, *Bible and Liturgy*, 52–53. Carl Clemen, *Primitive*

Christianity and Its Non-Jewish Sources (Edinburgh: Clark, 1912), 173–74, suggests Zoroastrian beliefs in the afterlife, including the righteous receiving heavenly garments (see *Bundahishn* 30:28), as a possible source for Christian and Jewish beliefs. James Moulton, *Early Zoroastrianism* (London: Williams and Norgate, 1913), 315, is more cautious on this point. On the other hand, there is no question of a bodily resurrection and the receipt of a heavenly robe in Zoroastrian tradition (see Mary Boyce, *Zoroastrians: Their Religious Beliefs and Practices* [London: Routledge & Kegan Paul, 1985], 27–28; Jal Cersetji Pavry, *The Zoroastrian Doctrine of a Future Life from Death to the Individual Judgment* [New York: Columbia University Press, 1929]). There is also an important Zoroastrian tradition of the *sudra,* the sacred garment (a muslin shirt with sleeves reaching to the hips), with a small pocket ("the pocket of good deeds"), and a sacred cord, the *kustī,* first assumed by Zoroastrian men and women no later than their fifteenth year and thereafter worn at all times. A man or woman who, "being more than fifteen years of age, walks without wearing the sacred girdle and the sacred shirt" was deemed the greatest of sinners. Those who did not wear the sacred shirt and cord were to be refused water and bread by other community members (see James Darmsteter, *The Zend-Avesta: The Vendîdâd* [Oxford: Clarendon, 1895], 195, 204; Boyce, *Zoroastrianism,* 31–33; Jivani J. Modi, *The Religious Ceremonies and Customs of the Parsees* [New York: Garland, 1979], 178–96).

75. Alfred C. Rush, *Death and Burial in Christian Antiquity* (Washington, D.C.: Catholic University of America, 1941), 217; see also Emil Freistedt, *Altchristliche Totengedächtnistage und Ihre Beziehung zum Jenseitsglauben und Totenkultus der Antike* (Münster: Aschendorff, 1928), 64–65. Rudolf Bultmann, "Die Bedeutung der neuerschlossenen mandäischen und manichäischen Quellen für das Verständnis des Johannesevangeliums," *Zeitschrift für die neutestamentlichen Wissenschaft* 24 (1925): 120, stresses the notion of earthly and heavenly garments in the early Christian tradition.

76. The *Passion of Perpetua and Felicitas* IV, 8; see Rush, *Death and Burial,* 217.

77. *Testament of Abraham* 20:10 (Rescension A); cf. Kaufmann Kohler, "The Pre-Talmudic Haggada II," *Jewish Quarterly Review* 7 (1895): 589–91; *Apocalypse of Moses* 37:4; *Life of Adam and Eve* 48:1–4; *Apocalypse of Thomas,* in *ANT,* 561.

78. See *Apocalypse of Moses* 20:1.

79. Ibid., 31:4, 37:1–6, 40:1–3; cf. *Testamentum Domini Nostri Jesu Christi* I, 28.

80. *Narrative of Zosimus* 13, cited in Wilhelm Lueken, *Michael: Eine*

Darstellung und Vergleichung der jüdischen und der morgenländisch-christlichen Tradition vom Erzengel Michael (Göttingen: Vandenhoeck und Ruprecht, 1898), 123.

81. See *Monument pour servir à l'histoire de l'Égypte chrétienne au IVe siècle: Historie de Saint Pakhôme et de ses communautés*, ed. and tr. E. Amélineau (Paris: Leroux, 1889), 122–23; cf. *Apocalypse of Thomas*, in *ANT*, 561.

82. E. A. Wallis Budge, *St. Michael the Archangel: Three Encomiums by Theodosius, Archbishop of Alexandria, Severus, Patriarch of Antioch, and Eustathius, Bishop of Trake* (London: Trench, Paul, and Trübner, 1894), 128 (Coptic Text), 102 (translation). A similar account is given in E. Amélineau, *Contes et romans de l'Égypte chrétienne* (Paris: Leroux, 1888), 1:6, where Michael appeared to an entire multitude and showed them the royal garment in which he received "the two pure souls"; cf. *The Book of the Resurrection of Christ by Bartholomew the Apostle*, in *ANT*, 185; *History of Joseph the Carpenter* 23, where, however, the soul is placed in a "silken napkin." In a sepulchral monument in Ely Cathedral is a depiction of Michael bearing a soul toward heaven in the fold of his garments, depicted in J. Romilly Allen, *Early Christian Symbolism in Great Britain and Ireland before the Thirteenth Century* (London: Whiting, 1887), 272, fig. 96; cf. also the twelfth-century Shaftesbury Psalter, in F. E. Halliday, *An Illustrated History of England* (New York: Viking, 1967), where there is a depiction of souls riding up towards heaven on a garment in the hands of the archangel Michael.

83. *1 Enoch* 71:1; cf. 71:10; *2 Enoch* [J] 37:1; *Apocalypse of Zephaniah* 8:3; Severus of Antioch, *Epistle (to Solon)* 96, in *Patrologia Orientalis*, 14:190; *Report of Pilate (Anaphora)*, in *ANT*, 154; *The Assumption: Latin Narrative of Pseudo-Melito* 3, in *ANT*, 210; in *Apocalypse of Peter (Akhmim Text)*, in *ANT*, 518; in *3 Enoch* 28:7, the "Holy One" is described as having a garment "white like snow"; *The Vercelli Acts of Peter* 16, in *ANT*, 318, "Peter . . . beheld Jesus clad in a vesture of brightness"; Goodenough, *Jewish Symbols*, 9:169.

84. *3 Enoch* 12:13.

85. Ibid., 10:1–2.

86. *Martyrdom and Ascension of Isaiah* 7:22.

87. *Exodus Rabbah* 38:8.

88. *History of the Rechabites* 14:3–5.

89. Garber, "Symbolism of Heavenly Robe," 51; cf. Edgar Haulotte, *Symbolique du vêtement selon la Bible* (Lyon: Aubier, 1966), 186.

90. Cf. Robin Scroggs, *The Last Adam* (Oxford: Blackwell, 1966), 26,

48–49, for a discussion of this verse. In the *Apocalypse of Moses* 21:6, Adam accuses Eve, "You have deprived me of the glory of God."

91. Cf. *Apocalypse of Moses* 39:2; *1 Enoch* 50:1; *4 Ezra* 7:122–25; *2 Apocalypse of Baruch* 51:1, 3; 54:15, 21; 1QS 4:23; CD 3:20; 17:15; see also Scroggs, *Last Adam*, 26–27, 54–56, and Haulotte, *Symbolique*, 188.

92. See Garber, "Symbolism of Heavenly Robe," 51–52.

Illustration Sources

Except where noted, the illustrations have been drawn for this volume by Michael Lyon.

Figure 1, page 8. Tabernacle of Moses and Temple of Solomon. Drawings based on biblical descriptions and current archaeological reconstructions.

Figure 2, page 30, and figure 3, page 31. 1870 photographs from stereographs by W. A. Faze, courtesy of the LDS Church Photo Archives.

Figure 4, page 38. Magic Flute scenic design by Gayl and Nessthaler, Vienna 1791, Historisiche Museum der Stadt, Vienna, from Jurgis Baltrušaitis, *La Quête d'Isis* (Paris: Flammarion, 1985), 43.

Figure 5, page 85. (A) Medamud Mound, redrawn from plans in Alexander Badawy, *A History of Egyptian Architecture*, 3 vols. (Berkeley: University of California Press, 1954), 1:116; (B) relief on foot end of stone sarcophagus, Museum of Marseilles, redrawn from Robert Lawlor, *Sacred Geometry* (London: Thames and Hudson, 1982), 60; (C) British Museum Papyrus 1008, redrawn from Andrzej Niwiński, *Theban Funerary Papyri* (Freiburg, Switzerland: Universitäts-Verlag, 1989), p. 29a.

Figure 6, page 87. (A) Central axis, Temple of Horus, Edfu, redrawn from Dieter Arnold, *Die Tempel Ägyptens: Gotterwohnungen, Kultstatten, Baudenkmaler* (Zurich:

Artemis & Winkler, 1992), 102; (B) Black granite shrine of Nectanebo, c. 370 B.C., redrawn from Emile Chassinat, *Le Temple d'Efou* (Cairo: Institut Francais d'Archéologie Oriental, 1984), I, 1, 9.

Figure 7, page 88. Moses before the Tabernacle, fresco, Dura Europos Synagogue, redrawn from Erwin Goodenough, *Jewish Symbols in the Greco-Roman Period*, 12 vols. (New York: Pantheon Books, 1954), vol. 11, ill. 331.

Figure 8, page 89. (A) Taj Mahal, redrawn (Tyler Moulton) from Roger Garaudy, *L'Islam, habite notre avenir* (Desclée De Brouwer, 1981), 54; (B) Map of Paradise, redrawn from Elizabeth Moynihan, *Paradise as a Garden in Persia and Mughal India* (New York: Braziller, 1979), 147.

Figure 9, page 90. Egyptian threshing floor, from Sir J. Gardner Wilkinson, *The Ancient Egyptians*, 2 vols. (New York: Harper & Brothers, 1854), 2:55.

Figure 10, page 91. Oracle of Trophonios, drawn from description in Pausanias, *Description of Greece, Boeotia* XXXIV, 5–14.

Figure 11, page 92. Great Pyramid, redrawn from Virginia Trimble, "Astronomical Investigation concerning the So-called Air-Shafts of Cheop's Pyramid," *Mitteilungen des Instituts für Orientforschung der deutschen Akademie der Wissenschaften zu Berlin* 10/2–3 (1964): 183.

Figure 12, page 93. Ziggurat of Ur, frontispiece by Marjorie Duffell in Sir Leonard Woolley, *The Ziggurat*, vol. 5 of *Ur Excavations* (Philadelphia: University of Pennsylvania Museum, 1939).

Figure 13, page 95. (A) Gudea with floorplan, diorite, Louvre, redrawn from H. W. Janson, *History of Art* (New Jersey: Prentice Hall, 1962), 55, fig. 77; restoration of head based on Gudea head, Museum of Fine Arts, Boston, ibid., fig. 78; detail of floorplan from W. Shaw Caldecott, *The*

Tabernacle (London: Religious Tract Society, 1906), 142; (B) kneeling god, redrawn from André Parrot, *Sumer und Akkad* (Munich: Beck, 1983), 248.

Figure 14, page 96. Frontispiece of *Iyyun Tefillah (Prayer Book)* (Prague: Landau, 1858), courtesy of the Jewish Museum/Art Resource, New York.

Figure 15, page 98. Ishtar temple, from Bruno Meissner, *Babylonien und Assyrien* (Heidelberg: Winters, 1925).

Figure 16, page 99, and figure 17, page 100. Abydos temple, redrawn from Henri Frankfort, *The Cenotaph of Seti I at Abydos* (London: Egyptian Exploration Society, 1933), plates 3, 73, 81.

Figure 18, pages 102–3. (A) Tomb of Sennedjem, drawn from plans in Bernard Bruyère, *La Tombe N° 1 de Sen-nedjem* (Cairo: L'Institut Français, 1959), plates 4, 5, 7, 13, 38; tomb murals from drawings by Abd el Wahab, p. XXXVI–XXXVII; (B) Tomb of Vicentius, redrawn from Johannes Leipoldt, *Die Religionen der Umwelt des Urchristentums* (Leipzig: Deichert, 1926), no. 166.

Figure 19, page 105. Vestments of the High Priest, redrawn from Moshe Levine, *Melekhet ha-Mishkan: Tabnit ha-Mishkan ve-kelav* (Tel Aviv: Melekhet ha-Mishkan, 1968), 124–41.

Figure 20, page 106. (A) Stele of Hammurabi, redrawn from M. Gauthier, *Le Louvre* (Paris: Grange Battelière, 1972), 28; (B) Stele of Ur-Nammu, redrawn from André Parrot, *Sumer und Akkad* (Munich: Beck, 1983), 241.

Figure 21, page 108. White Obelisk, redrawn from 1853 drawing by C. D. Hodder in Edmond Sollberger, "The White Obelisk," *Iraq* 36 (1974): pl. XLII.

Figure 22, page 109. *Soreg* fragment, redrawn from

J. Boudet, *Jerusalem, A History* (New York: Putnam, 1965), 112.

Figure 23, page 120. Marduk fighting Tiamat, alabaster bas-relief, Nimrud, time of Assurnasirpal II, 883–859 B.C., British Museum, redrawn from Austen Henry Layard, *Monuments of Nineveh*, second series (London: Murray, 1885), vol. 2, pl. 5.

Figure 24, page 121. Persian tomb, redrawn from C. J. Edmonds, "A Tomb in Kurdistan," *Iraq* 1/2 (Nov. 1934): fig. 2.

Figure 25, page 128. Menorah drawing, redrawn from photo in Nahman Avigad, *The Herodian Quarter in Jerusalem* (Jerusalem: Keter, 1989), 47.

Figure 26, page 131. Giovanni di Paolo, *Creation of the World*, Metropolitan Museum of Art, Robert Lehman Collection, 1975.1.31, redrawn from museum postcard.

Figure 27, pages 134–35. Garden of Eden landscape and Tabernacle based on interpretation of scriptural descriptions.

Figure 28, page 140. (A) Bronze cherubim/sphinxes, Metropolitan Museum of Art, Rogers Fund 1953.120, redrawn from museum postcard; (B) king on cherubim throne, ivory plaque, adapted from Gordon Loud, *The Megiddo Ivories* (Chicago: University of Chicago Oriental Institute Publications, 1939), vol. 52, pl. 4.

Figure 29, page 154. Ur-Nammu carrying basket, bronze, Baghdad Museum, Iraq, redrawn from Percy Knauth, *The Metalsmiths* (New York: TimeLife, 1974), 35.

Figure 30, page 208. Temple oval at Khafajah, redrawn from restoration by H. D. Darby in Pinhas Delougaz, *The Temple Oval at Khafajah* (Chicago: University of Chicago Oriental Institute Publications, 1940), vol. 53, frontispiece.

Figure 31, page 214. Stele of Bel-Harran-Beli-Ussur,

redrawn from Eckhard Unger, *Die Stele des Bel-Harran-Beli-Ussur ein Denkmal der Zeit Salmanassars IV* (Constantinople: Ahmed Ihsan, 1917), pl. 1.

Figure 32, page 239. *Daijosai* of Hirohito, drawn by Tekisui Ishii in *Enthronement of the 124th Emperor of Japan*. Commemorative issue of the *Japan Advertiser*, November 1928, Tokyo, Benjamin W. Fleisher, publisher, p. 55.

Figure 33, page 245. Royal names of Ramses II, translation courtesy of John Gee.

Figure 34, page 247. Coronation of mock king based on contemporary artifacts and reconstruction painting by H. M. Herget, in Gilbert Grosvenor, ed., *Everyday Life in Ancient Times* (Washington, D.C.: National Geographic Society, 1951), 44; quotation from A. K. Grayson, *Assyrian and Babylonian Chronicles* (Locust Valley, NY: Augustin, 1970), 155; courtesy of John Gee.

Figure 35, page 255. (A) Stone lintel, Cairo Museum, redrawn from Vagn Poulsen, *Egyptian Art* (Greenwich, Connecticut: New York Graphic Society, 1968), 82; (B) ritual girdle, c. 1950 B.C., Cairo Museum, redrawn from C. Andrews, *Ancient Egyptian Jewelry* (London: British Museum, 1990), 141.

Figure 36, pages 258–59. Egyptian coronation scene, Karnac, Temple of Khonsu, from Champollion, *Monuments de l'Égypte*, 4 vols. (Paris: Didot, 1845), 4:pl. cccviii; Persian crown, Metropolitan Museum of Art, Fletcher Fund, 1965.126, redrawn from museum postcard; Nubian crown, redrawn from Walter Emory, *Lost Land Emerging* (New York: Scribner's, 1967), 140; Siamese crown from Thai royal crest; Chinese crown, redrawn from C. A. S. Williams, *Outlines of Chinese Symbolism* (Shanghai: Kelly &

Walsh, 1941), 88; Japanese crown, redrawn from newspaper photo of Emperor Akihito.

Figure 37, page 283. Birth of the Buddha, Tibetan *tanka*, Musée Guimet, redrawn from Heinz Bechert and Richard Gombrich, eds., *The World of Buddhism* (London: Thames & Hudson, 1984), 20, fig. 9.

Figure 38, page 284. Balawat gate relief, bronze, British Museum, redrawn from William S. Smith, *Interconnections in the Ancient Near East* (New Haven: Yale University Press, 1965), fig. 166a.

Figure 39, page 285. Palace mural from Mari, redrawn and heavily restored from *Horizon Book of Lost Worlds* (New York: American Heritage, 1962), 162–63.

Figure 40, pages 402–3. Astronomical structures: (1) Medicine wheel, redrawn from E. C. Krupp, *In Search of Ancient Astronomies* (New York: McGraw-Hill, 1978), 159; (2) Monk's Mound, redrawn from Joseph Campbell, *Mythologies of the Great Hunt* (New York: Harper & Row, 1988), 216; (3) High Bank Works, five miles south of Chillicothe, Ohio, redrawn from Ray Hively and Robert Horn, "Hopewellian Geometry and Astronomy at High Bank," *Archaeoastronomy* 7 (1984): S94, fig. 7; (4) La Venta, redrawn from Joseph Campbell, *The Mythic Image* (Princeton: Princeton University Press, 1974), 105; (5) Templo Major, Tenochtitlan, redrawn from E. C. Krupp, *Echoes of Ancient Skies* (New York: Harper & Row, 1983), 268; (6) Sacsahuaman, redrawn from *Builders of the Ancient World* (Washington, D.C.: National Geographic Society, 1986), 117; (7) Step Pyramid, redrawn from Jean-Philippe Lauer, *Les pyramides de Sakkarah* (Cairo: IFAO, 1977), fig. 6; (8) Sun altar, redrawn from Henri Frankfort, *City of Akhenaton* (London: Egyptian Exploration Society, 1933), pl. xxvi; (9) Kaaba, redrawn from Desmond Stewart, *Mecca*

(New York: Newsweek, 1980), 128; (10) Altar of Heaven, redrawn from Campbell, *The Mythic Image*, 98; (11) Tomb Pyramid of Prince Yide, redrawn from *World Atlas of Archaeology* (Boston: Hall, 1985), 274; (12) New Grange, redrawn from Krupp, *Echoes of Ancient Skies*, 124–25.

Figure 41, page 418–19. Second Temple, redrawn from Charles J. Melchior, Marquis de Vogue, *Le Temple de Jerusalem* (Paris: Noblet & Baudry, 1864).

Figure 42, page 523. (A) Ivory pomegranate, redrawn from Nahman Avigad, "The Inscribed Pomegranate from the 'House of the Lord,'" *Biblical Archaeologist* 53/3 (September 1990): 160; (B) inscribed bowl, redrawn from Yigael Yadin, *The Temple Scroll* (New York: Putnam, 1965), 112.

Figure 43, page 558. (A) brass coin of Domitian, from Seth W. Stevenson, *A Dictionary of Roman Coins* (London: Bell & Sons, 1889), 149; (B) Salt Lake Temple handclasp, redrawn from C. Mark Hamilton, *The Salt Lake Temple: A Monument to a People* (Salt Lake City: University Services, 1983), 157.

Figure 44, page 560. (A) inscribed clay cone, redrawn from *The Age of God-Kings* (Alexandria, VA: TimeLife Books, 1987), 43; (B) Egyptian clay cone, redrawn from Lepsius, *Denkmäler Textband* (Leipzig: Hinrichs, 1897), 1:9; (C) Sopdu falcon, redrawn from Alexandre Piankoff, *The Pyramid of Unas* (Princeton: Princeton University Press, 1968), pl. 8, line 480d; (D) Senmut tomb ceiling, redrawn from Charles K. Wilkinson, *Egyptian Wall Paintings* (New York: Metropolitan Museum of Art, 1983), 31; (E) Magic nail, from Richard Wünsch, *Antikes Zaubergerät aus Pergamon* (Berlin: Reimer, 1905), p. 3.

Figure 45, page 561. (A) Pole of Min, Dendera, redrawn from Robert D. Anderson, *Egypt in 1800:*

Napoleon's Description de L'Egypte (London: Barrie & Jenkins, 1987), pl. 40; (B) Irminsul, redrawn from Nold Egenter, *Sacred Symbols of Reed and Bamboo* (Bern: Lang, 1982), 85; (C) Voladores, redrawn from E. C. Krupp, *Echoes of the Ancient Skies* (New York: Harper & Row, 1983), 210; (D) Otaimatsu, redrawn from Egenter, *Sacred Symbols*, 14b.

Figure 46, page 573. (A) Spirit door of Djoser, redrawn by Tyler Moulton from Jean Leclant, *Ägypten*, 3 vols. (Munich: Beck, 1979), 1:58; (B) Temple of Seti I, Abydos, drawn from plans in Amice M. Calverly, *The Temple of King Sethos I at Abydos*, 4 vols. (Chicago: Chicago University Press, 1933), 1:pl. 1.

Figure 47, page 575. Tomb of Fan Yen-Shih, reconstructed from descriptions in Sir Aurel Stein, *Innermost Asia*, 3 vols. (Oxford: Clarendon, 1928), 2:663–66; 3:plan 34, Astana IX.2.

Figure 48, page 592. (A) Egyptian incense burner, redrawn from F. Ll. Griffith, *Beni Hasan* (London: Egypt Exploration Fund, 1900), pt. IV, pl. XVII; Steatite incense burner, redrawn from Herbert G. May, *Material Remains of the Megiddo Cult* (Chicago: University of Chicago Press, 1935), pl. XVII.

Figure 49, page 603. Thoth, sandstone bas-relief, Temple of Amon, Karnac, reign of Hatshepsut, redrawn from Isha Schwaller de Lubicz, *Her-Bak: Egyptian Initiate* (New York: Inner Traditions, 1978), 116.

Figure 50, pages 628–29. (1) Sanchi *stupa*, redrawn from Henry Millon, *Key Monuments of the History of Architecture* (New York: Abrams, 1965), 162; (2) silver *stupa*, Doris Wiener Collection, New York City, redrawn from Pratapaditya Pal, *Light of Asia, Buddha Sakyamuni in Asian Art* (Los Angeles: L.A. County Museum, 1984), 136; (3) Sung-Yüeh Ssu, Honan, China, from photographs; (4)

Ta-Yen T'a, Cháng-an, Shensi, from photographs; (5) Goju-no-to, Horyuji, Nara, from Heinz Bechert and Richard Gombrich, eds., *The World of Buddhism* (London: Thames & Hudson, 1984), 95; (6) Borobudur, Indonesia, redrawn from Adrian Snodgrass, *The Symbolism of the Stupa* (Ithaca, NY: Cornell University Press, 1985), 142.

Figure 51, page 631. Jung, Mandala painting from Aniela Jaffed, ed., *C. G. Jung: Word and Image* (Princeton: Princeton University Press, 1979), 91.

Figure 52, page 650. (A) Aaron, fresco in Dura Europos Synagogue, redrawn from Alfred Rubens, *A History of Jewish Costume* (London: Owen, 1981), 20; (B) High Priest, thirteenth-century Hebrew manuscript, British Library, redrawn from Jean Comay, *Temple of Jerusalem* (New York: Holt, Rinehart, 1975), 55; (C) High Priest, eighteenth-century German engraving, Rheinisches Bildarchiv, from Geoffrey Wigoder, *Encyclopedia of Judaism* (New York: Macmillan, 1989), 568.

Figure 53, page 660. Jew wearing *tallith*, Dutch engraving, 1725, from Alfred Rubens, *A History of Jewish Costumes* (London: Owen, 1981), 9.

Contributors

Michael A. Carter is associate administrative director of the missionary training centers of The Church of Jesus Christ of Latter-day Saints.

Andrew F. Ehat is a product manager with WordPerfect Corporation in Orem, Utah.

William J. Hamblin, Ph.D., is assistant professor of history at Brigham Young University.

Marion D. Hanks is a General Authority emeritus of The Church of Jesus Christ of Latter-day Saints and former president of the Salt Lake Temple.

Brian M. Hauglid is pursuing a Ph.D. in Arabic and Islamic studies at the University of Utah and teaches seminary for the Church Educational System.

John M. Lundquist, Ph.D., is the Susan and Douglas Dillon Chief Librarian of the Oriental Division of the New York Public Library.

Truman G. Madsen, Ph.D., is professor of philosophy at Brigham Young University.

Daniel B. McKinlay, M.T.S., M.A., and M.L.I.S., is an author and researcher in Provo, Utah.

Hugh W. Nibley, Ph.D., is professor emeritus of ancient scripture at Brigham Young University.

Jay A. Parry is a freelance writer and researcher in Salt Lake City, Utah.

Donald W. Parry, Ph.D., is a visiting assistant professor of Hebrew at Brigham Young University.

Stephen D. Ricks, Ph.D., is professor of Hebrew and Semitic languages and Associate Dean of General Education and Honors at Brigham Young University.

M. Catherine Thomas, Ph.D., is an instructor in ancient scripture at Brigham Young University.

John A. Tvedtnes, M.A., is a technical writer for GTE Health Systems. He has studied extensively at Hebrew University in Jerusalem.

John W. Welch, J.D., is professor of law at Brigham Young University and editor of *Brigham Young University Studies*.

Index of Passages

**BOOK OF
MORMON**

1 Nephi

Index of Subjects

Aaron and his sons, clothing of, 715, 731. *See also* High Priest
Aaronic Priesthood: keys of, 8–9, 50–51; purpose of, 312; and keys to ministry of angels, 482
Abinadi: and law of Moses, 306; denunciations of Noah by, 341
Ablutions in coronation ceremonies, 241–43
Abraham: searches for priesthood privileges, 388; and endowment, 584–85; investiture of, 668; meets angels, 679–80; celestial clothing for, 682
Abundance: temples and, 97, 186; in garden and temple, 127, 145–46
Access to temples, 110–11
Adad, 155, 164, 186
Adam: and Eve give commandments, 9–10; cast out, 388; receives garment, 544–55; time not measured until Fall of, 545–46, 547; lives with animals, 547; enters the Garden, 548; duties of, 548–49; offers sacrifice, 550–51; receives the gospel, 551–52; and story of endowment, 577, 581–83. *See also* Fall of Adam; Garment of Adam
Adams, Robert M., 181–82, 189; on writing, 192; on role of religion, 203
Adultery, covenant to eschew, 338

Aerial space: above the sanctuary, 418; sanctity of, 426
"Afflict" souls, 353
Afterlife, temple associated with, 103–4, 187
Agency, free, 44
Agricultural practices, 198
Ahlstrom, G. W., 328
Airspace of heathen lands, 429
Akiba, Rabbi, on clothing with garments, 714
Akihito, coronation of, 138–39
Akītu festival, 119
Albright, W. F., 217–18
Altar, 455; solitary, 320
Ammi, Rabbi, 424–25
Ammon delivers final covenant speech, 342
Ammonites remain separate, 362
Amulek: and eternal sacrifice, 307; and God's dwelling place, 347
An, 155, 164
Ancestors, rites and worship of, 187
Ancient America: records about, 400; ruins of, 400
Ancient civilization, hierocentricity of, 407
Ancient order of things, 9, 51
Angelic host in celestial ascent, 451–52
Angell, Truman, 159–60
Angels, 39, 75; key to ministering, 482; clothing of, 678–80
Animal life in the Garden, 151

781

of Church to come unto, 14–15;
temple a place of learning
about, 18–19; principles of life
of, 21–23; following the path
of, 25–26; endowment of the
disciples of, 56; faith in coming
unto, 60; as scapegoat, 64; at
Gethsemane, 66; atonement of,
and living death, 66–67; commitment to, and marriage, 68;
receives the ordinances, 68;
replaces temple, 69; the good
shepherd, 71; face-to-face communion with, 74; the passion
of, 76; as keeper of the gate,
77–78; circumsion of, 313;
appears at temple in Bountiful,
343; shedding of blood of, 351;
given new name of, 360;
Nephites enshrine words of,
371; and the exaltation of the
righteous dead, 459; joint heirship with, 484; is epitome of
the temple, 496; as expiatory
proxy, 500; as mediator, 525;
garments made white in blood
of, 689–91; clothing of, 691–94;
cleanses Saints, 703
Jewish and Christian relationships, 376
"Jewish festivals," 317
Jewish mysticism. *See* Celestial
ascent
Jews: and a temple at Jerusalem,
64–65; and the Exodus, 495;
perplexity of, 591–93; Jacob
Neusner on laws of Rabbinic,
591, 592–93; literalness of,
596–97
Job: and sacred girdle, 669–70;
and the garment of Adam, 729
Johanan, Rabbi, 430–31
John, Gospel of, 596–97

John on heavenly garments,
717–18
Johnson, Gregory, on the state,
192
John the Beloved, appears in
temple, 169
Joining, separating and, 46
Jonah, 11–13
Jones, Rufus: on the nature of
things, 4; on Saints, 26
Joseph: and garment of Adam,
658, 698, 712–13, 730; marriage
of, to Aseneth, 676–77
Joshua and garments of wisdom,
661–62
Joshua the high priest, investiture
of, 668–69
Judaism: modern, and creation
account, 122; ancient and mod-
ern, 310
Judgment, 43; seat, 363; final,
371–72
Judicial oaths, 341
Jung, Carl Gustav, 630–31

Kabbalism: and Jewish mysticism,
461–62; Christian, 462, 464; and
Freemasonry, 462–63
Kaminaljuyu: as a model, 194–95;
cultural evolution at, 200
Kapelrud, Arvid, 152, 209
Kearney, P. J., 137–38
Kelly, J. N. D., 499, 506, 508
Keys: of the priesthood, 8–9, 171;
of the kingdom, 494, 509
Khafaje, 204–5
Khazanov, Anatolii M., 195–96
Kimball, Heber C., 160
Kimball, Spencer W., 58–59; on
derelictions of Latter-day
Saints, 612
King: as a temple builder, 209;
replaced by gardener, 247; ide-
ology of, in ancient Israel, 275;

What Is F.A.R.M.S.?

The Foundation for Ancient Research and Mormon Studies (F.A.R.M.S.) encourages and supports research about the Book of Mormon, Another Testament of Jesus Christ, and other ancient scriptures.

F.A.R.M.S. is a nonprofit educational foundation, independent of all other organizations. Its main research interests include ancient history, language, literature, culture, geography, politics, and law relevant to the scriptures. Although such subjects are of secondary importance when compared with the spiritual and eternal messages of the scriptures, solid research and academic perspectives alone can supply certain kinds of useful information, even if only tentatively, concerning many significant and interesting questions about the ancient backgrounds, origins, composition, and meanings of scripture.

The Foundation works to make interim and final reports about this research available widely, promptly, and economically. As a service to teachers and students of the scriptures, research results are distributed both in scholarly and popular formats.

It is hoped that this information will help all interested people to "come unto Christ" (Jacob 1:7) and to understand and take more seriously these ancient witnesses of the atonement of Jesus Christ, the Son of God.

For more information about F.A.R.M.S., call toll free 1-800-327-6715, or write to F.A.R.M.S., P.O. Box 7113, University Station, Provo UT 84602.

Copublications of
Deseret Book Company
and the
Foundation for Ancient Research and Mormon Studies

❧

The Allegory of the Olive Tree
An Ancient American Setting for the Book of Mormon
By Study and Also by Faith: Essays in Honor of Hugh W. Nibley
Rediscovering the Book of Mormon
Reexploring the Book of Mormon
The Sermon at the Temple and the Sermon on the Mount
Warfare in the Book of Mormon

The Collected Works of Hugh Nibley

Old Testament and Related Studies
Enoch the Prophet
The World and the Prophets
Mormonism and Early Christianity
Lehi in the Desert/The World of the Jaredites/There Were Jaredites
An Approach to the Book of Mormon
Since Cumorah
The Prophetic Book of Mormon
Approaching Zion
The Ancient State
Tinkling Cymbals and Sounding Brass
Temple and Cosmos
Brother Brigham Challenges the Saints